STARTING OUT WITH PYTHON®

FOURTH EDITION

STARTING OUT WITH PYTHON®

FOURTH EDITION

Tony Gaddis
Haywood Community College

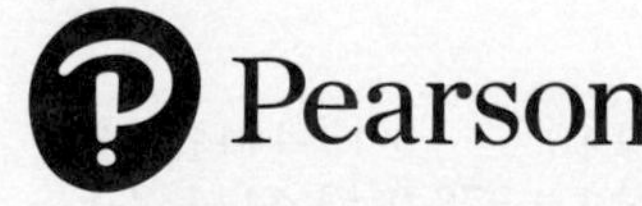

330 Hudson Street, New York, NY 10013

Senior Vice President Courseware Portfolio Management:	Marcia J. Horton
Director, Portfolio Management: Engineering, Computer Science & Global Editions:	Julian Partridge
Portfolio Manager:	Matt Goldstein
Portfolio Management Assistant:	Kristy Alaura
Field Marketing Manager:	Demetrius Hall
Product Marketing Manager:	Yvonne Vannatta
Managing Producer, ECS and Math:	Scott Disanno
Content Producer:	Sandra L. Rodriguez
Composition:	iEnergizer Aptara®, Ltd.
Cover Designer:	Joyce Wells
Cover Photo:	Westend61 GmbH/Alamy Stock Photo

Credits and acknowledgments borrowed from other sources and reproduced, with permission, appear on the Credits page in the endmatter of this textbook.

Pearson Education Ltd., London
Pearson Education Singapore, Pte. Ltd
Pearson Education Canada, Inc.
Pearson Education Japan
Pearson Education Australia PTY, Ltd
Pearson Education North Asia, Ltd., Hong Kong
Pearson Education de Mexico, S.A. de C.V.
Pearson Education Malaysia, Pte. Ltd.
Pearson Education, Inc., Hoboken

Library of Congress Cataloging-in-Publication Data
Names: Gaddis, Tony, author.
Title: Starting out with Python/Tony Gaddis, Haywood Community College.
Description: Fourth edition. | Boston : Pearson, [2018] | Includes index.
Identifiers: LCCN 2016058388 | ISBN 9780134444321 (alk. paper) | ISBN 0134444329 (alk. paper)
Subjects: LCSH: Python (Computer program language)
Classification: LCC QA76.73.P98 G34 2018 | DDC 005.13/3—dc23 LC record available at https://lccn.loc.gov/2016058388

2 17

ISBN 10: 0-13-444432-9
ISBN 13: 978-0-13-444432-1

Contents in a Glance

Contents

LOCATION OF VIDEONOTES IN THE TEXT

Preface

Welcome to *Starting Out with Python*, Fourth Edition. This book uses the Python language to teach programming concepts and problem-solving skills, without assuming any previous programming experience. With easy-to-understand examples, pseudocode, flowcharts, and other tools, the student learns how to design the logic of programs then implement those programs using Python. This book is ideal for an introductory programming course or a programming logic and design course using Python as the language.

As with all the books in the *Starting Out With* series, the hallmark of this text is its clear, friendly, and easy-to-understand writing. In addition, it is rich in example programs that are concise and practical. The programs in this book include short examples that highlight specific programming topics, as well as more involved examples that focus on problem solving. Each chapter provides one or more case studies that provide step-by-step analysis of a specific problem and shows the student how to solve it.

Control Structures First, Then Classes

Python is a fully object-oriented programming language, but students do not have to understand object-oriented concepts to start programming in Python. This text first introduces the student to the fundamentals of data storage, input and output, control structures, functions, sequences and lists, file I/O, and objects that are created from standard library classes. Then the student learns to write classes, explores the topics of inheritance and polymorphism, and learns to write recursive functions. Finally, the student learns to develop simple event-driven GUI applications.

Changes in the Fourth Edition

This book's clear writing style remains the same as in the previous edition. However, many additions and improvements have been made, which are summarized here:

- New sections on the Python Turtle Graphics library have been added to Chapters 2 through 5. The Turtle Graphics library, which is a standard part of Python, is a f[illegible] and motivating way to introduce programming concepts to students who hav[illegible] written code before. The library allows the student to write Python stat[illegible] draw graphics by moving a cursor on a canvas. The new sections that ha[illegible] to this edition are:
    - Chapter 2: Introduction to Turtle Graphics
    - Chapter 3: Determining the State of the Turtle
    - Chapter 4: Using loops to draw designs
    - Chapter 5: Modularizing Turtle Graphics Code with [illegible]

The new Turtle Graphics sections are designed with flexibility in mind. They can be assigned as optional material, incorporated into your existing syllabus, or skipped altogether.

- Chapter 2 has a new section on named constants. Although Python does not support true constants, you can create variable names that symbolize values that should not change as the program executes. This section teaches the student to avoid the use of "magic numbers," and to create symbolic names that his or her code more self-documenting and easier to maintain.
- Chapter 7 has a new section on using the `matplotlib` package to plot charts and graphs from lists. The new section describes how to install the `matplotlib` package, and use it to plot line graphs, bar charts, and pie charts.
- Chapter 13 has a new section on creating graphics in a GUI application with the `Canvas` widget. The new section describes how to use the `Canvas` widget to draw lines, rectangles, ovals, arcs, polygons, and text.
- Several new, more challenging, programming problems have been added throughout the book.
- Appendix E is a new appendix that discusses the various forms of the `import` statement.
- Appendix F is a new appendix that discusses installing third-party modules with the `pip` utility.

Brief Overview of Each Chapter

Chapter 1: Introduction to Computers and Programming

This chapter begins by giving a very concrete and easy-to-understand explanation of how computers work, how data is stored and manipulated, and why we write programs in high-level languages. An introduction to Python, interactive mode, script mode, and the IDLE environment are also given.

Chapter 2: Input, Processing, and Output

This chapter introduces the program development cycle, variables, data types, and simple programs that are written as sequence structures. The student learns to write simple programs that read input from the keyboard, perform mathematical operations, and produce screen output. Pseudocode and flowcharts are also introduced as tools for designing programs. The chapter also includes an optional introduction to the turtle graphics library.

Chapter 3: Decision Structures and Boolean Logic

In this chapter, the student learns about relational operators and Boolean expressions and is shown how to control the flow of a program with decision structures. The `if`, `if-else`, and `if-elif-else` statements are covered. Nested decision structures and logical operators are discussed as well. The chapter also includes an optional turtle graphics section, with a discus-on of how to use decision structures to test the state of the turtle.

ter 4: Repetition Structures

r shows the student how to create repetition structures using the `while` loop and unters, accumulators, running totals, and sentinels are discussed, as well as techniques for writing input validation loops. The chapter also includes an optional section on using loops to draw designs with the turtle graphics library.

Chapter 5: Functions

In this chapter, the student first learns how to write and call void functions. The chapter shows the benefits of using functions to modularize programs and discusses the top-down design approach. Then, the student learns to pass arguments to functions. Common library functions, such as those for generating random numbers, are discussed. After learning how to call library functions and use their return value, the student learns to define and call his or her own functions. Then the student learns how to use modules to organize functions. An optional section includes a discussion of modularizing turtle graphics code with functions.

Chapter 6: Files and Exceptions

This chapter introduces sequential file input and output. The student learns to read and write large sets of data and store data as fields and records. The chapter concludes by discussing exceptions and shows the student how to write exception-handling code.

Chapter 7: Lists and Tuples

This chapter introduces the student to the concept of a sequence in Python and explores the use of two common Python sequences: lists and tuples. The student learns to use lists for arraylike operations, such as storing objects in a list, iterating over a list, searching for items in a list, and calculating the sum and average of items in a list. The chapter discusses slicing and many of the list methods. One- and two-dimensional lists are covered. The chapter also includes a discussion of the `matplotlib` package, and how to use it to plot charts and graphs from lists.

Chapter 8: More About Strings

In this chapter, the student learns to process strings at a detailed level. String slicing and algorithms that step through the individual characters in a string are discussed, and several built-in functions and string methods for character and text processing are introduced.

Chapter 9: Dictionaries and Sets

This chapter introduces the dictionary and set data structures. The student learns to store data as key-value pairs in dictionaries, search for values, change existing values, add new key-value pairs, and delete key-value pairs. The student learns to store values as unique elements in sets and perform common set operations such as union, intersection, difference, and symmetric difference. The chapter concludes with a discussion of object serialization and introduces the student to the Python `pickle` module.

Chapter 10: Classes and Object-Oriented Programming

This chapter compares procedural and object-oriented programming practices. It covers the fundamental concepts of classes and objects. Attributes, methods, encapsulation and data hiding, `__init__` functions (which are similar to constructors), accessors, and mutators are discussed. The student learns how to model classes with UML and how to find the classes in a particular problem.

Chapter 11: Inheritance

The study of classes continues in this chapter with the subjects of inheritance and polymorphism. The topics covered include superclasses, subclasses, how `__init__` functions work in inheritance, method overriding, and polymorphism.

Chapter 12: Recursion

This chapter discusses recursion and its use in problem solving. A visual trace of recursive calls is provided, and recursive applications are discussed. Recursive algorithms for many tasks are presented, such as finding factorials, finding a greatest common denominator (GCD), and summing a range of values in a list, and the classic Towers of Hanoi example are presented.

Chapter 13: GUI Programming

This chapter discusses the basic aspects of designing a GUI application using the `tkinter` module in Python. Fundamental widgets, such as labels, buttons, entry fields, radio buttons, check buttons, and dialog boxes, are covered. The student also learns how events work in a GUI application and how to write callback functions to handle events. The Chapter includes a discussion of the `Canvas` widget, and how to use it to draw lines, rectangles, ovals, arcs, polygons, and text.

Appendix A: Installing Python

This appendix explains how to download and install the Python 3 interpreter.

Appendix B: Introduction to IDLE

This appendix gives an overview of the IDLE integrated development environment that comes with Python.

Appendix C: The ASCII Character Set

As a reference, this appendix lists the ASCII character set.

Appendix D: Predefined Named Colors

This appendix lists the predefined color names that can be used with the turtle graphics library, `matplotlib` and `tkinter`.

Appendix E: More About the `import` Statement

This appendix discusses various ways to use the `import` statement. For example, you can use the `import` statement to import a module, a class, a function, or to assign an alias to a module.

Appendix F: Installing Modules with the `pip` Utility

This appendix discusses how to use the `pip` utility to install third-party modules from the Python Package Index, or PyPI.

Appendix G: Answers to Checkpoints

This appendix gives the answers to the Checkpoint questions that appear throughout the text.

Organization of the Text

The text teaches programming in a step-by-step manner. Each chapter covers a major set of topics and builds knowledge as students progress through the book. Although the chapters can be easily taught in their existing sequence, you do have some flexibility in the order that you wish to cover them. Figure P-1 shows chapter dependencies. Each box represents a chapter or a group of chapters. An arrow points from a chapter to the chapter that must be covered before it.

Figure P-1 Chapter dependencies

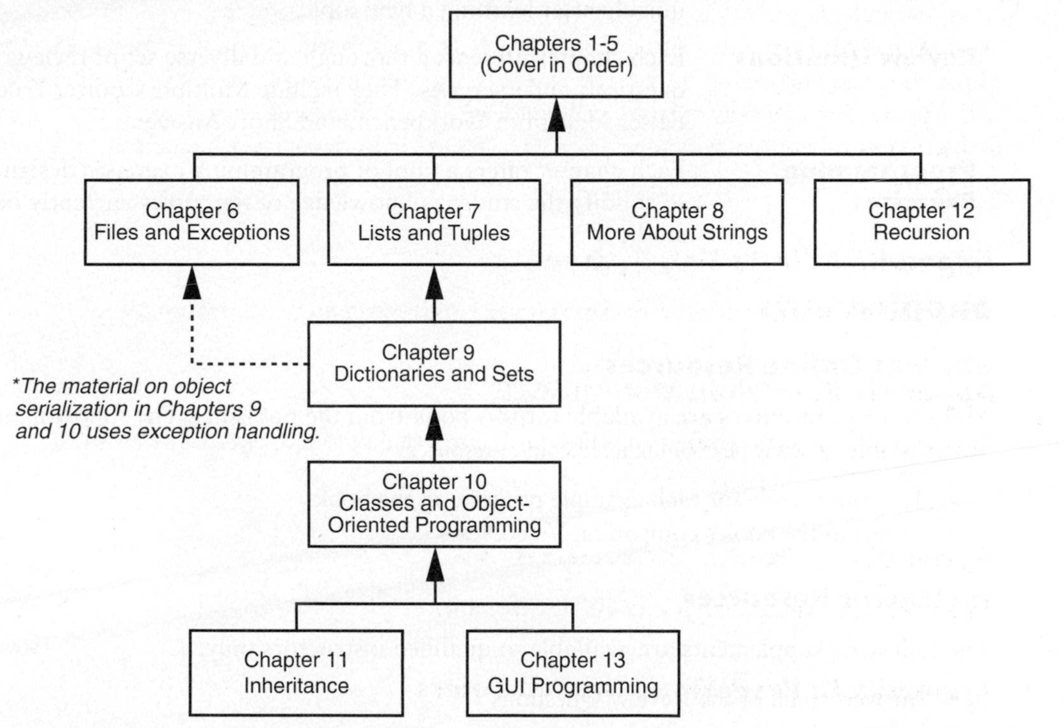

Features of the Text

Concept Statements Each major section of the text starts with a concept statement. This statement concisely summarizes the main point of the section.

Example Programs Each chapter has an abundant number of complete and partial example programs, each designed to highlight the current topic.

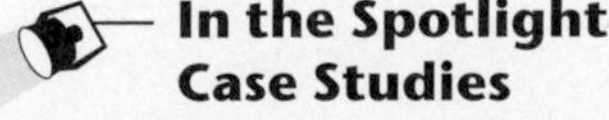

In the Spotlight Case Studies Each chapter has one or more *In the Spotlight* case studies that provide detailed, step-by-step analysis of problems and show the student how to solve them.

VideoNotes	Online videos developed specifically for this book are available for viewing at www.pearsonhighered.com/cs-resources. Icons appear throughout the text alerting the student to videos about specific topics.
Notes	Notes appear at several places throughout the text. They are short explanations of interesting or often misunderstood points relevant to the topic at hand.
Tips	Tips advise the student on the best techniques for approaching different programming problems.
Warnings	Warnings caution students about programming techniques or practices that can lead to malfunctioning programs or lost data.
Checkpoints	Checkpoints are questions placed at intervals throughout each chapter. They are designed to query the student's knowledge quickly after learning a new topic.
Review Questions	Each chapter presents a thorough and diverse set of review questions and exercises. They include Multiple Choice, True/False, Algorithm Workbench, and Short Answer.
Programming Exercises	Each chapter offers a pool of programming exercises designed to solidify the student's knowledge of the topics currently being studied.

Supplements

Student Online Resources

Many student resources are available for this book from the publisher. The following items are available at www.pearsonhighered.com/cs-resources

- The source code for each example program in the book
- Access to the book's companion VideoNotes

Instructor Resources

The following supplements are available to qualified instructors only:

- Answers to all of the Review Questions
- Solutions for the exercises
- PowerPoint presentation slides for each chapter
- Test bank

Visit the Pearson Education Instructor Resource Center (www.pearsonhighered.com/irc) or contact your local Pearson Education campus representative for information on how to access them.

Acknowledgments

I would like to thank the following faculty reviewers for their insight, expertise, and thoughtful recommendations:

Sonya Dennis
Morehouse College

Diane Innes
Sandhills Community College

John Kinuthia
Nazareth College of Rochester

Frank Liu
Sam Houston State University

Haris Ribic
SUNY at Binghamton

Anita Sutton
Germanna Community College

Christopher Urban
SUNY Institute of Technology

Nanette Veilleux
Simmons College

Brent Wilson
George Fox University

Reviewers of Previous Editions

Paul Amer
University of Delaware

James Atlas
University of Delaware

James Carrier
Guilford Technical Community College

John Cavazos
University of Delaware

Desmond K. H. Chun
Chabot Community College

Barbara Goldner
North Seattle Community College

Paul Gruhn
Manchester Community College

Bob Husson
Craven Community College

Diane Innes
Sandhills Community College

Daniel Jinguji
North Seattle Community College

Gary Marrer
Glendale Community College

Keith Mehl
Chabot College

Shyamal Mitra
University of Texas at Austin

Vince Offenback
North Seattle Community College

Smiljana Petrovic
Iona College

Raymond Pettit
Abilene Christian University

Janet Renwick
University of Arkansas–Fort Smith

Ken Robol
Beaufort Community College

Eric Shaffer
University of Illinois at Urbana-Champaign

Tom Stokke
University of North Dakota

Ann Ford Tyson
Florida State University

Karen Ughetta
Virginia Western Community College

Linda F. Wilson
Texas Lutheran University

I would also like to thank my family and friends for their support in all of my projects. I am extremely fortunate to have Matt Goldstein as my editor, and Kristy Alaura as editorial assistant. Their guidance and encouragement make it a pleasure to write chapters and meet deadlines. I am also fortunate to have Demetrius Hall as my marketing manager. His hard work is truly inspiring, and he does a great job of getting this book out to the academic community. The production team, led by Sandra Rodriguez, worked tirelessly to make this book a reality. Thanks to you all!

About the Author

Tony Gaddis is the principal author of the *Starting Out With* series of textbooks. Tony has nearly two decades of experience teaching computer science courses at Haywood Community College. He is a highly acclaimed instructor who was previously selected as the North Carolina Community College "Teacher of the Year" and has received the Teaching Excellence award from the National Institute for Staff and Organizational Development. The *Starting Out with* series includes introductory books covering C++, Java™, Microsoft® Visual Basic®, Microsoft® C#®, Python®, Programming Logic and Design, Alice, and App Inventor, all published by Pearson. More information about all these books can be found at www.pearsonhighered.com/gaddisbooks.

CHAPTER

1 Introduction to Computers and Programming

TOPICS

1.1 Introduction

Think about some of the different ways that people use computers. In school, students use computers for tasks such as writing papers, searching for articles, sending email, and participating in online classes. At work, people use computers to analyze data, make presentations, conduct business transactions, communicate with customers and coworkers, control machines in manufacturing facilities, and do many other things. At home, people use computers for tasks such as paying bills, shopping online, communicating with friends and family, and playing games. And don't forget that cell phones, tablets, smart phones, car navigation systems, and many other devices are computers too. The uses of computers are almost limitless in our everyday lives.

Computers can perform such a wide variety of tasks because they can be programmed. This means that computers are not designed to do just one job, but to do any job that their programs tell them to do. A *program* is a set of instructions that a computer follows to perform a task. For example, Figure 1-1 shows screens using Microsoft Word and PowerPoint, two commonly used programs.

Programs are commonly referred to as *software*. Software is essential to a computer because it controls everything the computer does. All of the software that we use to make our computers useful is created by individuals working as programmers or software developers. A *programmer*, or *software developer*, is a person with the training and skills necessary to design, create, and test computer programs. Computer programming is an exciting and rewarding career. Today, you will find programmers' work used in business, medicine, government, law enforcement, agriculture, academics, entertainment, and many other fields.

This book introduces you to the fundamental concepts of computer programming using the Python language. The Python language is a good choice for beginners because it is easy to learn

Figure 1-1 A word processing program and an image editing program

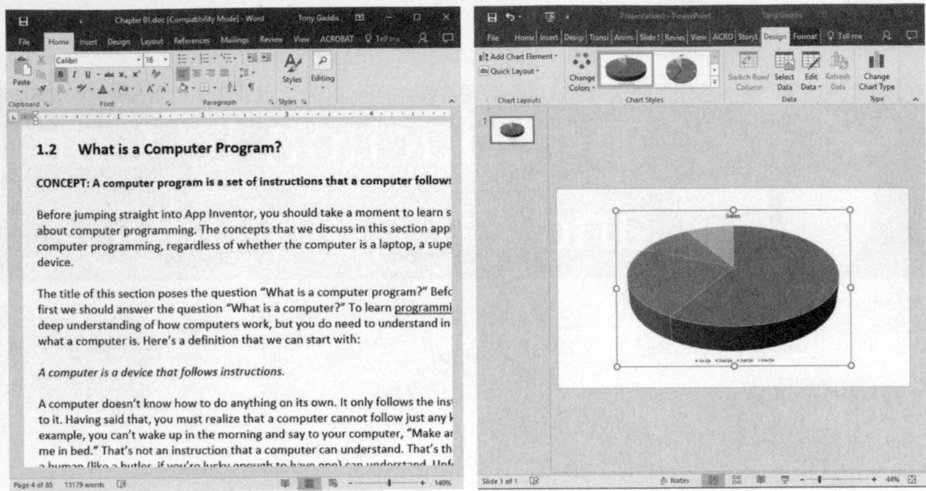

and programs can be written quickly using it. Python is also a powerful language, popular with professional software developers. In fact, it has been reported that Python is used by Google, NASA, YouTube, various game companies, the New York Stock Exchange, and many others.

Before we begin exploring the concepts of programming, you need to understand a few basic things about computers and how they work. This chapter will build a solid foundation of knowledge that you will continually rely on as you study computer science. First, we will discuss the physical components of which computers are commonly made. Next, we will look at how computers store data and execute programs. Finally, you will get a quick introduction to the software that you will use to write Python programs.

1.2 Hardware and Software

CONCEPT: **The physical devices of which a computer is made are referred to as the computer's hardware. The programs that run on a computer are referred to as software.**

Hardware

The term *hardware* refers to all of the physical devices, or *components*, of which a computer is made. A computer is not one single device, but a system of devices that all work together. Like the different instruments in a symphony orchestra, each device in a computer plays its own part.

If you have ever shopped for a computer, you've probably seen sales literature listing components such as microprocessors, memory, disk drives, video displays, graphics cards, and so on. Unless you already know a lot about computers, or at least have a friend that does, understanding what these different components do might be challenging. As shown in Figure 1-2, a typical computer system consists of the following major components:

- The central processing unit (CPU)
- Main memory

Figure 1-2 Typical components of a computer system

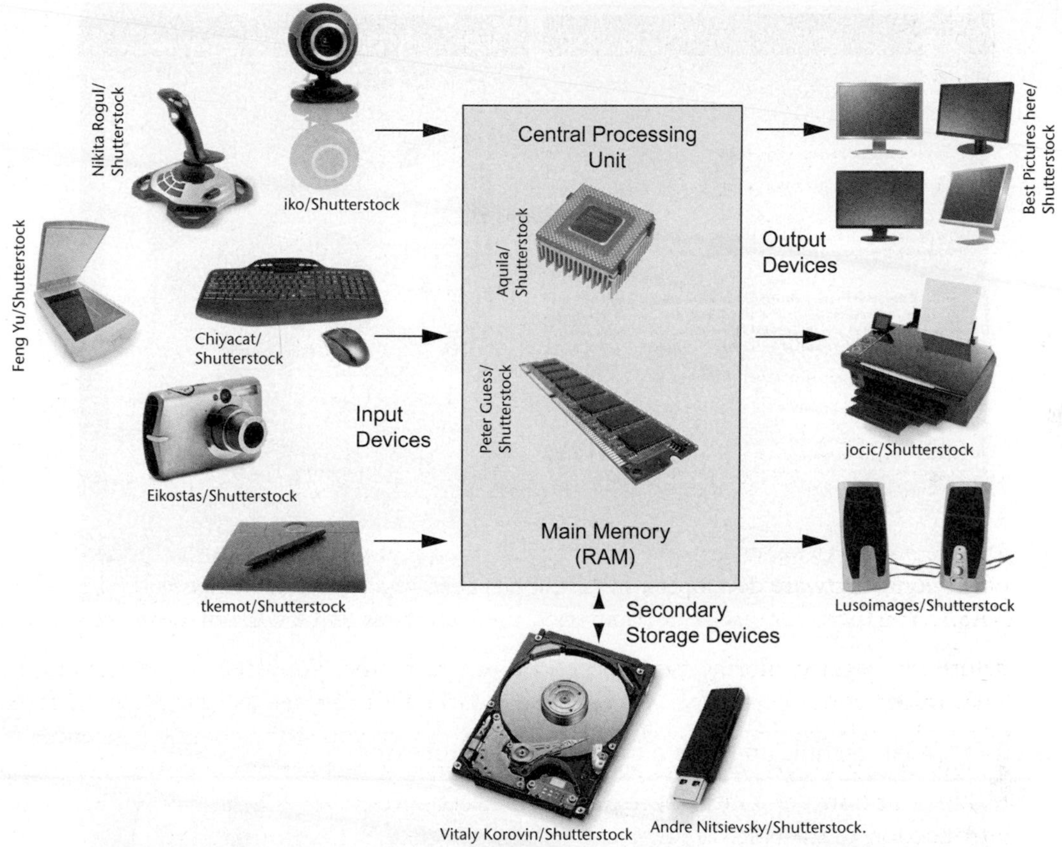

- Secondary storage devices
- Input devices
- Output devices

Let's take a closer look at each of these components.

The CPU

When a computer is performing the tasks that a program tells it to do, we say that the computer is *running* or *executing* the program. The *central processing unit,* or *CPU,* is the part of a computer that actually runs programs. The CPU is the most important component in a computer because without it, the computer could not run software.

In the earliest computers, CPUs were huge devices made of electrical and mechanical components such as vacuum tubes and switches. Figure 1-3 shows such a device. The two women in the photo are working with the historic ENIAC computer. The ENIAC, which is considered by many to be the world's first programmable electronic computer, was built in 1945 to calculate artillery ballistic tables for the U.S. Army. This machine, which was primarily one big CPU, was 8 feet tall, 100 feet long, and weighed 30 tons.

Today, CPUs are small chips known as *microprocessors*. Figure 1-4 shows a photo of a lab technician holding a modern microprocessor. In addition to being much smaller than the old electromechanical CPUs in early computers, microprocessors are also much more powerful.

Figure 1-3 The ENIAC computer

courtesy of U.S. Army Historic Computer Images

Figure 1-4 A lab technician holds a modern microprocessor

Creativa/Shutterstock

Main Memory

You can think of *main memory* as the computer's work area. This is where the computer stores a program while the program is running, as well as the data that the program is working with. For example, suppose you are using a word processing program to write an essay for one of your classes. While you do this, both the word processing program and the essay are stored in main memory.

Main memory is commonly known as *random-access memory,* or *RAM.* It is called this because the CPU is able to quickly access data stored at any random location in RAM. RAM is usually a *volatile* type of memory that is used only for temporary storage while a program is running. When the computer is turned off, the contents of RAM are erased. Inside your computer, RAM is stored in chips, similar to the ones shown in Figure 1-5.

Figure 1-5 Memory chips

Garsya/Shutterstock

Secondary Storage Devices

Secondary storage is a type of memory that can hold data for long periods of time, even when there is no power to the computer. Programs are normally stored in secondary memory and loaded into main memory as needed. Important data, such as word processing documents, payroll data, and inventory records, is saved to secondary storage as well.

The most common type of secondary storage device is the *disk drive.* A traditional disk drive stores data by magnetically encoding it onto a spinning circular disk. *Solid-state drives,* which store data in solid-state memory, are increasingly becoming popular. A solid-state drive has no moving parts and operates faster than a traditional disk drive. Most computers have some sort of secondary storage device, either a traditional disk drive or a solid-state drive, mounted inside their case. External storage devices, which connect to one of the computer's communication ports, are also available. External storage devices can be used to create backup copies of important data or to move data to another computer.

In addition to external storage devices, many types of devices have been created for copying data and for moving it to other computers. For example, *USB drives* are small devices that plug into the computer's USB (universal serial bus) port and appear to the system as a disk drive. These drives do not actually contain a disk, however. They store data in a special type of memory known as *flash memory.* USB drives, which are also known as *memory sticks* and *flash drives,* are inexpensive, reliable, and small enough to be carried in your pocket.

Optical devices such as the *CD* (compact disc) and the *DVD* (digital versatile disc) are also popular for data storage. Data is not recorded magnetically on an optical disc, but is encoded as a series of pits on the disc surface. CD and DVD drives use a laser to detect the pits and thus read the encoded data. Optical discs hold large amounts of data, and for that reason, recordable CD and DVD drives are commonly used for creating backup copies of data.

Input Devices

Input is any data the computer collects from people and from other devices. The component that collects the data and sends it to the computer is called an *input device*. Common input devices are the keyboard, mouse, touchscreen, scanner, microphone, and digital camera. Disk drives and optical drives can also be considered input devices, because programs and data are retrieved from them and loaded into the computer's memory.

Output Devices

Output is any data the computer produces for people or for other devices. It might be a sales report, a list of names, or a graphic image. The data is sent to an *output device*, which formats and presents it. Common output devices are video displays and printers. Disk drives can also be considered output devices because the system sends data to them in order to be saved.

Software

If a computer is to function, software is not optional. Everything computer does, from the time you turn the power switch on until you shut the system down, is under the control of software. There are two general categories of software: system software and application software. Most computer programs clearly fit into one of these two categories. Let's take a closer look at each.

System Software

The programs that control and manage the basic operations of a computer are generally referred to as *system software*. System software typically includes the following types of programs:

Operating Systems An *operating system* is the most fundamental set of programs on a computer. The operating system controls the internal operations of the computer's hardware, manages all of the devices connected to the computer, allows data to be saved to and retrieved from storage devices, and allows other programs to run on the computer. Popular operating systems for laptop and desktop computers include Windows, macOS, and Linux. Popular operating systems for mobile devices include Android and iOS.

Utility Programs A *utility program* performs a specialized task that enhances the computer's operation or safeguards data. Examples of utility programs are virus scanners, file compression programs, and data backup programs.

Software Development Tools *Software development tools* are the programs that programmers use to create, modify, and test software. Assemblers, compilers, and interpreters are examples of programs that fall into this category.

Application Software

Programs that make a computer useful for everyday tasks are known as *application software.* These are the programs that people normally spend most of their time running on their computers. Figure 1-1, at the beginning of this chapter, shows screens from two commonly used applications: Microsoft Word, a word processing program, and PowerPoint, a presentation program. Some other examples of application software are spreadsheet programs, email programs, web browsers, and game programs.

Checkpoint

1.1 What is a program?

1.2 What is hardware?

1.3 List the five major components of a computer system.

1.4 What part of the computer actually runs programs?

1.5 What part of the computer serves as a work area to store a program and its data while the program is running?

1.6 What part of the computer holds data for long periods of time, even when there is no power to the computer?

1.7 What part of the computer collects data from people and from other devices?

1.8 What part of the computer formats and presents data for people or other devices?

1.9 What fundamental set of programs control the internal operations of the computer's hardware?

1.10 What do you call a program that performs a specialized task, such as a virus scanner, a file compression program, or a data backup program?

1.11 Word processing programs, spreadsheet programs, email programs, web browsers, and game programs belong to what category of software?

1.3 How Computers Store Data

CONCEPT: All data that is stored in a computer is converted to sequences of 0s and 1s.

A computer's memory is divided into tiny storage locations known as *bytes*. One byte is only enough memory to store a letter of the alphabet or a small number. In order to do anything meaningful, a computer has to have lots of bytes. Most computers today have millions, or even billions, of bytes of memory.

Each byte is divided into eight smaller storage locations known as bits. The term *bit* stands for *binary digit*. Computer scientists usually think of bits as tiny switches that can be either on or off. Bits aren't actual "switches," however, at least not in the conventional sense. In most computer systems, bits are tiny electrical components that can hold either a positive or a negative charge. Computer scientists think of a positive charge as a switch in the *on* position, and a negative charge as a switch in the *off* position. Figure 1-6 shows the way that a computer scientist might think of a byte of memory: as a collection of switches that are each flipped to either the on or off position.

Figure 1-6 Think of a byte as eight switches

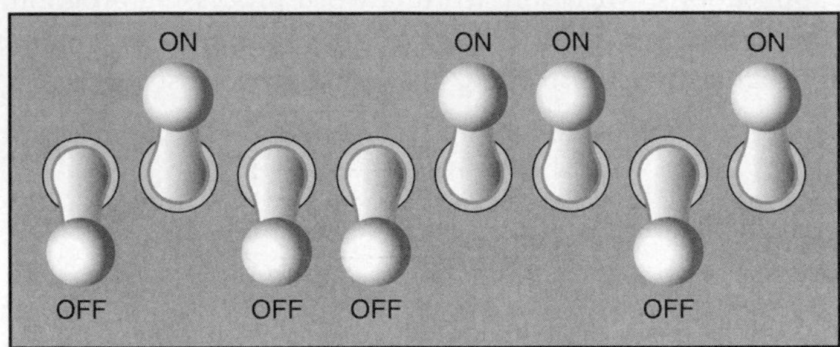

When a piece of data is stored in a byte, the computer sets the eight bits to an on/off pattern that represents the data. For example, the pattern on the left in Figure 1-7 shows how the number 77 would be stored in a byte, and the pattern on the right shows how the letter A would be stored in a byte. We explain below how these patterns are determined.

Figure 1-7 Bit patterns for the number 77 and the letter A

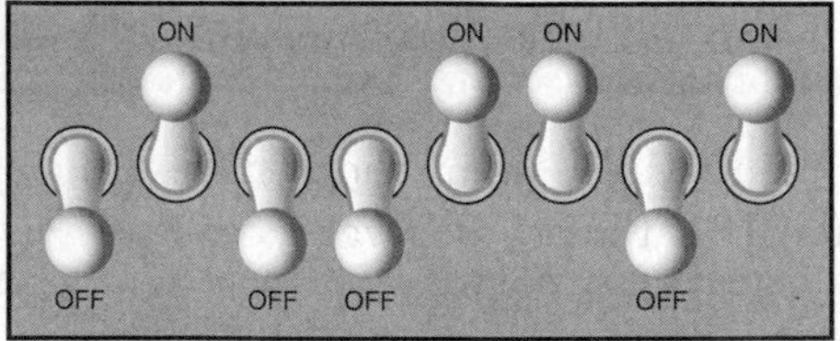

The number 77 stored in a byte.

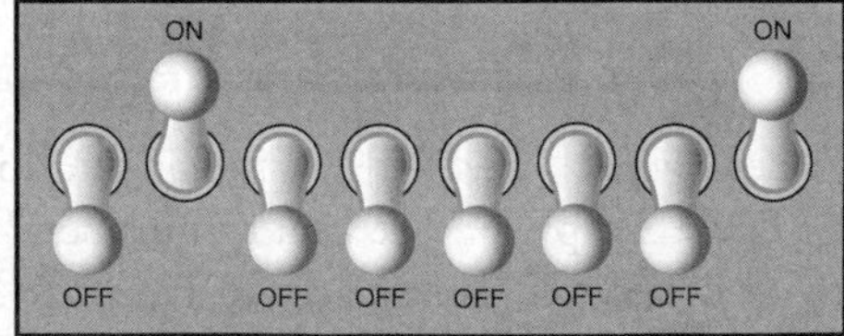

The letter A stored in a byte.

Storing Numbers

A bit can be used in a very limited way to represent numbers. Depending on whether the bit is turned on or off, it can represent one of two different values. In computer systems, a bit that is turned off represents the number 0, and a bit that is turned on represents the number 1. This corresponds perfectly to the *binary numbering system*. In the binary numbering system (or *binary*, as it is usually called), all numeric values are written as sequences of 0s and 1s. Here is an example of a number that is written in binary:

10011101

The position of each digit in a binary number has a value assigned to it. Starting with the rightmost digit and moving left, the position values are 2^0, 2^1, 2^2, 2^3, and so forth, as shown in Figure 1-8. Figure 1-9 shows the same diagram with the position values calculated. Starting with the rightmost digit and moving left, the position values are 1, 2, 4, 8, and so forth.

Figure 1-8 The values of binary digits as powers of 2

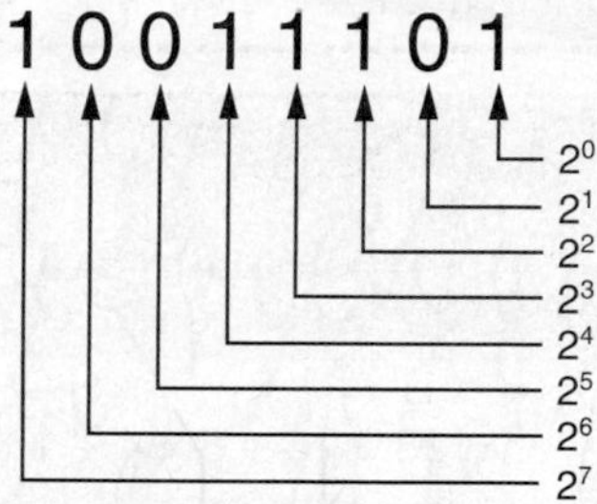

Figure 1-9 The values of binary digits

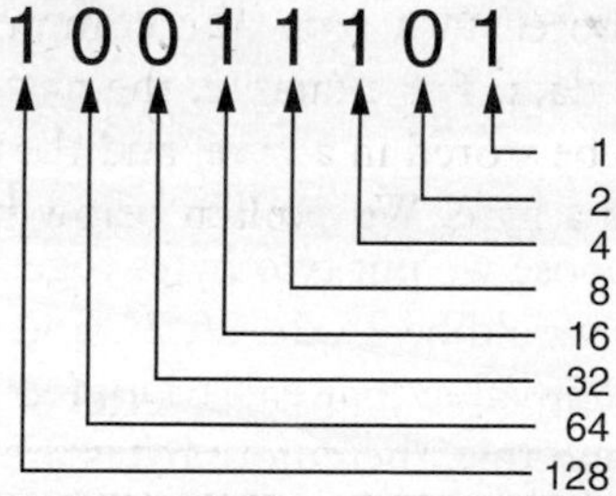

To determine the value of a binary number, you simply add up the position values of all the 1s. For example, in the binary number 10011101, the position values of the 1s are 1, 4, 8, 16, and 128. This is shown in Figure 1-10. The sum of all of these position values is 157. So, the value of the binary number 10011101 is 157.

Figure 1-10 Determining the value of 10011101

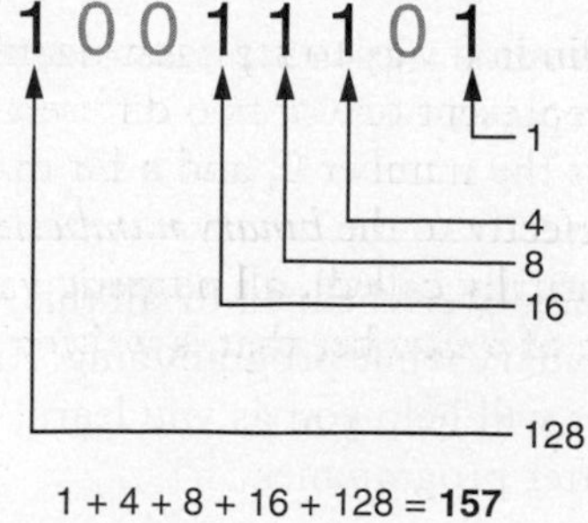

Figure 1-11 shows how you can picture the number 157 stored in a byte of memory. Each 1 is represented by a bit in the on position, and each 0 is represented by a bit in the off position.

Figure 1-11 The bit pattern for 157

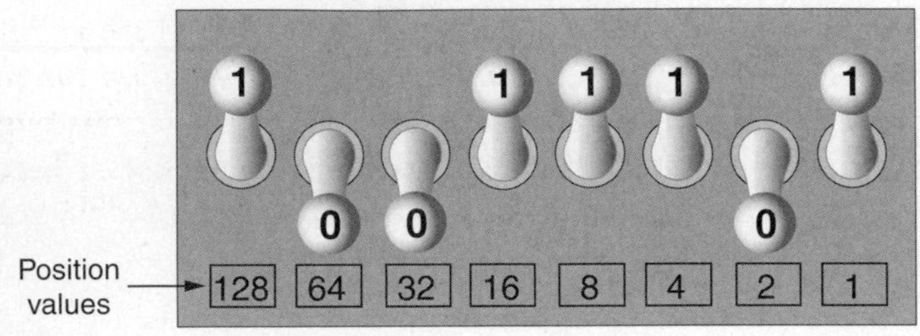

128 + 16 + 8 + 4 + 1 = **157**

When all of the bits in a byte are set to 0 (turned off), then the value of the byte is 0. When all of the bits in a byte are set to 1 (turned on), then the byte holds the largest value that can be stored in it. The largest value that can be stored in a byte is 1 + 2 + 4 + 8 + 16 + 32 + 64 + 128 = 255. This limit exists because there are only eight bits in a byte.

What if you need to store a number larger than 255? The answer is simple: use more than one byte. For example, suppose we put two bytes together. That gives us 16 bits. The position values of those 16 bits would be 2^0, 2^1, 2^2, 2^3, and so forth, up through 21^5. As shown in Figure 1-12, the maximum value that can be stored in two bytes is 65,535. If you need to store a number larger than this, then more bytes are necessary.

Figure 1-12 Two bytes used for a large number

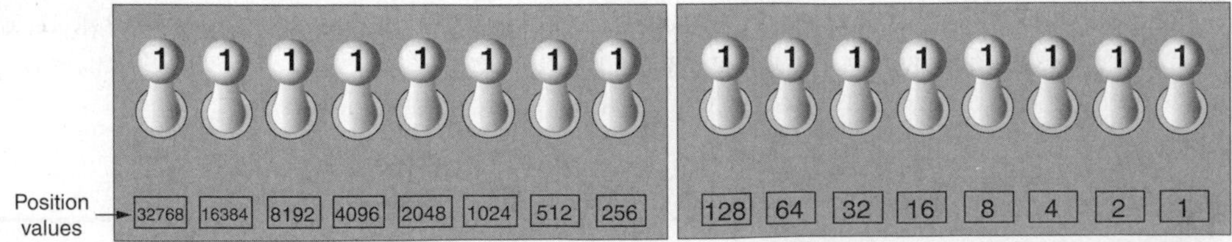

32768 + 16384 + 8192 + 4096 + 2048 + 1024 + 512 + 256 + 128 + 64 + 32 + 16 + 8 + 4 + 2 + 1 = **65535**

TIP: In case you're feeling overwhelmed by all this, relax! You will not have to actually convert numbers to binary while programming. Knowing that this process is taking place inside the computer will help you as you learn, and in the long term this knowledge will make you a better programmer.

Storing Characters

Any piece of data that is stored in a computer's memory must be stored as a binary number. That includes characters, such as letters and punctuation marks. When a character is stored in memory, it is first converted to a numeric code. The numeric code is then stored in memory as a binary number.

Over the years, different coding schemes have been developed to represent characters in computer memory. Historically, the most important of these coding schemes is *ASCII,* which stands for the *American Standard Code for Information Interchange.* ASCII is a set of 128 numeric codes that represent the English letters, various punctuation marks, and other characters. For example, the ASCII code for the uppercase letter A is 65. When you type an uppercase A on your computer keyboard, the number 65 is stored in memory (as a binary number, of course). This is shown in Figure 1-13.

Figure 1-13 The letter A is stored in memory as the number 65

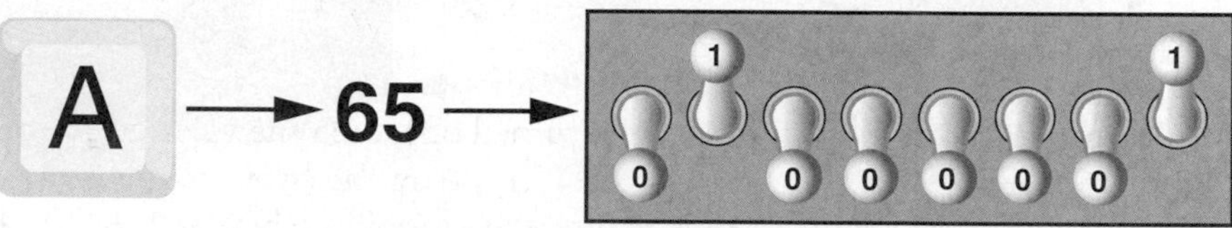

TIP: The acronym ASCII is pronounced "askee."

In case you are curious, the ASCII code for uppercase B is 66, for uppercase C is 67, and so forth. Appendix C shows all of the ASCII codes and the characters they represent.

The ASCII character set was developed in the early 1960s and was eventually adopted by almost all computer manufacturers. ASCII is limited, however, because it defines codes for only 128 characters. To remedy this, the Unicode character set was developed in the early 1990s. *Unicode* is an extensive encoding scheme that is compatible with ASCII, but can also represent characters for many of the languages in the world. Today, Unicode is quickly becoming the standard character set used in the computer industry.

Advanced Number Storage

Earlier, you read about numbers and how they are stored in memory. While reading that section, perhaps it occurred to you that the binary numbering system can be used to represent only integer numbers, beginning with 0. Negative numbers and real numbers (such as 3.14159) cannot be represented using the simple binary numbering technique we discussed.

Computers are able to store negative numbers and real numbers in memory, but to do so they use encoding schemes along with the binary numbering system. Negative numbers are encoded using a technique known as *two's complement,* and real numbers are encoded in *floating-point notation.* You don't need to know how these encoding schemes work, only that they are used to convert negative numbers and real numbers to binary format.

Other Types of Data

Computers are often referred to as digital devices. The term *digital* can be used to describe anything that uses binary numbers. *Digital data* is data that is stored in binary format, and a *digital device* is any device that works with binary data. In this section, we have discussed how numbers and characters are stored in binary, but computers also work with many other types of digital data.

For example, consider the pictures that you take with your digital camera. These images are composed of tiny dots of color known as *pixels*. (The term pixel stands for *picture element*.) As shown in Figure 1-14, each pixel in an image is converted to a numeric code that represents the pixel's color. The numeric code is stored in memory as a binary number.

Figure 1-14 A digital image is stored in binary format

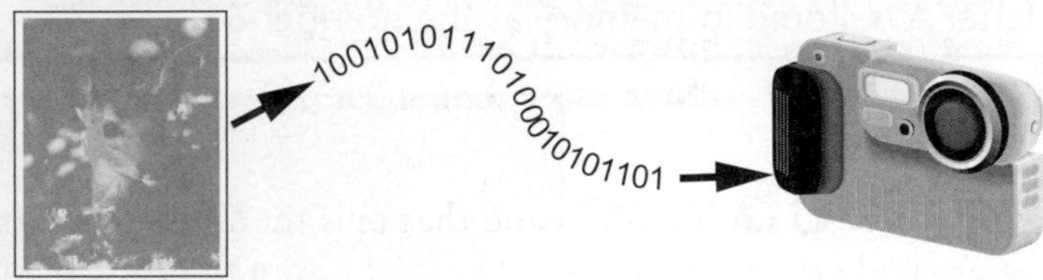

The music that you play on your CD player, iPod, or MP3 player is also digital. A digital song is broken into small pieces known as *samples*. Each sample is converted to a binary number, which can be stored in memory. The more samples that a song is divided into, the more it sounds like the original music when it is played back. A CD quality song is divided into more than 44,000 samples per second!

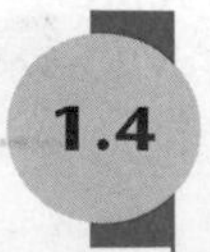

Checkpoint

1.12 What amount of memory is enough to store a letter of the alphabet or a small number?

1.13 What do you call a tiny "switch" that can be set to either on or off?

1.14 In what numbering system are all numeric values written as sequences of 0s and 1s?

1.15 What is the purpose of ASCII?

1.16 What encoding scheme is extensive enough to represent the characters of many of the languages in the world?

1.17 What do the terms "digital data" and "digital device" mean?

1.4 How a Program Works

CONCEPT: A computer's CPU can only understand instructions that are written in machine language. Because people find it very difficult to write entire programs in machine language, other programming languages have been invented.

Earlier, we stated that the CPU is the most important component in a computer because it is the part of the computer that runs programs. Sometimes the CPU is called the "computer's brain" and is described as being "smart." Although these are common metaphors, you should understand that the CPU is not a brain, and it is not smart. The CPU is an electronic device that is designed to do specific things. In particular, the CPU is designed to perform operations such as the following:

- Reading a piece of data from main memory
- Adding two numbers
- Subtracting one number from another number
- Multiplying two numbers
- Dividing one number by another number
- Moving a piece of data from one memory location to another
- Determining whether one value is equal to another value

As you can see from this list, the CPU performs simple operations on pieces of data. The CPU does nothing on its own, however. It has to be told what to do, and that's the purpose of a program. A program is nothing more than a list of instructions that cause the CPU to perform operations.

Each instruction in a program is a command that tells the CPU to perform a specific operation. Here's an example of an instruction that might appear in a program:

```
10110000
```

To you and me, this is only a series of 0s and 1s. To a CPU, however, this is an instruction to perform an operation.[1] It is written in 0s and 1s because CPUs only understand instructions that are written in *machine language,* and machine language instructions always have an underlying binary structure.

A machine language instruction exists for each operation that a CPU is capable of performing. For example, there is an instruction for adding numbers, there is an instruction for subtracting one number from another, and so forth. The entire set of instructions that a CPU can execute is known as the CPU's *instruction set.*

NOTE: There are several microprocessor companies today that manufacture CPUs. Some of the more well-known microprocessor companies are Intel, AMD, and Motorola. If you look carefully at your computer, you might find a tag showing a logo for its microprocessor.

Each brand of microprocessor has its own unique instruction set, which is typically understood only by microprocessors of the same brand. For example, Intel microprocessors understand the same instructions, but they do not understand instructions for Motorola microprocessors.

---

[1] The example shown is an actual instruction for an Intel microprocessor. It tells the microprocessor to move a value into the CPU.

The machine language instruction that was previously shown is an example of only one instruction. It takes a lot more than one instruction, however, for the computer to do anything meaningful. Because the operations that a CPU knows how to perform are so basic in nature, a meaningful task can be accomplished only if the CPU performs many operations. For example, if you want your computer to calculate the amount of interest that you will earn from your savings account this year, the CPU will have to perform a large number of instructions, carried out in the proper sequence. It is not unusual for a program to contain thousands or even millions of machine language instructions.

Programs are usually stored on a secondary storage device such as a disk drive. When you install a program on your computer, the program is typically copied to your computer's disk drive from a CD-ROM, or downloaded from a website.

Although a program can be stored on a secondary storage device such as a disk drive, it has to be copied into main memory, or RAM, each time the CPU executes it. For example, suppose you have a word processing program on your computer's disk. To execute the program, you use the mouse to double-click the program's icon. This causes the program to be copied from the disk into main memory. Then, the computer's CPU executes the copy of the program that is in main memory. This process is illustrated in Figure 1-15.

Figure 1-15 A program is copied into main memory and then executed

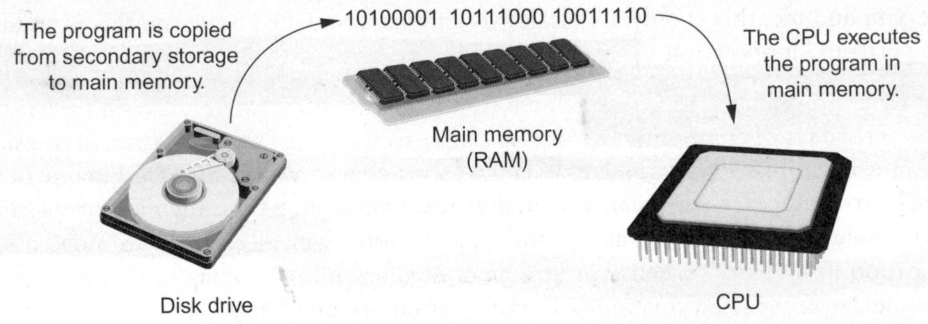

When a CPU executes the instructions in a program, it is engaged in a process that is known as the *fetch-decode-execute cycle*. This cycle, which consists of three steps, is repeated for each instruction in the program. The steps are:

1. **Fetch.** A program is a long sequence of machine language instructions. The first step of the cycle is to fetch, or read, the next instruction from memory into the CPU.
2. **Decode.** A machine language instruction is a binary number that represents a command that tells the CPU to perform an operation. In this step, the CPU decodes the instruction that was just fetched from memory, to determine which operation it should perform.
3. **Execute.** The last step in the cycle is to execute, or perform, the operation.

Figure 1-16 illustrates these steps.

Figure 1-16 The fetch-decode-execute cycle

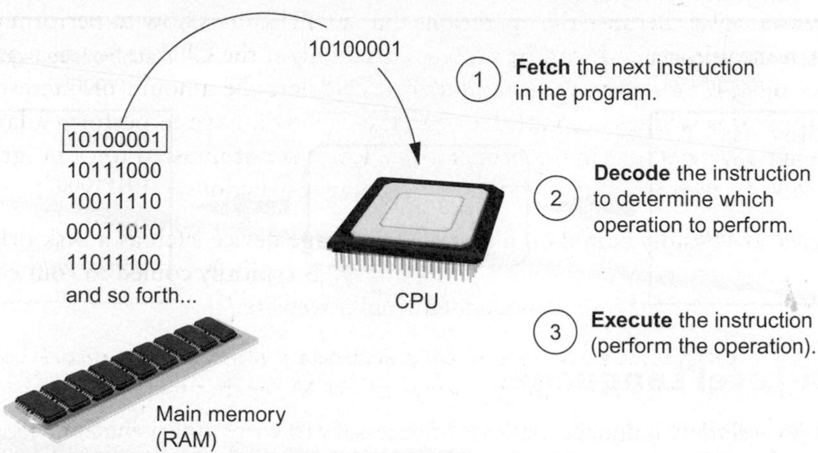

From Machine Language to Assembly Language

Computers can only execute programs that are written in machine language. As previously mentioned, a program can have thousands or even millions of binary instructions, and writing such a program would be very tedious and time consuming. Programming in machine language would also be very difficult, because putting a 0 or a 1 in the wrong place will cause an error.

Although a computer's CPU only understands machine language, it is impractical for people to write programs in machine language. For this reason, *assembly language* was created in the early days of computing[2] as an alternative to machine language. Instead of using binary numbers for instructions, assembly language uses short words that are known as *mnemonics*. For example, in assembly language, the mnemonic `add` typically means to add numbers, `mul` typically means to multiply numbers, and `mov` typically means to move a value to a location in memory. When a programmer uses assembly language to write a program, he or she can write short mnemonics instead of binary numbers.

> **NOTE:** There are many different versions of assembly language. It was mentioned earlier that each brand of CPU has its own machine language instruction set. Each brand of CPU typically has its own assembly language as well.

Assembly language programs cannot be executed by the CPU, however. The CPU only understands machine language, so a special program known as an *assembler* is used to translate an assembly language program to a machine language program. This process is shown in Figure 1-17. The machine language program that is created by the assembler can then be executed by the CPU.

---

[2] The first assembly language was most likely that developed in the 1940s at Cambridge University for use with a historic computer known as the EDSAC.

Figure 1-17 An assembler translates an assembly language program to a machine language program

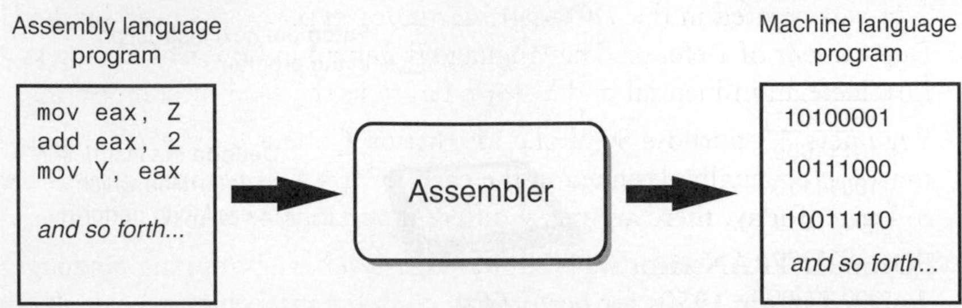

High-Level Languages

Although assembly language makes it unnecessary to write binary machine language instructions, it is not without difficulties. Assembly language is primarily a direct substitute for machine language, and like machine language, it requires that you know a lot about the CPU. Assembly language also requires that you write a large number of instructions for even the simplest program. Because assembly language is so close in nature to machine language, it is referred to as a *low-level language.*

In the 1950s, a new generation of programming languages known as *high-level languages* began to appear. A high-level language allows you to create powerful and complex programs without knowing how the CPU works and without writing large numbers of low-level instructions. In addition, most high-level languages use words that are easy to understand. For example, if a programmer were using COBOL (which was one of the early high-level languages created in the 1950s), he or she would write the following instruction to display the message *Hello world* on the computer screen:

```
DISPLAY "Hello world"
```

Python is a modern, high-level programming language that we will use in this book. In Python you would display the message *Hello world* with the following instruction:

```
print('Hello world')
```

Doing the same thing in assembly language would require several instructions and an intimate knowledge of how the CPU interacts with the computer's output device. As you can see from this example, high-level languages allow programmers to concentrate on the tasks they want to perform with their programs, rather than the details of how the CPU will execute those programs.

Since the 1950s, thousands of high-level languages have been created. Table 1-1 lists several of the more well-known languages.

Key Words, Operators, and Syntax: An Overview

Each high-level language has its own set of predefined words that the programmer must use to write a program. The words that make up a high-level programming language are known as *key words* or *reserved words*. Each key word has a specific meaning, and cannot be used for any other purpose. Table 1-2 shows all of the Python key words.

Table 1-1 Programming languages

Language	Description
Ada	Ada was created in the 1970s, primarily for applications used by the U.S. Department of Defense. The language is named in honor of Countess Ada Lovelace, an influential and historic figure in the field of computing.
BASIC	**B**eginners **A**ll-purpose **S**ymbolic **I**nstruction **C**ode is a general-purpose language that was originally designed in the early 1960s to be simple enough for beginners to learn. Today, there are many different versions of BASIC.
FORTRAN	**FOR**mula **TRAN**slator was the first high-level programming language. It was designed in the 1950s for performing complex mathematical calculations.
COBOL	**C**ommon **B**usiness-**O**riented **L**anguage was created in the 1950s and was designed for business applications.
Pascal	Pascal was created in 1970 and was originally designed for teaching programming. The language was named in honor of the mathematician, physicist, and philosopher Blaise Pascal.
C and C++	C and C++ (pronounced "c plus plus") are powerful, general-purpose languages developed at Bell Laboratories. The C language was created in 1972, and the C++ language was created in 1983.
C#	Pronounced "c sharp." This language was created by Microsoft around the year 2000 for developing applications based on the Microsoft .NET platform.
Java	Java was created by Sun Microsystems in the early 1990s. It can be used to develop programs that run on a single computer or over the Internet from a web server.
JavaScript	JavaScript, created in the 1990s, can be used in Web pages. Despite its name, JavaScript is not related to Java.
Python	Python, the language we use in this book, is a general-purpose language created in the early 1990s. It has become popular in business and academic applications.
Ruby	Ruby is a general-purpose language that was created in the 1990s. It is increasingly becoming a popular language for programs that run on Web servers.
Visual Basic	Visual Basic (commonly known as VB) is a Microsoft programming language and software development environment that allows programmers to create Windows-based applications quickly. VB was originally created in the early 1990s.

Table 1-2 The Python key words

`and`	`del`	`from`	`None`	`True`
`as`	`elif`	`global`	`nonlocal`	`try`
`assert`	`else`	`if`	`not`	`while`
`break`	`except`	`import`	`or`	`with`
`class`	`False`	`in`	`pass`	`yield`
`continue`	`finally`	`is`	`raise`	
`def`	`for`	`lambda`	`return`	

In addition to key words, programming languages have *operators* that perform various operations on data. For example, all programming languages have math operators that perform arithmetic. In Python, as well as most other languages, the + sign is an operator that adds two numbers. The following adds 12 and 75:

```
12 + 75
```

There are numerous other operators in the Python language, many of which you will learn about as you progress through this text.

In addition to key words and operators, each language also has its own *syntax*, which is a set of rules that must be strictly followed when writing a program. The syntax rules dictate how key words, operators, and various punctuation characters must be used in a program. When you are learning a programming language, you must learn the syntax rules for that particular language.

The individual instructions that you use to write a program in a high-level programming language are called *statements*. A programming statement can consist of key words, operators, punctuation, and other allowable programming elements, arranged in the proper sequence to perform an operation.

Compilers and Interpreters

Because the CPU understands only machine language instructions, programs that are written in a high-level language must be translated into machine language. Depending on the language in which a program has been written, the programmer will use either a compiler or an interpreter to make the translation.

A *compiler* is a program that translates a high-level language program into a separate machine language program. The machine language program can then be executed any time it is needed. This is shown in Figure 1-18. As shown in the figure, compiling and executing are two different processes.

Figure 1-18 Compiling a high-level program and executing it

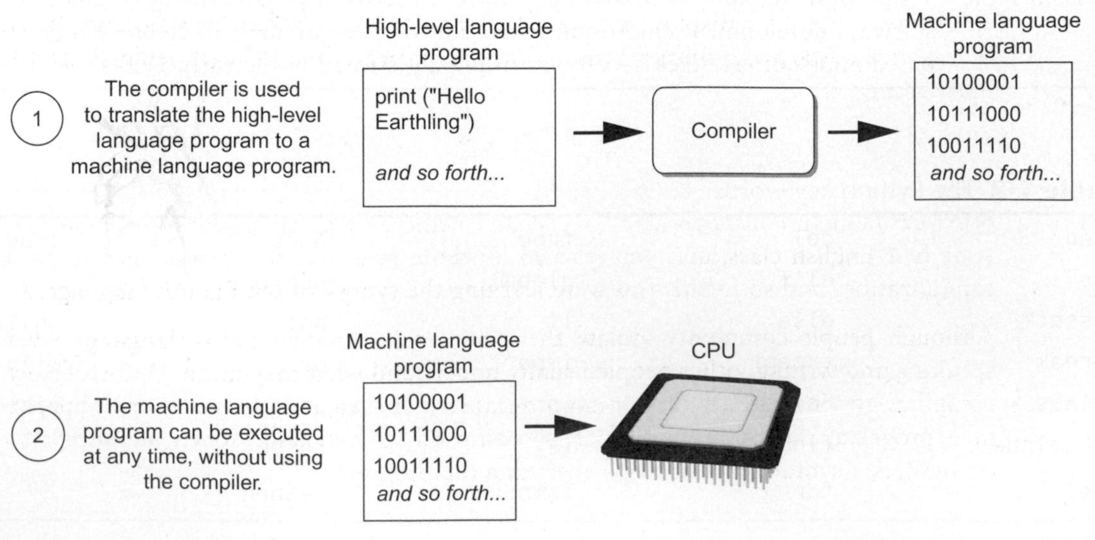

The Python language uses an *interpreter*, which is a program that both translates and executes the instructions in a high-level language program. As the interpreter reads each individual instruction in the program, it converts it to machine language instructions then immediately executes them. This process repeats for every instruction in the program. This process is illustrated in Figure 1-19. Because interpreters combine translation and execution, they typically do not create separate machine language programs.

Figure 1-19 Executing a high-level program with an interpreter

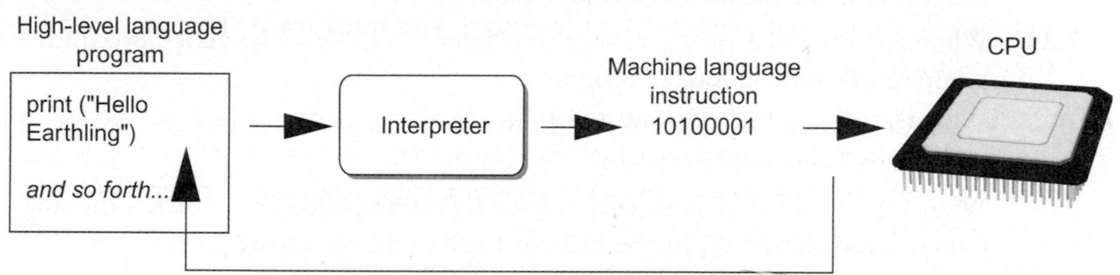

The interpreter translates each high-level instruction to its equivalent machine language instructions then immediately executes them.

This process is repeated for each high-level instruction.

The statements that a programmer writes in a high-level language are called *source code*, or simply *code*. Typically, the programmer types a program's code into a text editor then saves the code in a file on the computer's disk. Next, the programmer uses a compiler to translate the code into a machine language program, or an interpreter to translate and execute the code. If the code contains a syntax error, however, it cannot be translated. A *syntax error* is a mistake such as a misspelled key word, a missing punctuation character, or the incorrect use of an operator. When this happens, the compiler or interpreter displays an error message indicating that the program contains a syntax error. The programmer corrects the error then attempts once again to translate the program.

NOTE: Human languages also have syntax rules. Do you remember when you took your first English class, and you learned all those rules about commas, apostrophes, capitalization, and so forth? You were learning the syntax of the English language.

Although people commonly violate the syntax rules of their native language when speaking and writing, other people usually understand what they mean. Unfortunately, compilers and interpreters do not have this ability. If even a single syntax error appears in a program, the program cannot be compiled or executed. When an interpreter encounters a syntax error, it stops executing the program.

Checkpoint

1.18 A CPU understands instructions that are written only in what language?

1.19 A program has to be copied into what type of memory each time the CPU executes it?

1.20 When a CPU executes the instructions in a program, it is engaged in what process?

1.21 What is assembly language?

1.22 What type of programming language allows you to create powerful and complex programs without knowing how the CPU works?

1.23 Each language has a set of rules that must be strictly followed when writing a program. What is this set of rules called?

1.24 What do you call a program that translates a high-level language program into a separate machine language program?

1.25 What do you call a program that both translates and executes the instructions in a high-level language program?

1.26 What type of mistake is usually caused by a misspelled key word, a missing punctuation character, or the incorrect use of an operator?

1.5 Using Python

CONCEPT: The Python interpreter can run Python programs that are saved in files or interactively execute Python statements that are typed at the keyboard. Python comes with a program named IDLE that simplifies the process of writing, executing, and testing programs.

Installing Python

Before you can try any of the programs shown in this book, or write any programs of your own, you need to make sure that Python is installed on your computer and properly configured. If you are working in a computer lab, this has probably been done already. If you are using your own computer, you can follow the instructions in Appendix A to download and install Python.

The Python Interpreter

You learned earlier that Python is an interpreted language. When you install the Python language on your computer, one of the items that is installed is the Python interpreter. The *Python interpreter* is a program that can read Python programming statements and execute them. (Sometimes, we will refer to the Python interpreter simply as the interpreter.)

You can use the interpreter in two modes: interactive mode and script mode. In *interactive mode,* the interpreter waits for you to type Python statements on the keyboard. Once you type a statement, the interpreter executes it and then waits for you to type another statement. In *script mode,* the interpreter reads the contents of a file that contains Python statements. Such a file is known as a *Python program* or a *Python script.* The interpreter executes each statement in the Python program as it reads it.

Interactive Mode

Once Python has been installed and set up on your system, you start the interpreter in interactive mode by going to the operating system's command line and typing the following command:

```
python
```

If you are using Windows, you can alternatively type *python* in the Windows search box. In the search results, you will see a program named something like *Python 3.5*. (The "3.5" is the version of Python that is installed. At the time this is being written, Python 3.5 is the latest version.) Clicking this item will start the Python interpreter in interactive mode.

NOTE: When the Python interpreter is running in interactive mode, it is commonly called the *Python shell*.

When the Python interpreter starts in interactive mode, you will see something like the following displayed in a console window:

```
Python 3.5.1 (v3.5.1:37a07cee5969, Dec  6 2015, 01:38:48)
[MSC v.1900 32 bit (Intel)] on win32
Type "help", "copyright", "credits" or "license"
for more information.
>>>
```

The >>> that you see is a prompt that indicates the interpreter is waiting for you to type a Python statement. Let's try it out. One of the simplest things that you can do in Python is print a message on the screen. For example, the following statement prints the message *Python programming is fun!* on the screen:

```
print('Python programming is fun!')
```

You can think of this as a command that you are sending to the Python interpreter. If you type the statement exactly as it is shown, the message *Python programming is fun!* is printed on the screen. Here is an example of how you type this statement at the interpreter's prompt:

```
>>> print('Python programming is fun!') [Enter]
```

After typing the statement, you press the Enter key, and the Python interpreter executes the statement, as shown here:

```
>>> print('Python programming is fun!') [Enter]
Python programming is fun!
>>>
```

After the message is displayed, the >>> prompt appears again, indicating the interpreter is waiting for you to enter another statement. Let's look at another example. In the following sample session, we have entered two statements:

```
>>> print('To be or not to be') Enter
To be or not to be
>>> print('That is the question.') Enter
That is the question.
>>>
```

If you incorrectly type a statement in interactive mode, the interpreter will display an error message. This will make interactive mode useful to you while you learn Python. As you learn new parts of the Python language, you can try them out in interactive mode and get immediate feedback from the interpreter.

To quit the Python interpreter in interactive mode on a Windows computer, press Ctrl-Z (pressing both keys together) followed by Enter. On a Mac, Linux, or UNIX computer, press Ctrl-D.

NOTE: In Chapter 2, we will discuss the details of statements like the ones previously shown. If you want to try them now in interactive mode, make sure you type them exactly as shown.

Writing Python Programs and Running Them in Script Mode

Although interactive mode is useful for testing code, the statements that you enter in interactive mode are not saved as a program. They are simply executed and their results displayed on the screen. If you want to save a set of Python statements as a program, you save those statements in a file. Then, to execute the program, you use the Python interpreter in script mode.

For example, suppose you want to write a Python program that displays the following three lines of text:

```
Nudge nudge
Wink wink
Know what I mean?
```

To write the program you would use a simple text editor like Notepad (which is installed on all Windows computers) to create a file containing the following statements:

```
print('Nudge nudge')
print('Wink wink')
print('Know what I mean?')
```

NOTE: It is possible to use a word processor to create a Python program, but you must be sure to save the program as a plain text file. Otherwise, the Python interpreter will not be able to read its contents.

When you save a Python program, you give it a name that ends with the .py extension, which identifies it as a Python program. For example, you might save the program previously shown with the name test.py. To run the program, you would go to the directory in which the file is saved and type the following command at the operating system command line:

```
python test.py
```

This starts the Python interpreter in script mode and causes it to execute the statements in the file test.py. When the program finishes executing, the Python interpreter exits.

The IDLE Programming Environment

VideoNote **Using Interactive Mode in IDLE**

The previous sections described how the Python interpreter can be started in interactive mode or script mode at the operating system command line. As an alternative, you can use an *integrated development environment*, which is a single program that gives you all of the tools you need to write, execute, and test a program.

Recent versions of Python include a program named *IDLE*, which is automatically installed when the Python language is installed. (IDLE stands for Integrated DeveLopment Environment.) When you run IDLE, the window shown in Figure 1-20 appears. Notice the >>> prompt appears in the IDLE window, indicating that the interpreter is running in interactive mode. You can type Python statements at this prompt and see them executed in the IDLE window.

IDLE also has a built-in text editor with features specifically designed to help you write Python programs. For example, the IDLE editor "colorizes" code so key words and other

Figure 1-20 IDLE

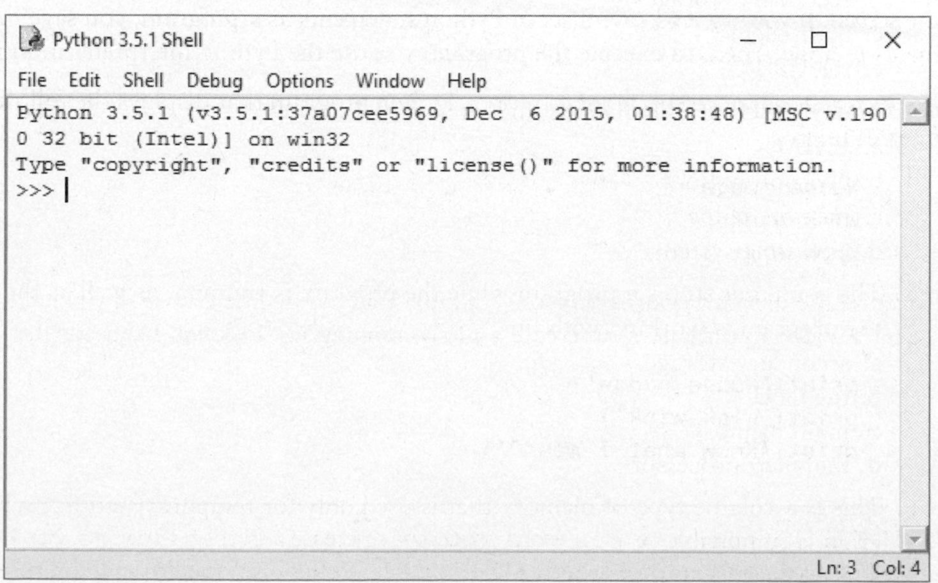

parts of a program are displayed in their own distinct colors. This helps make programs easier to read. In IDLE, you can write programs, save them to disk, and execute them. Appendix B provides a quick introduction to IDLE and leads you through the process of creating, saving, and executing a Python program.

NOTE: Although IDLE is installed with Python, there are several other Python IDEs available. Your instructor might prefer that you use a specific one in class.

Review Questions

Multiple Choice

1. A(n) __________ is a set of instructions that a computer follows to perform a task.
   a. compiler
   b. program
   c. interpreter
   d. programming language
2. The physical devices that a computer is made of are referred to as __________.
   a. hardware
   b. software
   c. the operating system
   d. tools
3. The part of a computer that runs programs is called __________.
   a. RAM
   b. secondary storage
   c. main memory
   e. the CPU
4. Today, CPUs are small chips known as __________.
   a. ENIACs
   b. microprocessors
   c. memory chips
   d. operating systems
5. The computer stores a program while the program is running, as well as the data that the program is working with, in __________.
   a. secondary storage
   b. the CPU
   c. main memory
   d. the microprocessor
6. This is a volatile type of memory that is used only for temporary storage while a program is running.
   a. RAM
   b. secondary storage
   c. the disk drive
   d. the USB drive

7. A type of memory that can hold data for long periods of time, even when there is no power to the computer, is called __________.
   a. RAM
   b. main memory
   c. secondary storage
   d. CPU storage
8. A component that collects data from people or other devices and sends it to the computer is called __________.
   a. an output device
   b. an input device
   c. a secondary storage device
   d. main memory
9. A video display is a(n) __________ device.
   a. output
   b. input
   c. secondary storage
   d. main memory
10. A __________ is enough memory to store a letter of the alphabet or a small number.
   a. byte
   b. bit
   c. switch
   d. transistor
11. A byte is made up of eight __________.
   a. CPUs
   b. instructions
   c. variables
   d. bits
12. In the __________ numbering system, all numeric values are written as sequences of 0s and 1s.
   a. hexadecimal
   b. binary
   c. octal
   d. decimal
13. A bit that is turned off represents the following value: __________.
   a. 1
   b. –1
   c. 0
   d. "no"
14. A set of 128 numeric codes that represent the English letters, various punctuation marks, and other characters is __________.
   a. binary numbering
   b. ASCII
   c. Unicode
   d. ENIAC

15. An extensive encoding scheme that can represent characters for many languages in the world is __________.
    a. binary numbering
    b. ASCII
    c. Unicode
    d. ENIAC
16. Negative numbers are encoded using the __________ technique.
    a. two's complement
    b. floating point
    c. ASCII
    d. Unicode
17. Real numbers are encoded using the __________ technique.
    a. two's complement
    b. floating point
    c. ASCII
    d. Unicode
18. The tiny dots of color that digital images are composed of are called __________.
    a. bits
    b. bytes
    c. color packets
    d. pixels
19. If you were to look at a machine language program, you would see __________.
    a. Python code
    b. a stream of binary numbers
    c. English words
    d. circuits
20. In the __________ part of the fetch-decode-execute cycle, the CPU determines which operation it should perform.
    a. fetch
    b. decode
    c. execute
    d. deconstruct
21. Computers can only execute programs that are written in __________.
    a. Java
    b. assembly language
    c. machine language
    d. Python
22. The __________ translates an assembly language program to a machine language program.
    a. assembler
    b. compiler
    c. translator
    d. interpreter

23. The words that make up a high-level programming language are called __________.
    a. binary instructions
    b. mnemonics
    c. commands
    d. key words
24. The rules that must be followed when writing a program are called __________.
    a. syntax
    b. punctuation
    c. key words
    d. operators
25. A(n) __________ program translates a high-level language program into a separate machine language program.
    a. assembler
    b. compiler
    c. translator
    d. utility

True or False

1. Today, CPUs are huge devices made of electrical and mechanical components such as vacuum tubes and switches.
2. Main memory is also known as RAM.
3. Any piece of data that is stored in a computer's memory must be stored as a binary number.
4. Images, like the ones created with your digital camera, cannot be stored as binary numbers.
5. Machine language is the only language that a CPU understands.
6. Assembly language is considered a high-level language.
7. An interpreter is a program that both translates and executes the instructions in a high-level language program.
8. A syntax error does not prevent a program from being compiled and executed.
9. Windows, Linux, Android, iOS, and macOS are all examples of application software.
10. Word processing programs, spreadsheet programs, email programs, web browsers, and games are all examples of utility programs.

Short Answer

1. Why is the CPU the most important component in a computer?
2. What number does a bit that is turned on represent? What number does a bit that is turned off represent?
3. What would you call a device that works with binary data?
4. What are the words that make up a high-level programming language called?
5. What are the short words that are used in assembly language called?
6. What is the difference between a compiler and an interpreter?
7. What type of software controls the internal operations of the computer's hardware?

Exercises

1. To make sure that you can interact with the Python interpreter, try the following steps on your computer:

   - Start the Python interpreter in interactive mode.
   - At the >>> prompt, type the following statement then press Enter:

   ```
   print('This is a test of the Python interpreter.') Enter
   ```

   - After pressing the Enter key, the interpreter will execute the statement. If you typed everything correctly, your session should look like this:

   ```
   >>> print('This is a test of the Python interpreter.') Enter
   This is a test of the Python interpreter.
   >>>
   ```

   - If you see an error message, enter the statement again, and make sure you type it exactly as shown.
   - Exit the Python interpreter. (In Windows, press Ctrl-Z followed by Enter. On other systems, press Ctrl-D.)

VideoNote
Performing Exercise 2

2. To make sure that you can interact with IDLE, try the following steps on your computer:

   - Start IDLE. To do this in Windows, type *IDLE* in the Windows search box. Click the IDLE desktop app, which will be displayed in the search results.
   - When IDLE starts, it should appear similar to the window previously shown in Figure 1-20. At the >>> prompt, type the following statement then press Enter:

   ```
   print('This is a test of IDLE.') Enter
   ```

   - After pressing the Enter key, the Python interpreter will execute the statement. If you typed everything correctly, your session should look like this:

   ```
   >>> print('This is a test of IDLE.') Enter
   This is a test of IDLE.
   >>>
   ```

   - If you see an error message, enter the statement again and make sure you type it exactly as shown.
   - Exit IDLE by clicking File, then Exit (or pressing Ctrl-Q on the keyboard).

3. Use what you've learned about the binary numbering system in this chapter to convert the following decimal numbers to binary:

   11
   65
   100
   255

4. Use what you've learned about the binary numbering system in this chapter to convert the following binary numbers to decimal:

   1101
   1000
   101011

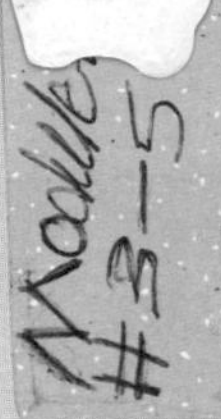

5. Look at the ASCII chart in Appendix C and determine the codes for each letter of your first name.
6. Use the Internet to research the history of the Python programming language, and answer the following questions:
   - Who was the creator of Python?
   - When was Python created?
   - In the Python programming community, the person who created Python is commonly referred to as the "BDFL." What does this mean?

CHAPTER 2

Input, Processing, and Output

TOPICS

2.1 Designing a Program

CONCEPT: Programs must be carefully designed before they are written. During the design process, programmers use tools such as pseudocode and flowcharts to create models of programs.

The Program Development Cycle

In Chapter 1, you learned that programmers typically use high-level languages such as Python to create programs. There is much more to creating a program than writing code, however. The process of creating a program that works correctly typically requires the five phases shown in Figure 2-1. The entire process is known as the *program development cycle*.

Figure 2-1 The program development cycle

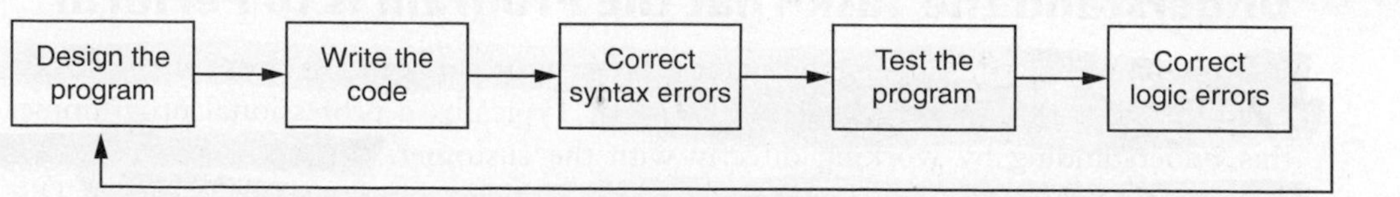

Let's take a closer look at each stage in the cycle.

1. **Design the Program.** All professional programmers will tell you that a program should be carefully designed before the code is actually written. When programmers begin a

new project, they should never jump right in and start writing code as the first step. They start by creating a design of the program. There are several ways to design a program, and later in this section, we will discuss some techniques that you can use to design your Python programs.

2. **Write the Code.** After designing the program, the programmer begins writing code in a high-level language such as Python. Recall from Chapter 1 that each language has its own rules, known as syntax, that must be followed when writing a program. A language's syntax rules dictate things such as how key words, operators, and punctuation characters can be used. A syntax error occurs if the programmer violates any of these rules.
3. **Correct Syntax Errors.** If the program contains a syntax error, or even a simple mistake such as a misspelled key word, the compiler or interpreter will display an error message indicating what the error is. Virtually all code contains syntax errors when it is first written, so the programmer will typically spend some time correcting these. Once all of the syntax errors and simple typing mistakes have been corrected, the program can be compiled and translated into a machine language program (or executed by an interpreter, depending on the language being used).
4. **Test the Program.** Once the code is in an executable form, it is then tested to determine whether any logic errors exist. A *logic error* is a mistake that does not prevent the program from running, but causes it to produce incorrect results. (Mathematical mistakes are common causes of logic errors.)
5. **Correct Logic Errors.** If the program produces incorrect results, the programmer *debugs* the code. This means that the programmer finds and corrects logic errors in the program. Sometimes during this process, the programmer discovers that the program's original design must be changed. In this event, the program development cycle starts over and continues until no errors can be found.

More About the Design Process

The process of designing a program is arguably the most important part of the cycle. You can think of a program's design as its foundation. If you build a house on a poorly constructed foundation, eventually you will find yourself doing a lot of work to fix the house! A program's design should be viewed no differently. If your program is designed poorly, eventually you will find yourself doing a lot of work to fix the program.

The process of designing a program can be summarized in the following two steps:

1. Understand the task that the program is to perform.
2. Determine the steps that must be taken to perform the task.

Let's take a closer look at each of these steps.

Understand the Task That the Program Is to Perform

It is essential that you understand what a program is supposed to do before you can determine the steps that the program will perform. Typically, a professional programmer gains this understanding by working directly with the customer. We use the term *customer* to describe the person, group, or organization that is asking you to write a program. This could be a customer in the traditional sense of the word, meaning someone who is paying you to write a program. It could also be your boss, or the manager of a department within your company. Regardless of whom it is, the customer will be relying on your program to perform an important task.

To get a sense of what a program is supposed to do, the programmer usually interviews the customer. During the interview, the customer will describe the task that the program should perform, and the programmer will ask questions to uncover as many details as possible about the task. A follow-up interview is usually needed because customers rarely mention everything they want during the initial meeting, and programmers often think of additional questions.

The programmer studies the information that was gathered from the customer during the interviews and creates a list of different software requirements. A *software requirement* is simply a single task that the program must perform in order to satisfy the customer. Once the customer agrees that the list of requirements is complete, the programmer can move to the next phase.

TIP: If you choose to become a professional software developer, your customer will be anyone who asks you to write programs as part of your job. As long as you are a student, however, your customer is your instructor! In every programming class that you will take, it's practically guaranteed that your instructor will assign programming problems for you to complete. For your academic success, make sure that you understand your instructor's requirements for those assignments and write your programs accordingly.

Determine the Steps That Must Be Taken to Perform the Task

Once you understand the task that the program will perform, you begin by breaking down the task into a series of steps. This is similar to the way you would break down a task into a series of steps that another person can follow. For example, suppose someone asks you how to boil water. You might break down that task into a series of steps as follows:

1. Pour the desired amount of water into a pot.
2. Put the pot on a stove burner.
3. Turn the burner to high.
4. Watch the water until you see large bubbles rapidly rising. When this happens, the water is boiling.

This is an example of an *algorithm,* which is a set of well-defined logical steps that must be taken to perform a task. Notice the steps in this algorithm are sequentially ordered. Step 1 should be performed before step 2, and so on. If a person follows these steps exactly as they appear, and in the correct order, he or she should be able to boil water successfully.

A programmer breaks down the task that a program must perform in a similar way. An algorithm is created, which lists all of the logical steps that must be taken. For example, suppose you have been asked to write a program to calculate and display the gross pay for an hourly paid employee. Here are the steps that you would take:

1. Get the number of hours worked.
2. Get the hourly pay rate.
3. Multiply the number of hours worked by the hourly pay rate.
4. Display the result of the calculation that was performed in step 3.

Of course, this algorithm isn't ready to be executed on the computer. The steps in this list have to be translated into code. Programmers commonly use two tools to help them accomplish this: pseudocode and flowcharts. Let's look at each of these in more detail.

Pseudocode

Because small mistakes like misspelled words and forgotten punctuation characters can cause syntax errors, programmers have to be mindful of such small details when writing code. For this reason, programmers find it helpful to write a program in pseudocode (pronounced "sue doe code") before they write it in the actual code of a programming language such as Python.

The word "pseudo" means fake, so *pseudocode* is fake code. It is an informal language that has no syntax rules and is not meant to be compiled or executed. Instead, programmers use pseudocode to create models, or "mock-ups," of programs. Because programmers don't have to worry about syntax errors while writing pseudocode, they can focus all of their attention on the program's design. Once a satisfactory design has been created with pseudocode, the pseudocode can be translated directly to actual code. Here is an example of how you might write pseudocode for the pay calculating program that we discussed earlier:

Input the hours worked
Input the hourly pay rate
Calculate gross pay as hours worked multiplied by pay rate
Display the gross pay

Each statement in the pseudocode represents an operation that can be performed in Python. For example, Python can read input that is typed on the keyboard, perform mathematical calculations, and display messages on the screen.

Flowcharts

Flowcharting is another tool that programmers use to design programs. A *flowchart* is a diagram that graphically depicts the steps that take place in a program. Figure 2-2 shows how you might create a flowchart for the pay calculating program.

Notice there are three types of symbols in the flowchart: ovals, parallelograms, and a rectangle. Each of these symbols represents a step in the program, as described here:

- The ovals, which appear at the top and bottom of the flowchart, are called *terminal symbols*. The *Start* terminal symbol marks the program's starting point, and the *End* terminal symbol marks the program's ending point.
- Parallelograms are used as *input symbols* and *output symbols*. They represent steps in which the program reads input or displays output.
- Rectangles are used as *processing symbols*. They represent steps in which the program performs some process on data, such as a mathematical calculation.

The symbols are connected by arrows that represent the "flow" of the program. To step through the symbols in the proper order, you begin at the *Start* terminal and follow the arrows until you reach the *End* terminal.

Checkpoint

2.1 Who is a programmer's customer?

2.2 What is a software requirement?

2.3 What is an algorithm?

2.4 What is pseudocode?

Figure 2-2 Flowchart for the pay calculating program

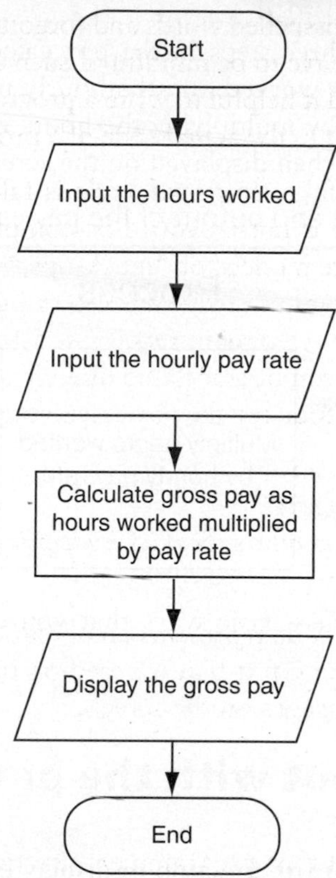

2.5 What is a flowchart?

2.6 What do each of the following symbols mean in a flowchart?
- Oval
- Parallelogram
- Rectangle

2.2 Input, Processing, and Output

CONCEPT: Input is data that the program receives. When a program receives data, it usually processes it by performing some operation with it. The result of the operation is sent out of the program as output.

Computer programs typically perform the following three-step process:

1. Input is received.
2. Some process is performed on the input.
3. Output is produced.

Input is any data that the program receives while it is running. One common form of input is data that is typed on the keyboard. Once input is received, some process, such as a mathematical calculation, is usually performed on it. The results of the process are then sent out of the program as output.

Figure 2-3 illustrates these three steps in the pay calculating program that we discussed earlier. The number of hours worked and the hourly pay rate are provided as input. The program processes this data by multiplying the hours worked by the hourly pay rate. The results of the calculation are then displayed on the screen as output.

Figure 2-3 The input, processing, and output of the pay calculating program

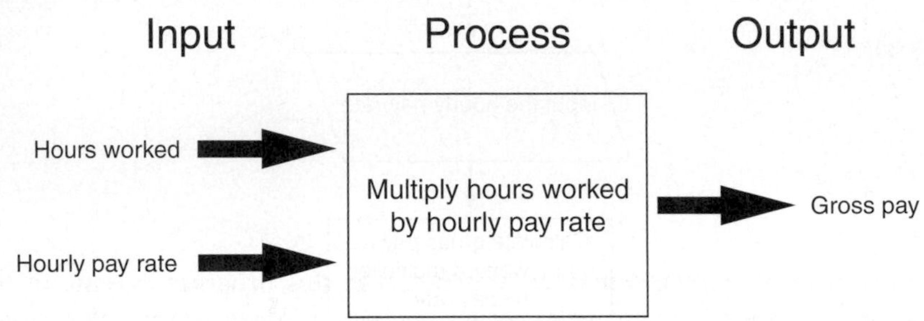

In this chapter, we will discuss basic ways that you can perform input, processing, and output using Python.

2.3 Displaying Output with the `print` Function

CONCEPT: You use the `print` function to display output in a Python program.

VideoNote The `print` Function

A *function* is a piece of prewritten code that performs an operation. Python has numerous built-in functions that perform various operations. Perhaps the most fundamental built-in function is the `print` function, which displays output on the screen. Here is an example of a statement that executes the `print` function:

```
print('Hello world')
```

In interactive mode, if you type this statement and press the Enter key, the message *Hello world* is displayed. Here is an example:

```
>>> print('Hello world') Enter
Hello world
>>>
```

When programmers execute a function, they say that they are *calling* the function. When you call the `print` function, you type the word `print`, followed by a set of parentheses. Inside the parentheses, you type an *argument*, which is the data that you want displayed on the screen. In the previous example, the argument is `'Hello world'`. Notice the quote marks are not displayed when the statement executes. The quote marks simply specify the beginning and the end of the text that you wish to display.

Suppose your instructor tells you to write a program that displays your name and address on the computer screen. Program 2-1 shows an example of such a program, with the output that it will produce when it runs. (The line numbers that appear in a program listing in this book are *not* part of the program. We use the line numbers in our discussion to refer to parts of the program.)

Program 2-1 (output.py)

```
print('Kate Austen')
print('123 Full Circle Drive')
print('Asheville, NC 28899')
```

Program Output

```
Kate Austen
123 Full Circle Drive
Asheville, NC 28899
```

It is important to understand that the statements in this program execute in the order that they appear, from the top of the program to the bottom. When you run this program, the first statement will execute, followed by the second statement, and followed by the third statement.

Strings and String Literals

Programs almost always work with data of some type. For example, Program 2-1 uses the following three pieces of data:

```
'Kate Austen'
'123 Full Circle Drive
'Asheville, NC 28899'
```

These pieces of data are sequences of characters. In programming terms, a sequence of characters that is used as data is called a *string*. When a string appears in the actual code of a program, it is called a *string literal*. In Python code, string literals must be enclosed in quote marks. As mentioned earlier, the quote marks simply mark where the string data begins and ends.

In Python, you can enclose string literals in a set of single-quote marks (`'`) or a set of double-quote marks (`"`). The string literals in Program 2-1 are enclosed in single-quote marks, but the program could also be written as shown in Program 2-2.

Program 2-2 (double_quotes.py)

```
print("Kate Austen")
print("123 Full Circle Drive")
print("Asheville, NC 28899")
```

Program Output

```
Kate Austen
123 Full Circle Drive
Asheville, NC 28899
```

If you want a string literal to contain either a single-quote or an apostrophe as part of the string, you can enclose the string literal in double-quote marks. For example, Program 2-3 prints two strings that contain apostrophes.

Program 2-3 (apostrophe.py)

```
print("Don't fear!")
print("I'm here!")
```

Program Output

```
Don't fear!
I'm here!
```

Likewise, you can use single-quote marks to enclose a string literal that contains double-quotes as part of the string. Program 2-4 shows an example.

Program 2-4 (display_quote.py)

```
print('Your assignment is to read "Hamlet" by tomorrow.')
```

Program Output

```
Your assignment is to read "Hamlet" by tomorrow.
```

Python also allows you to enclose string literals in triple quotes (either `"""` or `'''`). Triple-quoted strings can contain both single quotes and double quotes as part of the string. The following statement shows an example:

```
print("""I'm reading "Hamlet" tonight.""")
```

This statement will print

```
I'm reading "Hamlet" tonight.
```

Triple quotes can also be used to surround multiline strings, something for which single and double quotes cannot be used. Here is an example:

```
print("""One
Two
Three""")
```

This statement will print

```
One
Two
Three
```

Checkpoint

2.7 Write a statement that displays your name.

2.8 Write a statement that displays the following text:

```
Python's the best!
```

2.9 Write a statement that displays the following text:

```
The cat said "meow."
```

2.4 Comments

CONCEPT: Comments are notes of explanation that document lines or sections of a program. Comments are part of the program, but the Python interpreter ignores them. They are intended for people who may be reading the source code.

Comments are short notes placed in different parts of a program, explaining how those parts of the program work. Although comments are a critical part of a program, they are ignored by the Python interpreter. Comments are intended for any person reading a program's code, not the computer.

In Python, you begin a comment with the # character. When the Python interpreter sees a # character, it ignores everything from that character to the end of the line. For example, look at Program 2-5. Lines 1 and 2 are comments that briefly explain the program's purpose.

Program 2-5 (comment1.py)

```
1 # This program displays a person's
2 # name and address.
3 print('Kate Austen')
4 print('123 Full Circle Drive')
5 print('Asheville, NC 28899')
```

Program Output

```
Kate Austen
123 Full Circle Drive
Asheville, NC 28899
```

Programmers commonly write end-line comments in their code. An *end-line comment* is a comment that appears at the end of a line of code. It usually explains the statement that appears in that line. Program 2-6 shows an example. Each line ends with a comment that briefly explains what the line does.

Program 2-6 (comment2.py)

```
print('Kate Austen')              # Display the name.
print('123 Full Circle Drive')    # Display the address.
print('Asheville, NC 28899')      # Display the city, state, and ZIP.
```

Program Output

```
Kate Austen
123 Full Circle Drive
Asheville, NC 28899
```

As a beginning programmer, you might be resistant to the idea of liberally writing comments in your programs. After all, it can seem more productive to write code that actually does something! It is crucial that you take the extra time to write comments, however. They will almost certainly save you and others time in the future when you have to modify or debug the program. Large and complex programs can be almost impossible to read and understand if they are not properly commented.

2.5 Variables

CONCEPT: **A variable is a name that represents a value stored in the computer's memory.**

Programs usually store data in the computer's memory and perform operations on that data. For example, consider the typical online shopping experience: you browse a website and add the items that you want to purchase to the shopping cart. As you add items to the shopping cart, data about those items is stored in memory. Then, when you click the checkout button, a program running on the website's computer calculates the cost of all the items you have in your shopping cart, applicable sales taxes, shipping costs, and the total of all these charges. When the program performs these calculations, it stores the results in the computer's memory.

Programs use variables to access and manipulate data that is stored in memory. A *variable* is a name that represents a value in the computer's memory. For example, a program that calculates the sales tax on a purchase might use the variable name `tax` to represent that value in memory. And a program that calculates the distance between two cities might use the variable name `distance` to represent that value in memory. When a variable represents a value in the computer's memory, we say that the variable *references* the value.

Creating Variables with Assignment Statements

You use an *assignment statement* to create a variable and make it reference a piece of data. Here is an example of an assignment statement:

```
age = 25
```

After this statement executes, a variable named `age` will be created, and it will reference the value 25. This concept is shown in Figure 2-4. In the figure, think of the value 25 as being stored somewhere in the computer's memory. The arrow that points from `age` to the value 25 indicates that the name `age` references the value.

Figure 2-4 The age variable references the value 25

An assignment statement is written in the following general format:

```
variable = expression
```

The equal sign (=) is known as the *assignment operator*. In the general format, `variable` is the name of a variable and `expression` is a value, or any piece of code that results in a value. After an assignment statement executes, the variable listed on the left side of the = operator will reference the value given on the right side of the = operator.

To experiment with variables, you can type assignment statements in interactive mode, as shown here:

```
>>> width = 10 [Enter]
>>> length = 5 [Enter]
>>>
```

The first statement creates a variable named `width` and assigns it the value 10. The second statement creates a variable named `length` and assigns it the value 5. Next, you can use the `print` function to display the values referenced by these variables, as shown here:

```
>>> print(width) [Enter]
10
>>> print(length) [Enter]
5
>>>
```

When you pass a variable as an argument to the `print` function, you do not enclose the variable name in quote marks. To demonstrate why, look at the following interactive session:

```
>>> print('width') [Enter]
width
>>> print(width) [Enter]
10
>>>
```

In the first statement, you passed `'width'` as an argument to the `print` function, and the function printed the string `width`. In the second statement, you passed `width` (with no quote marks) as an argument to the `print function`, and the function displayed the value referenced by the `width` variable.

In an assignment statement, the variable that is receiving the assignment must appear on the left side of the = operator. As shown in the following interactive session, an error occurs if the item on the left side of the = operator is not a variable:

```
>>> 25 = age [Enter]
SyntaxError: can't assign to literal
>>>
```

The code in Program 2-7 demonstrates a variable. Line 2 creates a variable named `room` and assigns it the value 503. The statements in lines 3 and 4 display a message. Notice line 4 displays the value that is referenced by the `room` variable.

Program 2-7 (variable_demo.py)

```
1  # This program demonstrates a variable.
2  room = 503
3  print('I am staying in room number')
4  print(room)
```

Program Output

```
I am staying in room number
503
```

Program 2-8 shows a sample program that uses two variables. Line 2 creates a variable named `top_speed`, assigning it the value 160. Line 3 creates a variable named `distance`, assigning it the value 300. This is illustrated in Figure 2-5.

Program 2-8 (variable_demo2.py)

```
1  # Create two variables: top_speed and distance.
2  top_speed = 160
3  distance = 300
4
5  # Display the values referenced by the variables.
6  print('The top speed is')
7  print(top_speed)
8  print('The distance traveled is')
9  print(distance)
```

Program Output

```
The top speed is
160
The distance traveled is
300
```

Figure 2-5 Two variables

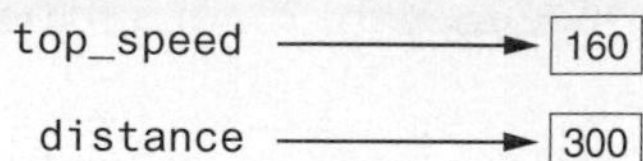

WARNING! You cannot use a variable until you have assigned a value to it. An error will occur if you try to perform an operation on a variable, such as printing it, before it has been assigned a value.

Sometimes a simple typing mistake will cause this error. One example is a misspelled variable name, as shown here:

```
temperature = 74.5 # Create a variable
print(tempereture) # Error! Misspelled variable name
```

In this code, the variable `temperature` is created by the assignment statement. The variable name is spelled differently in the `print` statement, however, which will cause an error. Another example is the inconsistent use of uppercase and lowercase letters in a variable name. Here is an example:

```
temperature = 74.5 # Create a variable
print(Temperature) # Error! Inconsistent use of case
```

In this code, the variable `temperature` (in all lowercase letters) is created by the assignment statement. In the `print` statement, the name `Temperature` is spelled with an uppercase T. This will cause an error because variable names are case sensitive in Python.

Variable Naming Rules

Although you are allowed to make up your own names for variables, you must follow these rules:

- You cannot use one of Python's key words as a variable name. (See Table 1-2 for a list of the key words.)
- A variable name cannot contain spaces.
- The first character must be one of the letters a through z, A through Z, or an underscore character (_).
- After the first character you may use the letters a through z or A through Z, the digits 0 through 9, or underscores.
- Uppercase and lowercase characters are distinct. This means the variable name `ItemsOrdered` is not the same as `itemsordered`.

In addition to following these rules, you should always choose names for your variables that give an indication of what they are used for. For example, a variable that holds the temperature might be named `temperature`, and a variable that holds a car's speed might be named `speed`. You may be tempted to give variables names such as `x` and `b2`, but names like these give no clue as to what the variable's purpose is.

Because a variable's name should reflect the variable's purpose, programmers often find themselves creating names that are made of multiple words. For example, consider the following variable names:

```
grosspay
payrate
hotdogssoldtoday
```

Unfortunately, these names are not easily read by the human eye because the words aren't separated. Because we can't have spaces in variable names, we need to find another way to separate the words in a multiword variable name and make it more readable to the human eye.

One way to do this is to use the underscore character to represent a space. For example, the following variable names are easier to read than those previously shown:

```
gross_pay
pay_rate
hot_dogs_sold_today
```

This style of naming variables is popular among Python programmers, and is the style we will use in this book. There are other popular styles, however, such as the *camelCase* naming convention. camelCase names are written in the following manner:

- The variable name begins with lowercase letters.
- The first character of the second and subsequent words is written in uppercase.

For example, the following variable names are written in camelCase:

```
grossPay
payRate
hotDogsSoldToday
```

NOTE: This style of naming is called camelCase because the uppercase characters that appear in a name may suggest a camel's humps.

Table 2-1 lists several sample variable names and indicates whether each is legal or illegal in Python.

Table 2-1 Sample variable names

Variable Name	Legal or Illegal?
`units_per_day`	Legal
`dayOfWeek`	Legal
`3dGraph`	Illegal. Variable names cannot begin with a digit.
`June1997`	Legal
`Mixture#3`	Illegal. Variable names may only use letters, digits, or underscores.

Displaying Multiple Items with the `print` Function

If you refer to Program 2-7, you will see that we used the following two statements in lines 3 and 4:

```
print('I am staying in room number')
print(room)
```

We called the `print` function twice because we needed to display two pieces of data. Line 3 displays the string literal `'I am staying in room number'`, and line 4 displays the value referenced by the `room` variable.

This program can be simplified, however, because Python allows us to display multiple items with one call to the `print` function. We simply have to separate the items with commas as shown in Program 2-9.

Program 2-9 (variable_demo3.py)

```
1  # This program demonstrates a variable.
2  room = 503
3  print('I am staying in room number', room)
```

Program Output

```
I am staying in room number 503
```

In line 3, we passed two arguments to the `print` function. The first argument is the string literal `'I am staying in room number'`, and the second argument is the `room` variable. When the `print` function executed, it displayed the values of the two arguments in the order that we passed them to the function. Notice the `print` function automatically printed a space separating the two items. When multiple arguments are passed to the `print` function, they are automatically separated by a space when they are displayed on the screen.

Variable Reassignment

Variables are called "variable" because they can reference different values while a program is running. When you assign a value to a variable, the variable will reference that value until you assign it a different value. For example, look at Program 2-10. The statement in line 3 creates a variable named `dollars` and assigns it the value 2.75. This is shown in the top part of Figure 2-6. Then, the statement in line 8 assigns a different value, 99.95, to the `dollars` variable. The bottom part of Figure 2-6 shows how this changes the `dollars` variable. The old value, 2.75, is still in the computer's memory, but it can no longer be used because it isn't referenced by a variable. When a value in memory is no longer referenced by a variable, the Python interpreter automatically removes it from memory through a process known as *garbage collection.*

Program 2-10 (variable_demo4.py)

```
1  # This program demonstrates variable reassignment.
2  # Assign a value to the dollars variable.
3  dollars = 2.75
```

(program continues)

Program 2-10 *(continued)*

```
4 print('I have', dollars, 'in my account.')
5
6 # Reassign dollars so it references
7 # a different value.
8 dollars = 99.95
9 print('But now I have', dollars, 'in my account!')
```

Program Output

```
I have 2.75 in my account.
But now I have 99.95 in my account!
```

Figure 2-6 Variable reassignment in Program 2-10

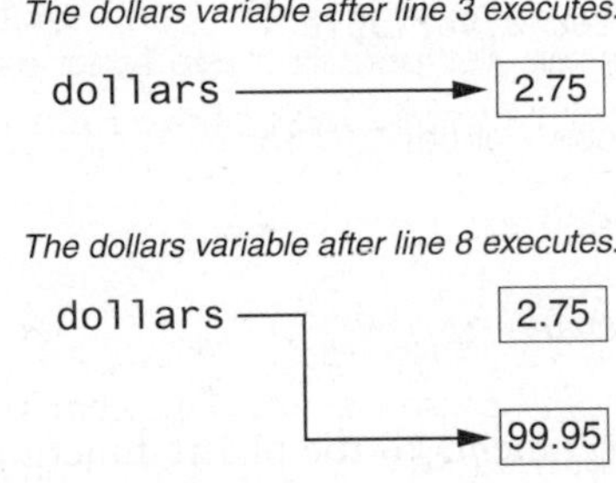

Numeric Data Types and Literals

In Chapter 1, we discussed the way that computers store data in memory. (See Section 1.3) You might recall from that discussion that computers use a different technique for storing real numbers (numbers with a fractional part) than for storing integers. Not only are these types of numbers stored differently in memory, but similar operations on them are carried out in different ways.

Because different types of numbers are stored and manipulated in different ways, Python uses *data types* to categorize values in memory. When an integer is stored in memory, it is classified as an `int`, and when a real number is stored in memory, it is classified as a `float`.

Let's look at how Python determines the data type of a number. Several of the programs that you have seen so far have numeric data written into their code. For example, the following statement, which appears in Program 2-9, has the number 503 written into it:

```
room = 503
```

This statement causes the value 503 to be stored in memory, and it makes the `room` variable reference it. The following statement, which appears in Program 2-10, has the number 2.75 written into it:

```
dollars = 2.75
```

This statement causes the value 2.75 to be stored in memory, and it makes the `dollars` variable reference it. A number that is written into a program's code is called a *numeric literal.*

When the Python interpreter reads a numeric literal in a program's code, it determines its data type according to the following rules:

- A numeric literal that is written as a whole number with no decimal point is considered an `int`. Examples are `7`, `124`, and `-9`.
- A numeric literal that is written with a decimal point is considered a `float`. Examples are `1.5`, `3.14159`, and `5.0`.

So, the following statement causes the number 503 to be stored in memory as an `int`:

```
room = 503
```

And the following statement causes the number 2.75 to be stored in memory as a `float`:

```
dollars = 2.75
```

When you store an item in memory, it is important for you to be aware of the item's data type. As you will see, some operations behave differently depending on the type of data involved, and some operations can only be performed on values of a specific data type.

As an experiment, you can use the built-in `type` function in interactive mode to determine the data type of a value. For example, look at the following session:

```
>>> type(1) Enter
<class 'int'>
>>>
```

In this example, the value 1 is passed as an argument to the `type` function. The message that is displayed on the next line, `<class 'int'>`, indicates that the value is an `int`. Here is another example:

```
>>> type(1.0) Enter
<class 'float'>
>>>
```

In this example, the value 1.0 is passed as an argument to the `type` function. The message that is displayed on the next line, `<class 'float'>`, indicates that the value is a `float`.

WARNING! You cannot write currency symbols, spaces, or commas in numeric literals. For example, the following statement will cause an error:

```
value = $4,567.99 # Error!
```

This statement must be written as:

```
value = 4567.99 # Correct
```

Storing Strings with the `str` Data Type

In addition to the `int` and `float` data types, Python also has a data type named `str`, which is used for storing strings in memory. The code in Program 2-11 shows how strings can be assigned to variables.

Program 2-11 (string_variable.py)

```
# Create variables to reference two strings.
first_name = 'Kathryn'
last_name = 'Marino'

# Display the values referenced by the variables.
print(first_name, last_name)
```

Program Output

```
Kathryn Marino
```

Reassigning a Variable to a Different Type

Keep in mind that in Python, a variable is just a name that refers to a piece of data in memory. It is a mechanism that makes it easy for you, the programmer, to store and retrieve data. Internally, the Python interpreter keeps track of the variable names that you create and the pieces of data to which those variable names refer. Any time you need to retrieve one of those pieces of data, you simply use the variable name that refers to it.

A variable in Python can refer to items of any type. After a variable has been assigned an item of one type, it can be reassigned an item of a different type. To demonstrate, look at the following interactive session. (We have added line numbers for easier reference.)

```
1 >>> x = 99 Enter
2 >>> print(x) Enter
3 99
4 >>> x = 'Take me to your leader' Enter
5 >>> print(x) Enter
6 Take me to your leader.
7 >>>
```

The statement in line 1 creates a variable named `x` and assigns it the `int` value 99. Figure 2-7 shows how the variable `x` references the value 99 in memory. The statement in line 2 calls the `print` function, passing `x` as an argument. The output of the `print` function is shown in line 3. Then, the statement in line 4 assigns a string to the `x` variable. After this statement executes, the `x` variable no longer refers to an `int`, but to the string `'Take me to your leader'`. This is shown in Figure 2-8. Line 5 calls the `print` function again, passing `x` as an argument. Line 6 shows the `print` function's output.

Figure 2-7 The variable x references an integer

Figure 2-8 The variable x references a string

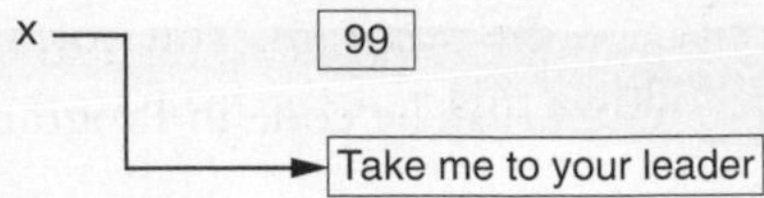

Checkpoint

2.10 What is a variable?

2.11 Which of the following are illegal variable names in Python, and why?

```
x
99bottles
july2009
theSalesFigureForFiscalYear
r&d
grade_report
```

2.12 Is the variable name `Sales` the same as `sales`? Why or why not?

2.13 Is the following assignment statement valid or invalid? If it is invalid, why?

```
72 = amount
```

2.14 What will the following code display?

```
val = 99
print('The value is', 'val')
```

2.15 Look at the following assignment statements:

```
value1 = 99
value2 = 45.9
value3 = 7.0
value4 = 7
value5 = 'abc'
```

After these statements execute, what is the Python data type of the values referenced by each variable?

2.16 What will be displayed by the following program?

```
my_value = 99
my_value = 0
print(my_value)
```

2.6 Reading Input from the Keyboard

CONCEPT: Programs commonly need to read input typed by the user on the keyboard. We will use the Python functions to do this.

VideoNote **Reading Input from the Keyboard**

Most of the programs that you will write will need to read input and then perform an operation on that input. In this section, we will discuss a basic input operation: reading data that has been typed on the keyboard. When a program reads data from the keyboard, usually it stores that data in a variable so it can be used later by the program.

In this book, we use Python's built-in `input` function to read input from the keyboard. The `input` function reads a piece of data that has been entered at the keyboard and returns that piece of data, as a string, back to the program. You normally use the `input` function in an assignment statement that follows this general format:

```
variable = input(prompt)
```

In the general format, `prompt` is a string that is displayed on the screen. The string's purpose is to instruct the user to enter a value; `variable` is the name of a `variable` that references the data that was entered on the keyboard. Here is an example of a statement that uses the `input` function to read data from the keyboard:

```
name = input('What is your name? ')
```

When this statement executes, the following things happen:

- The string `'What is your name? '` is displayed on the screen.
- The program pauses and waits for the user to type something on the keyboard and then to press the Enter key.
- When the Enter key is pressed, the data that was typed is returned as a string and assigned to the `name` variable.

To demonstrate, look at the following interactive session:

```
>>> name = input('What is your name? ') [Enter]
What is your name?  Holly  [Enter]
>>> print(name) [Enter]
Holly
>>>
```

When the first statement was entered, the interpreter displayed the prompt `'What is your name? '` and waited for the user to enter some data. The user entered **`Holly`** and pressed the Enter key. As a result, the string `'Holly'` was assigned to the `name` variable. When the second statement was entered, the interpreter displayed the value referenced by the `name` variable.

Program 2-12 shows a complete program that uses the `input` function to read two strings as input from the keyboard.

Program 2-12 (string_input.py)

```
1  # Get the user's first name.
2  first_name = input('Enter your first name: ')
3
4  # Get the user's last name.
5  last_name = input('Enter your last name: ')
6
7  # Print a greeting to the user.
8  print('Hello', first_name, last_name)
```

Program Output (with input shown in bold)

```
Enter your first name: Vinny [Enter]
Enter your last name: Brown [Enter]
Hello Vinny Brown
```

Take a closer look in line 2 at the string we used as a prompt:

```
'Enter your first name: '
```

Notice the last character in the string, inside the quote marks, is a space. The same is true for the following string, used as prompt in line 5:

```
'Enter your last name: '
```

We put a space character at the end of each string because the `input` function does not automatically display a space after the prompt. When the user begins typing characters, they appear on the screen immediately after the prompt. Making the last character in the prompt a space visually separates the prompt from the user's input on the screen.

Reading Numbers with the `input` Function

The `input` function always returns the user's input as a string, even if the user enters numeric data. For example, suppose you call the `input` function, type the number 72, and press the Enter key. The value that is returned from the `input` function is the string `'72'`. This can be a problem if you want to use the value in a math operation. Math operations can be performed only on numeric values, not strings.

Fortunately, Python has built-in functions that you can use to convert a string to a numeric type. Table 2-2 summarizes two of these functions.

Table 2-2 Data conversion functions

Function	Description
`int(`*`item`*`)`	You pass an argument to the `int()` function and it returns the argument's value converted to an `int`.
`float(`*`item`*`)`	You pass an argument to the `float()` function and it returns the argument's value converted to a `float`.

For example, suppose you are writing a payroll program and you want to get the number of hours that the user has worked. Look at the following code:

```
string_value = input('How many hours did you work? ')
hours = int(string_value)
```

The first statement gets the number of hours from the user and assigns that value as a string to the `string_value` variable. The second statement calls the `int()` function, passing `string_value` as an argument. The value referenced by `string_value` is converted to an `int` and assigned to the `hours` variable.

This example illustrates how the `int()` function works, but it is inefficient because it creates two variables: one to hold the string that is returned from the `input` function, and another to hold the integer that is returned from the `int()` function. The following code shows a better approach. This one statement does all the work that the previously shown two statements do, and it creates only one variable:

```
hours = int(input('How many hours did you work? '))
```

This one statement uses *nested function* calls. The value that is returned from the `input` function is passed as an argument to the `int()` function. This is how it works:

- It calls the `input` function to get a value entered at the keyboard.
- The value that is returned from the `input` function (a string) is passed as an argument to the `int()` function.
- The `int` value that is returned from the `int()` function is assigned to the `hours` variable.

After this statement executes, the `hours` variable is assigned the value entered at the keyboard, converted to an `int`.

Let's look at another example. Suppose you want to get the user's hourly pay rate. The following statement prompts the user to enter that value at the keyboard, converts the value to a `float`, and assigns it to the `pay_rate` variable:

```
pay_rate = float(input('What is your hourly pay rate? '))
```

This is how it works:

- It calls the `input` function to get a value entered at the keyboard.
- The value that is returned from the `input` function (a string) is passed as an argument to the `float()` function.
- The `float` value that is returned from the `float()` function is assigned to the `pay_rate` variable.

After this statement executes, the `pay_rate` variable is assigned the value entered at the keyboard, converted to a `float`.

Program 2-13 shows a complete program that uses the `input` function to read a string, an `int`, and a `float`, as input from the keyboard.

Program 2-13 (input.py)

```
# Get the user's name, age, and income.
name = input('What is your name? ')
age = int(input('What is your age? '))
income = float(input('What is your income? '))

# Display the data.
print('Here is the data you entered:')
print('Name:', name)
print('Age:', age)
print('Income:', income)
```

Program Output (with input shown in bold)

```
What is your name? Chris Enter
What is your age? 25 Enter
What is your income? 75000.0
Here is the data you entered:
Name: Chris
Age: 25
Income: 75000.0
```

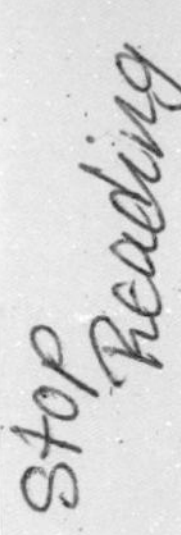

Let's take a closer look at the code:

- Line 2 prompts the user to enter his or her name. The value that is entered is assigned, as a string, to the `name` variable.
- Line 3 prompts the user to enter his or her age. The value that is entered is converted to an `int` and assigned to the `age` variable.
- Line 4 prompts the user to enter his or her income. The value that is entered is converted to a `float` and assigned to the `income` variable.
- Lines 7 through 10 display the values that the user entered.

The `int()` and `float()` functions work only if the item that is being converted contains a valid numeric value. If the argument cannot be converted to the specified data type, an error known as an exception occurs. An *exception* is an unexpected error that occurs while a program is running, causing the program to halt if the error is not properly dealt with. For example, look at the following interactive mode session:

```
>>> age = int(input('What is your age? ')) Enter
What is your age?  xyz  Enter
Traceback (most recent call last):
    File "<pyshell#81>", line 1, in <module>
        age = int(input('What is your age? '))
ValueError: invalid literal for int() with base 10: 'xyz'
>>>
```

NOTE: In this section, we mentioned the user. The *user* is simply any hypothetical person that is using a program and providing input for it. The user is sometimes called the *end user*.

Checkpoint

2.17 You need the user of a program to enter a customer's last name. Write a statement that prompts the user to enter this data and assigns the input to a variable.

2.18 You need the user of a program to enter the amount of sales for the week. Write a statement that prompts the user to enter this data and assigns the input to a variable.

2.7 Performing Calculations

CONCEPT: Python has numerous operators that can be used to perform mathematical calculations.

Most real-world algorithms require calculations to be performed. A programmer's tools for performing calculations are *math operators*. Table 2-3 lists the math operators that are provided by the Python language.

Programmers use the operators shown in Table 2-3 to create math expressions. A *math expression* performs a calculation and gives a value. The following is an example of a simple math expression:

```
12 + 2
```

Table 2-3 Python math operators

Symbol	Operation	Description
+	Addition	Adds two numbers
−	Subtraction	Subtracts one number from another
*	Multiplication	Multiplies one number by another
/	Division	Divides one number by another and gives the result as a floating-point number
//	Integer division	Divides one number by another and gives the result as a whole number
%	Remainder	Divides one number by another and gives the remainder
**	Exponent	Raises a number to a power

The values on the right and left of the + operator are called *operands*. These are values that the + operator adds together. If you type this expression in interactive mode, you will see that it gives the value 14:

```
>>> 12 + 2 [Enter]
14
>>>
```

Variables may also be used in a math expression. For example, suppose we have two variables named `hours` and `pay_rate`. The following math expression uses the * operator to multiply the value referenced by the `hours` variable by the value referenced by the `pay_rate` variable:

```
hours * pay_rate
```

When we use a math expression to calculate a value, normally we want to save that value in memory so we can use it again in the program. We do this with an assignment statement. Program 2-14 shows an example.

Program 2-14 (simple_math.py)

```
# Assign a value to the salary variable.
salary = 2500.0

# Assign a value to the bonus variable.
bonus = 1200.0

# Calculate the total pay by adding salary
# and bonus. Assign the result to pay.
pay = salary + bonus

# Display the pay.
print('Your pay is', pay)
```

Program Output

```
Your pay is 3700.0
```

Line 2 assigns 2500.0 to the `salary` variable, and line 5 assigns 1200.0 to the `bonus` variable. Line 9 assigns the result of the expression `salary + bonus` to the `pay` variable. As you can see from the program output, the `pay` variable holds the value 3700.0.

In the Spotlight:
Calculating a Percentage

If you are writing a program that works with a percentage, you have to make sure that the percentage's decimal point is in the correct location before doing any math with the percentage. This is especially true when the user enters a percentage as input. Most users enter the number 50 to mean 50 percent, 20 to mean 20 percent, and so forth. Before you perform any calculations with such a percentage, you have to divide it by 100 to move its decimal point two places to the left.

Let's step through the process of writing a program that calculates a percentage. Suppose a retail business is planning to have a storewide sale where the prices of all items will be 20 percent off. We have been asked to write a program to calculate the sale price of an item after the discount is subtracted. Here is the algorithm:

1. *Get the original price of the item.*
2. *Calculate 20 percent of the original price. This is the amount of the discount.*
3. *Subtract the discount from the original price. This is the sale price.*
4. *Display the sale price.*

In step 1, we get the original price of the item. We will prompt the user to enter this data on the keyboard. In our program we will use the following statement to do this. Notice the value entered by the user will be stored in a variable named `original_price`.

```
original_price = float(input("Enter the item's original price: "))
```

In step 2, we calculate the amount of the discount. To do this, we multiply the original price by 20 percent. The following statement performs this calculation and assigns the result to the `discount` variable:

```
discount = original_price * 0.2
```

In step 3, we subtract the discount from the original price. The following statement does this calculation and stores the result in the `sale_price` variable:

```
sale_price = original_price - discount
```

Last, in step 4, we will use the following statement to display the sale price:

```
print('The sale price is', sale_price)
```

Program 2-15 shows the entire program, with example output.

Program 2-15 (sale_price.py)

```
# This program gets an item's original price and
# calculates its sale price, with a 20% discount.

```

(program continues)

Program 2-15 *(continued)*

```
# Get the item's original price.
original_price = float(input("Enter the item's original price: "))

# Calculate the amount of the discount.
discount = original_price * 0.2

# Calculate the sale price.
sale_price = original_price - discount

# Display the sale price.
print('The sale price is', sale_price)
```

Program Output (with input shown in bold)

```
Enter the item's original price: 100.00 [Enter]
The sale price is 80.0
```

Floating-Point and Integer Division

Notice in Table 2-3 that Python has two different division operators. The / operator performs floating-point division, and the // operator performs integer division. Both operators divide one number by another. The difference between them is that the / operator gives the result as a floating-point value, and the // operator gives the result as a whole number. Let's use the interactive mode interpreter to demonstrate:

```
>>> 5 / 2 [Enter]
2.5
>>>
```

In this session, we used the / operator to divide 5 by 2. As expected, the result is 2.5. Now let's use the // operator to perform integer division:

```
>>> 5 // 2 [Enter]
2
>>>
```

As you can see, the result is 2. The // operator works like this:

- When the result is positive, it is *truncated*, which means that its fractional part is thrown away.
- When the result is negative, it is rounded *away from zero* to the nearest integer.

The following interactive session demonstrates how the // operator works when the result is negative:

```
>>> -5 // 2 [Enter]
-3
>>>
```

Operator Precedence

You can write statements that use complex mathematical expressions involving several operators. The following statement assigns the sum of 17, the variable x, 21, and the variable y to the variable answer:

```
answer = 17 + x + 21 + y
```

Some expressions are not that straightforward, however. Consider the following statement:

```
outcome = 12.0 + 6.0 / 3.0
```

What value will be assigned to outcome? The number 6.0 might be used as an operand for either the addition or division operator. The outcome variable could be assigned either 6.0 or 14.0, depending on when the division takes place. Fortunately, the answer can be predicted because Python follows the same order of operations that you learned in math class.

First, operations that are enclosed in parentheses are performed first. Then, when two operators share an operand, the operator with the higher *precedence* is applied first. The precedence of the math operators, from highest to lowest, are:

1. Exponentiation: **
2. Multiplication, division, and remainder: * / // %
3. Addition and subtraction: + −

Notice the multiplication (*), floating-point division (/), integer division (//), and remainder (%) operators have the same precedence. The addition (+) and subtraction (−) operators also have the same precedence. When two operators with the same precedence share an operand, the operators execute from left to right.

Now, let's go back to the previous math expression:

```
outcome = 12.0 + 6.0 / 3.0
```

The value that will be assigned to outcome is 14.0 because the division operator has a higher *precedence* than the addition operator. As a result, the division takes place before the addition. The expression can be diagrammed as shown in Figure 2-9.

Figure 2-9 Operator precedence

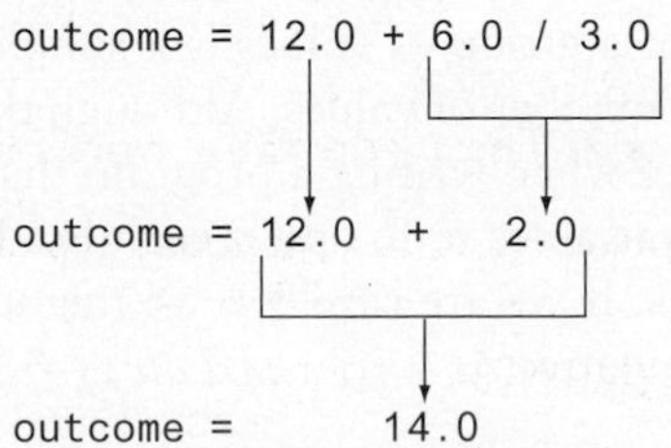

Table 2-4 shows some other sample expressions with their values.

Table 2-4 Some expressions

Expression	Value
`5 + 2 * 4`	13
`10 / 2 - 3`	2.0
`8 + 12 * 2 - 4`	28
`6 - 3 * 2 + 7 - 1`	6

NOTE: There is an exception to the left-to-right rule. When two `**` operators share an operand, the operators execute right-to-left. For example, the expression `2**3**4` is evaluated as `2**(3**4)`.

Grouping with Parentheses

Parts of a mathematical expression may be grouped with parentheses to force some operations to be performed before others. In the following statement, the variables `a` and `b` are added together, and their sum is divided by 4:

```
result = (a + b) / 4
```

Without the parentheses, however, `b` would be divided by 4 and the result added to `a`. Table 2-5 shows more expressions and their values.

Table 2-5 More expressions and their values

Expression	Value
`(5 + 2) * 4`	28
`10 / (5 - 3)`	5.0
`8 + 12 * (6 - 2)`	56
`(6 - 3) * (2 + 7) / 3`	9.0

In the Spotlight:
Calculating an Average

Determining the average of a group of values is a simple calculation: add all of the values then divide the sum by the number of values. Although this is a straightforward calculation, it is easy to make a mistake when writing a program that calculates an average. For example, let's assume that the variables `a`, `b`, and `c` each hold a value and we want to calculate the average of those values. If we are careless, we might write a statement such as the following to perform the calculation:

```
average = a + b + c / 3.0
```

Can you see the error in this statement? When it executes, the division will take place first. The value in `c` will be divided by 3, then the result will be added to `a + b`. That is not the correct way to calculate an average. To correct this error, we need to put parentheses around `a + b + c`, as shown here:

```
average = (a + b + c) / 3.0
```

Let's step through the process of writing a program that calculates an average. Suppose you have taken three tests in your computer science class, and you want to write a program that will display the average of the test scores. Here is the algorithm:

1. *Get the first test score.*
2. *Get the second test score.*
3. *Get the third test score.*
4. *Calculate the average by adding the three test scores and dividing the sum by 3.*
5. *Display the average.*

In steps 1, 2, and 3 we will prompt the user to enter the three test scores. We will store those test scores in the variables `test1`, `test2`, and `test3`. In step 4, we will calculate the average of the three test scores. We will use the following statement to perform the calculation and store the result in the `average` variable:

```
average = (test1 + test2 + test3) / 3.0
```

Last, in step 5, we display the average. Program 2-16 shows the program.

Program 2-16 (test_score_average.py)

```
# Get three test scores and assign them to the
# test1, test2, and test3 variables.
test1 = float(input('Enter the first test score: '))
test2 = float(input('Enter the second test score: '))
test3 = float(input('Enter the third test score: '))

# Calculate the average of the three scores
# and assign the result to the average variable.
average = (test1 + test2 + test3) / 3.0

# Display the average.
print('The average score is', average)
```

Program Output (with input shown in bold)

```
Enter the first test score: 90 Enter
Enter the second test score: 80 Enter
Enter the third test score: 100 Enter
The average score is 90.0
```

The Exponent Operator

In addition to the basic math operators for addition, subtraction, multiplication, and division, Python also provides an exponent operator. Two asterisks written together (`**`) is the exponent operator, and its purpose is to raise a number to a power. For example, the following statement raises the `length` variable to the power of 2 and assigns the result to the `area` variable:

```
area = length**2
```

The following session with the interactive interpreter shows the values of the expressions 4**2, 5**3, and 2**10:

```
>>> 4**2 Enter
16
>>> 5**3 Enter
125
>>> 2**10 Enter
1024
>>>
```

The Remainder Operator

In Python, the % symbol is the remainder operator. (This is also known as the *modulus operator.*) The remainder operator performs division, but instead of returning the quotient, it returns the remainder. The following statement assigns 2 to leftover:

```
leftover = 17 % 3
```

This statement assigns 2 to leftover because 17 divided by 3 is 5 with a remainder of 2. The remainder operator is useful in certain situations. It is commonly used in calculations that convert times or distances, detect odd or even numbers, and perform other specialized operations. For example, Program 2-17 gets a number of seconds from the user, and it converts that number of seconds to hours, minutes, and seconds. For example, it would convert 11,730 seconds to 3 hours, 15 minutes, and 30 seconds.

Program 2-17 (time_converter.py)

```
# Get a number of seconds from the user.
total_seconds = float(input('Enter a number of seconds: '))

# Get the number of hours.
hours = total_seconds // 3600

# Get the number of remaining minutes.
minutes = (total_seconds // 60) % 60

# Get the number of remaining seconds.
seconds = total_seconds % 60

# Display the results.
print('Here is the time in hours, minutes, and seconds:')
print('Hours:', hours)
print('Minutes:', minutes)
print('Seconds:', seconds)
```

Program Output (with input shown in bold)

```
Enter a number of seconds: 11730 Enter
Here is the time in hours, minutes, and seconds:
```

```
Hours: 3.0
Minutes: 15.0
Seconds: 30.0
```

Let's take a closer look at the code:

- Line 2 gets a number of seconds from the user, converts the value to a `float`, and assigns it to the `total_seconds` variable.
- Line 5 calculates the number of hours in the specified number of seconds. There are 3600 seconds in an hour, so this statement divides `total_seconds` by 3600. Notice we used the integer division operator (`//`) operator. This is because we want the number of hours with no fractional part.
- Line 8 calculates the number of remaining minutes. This statement first uses the `//` operator to divide `total_seconds` by 60. This gives us the total number of minutes. Then, it uses the `%` operator to divide the total number of minutes by 60 and get the remainder of the division. The result is the number of remaining minutes.
- Line 11 calculates the number of remaining seconds. There are 60 seconds in a minute, so this statement uses the `%` operator to divide the `total_seconds` by 60 and get the remainder of the division. The result is the number of remaining seconds.
- Lines 14 through 17 display the number of hours, minutes, and seconds.

Converting Math Formulas to Programming Statements

You probably remember from algebra class that the expression $2xy$ is understood to mean 2 times x times y. In math, you do not always use an operator for multiplication. Python, as well as other programming languages, requires an operator for any mathematical operation. Table 2-6 shows some algebraic expressions that perform multiplication and the equivalent programming expressions.

Table 2-6 Algebraic expressions

Algebraic Expression	Operation Being Performed	Programming Expression
$6B$	6 times B	`6 * B`
(3)(12)	3 times 12	`3 * 12`
$4xy$	4 times x times y	`4 * x * y`

When converting some algebraic expressions to programming expressions, you may have to insert parentheses that do not appear in the algebraic expression. For example, look at the following formula:

$$x = \frac{a + b}{c}$$

To convert this to a programming statement, $a + b$ will have to be enclosed in parentheses:

```
x = (a + b)/c
```

Table 2-7 shows additional algebraic expressions and their Python equivalents.

Table 2-7 Algebraic and programming expressions

Algebraic Expression	Python Statement
$y = 3\frac{x}{2}$	`y = 3 * x / 2`
$z = 3bc + 4$	`z = 3 * b * c + 4`
$a = \frac{x + 2}{b - 1}$	`a = (x + 2) / (b - 1)`

In the Spotlight:
Converting a Math Formula to a Programming Statement

Suppose you want to deposit a certain amount of money into a savings account and leave it alone to draw interest for the next 10 years. At the end of 10 years, you would like to have $10,000 in the account. How much do you need to deposit today to make that happen? You can use the following formula to find out:

$$P = \frac{F}{(1 + r)^n}$$

The terms in the formula are as follows:

- P is the present value, or the amount that you need to deposit today.
- F is the future value that you want in the account. (In this case, F is $10,000.)
- r is the annual interest rate.
- n is the number of years that you plan to let the money sit in the account.

It would be convenient to write a computer program to perform the calculation because then we can experiment with different values for the variables. Here is an algorithm that we can use:

1. *Get the desired future value.*
2. *Get the annual interest rate.*
3. *Get the number of years that the money will sit in the account.*
4. *Calculate the amount that will have to be deposited.*
5. *Display the result of the calculation in step 4.*

In steps 1 through 3, we will prompt the user to enter the specified values. We will assign the desired future value to a variable named `future_value`, the annual interest rate to a variable named `rate`, and the number of years to a variable named `years`.

In step 4, we calculate the present value, which is the amount of money that we will have to deposit. We will convert the formula previously shown to the following statement. The statement stores the result of the calculation in the `present_value` variable.

```
present_value = future_value / (1.0 + rate)**years
```

In step 5, we display the value in the `present_value` variable. Program 2-18 shows the program.

Program 2-18 (future_value.py)

```
# Get the desired future value.
future_value = float(input('Enter the desired future value: '))

# Get the annual interest rate.
rate = float(input('Enter the annual interest rate: '))

# Get the number of years that the money will appreciate.
years = int(input('Enter the number of years the money will grow: '))

# Calculate the amount needed to deposit.
present_value = future_value / (1.0 + rate)**years

# Display the amount needed to deposit.
print('You will need to deposit this amount:', present_value)
```

Program Output

```
Enter the desired future value: 10000.0 Enter
Enter the annual interest rate: 0.05 Enter
Enter the number of years the money will grow: 10 Enter
You will need to deposit this amount: 6139.13253541
```

NOTE: Unlike the output shown for this program, dollar amounts are usually rounded to two decimal places. Later in this chapter, you will learn how to format numbers so they are rounded to a specified number of decimal places.

Mixed-Type Expressions and Data Type Conversion

When you perform a math operation on two operands, the data type of the result will depend on the data type of the operands. Python follows these rules when evaluating mathematical expressions:

- When an operation is performed on two `int` values, the result will be an `int`.
- When an operation is performed on two `float` values, the result will be a `float`.
- When an operation is performed on an `int` and a `float`, the `int` value will be temporarily converted to a `float` and the result of the operation will be a `float`. (An expression that uses operands of different data types is called a *mixed-type expression*.)

The first two situations are straightforward: operations on `ints` produce `ints`, and operations on `floats` produce `floats`. Let's look at an example of the third situation, which involves mixed-type expressions:

```
my_number = 5 * 2.0
```

When this statement executes, the value 5 will be converted to a `float` (5.0) then multiplied by 2.0. The result, 10.0, will be assigned to `my_number`.

The `int` to `float` conversion that takes place in the previous statement happens implicitly. If you need to explicitly perform a conversion, you can use either the `int()` or `float()` functions. For example, you can use the `int()` function to convert a floating-point value to an integer, as shown in the following code:

```
fvalue = 2.6
ivalue = int(fvalue)
```

The first statement assigns the value 2.6 to the `fvalue` variable. The second statement passes `fvalue` as an argument to the `int()` function. The `int()` function returns the value 2, which is assigned to the `ivalue` variable. After this code executes, the `fvalue` variable is still assigned the value 2.6, but the `ivalue` variable is assigned the value 2.

As demonstrated in the previous example, the `int()` function converts a floating-point argument to an integer by truncating it. As previously mentioned, that means it throws away the number's fractional part. Here is an example that uses a negative number:

```
fvalue = -2.9
ivalue = int(fvalue)
```

In the second statement, the value –2 is returned from the `int()` function. After this code executes, the `fvalue` variable references the value –2.9, and the `ivalue` variable references the value –2.

You can use the `float()` function to explicitly convert an `int` to a `float`, as shown in the following code:

```
ivalue = 2
fvalue = float(ivalue)
```

After this code executes, the `ivalue` variable references the integer value 2, and the `fvalue` variable references the floating-point value 2.0.

Breaking Long Statements into Multiple Lines

Most programming statements are written on one line. If a programming statement is too long, however, you will not be able to view all of it in your editor window without scrolling horizontally. In addition, if you print your program code on paper and one of the statements is too long to fit on one line, it will wrap around to the next line and make the code difficult to read.

Python allows you to break a statement into multiple lines by using the *line continuation character,* which is a backslash (`\`). You simply type the backslash character at the point you want to break the statement, then press the Enter key.

For example, here is a statement that performs a mathematical calculation and has been broken up to fit on two lines:

```
result = var1 * 2 + var2 * 3 + \
         var3 * 4 + var4 * 5
```

The line continuation character that appears at the end of the first line tells the interpreter that the statement is continued on the next line.

Python also allows you to break any part of a statement that is enclosed in parentheses into multiple lines without using the line continuation character. For example, look at the following statement:

```
print("Monday's sales are", monday,
      "and Tuesday's sales are", tuesday,
      "and Wednesday's sales are", wednesday)
```

The following code shows another example:

```
total = (value1 + value2 +
         value3 + value4 +
         value5 + value6)
```

Checkpoint

2.19 Complete the following table by writing the value of each expression in the Value column:

Expression	Value
`6 + 3 * 5`	______
`12 / 2 - 4`	______
`9 + 14 * 2 - 6`	______
`(6 + 2) * 3`	______
`14 / (11 - 4)`	______
`9 + 12 * (8 - 3)`	______

2.20 What value will be assigned to `result` after the following statement executes?

```
result = 9 // 2
```

2.21 What value will be assigned to `result` after the following statement executes?

```
result = 9 % 2
```

2.8 More About Data Output

So far, we have discussed only basic ways to display data. Eventually, you will want to exercise more control over the way data appear on the screen. In this section, you will learn more details about the Python `print` function, and you'll see techniques for formatting output in specific ways.

Suppressing the `print` Function's Ending Newline

The `print` function normally displays a line of output. For example, the following three statements will produce three lines of output:

```
print('One')
print('Two')
print('Three')
```

Each of the statements shown here displays a string and then prints a *newline character*. You do not see the newline character, but when it is displayed, it causes the output to advance to the next line. (You can think of the newline character as a special command that causes the computer to start a new line of output.)

If you do not want the print function to start a new line of output when it finishes displaying its output, you can pass the special argument end=' ' to the function, as shown in the following code:

```
print('One', end=' ')
print('Two', end=' ')
print('Three')
```

Notice in the first two statements, the argument end=' ' is passed to the print function. This specifies that the print function should print a space instead of a newline character at the end of its output. Here is the output of these statements:

```
One Two Three
```

Sometimes, you might not want the print function to print anything at the end of its output, not even a space. If that is the case, you can pass the argument end='' to the print function, as shown in the following code:

```
print('One', end='')
print('Two', end='')
print('Three')
```

Notice in the argument end='' there is no space between the quote marks. This specifies that the print function should print nothing at the end of its output. Here is the output of these statements:

```
OneTwoThree
```

Specifying an Item Separator

When multiple arguments are passed to the print function, they are automatically separated by a space when they are displayed on the screen. Here is an example, demonstrated in interactive mode:

```
>>> print('One', 'Two', 'Three') Enter
One Two Three
>>>
```

If you do not want a space printed between the items, you can pass the argument sep='' to the print function, as shown here:

```
>>> print('One', 'Two', 'Three', sep='') Enter
OneTwoThree
>>>
```

You can also use this special argument to specify a character other than the space to separate multiple items. Here is an example:

```
>>> print('One', 'Two', 'Three', sep='*') Enter
One*Two*Three
>>>
```

Notice in this example, we passed the argument sep='*' to the print function. This specifies that the printed items should be separated with the * character. Here is another example:

```
>>> print('One', 'Two', 'Three', sep='~~~') Enter
One~~~Two~~~Three
>>>
```

Escape Characters

An *escape character* is a special character that is preceded with a backslash (\), appearing inside a string literal. When a string literal that contains escape characters is printed, the escape characters are treated as special commands that are embedded in the string.

For example, \n is the newline escape character. When the \n escape character is printed, it isn't displayed on the screen. Instead, it causes output to advance to the next line. For example, look at the following statement:

```
print('One\nTwo\nThree')
```

When this statement executes, it displays

```
One
Two
Three
```

Python recognizes several escape characters, some of which are listed in Table 2-8.

Table 2-8 Some of Python's escape characters

Escape Character	Effect
\n	Causes output to be advanced to the next line.
\t	Causes output to skip over to the next horizontal tab position.
\'	Causes a single quote mark to be printed.
\"	Causes a double quote mark to be printed.
\\	Causes a backslash character to be printed.

The \t escape character advances the output to the next horizontal tab position. (A tab position normally appears after every eighth character.) The following statements are illustrative:

```
print('Mon\tTues\tWed')
print('Thur\tFri\tSat')
```

This statement prints Monday, then advances the output to the next tab position, then prints Tuesday, then advances the output to the next tab position, then prints Wednesday. The output will look like this:

```
Mon     Tues    Wed
Thur    Fri     Sat
```

You can use the \' and \" escape characters to display quotation marks. The following statements are illustrative:

```
print("Your assignment is to read \"Hamlet\" by tomorrow.")
print('I\'m ready to begin.')
```

These statements display the following:

```
Your assignment is to read "Hamlet" by tomorrow.
I'm ready to begin.
```

You can use the `\\` escape character to display a backslash, as shown in the following:

```
print('The path is C:\\temp\\data.')
```

This statement will display

```
The path is C:\temp\data.
```

Displaying Multiple Items with the + Operator

Earlier in this chapter, you saw that the + operator is used to add two numbers. When the + operator is used with two strings, however, it performs *string concatenation*. This means that it appends one string to another. For example, look at the following statement:

```
print('This is ' + 'one string.')
```

This statement will print

```
This is one string.
```

String concatenation can be useful for breaking up a string literal so a lengthy call to the `print` function can span multiple lines. Here is an example:

```
print('Enter the amount of ' +
      'sales for each day and ' +
      'press Enter.')
```

This statement will display the following:

```
Enter the amount of sales for each day and press Enter.
```

Formatting Numbers

You might not always be happy with the way that numbers, especially floating-point numbers, are displayed on the screen. When a floating-point number is displayed by the `print` function, it can appear with up to 12 significant digits. This is shown in the output of Program 2-19.

Program 2-19 (no_formatting.py)

```
# This program demonstrates how a floating-point
# number is displayed with no formatting.
amount_due = 5000.0
monthly_payment = amount_due / 12.0
print(‘The monthly payment is’, monthly_payment)
```

Program Output

```
The monthly payment is 416.666666667
```

Because this program displays a dollar amount, it would be nice to see that amount rounded to two decimal places. Fortunately, Python gives us a way to do just that, and more, with the built-in `format` function.

When you call the built-in `format` function, you pass two arguments to the function: a numeric value and a format specifier. The *format specifier* is a string that contains special characters specifying how the numeric value should be formatted. Let's look at an example:

```
format(12345.6789, '.2f')
```

The first argument, which is the floating-point number 12345.6789, is the number that we want to format. The second argument, which is the string `'.2f'`, is the format specifier. Here is the meaning of its contents:

- The `.2` specifies the precision. It indicates that we want to round the number to two decimal places.
- The `f` specifies that the data type of the number we are formatting is a floating-point number.

The `format` function returns a string containing the formatted number. The following interactive mode session demonstrates how you use the `format` function along with the `print` function to display a formatted number:

```
>>> print(format(12345.6789, '.2f')) Enter
12345.68
>>>
```

Notice the number is rounded to two decimal places. The following example shows the same number, rounded to one decimal place:

```
>>> print(format(12345.6789, '.1f')) Enter
12345.7
>>>
```

Here is another example:

```
>>> print('The number is', format(1.234567, '.2f')) Enter
The number is 1.23
>>>
```

Program 2-20 shows how we can modify Program 2-19 so it formats its output using this technique.

Program 2-20 **(formatting.py)**

```
# This program demonstrates how a floating-point
# number can be formatted.
amount_due = 5000.0
monthly_payment = amount_due / 12
print('The monthly payment is',
      format(monthly_payment, '.2f'))
```

Program Output

```
The monthly payment is 416.67
```

Formatting in Scientific Notation

If you prefer to display floating-point numbers in scientific notation, you can use the letter `e` or the letter `E` instead of `f`. Here are some examples:

```
>>> print(format(12345.6789, 'e')) Enter
1.234568e+04
>>> print(format(12345.6789, '.2e')) Enter
1.23e+04
>>>
```

The first statement simply formats the number in scientific notation. The number is displayed with the letter `e` indicating the exponent. (If you use uppercase `E` in the format specifier, the result will contain an uppercase `E` indicating the exponent.) The second statement additionally specifies a precision of two decimal places.

Inserting Comma Separators

If you want the number to be formatted with comma separators, you can insert a comma into the format specifier, as shown here:

```
>>> print(format(12345.6789, ',.2f')) Enter
12,345.68
>>>
```

Here is an example that formats an even larger number:

```
>>> print(format(123456789.456, ',.2f')) Enter
123,456,789.46
>>>
```

Notice in the format specifier, the comma is written before (to the left of) the precision designator. Here is an example that specifies the comma separator, but does not specify precision:

```
>>> print(format(12345.6789, ',f')) Enter
12,345.678900
>>>
```

Program 2-21 demonstrates how the comma separator and a precision of two decimal places can be used to format larger numbers as currency amounts.

Program 2-21 (dollar_display.py)

```
# This program demonstrates how a floating-point
# number can be displayed as currency.
monthly_pay = 5000.0
annual_pay = monthly_pay * 12
print('Your annual pay is $',
      format(annual_pay, ',.2f'),
      sep='')
```

Program Output

```
Your annual pay is $60,000.00
```

Notice in line 7, we passed the argument `sep=''` to the `print` function. As we mentioned earlier, this specifies that no space should be printed between the items that are being displayed. If we did not pass this argument, a space would be printed after the $ sign.

Specifying a Minimum Field Width

The format specifier can also include a minimum field width, which is the minimum number of spaces that should be used to display the value. The following example prints a number in a field that is 12 spaces wide:

```
>>> print('The number is', format(12345.6789, '12,.2f')) Enter
The number is 12,345.68
>>>
```

In this example, the 12 that appears in the format specifier indicates that the number should be displayed in a field that is a minimum of 12 spaces wide. In this case, the number that is displayed is shorter than the field that it is displayed in. The number `12,345.68` uses only 9 spaces on the screen, but it is displayed in a field that is 12 spaces wide. When this is the case, the number is right justified in the field. If a value is too large to fit in the specified field width, the field is automatically enlarged to accommodate it.

Note in the previous example, the field width designator is written before (to the left of) the comma separator. Here is an example that specifies field width and precision, but does not use comma separators:

```
>>> print('The number is', format(12345.6789, '12.2f')) Enter
The number is     12345.68
>>>
```

Field widths can help when you need to print numbers aligned in columns. For example, look at Program 2-22. Each of the variables is displayed in a field that is seven spaces wide.

Program 2-22 (columns.py)

```
# This program displays the following
# floating-point numbers in a column
# with their decimal points aligned.
num1 = 127.899
num2 = 3465.148
num3 = 3.776
num4 = 264.821
num5 = 88.081
num6 = 799.999

# Display each number in a field of 7 spaces
# with 2 decimal places.
print(format(num1, '7.2f'))
print(format(num2, '7.2f'))
```

(program continues)

Program 2-22 *(continued)*

```
print(format(num3, '7.2f'))
print(format(num4, '7.2f'))
print(format(num5, '7.2f'))
print(format(num6, '7.2f'))
```

Program Output

```
 127.90
3465.15
   3.78
 264.82
  88.08
 800.00
```

Formatting a Floating-Point Number as a Percentage

Instead of using `f` as the type designator, you can use the `%` symbol to format a floating-point number as a percentage. The `%` symbol causes the number to be multiplied by 100 and displayed with a `%` sign following it. Here is an example:

```
>>> print(format(0.5, '%')) Enter
50.000000%
>>>
```

Here is an example that specifies 0 as the precision:

```
>>> print(format(0.5, '.0%')) Enter
50%
>>>
```

Formatting Integers

All the previous examples demonstrated how to format floating-point numbers. You can also use the `format` function to format integers. There are two differences to keep in mind when writing a format specifier that will be used to format an integer:

- You use `d` as the type designator.
- You cannot specify precision.

Let's look at some examples in the interactive interpreter. In the following session, the number 123456 is printed with no special formatting:

```
>>> print(format(123456, 'd')) Enter
123456
>>>
```

In the following session, the number 123456 is printed with a comma separator:

```
>>> print(format(123456, ',d')) Enter
123,456
>>>
```

In the following session, the number 123456 is printed in a field that is 10 spaces wide:

```
>>> print(format(123456, '10d')) Enter
    123456
>>>
```

In the following session, the number 123456 is printed with a comma separator in a field that is 10 spaces wide:

```
>>> print(format(123456, '10,d')) Enter
   123,456
>>>
```

Checkpoint

2.22 How do you suppress the `print` function's ending newline?

2.23 How can you change the character that is automatically displayed between multiple items that are passed to the `print` function?

2.24 What is the `'\n'` escape character?

2.25 What does the + operator do when it is used with two strings?

2.26 What does the statement `print(format(65.4321, '.2f'))` display?

2.27 What does the statement `print(format(987654.129, ',.2f'))` display?

2.9 Named Constants

CONCEPT: A named constant is a name that represents a value that cannot be changed during the program's execution.

Imagine, for a moment, that you are a programmer working for a bank. You are updating an existing program that calculates data pertaining to loans, and you see the following line of code:

```
amount = balance * 0.069
```

Because someone else wrote the program, you aren't sure what the number 0.069 is. It appears to be an interest rate, but it could be a number that is used to calculate some sort of fee. You simply can't determine the purpose of the number 0.069 by reading this line of code. This is an example of a magic number. A *magic number* is an unexplained value that appears in a program's code.

Magic numbers can be problematic, for a number of reasons. First, as illustrated in our example, it can be difficult for someone reading the code to determine the purpose of the number. Second, if the magic number is used in multiple places in the program, it can take painstaking effort to change the number in each location, should the need arise. Third, you take the risk of making a typographical mistake each time you type the magic number in the program's code. For example, suppose you intend to type 0.069, but you accidentally type .0069. This mistake will cause mathematical errors that can be difficult to find.

These problems can be addressed by using named constants to represent magic numbers. A *named constant* is a name that represents a value that does not change during the program's execution. The following is an example of how we will declare named constants in our code:

```
INTEREST_RATE = 0.069
```

This creates a named constant named `INTEREST_RATE` that is assigned the value 0.069. Notice the named constant is written in all uppercase letters. This is a standard practice in most programming languages because it makes named constants easily distinguishable from regular variables.

One advantage of using named constants is that they make programs more self-explanatory. The following statement:

```
amount = balance * 0.069
```

can be changed to read

```
amount = balance * INTEREST_RATE
```

A new programmer can read the second statement and know what is happening. It is evident that balance is being multiplied by the interest rate.

Another advantage to using named constants is that widespread changes can easily be made to the program. Let's say the interest rate appears in a dozen different statements throughout the program. When the rate changes, the initialization value in the declaration of the named constant is the only value that needs to be modified. If the rate increases to 7.2 percent, the declaration can be changed to:

```
INTEREST_RATE = 0.072
```

The new value of 0.072 will then be used in each statement that uses the `INTEREST_RATE` constant.

Another advantage to using named constants is that they help to prevent the typographical errors that are common when using magic numbers. For example, if you accidentally type .0069 instead of 0.069 in a math statement, the program will calculate the wrong value. However, if you misspell `INTEREST_RATE`, the Python interpreter will display a message indicating that the name is not defined.

Checkpoint

2.28 What are three advantages of using named constants?

2.29 Write a Python statement that defines a named constant for a 10 percent discount.

2.10 Introduction to Turtle Graphics

CONCEPT: Turtle graphics is an interesting and easy way to learn basic programming concepts. The Python turtle graphics system simulates a "turtle" that obeys commands to draw simple graphics.

In the late 1960s, MIT professor Seymour Papert used a robotic "turtle" to teach programming. The turtle was tethered to a computer where a student could enter commands, causing the turtle to move. The turtle also had a pen that could be raised and lowered, so it could be placed on a sheet of paper and programmed to draw images. Python has a *turtle graphics* system that simulates a robotic turtle. The system displays a small cursor (the turtle) on the screen. You can use Python statements to move the turtle around the screen, drawing lines and shapes.

The first step in using Python's turtle graphics system is to write the following statement:

VideoNote **Introduction to Turtle Graphics**

```
import turtle
```

This statement is necessary because the turtle graphics system is not built into the Python interpreter. Instead, it is stored in a file known as the *turtle module*. The `import turtle` statement loads the turtle module into memory so the Python interpreter can use it.

If you are writing a Python program that uses turtle graphics, you will write the `import` statement at the top of the program. If you want to experiment with turtle graphics in interactive mode, you can type the statement into the Python shell, as shown here:

```
>>> import turtle
>>>
```

Drawing Lines with the Turtle

The Python turtle is initially positioned in the center of a graphics window that serves as its canvas. In interactive mode, you can enter the `turtle.showturtle()` command to display the turtle in its window. Here is an example session that imports the `turtle` module, and then shows the turtle:

```
>>> import turtle
>>> turtle.showturtle()
```

This causes a graphics window similar to the one shown in Figure 2-10 to appear. Notice the turtle doesn't look like a turtle at all. Instead, it looks like an arrowhead (➤). This is important, because it points in the direction that the turtle is currently facing. If we instruct the turtle to move forward, it will move in the direction that the arrowhead is pointing. Let's try it out. You can use the `turtle.forward(n)` command to move the turtle forward *n* pixels. (Just type the desired number of pixels in place of *n*.) For example, the command `turtle.forward(200)` moves the turtle forward 200 pixels. Here is an example of a complete session in the Python shell:

```
>>> import turtle
>>> turtle.forward(200)
>>>
```

Figure 2-11 shows the output of this interactive session. Notice a line was drawn by turtle as it moved forward.

Turning the Turtle

When the turtle first appears, its default heading is 0 degrees (East). This is shown in Figure 2-12.

Figure 2-10 The turtle's graphics window

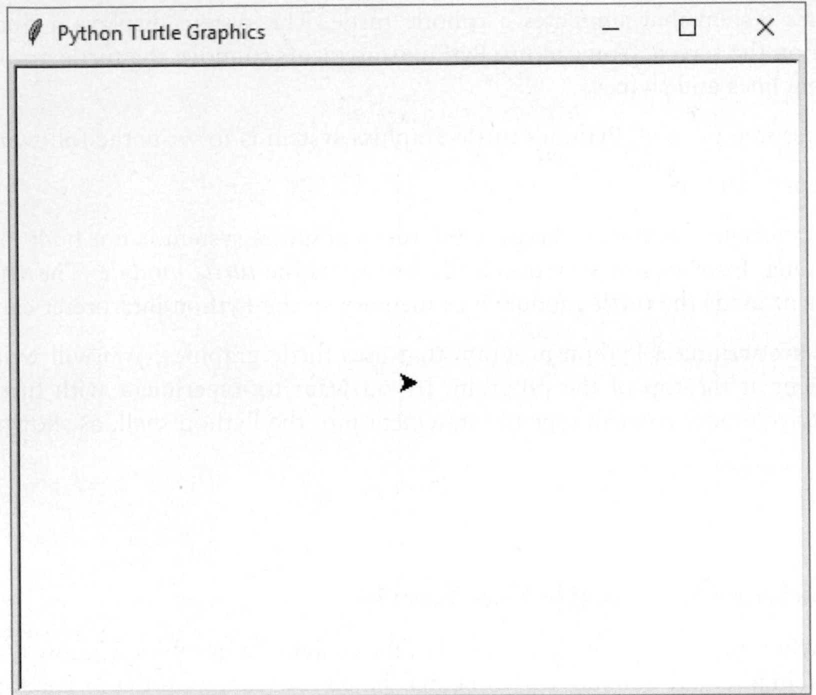

Figure 2-11 The turtle moving forward 200 pixels

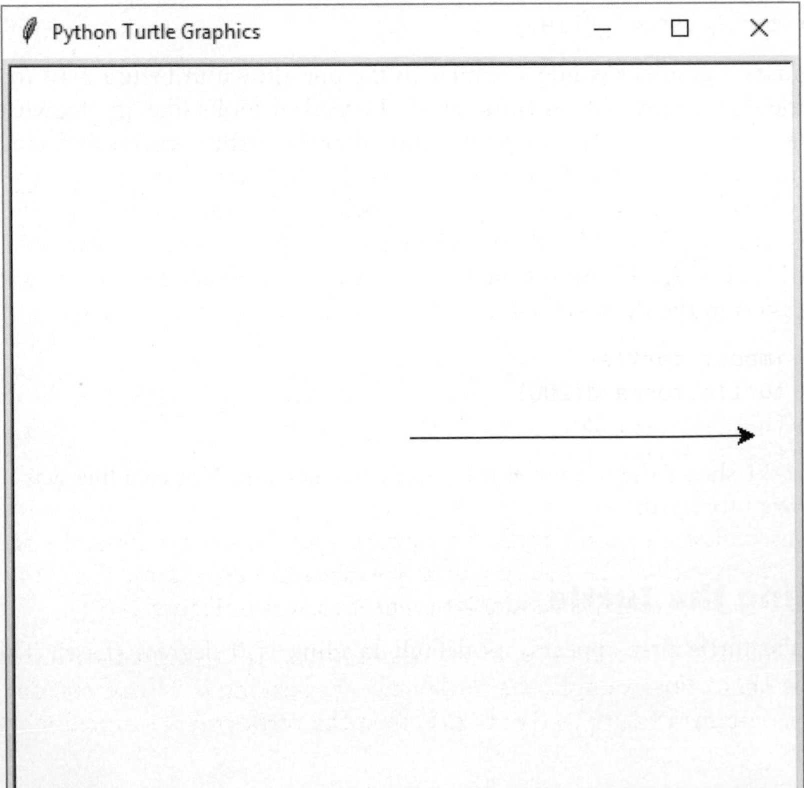

Figure 2-12 The turtle's heading

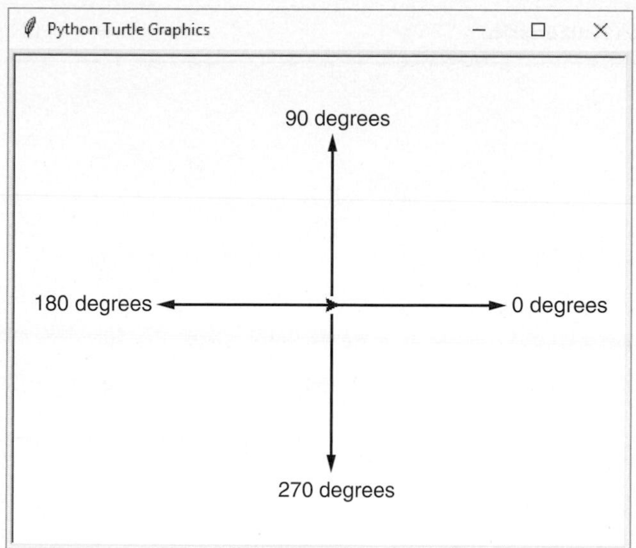

You can turn the turtle so it faces a different direction by using either the `turtle.right(`*`angle`*`)` command, or the `turtle.left(`*`angle`*`)` command. The `turtle.right(`*`angle`*`)` command turns the turtle right by *`angle`* degrees, and the `turtle.left(`*`angle`*`)` command turns the turtle left by *`angle`* degrees. Here is an example session that uses the `turtle.right(`*`angle`*`)` command:

```
>>> import turtle
>>> turtle.forward(200)
>>> turtle.right(90)
>>> turtle.forward(200)
>>>
```

This session first moves the turtle forward 200 pixels. Then it turns the turtle right by 90 degrees (the turtle will be pointing down). Then it moves the turtle forward by 200 pixels. The session's output is shown in Figure 2-13.

Here is an example session that uses the `turtle.left(`*`angle`*`)` command:

```
>>> import turtle
>>> turtle.forward(100)
>>> turtle.left(120)
>>> turtle.forward(150)
>>>
```

This session first moves the turtle forward 100 pixels. Then it turns the turtle left by 120 degrees (the turtle will be pointing in a Northwestern direction). Then it moves the turtle forward by 150 pixels. The session's output is shown in Figure 2-14.

Keep in mind that the `turtle.right` and `turtle.left` commands turn the turtle *by* a specified angle. For example, the turtle's current heading is 90 degrees (due north). If you enter the command `turtle.left(20)`, then the turtle will be turned left by 20 degrees.

Figure 2-13 The turtle turns right

Figure 2-14 The turtle turns left

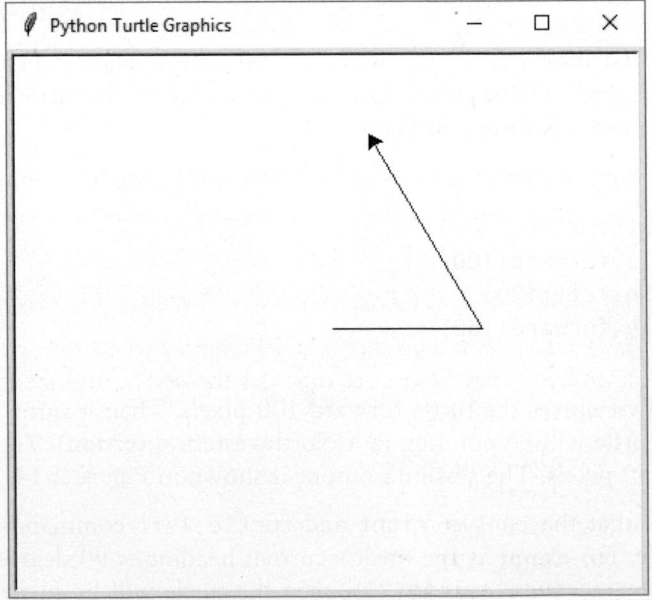

This means the turtle's heading will be 110 degrees. For another example, look at the following interactive session:

```
>>> import turtle
>>> turtle.forward(50)
>>> turtle.left(45)
>>> turtle.forward(50)
>>> turtle.left(45)
>>> turtle.forward(50)
>>> turtle.left(45)
>>> turtle.forward(50)
>>>
```

Figure 2-15 shows the session's output. At the beginning of this session, the turtle's heading is 0 degrees. In the third line, the turtle is turned left by 45 degrees. In the fifth line, the turtle is turned left again by an additional 45 degrees. In the seventh line, the turtle is once again turned left by 45 degrees. After all of these 45 degree turns, the turtle's heading will finally be 135 degrees.

Figure 2-15 Turning the turtle by 45 degree angles

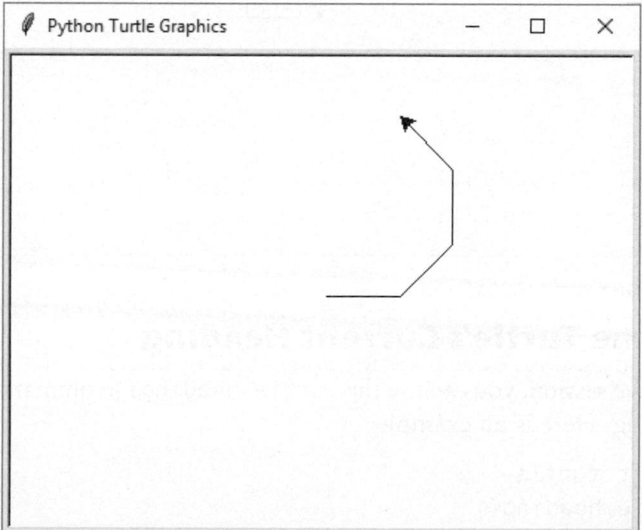

Setting the Turtle's Heading to a Specific Angle

You can use the `turtle.setheading(`*`angle`*`)` command to set the turtle's heading to a specific angle. Simply specify the desired angle as the *`angle`* argument. The following interactive session shows an example:

```
>>> import turtle
>>> turtle.forward(50)
>>> turtle.setheading(90)
>>> turtle.forward(100)
>>> turtle.setheading(180)
```

```
>>> turtle.forward(50)
>>> turtle.setheading(270)
>>> turtle.forward(100)
>>>
```

As usual, the turtle's initial heading is 0 degrees. In the third line, the turtle's heading is set to 90 degrees. Then, in the fifth line, the turtle's heading is set to 180 degrees. Then, in the seventh line, the turtle's heading is set to 270 degrees. The session's output is shown in Figure 2-16.

Figure 2-16 Setting the turtle's heading

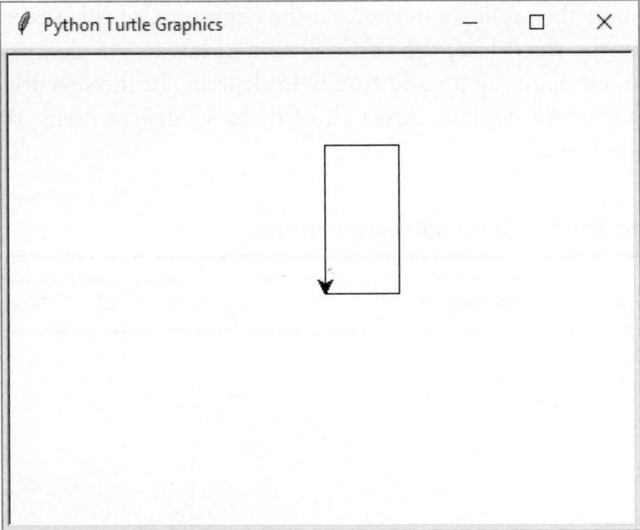

Getting the Turtle's Current Heading

In an interactive session, you can use the `turtle.heading()` command to display the turtle's current heading. Here is an example:

```
>>> import turtle
>>> turtle.heading()
0.0
>>> turtle.setheading(180)
>>> turtle.heading()
180.0
>>>
```

Moving the Pen Up and Down

The original robotic turtle sat on a large sheet of paper, and had a pen that could be raised and lowered. When the pen was down, it was in contact with the paper and would draw a line as the turtle moved. When the pen was up, it was not touching the paper, so the turtle could move without drawing a line.

In Python, you can use the `turtle.penup()` command to raise the pen, and the `turtle.pendown()` command to lower the pen. When the pen is up, you can move the turtle without drawing a line. When the pen is down, the turtle leaves a line when it is moved. (By default, the pen is down.) The following session shows an example. The session's output is shown in Figure 2-17.

```
>>> import turtle
>>> turtle.forward(50)
>>> turtle.penup()
>>> turtle.forward(25)
>>> turtle.pendown()
>>> turtle.forward(50)
>>> turtle.penup()
>>> turtle.forward(25)
>>> turtle.pendown()
>>> turtle.forward(50)
>>>
```

Figure 2-17 Raising and lowering the pen

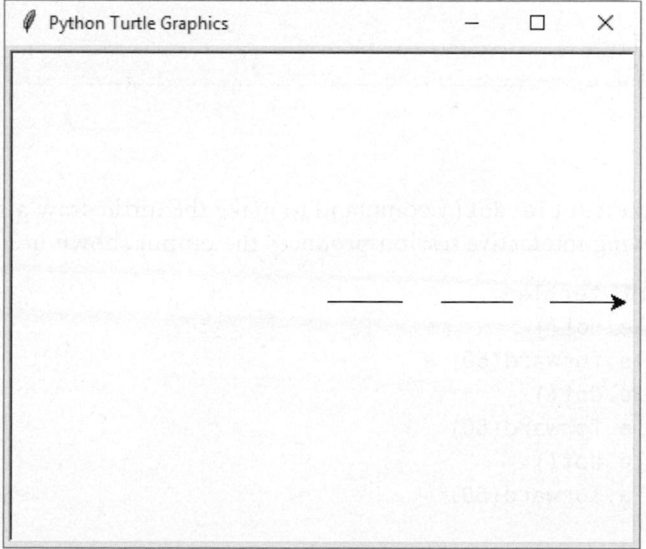

Drawing Circles and Dots

You can use the `turtle.circle(`*`radius`*`)` command to make the turtle draw a circle with a radius of *`radius`* pixels. For example, the command `turtle.circle(100)` causes the turtle to draw a circle with a radius of 100 pixels. The following interactive session displays the output shown in Figure 2-18:

```
>>> import turtle
>>> turtle.circle(100)
>>>
```

Figure 2-18 A circle

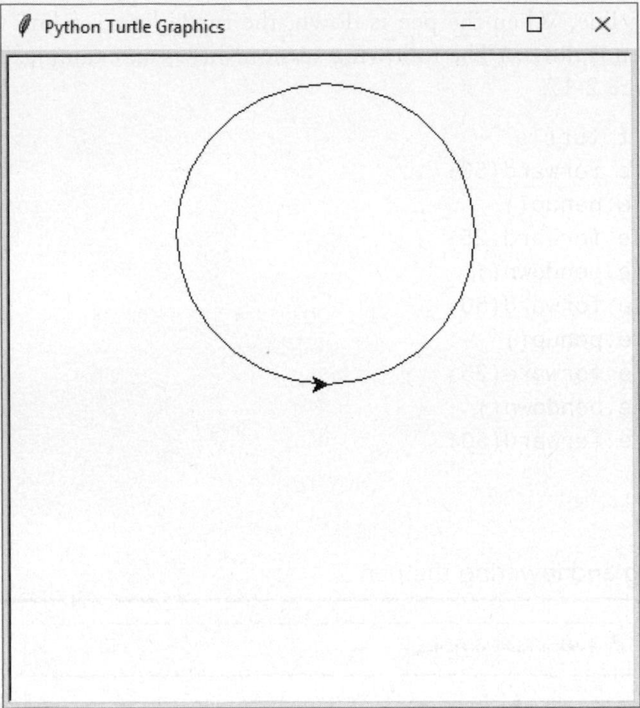

You can use the `turtle.dot()` command to make the turtle draw a simple dot. For example, the following interactive session produces the output shown in Figure 2-19:

```
>>> import turtle
>>> turtle.dot()
>>> turtle.forward(50)
>>> turtle.dot()
>>> turtle.forward(50)
>>> turtle.dot()
>>> turtle.forward(50)
>>>
```

Changing the Pen Size

You can use the `turtle.pensize(`*`width`*`)` command to change the width of the turtle's pen, in pixels. The *`width`* argument is an integer specifying the pen's width. For example, the following interactive session sets the pen's width to 5 pixels, then draws a circle:

```
>>> import turtle
>>> turtle.pencsize(5)
>>> turtle.circle(100)
>>>
```

Figure 2-19 Drawing dots

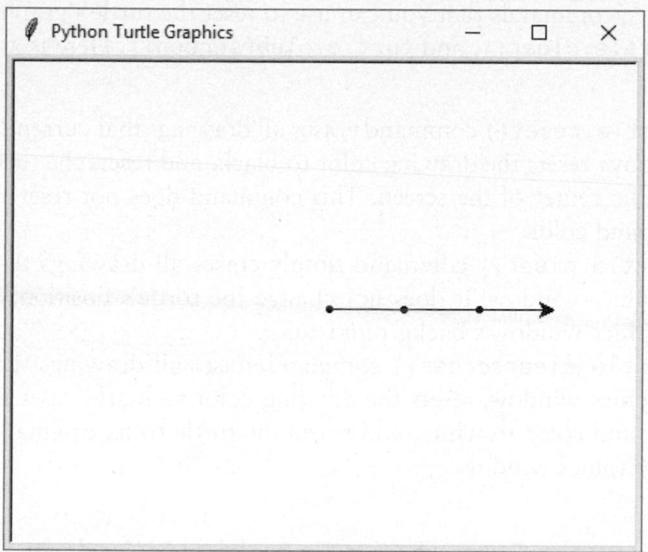

Changing the Drawing Color

You can use the `turtle.pencolor(color)` command to change the turtle's drawing color. The *`color`* argument is the name of a color, as a string. For example, the following interactive session changes the drawing color to red, then draws a circle:

```
>>> import turtle
>>> turtle.pencolor('red')
>>> turtle.circle(100)
>>>
```

There are numerous predefined color names that you can use with the `turtle.pencolor` command, and Appendix D shows the complete list. Some of the more common colors are `'red'`, `'green'`, `'blue'`, `'yellow'`, and `'cyan'`.

Changing the Background Color

You can use the `turtle.bgcolor(color)` command to change the background color of the turtle's graphics window. The *`color`* argument is the name of a color, as a string. For example, the following interactive session changes the background color to gray, changes the drawing color to red, then draws a circle:

```
>>> import turtle
>>> turtle.bgcolor('gray')
>>> turtle.pencolor('red')
>>> turtle.circle(100)
>>>
```

As previously mentioned, there are numerous predefined color names, and Appendix D shows the complete list.

Resetting the Screen

There are three commands that you can use to reset the turtle's graphics window: `turtle.reset()`, `turtle.clear()`, and `turtle.clearscreen()`. Here is a summary of the commands:

- The `turtle.reset()` command erases all drawings that currently appear in the graphics window, resets the drawing color to black, and resets the turtle to its original position in the center of the screen. This command does not reset the graphics window's background color.
- The `turtle.clear()` command simply erases all drawings that currently appear in the graphics window. It does not change the turtle's position, the drawing color, or the graphics window's background color.
- The `turtle.clearscreen()` command erases all drawings that currently appear in the graphics window, resets the drawing color to black, reset the graphics window's background color to white, and resets the turtle to its original position in the center of the graphics window.

Specifying the Size of the Graphics Window

You can use the `turtle.setup(width, height)` command to specify a size for the graphics window. The *`width`* and *`height`* arguments are the width and height, in pixels. For example, the following interactive session creates a graphics window that is 640 pixels wide and 480 pixels high:

```
>>> import turtle
>>> turtle.setup(640, 480)
>>>
```

Moving the Turtle to a Specific Location

A Cartesian coordinate system is used to identify the position of each pixel in the turtle's graphics window, as illustrated in Figure 2-20. Each pixel has an *X* coordinate and a *Y* coordinate. The *X* coordinate identifies the pixel's horizontal position, and the *Y* coordinate identifies its vertical position. Here are the important things to know:

- The pixel in the center of the graphics window is at the position (0, 0), which means that its *X* coordinate is 0 and its *Y* coordinate is 0.
- The *X* coordinates increase in value as we move toward the right side of the window, and they decrease in value as we move toward the left side of the window.
- The *Y* coordinates increase in value as we move toward the top of the window, and decrease in value as we move toward the bottom of the window.
- Pixels that are located to the right of the center point have positive *X* coordinates, and pixels that are located to the left of the center point have negative *X* coordinates.
- Pixels that are located above the center point have positive *Y* coordinates, and pixels that are located below the center point have negative *Y* coordinates.

You can use the `turtle.goto(x, y)` command to move the turtle from its current location to a specific position in the graphics window. The *x* and *y* arguments are the coordinates of the position to which to move the turtle. If the turtle's pen is down, a line will be drawn

Figure 2-20 Cartesian coordinate system

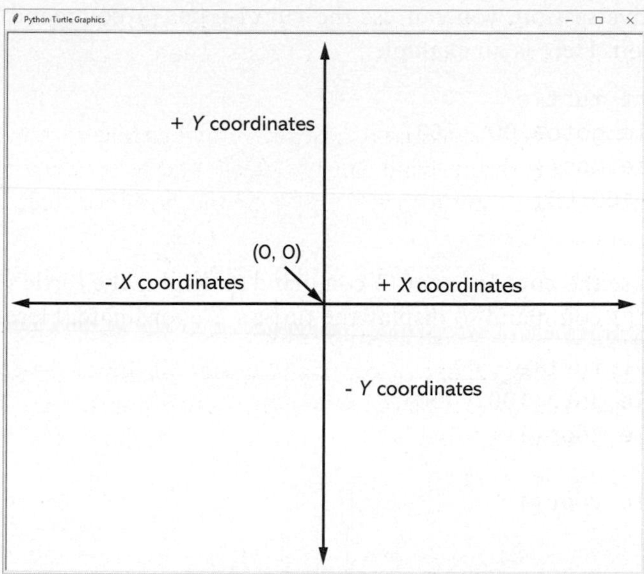

as the turtle moves. For example, the following interactive session draws the lines shown in Figure 2-21:

```
>>> import turtle
>>> turtle.goto(0, 100)
>>> turtle.goto(-100, 0)
>>> turtle.goto(0, 0)
>>>
```

Figure 2-21 Moving the turtle

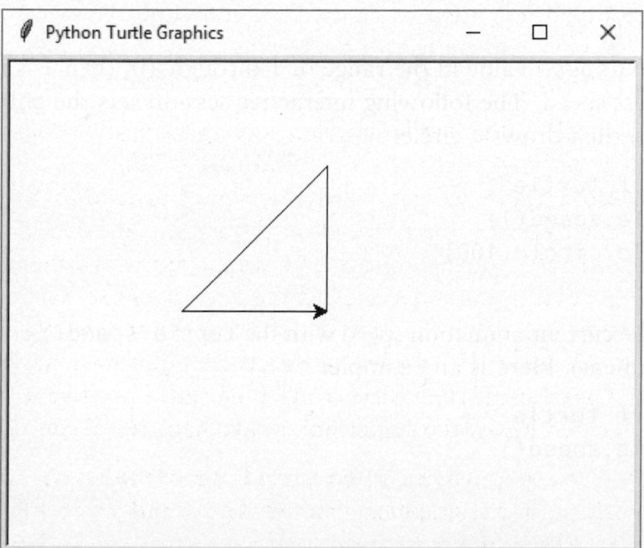

Getting the Turtle's Current Position

In an interactive session, you can use the `turtle.pos()` command to display the turtle's current position. Here is an example:

```
>>> import turtle
>>> turtle.goto(100, 150)
>>> turtle.pos()
(100.00, 150.00)
>>>
```

You can also use the `turtle.xcor()` command to display the turtle's *X* coordinate, and the `turtle.ycor()` command to display the turtle's *Y* coordinate. Here is an example:

```
>>> import turtle
>>> turtle.goto(100, 150)
>>> turtle.xcor()
100
>>> turtle.ycor()
150
>>>
```

Controlling the Turtle's Animation Speed

You can use the `turtle.speed(speed)` command to change the speed at which the turtle moves. The *speed* argument is a number in the range of 0 through 10. If you specify 0, then the turtle will make all of its moves instantly (animation is disabled). For example, the following interactive session disables the turtle's animation, then draws a circle. As a result, the circle will be instantly drawn:

```
>>> import turtle
>>> turtle.speed(0)
>>> turtle.circle(100)
>>>
```

If you specify a *speed* value in the range of 1 through 10, then 1 is the slowest speed, and 10 is the fastest speed. The following interactive session sets the animation speed to 1 (the slowest speed) then draws a circle:

```
>>> import turtle
>>> turtle.speed(1)
>>> turtle.circle(100)
>>>
```

You can get the current animation speed with the `turtle.speed()` command (do not specify a *speed* argument). Here is an example:

```
>>> import turtle
>>> turtle.speed()
3
>>>
```

Hiding the Turtle

If you don't want the turtle to be displayed, you can use the `turtle.hideturtle()` command to hide it. This command does not change the way graphics are drawn, it simply hides the turtle icon. When you want to display the turtle again, use the `turtle.showturtle()` command.

Displaying Text in the Graphics Window

You can use the `turtle.write(text)` command to display text in the graphics window. The `text` argument is a string that you want to display. When the string is displayed, the lower-left corner of the first character will be positioned at the turtle's `X` and `Y` coordinates. The following interactive session demonstrates this. The session's output is shown in Figure 2-22.

```
>>> import turtle
>>> turtle.write('Hello World')
>>>
```

Figure 2-22 Text displayed in the graphics window

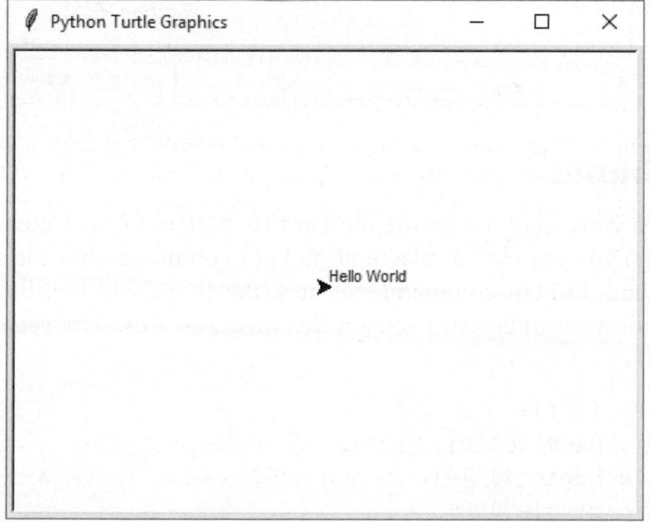

The following interactive session shows another example in which the turtle is moved to specific locations to display text. The session's output is shown in Figure 2-23.

```
>>> import turtle
>>> turtle.setup(300, 300)
>>> turtle.penup()
>>> turtle.hideturtle()
>>> turtle.goto(-120, 120)
>>> turtle.write("Top Left")
>>> turtle.goto(70, -120)
>>> turtle.write("Bottom Right")
>>>
```

Figure 2-23 Text displayed at specific locations in the graphics window

Filling Shapes

To fill a shape with a color, you use the `turtle.begin_fill()` command before drawing the shape, then you use the `turtle.end_fill()` command after the shape is drawn. When the `turtle.end_fill()` command executes, the shape will be filled with the current fill color. The following interactive session demonstrates this. The session's output is shown in Figure 2-24.

```
>>> import turtle
>>> turtle.hideturtle()
>>> turtle.begin_fill()
>>> turtle.circle(100)
>>> turtle.end_fill()
>>>
```

The circle that is drawn in Figure 2-24 is filled with black, which is the default color. You can change the fill color with the `turtle.fillcolor(`*`color`*`)` command. The *`color`* argument is the name of a color, as a string. For example, the following interactive session changes the drawing color to red, then draws a circle:

```
>>> import turtle
>>> turtle.hideturtle()
>>> turtle.fillcolor('red')
>>> turtle.begin_fill()
>>> turtle.circle(100)
>>> turtle.end_fill()
>>>
```

Figure 2-24 A filled circle

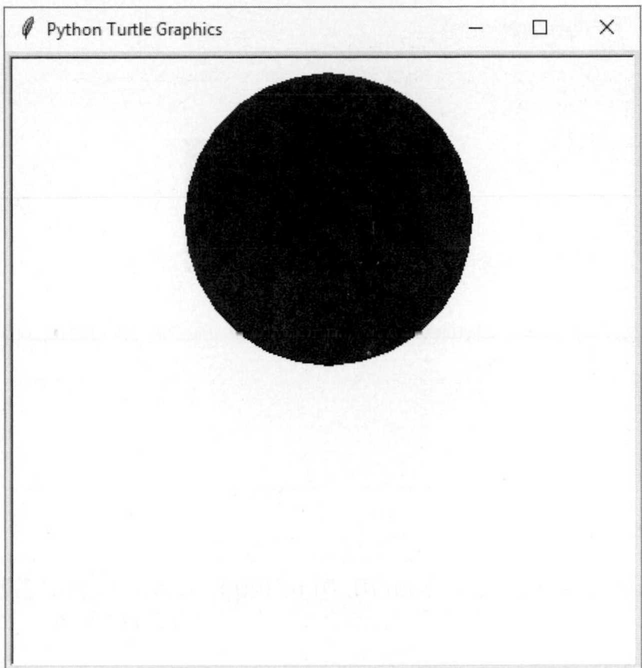

There are numerous predefined color names that you can use with the `turtle.fillcolor` command, and Appendix D shows the complete list. Some of the more common colors are `'red'`, `'green'`, `'blue'`, `'yellow'`, and `'cyan'`.

The following interactive session demonstrates how to draw a square that is filled with the color blue. The session's output is shown in Figure 2-25.

```
>>> import turtle
>>> turtle.hideturtle()
>>> turtle.fillcolor('blue')
>>> turtle.begin_fill()
>>> turtle.forward(100)
>>> turtle.left(90)
>>> turtle.forward(100)
>>> turtle.left(90)
>>> turtle.forward(100)
>>> turtle.left(90)
>>> turtle.forward(100)
>>> turtle.end_fill()
>>>
```

If you fill a shape that is not enclosed, the shape will be filled as if you had drawn a line connecting the starting point with the ending point. For example, the following interactive session draws two lines. The first is from (0, 0) to (120, 120), and the second is from (120, 120) to (200, −100). When the `turtle.end_fill()` command executes, the shape

Figure 2-25 A filled square

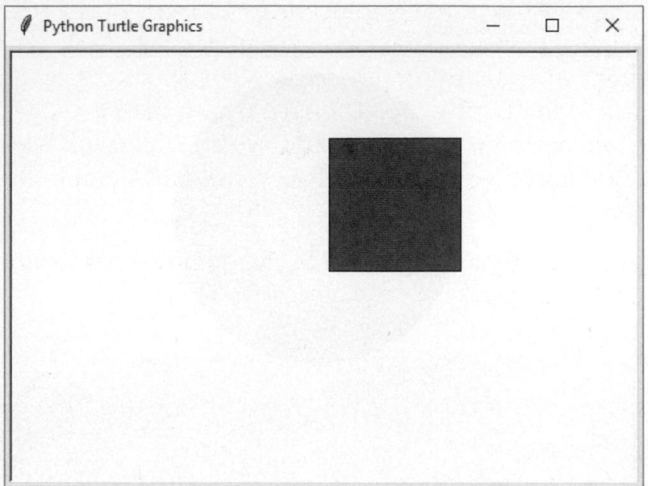

is filled as if there were a line from (0, 0) to (200, −120). Figure 2-26 shows the session's output.

```
>>> import turtle
>>> turtle.hideturtle()
>>> turtle.begin_fill()
>>> turtle.goto(120, 120)
>>> turtle.goto(200, -100)
>>> turtle.end_fill()
>>>
```

Figure 2-26 Shape filled

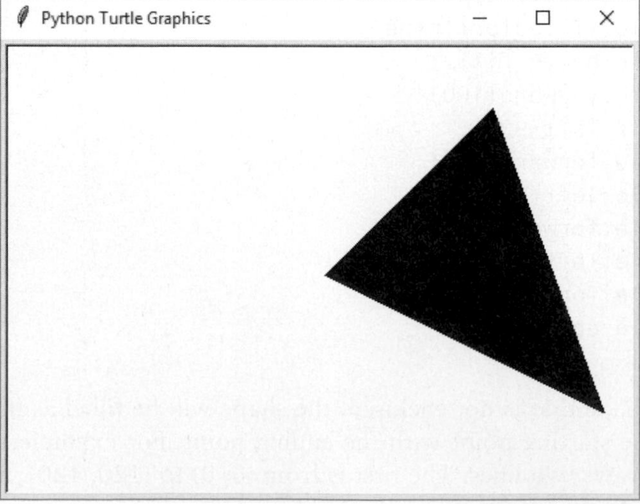

Using `turtle.done()` to Keep the Graphics Window Open

If you are running a Python turtle graphics program from an environment other that IDLE (for example, at the command line), you may notice the graphics window disappears as soon as your program ends. To prevent the window from closing after the program ends, you will need to add the `turtle.done()` statement to the very end of your turtle graphics programs. This will cause the graphics window to remain open, so you can see its contents after the program finishes executing. To close the window, simply click the window's standard "close" button.

If you are running your programs from IDLE, it is not necessary to have the `turtle.done()` statement in your programs.

In the Spotlight:

The Orion Constellation Program

Orion is one of the most famous constellations in the night sky. The diagram in Figure 2-27 shows the approximate positions of several stars in the constellation. The topmost stars are Orion's shoulders, the row of three stars in the middle are Orion's belt, and the bottom two stars are Orion's knees. The diagram in Figure 2-28 shows the names of each of these stars, and Figure 2-29 shows the lines that are typically used to connect the stars.

Figure 2-27 Stars in the Orion constellation

Figure 2-28 Names of the stars

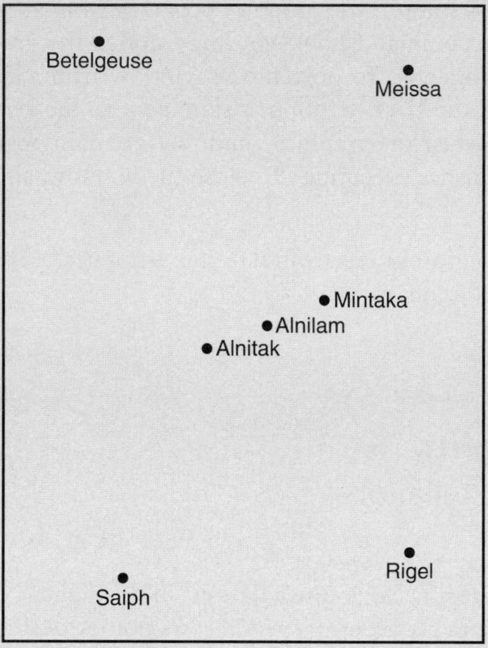

Figure 2-29 Constellation lines

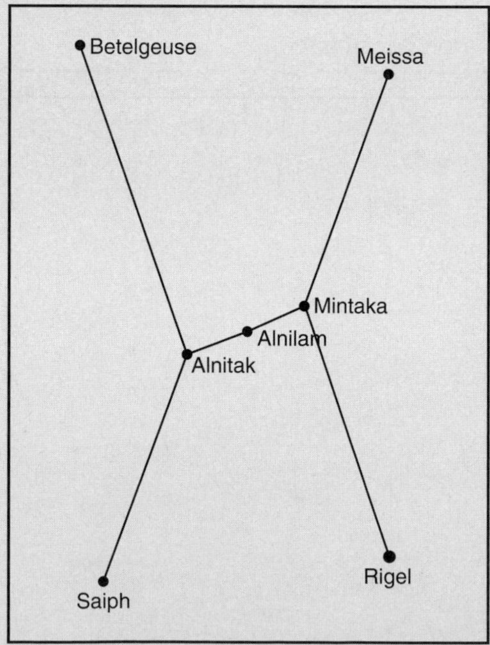

In this section, we will develop a program that displays the stars, the star names, and the constellation lines as they are shown in Figure 2-29. The program will display the constellation in a graphics window that is 500 pixels wide and 600 pixels high. The program will display dots to represent the stars. We will use a piece of graph paper, as shown in Figure 2-30, to sketch the positions of the dots and determine their coordinates.

Figure 2-30 Hand sketch of the Orion constellation

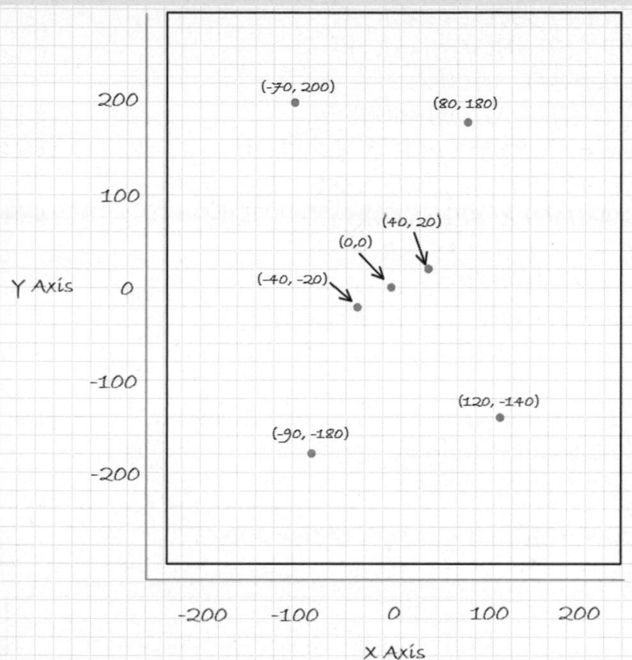

We will be using the coordinates that are identified in Figure 2-30 multiple times in our program. As you can imagine, keeping track of the correct coordinates for each star can be difficult and tedious. To make things more simple in our code, we will create the following named constants to represent each star's coordinates:

```
LEFT_SHOULDER_X = -70
LEFT_SHOULDER_Y = 200

RIGHT_SHOULDER_X = 80
RIGHT_SHOULDER_Y = 180

LEFT_BELTSTAR_X = -40
LEFT_BELTSTAR_Y = -20

MIDDLE_BELTSTAR_X = 0
MIDDLE_BELTSTAR_Y = 0

RIGHT_BELTSTAR_X = 40
RIGHT_BELTSTAR_Y = 20

LEFT_KNEE_X = -90
LEFT_KNEE_Y = -180

RIGHT_KNEE_X = 120
RIGHT_KNEE_Y = -140
```

Now that we have identified the coordinates for the stars and created named constants to represent them, we can write pseudocode for the first part of the program, which displays the stars:

```
Set the graphics window size to 500 pixels wide by 600 pixels high

Draw a dot at (LEFT_SHOULDER_X,
               LEFT_SHOULDER_Y)                      # Left shoulder
Draw a dot at (RIGHT_SHOULDER_X,
               RIGHT_SHOULDER_Y)                     # Right shoulder
Draw a dot at (LEFT_BELTSTAR_X, LEFT_BELTSTAR_Y)     # Leftmost star in the belt
Draw a dot at (MIDDLE_BELTSTAR_X,
               MIDDLE_BELTSTAR_Y)                    # Middle star in the belt
Draw a dot at (RIGHT_BELTSTAR_X,
               RIGHT_BELTSTAR_Y)                     # Rightmost star in the belt
Draw a dot at (LEFT_KNEE_X, LEFT_KNEE_Y)             # Left knee
Draw a dot at (RIGHT_KNEE_X, RIGHT_KNEE_Y)           # Right knee
```

Next, we will display the names of each star, as sketched in Figure 2-31. The pseudocode for displaying these names follows.

Figure 2-31 Orion sketch with the names of the stars

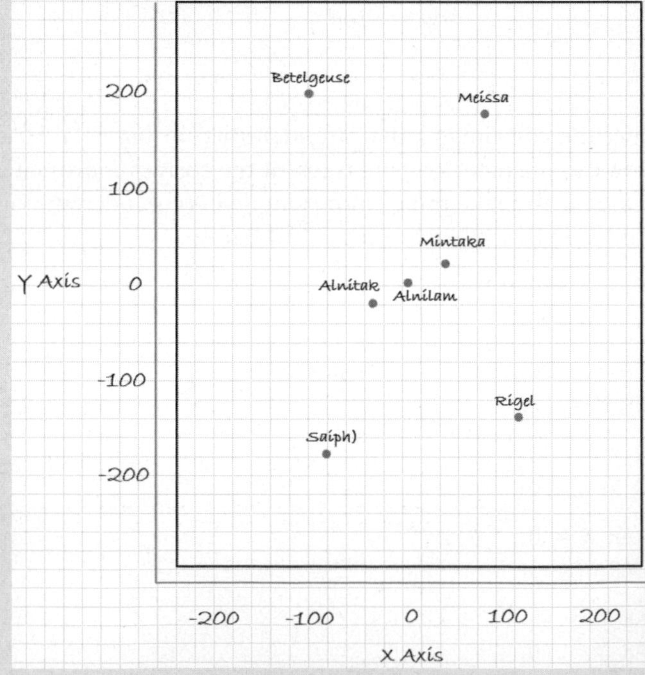

```
Display the text "Betelgeuse" at (LEFT_SHOULDER_X,
                                  LEFT_SHOULDER_Y)        # Left shoulder
Display the text "Meissa" at (RIGHT_SHOULDER_X,
                              RIGHT_SHOULDER_Y)           # Right shoulder
Display the text "Alnitak" at (LEFT_BELTSTAR_X,
                               LEFT_ BELTSTAR_Y)          # Leftmost star in the belt
Display the text "Alnilam" at (MIDDLE_BELTSTAR_X,
                               MIDDLE_BELTSTAR_Y)         # Middle star in the belt
Display the text "Mintaka" at (RIGHT_BELTSTAR_X,
                               RIGHT_BELTSTAR_Y)          # Rightmost star in the belt
Display the text "Saiph" at (LEFT_KNEE_X,
                             LEFT_ KNEE_Y)                # Left knee
Display the text "Rigel" at (RIGHT_KNEE_X,
                             RIGHT_ KNEE_Y)               # Right knee
```

Next, we will display the lines that connect the stars, as sketched in Figure 2-32. The pseudocode for displaying these lines follows.

Figure 2-32 Orion sketch with the names of the stars and constellation lines

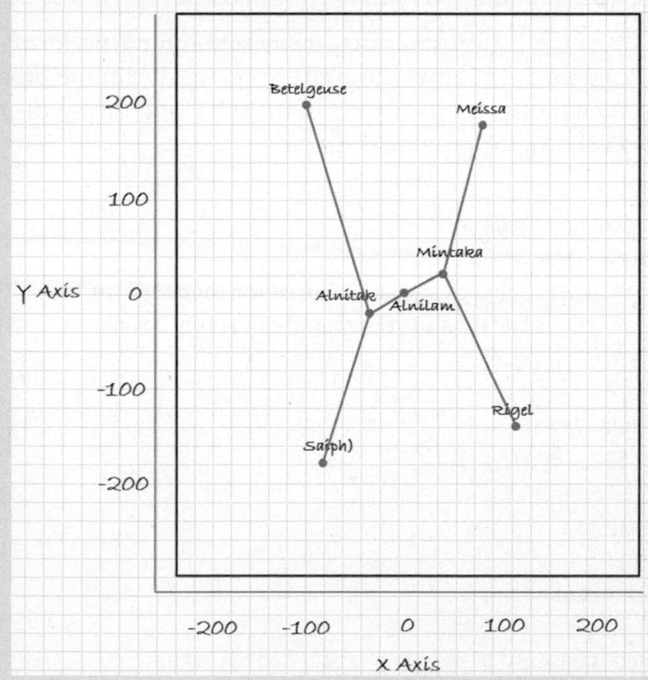

 # Left shoulder to left belt star
Draw a line from (LEFT_SHOULDER_X, LEFT_SHOULDER_Y) to (LEFT_BELTSTAR_X, LEFT_BELTSTAR_Y)

 # Right shoulder to right belt star
Draw a line from (RIGHT_SHOULDER_X, RIGHT_SHOULDER_Y) to (RIGHT_BELTSTAR_X, RIGHT_BELTSTAR_Y)

 # Left belt star to middle belt star
Draw a line from (LEFT_BELTSTAR_X, LEFT_BELTSTAR_Y) to (MIDDLE_BELTSTAR_X, MIDDLE_BELTSTAR_Y)

 # Middle belt star to right belt star
Draw a line from (MIDDLE_BELTSTAR_X, MIDDLE_BELTSTAR_Y) to (RIGHT_BELTSTAR_X, RIGHT_BELTSTAR_Y)

 # Left belt star to left knee
Draw a line from (LEFT_BELTSTAR_X, LEFT_BELTSTAR_Y) to (LEFT_KNEE_X, LEFT_KNEE_Y)

 # Right belt star to right knee
Draw a line from (RIGHT_BELTSTAR_X, RIGHT_BELTSTAR_Y) to (RIGHT_KNEE_X, RIGHT_KNEE_Y)

Now that we know the logical steps that the program must perform, we are ready to start writing code. Program 2-23 shows the entire program. When the program runs, it first displays the stars, then it displays the names of the stars, and then it displays the constellation lines. Figure 2-33 shows the program's output.

Program 2-23 (orion.py)

```
# This program draws the stars of the Orion constellation,
# the names of the stars, and the constellation lines.
import turtle

# Set the window size.
turtle.setup(500, 600)

# Setup the turtle.
turtle.penup()
turtle.hideturtle()

# Create named constants for the star coordinates.
LEFT_SHOULDER_X = -70
LEFT_SHOULDER_Y = 200

RIGHT_SHOULDER_X = 80
RIGHT_SHOULDER_Y = 180

LEFT_BELTSTAR_X = -40
```

```
LEFT_BELTSTAR_Y = -20

MIDDLE_BELTSTAR_X = 0
MIDDLE_BELTSTAR_Y = 0

RIGHT_BELTSTAR_X = 40
RIGHT_BELTSTAR_Y = 20

LEFT_KNEE_X = -90
LEFT_KNEE_Y = -180

RIGHT_KNEE_X = 120
RIGHT_KNEE_Y = -140

# Draw the stars.
turtle.goto(LEFT_SHOULDER_X, LEFT_SHOULDER_Y)           # Left shoulder
turtle.dot()
turtle.goto(RIGHT_SHOULDER_X, RIGHT_SHOULDER_Y)         # Right shoulder
turtle.dot()
turtle.goto(LEFT_BELTSTAR_X, LEFT_BELTSTAR_Y)           # Left belt star
turtle.dot()
turtle.goto(MIDDLE_BELTSTAR_X, MIDDLE_BELTSTAR_Y)       # Middle belt star
turtle.dot()
turtle.goto(RIGHT_BELTSTAR_X, RIGHT_BELTSTAR_Y)         # Right belt star
turtle.dot()
turtle.goto(LEFT_KNEE_X, LEFT_KNEE_Y)                   # Left knee
turtle.dot()
turtle.goto(RIGHT_KNEE_X, RIGHT_KNEE_Y)                 # Right knee
turtle.dot()

# Display the star names
turtle.goto(LEFT_SHOULDER_X, LEFT_SHOULDER_Y)           # Left shoulder
turtle.write('Betegeuse')
turtle.goto(RIGHT_SHOULDER_X, RIGHT_SHOULDER_Y)         # Right shoulder
turtle.write('Meissa')
turtle.goto(LEFT_BELTSTAR_X, LEFT_BELTSTAR_Y)           # Left belt star
turtle.write('Alnitak')
turtle.goto(MIDDLE_BELTSTAR_X, MIDDLE_BELTSTAR_Y)       # Middle belt star
turtle.write('Alnilam')
turtle.goto(RIGHT_BELTSTAR_X, RIGHT_BELTSTAR_Y)         # Right belt star
turtle.write('Mintaka')
turtle.goto(LEFT_KNEE_X, LEFT_KNEE_Y)                   # Left knee
turtle.write('Saiph')
turtle.goto(RIGHT_KNEE_X, RIGHT_KNEE_Y)                 # Right knee
turtle.write('Rigel')

# Draw a line from the left shoulder to left belt star
turtle.goto(LEFT_SHOULDER_X, LEFT_SHOULDER_Y)
turtle.pendown()
```

(program continues)

Program 2-23 *(continued)*

```
turtle.goto(LEFT_BELTSTAR_X, LEFT_BELTSTAR_Y)
turtle.penup()

# Draw a line from the right shoulder to right belt star
turtle.goto(RIGHT_SHOULDER_X, RIGHT_SHOULDER_Y)
turtle.pendown()
turtle.goto(RIGHT_BELTSTAR_X, RIGHT_BELTSTAR_Y)
turtle.penup()

# Draw a line from the left belt star to middle belt star
turtle.goto(LEFT_BELTSTAR_X, LEFT_BELTSTAR_Y)
turtle.pendown()
turtle.goto(MIDDLE_BELTSTAR_X, MIDDLE_BELTSTAR_Y)
turtle.penup()

# Draw a line from the middle belt star to right belt star
turtle.goto(MIDDLE_BELTSTAR_X, MIDDLE_BELTSTAR_Y)
turtle.pendown()
turtle.goto(RIGHT_BELTSTAR_X, RIGHT_BELTSTAR_Y)
turtle.penup()

# Draw a line from the left belt star to left knee
turtle.goto(LEFT_BELTSTAR_X, LEFT_BELTSTAR_Y)
turtle.pendown()
turtle.goto(LEFT_KNEE_X, LEFT_KNEE_Y)
turtle.penup()

# Draw a line from the right belt star to right knee
turtle.goto(RIGHT_BELTSTAR_X, RIGHT_BELTSTAR_Y)
turtle.pendown()
turtle.goto(RIGHT_KNEE_X, RIGHT_KNEE_Y)

# Keep the window open. (Not necessary with IDLE.)
turtle.done()
```

Figure 2-33 Output of the orion.py program

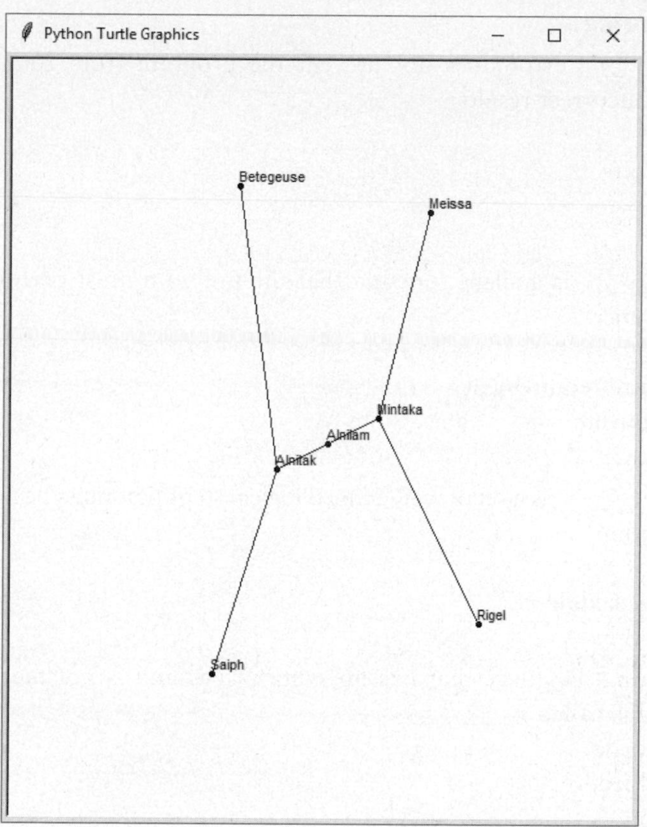

Checkpoint

2.30 What is the turtle's default heading when it first appears?

2.31 How do you move the turtle forward?

2.32 How would you turn the turtle right by 45 degrees?

2.33 How would you move the turtle to a new location without drawing a line?

2.34 What command would you use to display the turtle's current heading?

2.35 What command would you use to draw a circle with a radius of 100 pixels?

2.36 What command would you use to change the turtle's pen size to 8 pixels?

2.37 What command would you use to change the turtle's drawing color to blue?

2.38 What command would you use to change the background color of the turtle's graphics window to black?

2.39 What command would you use to set the size of the turtle's graphics window to 500 pixels wide by 200 pixels high?

2.40 What command would you use to move the turtle to the location (100, 50)?

2.41 What command would you use to display the coordinates of the turtle's current position?

2.42 Which of the following commands will make the animation speed faster? `turtle.speed(1)` or `turtle.speed(10)`

2.43 What command would you use to disable the turtle's animation?

2.44 Describe how to draw a shape that is filled with a color.

2.45 How do you display text in the turtle's graphics window?

Review Questions

Multiple Choice

1. A __________ error does not prevent the program from running, but causes it to produce incorrect results.
   a. syntax
   b. hardware
   c. logic
   d. fatal
2. A __________ is a single function that the program must perform in order to satisfy the customer.
   a. task
   b. software requirement
   c. prerequisite
   d. predicate
3. A(n) __________ is a set of well-defined logical steps that must be taken to perform a task.
   a. logarithm
   b. plan of action
   c. logic schedule
   d. algorithm
4. An informal language that has no syntax rules and is not meant to be compiled or executed is called __________.
   a. faux code
   b. pseudocode
   c. Python
   d. a flowchart
5. A __________ is a diagram that graphically depicts the steps that take place in a program.
   a. flowchart
   b. step chart
   c. code graph
   d. program graph
6. A __________ is a sequence of characters.
   a. char sequence
   b. character collection
   c. string
   d. text block
7. A __________ is a name that references a value in the computer's memory.
   a. variable
   b. register
   c. RAM slot
   d. byte
8. A __________ is any hypothetical person using a program and providing input for it.
   a. designer
   b. user
   c. guinea pig
   d. test subject

9. A string literal in Python must be enclosed in __________.
   a. parentheses.
   b. single-quotes.
   c. double-quotes.
   d. either single-quotes or double-quotes.
10. Short notes placed in different parts of a program explaining how those parts of the program work are called __________.
    a. comments
    b. reference manuals
    c. tutorials
    d. external documentation
11. A(n) __________ makes a variable reference a value in the computer's memory.
    a. variable declaration
    b. assignment statement
    c. math expression
    d. string literal
12. This symbol marks the beginning of a comment in Python.
    a. `&`
    b. `*`
    c. `**`
    d. `#`
13. Which of the following statements will cause an error?
    a. `x = 17`
    b. `17 = x`
    c. `x = 99999`
    d. `x = '17'`
14. In the expression 12 + 7, the values on the right and left of the + symbol are called __________.
    a. operands
    b. operators
    c. arguments
    d. math expressions
15. This operator performs integer division.
    a. `//`
    b. `%`
    c. `**`
    d. `/`
16. This is an operator that raises a number to a power.
    a. `%`
    b. `*`
    c. `**`
    d. `/`
17. This operator performs division, but instead of returning the quotient it returns the remainder.
    a. `%`
    b. `*`
    c. `**`
    d. `/`

18. Suppose the following statement is in a program: `price = 99.0`. After this statement executes, the price variable will reference a value of which data type?
    a. `int`
    b. `float`
    c. `currency`
    d. `str`
19. Which built-in function can be used to read input that has been typed on the keyboard?
    a. `input()`
    b. `get_input()`
    c. `read_input()`
    d. `keyboard()`
20. Which built-in function can be used to convert an `int` value to a `float`?
    a. `int_to_float()`
    b. `float()`
    c. `convert()`
    d. `int()`
21. A magic number is _______________.
    a. a number that is mathematically undefined
    b. an unexplained value that appears in a program's code
    c. a number that cannot be divided by 1
    d. a number that causes computers to crash
22. A __________ is a name that represents a value that does not change during the program's execution.
    a. named literal
    b. named constant
    c. variable signature
    d. key term

True or False

1. Programmers must be careful not to make syntax errors when writing pseudocode programs.
2. In a math expression, multiplication and division take place before addition and subtraction.
3. Variable names can have spaces in them.
4. In Python, the first character of a variable name cannot be a number.
5. If you print a variable that has not been assigned a value, the number 0 will be displayed.

Short Answer

1. What does a professional programmer usually do first to gain an understanding of a problem?
2. What is pseudocode?
3. Computer programs typically perform what three steps?
4. If a math expression adds a `float` to an `int`, what will the data type of the result be?
5. What is the difference between floating-point division and integer division?
6. What is a magic number? Why are magic numbers problematic?

7. Assume a program uses the named constant `PI` to represent the value 3.14159. The program uses the named constant in several statements. What is the advantage of using the named constant instead of the actual value 3.14159 in each statement?

Algorithm Workbench

1. Write Python code that prompts the user to enter his or her height and assigns the user's input to a variable named `height`.
2. Write Python code that prompts the user to enter his or her favorite color and assigns the user's input to a variable named `color`.
3. Write assignment statements that perform the following operations with the variables `a`, `b`, and `c`:
   a. Adds 2 to `a` and assigns the result to `b`
   b. Multiplies `b` times 4 and assigns the result to `a`
   c. Divides `a` by 3.14 and assigns the result to `b`
   d. Subtracts 8 from `b` and assigns the result to `a`
4. Assume the variables `result`, `w`, `x`, `y`, and `z` are all integers, and that `w = 5, x = 4, y = 8, and z = 2`. What value will be stored in `result` after each of the following statements execute?
   a. `result = x + y`
   b. `result = z * 2`
   c. `result = y / x`
   d. `result = y - z`
   e. `result = w // z`
5. Write a Python statement that assigns the sum of 10 and 14 to the variable `total`.
6. Write a Python statement that subtracts the variable `down_payment` from the variable `total` and assigns the result to the variable `due`.
7. Write a Python statement that multiplies the variable `subtotal` by 0.15 and assigns the result to the variable `total`.
8. What would the following display?
```
a = 5
b = 2
c = 3
result = a + b * c
print(result)
```
9. What would the following display?
```
num = 99
num = 5
print(num)
```
10. Assume the variable `sales` references a `float` value. Write a statement that displays the value rounded to two decimal points.
11. Assume the following statement has been executed:
```
number = 1234567.456
```
   Write a Python statement that displays the value referenced by the `number` variable formatted as
```
1,234,567.5
```
12. What will the following statement display?
```
print('George', 'John', 'Paul', 'Ringo', sep='@')
```

13. Write a turtle graphics statement that draws a circle with a radius of 75 pixels.
14. Write the turtle graphics statements to draw a square that is 100 pixels wide on each side and filled with the color blue.
15. Write the turtle graphics statements to draw a square that is 100 pixels wide on each side and a circle that is centered inside the square. The circle's radius should be 80 pixels. The circle should be filled with the color red. (The square should not be filled with a color.)

Programming Exercises

1. Personal Information

Write a program that displays the following information:

- Your name
- Your address, with city, state, and ZIP
- Your telephone number
- Your college major

2. Sales Prediction

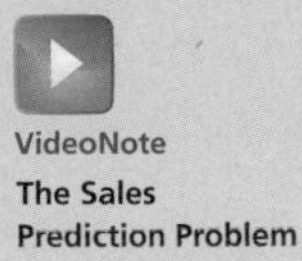

VideoNote The Sales Prediction Problem

A company has determined that its annual profit is typically 23 percent of total sales. Write a program that asks the user to enter the projected amount of total sales, then displays the profit that will be made from that amount.

Hint: Use the value 0.23 to represent 23 percent.

3. Land Calculation

One acre of land is equivalent to 43,560 square feet. Write a program that asks the user to enter the total square feet in a tract of land and calculates the number of acres in the tract.

Hint: Divide the amount entered by 43,560 to get the number of acres.

4. Total Purchase

A customer in a store is purchasing five items. Write a program that asks for the price of each item, then displays the subtotal of the sale, the amount of sales tax, and the total. Assume the sales tax is 7 percent.

5. Distance Traveled

Assuming there are no accidents or delays, the distance that a car travels down the interstate can be calculated with the following formula:

$$Distance = Speed \times Time$$

A car is traveling at 70 miles per hour. Write a program that displays the following:

- The distance the car will travel in 6 hours
- The distance the car will travel in 10 hours
- The distance the car will travel in 15 hours

6. Sales Tax

Write a program that will ask the user to enter the amount of a purchase. The program should then compute the state and county sales tax. Assume the state sales tax is 5 percent and the county sales tax is 2.5 percent. The program should display the amount of the purchase, the state sales tax, the county sales tax, the total sales tax, and the total of the sale (which is the sum of the amount of purchase plus the total sales tax).

Hint: Use the value 0.025 to represent 2.5 percent, and 0.05 to represent 5 percent.

7. Miles-per-Gallon

A car's miles-per-gallon (MPG) can be calculated with the following formula:

$$MPG = \text{Miles driven} \div \text{Gallons of gas used}$$

Write a program that asks the user for the number of miles driven and the gallons of gas used. It should calculate the car's MPG and display the result.

8. Tip, Tax, and Total

Write a program that calculates the total amount of a meal purchased at a restaurant. The program should ask the user to enter the charge for the food, then calculate the amounts of a 18 percent tip and 7 percent sales tax. Display each of these amounts and the total.

9. Celsius to Fahrenheit Temperature Converter

Write a program that converts Celsius temperatures to Fahrenheit temperatures. The formula is as follows:

$$F = \frac{9}{5}C + 32$$

The program should ask the user to enter a temperature in Celsius, then display the temperature converted to Fahrenheit.

10. Ingredient Adjuster

A cookie recipe calls for the following ingredients:

- 1.5 cups of sugar
- 1 cup of butter
- 2.75 cups of flour

The recipe produces 48 cookies with this amount of the ingredients. Write a program that asks the user how many cookies he or she wants to make, then displays the number of cups of each ingredient needed for the specified number of cookies.

11. Male and Female Percentages

Write a program that asks the user for the number of males and the number of females registered in a class. The program should display the percentage of males and females in the class.

Hint: Suppose there are 8 males and 12 females in a class. There are 20 students in the class. The percentage of males can be calculated as 8 ÷ 20 = 0.4, or 40%. The percentage of females can be calculated as 12 ÷ 20 = 0.6, or 60%.

12. Stock Transaction Program

Last month, Joe purchased some stock in Acme Software, Inc. Here are the details of the purchase:

- The number of shares that Joe purchased was 2,000.
- When Joe purchased the stock, he paid $40.00 per share.
- Joe paid his stockbroker a commission that amounted to 3 percent of the amount he paid for the stock.

Two weeks later, Joe sold the stock. Here are the details of the sale:

- The number of shares that Joe sold was 2,000.

- He sold the stock for \$42.75 per share.
- He paid his stockbroker another commission that amounted to 3 percent of the amount he received for the stock.

Write a program that displays the following information:

- The amount of money Joe paid for the stock.
- The amount of commission Joe paid his broker when he bought the stock.
- The amount for which Joe sold the stock.
- The amount of commission Joe paid his broker when he sold the stock.
- Display the amount of money that Joe had left when he sold the stock and paid his broker (both times). If this amount is positive, then Joe made a profit. If the amount is negative, then Joe lost money.

13. Planting Grapevines

A vineyard owner is planting several new rows of grapevines, and needs to know how many grapevines to plant in each row. She has determined that after measuring the length of a future row, she can use the following formula to calculate the number of vines that will fit in the row, along with the trellis end-post assemblies that will need to be constructed at each end of the row:

$$V = \frac{R - 2E}{S}$$

The terms in the formula are:

V is the number of grapevines that will fit in the row.
R is the length of the row, in feet.
E is the amount of space, in feet, used by an end-post assembly.
S is the space between vines, in feet.

Write a program that makes the calculation for the vineyard owner. The program should ask the user to input the following:

- The length of the row, in feet
- The amount of space used by an end-post assembly, in feet
- The amount of space between the vines, in feet

Once the input data has been entered, the program should calculate and display the number of grapevines that will fit in the row.

14. Compound Interest

When a bank account pays compound interest, it pays interest not only on the principal amount that was deposited into the account, but also on the interest that has accumulated over time. Suppose you want to deposit some money into a savings account, and let the account earn compound interest for a certain number of years. The formula for calculating the balance of the account after a specified number of years is:

$$A = P\left(1 + \frac{r}{n}\right)^{nt}$$

The terms in the formula are:

A is the amount of money in the account after the specified number of years.
P is the principal amount that was originally deposited into the account.
r is the annual interest rate.
n is the number of times per year that the interest is compounded.
t is the specified number of years.

Write a program that makes the calculation for you. The program should ask the user to input the following:

- The amount of principal originally deposited into the account
- The annual interest rate paid by the account
- The number of times per year that the interest is compounded (For example, if interest is compounded monthly, enter 12. If interest is compounded quarterly, enter 4.)
- The number of years the account will be left to earn interest

Once the input data has been entered, the program should calculate and display the amount of money that will be in the account after the specified number of years.

NOTE: The user should enter the interest rate as a percentage. For example, 2 percent would be entered as 2, not as .02. The program will then have to divide the input by 100 to move the decimal point to the correct position.

15. Turtle Graphics Drawings

Use the turtle graphics library to write programs that reproduce each of the designs shown in Figure 2-34.

Figure 2-34 Designs

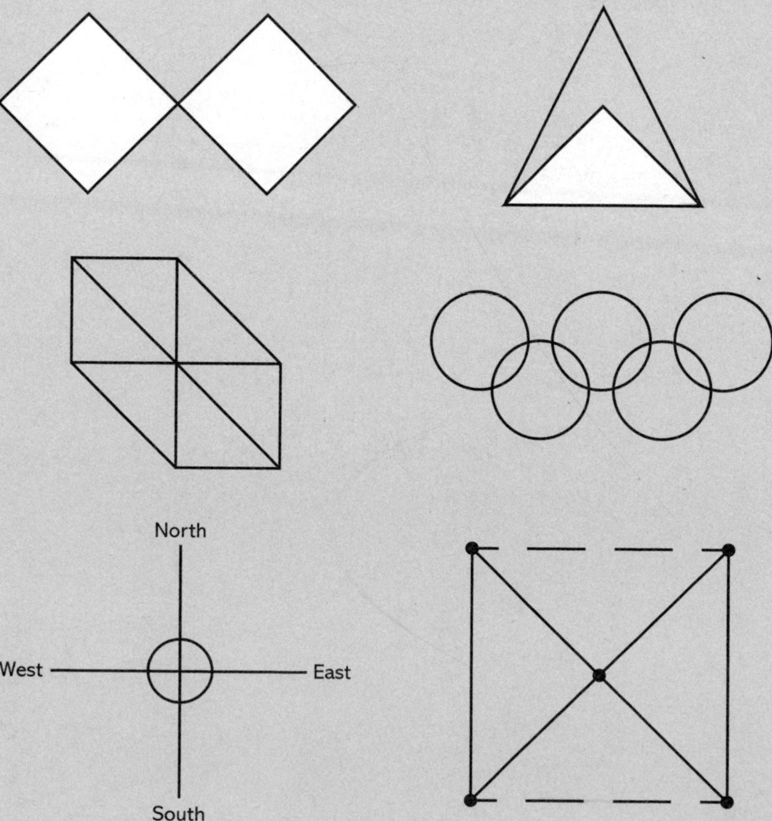

CHAPTER 3

Decision Structures and Boolean Logic

TOPICS

3.1 The if Statement

CONCEPT: The `if` statement is used to create a decision structure, which allows a program to have more than one path of execution. The `if` statement causes one or more statements to execute only when a Boolean expression is true.

A *control structure* is a logical design that controls the order in which a set of statements execute. So far in this book, we have used only the simplest type of control structure: the sequence structure. A *sequence structure* is a set of statements that execute in the order in which they appear. For example, the following code is a sequence structure because the statements execute from top to bottom:

VideoNote
The if Statement

```
name = input('What is your name? ')
age = int(input('What is your age? '))
print('Here is the data you entered:')
print('Name:', name)
print('Age:', age)
```

Although the sequence structure is heavily used in programming, it cannot handle every type of task. This is because some problems simply cannot be solved by performing a set of ordered steps, one after the other. For example, consider a pay calculating program that determines whether an employee has worked overtime. If the employee has worked more than 40 hours, he or she gets paid extra for all the hours over 40. Otherwise, the overtime calculation should be skipped. Programs like this require a different type of control structure: one that can execute a set of statements only under certain circumstances. This can be accomplished with a *decision structure*. (Decision structures are also known as *selection structures*.)

In a decision structure's simplest form, a specific action is performed only if a certain condition exists. If the condition does not exist, the action is not performed. The flowchart shown in Figure 3-1 shows how the logic of an everyday decision can be diagrammed as a decision structure. The diamond symbol represents a true/false condition. If the condition is true, we follow one path, which leads to an action being performed. If the condition is false, we follow another path, which skips the action.

Figure 3-1 A simple decision structure

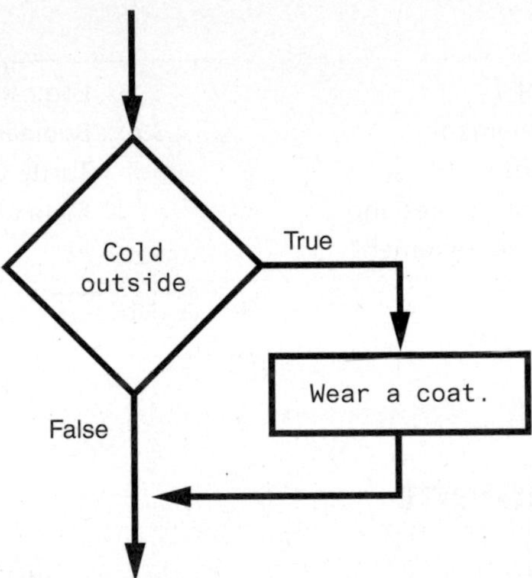

In the flowchart, the diamond symbol indicates some condition that must be tested. In this case, we are determining whether the condition `Cold outside` is true or false. If this condition is true, the action `Wear a coat` is performed. If the condition is false, the action is skipped. The action is *conditionally executed* because it is performed only when a certain condition is true.

Programmers call the type of decision structure shown in Figure 3-1 a *single alternative decision structure*. This is because it provides only one alternative path of execution. If the condition in the diamond symbol is true, we take the alternative path. Otherwise, we exit the structure. Figure 3-2 shows a more elaborate example, where three actions are taken only when it is cold outside. It is still a single alternative decision structure, because there is one alternative path of execution.

In Python, we use the `if` statement to write a single alternative decision structure. Here is the general format of the `if` statement:

```
if condition:
    statement
    statement
    etc.
```

Figure 3-2 A decision structure that performs three actions if it is cold outside

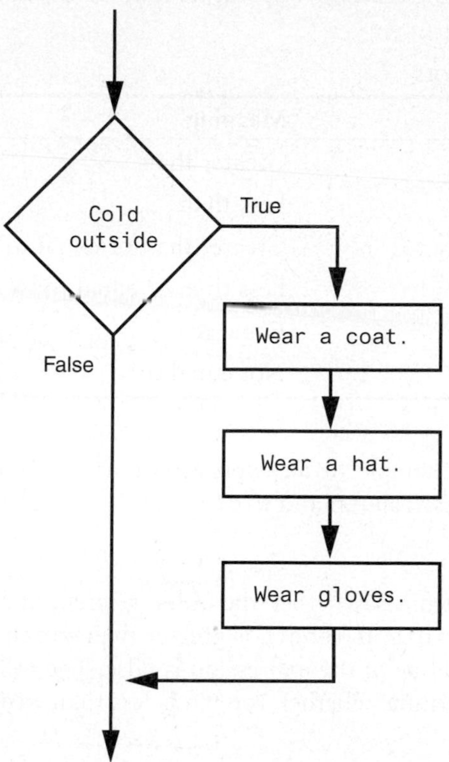

For simplicity, we will refer to the first line as the *`if` clause*. The `if` clause begins with the word `if`, followed by a *`condition`*, which is an expression that will be evaluated as either true or false. A colon appears after the *`condition`*. Beginning at the next line is a block of statements. A *block* is simply a set of statements that belong together as a group. Notice in the general format that all of the statements in the block are indented. This indentation is required because the Python interpreter uses it to tell where the block begins and ends.

When the `if` statement executes, the *`condition`* is tested. If the *`condition`* is true, the statements that appear in the block following the `if` clause are executed. If the condition is false, the statements in the block are skipped.

Boolean Expressions and Relational Operators

As previously mentioned, the `if` statement tests an expression to determine whether it is true or false. The expressions that are tested by the `if` statement are called *Boolean expressions*, named in honor of the English mathematician George Boole. In the 1800s, Boole invented a system of mathematics in which the abstract concepts of true and false can be used in computations.

Typically, the Boolean expression that is tested by an `if` statement is formed with a relational operator. A *relational operator* determines whether a specific relationship exists between two values. For example, the greater than operator (>) determines whether one value is greater than another. The equal to operator (==) determines whether two values are equal. Table 3-1 lists the relational operators that are available in Python.

Table 3-1 Relational operators

Operator	Meaning
`>`	Greater than
`<`	Less than
`>=`	Greater than or equal to
`<=`	Less than or equal to
`==`	Equal to
`!=`	Not equal to

The following is an example of an expression that uses the greater than (>) operator to compare two variables, `length` and `width`:

```
length > width
```

This expression determines whether the value referenced by `length` is greater than the value referenced by `width`. If `length` is greater than `width`, the value of the expression is true. Otherwise, the value of the expression is false. The following expression uses the less than operator to determine whether `length` is less than `width`:

```
length < width
```

Table 3-2 shows examples of several Boolean expressions that compare the variables `x` and `y`.

Table 3-2 Boolean expressions using relational operators

Expression	Meaning
`x > y`	Is `x` greater than `y`?
`x < y`	Is `x` less than `y`?
`x >= y`	Is `x` greater than or equal to `y`?
`x <= y`	Is `x` less than or equal to `y`?
`x == y`	Is `x` equal to `y`?
`x != y`	Is `x` not equal to `y`?

You can use the Python interpreter in interactive mode to experiment with these operators. If you type a Boolean expression at the >>> prompt, the interpreter will evaluate the expression and display its value as either `True` or `False`. For example, look at the following interactive session. (We have added line numbers for easier reference.)

```
>>> x = 1 [Enter]
>>> y = 0 [Enter]
>>> x > y [Enter]
```

```
4  True
5  >>> y > x
6  False
7  >>>
```

The statement in line 1 assigns the value 1 to the variable x. The statement in line 2 assigns the value 0 to the variable y. In line 3, we type the Boolean expression x > y. The value of the expression (True) is displayed in line 4. Then, in line 5, we type the Boolean expression y > x. The value of the expression (False) is displayed in line 6.

The following interactive session demonstrates the < operator:

```
1  >>> x = 1 Enter
2  >>> y = 0 Enter
3  >>> y < x Enter
4  True
5  >>> x < y Enter
6  False
7  >>>
```

The statement in line 1 assigns the value 1 to the variable x. The statement in line 2 assigns the value 0 to the variable y. In line 3, we type the Boolean expression y < x. The value of the expression (True) is displayed in line 4. Then, in line 5, we type the Boolean expression x < y. The value of the expression (False) is displayed in line 6.

The >= and <= Operators

Two of the operators, >= and <=, test for more than one relationship. The >= operator determines whether the operand on its left is greater than *or* equal to the operand on its right. The <= operator determines whether the operand on its left is less than *or* equal to the operand on its right.

For example, look at the following interactive session:

```
1  >>> x = 1 Enter
2  >>> y = 0 Enter
3  >>> z = 1 Enter
4  >>> x >= y Enter
5  True
6  >>> x >= z Enter
7  True
8  >>> x <= z Enter
9  True
10 >>> x <= y Enter
11 False
12 >>>
```

In lines 1 through 3, we assign values to the variables x, y, and z. In line 4, we enter the Boolean expression x >= y, which is True. In line 6, we enter the Boolean expression x >= z, which is True. In line 8, we enter the Boolean expression x <= z, which is True. In line 10, we enter the Boolean expression x <= y, which is False.

The == Operator

The == operator determines whether the operand on its left is equal to the operand on its right. If the values referenced by both operands are the same, the expression is true. Assuming a is 4, the expression `a == 4` is true, and the expression `a == 2` is false.

The following interactive session demonstrates the == operator:

```
>>> x = 1 Enter
>>> y = 0 Enter
>>> z = 1 Enter
>>> x == y Enter
False
>>> x == z Enter
True
>>>
```

NOTE: The equality operator is two = symbols together. Don't confuse this operator with the assignment operator, which is one = symbol.

The != Operator

The `!=` operator is the not-equal-to operator. It determines whether the operand on its left is not equal to the operand on its right, which is the opposite of the == operator. As before, assuming a is 4, b is 6, and c is 4, both `a != b` and `b != c` are true because a is not equal to b and b is not equal to c. However, `a != c` is false because a is equal to c.

The following interactive session demonstrates the `!=` operator:

```
>>> x = 1 Enter
>>> y = 0 Enter
>>> z = 1 Enter
>>> x != y Enter
True
>>> x != z Enter
False
>>>
```

Putting It All Together

Let's look at the following example of the `if` statement:

```
if sales > 50000:
    bonus = 500.0
```

This statement uses the > operator to determine whether `sales` is greater than 50,000. If the expression `sales > 50000` is true, the variable bonus is assigned 500.0. If the expression is false, however, the assignment statement is skipped. Figure 3-3 shows a flowchart for this section of code.

Figure 3-3 Example decision structure

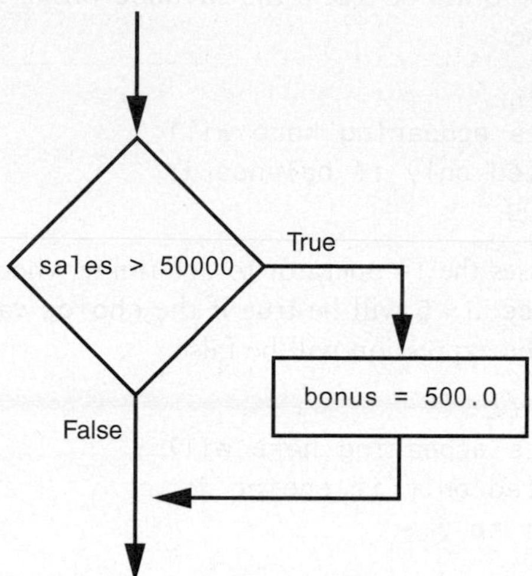

The following example conditionally executes a block containing three statements. Figure 3-4 shows a flowchart for this section of code:

```
if sales > 50000:
    bonus = 500.0
    commission_rate = 0.12
    print('You met your sales quota!')
```

Figure 3-4 Example decision structure

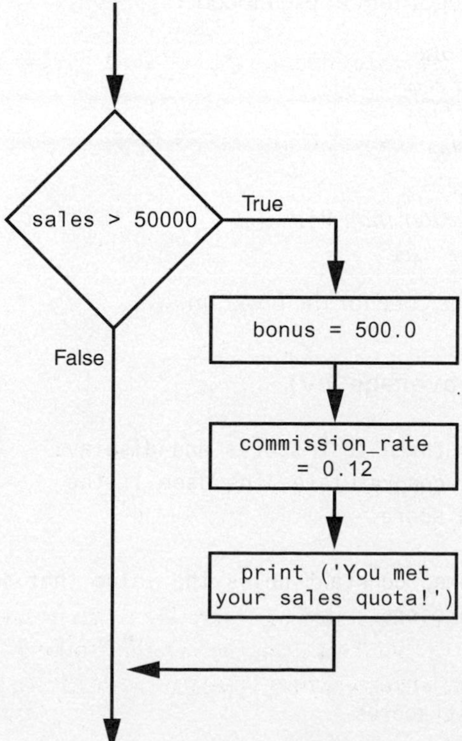

The following code uses the == operator to determine whether two values are equal. The expression `balance == 0` will be true if the `balance` variable is assigned 0. Otherwise, the expression will be false.

```
if balance == 0:
    # Statements appearing here will
    # be executed only if balance is
    # equal to 0.
```

The following code uses the != operator to determine whether two values are *not* equal. The expression `choice != 5` will be true if the `choice` variable does not reference the value 5. Otherwise, the expression will be false.

```
if choice != 5:
    # Statements appearing here will
    # be executed only if choice is
    # not equal to 5.
```

In the Spotlight:
Using the `if` Statement

Kathryn teaches a science class and her students are required to take three tests. She wants to write a program that her students can use to calculate their average test score. She also wants the program to congratulate the student enthusiastically if the average is greater than 95. Here is the algorithm in pseudocode:

Get the first test score
Get the second test score
Get the third test score
Calculate the average
Display the average
If the average is greater than 95:
    Congratulate the user

Program 3-1 shows the code for the program.

Program 3-1 (test_average.py)

```
# This program gets three test scores and displays
# their average. It congratulates the user if the
# average is a high score.

# The HIGH_SCORE named constant holds the value that is
# considered a high score.
HIGH_SCORE = 95

# Get the three test scores.
```

```
test1 = int(input('Enter the score for test 1: ' ))
test2 = int(input('Enter the score for test 2: ' ))
test3 = int(input('Enter the score for test 3: ' ))

# Calculate the average test score.
average = (test1 + test2 + test3) / 3

# Print the average.
print('The average score is', average)

# If the average is a high score,
# congratulate the user.
if average >= HIGH_SCORE:
    print('Congratulations!')
    print('That is a great average!')
```

Program Output (with input shown in bold)

```
Enter the score for test 1: 82 Enter
Enter the score for test 2: 76 Enter
Enter the score for test 3: 91 Enter
The average score is 83.0
```

Program Output (with input shown in bold)

```
Enter the score for test 1: 93 Enter
Enter the score for test 2: 99 Enter
Enter the score for test 3: 96 Enter
The average score is 96.0
Congratulations!
That is a great average!
```

Checkpoint

3.1 What is a control structure?

3.2 What is a decision structure?

3.3 What is a single alternative decision structure?

3.4 What is a Boolean expression?

3.5 What types of relationships between values can you test with relational operators?

3.6 Write an `if` statement that assigns 0 to `x` if `y` is equal to 20.

3.7 Write an `if` statement that assigns 0.2 to `commissionRate` if `sales` is greater than or equal to 10000.

3.2 The if-else Statement

CONCEPT: An if-else statement will execute one block of statements if its condition is true, or another block if its condition is false.

VideoNote
The if-else Statement

The previous section introduced the single alternative decision structure (the if statement), which has one alternative path of execution. Now, we will look at the *dual alternative decision structure*, which has two possible paths of execution—one path is taken if a condition is true, and the other path is taken if the condition is false. Figure 3-5 shows a flowchart for a dual alternative decision structure.

Figure 3-5 A dual alternative decision structure

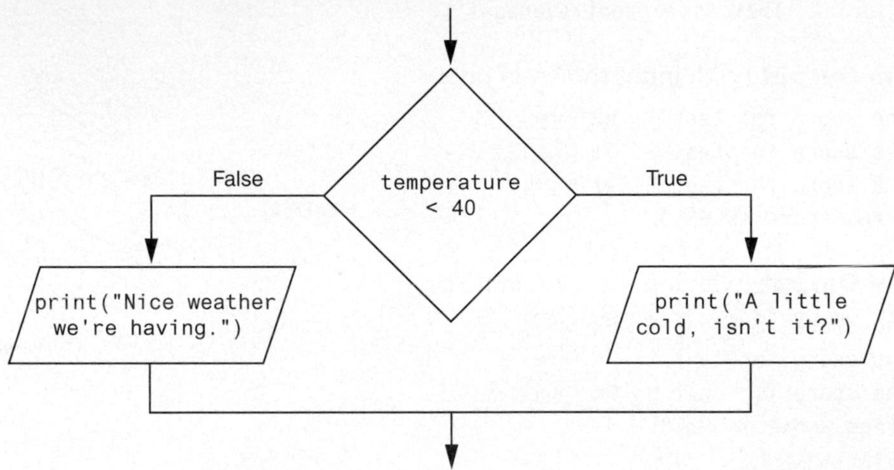

The decision structure in the flowchart tests the condition `temperature < 40`. If this condition is true, the statement `print("A little cold, isn't it?")` is performed. If the condition is false, the statement `print("Nice weather we're having.")` is performed.

In code, we write a dual alternative decision structure as an if-else statement. Here is the general format of the if-else statement:

```
if condition:
     statement
     statement
     etc.
else:
     statement
     statement
     etc.
```

When this statement executes, the *condition* is tested. If it is true, the block of indented statements following the if clause is executed, then control of the program jumps to the statement that follows the if-else statement. If the condition is false, the block of indented statements following the else clause is executed, then control of the program jumps to the statement that follows the if-else statement. This action is described in Figure 3-6.

Figure 3-6 Conditional execution in an if-else statement

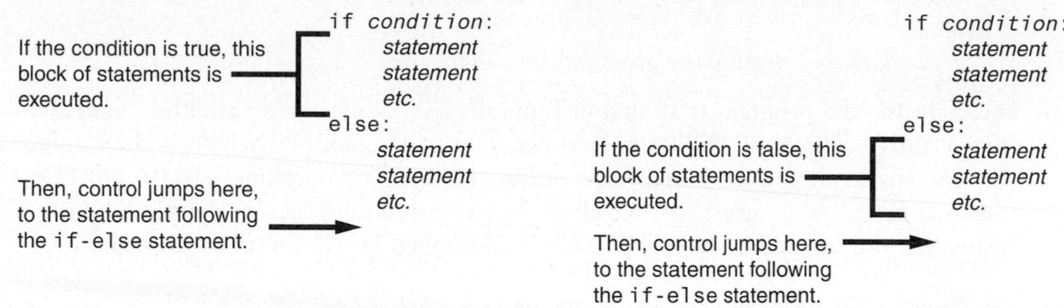

The following code shows an example of an if-else statement. This code matches the flowchart that was shown in Figure 3-5.

```
if temperature < 40:
    print("A little cold, isn't it?")
else:
    print("Nice weather we're having.")
```

Indentation in the if-else Statement

When you write an if-else statement, follow these guidelines for indentation:

- Make sure the if clause and the else clause are aligned.
- The if clause and the else clause are each followed by a block of statements. Make sure the statements in the blocks are consistently indented.

This is shown in Figure 3-7.

Figure 3-7 Indentation with an if-else statement

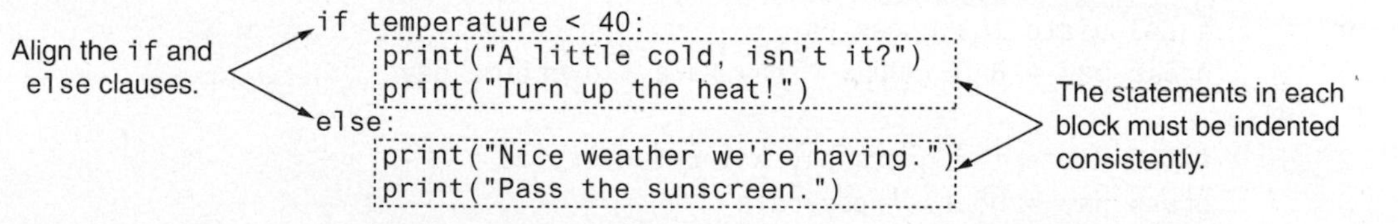

In the Spotlight:

Using the if-else Statement

Chris owns an auto repair business and has several employees. If any employee works over 40 hours in a week, he pays them 1.5 times their regular hourly pay rate for all hours over 40. He has asked you to design a simple payroll program that calculates an employee's gross pay, including any overtime wages. You design the following algorithm:

Get the number of hours worked.
Get the hourly pay rate.

If the employee worked more than 40 hours:
Calculate and display the gross pay with overtime.
Else:
Calculate and display the gross pay as usual.

The code for the program is shown in Program 3-2. Notice two variables are created in lines 3 and 4. The `BASE_HOURS` named constant is assigned 40, which is the number of hours an employee can work in a week without getting paid overtime. The `OT_MULTIPLIER` named constant is assigned 1.5, which is the pay rate multiplier for overtime hours. This means that the employee's hourly pay rate is multiplied by 1.5 for all overtime hours.

Program 3-2 (auto_repair_payroll.py)

```
1  # Named constants to represent the base hours and
2  # the overtime multiplier.
3  BASE_HOURS = 40       # Base hours per week
4  OT_MULTIPLIER = 1.5  # Overtime multiplier
5
6  # Get the hours worked and the hourly pay rate.
7  hours = float(input('Enter the number of hours worked: '))
8  pay_rate = float(input('Enter the hourly pay rate: '))
9
10 # Calculate and display the gross pay.
11 if hours > BASE_HOURS:
12     # Calculate the gross pay with overtime.
13     # First, get the number of overtime hours worked.
14     overtime_hours = hours - BASE_HOURS
15
16     # Calculate the amount of overtime pay.
17     overtime_pay = overtime_hours * pay_rate * OT_MULTIPLIER
18
19     # Calculate the gross pay.
20     gross_pay = BASE_HOURS * pay_rate + overtime_pay
21 else:
22     # Calculate the gross pay without overtime.
23     gross_pay = hours * pay_rate
24
25 # Display the gross pay.
26 print('The gross pay is $', format(gross_pay, ',.2f'), sep='')
```

Program Output (with input shown in bold)

Enter the number of hours worked: **40** [Enter]
Enter the hourly pay rate: **20** [Enter]
The gross pay is $800.00.

Program Output (with input shown in bold)

Enter the number of hours worked: **50** [Enter]
Enter the hourly pay rate: **20** [Enter]
The gross pay is $1,100.00.

Checkpoint

3.8 How does a dual alternative decision structure work?

3.9 What statement do you use in Python to write a dual alternative decision structure?

3.10 When you write an `if-else` statement, under what circumstances do the statements that appear after the `else` clause execute?

3.3 Comparing Strings

CONCEPT: Python allows you to compare strings. This allows you to create decision structures that test the value of a string.

You saw in the preceding examples how numbers can be compared in a decision structure. You can also compare strings. For example, look at the following code:

```
name1 = 'Mary'
name2 = 'Mark'
if name1 == name2:
    print('The names are the same.')
else:
    print('The names are NOT the same.')
```

The `==` operator compares `name1` and `name2` to determine whether they are equal. Because the strings `'Mary'` and `'Mark'` are not equal, the `else` clause will display the message `'The names are NOT the same.'`

Let's look at another example. Assume the `month` variable references a string. The following code uses the `!=` operator to determine whether the value referenced by `month` is not equal to `'October'`:

```
if month != 'October':
    print('This is the wrong time for Octoberfest!')
```

Program 3-3 is a complete program demonstrating how two strings can be compared. The program prompts the user to enter a password, then determines whether the string entered is equal to `'prospero'`.

Program 3-3 (password.py)

```
# This program compares two strings.
# Get a password from the user.
password = input('Enter the password: ')

# Determine whether the correct password
# was entered.
if password == 'prospero':
    print('Password accepted.')
else:
    print('Sorry, that is the wrong password.')
```

Program Output (with input shown in bold)

```
Enter the password: ferdinand [Enter]
Sorry, that is the wrong password.
```

Program Output (with input shown in bold)

```
Enter the password: prospero [Enter]
Password accepted.
```

String comparisons are case sensitive. For example, the strings `'saturday'` and `'Saturday'` are not equal because the `"s"` is lowercase in the first string, but uppercase in the second string. The following sample session with Program 4-3 shows what happens when the user enters `Prospero` as the password (with an uppercase `P`).

Program Output (with input shown in bold)

```
Enter the password: Prospero [Enter]
Sorry, that is the wrong password.
```

TIP: In Chapter 8, you will learn how to manipulate strings so case-insensitive comparisons can be performed.

Other String Comparisons

In addition to determining whether strings are equal or not equal, you can also determine whether one string is greater than or less than another string. This is a useful capability because programmers commonly need to design programs that sort strings in some order.

Recall from Chapter 1 that computers do not actually store characters, such as A, B, C, and so on, in memory. Instead, they store numeric codes that represent the characters. Chapter 1 mentioned that ASCII (the American Standard Code for Information Interchange) is a commonly used character coding system. You can see the set of ASCII codes in Appendix C, but here are some facts about it:

- The uppercase characters A through Z are represented by the numbers 65 through 90.
- The lowercase characters a through z are represented by the numbers 97 through 122.
- When the digits 0 through 9 are stored in memory as characters, they are represented by the numbers 48 through 57. (For example, the string `'abc123'` would be stored in memory as the codes 97, 98, 99, 49, 50, and 51.)
- A blank space is represented by the number 32.

In addition to establishing a set of numeric codes to represent characters in memory, ASCII also establishes an order for characters. The character "A" comes before the character "B", which comes before the character "C", and so on.

When a program compares characters, it actually compares the codes for the characters. For example, look at the following `if` statement:

```
if 'a' < 'b':
    print('The letter a is less than the letter b.')
```

This code determines whether the ASCII code for the character `'a'` is less than the ASCII code for the character `'b'`. The expression `'a' < 'b'` is true because the code for `'a'` is less than the code for `'b'`. So, if this were part of an actual program it would display the message `'The letter a is less than the letter b.'`

Let's look at how strings containing more than one character are typically compared. Suppose a program uses the strings `'Mary'` and `'Mark'` as follows:

```
name1 = 'Mary'
name2 = 'Mark'
```

Figure 3-8 shows how the individual characters in the strings `'Mary'` and `'Mark'` would actually be stored in memory, using ASCII codes.

Figure 3-8 Character codes for the strings `'Mary'` and `'Mark'`

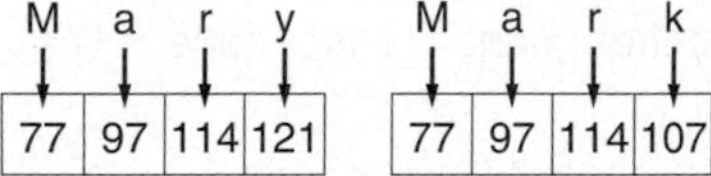

When you use relational operators to compare these strings, the strings are compared character-by-character. For example, look at the following code:

```
name1 = 'Mary'
name2 = 'Mark'
if name1 > name2:
    print('Mary is greater than Mark')
else:
    print('Mary is not greater than Mark')
```

The > operator compares each character in the strings `'Mary'` and `'Mark'`, beginning with the first, or leftmost, characters. This is shown in Figure 3-9.

Figure 3-9 Comparing each character in a string

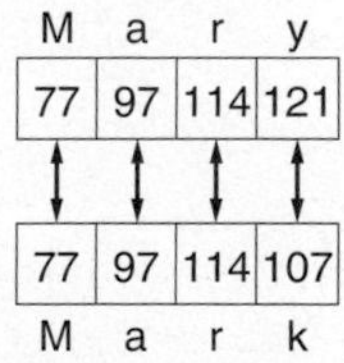

Here is how the comparison takes place:

1. The `'M'` in `'Mary'` is compared with the `'M'` in `'Mark'`. Since these are the same, the next characters are compared.
2. The `'a'` in `'Mary'` is compared with the `'a'` in `'Mark'`. Since these are the same, the next characters are compared.
3. The `'r'` in `'Mary'` is compared with the `'r'` in `'Mark'`. Since these are the same, the next characters are compared.
4. The `'y'` in `'Mary'` is compared with the `'k'` in `'Mark'`. Since these are not the same, the two strings are not equal. The character `'y'` has a higher ASCII code (121) than `'k'` (107), so it is determined that the string `'Mary'` is greater than the string `'Mark'`.

If one of the strings in a comparison is shorter than the other, only the corresponding characters will be compared. If the corresponding characters are identical, then the shorter string is considered less than the longer string. For example, suppose the strings `'High'` and `'Hi'` were being compared. The string `'Hi'` would be considered less than `'High'` because it is shorter.

Program 3-4 shows a simple demonstration of how two strings can be compared with the < operator. The user is prompted to enter two names, and the program displays those two names in alphabetical order.

Program 3-4 (sort_names.py)

```
# This program compares strings with the < operator.
# Get two names from the user.
name1 = input('Enter a name (last name first): ')
name2 = input('Enter another name (last name first): ')

# Display the names in alphabetical order.
print('Here are the names, listed alphabetically.')

if name1 < name2:
    print(name1)
    print(name2)
else:
    print(name2)
    print(name1)
```

Program Output (with input shown in bold)

Enter a name (last name first): **Jones, Richard** [Enter]
Enter another name (last name first) **Costa, Joan** [Enter]
Here are the names, listed alphabetically:
Costa, Joan
Jones, Richard

Checkpoint

3.11 What would the following code display?

```
if 'z' < 'a':
    print('z is less than a.')
else:
    print('z is not less than a.')
```

3.12 What would the following code display?

```
s1 = 'New York'
s2 = 'Boston'
```

```
if s1 > s2:
    print(s2)
    print(s1)
else:
    print(s1)
    print(s2)
```

3.4 Nested Decision Structures and the if-elif-else Statement

CONCEPT: To test more than one condition, a decision structure can be nested inside another decision structure.

In Section 3.1, we mentioned that a control structure determines the order in which a set of statements execute. Programs are usually designed as combinations of different control structures. For example, Figure 3-10 shows a flowchart that combines a decision structure with two sequence structures.

Figure 3-10 Combining sequence structures with a decision structure

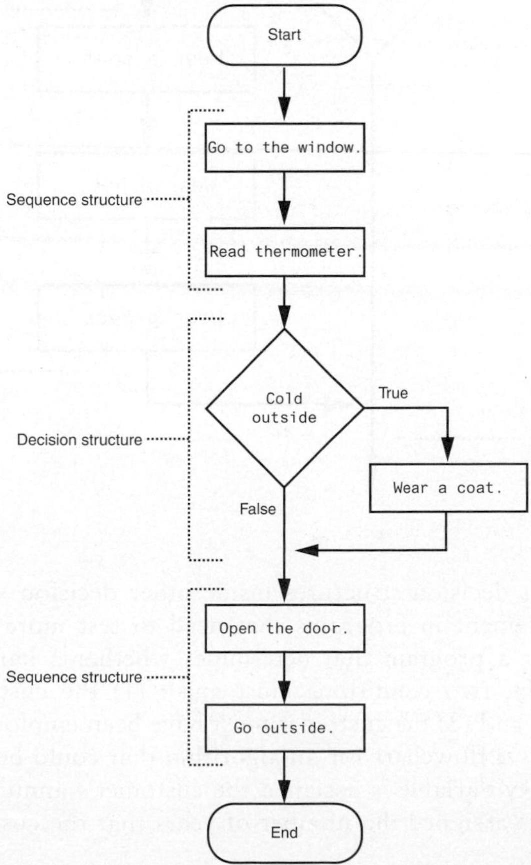

The flowchart in the figure starts with a sequence structure. Assuming you have an outdoor thermometer in your window, the first step is `Go to the window`, and the next step is `Read thermometer`. A decision structure appears next, testing the condition `Cold outside`. If this is true, the action `Wear a coat` is performed. Another sequence structure appears next. The step `Open the door` is performed, followed by `Go outside`.

Quite often, structures must be nested inside other structures. For example, look at the partial flowchart in Figure 3-11. It shows a decision structure with a sequence structure nested inside it. The decision structure tests the condition `Cold outside`. If that condition is true, the steps in the sequence structure are executed.

Figure 3-11 A sequence structure nested inside a decision structure

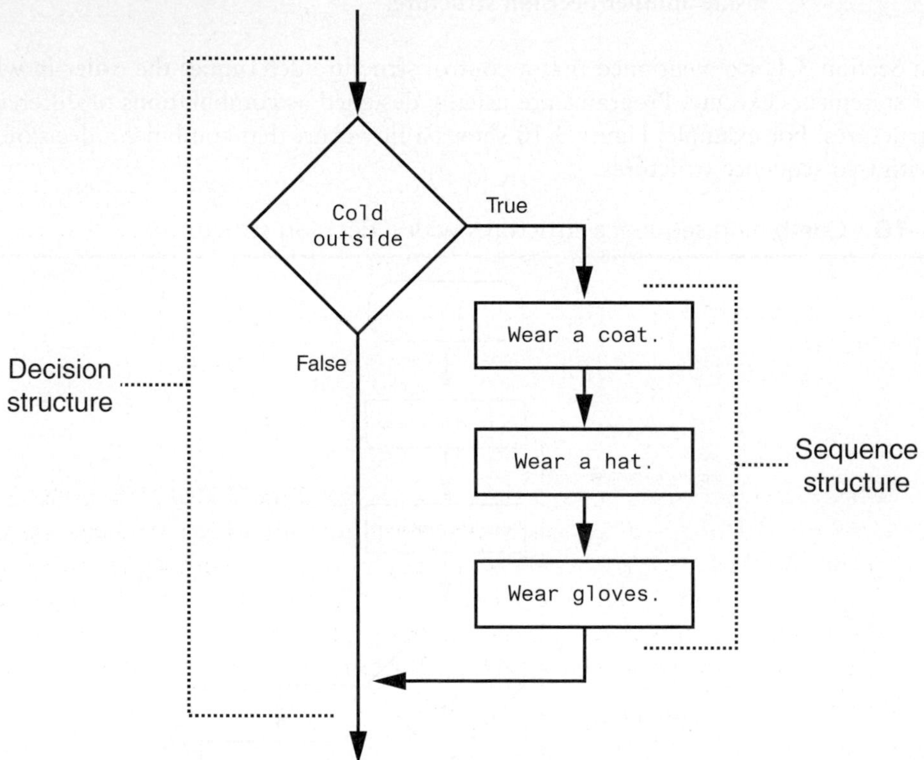

You can also nest decision structures inside other decision structures. In fact, this is a common requirement in programs that need to test more than one condition. For example, consider a program that determines whether a bank customer qualifies for a loan. To qualify, two conditions must exist: (1) the customer must earn at least $30,000 per year, and (2) the customer must have been employed for at least two years. Figure 3-12 shows a flowchart for an algorithm that could be used in such a program. Assume the `salary` variable is assigned the customer's annual salary, and the `years_on_job` variable is assigned the number of years that the customer has worked on his or her current job.

Figure 3-12 A nested decision structure

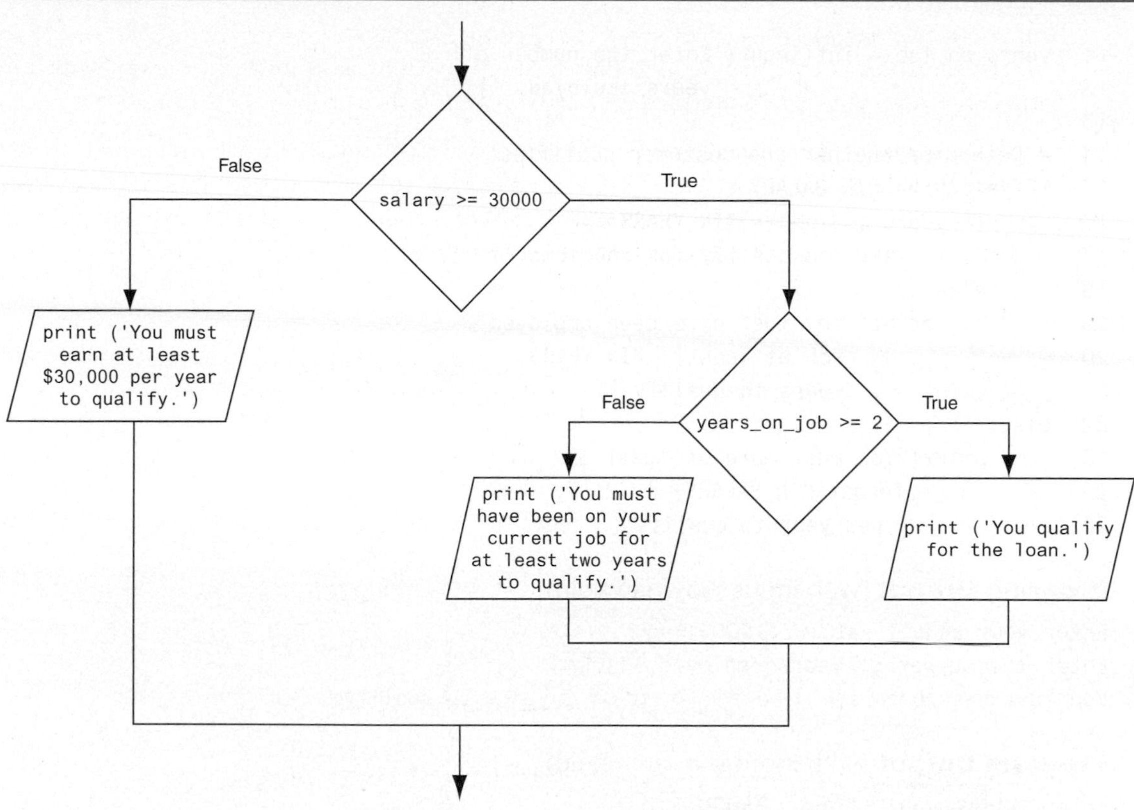

If we follow the flow of execution, we see that the condition `salary >= 30000` is tested. If this condition is false, there is no need to perform further tests; we know the customer does not qualify for the loan. If the condition is true, however, we need to test the second condition. This is done with a nested decision structure that tests the condition `years_on_job >= 2`. If this condition is true, then the customer qualifies for the loan. If this condition is false, then the customer does not qualify. Program 3-5 shows the code for the complete program.

Program 3-5 (loan_qualifier.py)

```
# This program determines whether a bank customer
# qualifies for a loan.

MIN_SALARY = 30000.0 # The minimum annual salary
MIN_YEARS = 2        # The minimum years on the job

# Get the customer's annual salary.
salary = float(input('Enter your annual salary: '))

# Get the number of years on the current job.
```

(program continues)

Program 3-5 *(continued)*

```
11  years_on_job = int(input('Enter the number of' +
12                           'years employed: '))
13
14  # Determine whether the customer qualifies.
15  if salary >= MIN_SALARY:
16      if years_on_job >= MIN_YEARS:
17          print('You qualify for the loan.')
18      else:
19          print('You must have been employed',
20                'for at least', MIN_YEARS,
21                'years to qualify.')
22  else:
23      print('You must earn at least $',
24            format(MIN_SALARY, ',.2f'),
25            ' per year to qualify.', sep='')
```

Program Output (with input shown in bold)

```
Enter your annual salary: 35000 Enter
Enter the number of years employed: 1 Enter
You must have been employed for at least 2 years to qualify.
```

Program Output (with input shown in bold)

```
Enter your annual salary: 25000 Enter
Enter the number of years employed: 5 Enter
You must earn at least $30,000.00 per year to qualify.
```

Program Output (with input shown in bold)

```
Enter your annual salary: 35000 Enter
Enter the number of years employed: 5 Enter
You qualify for the loan.
```

Look at the `if-else` statement that begins in line 15. It tests the condition `salary >= MIN_SALARY`. If this condition is true, the `if-else` statement that begins in line 16 is executed. Otherwise the program jumps to the `else` clause in line 22 and executes the statement in lines 23 through 25.

It's important to use proper indentation in a nested decision structure. Not only is proper indentation required by the Python interpreter, but it also makes it easier for you, the human reader of your code, to see which actions are performed by each part of the structure. Follow these rules when writing nested `if` statements:

- Make sure each `else` clause is aligned with its matching `if` clause. This is shown in Figure 3-13.
- Make sure the statements in each block are consistently indented. The shaded parts of Figure 3-14 show the nested blocks in the decision structure. Notice each statement in each block is indented the same amount.

Figure 3-13 Alignment of if and else clauses


```
if salary >= MIN_SALARY:
    if years_on_job >= MIN_YEARS:
        print('You qualify for the loan.')
    else:
        print('You must have been employed',
              'for at least', MIN_YEARS,
              'years to qualify.')
else:
    print('You must earn at least $',
          format(MIN_SALARY, ',.2f'),
          ' per year to qualify.', sep='')
```

Figure 3-14 Nested blocks

```
if salary >= MIN_SALARY:
    if years_on_job >= MIN_YEARS:
        print('You qualify for the loan.')
    else:
        print('You must have been employed',
              'for at least', MIN_YEARS,
              'years to qualify.')
else:
    print('You must earn at least $',
          format(MIN_SALARY, ',.2f'),
          ' per year to qualify.', sep='')
```

Testing a Series of Conditions

In the previous example, you saw how a program can use nested decision structures to test more than one condition. It is not uncommon for a program to have a series of conditions to test, then perform an action depending on which condition is true. One way to accomplish this is to have a decision structure with numerous other decision structures nested inside it. For example, consider the program presented in the following *In the Spotlight* section.

In the Spotlight:
Multiple Nested Decision Structures

Dr. Suarez teaches a literature class and uses the following 10-point grading scale for all of his exams:

Test Score	Grade
90 and above	A
80–89	B
70–79	C
60–69	D
Below 60	F

He has asked you to write a program that will allow a student to enter a test score and then display the grade for that score. Here is the algorithm that you will use:

1. Ask the user to enter a test score.
2. Determine the grade in the following manner:

If the score is greater than or equal to 90, then the grade is A.
Else, if the score is greater than or equal to 80, then the grade is B.
Else, if the score is greater than or equal to 70, then the grade is C.
Else, if the score is greater than or equal to 60, then the grade is D.
Else, the grade is F.

You decide that the process of determining the grade will require several nested decision structures, as shown in Figure 3-15. Program 3-6 shows the code for the program. The code for the nested decision structures is in lines 14 through 26.

Figure 3-15 Nested decision structure to determine a grade

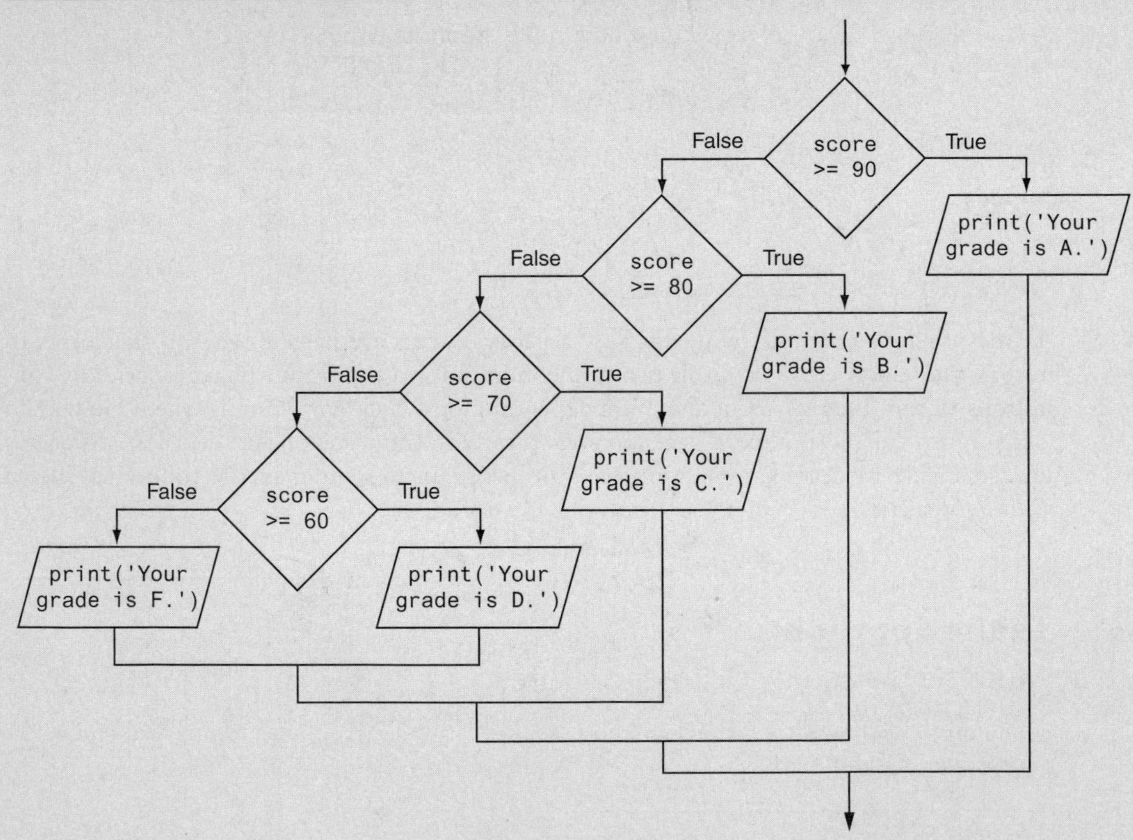

Program 3-6 (grader.py)

```
1  # This program gets a numeric test score from the
2  # user and displays the corresponding letter grade.
3
```

```
# Named constants to represent the grade thresholds
A_SCORE = 90
B_SCORE = 80
C_SCORE = 70
D_SCORE = 60

# Get a test score from the user.
score = int(input('Enter your test score: '))

# Determine the grade.
if score >= A_SCORE:
    print('Your grade is A.')
else:
    if score >= B_SCORE:
        print('Your grade is B.')
    else:
        if score >= C_SCORE:
            print('Your grade is C.')
        else:
            if score >= D_SCORE:
                print('Your grade is D.')
            else:
                print('Your grade is F.')
```

Program Output (with input shown in bold)

```
Enter your test score: 78 Enter
Your grade is C.
```

Program Output (with input shown in bold)

```
Enter your test score: 84 Enter
Your grade is B.
```

The `if-elif-else` Statement

Even though Program 3-6 is a simple example, the logic of the nested decision structure is fairly complex. Python provides a special version of the decision structure known as the `if-elif-else` statement, which makes this type of logic simpler to write. Here is the general format of the `if-elif-else` statement:

```
if condition_1:
    statement
    statement
    etc.
elif condition_2:
    statement
    statement
    etc.
```

Insert as many `elif` *clauses as necessary . . .*

```
else:
     statement
     statement
     etc.
```

When the statement executes, *condition_1* is tested. If *condition_1* is true, the block of statements that immediately follow is executed, up to the `elif` clause. The rest of the structure is ignored. If *condition_1* is false, however, the program jumps to the very next `elif` clause and tests *condition_2*. If it is true, the block of statements that immediately follow is executed, up to the next `elif` clause. The rest of the structure is then ignored. This process continues until a condition is found to be true, or no more `elif` clauses are left. If no condition is true, the block of statements following the `else` clause is executed.

The following is an example of the `if-elif-else` statement. This code works the same as the nested decision structure in lines 14 through 26 of Program 3-6.

```
if score >= A_SCORE:
    print('Your grade is A.')
elif score >= B_SCORE:
    print('Your grade is B.')
elif score >= C_SCORE:
    print('Your grade is C.')
elif score >= D_SCORE:
    print('Your grade is D.')
else:
    print('Your grade is F.')
```

Notice the alignment and indentation that is used with the `if-elif-else` statement: The `if`, `elif`, and `else` clauses are all aligned, and the conditionally executed blocks are indented.

The `if-elif-else` statement is never required because its logic can be coded with nested `if-else` statements. However, a long series of nested `if-else` statements has two particular disadvantages when you are debugging code:

- The code can grow complex and become difficult to understand.
- Because of the required indentation, a long series of nested `if-else` statements can become too long to be displayed on the computer screen without horizontal scrolling. Also, long statements tend to "wrap around" when printed on paper, making the code even more difficult to read.

The logic of an `if-elif-else` statement is usually easier to follow than a long series of nested `if-else` statements. And, because all of the clauses are aligned in an `if-elif-else` statement, the lengths of the lines in the statement tend to be shorter.

Checkpoint

3.13 Convert the following code to an `if-elif-else` statement:

```
if number == 1:
    print('One')
```

```
else:
    if number == 2:
        print('Two')
    else:
        if number == 3:
            print('Three')
        else:
            print('Unknown')
```

3.5 Logical Operators

CONCEPT: The logical and operator and the logical or operator allow you to connect multiple Boolean expressions to create a compound expression. The logical not operator reverses the truth of a Boolean expression.

Python provides a set of operators known as *logical operators*, which you can use to create complex Boolean expressions. Table 3-3 describes these operators.

Table 3-3 Logical operators

Operator	Meaning
`and`	The `and` operator connects two Boolean expressions into one compound expression. Both subexpressions must be true for the compound expression to be true.
`or`	The `or` operator connects two Boolean expressions into one compound expression. One or both subexpressions must be true for the compound expression to be true. It is only necessary for one of the subexpressions to be true, and it does not matter which.
`not`	The `not` operator is a unary operator, meaning it works with only one operand. The operand must be a Boolean expression. The `not` operator reverses the truth of its operand. If it is applied to an expression that is true, the operator returns false. If it is applied to an expression that is false, the operator returns true.

Table 3-4 shows examples of several compound Boolean expressions that use logical operators.

Table 3-4 Compound Boolean expressions using logical operators

Expression	Meaning
`x > y and a < b`	Is `x` greater than `y` AND is `a` less than `b`?
`x == y or x == z`	Is `x` equal to `y` OR is `x` equal to `z`?
`not (x > y)`	Is the expression `x > y` NOT true?

The and Operator

The and operator takes two Boolean expressions as operands and creates a compound Boolean expression that is true only when both subexpressions are true. The following is an example of an `if` statement that uses the and operator:

```
if temperature < 20 and minutes > 12:
    print('The temperature is in the danger zone.')
```

In this statement, the two Boolean expressions `temperature < 20` and `minutes > 12` are combined into a compound expression. The `print` function will be called only if `temperature` is less than 20 and `minutes` is greater than 12. If either of the Boolean subexpressions is false, the compound expression is false and the message is not displayed.

Table 3-5 shows a truth table for the and operator. The truth table lists expressions showing all the possible combinations of true and false connected with the and operator. The resulting values of the expressions are also shown.

Table 3-5 Truth table for the and operator

Expression	Value of the Expression
true and false	false
false and true	false
false and false	false
true and true	true

As the table shows, both sides of the and operator must be true for the operator to return a true value.

The or Operator

The or operator takes two Boolean expressions as operands and creates a compound Boolean expression that is true when either of the subexpressions is true. The following is an example of an `if` statement that uses the or operator:

```
if temperature < 20 or temperature > 100:
    print('The temperature is too extreme')
```

The `print` function will be called only if `temperature` is less than 20 or `temperature` is greater than 100. If either subexpression is true, the compound expression is true. Table 3-6 shows a truth table for the or operator.

Table 3-6 Truth table for the or operator

Expression	Value of the Expression
true or false	true
false or true	true
false or false	false
true or true	true

All it takes for an or expression to be true is for one side of the or operator to be true. It doesn't matter if the other side is false or true.

Short-Circuit Evaluation

Both the and and or operators perform *short-circuit evaluation*. Here's how it works with the and operator: If the expression on the left side of the and operator is false, the expression on the right side will not be checked. Because the compound expression will be false if only one of the subexpressions is false, it would waste CPU time to check the remaining expression. So, when the and operator finds that the expression on its left is false, it short-circuits and does not evaluate the expression on its right.

Here's how short-circuit evaluation works with the or operator: If the expression on the left side of the or operator is true, the expression on the right side will not be checked. Because it is only necessary for one of the expressions to be true, it would waste CPU time to check the remaining expression.

The not Operator

The not operator is a unary operator that takes a Boolean expression as its operand and reverses its logical value. In other words, if the expression is true, the not operator returns false, and if the expression is false, the not operator returns true. The following is an if statement using the not operator:

```
if not(temperature > 100):
    print('This is below the maximum temperature.')
```

First, the expression (temperature > 100) is tested and a value of either true or false is the result. Then the not operator is applied to that value. If the expression (temperature > 100) is true, the not operator returns false. If the expression (temperature > 100) is false, the not operator returns true. The previous code is equivalent to asking: "Is the temperature not greater than 100?"

NOTE: In this example, we have put parentheses around the expression temperature > 100. This is to make it clear that we are applying the not operator to the value of the expression temperature > 100, not just to the temperature variable.

Table 3-7 shows a truth table for the not operator.

Table 3-7 Truth table for the not operator

Expression	Value of the Expression
not true	false
not false	true

The Loan Qualifier Program Revisited

In some situations the and operator can be used to simplify nested decision structures. For example, recall that the loan qualifier program in Program 3-5 uses the following nested `if-else` statements:

```
if salary >= MIN_SALARY:
    if years_on_job >= MIN_YEARS:
        print('You qualify for the loan.')
    else:
        print('You must have been employed',
              'for at least', MIN_YEARS,
              'years to qualify.')
else:
    print('You must earn at least $',
          format(MIN_SALARY, ',.2f'),
          ' per year to qualify.', sep='')
```

The purpose of this decision structure is to determine that a person's salary is at least $30,000 and that he or she has been at their current job for at least two years. Program 3-7 shows a way to perform a similar task with simpler code.

Program 3-7 (`loan_qualifier2.py`)

```
# This program determines whether a bank customer
# qualifies for a loan.

MIN_SALARY = 30000.0 # The minimum annual salary
MIN_YEARS = 2        # The minimum years on the job

# Get the customer's annual salary.
salary = float(input('Enter your annual salary: '))

# Get the number of years on the current job.
years_on_job = int(input('Enter the number of ' +
                         'years employed: '))

# Determine whether the customer qualifies.
if salary >= MIN_SALARY and years_on_job >= MIN_YEARS:
    print('You qualify for the loan.')
else:
    print('You do not qualify for this loan.')
```

Program Output (with input shown in bold)

```
Enter your annual salary: 35000 Enter
Enter the number of years employed: 1 Enter
You do not qualify for this loan.
```

Program Output (with input shown in bold)

```
Enter your annual salary: 25000 Enter
Enter the number of years employed: 5 Enter
You do not qualify for this loan.
```

Program Output (with input shown in bold)

```
Enter your annual salary: 35000 Enter
Enter the number of years employed: 5 Enter
You qualify for the loan.
```

The `if-else` statement in lines 15 through 18 tests the compound expression `salary >= MIN_SALARY and years_on_job >= MIN_YEARS`. If both subexpressions are true, the compound expression is true and the message "You qualify for the loan" is displayed. If either of the subexpressions is false, the compound expression is false and the message "You do not qualify for this loan" is displayed.

NOTE: A careful observer will realize that Program 3-7 is similar to Program 3-5, but it is not equivalent. If the user does not qualify for the loan, Program 3-7 displays only the message "You do not qualify for this loan" whereas Program 3-5 displays one of two possible messages explaining why the user did not qualify.

Yet Another Loan Qualifier Program

Suppose the bank is losing customers to a competing bank that isn't as strict about to whom it loans money. In response, the bank decides to change its loan requirements. Now, customers have to meet only one of the previous conditions, not both. Program 3-8 shows the code for the new loan qualifier program. The compound expression that is tested by the `if-else` statement in line 15 now uses the `or` operator.

Program 3-8 (`loan_qualifier3.py`)

```
1  # This program determines whether a bank customer
2  # qualifies for a loan.
3
4  MIN_SALARY = 30000.0 # The minimum annual salary
5  MIN_YEARS = 2        # The minimum years on the job
6
7  # Get the customer's annual salary.
8  salary = float(input('Enter your annual salary: '))
9
10 # Get the number of years on the current job.
11 years_on_job = int(input('Enter the number of ' +
12                          'years employed: '))
13
```

(program continues)

Program 3-8 *(continued)*

```
# Determine whether the customer qualifies.
if salary >= MIN_SALARY or years_on_job >= MIN_YEARS:
    print('You qualify for the loan.')
else:
    print('You do not qualify for this loan.')
```

Program Output (with input shown in bold)

```
Enter your annual salary: 35000 Enter
Enter the number of years employed: 1 Enter
You qualify for the loan.
```

Program Output (with input shown in bold)

```
Enter your annual salary: 25000 Enter
Enter the number of years employed: 5 Enter
You qualify for the loan.
```

Program Output (with input shown in bold)

```
Enter your annual salary 12000 Enter
Enter the number of years employed: 1 Enter
You do not qualify for this loan.
```

Checking Numeric Ranges with Logical Operators

Sometimes you will need to design an algorithm that determines whether a numeric value is within a specific range of values or outside a specific range of values. When determining whether a number is inside a range, it is best to use the `and` operator. For example, the following `if` statement checks the value in `x` to determine whether it is in the range of 20 through 40:

```
if x >= 20 and x <= 40:
    print('The value is in the acceptable range.')
```

The compound Boolean expression being tested by this statement will be true only when `x` is greater than or equal to 20 and less than or equal to 40. The value in `x` must be within the range of 20 through 40 for this compound expression to be true.

When determining whether a number is outside a range, it is best to use the `or` operator. The following statement determines whether `x` is outside the range of 20 through 40:

```
if x < 20 or x > 40:
    print('The value is outside the acceptable range.')
```

It is important not to get the logic of the logical operators confused when testing for a range of numbers. For example, the compound Boolean expression in the following code would never test true:

```
# This is an error!
if x < 20 and x > 40:
    print('The value is outside the acceptable range.')
```

Obviously, `x` cannot be less than 20 and at the same time be greater than 40.

Checkpoint

3.14 What is a compound Boolean expression?

3.15 The following truth table shows various combinations of the values true and false connected by a logical operator. Complete the table by circling T or F to indicate whether the result of such a combination is true or false.

Logical Expression	Result (circle T or F)	
`True and False`	T	F
`True and True`	T	F
`False and True`	T	F
`False and False`	T	F
`True or False`	T	F
`True or True`	T	F
`False or True`	T	F
`False or False`	T	F
`not True`	T	F
`not False`	T	F

3.16 Assume the variables `a = 2`, `b = 4`, and `c = 6`. Circle T or F for each of the following conditions to indicate whether its value is true or false.

```
a == 4 or b > 2            T  F
6 <= c and a > 3           T  F
1 != b and c != 3          T  F
a >= -1 or a <= b          T  F
not (a > 2)                T  F
```

3.17 Explain how short-circuit evaluation works with the `and` and `or` operators.

3.18 Write an `if` statement that displays the message "The number is valid" if the value referenced by `speed` is within the range 0 through 200.

3.19 Write an `if` statement that displays the message "The number is not valid" if the value referenced by `speed` is outside the range 0 through 200.

3.6 Boolean Variables

CONCEPT: A Boolean variable can reference one of two values: `True` or `False`. Boolean variables are commonly used as flags, which indicate whether specific conditions exist.

So far in this book, we have worked with `int`, `float`, and `str` (string) variables. In addition to these data types, Python also provides a `bool` data type. The `bool` data type allows you to create variables that may reference one of two possible values: `True` or `False`. Here are examples of how we assign values to a `bool` variable:

```
hungry = True
sleepy = False
```

Boolean variables are most commonly used as flags. A *flag* is a variable that signals when some condition exists in the program. When the flag variable is set to `False`, it indicates the condition does not exist. When the flag variable is set to `True`, it means the condition does exist.

For example, suppose a salesperson has a quota of $50,000. Assuming `sales` references the amount that the salesperson has sold, the following code determines whether the quota has been met:

```
if sales >= 50000.0:
    sales_quota_met = True
else:
    sales_quota_met = False
```

As a result of this code, the `sales_quota_met` variable can be used as a flag to indicate whether the sales quota has been met. Later in the program, we might test the flag in the following way:

```
if sales_quota_met:
    print('You have met your sales quota!')
```

This code displays `'You have met your sales quota!'` if the `bool` variable `sales_quota_met` is `True`. Notice we did not have to use the == operator to explicitly compare the `sales_quota_met` variable with the value `True`. This code is equivalent to the following:

```
if sales_quota_met == True:
    print('You have met your sales quota!')
```

Checkpoint

3.20 What values can you assign to a `bool` variable?

3.21 What is a flag variable?

3.7 Turtle Graphics: Determining the State of the Turtle

CONCEPT: The turtle graphics library provides numerous functions that you can use in decision structures to determine the state of the turtle and conditionally perform actions.

You can use functions in the turtle graphics library to learn a lot about the current state of the turtle. In this section, we will discuss functions for determining the turtle's location, the direction in which it is heading, whether the pen is up or down, the current drawing color, and more.

Determining the Turtle's Location

Recall from Chapter 2 that you can use the `turtle.xcor()` and `turtle.ycor()` functions to get the turtle's current X and Y coordinates. The following code snippet uses an `if` statement to determine whether the turtle's *X* coordinate is greater than 249, or the turtle's *Y* coordinate is greater than 349. If so, the turtle is repositioned at (0, 0):

```
if turtle.xcor() > 249 or turtle.ycor() > 349:
    turtle.goto(0, 0)
```

Determining the Turtle's Heading

The `turtle.heading()` function returns the turtle's heading. By default, the heading is returned in degrees. The following interactive session demonstrates this:

```
>>> turtle.heading()
0.0
>>>
```

The following code snippet uses an `if` statement to determine whether the turtle's heading is between 90 degrees and 270 degrees. If so, the turtle's heading is set to 180 degrees:

```
if turtle.heading() >= 90 and turtle.heading() <= 270:
    turtle.setheading(180)
```

Determining Whether the Pen Is Down

The `turtle.isdown()` function returns `True` if the turtle's pen is down, or `False` otherwise. The following interactive session demonstrates this:

```
>>> turtle.isdown()
True
>>>
```

The following code snippet uses an `if` statement to determine whether the turtle's pen is down. If the pen is down, the code raises it:

```
if turtle.isdown():
    turtle.penup()
```

To determine whether the pen is up, you use the `not` operator along with the `turtle.isdown()` function. The following code snippet demonstrates this:

```
if not(turtle.isdown()):
    turtle.pendown()
```

Determining Whether the Turtle Is Visible

The `turtle.isvisible()` function returns `True` if the turtle is visible, or `False` otherwise. The following interactive session demonstrates this:

```
>>> turtle.isvisible()
True
>>>
```

The following code snippet uses an `if` statement to determine whether the turtle is visible. If the turtle is visible, the code hides it:

```
if turtle.isvisible():
    turtle.hideturtle()
```

Determining the Current Colors

When you execute the `turtle.pencolor()` function without passing it an argument, the function returns the pen's current drawing color as a string. The following interactive session demonstrates this:

```
>>> turtle.pencolor()
'black'
>>>
```

The following code snippet uses an `if` statement to determine whether the pen's current color is red. If the color is red, the code changes it to blue:

```
if turtle.pencolor() == 'red':
    turtle.pencolor('blue')
```

When you execute the `turtle.fillcolor()` function without passing it an argument, the function returns the current fill color as a string. The following interactive session demonstrates this:

```
>>> turtle.fillcolor()
'black'
>>>
```

The following code snippet uses an `if` statement to determine whether the current fill color is blue. If the fill color is blue, the code changes it to white:

```
if turtle.fillcolor() == 'blue':
    turtle.fillcolor('white')
```

When you execute the `turtle.bgcolor()` function without passing it an argument, the function returns the current background color of the turtle's graphics window as a string. The following interactive session demonstrates this:

```
>>> turtle.bgcolor()
'white'
>>>
```

The following code snippet uses an `if` statement to determine whether the current background color is white. If the background color is white, the code changes it to gray:

```
if turtle.bgcolor() == 'white':
    turtle.fillcolor('gray')
```

Determining the Pen Size

When you execute the `turtle.pensize()` function without passing it an argument, the function returns the pen's current size. The following interactive session demonstrates this:

```
>>> turtle.pensize()
1
>>>
```

The following code snippet uses an `if` statement to determine whether the pen's current size is less than 3. If the pen size is less than 3, the code changes it to 3:

```
if turtle.pensize() < 3:
    turtle.pensize(3)
```

Determining the Turtle's Animation Speed

When you execute the `turtle.speed()` function without passing it an argument, the function returns the turtle's current animation speed. The following interactive session demonstrates this:

```
>>> turtle.speed()
3
>>>
```

Recall from Chapter 2 that the turtle's animation speed is a value in the range of 0 to 10. If the speed is 0, then animation is disabled, and the turtle makes all of its moves instantly. If the speed is in the range of 1 through 10, then 1 is the slowest speed and 10 is the fastest speed.

The following code snippet determines whether the turtle's speed is greater than 0. If it is, then the speed is set to 0:

```
if turtle.speed() > 0:
    turtle.speed(0)
```

The following code snippet shows another example. It uses an `if-elif-else` statement to determine the turtle's speed, then set the pen color. If the speed is 0, the pen color is set to red. Otherwise, if the speed is greater than 5, the pen color is set to blue. Otherwise, the pen color is set to green:

```
if turtle.speed() == 0:
    turtle.pencolor('red')
elif turtle.speed() > 5:
    turtle.pencolor('blue')
else:
    turtle.pencolor('green')
```

In the Spotlight:
The Hit the Target Game

In this section, we're going to look at a Python program that uses turtle graphics to play a simple game. When the program runs, it displays the graphics screen shown in Figure 3-16. The small square that is drawn in the upper-right area of the window is the target. The object of the game is to launch the turtle like a projectile so it hits the target. You do this by entering an angle, and a force value in the Shell window. The program then sets the turtle's heading to the specified angle, and it uses the specified force value in a simple formula to calculate the distance that the turtle will travel. The greater the force value, the further the turtle will move. If the turtle stops inside the square, it has hit the target.

Figure 3-16 Hit the target game

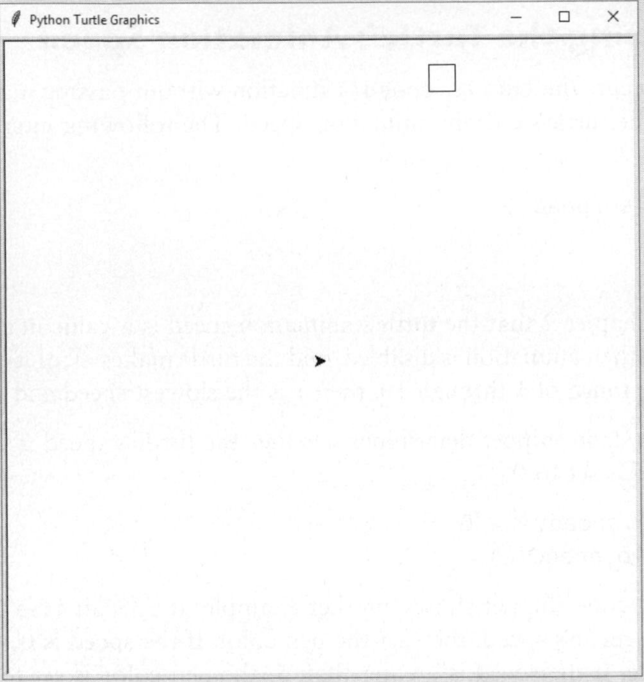

For example, Figure 3-17 shows a session with the program in which we entered 45 as the angle, and 8 as the force value. As you can see, the projectile (the turtle) missed the target. In Figure 3-18, we ran the program again, entering 67 as the angle and 9.8 as the force value. These values caused the projectile to hit the target. Program 3-9 shows the program's code.

Figure 3-17 Missing the target

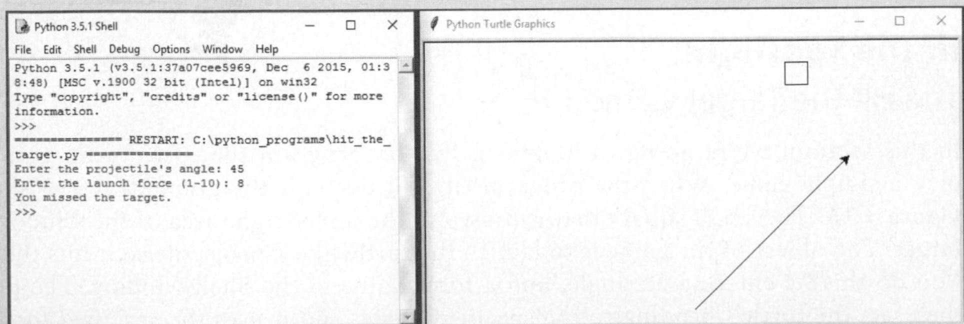

Figure 3-18 Hitting the target

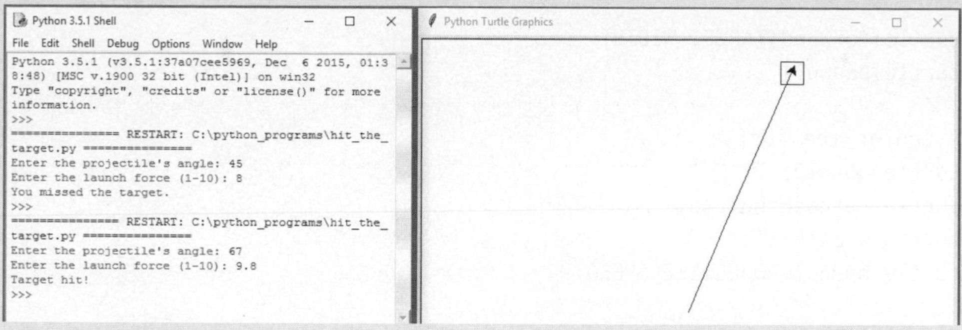

Program 3-9 (hit_the_target.py)

```
# Hit the Target Game
import turtle

# Named constants
SCREEN_WIDTH = 600        # Screen width
SCREEN_HEIGHT = 600       # Screen height
TARGET_LLEFT_X = 100      # Target's lower-left X
TARGET_LLEFT_Y = 250      # Target's lower-left Y
TARGET_WIDTH = 25         # Width of the target
FORCE_FACTOR = 30         # Arbitrary force factor
PROJECTILE_SPEED = 1      # Projectile's animation speed
NORTH = 90                # Angle of north direction
SOUTH = 270               # Angle of south direction
EAST = 0                  # Angle of east direction
WEST = 180                # Angle of west direction

# Setup the window.
turtle.setup(SCREEN_WIDTH, SCREEN_HEIGHT)

# Draw the target.
turtle.hideturtle()
turtle.speed(0)
turtle.penup()
turtle.goto(TARGET_LLEFT_X, TARGET_LLEFT_Y)
turtle.pendown()
turtle.setheading(EAST)
turtle.forward(TARGET_WIDTH)
turtle.setheading(NORTH)
turtle.forward(TARGET_WIDTH)
turtle.setheading(WEST)
turtle.forward(TARGET_WIDTH)
turtle.setheading(SOUTH)
```

(program continues)

Program 3-9 *(continued)*

```
33 turtle.forward(TARGET_WIDTH)
34 turtle.penup()
35
36 # Center the turtle.
37 turtle.goto(0, 0)
38 turtle.setheading(EAST)
39 turtle.showturtle()
40 turtle.speed(PROJECTILE_SPEED)
41
42 # Get the angle and force from the user.
43 angle = float(input("Enter the projectile's angle: "))
44 force = float(input("Enter the launch force (1-10): "))
45
46 # Calculate the distance.
47 distance = force * FORCE_FACTOR
48
49 # Set the heading.
50 turtle.setheading(angle)
51
52 # Launch the projectile.
53 turtle.pendown()
54 turtle.forward(distance)
55
56 # Did it hit the target?
57 if (turtle.xcor() >= TARGET_LLEFT_X and
58     turtle.xcor() <= (TARGET_LLEFT_X + TARGET_WIDTH) and
59     turtle.ycor() >= TARGET_LLEFT_Y and
60     turtle.ycor() <= (TARGET_LLEFT_Y + TARGET_WIDTH)):
61         print('Target hit!')
62 else:
63         print('You missed the target.')
```

Let's take a closer look at the code. Lines 5 through 15 define the following named constants:

- Lines 5 and 6 define the `SCREEN_WIDTH` and `SCREEN_HEIGHT` constants. We will use these in line 14 to set the size of the graphics window to 600 pixels wide by 600 pixels high.
- Lines 7 and 8 define the `TARGET_LLEFT_X` and `TARGET_LLEFT_Y` constants. These are arbitrary values used as the (*X*, *Y*) coordinates of the target's lower-left corner.
- Line 9 defines the `TARGET_WIDTH` constant, which is the width (and the height) of the target.
- Line 10 defines the `FORCE_FACTOR` constant, which is an arbitrary number that we use in our formula to calculate the distance that the projectile travels when it is launched.
- Line 11 defines the `PROJECTILE_SPEED` constant, which we will use as the turtle's animation speed when the projectile is launched.
- Lines 12–15 define the `NORTH`, `SOUTH`, `EAST`, and `WEST` constants, which we will use as the angles for north, south, east, and west, when we draw the target.

Lines 21 through 34 draw the rectangular target:

- Line 21 hides the turtle because we don't need to see it until the target is drawn.
- Line 22 sets the turtle's animation speed to 0, which disables the turtle's animation. We do this because we want the rectangular target to appear instantly.
- Line 23 raises the turtle's pen, so it does not draw a line as we move it from its default location (at the center of the window) to the point where we will begin drawing the target.
- Line 24 moves the turtle to the location of the target's lower-left corner.
- Line 25 lowers the turtle's pen so that the turtle will draw as we move it.
- Line 26 sets the turtle's heading at 0 degrees, pointing it toward east.
- Line 27 moves the turtle forward 25 pixels, drawing the bottom edge of the target.
- Line 28 sets the turtle's heading at 90 degrees, pointing it toward north.
- Line 29 moves the turtle forward 25 pixels, drawing the right edge of the target.
- Line 30 sets the turtle's heading at 180 degrees, pointing it toward west.
- Line 31 moves the turtle forward 25 pixels, drawing the top edge of the target.
- Line 32 sets the turtle's heading at 270 degrees, pointing it toward south.
- Line 33 moves the turtle forward 25 pixels, drawing the left edge of the target.
- Line 34 raises the turtle's pen, so it does not draw a line when we move the turtle back to the center of the window.

Lines 37 through 40 move the turtle back to the center of the window:

- Line 37 moves the turtle to (0, 0).
- Line 38 sets the turtle's heading at 0 degrees, pointing it toward east.
- Line 39 shows the turtle.
- Line 40 sets the turtle's animation speed to 1, which is slow enough to see the projectile move when it is launched.

Lines 43 and 44 get the angle and force value from the user:

- Line 43 prompts the user to enter the projectile's angle. The value that is entered is converted to a `float` and assigned to the `angle` variable.
- Line 44 prompts the user to enter the force value, in the range of 1–10. The value that is entered is converted to a `float` and assigned to the `force` variable. The force value is a number that we will use in line 47 to calculate the distance that the projectile will travel. The greater the force value, the further the projectile will move.

Line 47 calculates the distance the turtle will move, and assigns that value to the `distance` variable. The distance is calculated by multiplying the user's force value by the `FORCE_FACTOR` constant, which is 30. We picked 30 as the constant's value because the distance from the turtle to the edge of the window is 300 pixels (or just a bit more, depending on the turtle's heading). If the user enters 10 for the force value, the turtle will move to the edge of the screen.

Line 50 sets the turtle's heading to the angle that the user entered in line 43.

Lines 53 and 54 launch the turtle:

- Line 53 lowers the turtle's pen, so it draws a line as it moves.
- Line 54 moves the turtle forward by the distance that was calculated in line 54.

The last thing to do is determine whether the turtle hit the target. If the turtle is inside the target, all of the following will be true:

- The turtle's *X* coordinate will be greater than or equal to `TARGET_LLEFT_X`
- The turtle's *X* coordinate will be less than or equal to `TARGET_LLEFT_X + TARGET_WIDTH`
- The turtle's *Y* coordinate will be greater than or equal to `TARGET_LLEFT_Y`
- The turtle's *Y* coordinate will be less than or equal to `TARGET_LLEFT_Y + TARGET_WIDTH`

The `if-else` statement in lines 57 through 63 determines whether all of these conditions are true. If they are true, the message `'Target hit!'` is displayed in line 61. Otherwise, the message `'You missed the target.'` is displayed in line 63.

Checkpoint

3.22 How do you get the turtle's *X* and *Y* coordinates?

3.23 How would you determine whether the turtle's pen is up?

3.24 How do you get the turtle's current heading?

3.25 How do you determine whether the turtle is visible?

3.26 How do you determine the turtle's pen color? How do you determine the current fill color? How do you determine the current background color of the turtle's graphics window?

3.27 How do you determine the current pen size?

3.28 How do you determine the turtle's current animation speed?

Review Questions

Multiple Choice

1. A __________ structure can execute a set of statements only under certain circumstances.
   a. sequence
   b. circumstantial
   c. decision
   d. Boolean
2. A __________ structure provides one alternative path of execution.
   a. sequence
   b. single alternative decision
   c. one path alternative
   d. single execution decision

3. A(n) __________ expression has a value of either True or False.
   a. binary
   b. decision
   c. unconditional
   d. Boolean
4. The symbols >, <, and == are all __________ operators.
   a. relational
   b. logical
   c. conditional
   d. ternary
5. A(n) __________ structure tests a condition and then takes one path if the condition is true, or another path if the condition is false.
   a. `if` statement
   b. single alternative decision
   c. dual alternative decision
   d. sequence
6. You use a(n) __________ statement to write a single alternative decision structure.
   a. `test-jump`
   b. `if`
   c. `if-else`
   d. `if-call`
7. You use a(n) __________ statement to write a dual alternative decision structure.
   a. `test-jump`
   b. `if`
   c. `if-else`
   d. `if-call`
8. `and`, `or`, and `not` are __________ operators.
   a. relational
   b. logical
   c. conditional
   d. ternary
9. A compound Boolean expression created with the __________ operator is true only if both of its subexpressions are true.
   a. `and`
   b. `or`
   c. `not`
   d. `both`
10. A compound Boolean expression created with the __________ operator is true if either of its subexpressions is true.
    a. `and`
    b. `or`
    c. `not`
    d. `either`

11. The __________ operator takes a Boolean expression as its operand and reverses its logical value.
    a. `and`
    b. `or`
    c. `not`
    d. `either`
12. A __________ is a Boolean variable that signals when some condition exists in the program.
    a. flag
    b. signal
    c. sentinel
    d. siren

True or False

1. You can write any program using only sequence structures.
2. A program can be made of only one type of control structure. You cannot combine structures.
3. A single alternative decision structure tests a condition and then takes one path if the condition is true, or another path if the condition is false.
4. A decision structure can be nested inside another decision structure.
5. A compound Boolean expression created with the `and` operator is true only when both subexpressions are true.

Short Answer

1. Explain what is meant by the term "conditionally executed."
2. You need to test a condition then execute one set of statements if the condition is true. If the condition is false, you need to execute a different set of statements. What structure will you use?
3. Briefly describe how the `and` operator works.
4. Briefly describe how the `or` operator works.
5. When determining whether a number is inside a range, which logical operator is it best to use?
6. What is a flag and how does it work?

Algorithm Workbench

1. Write an `if` statement that assigns 20 to the variable `y`, and assigns 40 to the variable `z` if the variable `x` is greater than 100.
2. Write an `if` statement that assigns 0 to the variable `b`, and assigns 1 to the variable `c` if the variable `a` is less than 10.
3. Write an `if-else` statement that assigns 0 to the variable `b` if the variable `a` is less than 10. Otherwise, it should assign 99 to the variable `b`.

4. The following code contains several nested `if-else` statements. Unfortunately, it was written without proper alignment and indentation. Rewrite the code and use the proper conventions of alignment and indentation.

```
if score >= A_score:
print('Your grade is A.')
else:
if score >= B_score:
print('Your grade is B.')
else:
if score >= C_score:
print('Your grade is C.')
else:
if score >= D_score:
print('Your grade is D.')
else:
print('Your grade is F.')
```

5. Write nested decision structures that perform the following: If `amount1` is greater than 10 and `amount2` is less than 100, display the greater of `amount1` and `amount2`.
6. Write an `if-else` statement that displays `'Speed is normal'` if the `speed` variable is within the range of 24 to 56. If the `speed` variable's value is outside this range, display `'Speed is abnormal'`.
7. Write an `if-else` statement that determines whether the `points` variable is outside the range of 9 to 51. If the variable's value is outside this range it should display "Invalid points." Otherwise, it should display "Valid points."
8. Write an `if` statement that uses the turtle graphics library to determine whether the turtle's heading is in the range of 0 degrees to 45 degrees (including 0 and 45 in the range). If so, raise the turtle's pen.
9. Write an `if` statement that uses the turtle graphics library to determine whether the turtle's pen color is red or blue. If so, set the pen size to 5 pixels.
10. Write an `if` statement that uses the turtle graphics library to determine whether the turtle is inside of a rectangle. The rectangle's upper-left corner is at (100, 100) and its lower-right corner is at (200, 200). If the turtle is inside the rectangle, hide the turtle.

Programming Exercises

1. Day of the Week

Write a program that asks the user for a number in the range of 1 through 7. The program should display the corresponding day of the week, where 1 = Monday, 2 = Tuesday, 3 = Wednesday, 4 = Thursday, 5 = Friday, 6 = Saturday, and 7 = Sunday. The program should display an error message if the user enters a number that is outside the range of 1 through 7.

VideoNote
The Areas of Rectangles Problem

2. Areas of Rectangles

The area of a rectangle is the rectangle's length times its width. Write a program that asks for the length and width of two rectangles. The program should tell the user which rectangle has the greater area, or if the areas are the same.

3. Age Classifier

Write a program that asks the user to enter a person's age. The program should display a message indicating whether the person is an infant, a child, a teenager, or an adult. Following are the guidelines:

- If the person is 1 year old or less, he or she is an infant.
- If the person is older than 1 year, but younger than 13 years, he or she is a child.
- If the person is at least 13 years old, but less than 20 years old, he or she is a teenager.
- If the person is at least 20 years old, he or she is an adult.

4. Roman Numerals

Write a program that prompts the user to enter a number within the range of 1 through 10. The program should display the Roman numeral version of that number. If the number is outside the range of 1 through 10, the program should display an error message. The following table shows the Roman numerals for the numbers 1 through 10:

Number	Roman Numeral
1	I
2	II
3	III
4	IV
5	V
6	VI
7	VII
8	VIII
9	IX
10	X

5. Mass and Weight

Scientists measure an object's mass in kilograms and its weight in newtons. If you know the amount of mass of an object in kilograms, you can calculate its weight in newtons with the following formula:

$$weight = mass \times 9.8$$

Write a program that asks the user to enter an object's mass, then calculates its weight. If the object weighs more than 500 newtons, display a message indicating that it is too heavy. If the object weighs less than 100 newtons, display a message indicating that it is too light.

6. Magic Dates

The date June 10, 1960, is special because when it is written in the following format, the month times the day equals the year:

6/10/60

Design a program that asks the user to enter a month (in numeric form), a day, and a two-digit year. The program should then determine whether the month times the day equals the year. If so, it should display a message saying the date is magic. Otherwise, it should display a message saying the date is not magic.

7. Color Mixer

The colors red, blue, and yellow are known as the primary colors because they cannot be made by mixing other colors. When you mix two primary colors, you get a secondary color, as shown here:

When you mix red and blue, you get purple.
When you mix red and yellow, you get orange.
When you mix blue and yellow, you get green.

Design a program that prompts the user to enter the names of two primary colors to mix. If the user enters anything other than "red," "blue," or "yellow," the program should display an error message. Otherwise, the program should display the name of the secondary color that results.

8. Hot Dog Cookout Calculator

Assume hot dogs come in packages of 10, and hot dog buns come in packages of 8. Write a program that calculates the number of packages of hot dogs and the number of packages of hot dog buns needed for a cookout, with the minimum amount of leftovers. The program should ask the user for the number of people attending the cookout and the number of hot dogs each person will be given. The program should display the following details:

- The minimum number of packages of hot dogs required
- The minimum number of packages of hot dog buns required
- The number of hot dogs that will be left over
- The number of hot dog buns that will be left over

9. Roulette Wheel Colors

On a roulette wheel, the pockets are numbered from 0 to 36. The colors of the pockets are as follows:

- Pocket 0 is green.
- For pockets 1 through 10, the odd-numbered pockets are red and the even-numbered pockets are black.
- For pockets 11 through 18, the odd-numbered pockets are black and the even-numbered pockets are red.
- For pockets 19 through 28, the odd-numbered pockets are red and the even-numbered pockets are black.
- For pockets 29 through 36, the odd-numbered pockets are black and the even-numbered pockets are red.

Write a program that asks the user to enter a pocket number and displays whether the pocket is green, red, or black. The program should display an error message if the user enters a number that is outside the range of 0 through 36.

10. Money Counting Game

Create a change-counting game that gets the user to enter the number of coins required to make exactly one dollar. The program should prompt the user to enter the number of pennies, nickels, dimes, and quarters. If the total value of the coins entered is equal to one dollar, the program should congratulate the user for winning the game. Otherwise, the program should display a message indicating whether the amount entered was more than or less than one dollar.

11. Book Club Points

Serendipity Booksellers has a book club that awards points to its customers based on the number of books purchased each month. The points are awarded as follows:

- If a customer purchases 0 books, he or she earns 0 points.
- If a customer purchases 2 books, he or she earns 5 points.
- If a customer purchases 4 books, he or she earns 15 points.
- If a customer purchases 6 books, he or she earns 30 points.
- If a customer purchases 8 or more books, he or she earns 60 points.

Write a program that asks the user to enter the number of books that he or she has purchased this month, then displays the number of points awarded.

12. Software Sales

A software company sells a package that retails for $99. Quantity discounts are given according to the following table:

Quantity	Discount
10–19	10%
20–49	20%
50–99	30%
100 or more	40%

Write a program that asks the user to enter the number of packages purchased. The program should then display the amount of the discount (if any) and the total amount of the purchase after the discount.

13. Shipping Charges

The Fast Freight Shipping Company charges the following rates:

Weight of Package	Rate per Pound
2 pounds or less	$1.50
Over 2 pounds but not more than 6 pounds	$3.00
Over 6 pounds but not more than 10 pounds	$4.00
Over 10 pounds	$4.75

Write a program that asks the user to enter the weight of a package then displays the shipping charges.

14. Body Mass Index

Write a program that calculates and displays a person's body mass index (BMI). The BMI is often used to determine whether a person is overweight or underweight for his or her height. A person's BMI is calculated with the following formula:

$$BMI = weight \times 703/height^2$$

where *weight* is measured in pounds and *height* is measured in inches. The program should ask the user to enter his or her weight and height, then display the user's BMI. The program should also display a message indicating whether the person has optimal weight, is underweight, or is overweight. A person's weight is considered to be optimal if his or her

BMI is between 18.5 and 25. If the BMI is less than 18.5, the person is considered to be underweight. If the BMI value is greater than 25, the person is considered to be overweight.

15. Time Calculator

Write a program that asks the user to enter a number of seconds and works as follows:

- There are 60 seconds in a minute. If the number of seconds entered by the user is greater than or equal to 60, the program should convert the number of seconds to minutes and seconds.
- There are 3,600 seconds in an hour. If the number of seconds entered by the user is greater than or equal to 3,600, the program should convert the number of seconds to hours, minutes, and seconds.
- There are 86,400 seconds in a day. If the number of seconds entered by the user is greater than or equal to 86,400, the program should convert the number of seconds to days, hours, minutes, and seconds.

16. February Days

The month of February normally has 28 days. But if it is a *leap year*, February has 29 days. Write a program that asks the user to enter a year. The program should then display the number of days in February that year. Use the following criteria to identify leap years:

1. Determine whether the year is divisible by 100. If it is, then it is a leap year if and only if it is also divisible by 400. For example, 2000 is a leap year, but 2100 is not.
2. If the year is not divisible by 100, then it is a leap year if and only if it is divisible by 4. For example, 2008 is a leap year, but 2009 is not.

Here is a sample run of the program:

```
Enter a year: 2008 [Enter]
In 2008 February has 29 days.
```

17. Wi-Fi Diagnostic Tree

Figure 3-19 shows a simplified flowchart for troubleshooting a bad Wi-Fi connection. Use the flowchart to create a program that leads a person through the steps of fixing a bad Wi-Fi connection. Here is an example of the program's output:

```
Reboot the computer and try to connect.
Did that fix the problem? no [Enter]
Reboot the router and try to connect.
Did that fix the problem? yes [Enter]
```

Notice the program ends as soon as a solution is found to the problem. Here is another example of the program's output:

```
Reboot the computer and try to connect.
Did that fix the problem? no [Enter]
Reboot the router and try to connect.
Did that fix the problem? no [Enter]
Make sure the cables between the router and modem are plugged in firmly.
Did that fix the problem? no [Enter]
Move the router to a new location.
Did that fix the problem? no [Enter]
Get a new router.
```

Figure 3-19 Troubleshooting a bad Wi-Fi connection

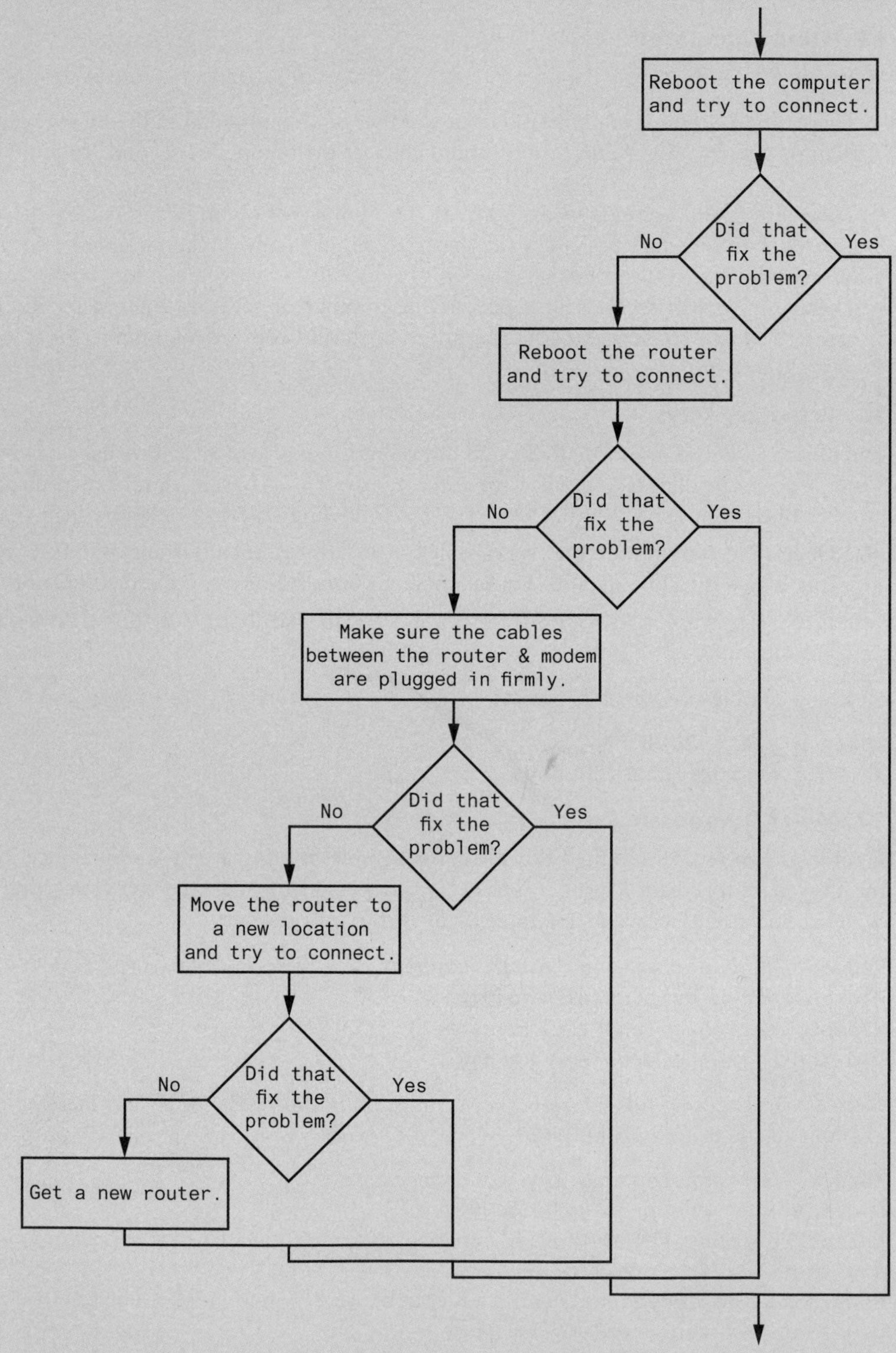

18. Restaurant Selector

You have a group of friends coming to visit for your high school reunion, and you want to take them out to eat at a local restaurant. You aren't sure if any of them have dietary restrictions, but your restaurant choices are as follows:

Joe's Gourmet Burgers—Vegetarian: No, Vegan: No, Gluten-Free: No
Main Street Pizza Company—Vegetarian: Yes, Vegan: No, Gluten-Free: Yes
Corner Café—Vegetarian: Yes, Vegan: Yes, Gluten-Free: Yes
Mama's Fine Italian—Vegetarian: Yes, Vegan: No, Gluten-Free: No
The Chef's Kitchen—Vegetarian: Yes, Vegan: Yes, Gluten-Free: Yes

Write a program that asks whether any members of your party are vegetarian, vegan, or gluten-free, to which then displays only the restaurants to which you may take the group. Here is an example of the program's output:

```
Is anyone in your party a vegetarian? yes [Enter]
Is anyone in your party a vegan? no [Enter]
Is anyone in your party gluten-free? yes [Enter]
Here are your restaurant choices:
    Main Street Pizza Company
    Corner Cafe
    The Chef's Kitchen
```

Here is another example of the program's output:

```
Is anyone in your party a vegetarian? yes [Enter]
Is anyone in your party a vegan? yes [Enter]
Is anyone in your party gluten-free? yes [Enter]
Here are your restaurant choices:
    Corner Cafe
    The Chef's Kitchen
```

19. Turtle Graphics: Hit the Target Modification

Enhance the `hit_the_target.py` program that you saw in Program 3-9 so that, when the projectile misses the target, it displays hints to the user indicating whether the angle and/or the force value should be increased or decreased. For example, the program should display messages such as `'Try a greater angle'` and `'Use less force.'`

CHAPTER

4 Repetition Structures

TOPICS

4.1 Introduction to Repetition Structures

CONCEPT: A repetition structure causes a statement or set of statements to execute repeatedly.

Programmers commonly have to write code that performs the same task over and over. For example, suppose you have been asked to write a program that calculates a 10 percent sales commission for several salespeople. Although it would not be a good design, one approach would be to write the code to calculate one salesperson's commission, and then repeat that code for each salesperson. For example, look at the following:

```
# Get a salesperson's sales and commission rate.
sales = float(input('Enter the amount of sales: '))
comm_rate = float(input('Enter the commission rate: '))

# Calculate the commission.
commission = sales * comm_rate

# Display the commission.
print('The commission is $', format(commission, ',.2f'), sep='')

# Get another salesperson's sales and commission rate.
sales = float(input('Enter the amount of sales: '))
comm_rate = float(input('Enter the commission rate: '))

# Calculate the commission.
commission = sales * comm_rate
```

```
    # Display the commission.
    print('The commission is $', format(commission, ',.2f'), sep='')

    # Get another salesperson's sales and commission rate.
    sales = float(input('Enter the amount of sales: '))
    comm_rate = float(input('Enter the commission rate: '))

    # Calculate the commission.
    commission = sales * comm_rate
    # Display the commission.

    print('The commission is $', format(commission, ',.2f'), sep='')
```

And this code goes on and on . . .

As you can see, this code is one long sequence structure containing a lot of duplicated code. There are several disadvantages to this approach, including the following:

- The duplicated code makes the program large.
- Writing a long sequence of statements can be time consuming.
- If part of the duplicated code has to be corrected or changed, then the correction or change has to be done many times.

Instead of writing the same sequence of statements over and over, a better way to repeatedly perform an operation is to write the code for the operation once, then place that code in a structure that makes the computer repeat it as many times as necessary. This can be done with a *repetition structure*, which is more commonly known as a *loop*.

Condition-Controlled and Count-Controlled Loops

In this chapter, we will look at two broad categories of loops: condition-controlled and count-controlled. A *condition-controlled loop* uses a true/false condition to control the number of times that it repeats. A *count-controlled loop* repeats a specific number of times. In Python, you use the `while` statement to write a condition-controlled loop, and you use the `for` statement to write a count-controlled loop. In this chapter, we will demonstrate how to write both types of loops.

Checkpoint

4.1 What is a repetition structure?

4.2 What is a condition-controlled loop?

4.3 What is a count-controlled loop?

4.2 The `while` Loop: A Condition-Controlled Loop

VideoNote The `while` Loop

CONCEPT: A condition-controlled loop causes a statement or set of statements to repeat as long as a condition is true. In Python, you use the `while` statement to write a condition-controlled loop.

The `while` loop gets its name from the way it works: *while a condition is true, do some task*. The loop has two parts: (1) a condition that is tested for a true or false value, and (2) a statement or set of statements that is repeated as long as the condition is true. Figure 4-1 shows the logic of a `while` loop.

Figure 4-1 The logic of a `while` loop

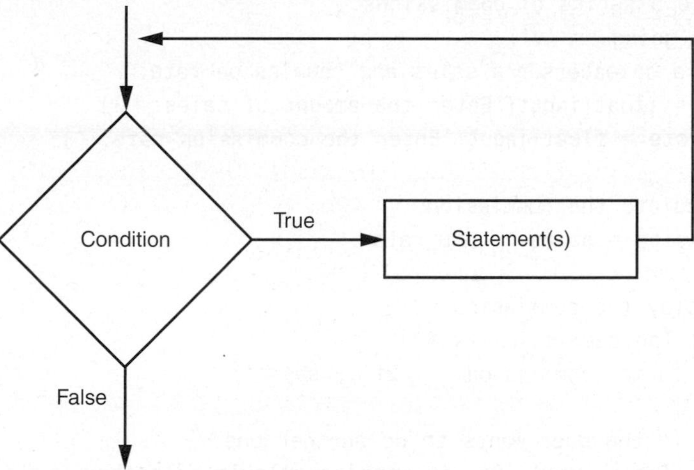

The diamond symbol represents the condition that is tested. Notice what happens if the condition is true: one or more statements are executed, and the program's execution flows back to the point just above the diamond symbol. The condition is tested again, and if it is true, the process repeats. If the condition is false, the program exits the loop. In a flowchart, you will always recognize a loop when you see a flow line going back to a previous part of the flowchart.

Here is the general format of the `while` loop in Python:

```
while condition:
    statement
    statement
    etc.
```

For simplicity, we will refer to the first line as the *`while` clause*. The `while` clause begins with the word `while`, followed by a Boolean *`condition`* that will be evaluated as either true or false. A colon appears after the *`condition`*. Beginning at the next line is a block of statements. (Recall from Chapter 3 that all of the statements in a block must be consistently indented. This indentation is required because the Python interpreter uses it to tell where the block begins and ends.)

When the `while` loop executes, the *`condition`* is tested. If the *`condition`* is true, the statements that appear in the block following the `while` clause are executed, and the loop starts over. If the *`condition`* is false, the program exits the loop. Program 4-1 shows how we might use a `while` loop to write the commission calculating program that was described at the beginning of this chapter.

Program 4-1 (commission.py)

```
1  # This program calculates sales commissions.
2
3  # Create a variable to control the loop.
4  keep_going = 'y'
5
6  # Calculate a series of commissions.
7  while keep_going == 'y':
8      # Get a salesperson's sales and commission rate.
9      sales = float(input('Enter the amount of sales: '))
10     comm_rate = float(input('Enter the commission rate: '))
11
12     # Calculate the commission.
13     commission = sales * comm_rate
14
15     # Display the commission.
16     print('The commission is $',
17           format(commission, ',.2f'), sep='')
18
19     # See if the user wants to do another one.
20     keep_going = input('Do you want to calculate another ' +
21                        'commission (Enter y for yes): ')
```

Program Output (with input shown in bold)

```
Enter the amount of sales: 10000.00 Enter
Enter the commission rate: 0.10 Enter
The commission is $1,000.00
Do you want to calculate another commission (Enter y for yes): y Enter
Enter the amount of sales: 20000.00 Enter
Enter the commission rate: 0.15 Enter
The commission is $3,000.00
Do you want to calculate another commission (Enter y for yes): y Enter
Enter the amount of sales: 12000.00 Enter
Enter the commission rate: 0.10 Enter
The commission is $1,200.00
Do you want to calculate another commission (Enter y for yes): n Enter
```

In line 4, we use an assignment statement to create a variable named `keep_going`. Notice the variable is assigned the value `'y'`. This initialization value is important, and in a moment you will see why.

Line 7 is the beginning of a `while` loop, which starts like this:

```
while keep_going == 'y':
```

Notice the condition that is being tested: `keep_going =='y'`. The loop tests this condition, and if it is true, the statements in lines 8 through 21 are executed. Then, the loop starts over at line 7. It tests the expression `keep_going =='y'` and if it is true, the statements in lines 8 through 21 are executed again. This cycle repeats until the expression `keep_going =='y'` is tested in line 7 and found to be false. When that happens, the program exits the loop. This is illustrated in Figure 4-2.

Figure 4-2 The `while` loop

This condition is tested.

```
while keep_going == 'y':

    # Get a salesperson's sales and commission rate.
    sales = float(input('Enter the amount of sales: '))
    comm_rate = float(input('Enter the commission rate: '))

    # Calculate the commission.
    commission = sales * comm_rate

    # Display the commission.
    print('The commission is $',
          format(commission, ',.2f'), sep='')

    # See if the user wants to do another one.
    keep_going = input('Do you want to calculate another ' +
                       'commission (Enter y for yes): ')
```

If the condition is true, these statements are executed, and then the loop starts over.

If the condition is false, these statements are skipped, and the program exits the loop.

In order for this loop to stop executing, something has to happen inside the loop to make the expression `keep_going == 'y'` false. The statement in lines 20 through 21 take care of this. This statement displays the prompt "Do you want to calculate another commission (Enter y for yes)." The value that is read from the keyboard is assigned to the `keep_going` variable. If the user enters y (and it must be a lowercase y), then the expression `keep_going == 'y'` will be true when the loop starts over. This will cause the statements in the body of the loop to execute again. But if the user enters anything other than lowercase y, the expression will be false when the loop starts over, and the program will exit the loop.

Now that you have examined the code, look at the program output in the sample run. First, the user entered 10000.00 for the sales and 0.10 for the commission rate. Then, the program displayed the commission for that amount, which is $1,000.00. Next the user is prompted "Do you want to calculate another commission? (Enter y for yes)." The user entered y, and the loop started the steps over. In the sample run, the user went through this process three times. Each execution of the body of a loop is known as an *iteration*. In the sample run, the loop iterated three times.

Figure 4-3 shows a flowchart for the `main` function. In the flowchart, we have a repetition structure, which is the `while` loop. The condition `keep_going =='y'` is tested, and if it is true, a series of statements are executed and the flow of execution returns to the point just above the conditional test.

Figure 4-3 Flowchart for Program 4-1

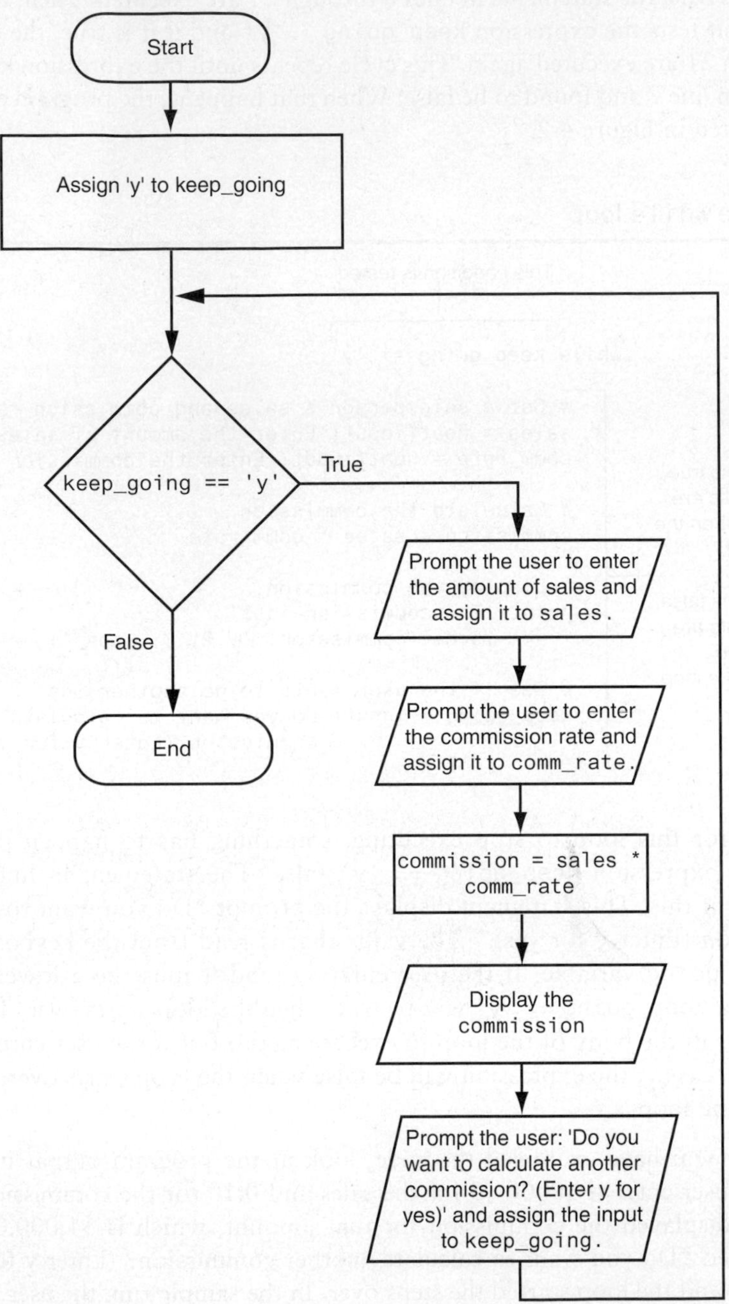

The while Loop Is a Pretest Loop

The while loop is known as a *pretest* loop, which means it tests its condition *before* performing an iteration. Because the test is done at the beginning of the loop, you usually have to perform some steps prior to the loop to make sure that the loop executes at least once. For example, the loop in Program 4-1 starts like this:

```
while keep_going == 'y':
```

The loop will perform an iteration only if the expression keep_going =='y' is true. This means that (a) the keep_going variable has to exist, and (b) it has to reference the value 'y'. To make sure the expression is true the first time that the loop executes, we assigned the value 'y' to the keep_going variable in line 4 as follows:

```
keep_going = 'y'
```

By performing this step we know that the condition keep_going =='y' will be true the first time the loop executes. This is an important characteristic of the while loop: it will never execute if its condition is false to start with. In some programs, this is exactly what you want. The following *In the Spotlight* section gives an example.

In the Spotlight:

Designing a Program with a while Loop

A project currently underway at Chemical Labs, Inc. requires that a substance be continually heated in a vat. A technician must check the substance's temperature every 15 minutes. If the substance's temperature does not exceed 102.5 degrees Celsius, then the technician does nothing. However, if the temperature is greater than 102.5 degrees Celsius, the technician must turn down the vat's thermostat, wait 5 minutes, and check the temperature again. The technician repeats these steps until the temperature does not exceed 102.5 degrees Celsius. The director of engineering has asked you to write a program that guides the technician through this process.

Here is the algorithm:

1. Get the substance's temperature.
2. Repeat the following steps as long as the temperature is greater than 102.5 degrees Celsius:
   a. Tell the technician to turn down the thermostat, wait 5 minutes, and check the temperature again.
   b. Get the substance's temperature.
3. After the loop finishes, tell the technician that the temperature is acceptable and to check it again in 15 minutes.

After reviewing this algorithm, you realize that steps 2(a) and 2(b) should not be performed if the test condition (temperature is greater than 102.5) is false to begin with. The while loop will work well in this situation, because it will not execute even once if its condition is false. Program 4-2 shows the code for the program.

Program 4-2 (temperature.py)

```
# This program assists a technician in the process
# of checking a substance's temperature.

# Named constant to represent the maximum
# temperature.
MAX_TEMP = 102.5

# Get the substance's temperature.
temperature = float(input("Enter the substance's Celsius temperature: "))

# As long as necessary, instruct the user to
# adjust the thermostat.
while temperature > MAX_TEMP:
    print('The temperature is too high.')
    print('Turn the thermostat down and wait')
    print('5 minutes. Then take the temperature')
    print('again and enter it.')
    temperature = float(input('Enter the new Celsius temperature: '))

# Remind the user to check the temperature again
# in 15 minutes.
print('The temperature is acceptable.')
print('Check it again in 15 minutes.')
```

Program Output (with input shown in bold)

```
Enter the substance's Celsius temperature: 104.7 Enter
The temperature is too high.
Turn the thermostat down and wait
5 minutes. Take the temperature
again and enter it.
Enter the new Celsius temperature: 103.2 Enter
The temperature is too high.
Turn the thermostat down and wait
5 minutes. Take the temperature
again and enter it.
Enter the new Celsius temperature: 102.1 Enter
The temperature is acceptable.
Check it again in 15 minutes.
```

Program Output (with input shown in bold)

```
Enter the substance's Celsius temperature: 102.1 [Enter]
The temperature is acceptable.
Check it again in 15 minutes.
```

Infinite Loops

In all but rare cases, loops must contain within themselves a way to terminate. This means that something inside the loop must eventually make the test condition false. The loop in Program 4-1 stops when the expression `keep_going == 'y'` is false. If a loop does not have a way of stopping, it is called an infinite loop. An *infinite loop* continues to repeat until the program is interrupted. Infinite loops usually occur when the programmer forgets to write code inside the loop that makes the test condition false. In most circumstances, you should avoid writing infinite loops.

Program 4-3 demonstrates an infinite loop. This is a modified version of the commission calculating program shown in Program 4-1. In this version, we have removed the code that modifies the `keep_going` variable in the body of the loop. Each time the expression `keep_going == 'y'` is tested in line 6, `keep_going` will reference the string `'y'`. As a consequence, the loop has no way of stopping. (The only way to stop this program is to press Ctrl+C on the keyboard to interrupt it.)

Program 4-3 (infinite.py)

```
 1  # This program demonstrates an infinite loop.
 2  # Create a variable to control the loop.
 3  keep_going = 'y'
 4
 5  # Warning! Infinite loop!
 6  while keep_going == 'y':
 7      # Get a salesperson's sales and commission rate.
 8      sales = float(input('Enter the amount of sales: '))
 9      comm_rate = float(input('Enter the commission rate: '))
10
11      # Calculate the commission.
12      commission = sales * comm_rate
13
14      # Display the commission.
15      print('The commission is $',
16            format(commission, ',.2f'), sep='')
```

Checkpoint

4.4 What is a loop iteration?

4.5 Does the `while` loop test its condition before or after it performs an iteration?

4.6 How many times will `'Hello World'` be printed in the following program?

```
count = 10
while count < 1:
     print('Hello World')
```

4.7 What is an infinite loop?

4.3 The for Loop: A Count-Controlled Loop

CONCEPT: A count-controlled loop iterates a specific number of times. In Python, you use the `for` statement to write a count-controlled loop.

VideoNote The for Loop

As mentioned at the beginning of this chapter, a count-controlled loop iterates a specific number of times. Count-controlled loops are commonly used in programs. For example, suppose a business is open six days per week, and you are going to write a program that calculates the total sales for a week. You will need a loop that iterates exactly six times. Each time the loop iterates, it will prompt the user to enter the sales for one day.

You use the `for` statement to write a count-controlled loop. In Python, the `for` statement is designed to work with a sequence of data items. When the statement executes, it iterates once for each item in the sequence. Here is the general format:

```
for variable in [value1, value2, etc.]:
    statement
    statement
    etc.
```

We will refer to the first line as the *for clause*. In the `for` clause, *`variable`* is the name of a variable. Inside the brackets a sequence of values appears, with a comma separating each value. (In Python, a comma-separated sequence of data items that are enclosed in a set of brackets is called a *list*. In Chapter 7, you will learn more about lists.) Beginning at the next line is a block of statements that is executed each time the loop iterates.

The `for` statement executes in the following manner: The *`variable`* is assigned the first value in the list, then the statements that appear in the block are executed. Then, *`variable`* is assigned the next value in the list, and the statements in the block are executed again. This continues until *`variable`* has been assigned the last value in the list. Program 4-4 shows a simple example that uses a `for` loop to display the numbers 1 through 5.

Program 4-4 (simple_loop1.py)

```
1 # This program demonstrates a simple for loop
2 # that uses a list of numbers.
3
4 print('I will display the numbers 1 through 5.')
5 for num in [1, 2, 3, 4, 5]:
6     print(num)
```

Program Output

```
I will display the numbers 1 through 5.
1
2
3
4
5
```

The first time the for loop iterates, the num variable is assigned the value 1 and then the statement in line 6 executes (displaying the value 1). The next time the loop iterates, num is assigned the value 2, and the statement in line 6 executes (displaying the value 2). This process continues, as shown in Figure 4-4, until num has been assigned the last value in the list. Because the list contains five values, the loop will iterate five times.

Figure 4-4 The for loop

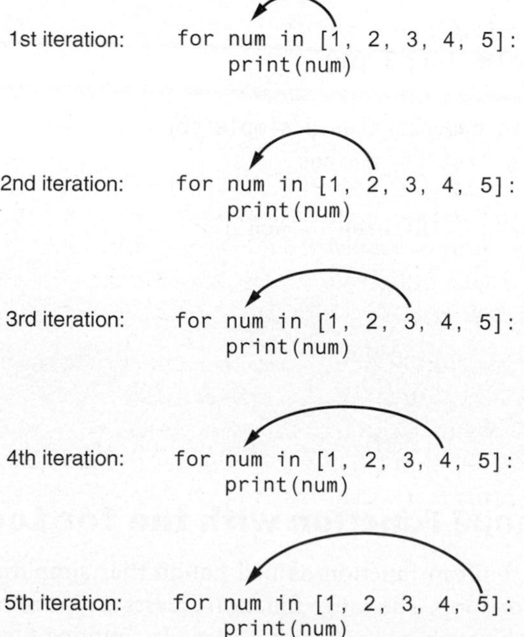

Python programmers commonly refer to the variable that is used in the `for` clause as the *target variable* because it is the target of an assignment at the beginning of each loop iteration.

The values that appear in the list do not have to be a consecutively ordered series of numbers. For example, Program 4-5 uses a `for` loop to display a list of odd numbers. There are five numbers in the list, so the loop iterates five times.

Program 4-5 (simple_loop2.py)

```
# This program also demonstrates a simple for
# loop that uses a list of numbers.

print('I will display the odd numbers 1 through 9.')
for num in [1, 3, 5, 7, 9]:
    print(num)
```

Program Output

```
I will display the odd numbers 1 through 9.
1
3
5
7
9
```

Program 4-6 shows another example. In this program, the `for` loop iterates over a list of strings. Notice the list (in line 4) contains the three strings 'Winken', 'Blinken', and 'Nod'. As a result, the loop iterates three times.

Program 4-6 (simple_loop3.py)

```
1 # This program also demonstrates a simple for
2 # loop that uses a list of strings.
3
4 for name in ['Winken', 'Blinken', 'Nod']:
5     print(name)
```

Program Output

```
Winken
Blinken
Nod
```

Using the range Function with the for Loop

Python provides a built-in function named `range` that simplifies the process of writing a count-controlled `for` loop. The range function creates a type of object known as an iterable. An *iterable* is an object that is similar to a list. It contains a sequence of values that can be iterated over with something like a loop. Here is an example of a `for` loop that uses the `range` function:

```
for num in range(5):
    print(num)
```

Notice instead of using a list of values, we call to the `range` function passing 5 as an argument. In this statement, the `range` function will generate an iterable sequence of integers in the range of 0 up to (but not including) 5. This code works the same as the following:

```
for num in [0, 1, 2, 3, 4]:
    print(num)
```

As you can see, the list contains five numbers, so the loop will iterate five times. Program 4-7 uses the `range` function with a `for` loop to display "Hello world" five times.

Program 4-7 (simple_loop4.py)

```
# This program demonstrates how the range
# function can be used with a for loop.

# Print a message five times.
for x in range(5):
    print('Hello world')
```

Program Output

```
Hello world
Hello world
Hello world
Hello world
Hello world
```

If you pass one argument to the `range` function, as demonstrated in Program 4-7, that argument is used as the ending limit of the sequence of numbers. If you pass two arguments to the `range` function, the first argument is used as the starting value of the sequence, and the second argument is used as the ending limit. Here is an example:

```
for num in range(1, 5):
    print(num)
```

This code will display the following:

```
1
2
3
4
```

By default, the `range` function produces a sequence of numbers that increase by 1 for each successive number in the list. If you pass a third argument to the `range` function, that argument is used as *step value*. Instead of increasing by 1, each successive number in the sequence will increase by the step value. Here is an example:

```
for num in range(1, 10, 2):
    print(num)
```

In this for statement, three arguments are passed to the range function:

- The first argument, 1, is the starting value for the sequence.
- The second argument, 10, is the ending limit of the list. This means that the last number in the sequence will be 9.
- The third argument, 2, is the step value. This means that 2 will be added to each successive number in the sequence.

This code will display the following:

```
1
3
5
7
9
```

Using the Target Variable Inside the Loop

In a for loop, the purpose of the target variable is to reference each item in a sequence of items as the loop iterates. In many situations it is helpful to use the target variable in a calculation or other task within the body of the loop. For example, suppose you need to write a program that displays the numbers 1 through 10 and their respective squares, in a table similar to the following:

Number	Square
1	1
2	4
3	9
4	16
5	25
6	36
7	49
8	64
9	81
10	100

This can be accomplished by writing a for loop that iterates over the values 1 through 10. During the first iteration, the target variable will be assigned the value 1, during the second iteration it will be assigned the value 2, and so forth. Because the target variable will reference the values 1 through 10 during the loop's execution, you can use it in the calculation inside the loop. Program 4-8 shows how this is done.

Program 4-8 (squares.py)

```
1  # This program uses a loop to display a
2  # table showing the numbers 1 through 10
3  # and their squares.
4
5  # Print the table headings.
6  print('Number\tSquare')
7  print('--------------')
8
9  # Print the numbers 1 through 10
10 # and their squares.
11 for number in range(1, 11):
12     square = number**2
13     print(number, '\t', square)
```

Program Output

```
Number  Square
--------------
1       1
2       4
3       9
4       16
5       25
6       36
7       49
8       64
9       81
10      100
```

First, take a closer look at line 6, which displays the table headings:

```
print('Number\tSquare')
```

Notice inside the string literal, the `\t` escape sequence between the words Number and Square. Recall from Chapter 2 that the `\t` escape sequence is like pressing the Tab key; it causes the output cursor to move over to the next tab position. This causes the space that you see between the words Number and Square in the sample output.

The `for` loop that begins in line 11 uses the `range` function to produce a sequence containing the numbers 1 through 10. During the first iteration, `number` will reference 1, during the second iteration `number` will reference 2, and so forth, up to 10. Inside the loop, the statement in line 12 raises `number` to the power of 2 (recall from Chapter 2 that `**` is the exponent operator) and assigns the result to the `square` variable. The statement in line 13 prints the value referenced by `number`, tabs over, then prints the value referenced by `square`. (Tabbing over with the `\t` escape sequence causes the numbers to be aligned in two columns in the output.)

Figure 4-5 shows how we might draw a flowchart for this program.

Figure 4-5 Flowchart for Program 4-8

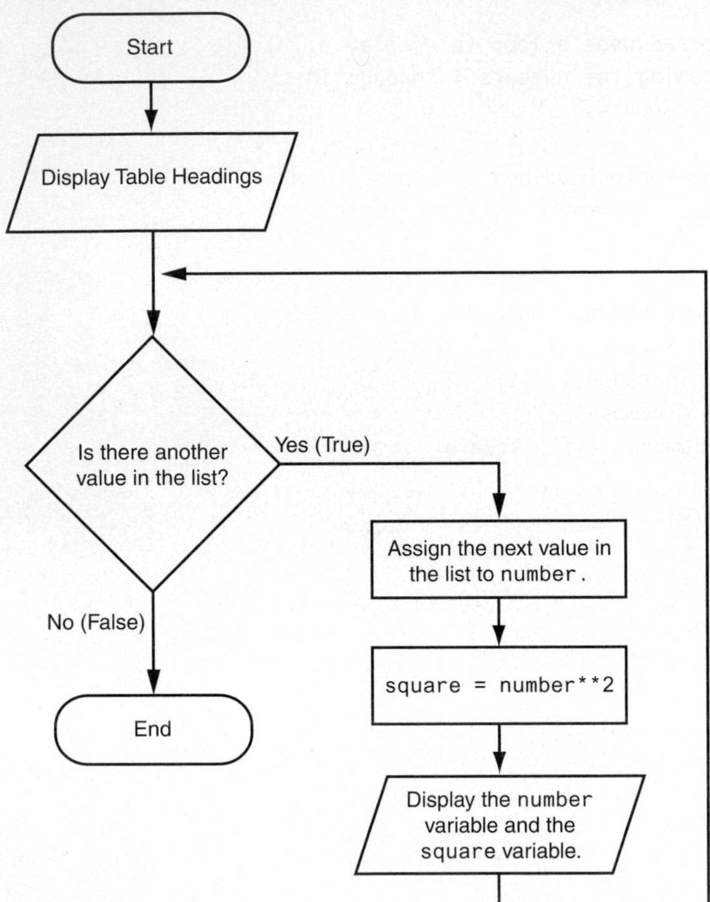

In the Spotlight:
Designing a Count-Controlled Loop with the `for` Statement

Your friend Amanda just inherited a European sports car from her uncle. Amanda lives in the United States, and she is afraid she will get a speeding ticket because the car's speedometer indicates kilometers per hour (KPH). She has asked you to write a program that displays a table of speeds in KPH with their values converted to miles per hour (MPH). The formula for converting KPH to MPH is:

$$MPH = KPH * 0.6214$$

In the formula, *MPH* is the speed in miles per hour, and *KPH* is the speed in kilometers per hour.

The table that your program displays should show speeds from 60 KPH through 130 KPH, in increments of 10, along with their values converted to MPH. The table should look something like this:

KPH	MPH
60	37.3
70	43.5
80	49.7
etc. . . .	
130	80.8

After thinking about this table of values, you decide that you will write a `for` loop. The list of values that the loop will iterate over will be the kilometer-per-hour speeds. In the loop, you will call the `range` function like this:

```
range(60, 131, 10)
```

The first value in the sequence will be 60. Notice the third argument specifies 10 as the step value. This means the numbers in the list will be 60, 70, 80, and so forth. The second argument specifies 131 as the sequence's ending limit, so the last number in the sequence will be 130.

Inside the loop, you will use the target variable to calculate a speed in miles per hour. Program 4-9 shows the program.

Program 4-9 (speed_converter.py)

```
# This program converts the speeds 60 kph
# through 130 kph (in 10 kph increments)
# to mph.

START_SPEED = 60               # Starting speed
END_SPEED = 131                # Ending speed
INCREMENT = 10                 # Speed increment
CONVERSION_FACTOR = 0.6214     # Conversion factor

# Print the table headings.
print('KPH\tMPH')
print('--------------')

# Print the speeds.
for kph in range(START_SPEED, END_SPEED, INCREMENT)
    mph = kph * CONVERSION_FACTOR
    print(kph, '\t', format(mph, '.1f'))
```

(program continues)

Program 4-9 *(continued)*

Program Output

```
KPH         MPH
----------------
60          37.3
70          43.5
80          49.7
90          55.9
100         62.1
110         68.4
120         74.6
130         80.8
```

Letting the User Control the Loop Iterations

In many cases, the programmer knows the exact number of iterations that a loop must perform. For example, recall Program 4-8, which displays a table showing the numbers 1 through 10 and their squares. When the code was written, the programmer knew that the loop had to iterate over the values 1 through 10.

Sometimes, the programmer needs to let the user control the number of times that a loop iterates. For example, what if you want Program 4-8 to be a bit more versatile by allowing the user to specify the maximum value displayed by the loop? Program 4-10 shows how you can accomplish this.

Program 4-10 **(user_squares1.py)**

```
# This program uses a loop to display a
# table of numbers and their squares.

# Get the ending limit.
print('This program displays a list of numbers')
print('(starting at 1) and their squares.')
end = int(input('How high should I go? '))

# Print the table headings.
print()
print('Number\tSquare')
print('--------------')

# Print the numbers and their squares.
for number in range(1, end + 1):
    square = number**2
    print(number, '\t', square)
```

Program Output (with input shown in bold)

```
This program displays a list of numbers
(starting at 1) and their squares.
How high should I go? 5 [Enter]

Number   Square
-----------------
1        1
2        4
3        9
4        16
5        25
```

This program asks the user to enter a value that can be used as the ending limit for the list. This value is assigned to the `end` variable in line 7. Then, the expression `end + 1` is used in line 15 as the second argument for the `range` function. (We have to add one to `end` because otherwise the sequence would go up to, but not include, the value entered by the user.)

Program 4-11 shows an example that allows the user to specify both the starting value and the ending limit of the sequence.

Program 4-11 (user_squares2.py)

```
# This program uses a loop to display a
# table of numbers and their squares.

# Get the starting value.
print('This program displays a list of numbers')
print('and their squares.')
start = int(input('Enter the starting number: '))

# Get the ending limit.
end = int(input('How high should I go? '))

# Print the table headings.
print()
print('Number\tSquare')
print('---------------')

# Print the numbers and their squares.
for number in range(start, end + 1):
    square = number**2
    print(number, '\t', square)
```

(program continues)

Program 4-11 *(continued)*

Program Output (with input shown in bold)

```
This program displays a list of numbers and their squares.
Enter the starting number: 5 [Enter]
How high should I go? 10 [Enter]

Number  Square
---------------
5       25
6       36
7       49
8       64
9       81
10      100
```

Generating an Iterable Sequence that Ranges from Highest to Lowest

In the examples you have seen so far, the `range` function was used to generate a sequence with numbers that go from lowest to highest. Alternatively, you can use the `range` function to generate sequences of numbers that go from highest to lowest. Here is an example:

```
range(10, 0, -1)
```

In this function call, the starting value is 10, the sequence's ending limit is 0, and the step value is −1. This expression will produce the following sequence:

```
10, 9, 8, 7, 6, 5, 4, 3, 2, 1
```

Here is an example of a `for` loop that prints the numbers 5 down to 1:

```
for num in range(5, 0, -1):
    print(num)
```

Checkpoint

4.8 Rewrite the following code so it calls the `range` function instead of using the list `[0, 1, 2, 3, 4, 5]`:

```
for x in [0, 1, 2, 3, 4, 5]:
    print('I love to program!')
```

4.9 What will the following code display?

```
for number in range(6):
    print(number)
```

4.10 What will the following code display?

```
for number in range(2, 6):
    print(number)
```

4.11 What will the following code display?

```
for number in range(0, 501, 100):
    print(number)
```

4.12 What will the following code display?

```
for number in range(10, 5, -1):
    print(number)
```

4.4 Calculating a Running Total

CONCEPT: A running total is a sum of numbers that accumulates with each iteration of a loop. The variable used to keep the running total is called an accumulator.

Many programming tasks require you to calculate the total of a series of numbers. For example, suppose you are writing a program that calculates a business's total sales for a week. The program would read the sales for each day as input and calculate the total of those numbers.

Programs that calculate the total of a series of numbers typically use two elements:

- A loop that reads each number in the series.
- A variable that accumulates the total of the numbers as they are read.

The variable that is used to accumulate the total of the numbers is called an *accumulator*. It is often said that the loop keeps a *running total* because it accumulates the total as it reads each number in the series. Figure 4-6 shows the general logic of a loop that calculates a running total.

Figure 4-6 Logic for calculating a running total

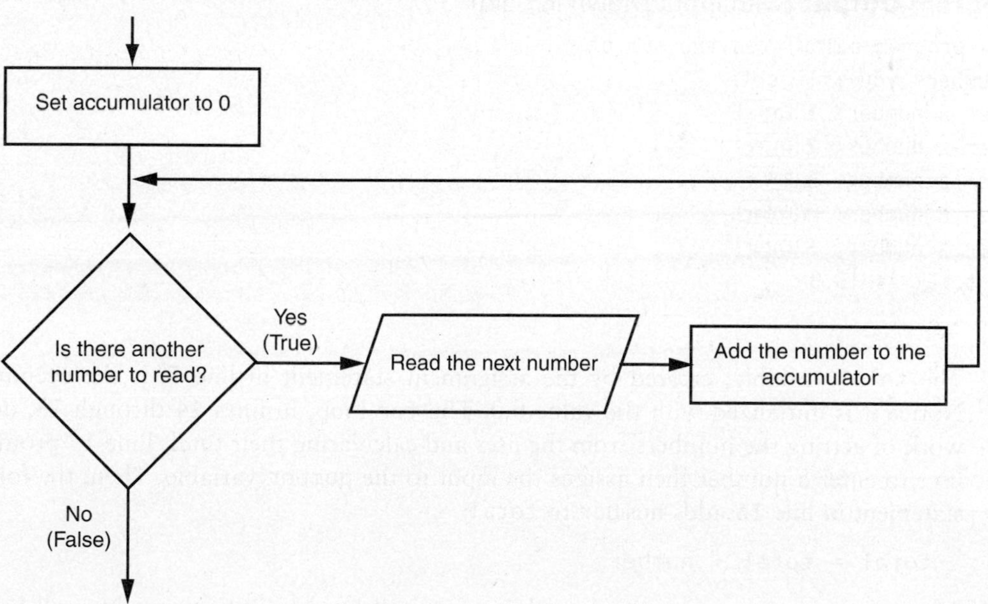

When the loop finishes, the accumulator will contain the total of the numbers that were read by the loop. Notice the first step in the flowchart is to set the accumulator variable to 0. This is a critical step. Each time the loop reads a number, it adds it to the accumulator. If the accumulator starts with any value other than 0, it will not contain the correct total when the loop finishes.

Let's look at a program that calculates a running total. Program 4-12 allows the user to enter five numbers, and displays the total of the numbers entered.

Program 4-12 (sum_numbers.py)

```
1  # This program calculates the sum of a series
2  # of numbers entered by the user.
3
4  MAX = 5 # The maximum number
5
6  # Initialize an accumulator variable.
7  total = 0.0
8
9  # Explain what we are doing.
10 print('This program calculates the sum of')
11 print(MAX, 'numbers you will enter.')
12
13 # Get the numbers and accumulate them.
14 for counter in range(MAX):
15     number = int(input('Enter a number: '))
16     total = total + number
17
18 # Display the total of the numbers.
19 print('The total is', total)
```

Program Output (with input shown in bold)

```
This program calculates the sum of
5 numbers you will enter.
Enter a number: 1 Enter
Enter a number: 2 Enter
Enter a number: 3 Enter
Enter a number: 4 Enter
Enter a number: 5 Enter
The total is 15.0
```

The `total` variable, created by the assignment statement in line 7, is the accumulator. Notice it is initialized with the value 0.0. The `for` loop, in lines 14 through 16, does the work of getting the numbers from the user and calculating their total. Line 15 prompts the user to enter a number then assigns the input to the `number` variable. Then, the following statement in line 16 adds `number` to `total`:

```
total = total + number
```

After this statement executes, the value referenced by the `number` variable will be added to the value in the `total` variable. It's important that you understand how this statement works. First, the interpreter gets the value of the expression on the right side of the = operator, which is `total + number`. Then, that value is assigned by the = operator to the `total` variable. The effect of the statement is that the value of the `number` variable is added to the `total` variable. When the loop finishes, the `total` variable will hold the sum of all the numbers that were added to it. This value is displayed in line 19.

The Augmented Assignment Operators

Quite often, programs have assignment statements in which the variable that is on the left side of the = operator also appears on the right side of the = operator. Here is an example:

```
x = x + 1
```

On the right side of the assignment operator, 1 is added to `x`. The result is then assigned to `x`, replacing the value that `x` previously referenced. Effectively, this statement adds 1 to `x`. You saw another example of this type of statement in Program 4-13:

```
total = total + number
```

This statement assigns the value of `total + number` to `total`. As mentioned before, the effect of this statement is that `number` is added to the value of `total`. Here is one more example:

```
balance = balance - withdrawal
```

This statement assigns the value of the expression `balance - withdrawal` to `balance`. The effect of this statement is that `withdrawal` is subtracted from `balance`.

Table 4-1 shows other examples of statements written this way.

Table 4-1 Various assignment statements (assume x = 6 in each statement)

Statement	What It Does	Value of x after the Statement
`x = x + 4`	Add 4 to `x`	10
`x = x - 3`	Subtracts 3 from `x`	3
`x = x * 10`	Multiplies `x` by 10	60
`x = x / 2`	Divides `x` by 2	3
`x = x % 4`	Assigns the remainder of `x / 4` to `x`	2

These types of operations are common in programming. For convenience, Python offers a special set of operators designed specifically for these jobs. Table 4-2 shows the *augmented assignment operators*.

Table 4-2 Augmented assignment operators

Operator	Example Usage	Equivalent To
+=	`x += 5`	`x = x + 5`
-=	`y -= 2`	`y = y - 2`
*=	`z *= 10`	`z = z * 10`
/=	`a /= b`	`a = a / b`
%=	`c %= 3`	`c = c % 3`

As you can see, the augmented assignment operators do not require the programmer to type the variable name twice. The following statement:

```
total = total + number
```

could be rewritten as

```
total += number
```

Similarly, the statement

```
balance = balance - withdrawal
```

could be rewritten as

```
balance -= withdrawal
```

Checkpoint

4.13 What is an accumulator?

4.14 Should an accumulator be initialized to any specific value? Why or why not?

4.15 What will the following code display?

```
total = 0
for count in range(1, 6):
    total = total + count
print(total)
```

4.16 What will the following code display?

```
number 1 = 10
number 2 = 5
number 1 = number 1 + number 2
print(number1)
print(number2)
```

4.17 Rewrite the following statements using augmented assignment operators:

a) `quantity = quantity + 1`
b) `days_left = days_left - 5`
c) `price = price * 10`
d) `price = price / 2`

4.5 Sentinels

CONCEPT: A sentinel is a special value that marks the end of a sequence of values.

Consider the following scenario: You are designing a program that will use a loop to process a long sequence of values. At the time you are designing the program, you do not know the number of values that will be in the sequence. In fact, the number of values in the sequence could be different each time the program is executed. What is the best way to design such a loop? Here are some techniques that you have seen already in this chapter, along with the disadvantages of using them when processing a long list of values:

- Simply ask the user, at the end of each loop iteration, if there is another value to process. If the sequence of values is long, however, asking this question at the end of each loop iteration might make the program cumbersome for the user.
- Ask the user at the beginning of the program how many items are in the sequence. This might also inconvenience the user, however. If the sequence is very long, and the user does not know the number of items it contains, it will require the user to count them.

When processing a long sequence of values with a loop, perhaps a better technique is to use a sentinel. A *sentinel* is a special value that marks the end of a sequence of items. When a program reads the sentinel value, it knows it has reached the end of the sequence, so the loop terminates.

For example, suppose a doctor wants a program to calculate the average weight of all her patients. The program might work like this: A loop prompts the user to enter either a patient's weight, or 0 if there are no more weights. When the program reads 0 as a weight, it interprets this as a signal that there are no more weights. The loop ends and the program displays the average weight.

A sentinel value must be distinctive enough that it will not be mistaken as a regular value in the sequence. In the example cited above, the doctor (or her medical assistant) enters 0 to signal the end of the sequence of weights. Because no patient's weight will be 0, this is a good value to use as a sentinel.

In the Spotlight:

Using a Sentinel

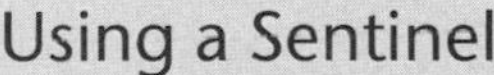

The county tax office calculates the annual taxes on property using the following formula:

$$\textit{property tax} = \textit{property value} \times 0.0065$$

Every day, a clerk in the tax office gets a list of properties and has to calculate the tax for each property on the list. You have been asked to design a program that the clerk can use to perform these calculations.

In your interview with the tax clerk, you learn that each property is assigned a lot number, and all lot numbers are 1 or greater. You decide to write a loop that uses the number 0 as a sentinel value. During each loop iteration, the program will ask the clerk to enter either a property's lot number, or 0 to end. The code for the program is shown in Program 4-13.

Program 4-13 (property_tax.py)

```
# This program displays property taxes.

TAX_FACTOR = 0.0065 # Represents the tax factor.

```

(program continues)

Program 4-13 *(continued)*

```
# Get the first lot number.
print('Enter the property lot number')
print('or enter 0 to end.')
lot = int(input('Lot number: '))

# Continue processing as long as the user
# does not enter lot number 0.
while lot ! = 0:
    # Get the property value.
    value = float(input('Enter the property value: '))

    # Calculate the property's tax.
    tax = value * TAX_FACTOR

    # Display the tax.
    print('Property tax: $', format(tax, ',.2f'), sep='')

    # Get the next lot number.
    print('Enter the next lot number or')
    print('enter 0 to end.')
    lot = int(input('Lot number: '))
```

Program Output (with input shown in bold)

```
Enter the property lot number
or enter 0 to end.
Lot number: 100 [Enter]
Enter the property value: 100000.00 [Enter]
Property tax: $650.00.
Enter the next lot number or
enter 0 to end.
Lot number: 200 [Enter]
Enter the property value: 5000.00 [Enter]
Property tax: $32.50.
Enter the next lot number or
enter 0 to end.
Lot number: 0 [Enter]
```

Checkpoint

4.18 What is a sentinel?

4.19 Why should you take care to choose a distinctive value as a sentinel?

4.6 Input Validation Loops

CONCEPT: Input validation is the process of inspecting data that has been input to a program, to make sure it is valid before it is used in a computation. Input validation is commonly done with a loop that iterates as long as an input variable references bad data.

One of the most famous sayings among computer programmers is "garbage in, garbage out." This saying, sometimes abbreviated as *GIGO,* refers to the fact that computers cannot tell the difference between good data and bad data. If a user provides bad data as input to a program, the program will process that bad data and, as a result, will produce bad data as output. For example, look at the payroll program in Program 4-14 and notice what happens in the sample run when the user gives bad data as input.

Program 4-14 (gross_pay.py)

```
# This program displays gross pay.
# Get the number of hours worked.
hours = int(input('Enter the hours worked this week: '))

# Get the hourly pay rate.
pay_rate = float(input('Enter the hourly pay rate: '))

# Calculate the gross pay.
gross_pay = hours * pay_rate

# Display the gross pay.
print('Gross pay: $', format(gross_pay, ',.2f'))
```

Program Output (with input shown in bold)

```
Enter the hours worked this week: 400 Enter
Enter the hourly pay rate: 20 Enter
The gross pay is $8,000.00
```

Did you spot the bad data that was provided as input? The person receiving the paycheck will be pleasantly surprised, because in the sample run the payroll clerk entered 400 as the number of hours worked. The clerk probably meant to enter 40, because there are not 400 hours in a week. The computer, however, is unaware of this fact, and the program processed the bad data just as if it were good data. Can you think of other types of input that can be given to this program that will result in bad output? One example is a negative number entered for the hours worked; another is an invalid hourly pay rate.

Sometimes stories are reported in the news about computer errors that mistakenly cause people to be charged thousands of dollars for small purchases, or to receive large tax refunds to which they were not entitled. These "computer errors" are rarely caused by the computer, however; they are more commonly caused by bad data that was read into a program as input.

The integrity of a program's output is only as good as the integrity of its input. For this reason, you should design your programs in such a way that bad input is never accepted. When input is given to a program, it should be inspected before it is processed. If the input is invalid, the program should discard it and prompt the user to enter the correct data. This process is known as *input validation.*

Figure 4-7 shows a common technique for validating an item of input. In this technique, the input is read, then a loop is executed. If the input data is bad, the loop executes its block of statements. The loop displays an error message so the user will know that the input was invalid, and then it reads the new input. The loop repeats as long as the input is bad.

Figure 4-7 Logic containing an input validation loop

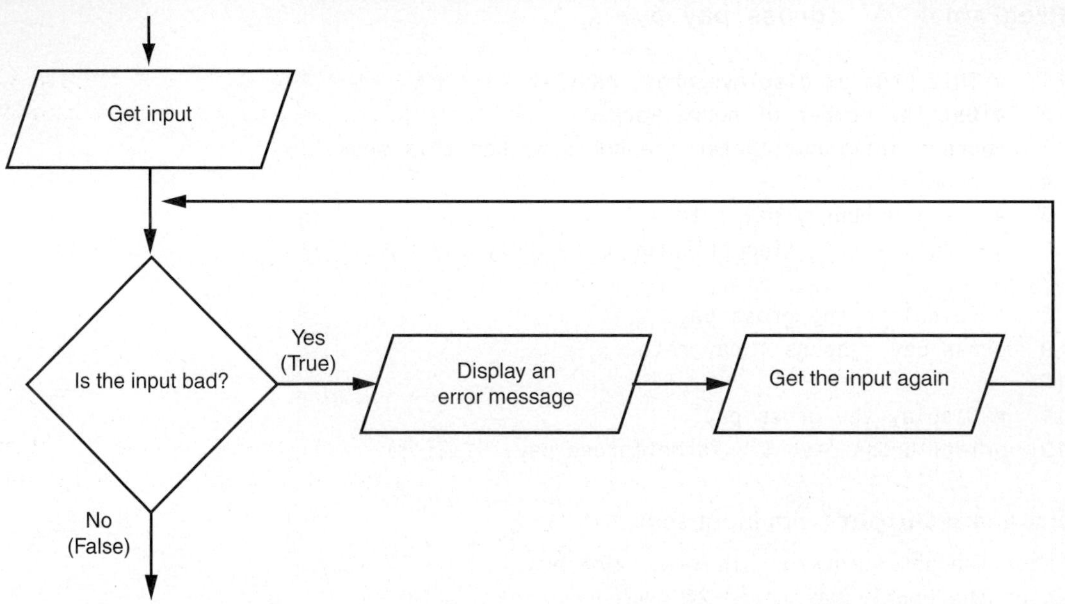

Notice the flowchart in Figure 4-7 reads input in two places: first just before the loop, and then inside the loop. The first input operation—just before the loop—is called a *priming read,* and its purpose is to get the first input value that will be tested by the validation loop. If that value is invalid, the loop will perform subsequent input operations.

Let's consider an example. Suppose you are designing a program that reads a test score and you want to make sure the user does not enter a value less than 0. The following code shows how you can use an input validation loop to reject any input value that is less than 0.

```
# Get a test score.
score = int(input('Enter a test score: '))
```

```
# Make sure it is not less than 0.
while score < 0:
    print('ERROR: The score cannot be negative.')
    score = int(input('Enter the correct score: '))
```

This code first prompts the user to enter a test score (this is the priming read), then the `while` loop executes. Recall that the `while` loop is a pretest loop, which means it tests the expression `score < 0` before performing an iteration. If the user entered a valid test score, this expression will be false, and the loop will not iterate. If the test score is invalid, however, the expression will be true, and the loop's block of statements will execute. The loop displays an error message and prompts the user to enter the correct test score. The loop will continue to iterate until the user enters a valid test score.

NOTE: An input validation loop is sometimes called an *error trap* or an *error handler.*

This code rejects only negative test scores. What if you also want to reject any test scores that are greater than 100? You can modify the input validation loop so it uses a compound Boolean expression, as shown next.

```
# Get a test score.
score = int(input('Enter a test score: '))
# Make sure it is not less than 0 or greater than 100.
while score < 0 or score > 100:
    print('ERROR: The score cannot be negative')
    print('or greater than 100.')
    score = int(input('Enter the correct score: '))
```

The loop in this code determines whether `score` is less than 0 or greater than 100. If either is true, an error message is displayed and the user is prompted to enter a correct score.

In the Spotlight:

Writing an Input Validation Loop

Samantha owns an import business, and she calculates the retail prices of her products with the following formula:

$$\textit{retail price} = \textit{wholesale cost} \times 2.5$$

She currently uses the program shown in Program 4-15 to calculate retail prices.

Program 4-15 (retail_no_validation.py)

```
# This program calculates retail prices.

MARK_UP = 2.5 # The markup percentage
another = 'y' # Variable to control the loop.

# Process one or more items.
while another == 'y' or another == 'Y':
    # Get the item's wholesale cost.
    wholesale = float(input("Enter the item's " +
                            "wholesale cost: "))

    # Calculate the retail price.
    retail = wholesale * MARK_UP

    # Display the retail price.
    print('Retail price: $', format(retail, ',.2f'), sep='')


    # Do this again?
    another = input('Do you have another item? ' +
                    '(Enter y for yes): ')
```

Program Output (with input shown in bold)

```
Enter the item's wholesale cost: 10.00 Enter
Retail price: $25.00.
Do you have another item? (Enter y for yes): y Enter
Enter the item's wholesale cost: 15.00 Enter
Retail price: $37.50.
Do you have another item? (Enter y for yes): y Enter
Enter the item's wholesale cost: 12.50 Enter
Retail price: $31.25.
Do you have another item? (Enter y for yes): n Enter
```

Samantha has encountered a problem when using the program, however. Some of the items that she sells have a wholesale cost of 50 cents, which she enters into the program as 0.50. Because the 0 key is next to the key for the negative sign, she sometimes accidentally enters a negative number. She has asked you to modify the program so it will not allow a negative number to be entered for the wholesale cost.

You decide to add an input validation loop to the `show_retail` function that rejects any negative numbers that are entered into the `wholesale` variable. Program 4-16 shows the revised program, with the new input validation code shown in lines 13 through 16.

Program 4-16 (retail_with_validation.py)

```
# This program calculates retail prices.

MARK_UP = 2.5 # The markup percentage
another = 'y' # Variable to control the loop.

# Process one or more items.
while another == 'y' or another == 'Y':
    # Get the item's wholesale cost.
    wholesale = float(input("Enter the item's " +
                            "wholesale cost: "))

    # Validate the wholesale cost.
    while wholesale < 0:
        print('ERROR: the cost cannot be negative.')
        wholesale = float(input('Enter the correct' +
                                'wholesale cost: '))

    # Calculate the retail price.
    retail = wholesale * MARK_UP

    # Display the retail price.
    print('Retail price: $', format(retail, ',.2f'), sep='')


    # Do this again?
    another = input('Do you have another item? ' +
                    '(Enter y for yes): ')
```

Program Output (with input shown in bold)

```
Enter the item's wholesale cost: -.50 [Enter]
ERROR: the cost cannot be negative.
Enter the correct wholesale cost: 0.50 [Enter]
Retail price: $1.25.
Do you have another item? (Enter y for yes): n [Enter]
```

Checkpoint

4.20 What does the phrase “garbage in, garbage out” mean?

4.21 Give a general description of the input validation process.

4.22 Describe the steps that are generally taken when an input validation loop is used to validate data.

4.23 What is a priming read? What is its purpose?

4.24 If the input that is read by the priming read is valid, how many times will the input validation loop iterate?

4.7 Nested Loops

CONCEPT: A loop that is inside another loop is called a nested loop.

A nested loop is a loop that is inside another loop. A clock is a good example of something that works like a nested loop. The second hand, minute hand, and hour hand all spin around the face of the clock. The hour hand, however, only makes 1 revolution for every 12 of the minute hand's revolutions. And it takes 60 revolutions of the second hand for the minute hand to make 1 revolution. This means that for every complete revolution of the hour hand, the second hand has revolved 720 times. Here is a loop that partially simulates a digital clock. It displays the seconds from 0 to 59:

```
for seconds in range(60):
    print(seconds)
```

We can add a `minutes` variable and nest the loop above inside another loop that cycles through 60 minutes:

```
for minutes in range(60):
    for seconds in range(60):
        print(minutes, ':', seconds)
```

To make the simulated clock complete, another variable and loop can be added to count the hours:

```
for hours in range(24):
    for minutes in range(60):
        for seconds in range(60):
            print(hours, ':', minutes, ':', seconds)
```

This code's output would be:

```
0:0:0
0:0:1
0:0:2
```

(The program will count through each second of 24 hours.)

```
23:59:59
```

The innermost loop will iterate 60 times for each iteration of the middle loop. The middle loop will iterate 60 times for each iteration of the outermost loop. When the outermost loop has iterated 24 times, the middle loop will have iterated 1,440 times and the innermost loop will have iterated 86,400 times! Figure 4-8 shows a flowchart for the complete clock simulation program previously shown.

Figure 4-8 Flowchart for a clock simulator

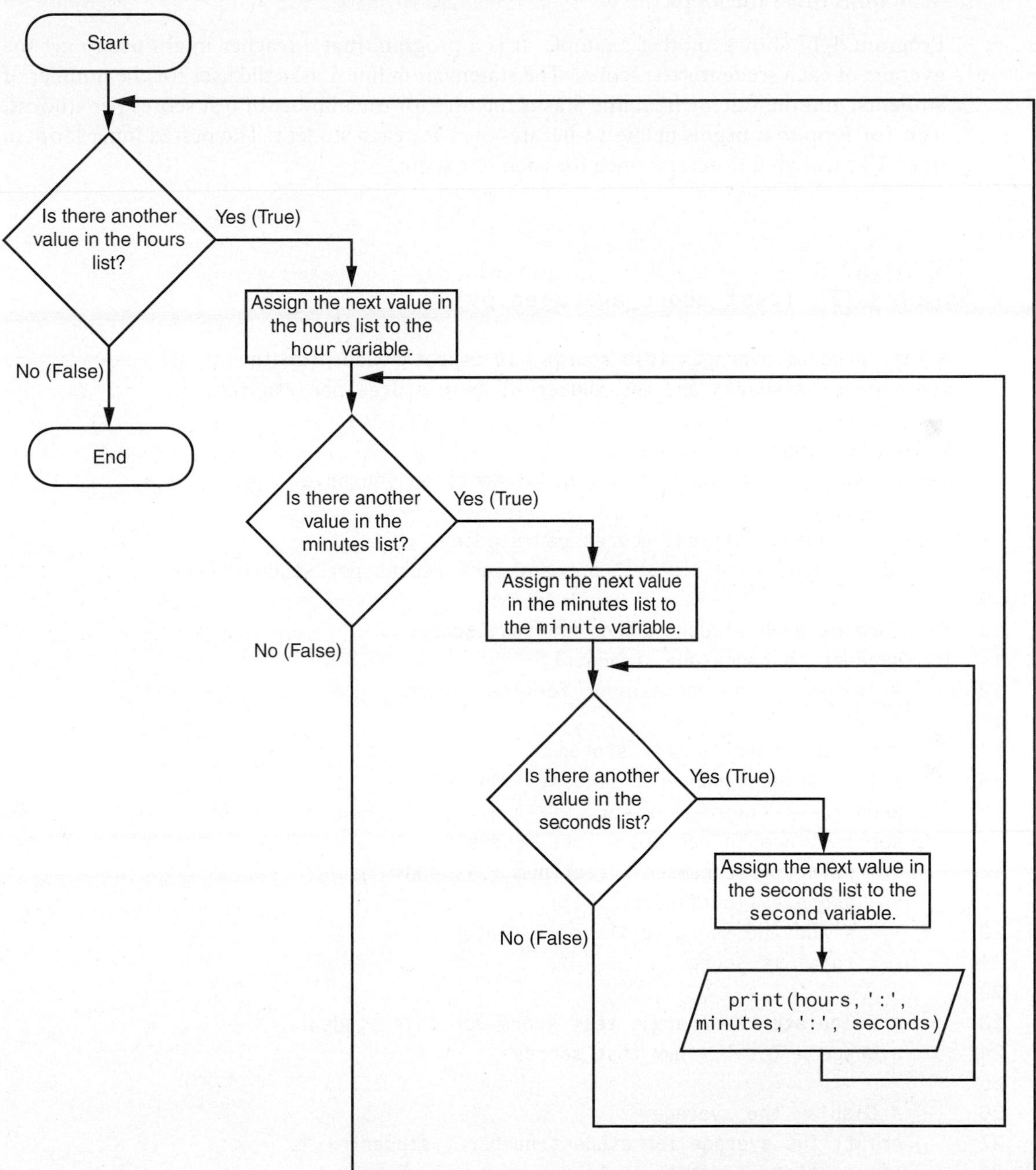

The simulated clock example brings up a few points about nested loops:

- An inner loop goes through all of its iterations for every single iteration of an outer loop.
- Inner loops complete their iterations faster than outer loops.

- To get the total number of iterations of a nested loop, multiply the number of iterations of all the loops.

Program 4-17 shows another example. It is a program that a teacher might use to get the average of each student's test scores. The statement in line 5 asks the user for the number of students, and the statement in line 8 asks the user for the number of test scores per student. The `for` loop that begins in line 11 iterates once for each student. The nested inner loop, in lines 17 through 21, iterates once for each test score.

Program 4-17 (test_score_averages.py)

```
 1  # This program averages test scores. It asks the user for the
 2  # number of students and the number of test scores per student.
 3
 4  # Get the number of students.
 5  num_students = int(input('How many students do you have? '))
 6
 7  # Get the number of test scores per student.
 8  num_test_scores = int(input('How many test scores per student? '))
 9
10  # Determine each student's average test score.
11  for student in range(num_students):
12      # Initialize an accumulator for test scores.
13      total = 0.0
14      # Get a student's test scores.
15      print('Student number', student + 1)
16      print('------------------')
17      for test_num in range(num_test_scores):
18          print('Test number', test_num + 1, end='')
19          score = float(input(': '))
20          # Add the score to the accumulator.
21          total += score
22
23      # Calculate the average test score for this student.
24      average = total / num_test_scores
25
26      # Display the average.
27      print('The average for student number', student + 1,
28            'is:', average)
29      print()
```

Program Output (with input shown in bold)

```
How many students do you have? 3 [Enter]
How many test scores per student? 3 [Enter]
```

```
Student number 1
----------------
Test number 1: 100 Enter
Test number 2: 95 Enter
Test number 3: 90 Enter
The average for student number 1 is: 95.0

Student number 2
----------------
Test number 1: 80 Enter
Test number 2: 81 Enter
Test number 3: 82 Enter
The average for student number 2 is: 81.0

Student number 3
----------------
Test number 1: 75 Enter
Test number 2: 85 Enter
Test number 3: 80 Enter
The average for student number 3 is: 80.0
```

In the Spotlight:

Using Nested Loops to Print Patterns

One interesting way to learn about nested loops is to use them to display patterns on the screen. Let's look at a simple example. Suppose we want to print asterisks on the screen in the following rectangular pattern:

```
******
******
******
******
******
******
******
******
```

If you think of this pattern as having rows and columns, you can see that it has eight rows, and each row has six columns. The following code can be used to display one row of asterisks:

```
for col in range(6):
    print('*', end='')
```

If we run this code in a program or in interactive mode, it produces the following output:

```
******
```

To complete the entire pattern, we need to execute this loop eight times. We can place the loop inside another loop that iterates eight times, as shown here:

```
1  for row in range(8):
2      for col in range(6):
3          print('*', end='')
4      print()
```

The outer loop iterates eight times. Each time it iterates, the inner loop iterates 6 times. (Notice in line 4, after each row has been printed, we call the `print()` function. We have to do that to advance the screen cursor to the next line at the end of each row. Without that statement, all the asterisks will be printed in one long row on the screen.)

We could easily write a program that prompts the user for the number of rows and columns, as shown in Program 4-18.

Program 4-18 (rectangluar_pattern.py)

```
# This program displays a rectangular pattern
# of asterisks.
rows = int(input('How many rows? '))
cols = int(input('How many columns? '))

for r in range(rows):
    for c in range(cols):
        print('*', end='')
    print()
```

Program Output (with input shown in bold)

```
How many rows? 5 [Enter]
How many columns? 10 [Enter]
**********
**********
**********
**********
**********
```

Let's look at another example. Suppose you want to print asterisks in a pattern that looks like the following triangle:

```
*
**
***
****
*****
******
*******
********
```

Once again, think of the pattern as being arranged in rows and columns. The pattern has a total of eight rows. In the first row, there is one column. In the second row, there are two columns. In the third row, there are three columns. This continues to the eighth row, which has eight columns. Program 4-19 shows the code that produces this pattern.

Program 4-19 (triangle_pattern.py)

```
1  # This program displays a triangle pattern.
2  BASE_SIZE = 8
3
4  for r in range(BASE_SIZE):
5      for c in range(r + 1):
6          print('*', end='')
7      print()
```

Program Output

```
*
**
***
****
*****
******
*******
********
```

First, let's look at the outer loop. In line 4, the expression `range(BASE_SIZE)` produces an iterable containing the following sequence of integers:

```
0, 1, 2, 3, 4, 5, 6, 7
```

As a result, the variable `r` is assigned the values 0 through 7 as the outer loop iterates. The inner loop's `range` expression, in line 5, is `range(r + 1)`. The inner loop executes as follows:

- During the outer loop's first iteration, the variable `r` is assigned 0. The expression `range(r + 1)` causes the inner loop to iterate one time, printing one asterisk.
- During the outer loop's second iteration, the variable `r` is assigned 1. The expression `range(r + 1)` causes the inner loop to iterate two times, printing two asterisks.
- During the outer loop's third iteration, the variable `r` is assigned 2. The expression `range(r + 1)` causes the inner loop to iterate three times, printing three asterisks, and so forth.

Let's look at another example. Suppose you want to display the following stair-step pattern:

```
#
 #
  #
   #
    #
     #
```

The pattern has six rows. In general, we can describe each row as having some number of spaces followed by a # character. Here's a row-by-row description:

First row:	0 spaces followed by a # character.
Second row:	1 space followed by a # character.
Third row:	2 spaces followed by a # character.
Fourth row:	3 spaces followed by a # character.
Fifth row:	4 spaces followed by a # character.
Sixth row:	5 spaces followed by a # character.

To display this pattern, we can write code containing a pair of nested loops that work in the following manner:

- The outer loop will iterate six times. Each iteration will perform the following:
  - The inner loop will display the correct number of spaces, side by side.
  - Then, a # character will be displayed.

Program 4-20 shows the Python code.

Program 4-20 (stair_step_pattern.py)

```
1  # This program displays a stair-step pattern.
2  NUM_STEPS = 6
3
4  for r in range(NUM_STEPS):
5      for c in range(r):
6          print(' ', end='')
7      print('#')
```

Program Output

```
#
 #
  #
   #
    #
     #
```

In line 1, the expression range(NUM_STEPS) produces an iterable containing the following sequence of integers:

```
0, 1, 2, 3, 4, 5
```

As a result, the outer loop iterates 6 times. As the outer loop iterates, variable r is assigned the values 0 through 5. The inner loop executes as follows:

- During the outer loop's first iteration, the variable r is assigned 0. A loop that is written as for c in range(0): iterates zero times, so the inner loop does not execute at this time.
- During the outer loop's second iteration, the variable r is assigned 1. A loop that is written as for c in range(1): iterates one time, so the inner loop iterates once, printing one space.
- During the outer loop's third iteration, the variable r is assigned 2. A loop that is written as for c in range(2): will iterate two times, so the inner loop iterates twice, printing two spaces, and so forth.

4.8 Turtle Graphics: Using Loops to Draw Designs

CONCEPT: You can use loops to draw graphics that range in complexity from simple shapes to elaborate designs.

You can use loops with the turtle to draw both simple shapes and elaborate designs. For example, the following `for` loop iterates four times to draw a square that is 100 pixels wide:

```
for x in range(4):
    turtle.forward(100)
    turtle.right(90)
```

The following code shows another example. This `for` loop iterates eight times to draw the octagon shown in Figure 4-9:

```
for x in range(8):
    turtle.forward(100)
    turtle.right(45)
```

Figure 4-9 Octagon

Program 4-21 shows an example of using a loop to draw concentric circles. The program's output is shown in Figure 4-10.

Program 4-21 (concentric_circles.py)

```
# Concentric circles
import turtle

# Named constants
NUM_CIRCLES = 20
STARTING_RADIUS = 20
```

(program continues)

Program 4-21 *(continued)*

```
OFFSET = 10
ANIMATION_SPEED = 0

# Setup the turtle.
turtle.speed(ANIMATION_SPEED)
turtle.hideturtle()

# Set the radius of the first circle
radius = STARTING_RADIUS

# Draw the circles.
for count in range(NUM_CIRCLES):
    # Draw the circle.
    turtle.circle(radius)

    # Get the coordinates for the next circle.
    x = turtle.xcor()
    y = turtle.ycor() - OFFSET

    # Calculate the radius for the next circle.
    radius = radius + OFFSET

    # Position the turtle for the next circle.
    turtle.penup()
    turtle.goto(x, y)
    turtle.pendown()
```

Figure 4-10 Concentric circles

You can create a lot of interesting designs with the turtle by repeatedly drawing a simple shape, with the turtle tilted at a slightly different angle each time it draws the shape. For example, the design shown in Figure 4-11 was created by drawing 36 circles with a loop. After each circle was drawn, the turtle was tilted left by 10 degrees. Program 4-22 shows the code that created the design.

Figure 4-11 A design created with circles

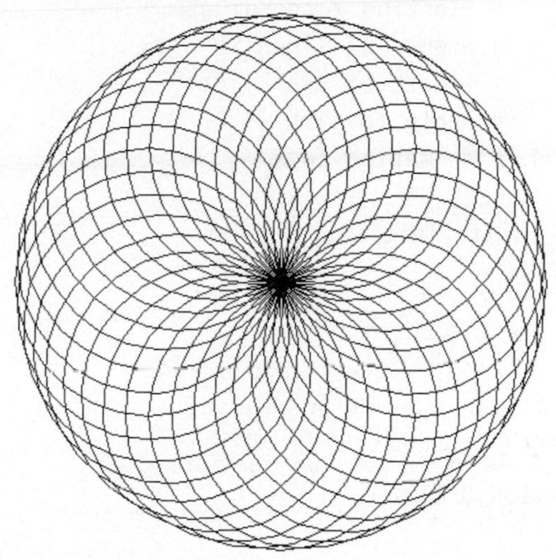

Program 4-22 (spiral_circles.py)

```
# This program draws a design using repeated circles.
import turtle

# Named constants
NUM_CIRCLES = 36     # Number of circles to draw
RADIUS = 100         # Radius of each circle
ANGLE = 10           # Angle to turn
ANIMATION_SPEED = 0 # Animation speed

# Set the animation speed.
turtle.speed(ANIMATION_SPEED)

# Draw 36 circles, with the turtle tilted
# by 10 degrees after each circle is drawn.
for x in range(NUM_CIRCLES):
    turtle.circle(RADIUS)
    turtle.left(ANGLE)
```

Program 4-23 shows another example. It draws a sequence of 36 straight lines to make the design shown in Figure 4-12.

Program 4-23 (spiral_lines.py)

```
# This program draws a design using repeated lines.
import turtle

# Named constants
START_X = -200          # Starting X coordinate
START_Y = 0             # Starting Y coordinate
NUM_LINES = 36          # Number of lines to draw
LINE_LENGTH = 400       # Length of each line
ANGLE = 170             # Angle to turn
ANIMATION_SPEED = 0 # Animation speed

# Move the turtle to its initial position.
turtle.hideturtle()
turtle.penup()
turtle.goto(START_X, START_Y)
turtle.pendown()

# Set the animation speed.
turtle.speed(ANIMATION_SPEED)

# Draw 36 lines, with the turtle tilted
# by 170 degrees after each line is drawn.
for x in range(NUM_LINES):
    turtle.forward(LINE_LENGTH)
    turtle.left(ANGLE)
```

Figure 4-12 Design created by Program 4-23

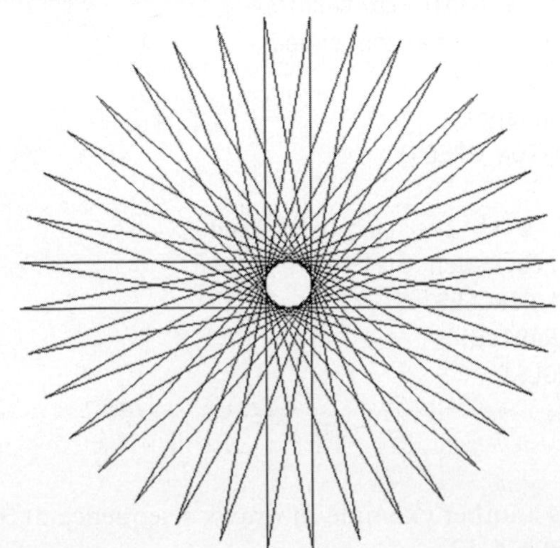

Review Questions

Multiple Choice

1. A __________ -controlled loop uses a true/false condition to control the number of times that it repeats.
   a. Boolean
   b. condition
   c. decision
   d. count
2. A __________ -controlled loop repeats a specific number of times.
   a. Boolean
   b. condition
   c. decision
   d. count
3. Each repetition of a loop is known as a(n) __________.
   a. cycle
   b. revolution
   c. orbit
   d. iteration
4. The `while` loop is a __________ type of loop.
   a. pretest
   b. no-test
   c. prequalified
   d. post-iterative
5. A(n) __________ loop has no way of ending and repeats until the program is interrupted.
   a. indeterminate
   b. interminable
   c. infinite
   d. timeless
6. The -= operator is an example of a(n) __________ operator.
   a. relational
   b. augmented assignment
   c. complex assignment
   d. reverse assignment
7. A(n) __________ variable keeps a running total.
   a. sentinel
   b. sum
   c. total
   d. accumulator
8. A(n) __________ is a special value that signals when there are no more items from a list of items to be processed. This value cannot be mistaken as an item from the list.
   a. sentinel
   b. flag
   c. signal
   d. accumulator

9. GIGO stands for ______________.
   a. great input, great output
   b. garbage in, garbage out
   c. GIGahertz Output
   d. GIGabyte Operation
10. The integrity of a program's output is only as good as the integrity of the program's ______________.
    a. compiler
    b. programming language
    c. input
    d. debugger
11. The input operation that appears just before a validation loop is known as the ______________.
    a. prevalidation read
    b. primordial read
    c. initialization read
    d. priming read
12. Validation loops are also known as ______________.
    a. error traps
    b. doomsday loops
    c. error avoidance loops
    d. defensive loops

True or False

1. A condition-controlled loop always repeats a specific number of times.
2. The `while` loop is a pretest loop.
3. The following statement subtracts 1 from `x`: `x = x - 1`
4. It is not necessary to initialize accumulator variables.
5. In a nested loop, the inner loop goes through all of its iterations for every single iteration of the outer loop.
6. To calculate the total number of iterations of a nested loop, add the number of iterations of all the loops.
7. The process of input validation works as follows: when the user of a program enters invalid data, the program should ask the user "Are you sure you meant to enter that?" If the user answers "yes," the program should accept the data.

Short Answer

1. What is a condition-controlled loop?
2. What is a count-controlled loop?
3. What is an infinite loop? Write the code for an infinite loop.
4. Why is it critical that accumulator variables are properly initialized?
5. What is the advantage of using a sentinel?
6. Why must the value chosen for use as a sentinel be carefully selected?
7. What does the phrase "garbage in, garbage out" mean?
8. Give a general description of the input validation process.

Algorithm Workbench

1. Write a `while` loop that lets the user enter a number. The number should be multiplied by 10, and the result assigned to a variable named `product`. The loop should iterate as long as `product` is less than 100.
2. Write a `while` loop that asks the user to enter two numbers. The numbers should be added and the sum displayed. The loop should ask the user if he or she wishes to perform the operation again. If so, the loop should repeat, otherwise it should terminate.
3. Write a `for` loop that displays the following set of numbers:

   `0, 10, 20, 30, 40, 50 . . . 1000`
4. Write a loop that asks the user to enter a number. The loop should iterate 10 times and keep a running total of the numbers entered.
5. Write a loop that calculates the total of the following series of numbers:

   $$\frac{1}{30} + \frac{2}{29} + \frac{3}{28} + \ldots \frac{30}{1}$$
6. Rewrite the following statements using augmented assignment operators.

   a. `x = x + 1`

   b. `x = x * 2`

   c. `x = x / 10`

   d. `x = x - 100`
7. Write a set of nested loops that display 10 rows of # characters. There should be 15 # characters in each row.
8. Write code that prompts the user to enter a positive nonzero number and validates the input.
9. Write code that prompts the user to enter a number in the range of 1 through 100 and validates the input.

Programming Exercises

1. Bug Collector

VideoNote
The Bug Collector Problem

A bug collector collects bugs every day for five days. Write a program that keeps a running total of the number of bugs collected during the five days. The loop should ask for the number of bugs collected for each day, and when the loop is finished, the program should display the total number of bugs collected.

2. Calories Burned

Running on a particular treadmill you burn 4.2 calories per minute. Write a program that uses a loop to display the number of calories burned after 10, 15, 20, 25, and 30 minutes.

3. Budget Analysis

Write a program that asks the user to enter the amount that he or she has budgeted for a month. A loop should then prompt the user to enter each of his or her expenses for the month and keep a running total. When the loop finishes, the program should display the amount that the user is over or under budget.

4. Distance Traveled

The distance a vehicle travels can be calculated as follows:

$$distance = speed \times time$$

For example, if a train travels 40 miles per hour for three hours, the distance traveled is 120 miles. Write a program that asks the user for the speed of a vehicle (in miles per hour) and the number of hours it has traveled. It should then use a loop to display the distance the vehicle has traveled for each hour of that time period. Here is an example of the desired output:

```
What is the speed of the vehicle in mph? 40 [Enter]
How many hours has it traveled? 3 [Enter]
Hour          Distance Traveled
--------------------------------
1                   40
2                   80
3                  120
```

5. Average Rainfall

Write a program that uses nested loops to collect data and calculate the average rainfall over a period of years. The program should first ask for the number of years. The outer loop will iterate once for each year. The inner loop will iterate twelve times, once for each month. Each iteration of the inner loop will ask the user for the inches of rainfall for that month. After all iterations, the program should display the number of months, the total inches of rainfall, and the average rainfall per month for the entire period.

6. Celsius to Fahrenheit Table

Write a program that displays a table of the Celsius temperatures 0 through 20 and their Fahrenheit equivalents. The formula for converting a temperature from Celsius to Fahrenheit is

$$F = \frac{9}{5}C + 32$$

where F is the Fahrenheit temperature, and C is the Celsius temperature. Your program must use a loop to display the table.

7. Pennies for Pay

Write a program that calculates the amount of money a person would earn over a period of time if his or her salary is one penny the first day, two pennies the second day, and continues to double each day. The program should ask the user for the number of days. Display a table showing what the salary was for each day, then show the total pay at the end of the period. The output should be displayed in a dollar amount, not the number of pennies.

8. Sum of Numbers

Write a program with a loop that asks the user to enter a series of positive numbers. The user should enter a negative number to signal the end of the series. After all the positive numbers have been entered, the program should display their sum.

9. Ocean Levels

Assuming the ocean's level is currently rising at about 1.6 millimeters per year, create an application that displays the number of millimeters that the ocean will have risen each year for the next 25 years.

10. Tuition Increase

At one college, the tuition for a full-time student is $8,000 per semester. It has been announced that the tuition will increase by 3 percent each year for the next 5 years. Write a program with a loop that displays the projected semester tuition amount for the next 5 years.

11. Weight Loss

If a moderately active person cuts their calorie intake by 500 calories a day, they can typically lose about 4 pounds a month. Write a program that lets the user enter their starting weight, then creates and displays a table showing what their expected weight will be at the end of each month for the next 6 months if they stay on this diet.

12. Calculating the Factorial of a Number

In mathematics, the notation $n!$ represents the factorial of the nonnegative integer n. The factorial of n is the product of all the nonnegative integers from 1 to n. For example,

$$7! = 1 \times 2 \times 3 \times 4 \times 5 \times 6 \times 7 = 5{,}040$$

and

$$4! = 1 \times 2 \times 3 \times 4 = 24$$

Write a program that lets the user enter a nonnegative integer then uses a loop to calculate the factorial of that number. Display the factorial.

13. Population

Write a program that predicts the approximate size of a population of organisms. The application should use text boxes to allow the user to enter the starting number of organisms, the average daily population increase (as a percentage), and the number of days the organisms will be left to multiply. For example, assume the user enters the following values:

Starting number of organisms: 2
Average daily increase: 30%
Number of days to multiply: 10

The program should display the following table of data:

Day Approximate	Population
1	2
2	2.6
3	3.38
4	4.394
5	5.7122
6	7.42586
7	9.653619
8	12.5497
9	16.31462
10	21.209

14. Write a program that uses nested loops to draw this pattern:

```
*******
******
*****
****
***
**
*
```

15. Write a program that uses nested loops to draw this pattern:

```
##
# #
#  #
#   #
#    #
#     #
```

16. Turtle Graphics: Repeating Squares

In this chapter, you saw an example of a loop that draws a square. Write a turtle graphics program that uses nested loops to draw 100 squares, to create the design shown in Figure 4-13.

Figure 4-13 Repeating squares

17. Turtle Graphics: Star Pattern

Use a loop with the turtle graphics library to draw the design shown in Figure 4-14.

Figure 4-14 Star pattern

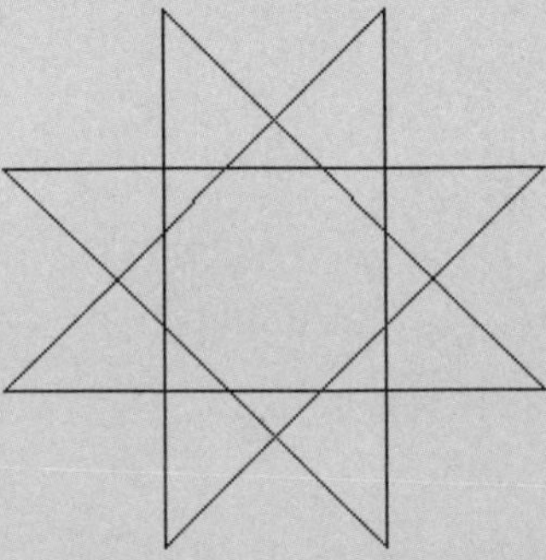

18. Turtle Graphics: Hypnotic Pattern

Use a loop with the turtle graphics library to draw the design shown in Figure 4-15.

Figure 4-15 Hypnotic pattern

19. Turtle Graphics: STOP Sign

In this chapter, you saw an example of a loop that draws an octagon. Write a program that uses the loop to draw an octagon with the word "STOP" displayed in its center. The STOP sign should be centered in the graphics window.

CHAPTER

5 Functions

TOPICS

5.1 Introduction to Functions

CONCEPT: A function is a group of statements that exist within a program for the purpose of performing a specific task.

In Chapter 2, we described a simple algorithm for calculating an employee's pay. In the algorithm, the number of hours worked is multiplied by an hourly pay rate. A more realistic payroll algorithm, however, would do much more than this. In a real-world application, the overall task of calculating an employee's pay would consist of several subtasks, such as the following:

- Getting the employee's hourly pay rate
- Getting the number of hours worked
- Calculating the employee's gross pay
- Calculating overtime pay
- Calculating withholdings for taxes and benefits
- Calculating the net pay
- Printing the paycheck

Most programs perform tasks that are large enough to be broken down into several subtasks. For this reason, programmers usually break down their programs into small manageable pieces known as functions. A *function* is a group of statements that exist within a program for the purpose of performing a specific task. Instead of writing a large program as one long sequence of statements, it can be written as several small functions, each one performing a specific part of the task. These small functions can then be executed in the desired order to perform the overall task.

This approach is sometimes called *divide and conquer* because a large task is divided into several smaller tasks that are easily performed. Figure 5-1 illustrates this idea by comparing two programs: one that uses a long complex sequence of statements to perform a task, and another that divides a task into smaller tasks, each of which is performed by a separate function.

When using functions in a program, you generally isolate each task within the program in its own function. For example, a realistic pay calculating program might have the following functions:

- A function that gets the employee's hourly pay rate
- A function that gets the number of hours worked
- A function that calculates the employee's gross pay
- A function that calculates the overtime pay
- A function that calculates the withholdings for taxes and benefits
- A function that calculates the net pay
- A function that prints the paycheck

A program that has been written with each task in its own function is called a *modularized program.*

Figure 5-1 Using functions to divide and conquer a large task

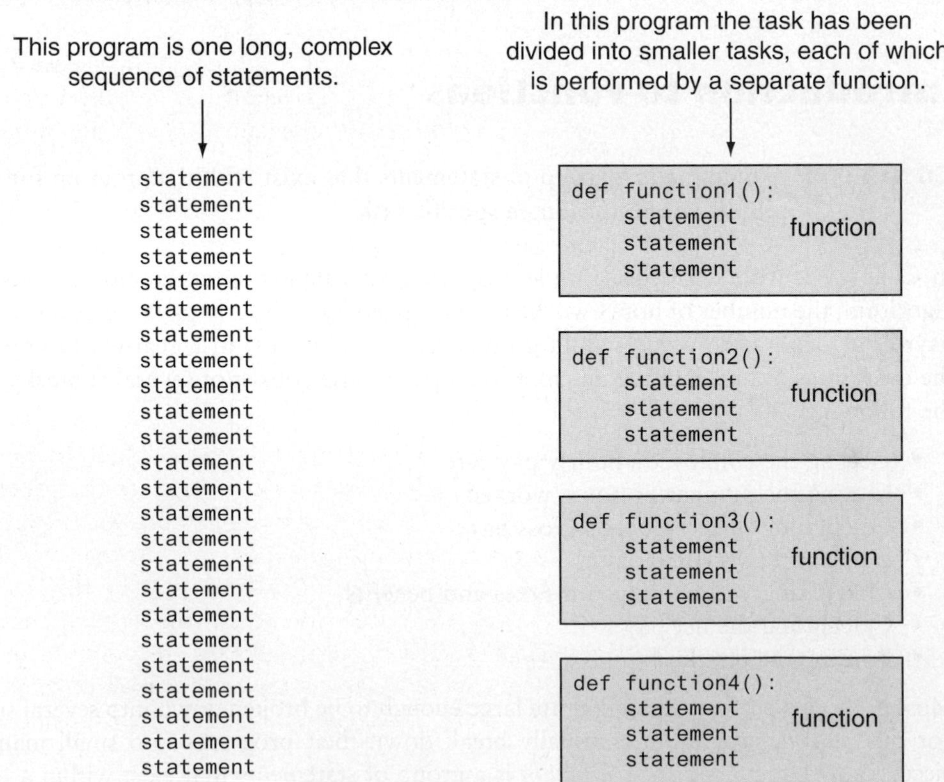

Benefits of Modularizing a Program with Functions

A program benefits in the following ways when it is broken down into functions:

Simpler Code

A program's code tends to be simpler and easier to understand when it is broken down into functions. Several small functions are much easier to read than one long sequence of statements.

Code Reuse

Functions also reduce the duplication of code within a program. If a specific operation is performed in several places in a program, a function can be written once to perform that operation, then be executed any time it is needed. This benefit of using functions is known as *code reuse* because you are writing the code to perform a task once, then reusing it each time you need to perform the task.

Better Testing

When each task within a program is contained in its own function, testing and debugging becomes simpler. Programmers can test each function in a program individually, to determine whether it correctly performs its operation. This makes it easier to isolate and fix errors.

Faster Development

Suppose a programmer or a team of programmers is developing multiple programs. They discover that each of the programs perform several common tasks, such as asking for a username and a password, displaying the current time, and so on. It doesn't make sense to write the code for these tasks multiple times. Instead, functions can be written for the commonly needed tasks, and those functions can be incorporated into each program that needs them.

Easier Facilitation of Teamwork

Functions also make it easier for programmers to work in teams. When a program is developed as a set of functions that each performs an individual task, then different programmers can be assigned the job of writing different functions.

Void Functions and Value-Returning Functions

In this chapter, you will learn to write two types of functions: void functions and value-returning functions. When you call a *void function*, it simply executes the statements it contains and then terminates. When you call a *value-returning function*, it executes the statements that it contains, then returns a value back to the statement that called it. The `input` function is an example of a value-returning function. When you call the `input` function, it gets the data that the user types on the keyboard and returns that data as a string. The `int` and `float` functions are also examples of value-returning functions. You pass an argument to the `int` function, and it returns that argument's value converted to an integer. Likewise, you pass an argument to the `float` function, and it returns that argument's value converted to a floating-point number.

The first type of function that you will learn to write is the void function.

Checkpoint

5.1 What is a function?

5.2 What is meant by the phrase "divide and conquer"?

5.3 How do functions help you reuse code in a program?

5.4 How can functions make the development of multiple programs faster?

5.5 How can functions make it easier for programs to be developed by teams of programmers?

5.2 Defining and Calling a Void Function

CONCEPT: The code for a function is known as a function definition. To execute the function, you write a statement that calls it.

Function Names

Before we discuss the process of creating and using functions, we should mention a few things about function names. Just as you name the variables that you use in a program, you also name the functions. A function's name should be descriptive enough so anyone reading your code can reasonably guess what the function does.

Python requires that you follow the same rules that you follow when naming variables, which we recap here:

- You cannot use one of Python's key words as a function name. (See Table 1-2 for a list of the key words.)
- A function name cannot contain spaces.
- The first character must be one of the letters a through z, A through Z, or an underscore character (_).
- After the first character you may use the letters a through z or A through Z, the digits 0 through 9, or underscores.
- Uppercase and lowercase characters are distinct.

Because functions perform actions, most programmers prefer to use verbs in function names. For example, a function that calculates gross pay might be named `calculate_gross_pay`. This name would make it evident to anyone reading the code that the function calculates something. What does it calculate? The gross pay, of course. Other examples of good function names would be `get_hours`, `get_pay_rate`, `calculate_overtime`, `print_check`, and so on. Each function name describes what the function does.

Defining and Calling a Function

VideoNote Defining and Calling a Function

To create a function, you write its *definition*. Here is the general format of a function definition in Python:

```
def function_name():
    statement
    statement
    etc.
```

The first line is known as the *function header*. It marks the beginning of the function definition. The function header begins with the key word def, followed by the name of the function, followed by a set of parentheses, followed by a colon.

Beginning at the next line is a set of statements known as a block. A *block* is simply a set of statements that belong together as a group. These statements are performed any time the function is executed. Notice in the general format that all of the statements in the block are indented. This indentation is required, because the Python interpreter uses it to tell where the block begins and ends.

Let's look at an example of a function. Keep in mind that this is not a complete program. We will show the entire program in a moment.

```
def message():
    print('I am Arthur,')
    print('King of the Britons.')
```

This code defines a function named message. The message function contains a block with two statements. Executing the function will cause these statements to execute.

Calling a Function

A function definition specifies what a function does, but it does not cause the function to execute. To execute a function, you must *call* it. This is how we would call the message function:

```
message()
```

When a function is called, the interpreter jumps to that function and executes the statements in its block. Then, when the end of the block is reached, the interpreter jumps back to the part of the program that called the function, and the program resumes execution at that point. When this happens, we say that the function *returns*. To fully demonstrate how function calling works, we will look at Program 5-1.

Program 5-1 (function_demo.py)

```
1 # This program demonstrates a function.
2 # First, we define a function named message.
3 def message():
4     print('I am Arthur,')
5     print('King of the Britons.')
6
7 # Call the message function.
8 message()
```

Program Output

```
I am Arthur,
King of the Britons.
```

Let's step through this program and examine what happens when it runs. First, the interpreter ignores the comments that appear in lines 1 and 2. Then, it reads the def statement in line 3. This causes a function named `message` to be created in memory, containing the block of statements in lines 4 and 5. (Remember, a function definition creates a function, but it does not cause the function to execute.) Next, the interpreter encounters the comment in line 7, which is ignored. Then it executes the statement in line 8, which is a function call. This causes the `message` function to execute, which prints the two lines of output. Figure 5-2 illustrates the parts of this program.

Figure 5-2 The function definition and the function call

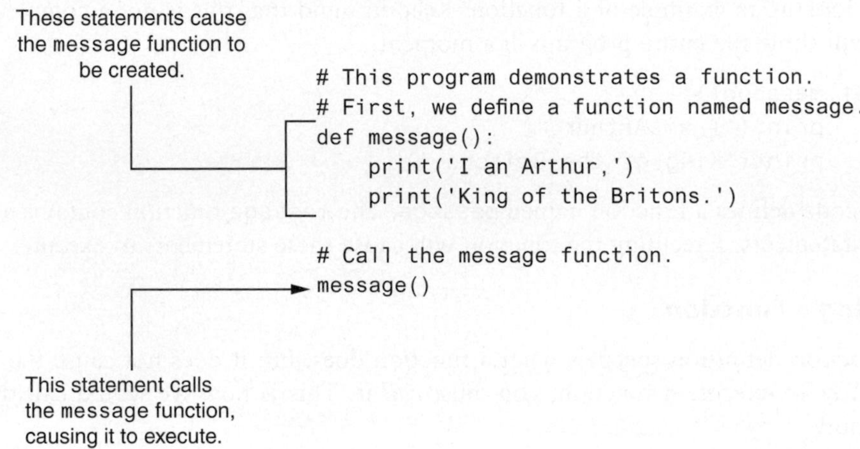

Program 5-1 has only one function, but it is possible to define many functions in a program. In fact, it is common for a program to have a `main` function that is called when the program starts. The `main` function then calls other functions in the program as they are needed. It is often said that the `main` function contains a program's *mainline logic,* which is the overall logic of the program. Program 5-2 shows an example of a program with two functions: `main` and `message`.

Program 5-2 (two_functions.py)

```
# This program has two functions. First we
# define the main function.
def main():
    print('I have a message for you.')
    message()
    print('Goodbye!')

# Next we define the message function.
def message():
    print('I am Arthur,')
    print('King of the Britons.')

# Call the main function.
main()
```

Program Output

```
I have a message for you.
I am Arthur,
King of the Britons.
Goodbye!
```

The definition of the `main` function appears in lines 3 through 6, and the definition of the `message` function appears in lines 9 through 11. The statement in line 14 calls the `main` function, as shown in Figure 5-3.

Figure 5-3 Calling the `main` function

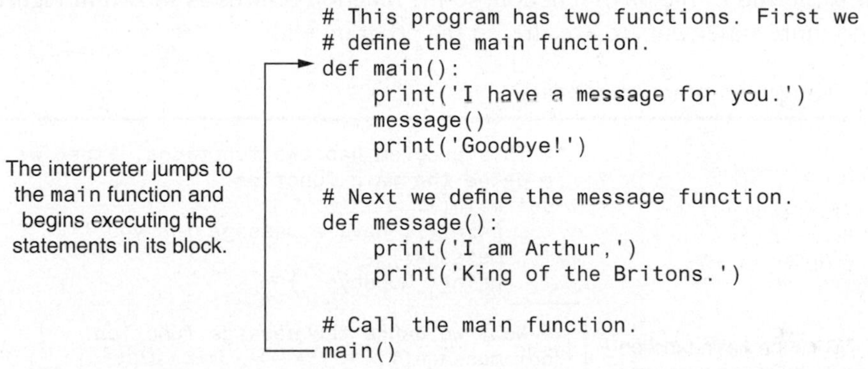

```
# This program has two functions. First we
# define the main function.
def main():
    print('I have a message for you.')
    message()
    print('Goodbye!')

# Next we define the message function.
def message():
    print('I am Arthur,')
    print('King of the Britons.')

# Call the main function.
main()
```

The interpreter jumps to the `main` function and begins executing the statements in its block.

The first statement in the `main` function calls the `print` function in line 4. It displays the string `'I have a message for you'`. Then, the statement in line 5 calls the `message` function. This causes the interpreter to jump to the `message` function, as shown in Figure 5-4. After the statements in the `message` function have executed, the interpreter returns to the `main` function and resumes with the statement that immediately follows the function call. As shown in Figure 5-5, this is the statement that displays the string `'Goodbye!'`.

Figure 5-4 Calling the `message` function

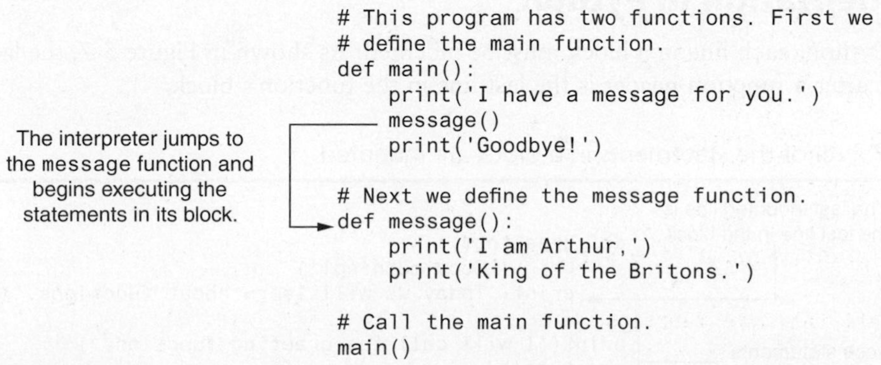

```
# This program has two functions. First we
# define the main function.
def main():
    print('I have a message for you.')
    message()
    print('Goodbye!')

# Next we define the message function.
def message():
    print('I am Arthur,')
    print('King of the Britons.')

# Call the main function.
main()
```

The interpreter jumps to the message function and begins executing the statements in its block.

Figure 5-5 The message function returns


```
# This program has two functions. First we
# define the main function.
def main():
    print('I have a message for you.')
    message()
    print('Goodbye!')

# Next we define the message function.
def message():
    print('I am Arthur,')
    print('King of the Britons.')

# Call the main function.
main()
```

That is the end of the `main` function, so the function returns as shown in Figure 5-6. There are no more statements to execute, so the program ends.

Figure 5-6 The `main` function returns


```
# This program has two functions. First we
# define the main function.
def main():
    print('I have a message for you.')
    message()
    print('Goodbye!')

# Next we define the message function.
def message():
    print('I am Arthur,')
    print('King of the Britons.')

# Call the main function.
main()
```

NOTE: When a program calls a function, programmers commonly say that the *control* of the program transfers to that function. This simply means that the function takes control of the program's execution.

Indentation in Python

In Python, each line in a block must be indented. As shown in Figure 5-7, the last indented line after a function header is the last line in the function's block.

Figure 5-7 All of the statements in a block are indented


```
def greeting():
    print('Good morning!')
    print('Today we will learn about functions.')

print('I will call the greeting function.')
greeting()
```

When you indent the lines in a block, make sure each line begins with the same number of spaces. Otherwise, an error will occur. For example, the following function definition will cause an error because the lines are all indented with different numbers of spaces:

```
def my_function():
   print('And now for')
print('something completely')
     print('different.')
```

In an editor, there are two ways to indent a line: (1) by pressing the Tab key at the beginning of the line, or (2) by using the spacebar to insert spaces at the beginning of the line. You can use either tabs or spaces when indenting the lines in a block, but don't use both. Doing so may confuse the Python interpreter and cause an error.

IDLE, as well as most other Python editors, automatically indents the lines in a block. When you type the colon at the end of a function header, all of the lines typed afterward will automatically be indented. After you have typed the last line of the block, you press the Backspace key to get out of the automatic indentation.

TIP: Python programmers customarily use four spaces to indent the lines in a block. You can use any number of spaces you wish, as long as all the lines in the block are indented by the same amount.

NOTE: Blank lines that appear in a block are ignored.

Checkpoint

5.6 A function definition has what two parts?

5.7 What does the phrase "calling a function" mean?

5.8 When a function is executing, what happens when the end of the function's block is reached?

5.9 Why must you indent the statements in a block?

5.3 Designing a Program to Use Functions

CONCEPT: Programmers commonly use a technique known as top-down design to break down an algorithm into functions.

Flowcharting a Program with Functions

In Chapter 2, we introduced flowcharts as a tool for designing programs. In a flowchart, a function call is shown with a rectangle that has vertical bars at each side, as shown in Figure 5-8. The name of the function that is being called is written on the symbol. The example shown in Figure 5-8 shows how we would represent a call to the `message` function.

Figure 5-8 Function call symbol

Programmers typically draw a separate flowchart for each function in a program. For example, Figure 5-9 shows how the `main` function and the `message` function in Program 5-2 would be flowcharted. When drawing a flowchart for a function, the starting terminal symbol usually shows the name of the function and the ending terminal symbol usually reads `Return`.

Figure 5-9 Flowchart for Program 5-2

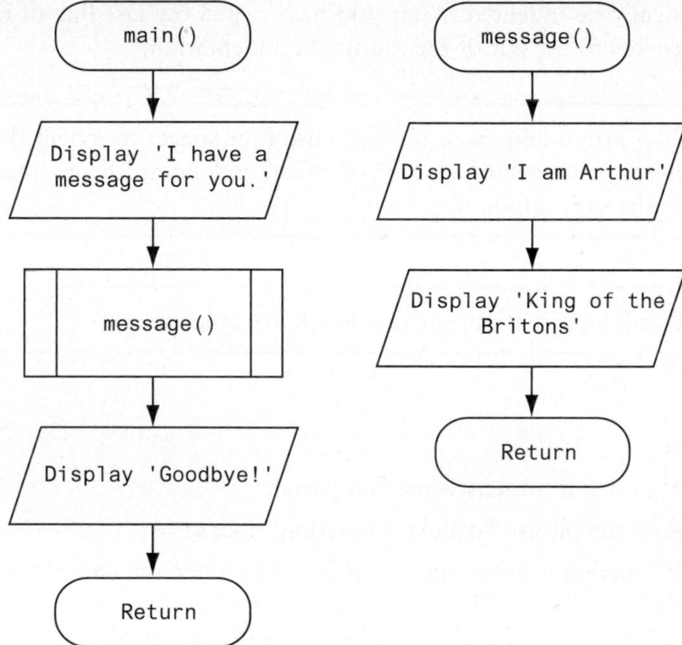

Top-Down Design

In this section, we have discussed and demonstrated how functions work. You've seen how control of a program is transferred to a function when it is called, then returns to the part of the program that called the function when the function ends. It is important that you understand these mechanical aspects of functions.

Just as important as understanding how functions work is understanding how to design a program that uses functions. Programmers commonly use a technique known as *top-down design* to break down an algorithm into functions. The process of top-down design is performed in the following manner:

- The overall task that the program is to perform is broken down into a series of subtasks.

- Each of the subtasks is examined to determine whether it can be further broken down into more subtasks. This step is repeated until no more subtasks can be identified.
- Once all of the subtasks have been identified, they are written in code.

This process is called top-down design because the programmer begins by looking at the topmost level of tasks that must be performed and then breaks down those tasks into lower levels of subtasks.

Hierarchy Charts

Flowcharts are good tools for graphically depicting the flow of logic inside a function, but they do not give a visual representation of the relationships between functions. Programmers commonly use *hierarchy charts* for this purpose. A hierarchy chart, which is also known as a *structure chart,* shows boxes that represent each function in a program. The boxes are connected in a way that illustrates the functions called by each function. Figure 5-10 shows an example of a hierarchy chart for a hypothetical pay calculating program.

Figure 5-10 A hierarchy chart

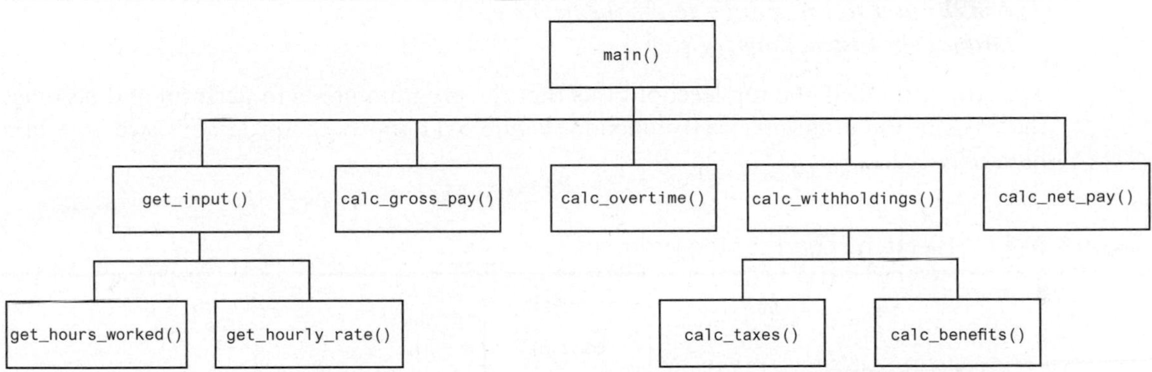

The chart shown in Figure 5-10 shows the `main` function as the topmost function in the hierarchy. The `main` function calls five other functions: `get_input`, `calc_gross_pay`, `calc_overtime`, `calc_withholdings`, and `calc_net_pay`. The `get_input` function calls two additional functions: `get_hours_worked` and `get_hourly_rate`. The `calc_withholdings` function also calls two functions: `calc_taxes` and `calc_benefits`.

Notice the hierarchy chart does not show the steps that are taken inside a function. Because they do not reveal any details about how functions work, they do not replace flowcharts or pseudocode.

In the Spotlight:

Defining and Calling Functions

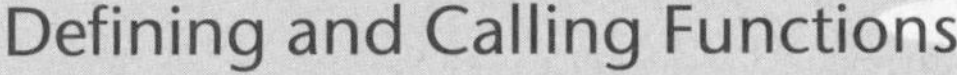

Professional Appliance Service, Inc. offers maintenance and repair services for household appliances. The owner wants to give each of the company's service technicians a small handheld computer that displays step-by-step instructions for many of the repairs that they perform. To see how this might work, the owner has asked you to develop a program that displays the following instructions for disassembling an Acme laundry dryer:

Step 1: Unplug the dryer and move it away from the wall.
Step 2: Remove the six screws from the back of the dryer.
Step 3: Remove the dryer's back panel.
Step 4: Pull the top of the dryer straight up.

During your interview with the owner, you determine that the program should display the steps one at a time. You decide that after each step is displayed, the user will be asked to press the Enter key to see the next step. Here is the algorithm in pseudocode:

Display a starting message, explaining what the program does.
Ask the user to press Enter to see step 1.
Display the instructions for step 1.
Ask the user to press Enter to see the next step.
Display the instructions for step 2.
Ask the user to press Enter to see the next step.
Display the instructions for step 3.
Ask the user to press Enter to see the next step.
Display the instructions for step 4.

This algorithm lists the top level of tasks that the program needs to perform and becomes the basis of the program's `main` function. Figure 5-11 shows the program's structure in a hierarchy chart.

Figure 5-11 Hierarchy chart for the program

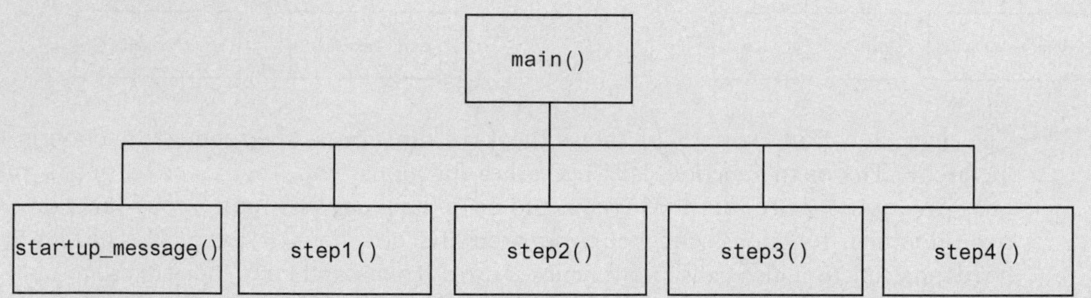

As you can see from the hierarchy chart, the `main` function will call several other functions. Here are summaries of those functions:

- `startup_message`. This function will display the starting message that tells the technician what the program does.
- `step1`. This function will display the instructions for step 1.
- `step2`. This function will display the instructions for step 2.
- `step3`. This function will display the instructions for step 3.
- `step4`. This function will display the instructions for step 4.

Between calls to these functions, the `main` function will instruct the user to press a key to see the next step in the instructions. Program 5-3 shows the code for the program.

Program 5-3 (acme_dryer.py)

```
# This program displays step-by-step instructions
# for disassembling an Acme dryer.
# The main function performs the program's main logic.
def main():
    # Display the start-up message.
    startup_message()
    input('Press Enter to see Step 1.')
    # Display step 1.
    step1()
    input('Press Enter to see Step 2.')
    # Display step 2.
    step2()
    input('Press Enter to see Step 3.')
    # Display step 3.
    step3()
    input('Press Enter to see Step 4.')
    # Display step 4.
    step4()

# The startup_message function displays the
# program's initial message on the screen.
def startup_message():
    print('This program tells you how to')
    print('disassemble an ACME laundry dryer.')
    print('There are 4 steps in the process.')
    print()

# The step1 function displays the instructions
# for step 1.
def step1():
    print('Step 1: Unplug the dryer and')
    print('move it away from the wall.')
    print()

# The step2 function displays the instructions
# for step 2.
def step2():
    print('Step 2: Remove the six screws')
    print('from the back of the dryer.')
    print()

# The step3 function displays the instructions
# for step 3.
def step3():
    print('Step 3: Remove the back panel')
```

(program continues)

Program 5-3 *(continued)*

```
46         print('from the dryer.')
47         print()
48
49     # The step4 function displays the instructions
50     # for step 4.
51     def step4():
52         print('Step 4: Pull the top of the')
53         print('dryer straight up.')
54
55     # Call the main function to begin the program.
56     main()
```

Program Output

```
This program tells you how to
disassemble an ACME laundry dryer.
There are 4 steps in the process.

Press Enter to see Step 1. Enter
Step 1: Unplug the dryer and
move it away from the wall.

Press Enter to see Step 2. Enter
Step 2: Remove the six screws
from the back of the dryer.

Press Enter to see Step 3. Enter
Step 3: Remove the back panel
from the dryer.

Press Enter to see Step 4. Enter
Step 4: Pull the top of the
dryer straight up.
```

Pausing Execution Until the User Presses Enter

Sometimes you want a program to pause so the user can read information that has been displayed on the screen. When the user is ready for the program to continue execution, he or she presses the Enter key and the program resumes. In Python, you can use the `input` function to cause a program to pause until the user presses the Enter key. Line 7 in Program 5-3 is an example:

```
input('Press Enter to see Step 1.')
```

This statement displays the prompt `'Press Enter to see Step 1.'` and pauses until the user presses the Enter key. The program also uses this technique in lines 10, 13, and 16.

5.4 Local Variables

CONCEPT: A local variable is created inside a function and cannot be accessed by statements that are outside the function. Different functions can have local variables with the same names because the functions cannot see each other's local variables.

Anytime you assign a value to a variable inside a function, you create a *local variable*. A local variable belongs to the function in which it is created, and only statements inside that function can access the variable. (The term *local* is meant to indicate that the variable can be used only locally, within the function in which it is created.)

An error will occur if a statement in one function tries to access a local variable that belongs to another function. For example, look at Program 5-4.

Program 5-4 (bad_local.py)

```
1  # Definition of the main function.
2  def main():
3      get_name()
4      print('Hello', name)      # This causes an error!
5
6  # Definition of the get_name function.
7  def get_name():
8      name = input('Enter your name: ')
9
10 # Call the main function.
11 main()
```

This program has two functions: `main` and `get_name`. In line 8, the `name` variable is assigned a value that is entered by the user. This statement is inside the `get_name` function, so the `name` variable is local to that function. This means that the `name` variable cannot be accessed by statements outside the `get_name` function.

The `main` function calls the `get_name` function in line 3. Then, the statement in line 4 tries to access the `name` variable. This results in an error because the `name` variable is local to the `get_name` function, and statements in the `main` function cannot access it.

Scope and Local Variables

A variable's *scope* is the part of a program in which the variable may be accessed. A variable is visible only to statements in the variable's scope. A local variable's scope is the function in which the variable is created. As you saw demonstrated in Program 5-4, no statement outside the function may access the variable.

In addition, a local variable cannot be accessed by code that appears inside the function at a point before the variable has been created. For example, look at the following function. It will cause an error because the `print` function tries to access the `val` variable, but this statement appears before the `val` variable has been created. Moving the assignment statement to a line before the `print` statement will fix this error.

```
def bad_function():
    print('The value is', val)    # This will cause an error!
    val = 99
```

Because a function's local variables are hidden from other functions, the other functions may have their own local variables with the same name. For example, look at Program 5-5. In addition to the `main` function, this program has two other functions: `texas` and `california`. These two functions each have a local variable named `birds`.

Program 5-5 (birds.py)

```
# This program demonstrates two functions that
# have local variables with the same name.

def main():
    # Call the texas function.
    texas()
    # Call the california function.
    california()

# Definition of the texas function. It creates
# a local variable named birds.
def texas():
    birds = 5000
    print('texas has', birds, 'birds.')

# Definition of the california function. It also
# creates a local variable named birds.
def california():
    birds = 8000
    print('california has', birds, 'birds.')

# Call the main function.
main()
```

Program Output

```
texas has 5000 birds.
california has 8000 birds.
```

Although there are two separate variables named `birds` in this program, only one of them is visible at a time because they are in different functions. This is illustrated in Figure 5-12. When the `texas` function is executing, the `birds` variable that is created in line 13 is visible. When the `california` function is executing, the `birds` variable that is created in line 19 is visible.

Figure 5-12 Each function has its own `birds` variable

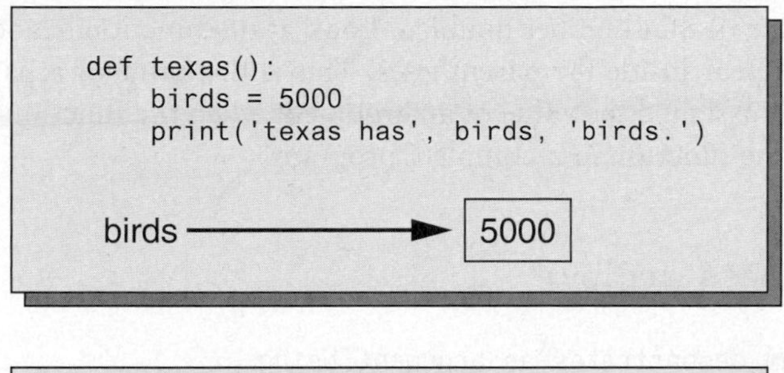


```
def california():
    birds = 8000
    print('california has', birds, 'birds.')
```

birds → 8000

Checkpoint

5.10 What is a local variable? How is access to a local variable restricted?

5.11 What is a variable's scope?

5.12 Is it permissible for a local variable in one function to have the same name as a local variable in a different function?

5.5 Passing Arguments to Functions

CONCEPT: An argument is any piece of data that is passed into a function when the function is called. A parameter is a variable that receives an argument that is passed into a function.

VideoNote Passing Arguments to a Function

Sometimes it is useful not only to call a function, but also to send one or more pieces of data into the function. Pieces of data that are sent into a function are known as *arguments*. The function can use its arguments in calculations or other operations.

If you want a function to receive arguments when it is called, you must equip the function with one or more parameter variables. A *parameter variable,* often simply called a *parameter,* is a special variable that is assigned the value of an argument when a function is called. Here is an example of a function that has a parameter variable:

```
def show_double(number):
    result = number * 2
    print(result)
```

This function's name is `show_double`. Its purpose is to accept a number as an argument and display the value of that number doubled. Look at the function header and notice the word `number` that appear inside the parentheses. This is the name of a parameter variable. This variable will be assigned the value of an argument when the function is called. Program 5-6 demonstrates the function in a complete program.

Program 5-6 (pass_arg.py)

```
1  # This program demonstrates an argument being
2  # passed to a function.
3
4  def main():
5      value = 5
6      show_double(value)
7
8  # The show_double function accepts an argument
9  # and displays double its value.
10 def show_double(number):
11     result = number * 2
12     print(result)
13
14 # Call the main function.
15 main()
```

Program Output

```
10
```

When this program runs, the `main` function is called in line 15. Inside the `main` function, line 5 creates a local variable named `value`, assigned the value 5. Then the following statement in line 6 calls the `show_double` function:

```
show_double(value)
```

Notice `value` appears inside the parentheses. This means that `value` is being passed as an argument to the `show_double` function, as shown in Figure 5-13 When this statement executes, the `show_double` function will be called, and the `number` parameter will be assigned the same `value` as the `value` variable. This is shown in Figure 5-14.

Figure 5-13 The value variable is passed as an argument

```
def main():
    value = 5
    show_double(value)

def show_double(number):
    result = number * 2
    print(result)
```

Figure 5-14 The value variable and the number parameter reference the same value

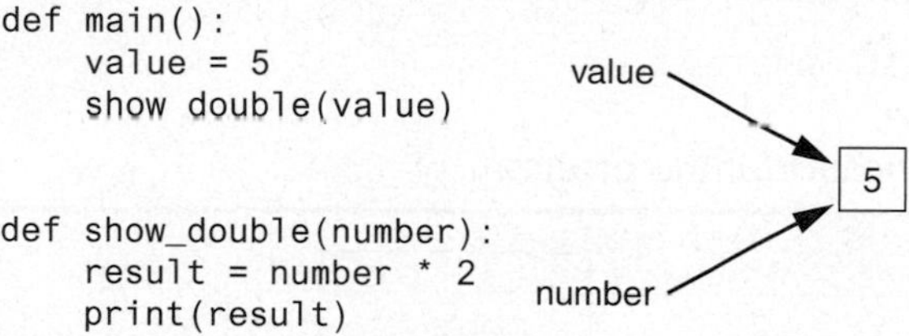

Let's step through the show_double function. As we do, remember that the number parameter variable will be assigned the value that was passed to it as an argument. In this program, that number is 5.

Line 11 assigns the value of the expression number * 2 to a local variable named result. Because number references the value 5, this statement assigns 10 to result. Line 12 displays the result variable.

The following statement shows how the show_double function can be called with a numeric literal passed as an argument:

```
show_double(50)
```

This statement executes the show_double function, assigning 50 to the number parameter. The function will print 100.

Parameter Variable Scope

Earlier in this chapter, you learned that a variable's scope is the part of the program in which the variable may be accessed. A variable is visible only to statements inside the variable's scope. A parameter variable's scope is the function in which the parameter is used. All of the statements inside the function can access the parameter variable, but no statement outside the function can access it.

In the Spotlight:

Passing an Argument to a Function

Your friend Michael runs a catering company. Some of the ingredients that his recipes require are measured in cups. When he goes to the grocery store to buy those ingredients, however, they are sold only by the fluid ounce. He has asked you to write a simple program that converts cups to fluid ounces.

You design the following algorithm:

1. *Display an introductory screen that explains what the program does.*
2. *Get the number of cups.*
3. *Convert the number of cups to fluid ounces and display the result.*

This algorithm lists the top level of tasks that the program needs to perform and becomes the basis of the program's `main` function. Figure 5-15 shows the program's structure in a hierarchy chart.

Figure 5-15 Hierarchy chart for the program

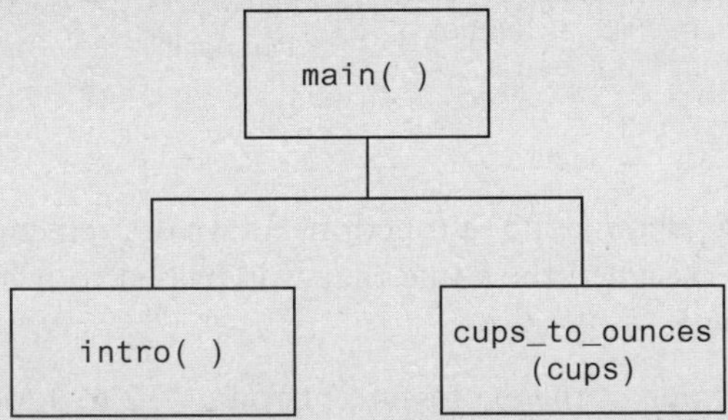

As shown in the hierarchy chart, the `main` function will call two other functions.

Here are summaries of those functions:

- `intro`. This function will display a message on the screen that explains what the program does.
- `cups_to_ounces`. This function will accept the number of cups as an argument and calculate and display the equivalent number of fluid ounces.

In addition to calling these functions, the `main` function will ask the user to enter the number of cups. This value will be passed to the `cups_to_ounces` function. The code for the program is shown in Program 5-7.

Program 5-7 (cups_to_ounces.py)

```
# This program converts cups to fluid ounces.

def main():
    # display the intro screen.
```

```
    intro()
    # Get the number of cups.
    cups_needed = int(input('Enter the number of cups: '))
    # Convert the cups to ounces.
    cups_to_ounces(cups_needed)

# The intro function displays an introductory screen.
def intro():
    print('This program converts measurements')
    print('in cups to fluid ounces. For your')
    print('reference the formula is:')
    print(' 1 cup = 8 fluid ounces')
    print()

# The cups_to_ounces function accepts a number of
# cups and displays the equivalent number of ounces.
def cups_to_ounces(cups):
    ounces = cups * 8
    print('That converts to', ounces, 'ounces.')

# Call the main function.
main()
```

Program Output (with input shown in bold)

```
This program converts measurements
in cups to fluid ounces. For your
reference the formula is:
    1 cup = 8 fluid ounces
Enter the number of cups: 4 [Enter]
That converts to 32 ounces.
```

Passing Multiple Arguments

Often it's useful to write functions that can accept multiple arguments. Program 5-8 shows a function named show_sum, that accepts two arguments. The function adds the two arguments and displays their sum.

Program 5-8 (multiple_args.py)

```
# This program demonstrates a function that accepts
# two arguments.

def main():
    print('The sum of 12 and 45 is')
```

(program continues)

Program 5-8 *(continued)*

```
 6      show_sum(12, 45)
 7
 8  # The show_sum function accepts two arguments
 9  # and displays their sum.
10  def show_sum(num1, num2):
11      result = num1 + num2
12      print(result)
13
14  # Call the main function.
15  main()
```

Program Output

```
The sum of 12 and 45 is
57
```

Notice two parameter variable names, num1 and num2, appear inside the parentheses in the show_sum function header. This is often referred to as a *parameter list*. Also notice a comma separates the variable names.

The statement in line 6 calls the show_sum function and passes two arguments: 12 and 45. These arguments are passed *by position* to the corresponding parameter variables in the function. In other words, the first argument is passed to the first parameter variable, and the second argument is passed to the second parameter variable. So, this statement causes 12 to be assigned to the num1 parameter and 45 to be assigned to the num2 parameter, as shown in Figure 5-16.

Figure 5-16 Two arguments passed to two parameters

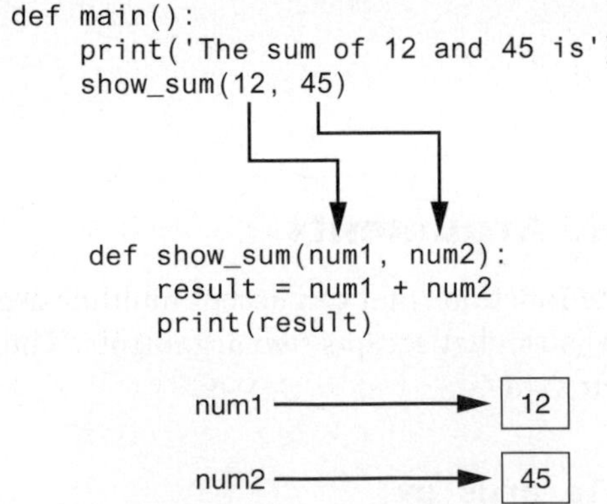

Suppose we were to reverse the order in which the arguments are listed in the function call, as shown here:

```
show_sum(45, 12)
```

This would cause 45 to be passed to the num1 parameter, and 12 to be passed to the num2 parameter. The following code shows another example. This time, we are passing variables as arguments.

```
value1 = 2
value2 = 3
show_sum(value1, value2)
```

When the `show_sum` function executes as a result of this code, the `num1` parameter will be assigned the value 2, and the `num2` parameter will be assigned the value 3.

Program 5-9 shows one more example. This program passes two strings as arguments to a function.

Program 5-9 (string_args.py)

```
# This program demonstrates passing two string
# arguments to a function.

def main():
    first_name = input('Enter your first name: ')
    last_name = input('Enter your last name: ')
    print('Your name reversed is')
    reverse_name(first_name, last_name)

def reverse_name(first, last):
    print(last, first)

# Call the main function.
main()
```

Program Output (with input shown in bold)

```
Enter your first name: Matt [Enter]
Enter your last name: Hoyle [Enter]
Your name reversed is
Hoyle Matt
```

Making Changes to Parameters

When an argument is passed to a function in Python, the function parameter variable will reference the argument's value. However, any changes that are made to the parameter variable will not affect the argument. To demonstrate this, look at Program 5-10.

Program 5-10 (change_me.py)

```
# This program demonstrates what happens when you
# change the value of a parameter.

```

(program continues)

Program 5-10 *(continued)*

```
4  def main():
5      value = 99
6      print('The value is', value)
7      change_me(value)
8      print('Back in main the value is', value)
9
10 def change_me(arg):
11     print('I am changing the value.')
12     arg = 0
13     print('Now the value is', arg)
14
15 # Call the main function.
16 main()
```

Program Output

```
The value is 99
I am changing the value.
Now the value is 0
Back in main the value is 99
```

The `main` function creates a local variable named `value` in line 5, assigned the value 99. The statement in line 6 displays `'The value is 99'`. The `value` variable is then passed as an argument to the `change_me` function in line 7. This means that in the `change_me` function, the `arg` parameter will also reference the value 99. This is shown in Figure 5-17.

Figure 5-17 The value variable is passed to the change_me function

```
def main():
    value = 99
    print('The value is', value)
    change_me(value)
    print('Back in main the value is', value)


def change_me(arg):
    print('I am changing the value.')
    arg = 0
    print('Now the value is', arg)
```


Inside the `change_me` function, in line 12, the `arg` parameter is assigned the value 0. This reassignment changes `arg`, but it does not affect the `value` variable in `main`. As shown in Figure 5-18, the two variables now reference different values in memory. The statement in line 13 displays `'Now the value is 0'` and the function ends.

Control of the program then returns to the `main` function. The next statement to execute is in line 8. This statement displays `'Back in main the value is 99'`. This proves that even though the parameter variable `arg` was changed in the `change_me` function, the argument (the `value` variable in `main`) was not modified.

Figure 5-18 The `value` variable is passed to the change_me function

```
def main():
    value = 99
    print('The value is', value)
    change_me(value)
    print('Back in main the value is', value)

def change_me(arg):
    print('I am changing the value.')
    arg = 0
    print('Now the value is', arg)
```

value → 99

arg → 0

The form of argument passing that is used in Python, where a function cannot change the value of an argument that was passed to it, is commonly called *pass by value*. This is a way that one function can communicate with another function. The communication channel works in only one direction, however. The calling function can communicate with the called function, but the called function cannot use the argument to communicate with the calling function. Later in this chapter, you will learn how to write a function that can communicate with the part of the program that called it by returning a value.

Keyword Arguments

Programs 5-8 and 5-9 demonstrate how arguments are passed by position to parameter variables in a function. Most programming languages match function arguments and parameters this way. In addition to this conventional form of argument passing, the Python language allows you to write an argument in the following format, to specify which parameter variable the argument should be passed to:

parameter_name=value

In this format, *parameter_name* is the name of a parameter variable, and `value` is the value being passed to that parameter. An argument that is written in accordance with this syntax is known as a *keyword argument.*

Program 5-11 demonstrates keyword arguments. This program uses a function named `show_interest` that displays the amount of simple interest earned by a bank account for a number of periods. The function accepts the arguments `principal` (for the account principal), `rate` (for the interest rate per period), and `periods` (for the number of periods). When the function is called in line 7, the arguments are passed as keyword arguments.

Program 5-11 (keyword_args.py)

```
1 # This program demonstrates keyword arguments.
2
3 def main():
4     # Show the amount of simple interest, using 0.01 as
5     # interest rate per period, 10 as the number of periods,
6     # and $10,000 as the principal.
7     show_interest(rate=0.01, periods=10, principal=10000.0)
```

(program continues)

Program 5-11 *(continued)*

```
 8
 9  # The show_interest function displays the amount of
10  # simple interest for a given principal, interest rate
11  # per period, and number of periods.
12
13  def show_interest(principal, rate, periods):
14      interest = principal * rate * periods
15      print('The simple interest will be $',
16            format(interest, ',.2f'),
17            sep='')
18
19  # Call the main function.
20  main()
```

Program Output

```
The simple interest will be $1000.00.
```

Notice in line 7 the order of the keyword arguments does not match the order of the parameters in the function header in line 13. Because a keyword argument specifies which parameter the argument should be passed into, its position in the function call does not matter.

Program 5-12 shows another example. This is a variation of the `string_args` program shown in Program 5-9. This version uses keyword arguments to call the `reverse_name` function.

Program 5-12 **(keyword_string_args.py)**

```
# This program demonstrates passing two strings as
# keyword arguments to a function.

def main():
    first_name = input('Enter your first name: ')
    last_name = input('Enter your last name: ')
    print('Your name reversed is')
    reverse_name(last=last_name, first=first_name)

def reverse_name(first, last):
    print(last, first)

# Call the main function.
main()
```

Program Output (with input shown in bold)

Enter your first name: **Matt** [Enter]
Enter your last name: **Hoyle** [Enter]
Your name reversed is
Hoyle Matt

Mixing Keyword Arguments with Positional Arguments

It is possible to mix positional arguments and keyword arguments in a function call, but the positional arguments must appear first, followed by the keyword arguments. Otherwise, an error will occur. Here is an example of how we might call the `show_interest` function of Program 5-10 using both positional and keyword arguments:

```
show_interest(10000.0, rate=0.01, periods=10)
```

In this statement, the first argument, `10000.0`, is passed by its position to the `principal` parameter. The second and third arguments are passed as keyword arguments. The following function call will cause an error, however, because a non-keyword argument follows a keyword argument:

```
# This will cause an ERROR!
show_interest(1000.0, rate=0.01, 10)
```

Checkpoint

5.13 What are the pieces of data that are passed into a function called?

5.14 What are the variables that receive pieces of data in a function called?

5.15 What is a parameter variable's scope?

5.16 When a parameter is changed, does this affect the argument that was passed into the parameter?

5.17 The following statements call a function named `show_data`. Which of the statements passes arguments by position, and which passes keyword arguments?
   a. `show_data(name='Kathryn', age=25)`
   b. `show_data('Kathryn', 25)`

5.6 Global Variables and Global Constants

CONCEPT: A global variable is accessible to all the functions in a program file.

You've learned that when a variable is created by an assignment statement inside a function, the variable is local to that function. Consequently, it can be accessed only by statements inside the function that created it. When a variable is created by an assignment statement that is written outside all the functions in a program file, the variable is *global*. A global variable can be accessed by any statement in the program file, including the statements in any function. For example, look at Program 5-13.

Program 5-13 (`global1.py`)

```
# Create a global variable.
my_value = 10

# The show_value function prints
# the value of the global variable.
```

(program continues)

Program 5-13 *(continued)*

```
 6 def show_value():
 7     print(my_value)
 8
 9 # Call the show_value function.
10 show_value()
```

Program Output

```
10
```

The assignment statement in line 2 creates a variable named `my_value`. Because this statement is outside any function, it is global. When the `show_value` function executes, the statement in line 7 prints the value referenced by `my_value`.

An additional step is required if you want a statement in a function to assign a value to a global variable. In the function, you must declare the global variable, as shown in Program 5-14.

Program 5-14 (`global2.py`)

```
 1 # Create a global variable.
 2 number = 0
 3
 4 def main():
 5     global number
 6     number = int(input('Enter a number: '))
 7     show_number()
 8
 9 def show_number():
10     print('The number you entered is', number)
11
12 # Call the main function.
13 main()
```

Program Output

```
Enter a number: 55 Enter
The number you entered is 55
```

The assignment statement in line 2 creates a global variable named `number`. Notice inside the `main` function, line 5 uses the `global` key word to declare the `number` variable. This statement tells the interpreter that the `main` function intends to assign a value to the global `number` variable. That's just what happens in line 6. The value entered by the user is assigned to `number`.

Most programmers agree that you should restrict the use of global variables, or not use them at all. The reasons are as follows:

- Global variables make debugging difficult. Any statement in a program file can change the value of a global variable. If you find that the wrong value is being stored in a global variable, you have to track down every statement that accesses it to determine where the bad value is coming from. In a program with thousands of lines of code, this can be difficult.

- Functions that use global variables are usually dependent on those variables. If you want to use such a function in a different program, most likely you will have to redesign it so it does not rely on the global variable.
- Global variables make a program hard to understand. A global variable can be modified by any statement in the program. If you are to understand any part of the program that uses a global variable, you have to be aware of all the other parts of the program that access the global variable.

In most cases, you should create variables locally and pass them as arguments to the functions that need to access them.

Global Constants

Although you should try to avoid the use of global variables, it is permissible to use global constants in a program. A *global constant* is a global name that references a value that cannot be changed. Because a global constant's value cannot be changed during the program's execution, you do not have to worry about many of the potential hazards that are associated with the use of global variables.

Although the Python language does not allow you to create true global constants, you can simulate them with global variables. If you do not declare a global variable with the `global` key word inside a function, then you cannot change the variable's assignment inside that function. The following *In the Spotlight* section demonstrates how global variables can be used in Python to simulate global constants.

In the Spotlight:

Using Global Constants

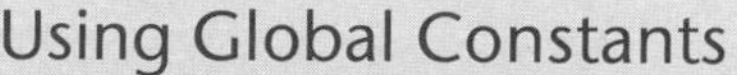

Marilyn works for Integrated Systems, Inc., a software company that has a reputation for providing excellent fringe benefits. One of their benefits is a quarterly bonus that is paid to all employees. Another benefit is a retirement plan for each employee. The company contributes 5 percent of each employee's gross pay and bonuses to their retirement plans. Marilyn wants to write a program that will calculate the company's contribution to an employee's retirement account for a year. She wants the program to show the amount of contribution for the employee's gross pay and for the bonuses separately. Here is an algorithm for the program:

Get the employee's annual gross pay.
Get the amount of bonuses paid to the employee.
Calculate and display the contribution for the gross pay.
Calculate and display the contribution for the bonuses.

The code for the program is shown in Program 5-15.

Program 5-15 (retirement.py)

```
1  # The following is used as a global constant
2  # the contribution rate.
3  CONTRIBUTION_RATE = 0.05
4
5  def main():
6      gross_pay = float(input('Enter the gross pay: '))
7      bonus = float(input('Enter the amount of bonuses: '))
8      show_pay_contrib(gross_pay)
9      show_bonus_contrib(bonus)
10
11 # The show_pay_contrib function accepts the gross
12 # pay as an argument and displays the retirement
13 # contribution for that amount of pay.
14 def show_pay_contrib(gross):
15     contrib = gross * CONTRIBUTION_RATE
16     print('Contribution for gross pay: $',
17           format(contrib, ',.2f'),
18           sep='')
19
20 # The show_bonus_contrib function accepts the
21 # bonus amount as an argument and displays the
22 # retirement contribution for that amount of pay.
23 def show_bonus_contrib(bonus):
24     contrib = bonus * CONTRIBUTION_RATE
25     print('Contribution for bonuses: $',
26           format(contrib, ',.2f'),
27           sep='')
28
29 # Call the main function.
30 main()
```

Program Output (with input shown in bold)

```
Enter the gross pay: 80000.00 [Enter]
Enter the amount of bonuses: 20000.00 [Enter]
Contribution for gross pay: $4000.00
Contribution for bonuses: $1000.00
```

First, notice the global declaration in line 3:

```
CONTRIBUTION_RATE = 0.05
```

`CONTRIBUTION_RATE` will be used as a global constant to represent the percentage of an employee's pay that the company will contribute to a retirement account. It is a common practice to write a constant's name in all uppercase letters. This serves as a reminder that the value referenced by the name is not to be changed in the program.

The `CONTRIBUTION_RATE` constant is used in the calculation in line 15 (in the `show_pay_contrib` function) and again in line 24 (in the `show_bonus_contrib` function).

Marilyn decided to use this global constant to represent the 5 percent contribution rate for two reasons:

- It makes the program easier to read. When you look at the calculations in lines 15 and 24 it is apparent what is happening.
- Occasionally the contribution rate changes. When this happens, it will be easy to update the program by changing the assignment statement in line 3.

Checkpoint

5.18 What is the scope of a global variable?

5.19 Give one good reason that you should not use global variables in a program.

5.20 What is a global constant? Is it permissible to use global constants in a program?

5.7 Introduction to Value-Returning Functions: Generating Random Numbers

CONCEPT: A value-returning function is a function that returns a value back to the part of the program that called it. Python, as well as most other programming languages, provides a library of prewritten functions that perform commonly needed tasks. These libraries typically contain a function that generates random numbers.

In the first part of this chapter, you learned about void functions. A void function is a group of statements that exist within a program for the purpose of performing a specific task. When you need the function to perform its task, you call the function. This causes the statements inside the function to execute. When the function is finished, control of the program returns to the statement appearing immediately after the function call.

A *value-returning function* is a special type of function. It is like a void function in the following ways.

- It is a group of statements that perform a specific task.
- When you want to execute the function, you call it.

When a value-returning function finishes, however, it returns a value back to the part of the program that called it. The value that is returned from a function can be used like any other value: it can be assigned to a variable, displayed on the screen, used in a mathematical expression (if it is a number), and so on.

Standard Library Functions and the `import` Statement

Python, as well as most programming languages, comes with a *standard library* of functions that have already been written for you. These functions, known as *library functions,* make a programmer's job easier because they perform many of the tasks that programmers commonly need to perform. In fact, you have already used several of Python's library functions. Some of the functions that you have used are `print`, `input`, and `range`. Python has many other library functions. Although we won't cover them all in this book, we will discuss library functions that perform fundamental operations.

Some of Python's library functions are built into the Python interpreter. If you want to use one of these built-in functions in a program, you simply call the function. This is the case with the `print`, `input`, `range`, and other functions about which you have already learned. Many of the functions in the standard library, however, are stored in files that are known as *modules*. These modules, which are copied to your computer when you install Python, help organize the standard library functions. For example, functions for performing math operations are stored together in a module, functions for working with files are stored together in another module, and so on.

In order to call a function that is stored in a module, you have to write an `import` statement at the top of your program. An `import` statement tells the interpreter the name of the module that contains the function. For example, one of the Python standard modules is named `math`. The `math` module contains various mathematical functions that work with floating-point numbers. If you want to use any of the `math` module's functions in a program, you should write the following `import` statement at the top of the program:

```
import math
```

This statement causes the interpreter to load the contents of the `math` module into memory and makes all the functions in the `math` module available to the program.

Because you do not see the internal workings of library functions, many programmers think of them as *black boxes*. The term "black box" is used to describe any mechanism that accepts input, performs some operation (that cannot be seen) using the input, and produces output. Figure 5-19 illustrates this idea.

Figure 5-19 A library function viewed as a black box

We will first demonstrate how value-returning functions work by looking at standard library functions that generate random numbers and some interesting programs that can be written with them. Then, you will learn to write your own value-returning functions and how to create your own modules. The last section in this chapter comes back to the topic of library functions, and looks at several other useful functions in the Python standard library.

Generating Random Numbers

Random numbers are useful for lots of different programming tasks. The following are just a few examples.

- Random numbers are commonly used in games. For example, computer games that let the player roll dice use random numbers to represent the values of the dice.

Programs that show cards being drawn from a shuffled deck use random numbers to represent the face values of the cards.

- Random numbers are useful in simulation programs. In some simulations, the computer must randomly decide how a person, animal, insect, or other living being will behave. Formulas can be constructed in which a random number is used to determine various actions and events that take place in the program.
- Random numbers are useful in statistical programs that must randomly select data for analysis.
- Random numbers are commonly used in computer security to encrypt sensitive data.

Python provides several library functions for working with random numbers. These functions are stored in a module named `random` in the standard library. To use any of these functions, you first need to write this `import` statement at the top of your program:

```
import random
```

This statement causes the interpreter to load the contents of the `random` module into memory. This makes all of the functions in the `random` module available to your program.[1]

The first random-number generating function that we will discuss is named `randint`. Because the `randint` function is in the `random` module, we will need to use *dot notation* to refer to it in our program. In dot notation, the function's name is `random.randint`. On the left side of the dot (period) is the name of the module, and on the right side of the dot is the name of the function.

The following statement shows an example of how you might call the `randint` function:

```
number = random.randint (1, 100)
```

The part of the statement that reads `random.randint(1, 100)` is a call to the `randint` function. Notice two arguments appear inside the parentheses: 1 and 100. These arguments tell the function to give an integer random number in the range of 1 through 100. (The values 1 and 100 are included in the range.) Figure 5-20 illustrates this part of the statement.

Figure 5-20 A statement that calls the random function

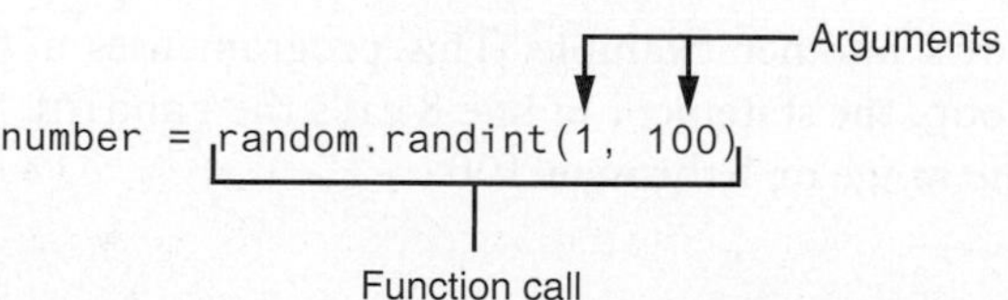

Notice the call to the `randint` function appears on the right side of an = operator. When the function is called, it will generate a random number in the range of 1 through 100 then *return* that number. The number that is returned will be assigned to the `number` variable, as shown in Figure 5-21.

[1] There are several ways to write an `import` statement in Python, and each variation works a little differently. Many Python programmers agree that the preferred way to import a module is the way shown in this book.

Figure 5-21 The random function returns a value

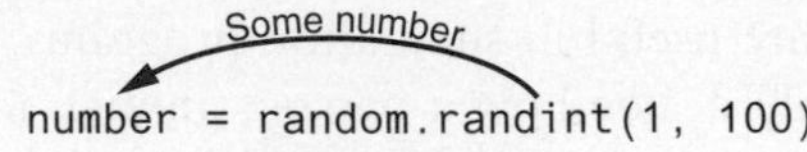

A random number in the range of 1 through 100 will be assigned to the number variable.

Program 5-16 shows a complete program that uses the `randint` function. The statement in line 2 generates a random number in the range of 1 through 10 and assigns it to the `number` variable. (The program output shows that the number 7 was generated, but this value is arbitrary. If this were an actual program, it could display any number from 1 to 10.)

Program 5-16 **(random_numbers.py)**

```
1  # This program displays a random number
2  # in the range of 1 through 10.
3  import random
4
5  def main():
6      # Get a random number.
7      number = random.randint(1, 10)
8      # Display the number.
9      print('The number is', number)
10
11 # Call the main function.
12 main()
```

Program Output

```
The number is 7
```

Program 5-17 shows another example. This program uses a `for` loop that iterates five times. Inside the loop, the statement in line 8 calls the `randint` function to generate a random number in the range of 1 through 100.

Program 5-17 **(random_numbers2.py)**

```
1  # This program displays five random
2  # numbers in the range of 1 through 100.
3  import random
4
5  def main():
6      for count in range(5):
7          # Get a random number.
8          number = random.randint(1, 100)
```

```
        # Display the number.
        print(number)

# Call the main function.
main()
```

Program Output

```
89
7
16
41
12
```

Both Program 5-16 and 5-17 call the `randint` function and assign its return value to the `number` variable. If you just want to display a random number, it is not necessary to assign the random number to a variable. You can send the `random` function's return value directly to the `print` function, as shown here:

```
print(random.randint(1, 10))
```

When this statement executes, the `randint` function is called. The function generates a random number in the range of 1 through 10. That value is returned and sent to the `print` function. As a result, a random number in the range of 1 through 10 will be displayed. Figure 5-22 illustrates this.

Figure 5-22 Displaying a random number

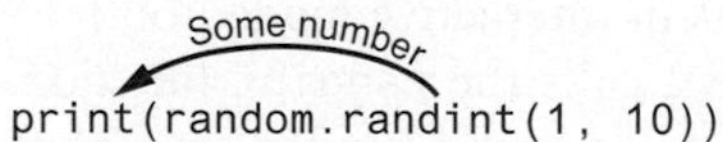

Program 5-18 shows how you could simplify Program 5-17. This program also displays five random numbers, but this program does not use a variable to hold those numbers. The `randint` function's return value is sent directly to the `print` function in line 7.

Program 5-18 (random_numbers3.py)

```
 1  # This program displays five random
 2  # numbers in the range of 1 through 100.
 3  import random
 4
 5  def main():
 6      for count in range(5):
 7          print(random.randint(1, 100))
 8
 9  # Call the main function.
10  main()
```

(program continues)

Program 5-18 *(continued)*

Program Output

```
89
7
16
41
12
```

Experimenting with Random Numbers in Interactive Mode

To get a feel for the way the `randint` function works with different arguments, you might want to experiment with it in interactive mode. To demonstrate, look at the following interactive session. (We have added line numbers for easier reference.)

```
1 >>> import random Enter
2 >>> random.randint(1, 10) Enter
3 5
4 >>> random.randint(1, 100) Enter
5 98
6 >>> random.randint(100, 200) Enter
7 181
8 >>>
```

Let's take a closer look at each line in the interactive session:

- The statement in line 1 imports the `random` module. (You have to write the appropriate `import` statements in interactive mode, too.)
- The statement in line 2 calls the `randint` function, passing 1 and 10 as arguments. As a result, the function returns a random number in the range of 1 through 10. The number that is returned from the function is displayed in line 3.
- The statement in line 4 calls the `randint` function, passing 1 and 100 as arguments. As a result, the function returns a random number in the range of 1 through 100. The number that is returned from the function is displayed in line 5.
- The statement in line 6 calls the `randint` function, passing 100 and 200 as arguments. As a result, the function returns a random number in the range of 100 through 200. The number that is returned from the function is displayed in line 7.

In the Spotlight:
Using Random Numbers

Dr. Kimura teaches an introductory statistics class and has asked you to write a program that he can use in class to simulate the rolling of dice. The program should randomly generate two numbers in the range of 1 through 6 and display them. In your interview with Dr. Kimura, you learn that he would like to use the program to simulate several rolls of the dice, one after the other. Here is the pseudocode for the program:

While the user wants to roll the dice:
    Display a random number in the range of 1 through 6
    Display another random number in the range of 1 through 6
    Ask the user if he or she wants to roll the dice again

You will write a `while` loop that simulates one roll of the dice and then asks the user if another roll should be performed. As long as the user answers "y" for yes, the loop will repeat. Program 5-19 shows the program.

Program 5-19 (dice.py)

```
# This program the rolling of dice.
import random

# Constants for the minimum and maximum random numbers
MIN = 1
MAX = 6

def main():
    # Create a variable to control the loop.
    again = 'y'

    # Simulate rolling the dice.
    while again == 'y' or again == 'Y':
        print('Rolling the dice ...')
        print('Their values are:')
        print(random.randint(MIN, MAX))
        print(random.randint(MIN, MAX))

        # Do another roll of the dice?
        again = input('Roll them again? (y = yes): ')

# Call the main function.
main()
```

Program Output (with input shown in bold)

```
Rolling the dice ...
Their values are:
3
1
Roll them again? (y = yes): y [Enter]
Rolling the dice ...
Their values are:
1
1
Roll them again? (y = yes): y [Enter]
Rolling the dice ...
Their values are:
5
6
Roll them again? (y = yes): y [Enter]
```

The `randint` function returns an integer value, so you can write a call to the function anywhere that you can write an integer value. You have already seen examples where the function's return value is assigned to a variable, and where the function's return value is sent to the `print` function. To further illustrate the point, here is a statement that uses the `randint` function in a math expression:

```
x = random.randint (1, 10) * 2
```

In this statement, a random number in the range of 1 through 10 is generated then multiplied by 2. The result is a random even integer from 2 to 20 assigned to the `x` variable. You can also test the return value of the function with an `if` statement, as demonstrated in the following *In the Spotlight* section.

In the Spotlight:

Using Random Numbers to Represent Other Values

Dr. Kimura was so happy with the dice rolling simulator that you wrote for him, he has asked you to write one more program. He would like a program that he can use to simulate ten coin tosses, one after the other. Each time the program simulates a coin toss, it should randomly display either "Heads" or "Tails".

You decide that you can simulate the tossing of a coin by randomly generating a number in the range of 1 through 2. You will write an `if` statement that displays "Heads" if the random number is 1, or "Tails" otherwise. Here is the pseudocode:

Repeat 10 times:
    If a random number in the range of 1 through 2 equals 1 then:
        Display 'Heads'
    Else:
        Display 'Tails'

Because the program should simulate 10 tosses of a coin you decide to use a `for` loop. The program is shown in Program 5-20.

Program 5-20 (coin_toss.py)

```
# This program simulates 10 tosses of a coin.
import random

# Constants
HEADS = 1
TAILS = 2
TOSSES = 10

```

```
def main():
    for toss in range(TOSSES):
        # Simulate the coin toss.
        if random.randint(HEADS, TAILS) == HEADS:
            print('Heads')
        else:
            print('Tails')

# Call the main function.
main()
```

Program Output

```
Tails
Tails
Heads
Tails
Heads
Heads
Heads
Tails
Heads
Tails
```

The `randrange`, `random`, and `uniform` Functions

The standard library's `random` module contains numerous functions for working with random numbers. In addition to the `randint` function, you might find the `randrange`, `random`, and `uniform` functions useful. (To use any of these functions, you need to write `import random` at the top of your program.)

If you remember how to use the `range` function (which we discussed in Chapter 4), then you will immediately be comfortable with the `randrange` function. The `randrange` function takes the same arguments as the `range` function. The difference is that the `randrange` function does not return a list of values. Instead, it returns a randomly selected value from a sequence of values. For example, the following statement assigns a random number in the range of 0 through 9 to the `number` variable:

```
number = random.randrange(10)
```

The argument, in this case 10, specifies the ending limit of the sequence of values. The function will return a randomly selected number from the sequence of values 0 up to, but not including, the ending limit. The following statement specifies both a starting value and an ending limit for the sequence:

```
number = random.randrange(5,10)
```

When this statement executes, a random number in the range of 5 through 9 will be assigned to number. The following statement specifies a starting value, an ending limit, and a step value:

```
number = random.randrange(0, 101, 10)
```

In this statement the `randrange` function returns a randomly selected value from the following sequence of numbers:

```
[0, 10, 20, 30, 40, 50, 60, 70, 80, 90, 100]
```

Both the `randint` and the `randrange` functions return an integer number. The `random` function, however, returns a random floating-point number. You do not pass any arguments to the `random` function. When you call it, it returns a random floating point number in the range of 0.0 up to 1.0 (but not including 1.0). Here is an example:

```
number = random.random()
```

The `uniform` function also returns a random floating-point number, but allows you to specify the range of values to select from. Here is an example:

```
number = random.uniform(1.0, 10.0)
```

In this statement, the `uniform` function returns a random floating-point number in the range of 1.0 through 10.0 and assigns it to the `number` variable.

Random Number Seeds

The numbers that are generated by the functions in the `random` module are not truly random. Although we commonly refer to them as random numbers, they are actually *pseudorandom numbers* that are calculated by a formula. The formula that generates random numbers has to be initialized with a value known as a *seed value*. The seed value is used in the calculation that returns the next random number in the series. When the `random` module is imported, it retrieves the system time from the computer's internal clock and uses that as the seed value. The system time is an integer that represents the current date and time, down to a hundredth of a second.

If the same seed value were always used, the random number functions would always generate the same series of pseudorandom numbers. Because the system time changes every hundredth of a second, it is a fairly safe bet that each time you import the `random` module, a different sequence of random numbers will be generated. However, there may be some applications in which you want to always generate the same sequence of random numbers. If that is the case, you can call the `random.seed` function to specify a seed value. Here is an example:

```
random.seed(10)
```

In this example, the value 10 is specified as the seed value. If a program calls the `random.seed` function, passing the same value as an argument each time it runs, it will always produce the same sequence of pseudorandom numbers. To demonstrate, look at the following interactive sessions. (We have added line numbers for easier reference.)

```
1 >>> import random [Enter]
2 >>> random.seed(10) [Enter]
3 >>> random.randint(1, 100) [Enter]
4 58
5 >>> random.randint(1, 100) [Enter]
6 43
```

```
7   >>> random.randint(1, 100) Enter
8   58
9   >>> random.randint(1, 100) Enter
10  21
11  >>>
```

In line 1, we import the random module. In line 2, we call the `random.seed` function, passing 10 as the seed value. In lines 3, 5, 7, and 9, we call `random.randint` function to get a pseudorandom number in the range of 1 through 100. As you can see, the function gave us the numbers 58, 43, 58, and 21. If we start a new interactive session and repeat these statements, we get the same sequence of pseudorandom numbers, as shown here:

```
1   >>> import random Enter
2   >>> random.seed(10) Enter
3   >>> random.randint(1, 100) Enter
4   58
5   >>> random.randint(1, 100) Enter
6   43
7   >>> random.randint(1, 100) Enter
8   58
9   >>> random.randint(1, 100) Enter
10  21
11  >>>
```

Checkpoint

5.21 How does a value-returning function differ from the void functions?

5.22 What is a library function?

5.23 Why are library functions like "black boxes"?

5.24 What does the following statement do?

```
x = random.randint(1, 100)
```

5.25 What does the following statement do?

```
print(random.randint(1, 20))
```

5.26 What does the following statement do?

```
print(random.randrange(10, 20))
```

5.27 What does the following statement do?

```
print(random.random())
```

5.28 What does the following statement do?

```
print(random.uniform(0.1, 0.5))
```

5.29 When the `random` module is imported, what does it use as a seed value for random number generation?

5.30 What happens if the same seed value is always used for generating random numbers?

5.8 Writing Your Own Value-Returning Functions

CONCEPT: A value-returning function has a `return` statement that returns a value back to the part of the program that called it.

VideoNote
Writing a Value-Returning Function

You write a value-returning function in the same way that you write a void function, with one exception: a value-returning function must have a `return` statement. Here is the general format of a value-returning function definition in Python:

```
def function_name():
    statement
    statement
    etc.
    return expression
```

One of the statements in the function must be a `return` statement, which takes the following form:

```
return expression
```

The value of the *`expression`* that follows the key word `return` will be sent back to the part of the program that called the function. This can be any value, variable, or expression that has a value (such as a math expression).

Here is a simple example of a value-returning function:

```
def sum(num1, num2):
    result = num 1 + num 2
    return result
```

Figure 5-23 illustrates various parts of the function.

Figure 5-23 Parts of the function

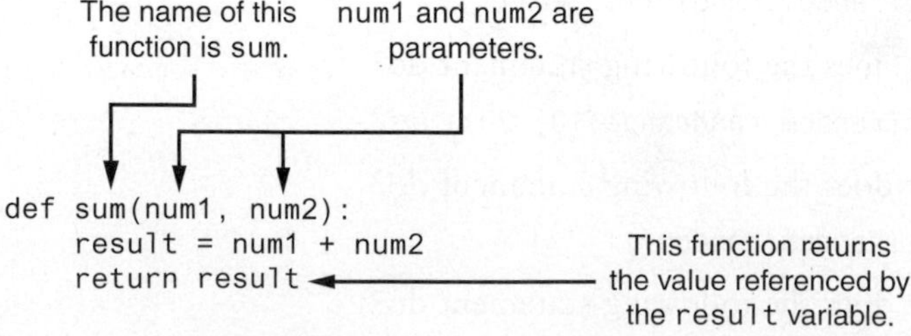

The purpose of this function is to accept two integer values as arguments and return their sum. Let's take a closer look at how it works. The first statement in the function's block assigns the value of `num1 + num2` to the `result` variable. Next, the `return` statement executes, which causes the function to end execution and sends the value referenced by the `result` variable back to the part of the program that called the function. Program 5-21 demonstrates the function.

Program 5-21 (total_ages.py)

```
1  # This program uses the return value of a function.
2
3  def main():
4      # Get the user's age.
5      first_age = int(input('Enter your age: '))
6
7      # Get the user's best friend's age.
8      second_age = int(input("Enter your best friend's age: "))
9
10     # Get the sum of both ages.
11     total = sum(first_age, second_age)
12
13     # Display the total age.
14     print('Together you are', total, 'years old.')
15
16 # The sum function accepts two numeric arguments and
17 # returns the sum of those arguments.
18 def sum(num1, num2):
19     result = num1 + num2
20     return result
21
22 # Call the main function.
23 main()
```

Program Output (with input shown in bold)

```
Enter your age: 22 [Enter]
Enter your best friend's age: 24 [Enter]
Together you are 46 years old.
```

In the `main` function, the program gets two values from the user and stores them in the `first_age` and `second_age` variables. The statement in line 11 calls the `sum` function, passing `first_age` and `second_age` as arguments. The value that is returned from the `sum` function is assigned to the `total` variable. In this case, the function will return 46. Figure 5-24 shows how the arguments are passed into the function, and how a value is returned back from the function.

Figure 5-24 Arguments are passed to the `sum` function and a value is returned

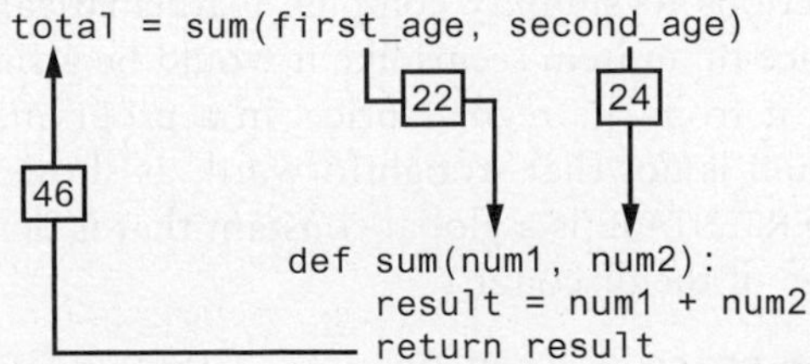

Making the Most of the `return` Statement

Look again at the sum function presented in Program 5-21:

```
def sum(num1, num2):
    result = num 1 + num 2
    return result
```

Notice two things happen inside this function: (1) the value of the expression num1 + num2 is assigned to the result variable, and (2) the value of the result variable is returned. Although this function does what it sets out to do, it can be simplified. Because the return statement can return the value of an expression, you can eliminate the result variable and rewrite the function as:

```
def sum(num1, num2):
    return num 1 + num 2
```

This version of the function does not store the value of num1 + num2 in a variable. Instead, it takes advantage of the fact that the return statement can return the value of an expression. This version of the function does the same thing as the previous version, but in only one step.

How to Use Value-Returning Functions

Value-returning functions provide many of the same benefits as void functions: they simplify code, reduce duplication, enhance your ability to test code, increase the speed of development, and ease the facilitation of teamwork.

Because value-returning functions return a value, they can be useful in specific situations. For example, you can use a value-returning function to prompt the user for input, and then it can return the value entered by the user. Suppose you've been asked to design a program that calculates the sale price of an item in a retail business. To do that, the program would need to get the item's regular price from the user. Here is a function you could define for that purpose:

```
def get_regular_price():
    price = float(input("Enter the item's regular price: "))
    return price
```

Then, elsewhere in the program, you could call that function, as shown here:

```
# Get the item's regular price.
reg_price = get_regular_price()
```

When this statement executes, the get_regular_price function is called, which gets a value from the user and returns it. That value is then assigned to the reg_price variable.

You can also use functions to simplify complex mathematical expressions. For example, calculating the sale price of an item seems like it would be a simple task: you calculate the discount and subtract it from the regular price. In a program, however, a statement that performs this calculation is not that straightforward, as shown in the following example. (Assume DISCOUNT_PERCENTAGE is a global constant that is defined in the program, and it specifies the percentage of the discount.)

```
sale_price = reg_price - (reg_price * DISCOUNT_PERCENTAGE)
```

At a glance, this statement isn't easy to understand because it performs so many steps: it calculates the discount amount, subtracts that value from `reg_price`, and assigns the result to `sale_price`. You could simplify the statement by breaking out part of the math expression and placing it in a function. Here is a function named `discount` that accepts an item's price as an argument and returns the amount of the discount:

```
def discount(price):
    return price * DISCOUNT_PERCENTAGE
```

You could then call the function in your calculation:

```
sale_price = reg_price - discount(reg_price)
```

This statement is easier to read than the one previously shown, and it is clearer that the discount is being subtracted from the regular price. Program 5-22 shows the complete sale price calculating program using the functions just described.

Program 5-22 (sale_price.py)

```
# This program calculates a retail item's
# sale price.

# DISCOUNT_PERCENTAGE is used as a global
# constant for the discount percentage.
DISCOUNT_PERCENTAGE = 0.20

# The main function.
def main():
    # Get the item's regular price.
    reg_price = get_regular_price()

    # Calculate the sale price.
    sale_price = reg_price - discount(reg_price)

    # Display the sale price.
    print('The sale price is $', format(sale_price, ',.2f'), sep='')

# The get_regular_price function prompts the
# user to enter an item's regular price and it
# returns that value.
def get_regular_price():
    price = float(input("Enter the item's regular price: "))
    return price

# The discount function accepts an item's price
# as an argument and returns the amount of the
# discount, specified by DISCOUNT_PERCENTAGE.
```

(program continues)

Program 5-22 *(continued)*

```
def discount(price):
    return price * DISCOUNT_PERCENTAGE

# Call the main function.
main()
```

Program Output (with input shown in bold)

```
Enter the item's regular price: 100.00 Enter
The sale price is $80.00
```

Using IPO Charts

An IPO chart is a simple but effective tool that programmers sometimes use for designing and documenting functions. IPO stands for *input, processing,* and *output,* and an *IPO chart* describes the input, processing, and output of a function. These items are usually laid out in columns: the input column shows a description of the data that is passed to the function as arguments, the processing column shows a description of the process that the function performs, and the output column describes the data that is returned from the function. For example, Figure 5-25 shows IPO charts for the `get_regular_price` and `discount` functions you saw in Program 5-22.

Figure 5-25 IPO charts for the `getRegularPrice` and `discount` functions

The `get_regular_price` Function

Input	Processing	Output
None	Prompts the user to enter an item's regular price	The item's regular price

The `discount` Function

Input	Processing	Output
An item's regular price	Calculates an item's discount by multiplying the regular price by the global constant `DISCOUNT_PERCENTAGE`	The item's discount

Notice the IPO charts provide only brief descriptions of a function's input, processing, and output, but do not show the specific steps taken in a function. In many cases, however, IPO charts include sufficient information so they can be used instead of a flowchart. The decision of whether to use an IPO chart, a flowchart, or both is often left to the programmer's personal preference.

In the Spotlight:
Modularizing with Functions

Hal owns a business named Make Your Own Music, which sells guitars, drums, banjos, synthesizers, and many other musical instruments. Hal's sales staff works strictly on commission. At the end of the month, each salesperson's commission is calculated according to Table 5-1.

Table 5-1 Sales commission rates

Sales This Month	Commission Rate
Less than $10,000	10%
$10,000–14,999	12%
$15,000–17,999	14%
$18,000–21,999	16%
$22,000 or more	18%

For example, a salesperson with $16,000 in monthly sales will earn a 14 percent commission ($2,240). Another salesperson with $18,000 in monthly sales will earn a 16 percent commission ($2,880). A person with $30,000 in sales will earn an 18 percent commission ($5,400).

Because the staff gets paid once per month, Hal allows each employee to take up to $2,000 per month in advance. When sales commissions are calculated, the amount of each employee's advanced pay is subtracted from the commission. If any salesperson's commissions are less than the amount of their advance, they must reimburse Hal for the difference. To calculate a salesperson's monthly pay, Hal uses the following formula:

$$pay = sales \times commission\ rate - advanced\ pay$$

Hal has asked you to write a program that makes this calculation for him. The following general algorithm outlines the steps the program must take.

1. *Get the salesperson's monthly sales.*
2. *Get the amount of advanced pay.*
3. *Use the amount of monthly sales to determine the commission rate.*
4. *Calculate the salesperson's pay using the formula previously shown. If the amount is negative, indicate that the salesperson must reimburse the company.*

Program 5-23 shows the code, which is written using several functions. Rather than presenting the entire program at once, let's first examine the main function and then each function separately. Here is the main function:

Program 5-23 (commission_rate.py) main function

```
1  # This program calculates a salesperson's pay
2  # at Make Your Own Music.
3  def main():
4      # Get the amount of sales.
5      sales = get_sales()
6
7      # Get the amount of advanced pay.
8      advanced_pay = get_advanced_pay()
9
10     # Determine the commission rate.
11     comm_rate = determine_comm_rate(sales)
12
13     # Calculate the pay.
14     pay = sales * comm_rate - advanced_pay
15
16     # Display the amount of pay.
17     print('The pay is $', format(pay, ',.2f'), sep='')
18
19     # Determine whether the pay is negative.
20     if pay < 0:
21         print('The Salesperson must reimburse')
22         print('the company.')
23
```

Line 5 calls the get_sales function, which gets the amount of sales from the user and returns that value. The value that is returned from the function is assigned to the sales variable. Line 8 calls the get_advanced_pay function, which gets the amount of advanced pay from the user and returns that value. The value that is returned from the function is assigned to the advanced_pay variable.

Line 11 calls the determine_comm_rate function, passing sales as an argument. This function returns the rate of commission for the amount of sales. That value is assigned to the comm_rate variable. Line 14 calculates the amount of pay, then line 17 displays that amount. The if statement in lines 20 through 22 determines whether the pay is negative, and if so, displays a message indicating that the salesperson must reimburse the company. The get_sales function definition is next.

Program 5-23 (commission_rate.py) get_sales function

```
24 # The get_sales function gets a salesperson's
25 # monthly sales from the user and returns that value.
26 def get_sales():
27     # Get the amount of monthly sales.
```

```
28         monthly_sales = float(input('Enter the monthly sales: '))
29
30         # Return the amount entered.
31         return monthly_sales
32
```

The purpose of the get_sales function is to prompt the user to enter the amount of sales for a salesperson and return that amount. Line 28 prompts the user to enter the sales and stores the user's input in the monthly_sales variable. Line 31 returns the amount in the monthly_sales variable. Next is the definition of the get_advanced_pay function.

Program 5-23 **(commission_rate.py) get_advanced_pay function**

```
33     # The get_advanced_pay function gets the amount of
34     # advanced pay given to the salesperson and returns
35     # that amount.
36     def get_advanced_pay():
37         # Get the amount of advanced pay.
38         print('Enter the amount of advanced pay, or')
39         print('enter 0 if no advanced pay was given.')
40         advanced = float(input('Advanced pay: '))
41
42         # Return the amount entered.
43         return advanced
44
```

The purpose of the get_advanced_pay function is to prompt the user to enter the amount of advanced pay for a salesperson and return that amount. Lines 38 and 39 tell the user to enter the amount of advanced pay (or 0 if none was given). Line 40 gets the user's input and stores it in the advanced variable. Line 43 returns the amount in the advanced variable. Defining the determine_comm_rate function comes next.

Program 5-23 **(commission_rate.py) determine_comm_rate function**

```
45     # The determine_comm_rate function accepts the
46     # amount of sales as an argument and returns the
47     # applicable commission rate.
48     def determine_comm_rate(sales):
49         # Determine the commission rate.
50         if sales < 10000.00:
51             rate = 0.10
52         elif sales >= 10000 and sales <= 14999.99:
53             rate = 0.12
54         elif sales >= 15000 and sales <= 17999.99:
55             rate = 0.14
56         elif sales >= 18000 and sales <= 21999.99:
57             rate = 0.16
```

(program continues)

Program 5-23 *(continued)*

```
58      else:
59          rate = 0.18
60
61      # Return the commission rate.
62      return rate
63
```

The `determine_comm_rate` function accepts the amount of sales as an argument, and it returns the applicable commission rate for that amount of sales. The `if-elif-else` statement in lines 50 through 59 tests the `sales` parameter and assigns the correct value to the local `rate` variable. Line 62 returns the value in the local `rate` variable.

Program Output (with input shown in bold)

```
Enter the monthly sales: 14650.00 [Enter]
Enter the amount of advanced pay, or
enter 0 if no advanced pay was given.
Advanced pay: 1000.00 [Enter]
The pay is $758.00
```

Program Output (with input shown in bold)

```
Enter the monthly sales: 9000.00 [Enter]
Enter the amount of advanced pay, or
enter 0 if no advanced pay was given.
Advanced pay: 0 [Enter]
The pay is $900.00
```

Program Output (with input shown in bold)

```
Enter the monthly sales: 12000.00 [Enter]
Enter the amount of advanced pay, or
enter 0 if no advanced pay was given.
Advanced pay: 2000.00 [Enter]
The pay is $-560.00
The salesperson must reimburse
the company.
```

Returning Strings

So far, you've seen examples of functions that return numbers. You can also write functions that return strings. For example, the following function prompts the user to enter his or her name, then returns the string that the user entered:

```
def get_name():
    # Get the user's name.
    name = input('Enter your name: ')
    # Return the name.
    return name
```

Returning Boolean Values

Python allows you to write *Boolean functions,* which return either `True` or `False`. You can use a Boolean function to test a condition, then return either `True` or `False` to indicate whether the condition exists. Boolean functions are useful for simplifying complex conditions that are tested in decision and repetition structures.

For example, suppose you are designing a program that will ask the user to enter a number, then determine whether that number is even or odd. The following code shows how you can make that determination:

```
number = int(input('Enter a number: '))
if (number % 2) == 0:
    print('The number is even.')
else:
    print('The number is odd.')
```

Let's take a closer look at the Boolean expression being tested by this `if-else` statement:

```
(number % 2) == 0
```

This expression uses the `%` operator, which was introduced in Chapter 2. This is called the remainder operator. It divides two numbers and returns the remainder of the division. So this code is saying, "If the remainder of `number` divided by 2 is equal to 0, then display a message indicating the number is even, or else display a message indicating the number is odd."

Because dividing an even number by 2 will always give a remainder of 0, this logic will work. The code would be easier to understand, however, if you could somehow rewrite it to say, "If the number is even, then display a message indicating it is even, or else display a message indicating it is odd." As it turns out, this can be done with a Boolean function. In this example, you could write a Boolean function named `is_even` that accepts a number as an argument and returns `True` if the number is even, or `False` otherwise. The following is the code for such a function:

```
def is_even(number):
    # Determine whether number is even. If it is,
    # set status to true. Otherwise, set status
    # to false.
    if (number % 2) == 0:
        status = True
    else:
        status = False
    # Return the value of the status variable.
    return status
```

Then, you can rewrite the `if-else` statement so it calls the `is_even` function to determine whether `number` is even:

```
number = int(input('Enter a number: '))
if is_even(number):
    print('The number is even.')
else:
    print('The number is odd.')
```

Not only is this logic easier to understand, but now you have a function that you can call in the program anytime you need to test a number to determine whether it is even.

Using Boolean Functions in Validation Code

You can also use Boolean functions to simplify complex input validation code. For instance, suppose you are writing a program that prompts the user to enter a product model number and should only accept the values 100, 200, and 300. You could design the input algorithm as follows:

```
# Get the model number.
model = int(input('Enter the model number: '))
# Validate the model number.
while model != 100 and model != 200 and model != 300:
    print('The valid model numbers are 100, 200 and 300.')
    model = int(input('Enter a valid model number: '))
```

The validation loop uses a long compound Boolean expression that will iterate as long as `model` does not equal 100 *and* `model` does not equal 200 *and* `model` does not equal 300. Although this logic will work, you can simplify the validation loop by writing a Boolean function to test the `model` variable then calling that function in the loop. For example, suppose you pass the `model` variable to a function you write named `is_invalid`. The function returns `True` if `model` is invalid, or `False` otherwise. You could rewrite the validation loop as follows:

```
# Validate the model number.
while is_invalid(model):
    print('The valid model numbers are 100, 200 and 300.')
    model = int(input('Enter a valid model number: '))
```

This makes the loop easier to read. It is evident now that the loop iterates as long as `model` is invalid. The following code shows how you might write the `is_invalid` function. It accepts a model number as an argument, and if the argument is not 100 and the argument is not 200 and the argument is not 300, the function returns `True` to indicate that it is invalid. Otherwise, the function returns `False`.

```
def is_invalid(mod_num):
    if mod_num != 100 and mod_num != 200 and mod_num != 300:
        status = True
    else:
        status = False
    return status
```

Returning Multiple Values

The examples of value-returning functions that we have looked at so far return a single value. In Python, however, you are not limited to returning only one value. You can specify multiple expressions separated by commas after the `return` statement, as shown in this general format:

```
return expression1, expression2, etc.
```

As an example, look at the following definition for a function named get_name. The function prompts the user to enter his or her first and last names. These names are stored in two local variables: first and last. The return statement returns both of the variables.

```
def get_name():
    # Get the user's first and last names.
    first = input('Enter your first name: ')
    last = input('Enter your last name: ')
    # Return both names.
    return first, last
```

When you call this function in an assignment statement, you need to use two variables on the left side of the = operator. Here is an example:

```
first_name, last_name = get_name()
```

The values listed in the return statement are assigned, in the order that they appear, to the variables on the left side of the = operator. After this statement executes, the value of the first variable will be assigned to first_name, and the value of the last variable will be assigned to last_name. Note the number of variables on the left side of the = operator must match the number of values returned by the function. Otherwise, an error will occur.

Checkpoint

5.31 What is the purpose of the return statement in a function?

5.32 Look at the following function definition:

```
def do_something(number):
    return number * 2
```

a. What is the name of the function?
b. What does the function do?
c. Given the function definition, what will the following statement display?

```
print(do_something(10))
```

5.33 What is a Boolean function?

5.9 The math Module

CONCEPT: The Python standard library's math module contains numerous functions that can be used in mathematical calculations.

The math module in the Python standard library contains several functions that are useful for performing mathematical operations. Table 5-2 lists many of the functions in the math module. These functions typically accept one or more values as arguments, perform a mathematical operation using the arguments, and return the result. (All of the functions listed in Table 5-2 return a float value, except the ceil and floor functions, which return int values.) For example, one of the functions is named sqrt. The sqrt function accepts an argument and returns the square root of the argument. Here is an example of how it is used:

```
result = math.sqrt(16)
```

This statement calls the sqrt function, passing 16 as an argument. The function returns the square root of 16, which is then assigned to the `result` variable. Program 5-24 demonstrates the `sqrt` function. Notice the `import math` statement in line 2. You need to write this in any program that uses the `math` module.

Program 5-24 (square_root.py)

```
1   # This program demonstrates the sqrt function.
2   import math
3
4   def main():
5       # Get a number.
6       number = float(input('Enter a number: '))
7
8       # Get the square root of the number.
9       square_root = math.sqrt(number)
10
11      # Display the square root.
12      print('The square root of', number, '0 is', square_root)
13
14  # Call the main function.
15  main()
```

Program Output (with input shown in bold)

```
Enter a number: 25 Enter
The square root of 25.0 is 5.0
```

Program 5-25 shows another example that uses the `math` module. This program uses the hypot function to calculate the length of a right triangle's hypotenuse.

Program 5-25 (hypotenuse.py)

```
# This program calculates the length of a right
# triangle's hypotenuse.
import math

def main():
    # Get the length of the triangle's two sides.
    a = float(input('Enter the length of side A: '))
    b = float(input('Enter the length of side B: '))

    # Calculate the length of the hypotenuse.
    c = math.hypot(a, b)

    # Display the length of the hypotenuse.
    print('The length of the hypotenuse is', c)

# Call the main function.
main()
```

Program Output (with input shown in bold)

```
Enter the length of side A: 5.0 Enter
Enter the length of side B: 12.0 Enter
The length of the hypotenuse is 13.0
```

Table 5-2 Many of the functions in the math module

math Module Function	Description
acos(x)	Returns the arc cosine of x, in radians.
asin(x)	Returns the arc sine of x, in radians.
atan(x)	Returns the arc tangent of x, in radians.
ceil(x)	Returns the smallest integer that is greater than or equal to x.
cos(x)	Returns the cosine of x in radians.
degrees(x)	Assuming x is an angle in radians, the function returns the angle converted to degrees.
exp(x)	Returns e^x
floor(x)	Returns the largest integer that is less than or equal to x.
hypot(x, y)	Returns the length of a hypotenuse that extends from (0, 0) to (x, y).
log(x)	Returns the natural logarithm of x.
log10(x)	Returns the base-10 logarithm of x.
radians(x)	Assuming x is an angle in degrees, the function returns the angle converted to radians.
sin(x)	Returns the sine of x in radians.
sqrt(x)	Returns the square root of x.
tan(x)	Returns the tangent of x in radians.

The math.pi and math.e Values

The math module also defines two variables, pi and e, which are assigned mathematical values for *pi* and *e*. You can use these variables in equations that require their values. For example, the following statement, which calculates the area of a circle, uses pi. (Notice we use dot notation to refer to the variable.)

```
area = math.pi * radius**2
```

Checkpoint

5.34 What import statement do you need to write in a program that uses the math module?

5.35 Write a statement that uses a math module function to get the square root of 100 and assigns it to a variable.

5.36 Write a statement that uses a math module function to convert 45 degrees to radians and assigns the value to a variable.

5.10 Storing Functions in Modules

CONCEPT: A module is a file that contains Python code. Large programs are easier to debug and maintain when they are divided into modules.

As your programs become larger and more complex, the need to organize your code becomes greater. You have already learned that a large and complex program should be divided into functions that each performs a specific task. As you write more and more functions in a program, you should consider organizing the functions by storing them in modules.

A module is simply a file that contains Python code. When you break a program into modules, each module should contain functions that perform related tasks. For example, suppose you are writing an accounting system. You would store all of the account receivable functions in their own module, all of the account payable functions in their own module, and all of the payroll functions in their own module. This approach, which is called *modularization*, makes the program easier to understand, test, and maintain.

Modules also make it easier to reuse the same code in more than one program. If you have written a set of functions that are needed in several different programs, you can place those functions in a module. Then, you can import the module in each program that needs to call one of the functions.

Let's look at a simple example. Suppose your instructor has asked you to write a program that calculates the following:

- The area of a circle
- The circumference of a circle
- The area of a rectangle
- The perimeter of a rectangle

There are obviously two categories of calculations required in this program: those related to circles, and those related to rectangles. You could write all of the circle-related functions in one module, and the rectangle-related functions in another module. Program 5-26 shows the `circle` module. The module contains two function definitions: `area` (which returns the area of a circle), and `circumference` (which returns the circumference of a circle).

Program 5-26 (circle.py)

```
# The circle module has functions that perform
# calculations related to circles.
import math

# The area function accepts a circle's radius as an
# argument and returns the area of the circle.
def area(radius):
    return math.pi * radius**2

```

```
# The circumference function accepts a circle's
# radius and returns the circle's circumference.
def circumference(radius):
    return 2 * math.pi * radius
```

Program 5-27 shows the `rectangle` module. The module contains two function definitions: `area` (which returns the area of a rectangle), and `perimeter` (which returns the perimeter of a rectangle.)

Program 5-27 (rectangle.py)

```
# The rectangle module has functions that perform
# calculations related to rectangles.

# The area function accepts a rectangle's width and
# length as arguments and returns the rectangle's area.
def area(width, length):
    return width * length

# The perimeter function accepts a rectangle's width
# and length as arguments and returns the rectangle's
# perimeter.
def perimeter(width, length):
    return 2 * (width + length)
```

Notice both of these files contain function definitions, but they do not contain code that calls the functions. That will be done by the program or programs that import these modules.

Before continuing, we should mention the following things about module names:

- A module's file name should end in `.py`. If the module's file name does not end in `.py`, you will not be able to import it into other programs.
- A module's name cannot be the same as a Python key word. An error would occur, for example, if you named a module `for`.

To use these modules in a program, you import them with the `import` statement. Here is an example of how we would import the `circle` module:

```
import circle
```

When the Python interpreter reads this statement it will look for the file `circle.py` in the same folder as the program that is trying to import it. If it finds the file, it will load it into memory. If it does not find the file, an error occurs.[2]

[2] Actually the Python interpreter is set up to look in various other predefined locations in your system when it does not find a module in the program's folder. If you choose to learn about the advanced features of Python, you can learn how to specify where the interpreter looks for modules.

Once a module is imported you can call its functions. Assuming `radius` is a variable that is assigned the radius of a circle, here is an example of how we would call the `area` and `circumference` functions:

```
my_area = circle.area(radius)
my_circum = circle.circumference(radius)
```

Program 5-28 shows a complete program that uses these modules.

Program 5-28 (geometry.py)

```
# This program allows the user to choose various
# geometry calculations from a menu. This program
# imports the circle and rectangle modules.
import circle
import rectangle

# Constants for the menu choices
AREA_CIRCLE_CHOICE = 1
CIRCUMFERENCE_CHOICE = 2
AREA_RECTANGLE_CHOICE = 3
PERIMETER_RECTANGLE_CHOICE = 4
QUIT_CHOICE = 5

# The main function.
def main():
    # The choice variable controls the loop
    # and holds the user's menu choice.
    choice = 0

    while choice != QUIT_CHOICE:
        # display the menu.
        display_menu()

        # Get the user's choice.
        choice = int(input('Enter your choice: '))

        # Perform the selected action.
        if choice == AREA_CIRCLE_CHOICE:
            radius = float(input("Enter the circle's radius: "))
            print('The area is', circle.area(radius))
        elif choice == CIRCUMFERENCE_CHOICE:
            radius = float(input("Enter the circle's radius: "))
            print('The circumference is',
                  circle.circumference(radius))
        elif choice == AREA_RECTANGLE_CHOICE:
            width = float(input("Enter the rectangle's width: "))
            length = float(input("Enter the rectangle's length: "))
            print('The area is', rectangle.area(width, length))
```

```
        elif choice == PERIMETER_RECTANGLE_CHOICE:
            width = float(input("Enter the rectangle's width: "))
            length = float(input("Enter the rectangle's length: "))
            print('The perimeter is',
                  rectangle.perimeter(width, length))
        elif choice == QUIT_CHOICE:
            print('Exiting the program. . .')
        else:
            print('Error: invalid selection.')

# The display_menu function displays a menu.
def display_menu():
    print('    MENU')
    print('1) Area of a circle')
    print('2) Circumference of a circle')
    print('3) Area of a rectangle')
    print('4) Perimeter of a rectangle')
    print('5) Quit')

# Call the main function.
main()
```

Program Output (with input shown in bold)

```
    MENU
1) Area of a circle
2) Circumference of a circle
3) Area of a rectangle
4) Perimeter of a rectangle
5) Quit
Enter your choice: 1 [Enter]
Enter the circle's radius: 10
The area is 314.159265359
    MENU
1) Area of a circle
2) Circumference of a circle
3) Area of a rectangle
4) Perimeter of a rectangle
5) Quit
Enter your choice: 2 [Enter]
Enter the circle's radius: 10
The circumference is 62.8318530718
    MENU
1) Area of a circle
2) Circumference of a circle
3) Area of a rectangle
4) Perimeter of a rectangle
5) Quit
```

(program output continues)

Program Output *(continued)*

```
Enter your choice: 3 Enter
Enter the rectangle's width: 5
Enter the rectangle's length: 10
The area is 50
        MENU
1) Area of a circle
2) Circumference of a circle
3) Area of a rectangle
4) Perimeter of a rectangle
5) Quit
Enter your choice: 4 Enter
Enter the rectangle's width: 5
Enter the rectangle's length: 10
The perimeter is 30
        MENU
1) Area of a circle
2) Circumference of a circle
3) Area of a rectangle
4) Perimeter of a rectangle
5) Quit
Enter your choice: 5 Enter
Exiting the program ...
```

Menu-Driven Programs

Program 5-28 is an example of a menu-driven program. A *menu-driven program* displays a list of the operations on the screen, and allows the user to select the operation that he or she wants the program to perform. The list of operations that is displayed on the screen is called a *menu*. When Program 5-28 is running, the user enters 1 to calculate the area of a circle, 2 to calculate the circumference of a circle, and so forth.

Once the user types a menu selection, the program uses a decision structure to determine which menu item the user selected. An `if-elif-else` statement is used in Program 5-28 (in lines 28 through 47) to carry out the user's desired action. The entire process of displaying a menu, getting the user's selection, and carrying out that selection is repeated by a `while` loop (which begins in line 14). The loop repeats until the user selects 5 (Quit) from the menu.

5.11 Turtle Graphics: Modularizing Code with Functions

CONCEPT: Commonly needed turtle graphics operations can be stored in functions and then called whenever needed.

Using the turtle to draw a shape usually requires several steps. For example, suppose you want to draw a 100-pixel wide square that is filled with the color blue. These are the steps that you would take:

```
turtle.fillcolor('blue')
turtle.begin_fill()
for count in range(4):
    turtle.forward(100)
    turtle.left(90)
turtle.end_fill()
```

Writing these six lines of code doesn't seem like a lot of work, but what if we need to draw a lot of blue squares, in different locations on the screen? Suddenly, we find ourselves writing similar lines of code, over and over. We can simplify our program (and save a lot of time) by writing a function that draws a square at a specified location, and then calling that function anytime we need it.

Program 5-29 demonstrates such a function. The `square` function is defined in lines 14 through 23. The `square` function has the following parameters:

- `x` and `y`: These are the (*X*, *Y*) coordinates of the square's lower-left corner.
- `width`: This is the width, in pixels, of each side of the square.
- `color`: This is the name of the fill color, as a string.

In the `main` function, we call the `square` function three times:

- In line 5, we draw a square, positioning its lower-left corner at (100, 0). The square is 50 pixels wide, and filled with the color red.
- In line 6, we draw a square, positioning its lower-left corner at (–150, –100). The square is 200 pixels wide, and filled with the color blue.
- In line 7, we draw a square, positioning its lower-left corner at (–200, 150). The square is 75 pixels wide, and filled with the color green.

The program draws the three squares shown in Figure 5-26.

Program 5-29 (draw_squares.py)

```
1   import turtle
2
3   def main():
4       turtle.hideturtle()
5       square(100, 0, 50, 'red')
6       square(-150, -100, 200, 'blue')
7       square(-200, 150, 75, 'green')
8
9   # The square function draws a square. The x and y parameters
10  # are the coordinates of the lower-left corner. The width
11  # parameter is the width of each side. The color parameter
12  # is the fill color, as a string.
13
14  def square(x, y, width, color):
15      turtle.penup()                # Raise the pen
16      turtle.goto(x, y)             # Move to the specified location
17      turtle.fillcolor(color)       # Set the fill color
18      turtle.pendown()              # Lower the pen
19      turtle.begin_fill()           # Start filling
```

(program continues)

Program 5-29 *(continued)*

```
    for count in range(4):          # Draw a square
        turtle.forward(width)
        turtle.left(90)
    turtle.end_fill()               # End filling

# Call the main function.
main()
```

Figure 5-26 Output of Program 5-29

Program 5-30 shows another example that uses a function to modularize the code for drawing a circle. The `circle` function is defined in lines 14 through 21. The `circle` function has the following parameters:

- `x` and `y`: These are the (*X*, *Y*) coordinates of the circle's center point.
- `radius`: This is the circle's radius, in pixels.
- `color`: This is the name of the fill color, as a string.

In the `main` function, we call the `circle` function three times:

- In line 5, we draw a circle, positioning its center point at (0, 0). The circle's radius is 100 pixels, and it is filled with the color red.
- In line 6, we draw a circle, positioning its center point at (–150, –75). The circle's radius is 50 pixels wide, and it is filled with the color blue.
- In line 7, we draw a circle, positioning its center point at (–200, 150). The circle's radius is 75 pixels, and it is filled with the color green.

The program draws the three circles shown in Figure 5-27.

Program 5-30 **(draw_circles.py)**

```
1  import turtle
2
3  def main():
```

```
    turtle.hideturtle()
    circle(0, 0, 100, 'red')
    circle(-150, -75, 50, 'blue')
    circle(-200, 150, 75, 'green')

# The circle function draws a circle. The x and y parameters
# are the coordinates of the center point. The radius
# parameter is the circle's radius. The color parameter
# is the fill color, as a string.

def circle(x, y, radius, color):
    turtle.penup()                 # Raise the pen
    turtle.goto(x, y - radius)     # Position the turtle
    turtle.fillcolor(color)        # Set the fill color
    turtle.pendown()               # Lower the pen
    turtle.begin_fill()            # Start filling
    turtle.circle(radius)          # Draw a circle
    turtle.end_fill()              # End filling

# Call the main function.
main()
```

Figure 5-27 Output of Program 5-30

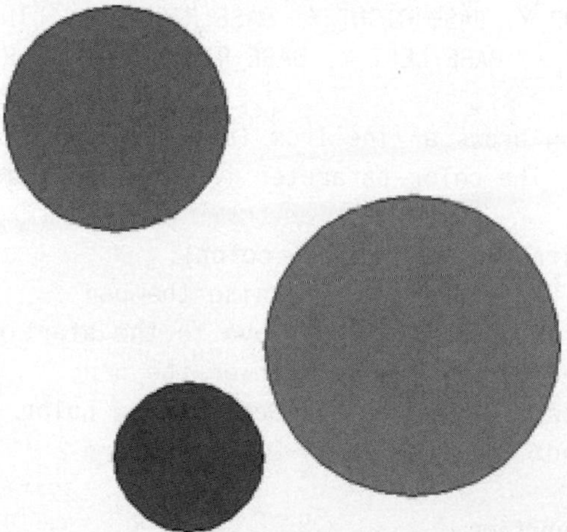

Program 5-31 shows another example that uses a function to modularize the code for drawing a line. The `line` function is defined in lines 20 through 25. The `line` function has the following parameters:

- `startX` and `startY`: These are the (*X*, *Y*) coordinates of the line's starting point.
- `endX` and `endY`: These are the (*X*, *Y*) coordinates of the line's ending point.
- `color`: This is the name of the line's color, as a string.

In the `main` function, we call the `circle` function three times to draw a triangle:

- In line 13, we draw a line from the triangle's top point (0, 100) to its left base point (–100, –100). The line's color is red.
- In line 14, we draw a line from the triangle's top point (0, 100) to its right base point (100, 100). The line's color is blue.
- In line 15, we draw a line from the triangle's left base point (–100, –100) to its right base point (100, 100). The line's color is green.

The program draws the triangle shown in Figure 5-28.

Program 5-31 (draw_lines.py)

```
1  import turtle
2
3  # Named constants for the triangle's points
4  TOP_X = 0
5  TOP_Y = 100
6  BASE_LEFT_X = -100
7  BASE_LEFT_Y = -100
8  BASE_RIGHT_X = 100
9  BASE_RIGHT_Y = -100
10
11 def main():
12     turtle.hideturtle()
13     line(TOP_X, TOP_Y, BASE_LEFT_X, BASE_LEFT_Y, 'red')
14     line(TOP_X, TOP_Y, BASE_RIGHT_X, BASE_RIGHT_Y, 'blue')
15     line(BASE_LEFT_X, BASE_LEFT_Y, BASE_RIGHT_X, BASE_RIGHT_Y, 'green')
16
17 # The line function draws a line from (startX, startY)
18 # to (endX, endY). The color parameter is the line's color.
19
20 def line(startX, startY, endX, endY, color):
21     turtle.penup()                 # Raise the pen
22     turtle.goto(startX, startY)    # Move to the starting point
23     turtle.pendown()               # Lower the pen
24     turtle.pencolor(color)         # Set the pen color
25     turtle.goto(endX, endY)        # Draw a square
26
27 # Call the main function.
28 main()
```

Figure 5-28 Output of Program 5-31

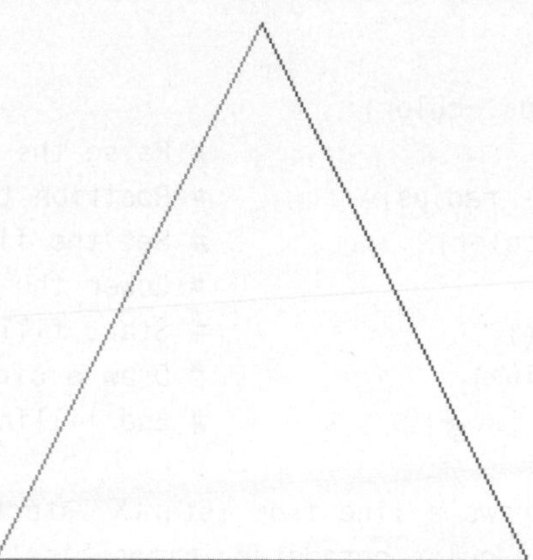

Storing Your Graphics Functions in a Module

As you write more and more turtle graphics functions, you should consider storing them in a module. Then, you can import the module into any program that needs to use them. For example, Program 5-32 shows a module named `my_graphics.py` that contains the `square`, `circle`, and `line` functions presented earlier. Program 5-33 shows how to import the module and call the functions it contains. Figure 5-29 shows the program's output.

Program 5-32 (my_graphics.py)

```
# Turtle graphics functions
import turtle

# The square function draws a square. The x and y parameters
# are the coordinates of the lower-left corner. The width
# parameter is the width of each side. The color parameter
# is the fill color, as a string.

def square(x, y, width, color):
    turtle.penup()              # Raise the pen
    turtle.goto(x, y)           # Move to the specified location
    turtle.fillcolor(color)     # Set the fill color
    turtle.pendown()            # Lower the pen
    turtle.begin_fill()         # Start filling
    for count in range(4):      # Draw a square
        turtle.forward(width)
        turtle.left(90)
    turtle.end_fill()           # End filling

# The circle function draws a circle. The x and y parameters
# are the coordinates of the center point. The radius
# parameter is the circle's radius. The color parameter
# is the fill color, as a string.
```

(program continues)

Program 5-32 *(continued)*

```

def circle(x, y, radius, color):
    turtle.penup()                    # Raise the pen
    turtle.goto(x, y - radius)        # Position the turtle
    turtle.fillcolor(color)           # Set the fill color
    turtle.pendown()                  # Lower the pen
    turtle.begin_fill()               # Start filling
    turtle.circle(radius)             # Draw a circle
    turtle.end_fill()                 # End filling

# The line function draws a line from (startX, startY)
# to (endX, endY). The color parameter is the line's color.

def line(startX, startY, endX, endY, color):
    turtle.penup()                    # Raise the pen
    turtle.goto(startX, startY)       # Move to the starting point
    turtle.pendown()                  # Lower the pen
    turtle.pencolor(color)            # Set the pen color
    turtle.goto(endX, endY)           # Draw a square
```

Program 5-33 (graphics_mod_demo.py)

```
import turtle
import my_graphics

# Named constants
X1 = 0
Y1 = 100
X2 = -100
Y2 = -100
X3 = 100
Y3 = -100
RADIUS = 50

def main():
    turtle.hideturtle()

    # Draw a square.
    my_graphics.square(X2, Y2, (X3 - X2), 'gray')

    # Draw some circles.
    my_graphics.circle(X1, Y1, RADIUS, 'blue')
    my_graphics.circle(X2, Y2, RADIUS, 'red')
    my_graphics.circle(X3, Y3, RADIUS, 'green')

    # Draw some lines.
```

```
    my_graphics.line(X1, Y1, X2, Y2, 'black')
    my_graphics.line(X1, Y1, X3, Y3, 'black')
    my_graphics.line(X2, Y2, X3, Y3, 'black')

main()
```

Figure 5-29 Output of Program 5-33

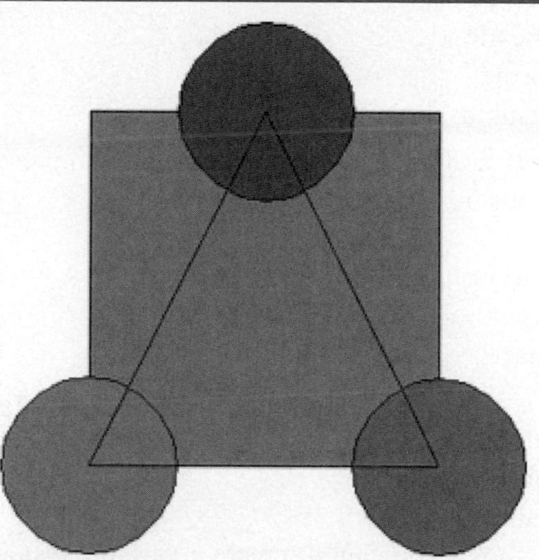

Review Questions

Multiple Choice

1. A group of statements that exist within a program for the purpose of performing a specific task is a(n) __________.
   a. block
   b. parameter
   c. function
   d. expression
2. A design technique that helps to reduce the duplication of code within a program and is a benefit of using functions is __________.
   a. code reuse
   b. divide and conquer
   c. debugging
   d. facilitation of teamwork
3. The first line of a function definition is known as the __________.
   a. body
   b. introduction
   c. initialization
   d. header

4. You __________ a function to execute it.
   a. define
   b. call
   c. import
   d. export
5. A design technique that programmers use to break down an algorithm into functions is known as __________.
   a. top-down design
   b. code simplification
   c. code refactoring
   d. hierarchical subtasking
6. A __________ is a diagram that gives a visual representation of the relationships between functions in a program.
   a. flowchart
   b. function relationship chart
   c. symbol chart
   d. hierarchy chart
7. A __________ is a variable that is created inside a function.
   a. global variable
   b. local variable
   c. hidden variable
   d. none of the above; you cannot create a variable inside a function
8. A(n) __________ is the part of a program in which a variable may be accessed.
   a. declaration space
   b. area of visibility
   c. scope
   d. mode
9. A(n) __________ is a piece of data that is sent into a function.
   a. argument
   b. parameter
   c. header
   d. packet
10. A(n) __________ is a special variable that receives a piece of data when a function is called.
   a. argument
   b. parameter
   c. header
   d. packet
11. A variable that is visible to every function in a program file is a __________.
   a. local variable
   b. universal variable
   c. program-wide variable
   d. global variable

12. When possible, you should avoid using _________ variables in a program.
    a. local
    b. global
    c. reference
    d. parameter
13. This is a prewritten function that is built into a programming language.
    a. standard function
    b. library function
    c. custom function
    d. cafeteria function
14. This standard library function returns a random integer within a specified range of values.
    a. `random`
    b. `randint`
    c. `random_integer`
    d. `uniform`
15. This standard library function returns a random floating-point number in the range of 0.0 up to 1.0 (but not including 1.0).
    a. `random`
    b. `randint`
    c. `random_integer`
    d. `uniform`
16. This standard library function returns a random floating-point number within a specified range of values.
    a. `random`
    b. `randint`
    c. `random_integer`
    d. `uniform`
17. This statement causes a function to end and sends a value back to the part of the program that called the function.
    a. `end`
    b. `send`
    c. `exit`
    d. `return`
18. This is a design tool that describes the input, processing, and output of a function.
    a. hierarchy chart
    b. IPO chart
    c. datagram chart
    d. data processing chart
19. This type of function returns either `True` or `False`.
    a. Binary
    b. `true_false`
    c. Boolean
    d. logical

20. This is a `math` module function.
    a. `derivative`
    b. `factor`
    c. `sqrt`
    d. `differentiate`

True or False

1. The phrase "divide and conquer" means that all of the programmers on a team should be divided and work in isolation.
2. Functions make it easier for programmers to work in teams.
3. Function names should be as short as possible.
4. Calling a function and defining a function mean the same thing.
5. A flowchart shows the hierarchical relationships between functions in a program.
6. A hierarchy chart does not show the steps that are taken inside a function.
7. A statement in one function can access a local variable in another function.
8. In Python, you cannot write functions that accept multiple arguments.
9. In Python, you can specify which parameter an argument should be passed into a function call.
10. You cannot have both keyword arguments and non-keyword arguments in a function call.
11. Some library functions are built into the Python interpreter.
12. You do not need to have an import statement in a program to use the functions in the `random` module.
13. Complex mathematical expressions can sometimes be simplified by breaking out part of the expression and putting it in a function.
14. A function in Python can return more than one value.
15. IPO charts provide only brief descriptions of a function's input, processing, and output, but do not show the specific steps taken in a function.

Short Answer

1. How do functions help you to reuse code in a program?
2. Name and describe the two parts of a function definition.
3. When a function is executing, what happens when the end of the function block is reached?
4. What is a local variable? What statements are able to access a local variable?
5. What is a local variable's scope?
6. Why do global variables make a program difficult to debug?
7. Suppose you want to select a random number from the following sequence:

   0, 5, 10, 15, 20, 25, 30

   What library function would you use?
8. What statement do you have to have in a value-returning function?
9. What three things are listed on an IPO chart?
10. What is a Boolean function?
11. What are the advantages of breaking a large program into modules?

Algorithm Workbench

1. Write a function named `times_ten`. The function should accept an argument and display the product of its argument multiplied times 10.
2. Examine the following function header, then write a statement that calls the function, passing 12 as an argument.

   ```
   def show_value(quantity):
   ```
3. Look at the following function header:

   ```
   def my_function(a, b, c):
   ```

   Now look at the following call to `my_function`:

   ```
   my_function(3, 2, 1)
   ```

   When this call executes, what value will be assigned to `a`? What value will be assigned to `b`? What value will be assigned to `c`?
4. What will the following program display?

   ```
   def main():
       x = 1
       y = 3.4
       print(x, y)
       change_us(x, y)
       print(x, y)
   def change_us(a, b):
       a = 0
       b = 0
       print(a, b)
   main()
   ```
5. Look at the following function definition:

   ```
   def my_function(a, b, c):
       d = (a + c) / b
       print(d)
   ```

   a. Write a statement that calls this function and uses keyword arguments to pass 2 into `a`, 4 into `b`, and 6 into `c`.

   b. What value will be displayed when the function call executes?
6. Write a statement that generates a random number in the range of 1 through 100 and assigns it to a variable named `rand`.
7. The following statement calls a function named `half`, which returns a value that is half that of the argument. (Assume the `number` variable references a `float` value.) Write code for the function.

   ```
   result = half(number)
   ```
8. A program contains the following function definition:

   ```
   def cube(num):
       return num * num * num
   ```

   Write a statement that passes the value 4 to this function and assigns its return value to the variable `result`.

9. Write a function named `times_ten` that accepts a number as an argument. When the function is called, it should return the value of its argument multiplied times 10.
10. Write a function named `get_first_name` that asks the user to enter his or her first name, and returns it.

Programming Exercises

VideoNote
The Kilometer Converter Problem

1. Kilometer Converter

Write a program that asks the user to enter a distance in kilometers, then converts that distance to miles. The conversion formula is as follows:

$$Miles = Kilometers \times 0.6214$$

2. Sales Tax Program Refactoring

Programming Exercise #6 in Chapter 2 was the Sales Tax program. For that exercise, you were asked to write a program that calculates and displays the county and state sales tax on a purchase. If you have already written that program, redesign it so the subtasks are in functions. If you have not already written that program, write it using functions.

3. How Much Insurance?

Many financial experts advise that property owners should insure their homes or buildings for at least 80 percent of the amount it would cost to replace the structure. Write a program that asks the user to enter the replacement cost of a building, then displays the minimum amount of insurance he or she should buy for the property.

4. Automobile Costs

Write a program that asks the user to enter the monthly costs for the following expenses incurred from operating his or her automobile: loan payment, insurance, gas, oil, tires, and maintenance. The program should then display the total monthly cost of these expenses, and the total annual cost of these expenses.

5. Property Tax

A county collects property taxes on the assessment value of property, which is 60 percent of the property's actual value. For example, if an acre of land is valued at $10,000, its assessment value is $6,000. The property tax is then 72¢ for each $100 of the assessment value. The tax for the acre assessed at $6,000 will be $43.20. Write a program that asks for the actual value of a piece of property and displays the assessment value and property tax.

6. Calories from Fat and Carbohydrates

A nutritionist who works for a fitness club helps members by evaluating their diets. As part of her evaluation, she asks members for the number of fat grams and carbohydrate grams that they consumed in a day. Then, she calculates the number of calories that result from the fat, using the following formula:

$$calories\ from\ fat = fat\ grams \times 9$$

Next, she calculates the number of calories that result from the carbohydrates, using the following formula:

$$\textit{calories from carbs} = \textit{carb grams} \times 4$$

The nutritionist asks you to write a program that will make these calculations.

7. Stadium Seating

There are three seating categories at a stadium. Class A seats cost \$20, Class B seats cost \$15, and Class C seats cost \$10. Write a program that asks how many tickets for each class of seats were sold, then displays the amount of income generated from ticket sales.

8. Paint Job Estimator

A painting company has determined that for every 112 square feet of wall space, one gallon of paint and eight hours of labor will be required. The company charges \$35.00 per hour for labor. Write a program that asks the user to enter the square feet of wall space to be painted and the price of the paint per gallon. The program should display the following data:

- The number of gallons of paint required
- The hours of labor required
- The cost of the paint
- The labor charges
- The total cost of the paint job

9. Monthly Sales Tax

A retail company must file a monthly sales tax report listing the total sales for the month, and the amount of state and county sales tax collected. The state sales tax rate is 5 percent and the county sales tax rate is 2.5 percent. Write a program that asks the user to enter the total sales for the month. From this figure, the application should calculate and display the following:

- The amount of county sales tax
- The amount of state sales tax
- The total sales tax (county plus state)

VideoNote
The Feet to Inches Problem

10. Feet to Inches

One foot equals 12 inches. Write a function named `feet_to_inches` that accepts a number of feet as an argument and returns the number of inches in that many feet. Use the function in a program that prompts the user to enter a number of feet then displays the number of inches in that many feet.

11. Math Quiz

Write a program that gives simple math quizzes. The program should display two random numbers that are to be added, such as:

```
  247
+ 129
```

The program should allow the student to enter the answer. If the answer is correct, a message of congratulations should be displayed. If the answer is incorrect, a message showing the correct answer should be displayed.

12. Maximum of Two Values

Write a function named `max` that accepts two integer values as arguments and returns the value that is the greater of the two. For example, if 7 and 12 are passed as arguments to the function, the function should return 12. Use the function in a program that prompts the user to enter two integer values. The program should display the value that is the greater of the two.

13. Falling Distance

When an object is falling because of gravity, the following formula can be used to determine the distance the object falls in a specific time period:

$$d = \frac{1}{2} gt^2$$

The variables in the formula are as follows: d is the distance in meters, g is 9.8, and t is the amount of time, in seconds, that the object has been falling.

Write a function named `falling_distance` that accepts an object's falling time (in seconds) as an argument. The function should return the distance, in meters, that the object has fallen during that time interval. Write a program that calls the function in a loop that passes the values 1 through 10 as arguments and displays the return value.

14. Kinetic Energy

In physics, an object that is in motion is said to have kinetic energy. The following formula can be used to determine a moving object's kinetic energy:

$$KE = \frac{1}{2} mv^2$$

The variables in the formula are as follows: KE is the kinetic energy, m is the object's mass in kilograms, and v is the object's velocity in meters per second.

Write a function named `kinetic_energy` that accepts an object's mass (in kilograms) and velocity (in meters per second) as arguments. The function should return the amount of kinetic energy that the object has. Write a program that asks the user to enter values for mass and velocity, then calls the `kinetic_energy` function to get the object's kinetic energy.

15. Test Average and Grade

Write a program that asks the user to enter five test scores. The program should display a letter grade for each score and the average test score. Write the following functions in the program:

- `calc_average`. This function should accept five test scores as arguments and return the average of the scores.
- `determine_grade`. This function should accept a test score as an argument and return a letter grade for the score based on the following grading scale:

Score	Letter Grade
90–100	A
80–89	B
70–79	C
60–69	D
Below 60	F

16. Odd/Even Counter

In this chapter, you saw an example of how to write an algorithm that determines whether a number is even or odd. Write a program that generates 100 random numbers and keeps a count of how many of those random numbers are even, and how many of them are odd.

17. Prime Numbers

A prime number is a number that is only evenly divisible by itself and 1. For example, the number 5 is prime because it can only be evenly divided by 1 and 5. The number 6, however, is not prime because it can be divided evenly by 1, 2, 3, and 6.

Write a Boolean function named `is_prime` which takes an integer as an argument and returns true if the argument is a prime number, or false otherwise. Use the function in a program that prompts the user to enter a number then displays a message indicating whether the number is prime.

TIP: Recall that the `%` operator divides one number by another and returns the remainder of the division. In an expression such as `num1 % num2`, the `%` operator will return 0 if `num1` is evenly divisible by `num2`.

18. Prime Number List

This exercise assumes that you have already written the `is_prime` function in Programming Exercise 17. Write another program that displays all of the prime numbers from 1 to 100. The program should have a loop that calls the `is_prime` function.

19. Future Value

Suppose you have a certain amount of money in a savings account that earns compound monthly interest, and you want to calculate the amount that you will have after a specific number of months. The formula is as follows:

$$F = P \times (1 + i)^t$$

The terms in the formula are:

- F is the future value of the account after the specified time period.
- P is the present value of the account.
- i is the monthly interest rate.
- t is the number of months.

Write a program that prompts the user to enter the account's present value, monthly interest rate, and the number of months that the money will be left in the account. The program should pass these values to a function that returns the future value of the account, after the specified number of months. The program should display the account's future value.

20. Random Number Guessing Game

Write a program that generates a random number in the range of 1 through 100, and asks the user to guess what the number is. If the user's guess is higher than the random number, the program should display "Too high, try again." If the user's guess is lower than the random number, the program should display "Too low, try again." If the user guesses the number, the application should congratulate the user and generate a new random number so the game can start over.

Optional Enhancement: Enhance the game so it keeps count of the number of guesses that the user makes. When the user correctly guesses the random number, the program should display the number of guesses.

21. Rock, Paper, Scissors Game

Write a program that lets the user play the game of Rock, Paper, Scissors against the computer. The program should work as follows:

1. When the program begins, a random number in the range of 1 through 3 is generated. If the number is 1, then the computer has chosen rock. If the number is 2, then the computer has chosen paper. If the number is 3, then the computer has chosen scissors. (Don't display the computer's choice yet.)
2. The user enters his or her choice of "rock," "paper," or "scissors" at the keyboard.
3. The computer's choice is displayed.
4. A winner is selected according to the following rules:
   - If one player chooses rock and the other player chooses scissors, then rock wins. (Rock smashes scissors.)
   - If one player chooses scissors and the other player chooses paper, then scissors wins. (Scissors cuts paper.)
   - If one player chooses paper and the other player chooses rock, then paper wins. (Paper wraps rock.)
   - If both players make the same choice, the game must be played again to determine the winner.

22. Turtle Graphics: Triangle Function

Write a function named `triangle` that uses the turtle graphics library to draw a triangle. The functions should take arguments for the *X* and *Y* coordinates of the triangle's vertices, and the color with which the triangle should be filled. Demonstrate the function in a program.

23. Turtle Graphics: Modular Snowman

Write a program that uses turtle graphics to display a snowman, similar to the one shown in Figure 5-30. In addition to a `main` function, the program should also have the following functions:

- `drawBase`. This function should draw the base of the snowman, which is the large snowball at the bottom.
- `drawMidSection`. This function should draw the middle snowball.
- `drawArms`. This function should draw the snowman's arms.
- `drawHead`. This function should draw the snowman's head, with eyes, mouth, and other facial features you desire.
- `drawHat`. This function should draw the snowman's hat.

Figure 5-30 Snowman

24. Turtle Graphics: Rectangular Pattern

In a program, write a function named `drawPattern` that uses the turtle graphics library to draw the rectangular pattern shown in Figure 5-31. The `drawPattern` function should accept two arguments: one that specifies the pattern's width, and another that specifies the pattern's height. (The example shown in Figure 5-31 shows how the pattern would appear when the width and the height are the same.) When the program runs, the program should ask the user for the width and height of the pattern, then pass these values as arguments to the `drawPattern` function.

Figure 5-31 Rectangular pattern

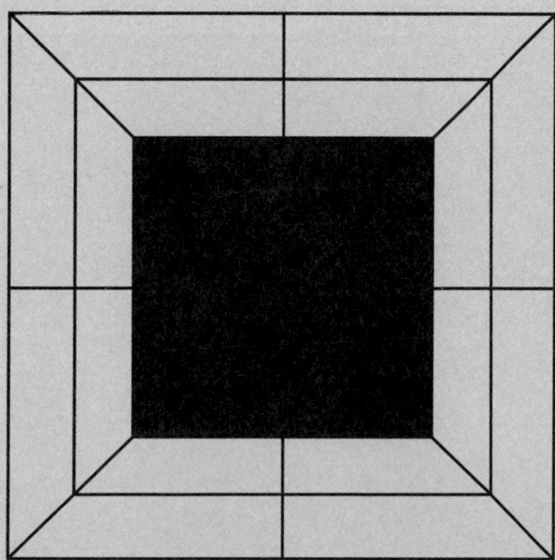

25. Turtle Graphics: Checkerboard

Write a turtle graphics program that uses the `square` function presented in this chapter, along with a loop (or loops) to draw the checkerboard pattern shown in Figure 5-32.

Figure 5-32 Checkerboard pattern

26. Turtle Graphics: City Skyline

Write a turtle graphics program that draws a city skyline similar to the one shown in Figure 5-33. The program's overall task is to draw an outline of some city buildings against a night sky. Modularize the program by writing functions that perform the following tasks:

- Draw the outline of buildings.
- Draw some windows on the buildings.
- Use randomly placed dots as the stars (make sure the stars appear on the sky, not on the buildings).

Figure 5-33 City skyline

CHAPTER 6 Files and Exceptions

TOPICS

6.1 Introduction to File Input and Output

CONCEPT: When a program needs to save data for later use, it writes the data in a file. The data can be read from the file at a later time.

The programs you have written so far require the user to reenter data each time the program runs, because data stored in RAM (referenced by variables) disappears once the program stops running. If a program is to retain data between the times it runs, it must have a way of saving it. Data is saved in a file, which is usually stored on a computer's disk. Once the data is saved in a file, it will remain there after the program stops running. Data stored in a file can be retrieved and used at a later time.

Most of the commercial software packages that you use on a day-to-day basis store data in files. The following are a few examples:

- **Word processors.** Word processing programs are used to write letters, memos, reports, and other documents. The documents are then saved in files so they can be edited and printed.
- **Image editors.** Image editing programs are used to draw graphics and edit images, such as the ones that you take with a digital camera. The images that you create or edit with an image editor are saved in files.
- **Spreadsheets.** Spreadsheet programs are used to work with numerical data. Numbers and mathematical formulas can be inserted into the rows and columns of the spreadsheet. The spreadsheet can then be saved in a file for use later.
- **Games.** Many computer games keep data stored in files. For example, some games keep a list of player names with their scores stored in a file. These games typically

display the players' names in order of their scores, from highest to lowest. Some games also allow you to save your current game status in a file so you can quit the game and then resume playing it later without having to start from the beginning.

- **Web browers.** Sometimes when you visit a Web page, the browser stores a small file known as a *cookie* on your computer. Cookies typically contain information about the browsing session, such as the contents of a shopping cart.

Programs that are used in daily business operations rely extensively on files. Payroll programs keep employee data in files, inventory programs keep data about a company's products in files, accounting systems keep data about a company's financial operations in files, and so on.

Programmers usually refer to the process of saving data in a file as "writing data" to the file. When a piece of data is written to a file, it is copied from a variable in RAM to the file. This is illustrated in Figure 6-1. The term *output file* is used to describe a file that data is written to. It is called an output file because the program stores output in it.

Figure 6-1 Writing data to a file

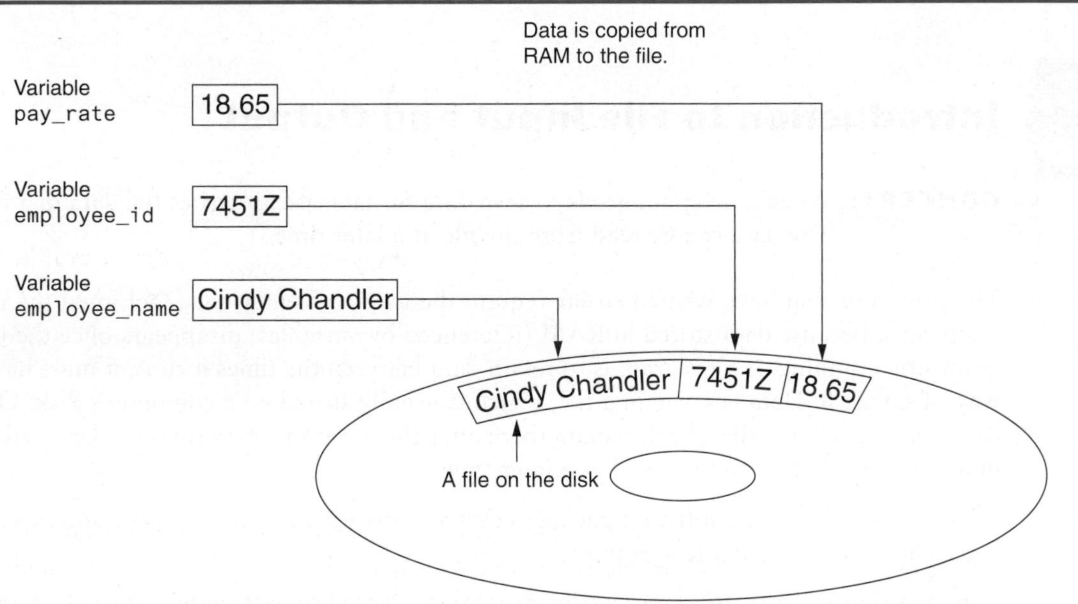

The process of retrieving data from a file is known as "reading data" from the file. When a piece of data is read from a file, it is copied from the file into RAM and referenced by a variable. Figure 6-2 illustrates this. The term *input file* is used to describe a file from which data is read. It is called an input file because the program gets input from the file.

Figure 6-2 Reading data from a file

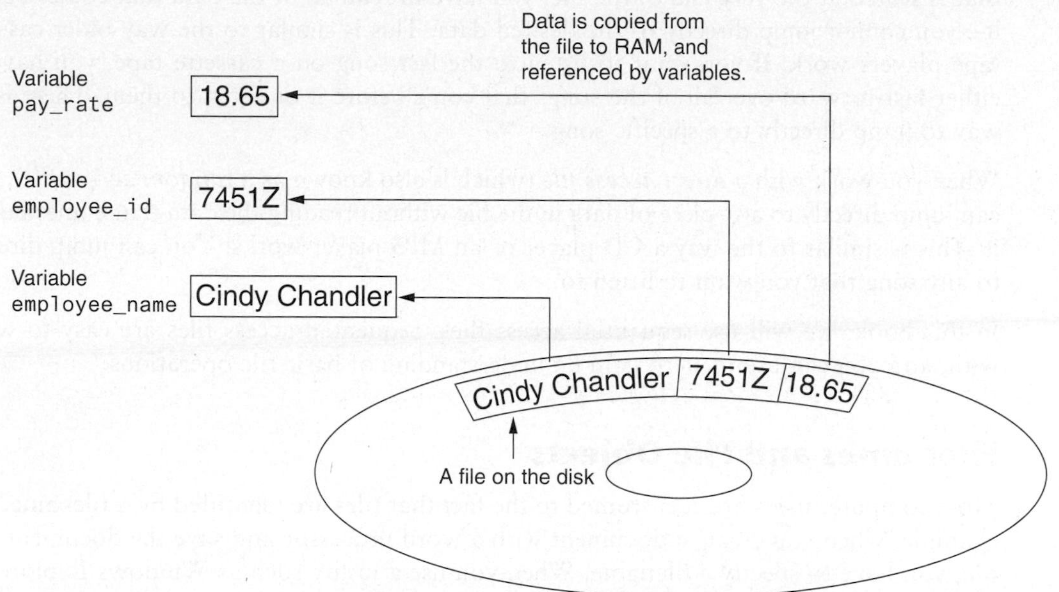

This chapter discusses how to write data to files and read data from files. There are always three steps that must be taken when a file is used by a program.

1. **Open the file.** Opening a file creates a connection between the file and the program. Opening an output file usually creates the file on the disk and allows the program to write data to it. Opening an input file allows the program to read data from the file.
2. **Process the file.** In this step, data is either written to the file (if it is an output file) or read from the file (if it is an input file).
3. **Close the file.** When the program is finished using the file, the file must be closed. Closing a file disconnects the file from the program.

Types of Files

In general, there are two types of files: text and binary. A *text file* contains data that has been encoded as text, using a scheme such as ASCII or Unicode. Even if the file contains numbers, those numbers are stored in the file as a series of characters. As a result, the file may be opened and viewed in a text editor such as Notepad. A *binary file* contains data that has not been converted to text. The data that is stored in a binary file is intended only for a program to read. As a consequence, you cannot view the contents of a binary file with a text editor.

Although Python allows you to work both text files and binary files, we will work only with text files in this book. That way, you will be able to use an editor to inspect the files that your programs create.

File Access Methods

Most programming languages provide two different ways to access data stored in a file: sequential access and direct access. When you work with a *sequential access file*, you access data from the beginning of the file to the end of the file. If you want to read a piece of data that is stored at the very end of the file, you have to read all of the data that comes before it—you cannot jump directly to the desired data. This is similar to the way older cassette tape players work. If you want to listen to the last song on a cassette tape, you have to either fast-forward over all of the songs that come before it or listen to them. There is no way to jump directly to a specific song.

When you work with a *direct access file* (which is also known as a *random access file*), you can jump directly to any piece of data in the file without reading the data that comes before it. This is similar to the way a CD player or an MP3 player works. You can jump directly to any song that you want to listen to.

In this book, we will use sequential access files. Sequential access files are easy to work with, and you can use them to gain an understanding of basic file operations.

Filenames and File Objects

Most computer users are accustomed to the fact that files are identified by a filename. For example, when you create a document with a word processor and save the document in a file, you have to specify a filename. When you use a utility such as Windows Explorer to examine the contents of your disk, you see a list of filenames. Figure 6-3 shows how three files named `cat.jpg`, `notes.txt`, and `resume.docx` might be graphically represented in Windows.

Figure 6-3 Three files

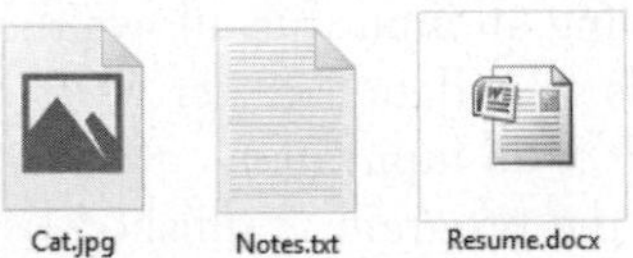

Each operating system has its own rules for naming files. Many systems support the use of *filename extensions*, which are short sequences of characters that appear at the end of a filename preceded by a period (which is known as a "dot"). For example, the files depicted in Figure 6-3 have the extensions `.jpg`, `.txt`, and `.doc`. The extension usually indicates the type of data stored in the file. For example, the `.jpg` extension usually indicates that the file contains a graphic image that is compressed according to the JPEG image standard. The `.txt` extension usually indicates that the file contains text. The `.doc` extension (as well as the `.docx` extension) usually indicates that the file contains a Microsoft Word document.

In order for a program to work with a file on the computer's disk, the program must create a file object in memory. A *file object* is an object that is associated with a specific file and provides a way for the program to work with that file. In the program, a variable references the file object. This variable is used to carry out any operations that are performed on the file. This concept is shown in Figure 6-4.

Figure 6-4 A variable name references a file object that is associated with a file

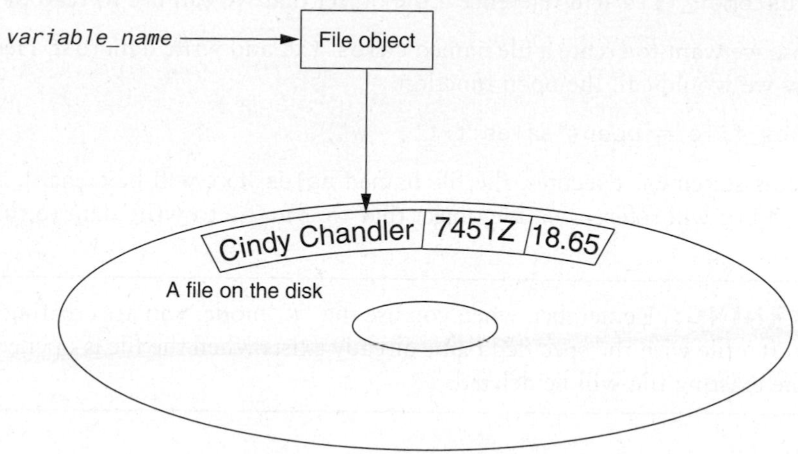

Opening a File

You use the open function in Python to open a file. The open function creates a file object and associates it with a file on the disk. Here is the general format of how the open function is used:

```
file_variable = open(filename, mode)
```

In the general format:

- *file_variable* is the name of the variable that will reference the file object.
- *filename* is a string specifying the name of the file.
- *mode* is a string specifying the mode (reading, writing, etc.) in which the file will be opened. Table 6-1 shows three of the strings that you can use to specify a mode. (There are other, more complex modes. The modes shown in Table 6-1 are the ones we will use in this book.)

Table 6-1 Some of the Python file modes

Mode	Description
'r'	Open a file for reading only. The file cannot be changed or written to.
'w'	Open a file for writing. If the file already exists, erase its contents. If it does not exist, create it.
'a'	Open a file to be written to. All data written to the file will be appended to its end. If the file does not exist, create it.

For example, suppose the file customers.txt contains customer data, and we want to open it for reading. Here is an example of how we would call the open function:

```
customer_file = open('customers.txt', 'r')
```

After this statement executes, the file named `customers.txt` will be opened, and the variable `customer_file` will reference a file object that we can use to read data from the file.

Suppose we want to create a file named `sales.txt` and write data to it. Here is an example of how we would call the open function:

```
sales_file = open('sales.txt', 'w')
```

After this statement executes, the file named `sales.txt` will be created, and the variable `sales_file` will reference a file object that we can use to write data to the file.

WARNING: Remember, when you use the `'w'` mode, you are creating the file on the disk. If a file with the specified name already exists when the file is opened, the contents of the existing file will be deleted.

Specifying the Location of a File

When you pass a file name that does not contain a path as an argument to the `open` function, the Python interpreter assumes the file's location is the same as that of the program. For example, suppose a program is located in the following folder on a Windows computer:

```
C:\Users\Blake\Documents\Python
```

If the program is running and it executes the following statement, the file `test.txt` is created in the same folder:

```
test_file = open('test.txt', 'w')
```

If you want to open a file in a different location, you can specify a path as well as a filename in the argument that you pass to the `open` function. If you specify a path in a string literal (particularly on a Windows computer), be sure to prefix the string with the letter `r`. Here is an example:

```
test_file = open(r'C:\Users\Blake\temp\test.txt', 'w')
```

This statement creates the file `test.txt` in the folder `C:\Users\Blake\temp`. The `r` prefix specifies that the string is a *raw string*. This causes the Python interpreter to read the backslash characters as literal backslashes. Without the `r` prefix, the interpreter would assume that the backslash characters were part of escape sequences, and an error would occur.

Writing Data to a File

So far in this book, you have worked with several of Python's library functions, and you have even written your own functions. Now, we will introduce you to another type of function, which is known as a method. A *method* is a function that belongs to an object and performs some operation using that object. Once you have opened a file, you use the file object's methods to perform operations on the file.

For example, file objects have a method named `write` that can be used to write data to a file. Here is the general format of how you call the `write` method:

```
file_variable.write(string)
```

In the format, `file_variable` is a variable that references a file object, and `string` is a string that will be written to the file. The file must be opened for writing (using the `'w'` or `'a'` mode) or an error will occur.

Let's assume `customer_file` references a file object, and the file was opened for writing with the `'w'` mode. Here is an example of how we would write the string 'Charles Pace' to the file:

```
customer_file.write('Charles Pace')
```

The following code shows another example:

```
name = 'Charles Pace'
customer_file.write(name)
```

The second statement writes the value referenced by the `name` variable to the file associated with `customer_file`. In this case, it would write the string 'Charles Pace' to the file. (These examples show a string being written to a file, but you can also write numeric values.)

Once a program is finished working with a file, it should close the file. Closing a file disconnects the program from the file. In some systems, failure to close an output file can cause a loss of data. This happens because the data that is written to a file is first written to a *buffer*, which is a small "holding section" in memory. When the buffer is full, the system writes the buffer's contents to the file. This technique increases the system's performance, because writing data to memory is faster than writing it to a disk. The process of closing an output file forces any unsaved data that remains in the buffer to be written to the file.

In Python, you use the file object's `close` method to close a file. For example, the following statement closes the file that is associated with `customer_file`:

```
customer_file.close()
```

Program 6-1 shows a complete Python program that opens an output file, writes data to it, then closes it.

Program 6-1 (file_write.py)

```
# This program writes three lines of data
# to a file.
def main():
    # Open a file named philosophers.txt.
    outfile = open('philosophers.txt', 'w')

    # Write the names of three philosphers
    # to the file.
    outfile.write('John Locke\n')
    outfile.write('David Hume\n')
    outfile.write('Edmund Burke\n')

    # Close the file.
    outfile.close()

# Call the main function.
main()
```

Line 5 opens the file `philosophers.txt` using the `'w'` mode. (This causes the file to be created and opens it for writing.) It also creates a file object in memory and assigns that object to the `outfile` variable.

The statements in lines 9 through 11 write three strings to the file. Line 9 writes the string `'John Locke\n'`, line 10 writes the string `'David Hume\n'`, and line 11 writes the string `'Edmund Burke\n'`. Line 14 closes the file. After this program runs, the three items shown in Figure 6-5 will be written to the `philosophers.txt` file.

Figure 6-5 Contents of the file `philosophers.txt`

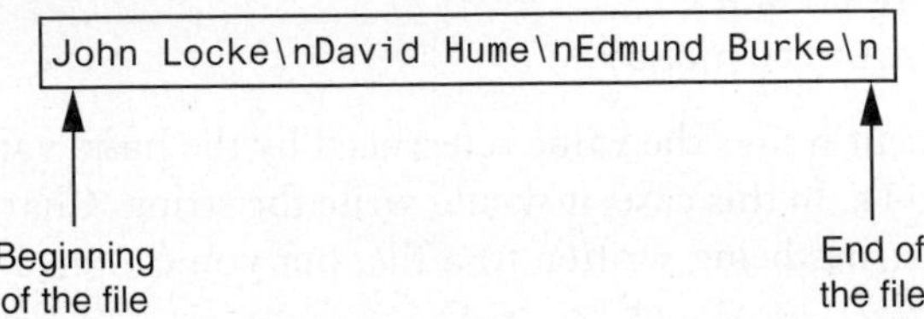

Notice each of the strings written to the file end with `\n`, which you will recall is the newline escape sequence. The `\n` not only separates the items that are in the file, but also causes each of them to appear in a separate line when viewed in a text editor. For example, Figure 6-6 shows the `philosophers.txt` file as it appears in Notepad.

Figure 6-6 Contents of `philosophers.txt` in Notepad

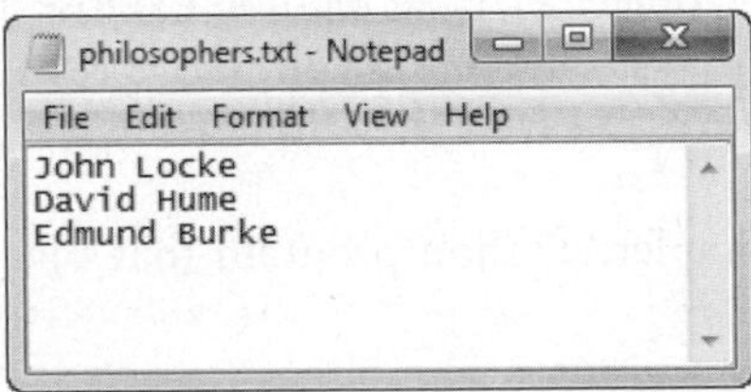

Reading Data From a File

If a file has been opened for reading (using the `'r'` mode) you can use the file object's `read` method to read its entire contents into memory. When you call the `read` method, it returns the file's contents as a string. For example, Program 6-2 shows how we can use the `read` method to read the contents of the `philosophers.txt` file we created earlier.

Program 6-2 (`file_read.py`)

```
# This program reads and displays the contents
# of the philosophers.txt file.
def main():
    # Open a file named philosophers.txt.
    infile = open('philosophers.txt', 'r')

    # Read the file's contents.
    file_contents = infile.read()

```

```
10         # Close the file.
11         infile.close()
12 
13         # Print the data that was read into
14         # memory.
15         print(file_contents)
16 
17     # Call the main function.
18     main()
```

Program Output

```
John Locke
David Hume
Edmund Burke
```

The statement in line 5 opens the `philosophers.txt` file for reading, using the `'r'` mode. It also creates a file object and assigns the object to the `infile` variable. Line 8 calls the `infile.read` method to read the file's contents. The file's contents are read into memory as a string and assigned to the `file_contents` variable. This is shown in Figure 6-7. Then the statement in line 15 prints the string that is referenced by the variable.

Figure 6-7 The `file_contents` variable references the string that was read from the file

```
file_contents ────────► John Locke\nDavid Hume\nEdmund Burke\n
```

Although the `read` method allows you to easily read the entire contents of a file with one statement, many programs need to read and process the items that are stored in a file one at a time. For example, suppose a file contains a series of sales amounts, and you need to write a program that calculates the total of the amounts in the file. The program would read each sale amount from the file and add it to an accumulator.

In Python, you can use the `readline` method to read a line from a file. (A line is simply a string of characters that are terminated with a `\n`.) The method returns the line as a string, including the `\n`. Program 6-3 shows how we can use the `readline` method to read the contents of the `philosophers.txt` file, one line at a time.

Program 6-3 (`line_read.py`)

```
# This program reads the contents of the
# philosophers.txt file one line at a time.
def main():
    # Open a file named philosophers.txt.
    infile = open('philosophers.txt', 'r')

    # Read three lines from the file.
    line1 = infile.readline()
    line2 = infile.readline()
    line3 = infile.readline()
```

(program continues)

Program 6-3 *(continued)*

```
11
12         # Close the file.
13         infile.close()
14
15         # Print the data that was read into
16         # memory.
17         print(line1)
18         print(line2)
19         print(line3)
20
21     # Call the main function.
22     main()
```

Program Output

```
John Locke

David Hume

Edmund Burke
```

Before we examine the code, notice that a blank line is displayed after each line in the output. This is because each item that is read from the file ends with a newline character (`\n`). Later, you will learn how to remove the newline character.

The statement in line 5 opens the `philosophers.txt` file for reading, using the `'r'` mode. It also creates a file object and assigns the object to the `infile` variable. When a file is opened for reading, a special value known as a *read position* is internally maintained for that file. A file's read position marks the location of the next item that will be read from the file. Initially, the read position is set to the beginning of the file. After the statement in line 5 executes, the read position for the `philosophers.txt` file will be positioned as shown in Figure 6-8.

Figure 6-8 Initial read position

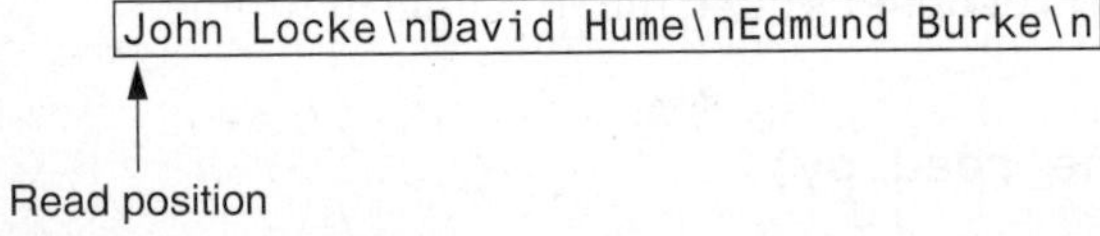

The statement in line 8 calls the `infile.readline` method to read the first line from the file. The line, which is returned as a string, is assigned to the `line1` variable. After this statement executes the `line1` variable will be assigned the string `'John Locke\n'`. In addition, the file's read position will be advanced to the next line in the file, as shown in Figure 6-9.

Figure 6-9 Read position advanced to the next line

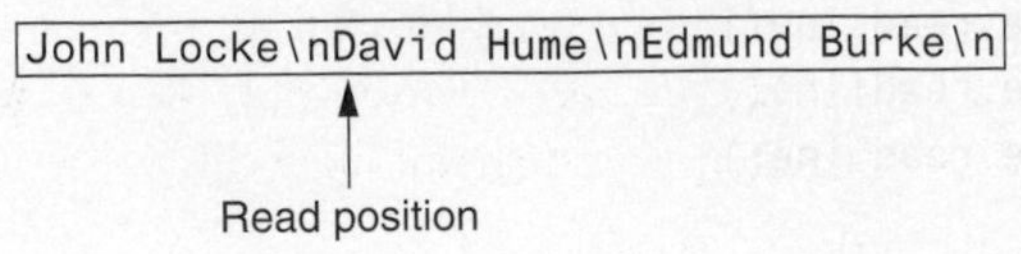

Then the statement in line 9 reads the next line from the file and assigns it to the `line2` variable. After this statement executes the `line2` variable will reference the string `'David Hume\n'`. The file's read position will be advanced to the next line in the file, as shown in Figure 6-10.

Figure 6-10 Read position advanced to the next line

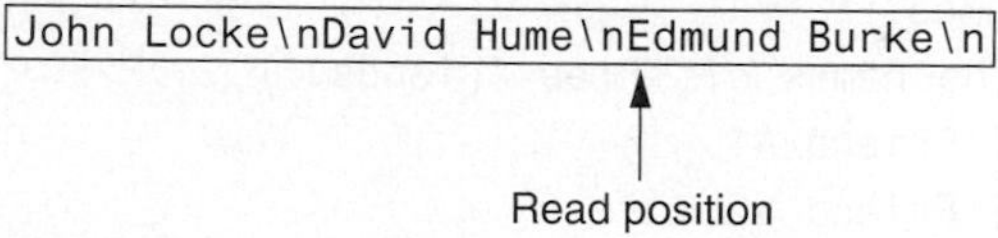

Then the statement in line 10 reads the next line from the file and assigns it to the `line3` variable. After this statement executes, the `line3` variable will reference the string `'Edmund Burke\n'`. After this statement executes, the read position will be advanced to the end of the file, as shown in Figure 6-11. Figure 6-12 shows the `line1`, `line2`, and `line3` variables and the strings they reference after these statements have executed.

Figure 6-11 Read position advanced to the end of the file

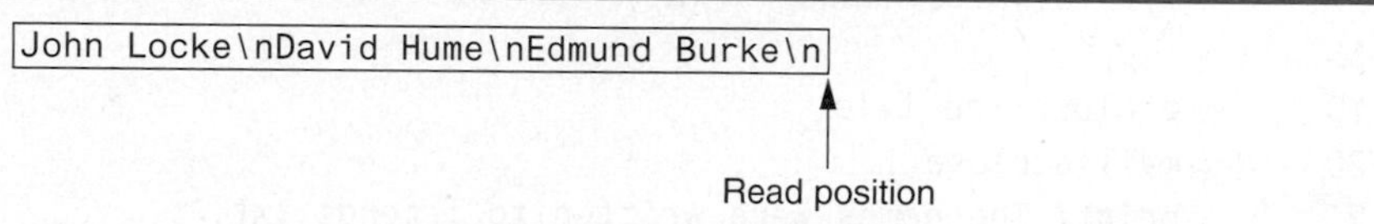

Figure 6-12 The strings referenced by the `line1`, `line2`, and `line3` variables

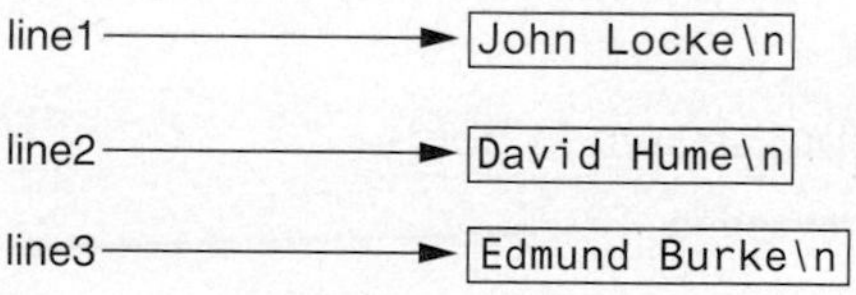

The statement in line 13 closes the file. The statements in lines 17 through 19 display the contents of the `line1`, `line2`, and `line3` variables.

NOTE: If the last line in a file is not terminated with a `\n`, the `readline` method will return the line without a `\n`.

Concatenating a Newline to a String

Program 6-1 wrote three string literals to a file, and each string literal ended with a `\n` escape sequence. In most cases, the data items that are written to a file are not string literals, but values in memory that are referenced by variables. This would be the case in a program that prompts the user to enter data and then writes that data to a file.

When a program writes data that has been entered by the user to a file, it is usually necessary to concatenate a `\n` escape sequence to the data before writing it. This ensures that each piece of data is written to a separate line in the file. Program 6-4 demonstrates how this is done.

Program 6-4 (write_names.py)

```
1  # This program gets three names from the user
2  # and writes them to a file.
3
4  def main():
5      # Get three names.
6      print('Enter the names of three friends.')
7      name1 = input('Friend #1: ')
8      name2 = input('Friend #2: ')
9      name3 = input('Friend #3: ')
10
11     # Open a file named friends.txt.
12     myfile = open('friends.txt', 'w')
13
14     # Write the names to the file.
15     myfile.write(name1 + '\n')
16     myfile.write(name2 + '\n')
17     myfile.write(name3 + '\n')
18
19     # Close the file.
20     myfile.close()
21     print('The names were written to friends.txt.')
22
23 # Call the main function.
24 main()
```

Program Output (with input shown in bold)

```
Enter the names of three friends.
Friend #1: Joe Enter
Friend #2: Rose Enter
Friend #3: Geri Enter
The names were written to friends.txt.
```

Lines 7 through 9 prompt the user to enter three names, and those names are assigned to the variables `name1`, `name2`, and `name3`. Line 12 opens a file named `friends.txt` for writing. Then, lines 15 through 17 write the names entered by the user, each with `'\n'` concatenated to it. As a result, each name will have the `\n` escape sequence added to it when written to the file. Figure 6-13 shows the contents of the file with the names entered by the user in the sample run.

Figure 6-13 The `friends.txt` file

```
Joe\nRose\nGeri\n
```

Reading a String and Stripping the Newline from It

Sometimes complications are caused by the `\n` that appears at the end of the strings that are returned from the `readline` method. For example, did you notice in the sample output of Program 6-3 that a blank line is printed after each line of output? This is because each of the strings that are printed in lines 17 through 19 end with a `\n` escape sequence. When the strings are printed, the `\n` causes an extra blank line to appear.

The `\n` serves a necessary purpose inside a file: it separates the items that are stored in the file. However, in many cases, you want to remove the `\n` from a string after it is read from a file. Each string in Python has a method named `rstrip` that removes, or "strips," specific characters from the end of a string. (It is named `rstrip` because it strips characters from the right side of a string.) The following code shows an example of how the `rstrip` method can be used.

```
name = 'Joanne Manchester\n'
name = name.rstrip('\n')
```

The first statement assigns the string `'Joanne Manchester\n'` to the `name` variable. (Notice the string ends with the `\n` escape sequence.) The second statement calls the `name.rstrip('\n')` method. The method returns a copy of the `name` string without the trailing `\n`. This string is assigned back to the `name` variable. The result is that the trailing `\n` is stripped away from the `name` string.

Program 6-5 is another program that reads and displays the contents of the `philosophers.txt` file. This program uses the `rstrip` method to strip the `\n` from the strings that are read from the file before they are displayed on the screen. As a result, the extra blank lines do not appear in the output.

Program 6-5 (`strip_newline.py`)

```
# This program reads the contents of the
# philosophers.txt file one line at a time.
def main():
    # Open a file named philosophers.txt.
    infile = open('philosophers.txt', 'r')

    # Read three lines from the file.
    line1 = infile.readline()
    line2 = infile.readline()
    line3 = infile.readline()

    # Strip the \n from each string.
    line1 = line1.rstrip('\n')
    line2 = line2.rstrip('\n')
    line3 = line3.rstrip('\n')

    # Close the file.
    infile.close()

    # Print the data that was read into
    # memory.
    print(line1)
```

(program continues)

Program 6-5 *(continued)*

```
    print(line2)
    print(line3)

# Call the main function.
main()
```

Program Output

```
John Locke
David Hume
Edmund Burke
```

Appending Data to an Existing File

When you use the `'w'` mode to open an output file and a file with the specified filename already exists on the disk, the existing file will be deleted and a new empty file with the same name will be created. Sometimes you want to preserve an existing file and append new data to its current contents. Appending data to a file means writing new data to the end of the data that already exists in the file.

In Python, you can use the `'a'` mode to open an output file in *append mode*, which means the following.

- If the file already exists, it will not be erased. If the file does not exist, it will be created.
- When data is written to the file, it will be written at the end of the file's current contents.

For example, assume the file `friends.txt` contains the following names, each in a separate line:

```
Joe
Rose
Geri
```

The following code opens the file and appends additional data to its existing contents.

```
myfile = open('friends.txt', 'a')
myfile.write('Matt\n')
myfile.write('Chris\n')
myfile.write('Suze\n')
myfile.close()
```

After this program runs, the file `friends.txt` will contain the following data:

```
Joe
Rose
Geri
Matt
Chris
Suze
```

Writing and Reading Numeric Data

Strings can be written directly to a file with the `write` method, but numbers must be converted to strings before they can be written. Python has a built-in function named `str` that converts a value to a string. For example, assuming the variable `num` is assigned the value 99, the expression `str(num)` will return the string `'99'`.

Program 6-6 shows an example of how you can use the `str` function to convert a number to a string, and write the resulting string to a file.

Program 6-6 (write_numbers.py)

```
 1  # This program demonstrates how numbers
 2  # must be converted to strings before they
 3  # are written to a text file.
 4
 5  def main():
 6      # Open a file for writing.
 7      outfile = open('numbers.txt', 'w')
 8
 9      # Get three numbers from the user.
10      num1 = int(input('Enter a number: '))
11      num2 = int(input('Enter another number: '))
12      num3 = int(input('Enter another number: '))
13
14      # Write the numbers to the file.
15      outfile.write(str(num1) + '\n')
16      outfile.write(str(num2) + '\n')
17      outfile.write(str(num3) + '\n')
18
19      # Close the file.
20      outfile.close()
21      print('Data written to numbers.txt')
22
23  # Call the main function.
24  main()
```

Program Output (with input shown in bold)

```
Enter a number: 22 [Enter]
Enter another number: 14 [Enter]
Enter another number: -99 [Enter]
Data written to numbers.txt
```

The statement in line 7 opens the file `numbers.txt` for writing. Then the statements in lines 10 through 12 prompt the user to enter three numbers, which are assigned to the variables `num1`, `num2`, and `num3`.

Take a closer look at the statement in line 15, which writes the value referenced by `num1` to the file:

```
outfile.write(str(num1) + '\n')
```

The expression `str(num1) + '\n'` converts the value referenced by `num1` to a string and concatenates the `\n` escape sequence to the string. In the program's sample run, the user entered 22 as the first number, so this expression produces the string `'22\n'`. As a result, the string `'22\n'` is written to the file.

Lines 16 and 17 perform the similar operations, writing the values referenced by `num2` and `num3` to the file. After these statements execute, the values shown in Figure 6-14 will be written to the file. Figure 6-15 shows the file viewed in Notepad.

Figure 6-14 Contents of the `numbers.txt` file

```
22\n14\n-99\n
```

Figure 6-15 The `numbers.txt` file viewed in Notepad

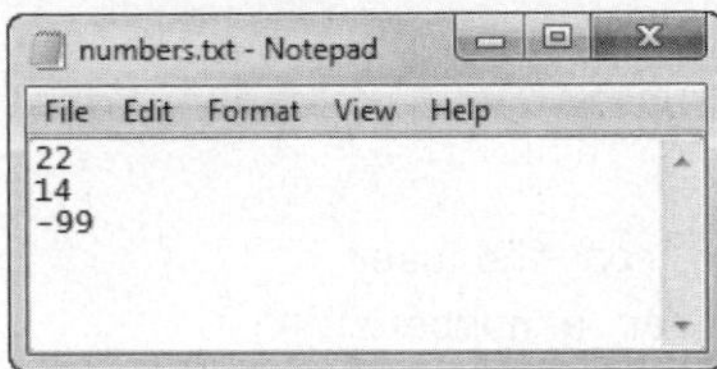

When you read numbers from a text file, they are always read as strings. For example, suppose a program uses the following code to read the first line from the `numbers.txt` file that was created by Program 6-6:

```
1  infile = open('numbers.txt', 'r')
2  value = infile.readline()
3  infile.close()
```

The statement in line 2 uses the `readline` method to read a line from the file. After this statement executes, the `value` variable will reference the string `'22\n'`. This can cause a problem if we intend to perform math with the `value` variable, because you cannot perform math on strings. In such a case you must convert the string to a numeric type.

Recall from Chapter 2 that Python provides the built-in function `int` to convert a string to an integer, and the built-in function `float` to convert a string to a floating-point number. For example, we could modify the code previously shown as follows:

```
1  infile = open('numbers.txt', 'r')
2  string_input = infile.readline()
3  value = int(string_input)
4  infile.close()
```

The statement in line 2 reads a line from the file and assigns it to the `string_input` variable. As a result, `string_input` will reference the string `'22\n'`. Then the statement in line 3 uses the `int` function to convert `string_input` to an integer, and assigns the result to `value`. After this statement executes, the `value` variable will reference the integer 22. (Both the `int` and `float` functions ignore any `\n` at the end of the string that is passed as an argument.)

This code demonstrates the steps involved in reading a string from a file with the `readline` method then converting that string to an integer with the `int` function. In many situations, however, the code can be simplified. A better way is to read the string from the file and convert it in one statement, as shown here:

```
1 infile = open('numbers.txt', 'r')
2 value = int(infile.readline())
3 infile.close()
```

Notice in line 2 a call to the `readline` method is used as the argument to the `int` function. Here's how the code works: the `readline` method is called, and it returns a string. That string is passed to the `int` function, which converts it to an integer. The result is assigned to the `value` variable.

Program 6-7 shows a more complete demonstration. The contents of the `numbers.txt` file are read, converted to integers, and added together.

Program 6-7 (read_numbers.py)

```
# This program demonstrates how numbers that are
# read from a file must be converted from strings
# before they are used in a math operation.

def main():
    # Open a file for reading.
    infile = open('numbers.txt', 'r')

    # Read three numbers from the file.
    num1 = int(infile.readline())
    num2 = int(infile.readline())
    num3 = int(infile.readline())

    # Close the file.
    infile.close()

    # Add the three numbers.
    total = num1 + num2 + num3

    # Display the numbers and their total.
    print('The numbers are:', num1, num2, num3)
    print('Their total is:', total)

# Call the main function.
main()
```

Program Output

```
The numbers are: 22 14 -99
Their total is: -63
```

Checkpoint

6.1 What is an output file?

6.2 What is an input file?

6.3 What three steps must be taken by a program when it uses a file?

6.4 In general, what are the two types of files? What is the difference between these two types of files?

6.5 What are the two types of file access? What is the difference between these two?

6.6 When writing a program that performs an operation on a file, what two file-associated names do you have to work with in your code?

6.7 If a file already exists, what happens to it if you try to open it as an output file (using the `'w'` mode)?

6.8 What is the purpose of opening a file?

6.9 What is the purpose of closing a file?

6.10 What is a file's read position? Initially, where is the read position when an input file is opened?

6.11 In what mode do you open a file if you want to write data to it, but you do not want to erase the file's existing contents? When you write data to such a file, to what part of the file is the data written?

6.2 Using Loops to Process Files

CONCEPT: Files usually hold large amounts of data, and programs typically use a loop to process the data in a file.

VideoNote Using Loops to Process Files

Although some programs use files to store only small amounts of data, files are typically used to hold large collections of data. When a program uses a file to write or read a large amount of data, a loop is typically involved. For example, look at the code in Program 6-8. This program gets sales amounts for a series of days from the user and writes those amounts to a file named `sales.txt`. The user specifies the number of days of sales data he or she needs to enter. In the sample run of the program, the user enters sales amounts for five days. Figure 6-16 shows the contents of the `sales.txt` file containing the data entered by the user in the sample run.

Program 6-8 (write_sales.py)

```
# This program prompts the user for sales amounts
# and writes those amounts to the sales.txt file.

def main():
    # Get the number of days.
    num_days = int(input('For how many days do ' +
                         'you have sales? '))

```

```python
    # Open a new file named sales.txt.
    sales_file = open('sales.txt', 'w')

    # Get the amount of sales for each day and write
    # it to the file.
    for count in range(1, num_days + 1):
        # Get the sales for a day.
        sales = float(input('Enter the sales for day #' +
                            str(count) + ': '))

        # Write the sales amount to the file.
        sales_file.write(str(sales) + '\n')

    # Close the file.
    sales_file.close()
    print('Data written to sales.txt.')

# Call the main function.
main()
```

Program Output (with input shown in bold)

For how many days do you have sales? **5** Enter
Enter the sales for day #1: **1000.0** Enter
Enter the sales for day #2: **2000.0** Enter
Enter the sales for day #3: **3000.0** Enter
Enter the sales for day #4: **4000.0** Enter
Enter the sales for day #5: **5000.0** Enter
Data written to sales.txt.

Figure 6-16 Contents of the `sales.txt` file

```
1000.0\n2000.0\n3000.0\n4000.0\n5000.0\n
```

Reading a File with a Loop and Detecting the End of the File

Quite often, a program must read the contents of a file without knowing the number of items that are stored in the file. For example, the `sales.txt` file that was created by Program 6-8 can have any number of items stored in it, because the program asks the user for the number of days for which he or she has sales amounts. If the user enters 5 as the number of days, the program gets 5 sales amounts and writes them to the file. If the user enters 100 as the number of days, the program gets 100 sales amounts and writes them to the file.

This presents a problem if you want to write a program that processes all of the items in the file, however many there are. For example, suppose you need to write a program that reads all of the amounts in the `sales.txt` file and calculates their total. You can use a loop to read the items in the file, but you need a way of knowing when the end of the file has been reached.

In Python, the `readline` method returns an empty string (`''`) when it has attempted to read beyond the end of a file. This makes it possible to write a `while` loop that determines when the end of a file has been reached. Here is the general algorithm, in pseudocode:

Open the file
Use `readline` *to read the first line from the file*
While the value returned from `readline` *is not an empty string:*
  Process the item that was just read from the file
  Use `readline` *to read the next line from the file.*
Close the file

NOTE: In this algorithm, we call the `readline` method just before entering the `while` loop. The purpose of this method call is to get the first line in the file, so it can be tested by the loop. This initial read operation is called a *priming read.*

Figure 6-17 shows this algorithm in a flowchart.

Figure 6-17 General logic for detecting the end of a file

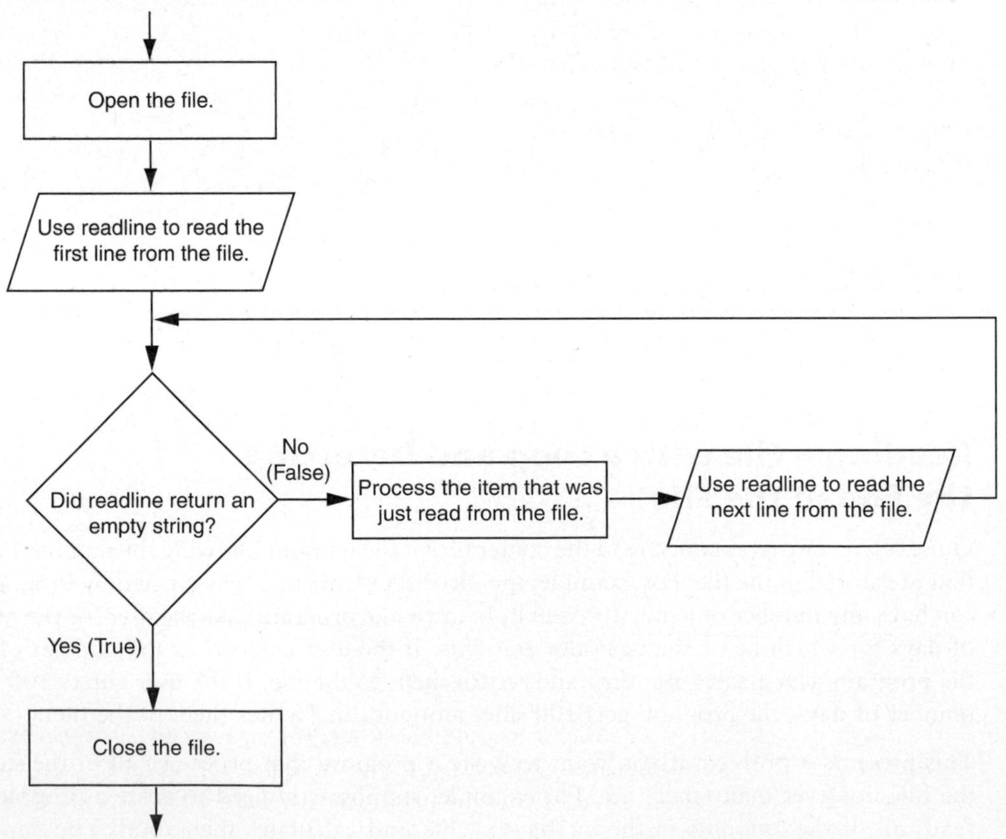

Program 6-9 demonstrates how this can be done in code. The program reads and displays all of the values in the `sales.txt` file.

Program 6-9 (read_sales.py)

```
# This program reads all of the values in
# the sales.txt file.

def main():
    # Open the sales.txt file for reading.
    sales_file = open('sales.txt', 'r')

    # Read the first line from the file, but
    # don't convert to a number yet. We still
    # need to test for an empty string.
    line = sales_file.readline()

    # As long as an empty string is not returned
    # from readline, continue processing.
    while line != '':
        # Convert line to a float.
        amount = float(line)

        # Format and display the amount.
        print(format(amount, '.2f'))

        # Read the next line.
        line = sales_file.readline()

    # Close the file.
    sales_file.close()

# Call the main function.
main()
```

Program Output

```
1000.00
2000.00
3000.00
4000.00
5000.00
```

Using Python's `for` Loop to Read Lines

In the previous example, you saw how the `readline` method returns an empty string when the end of the file has been reached. Most programming languages provide a similar technique for detecting the end of a file. If you plan to learn programming languages other than Python, it is important for you to know how to construct this type of logic.

The Python language also allows you to write a `for` loop that automatically reads the lines in a file without testing for any special condition that signals the end of the file. The loop does not require a priming read operation, and it automatically stops when the end of the file has been reached. When you simply want to read the lines in a file, one after the other, this technique is simpler and more elegant than writing a `while` loop that explicitly tests for an end of the file condition. Here is the general format of the loop:

```
for variable in file_object:
    statement
    statement
    etc.
```

In the general format, *`variable`* is the name of a variable, and *`file_object`* is a variable that references a file object. The loop will iterate once for each line in the file. The first time the loop iterates, *`variable`* will reference the first line in the file (as a string), the second time the loop iterates, *`variable`* will reference the second line, and so forth. Program 6-10 provides a demonstration. It reads and displays all of the items in the `sales.txt` file.

Program 6-10 (read_sales2.py)

```
# This program uses the for loop to read
# all of the values in the sales.txt file.

def main():
    # Open the sales.txt file for reading.
    sales_file = open('sales.txt', 'r')

    # Read all the lines from the file.
    for line in sales_file:
        # Convert line to a float.
        amount = float(line)
        # Format and display the amount.
        print(format(amount, '.2f'))

    # Close the file.
    sales_file.close()

# Call the main function.
main()
```

Program Output

```
1000.00
2000.00
3000.00
4000.00
5000.00
```

In the Spotlight:
Working with Files

Kevin is a freelance video producer who makes TV commercials for local businesses. When he makes a commercial, he usually films several short videos. Later, he puts these short videos together to make the final commercial. He has asked you to write the following two programs.

1. A program that allows him to enter the running time (in seconds) of each short video in a project. The running times are saved to a file.
2. A program that reads the contents of the file, displays the running times, and then displays the total running time of all the segments.

Here is the general algorithm for the first program, in pseudocode:

Get the number of videos in the project.
Open an output file.
For each video in the project:
  Get the video's running time.
  Write the running time to the file.
Close the file.

Program 6-11 shows the code for the first program.

Program 6-11 (save_running_times.py)

```
# This program saves a sequence of video running times
# to the video_times.txt file.

def main():
    # Get the number of videos in the project.
    num_videos = int(input('How many videos are in the project? '))

    # Open the file to hold the running times.
    video_file = open('video_times.txt', 'w')

    # Get each video's running time and write
    # it to the file.
    print('Enter the running times for each video.')
    for count in range(1, num_videos + 1):
        run_time = float(input('Video #' + str(count) + ': '))
        video_file.write(str(run_time) + '\n')

    # Close the file.
    video_file.close()
    print('The times have been saved to video_times.txt.')

# Call the main function.
main()
```

(program continues)

Program 6-11 *(continued)*

Program Output (with input shown in bold)

```
How many videos are in the project? 6 [Enter]
Enter the running times for each video.
Video #1: 24.5 [Enter]
Video #2: 12.2 [Enter]
Video #3: 14.6 [Enter]
Video #4: 20.4 [Enter]
Video #5: 22.5 [Enter]
Video #6: 19.3 [Enter]
The times have been saved to video_times.txt.
```

Here is the general algorithm for the second program:

Initialize an accumulator to 0.
Initialize a count variable to 0.
Open the input file.
For each line in the file:
    Convert the line to a floating-point number. (This is the running time for a video.)
    Add one to the count variable. (This keeps count of the number of videos.)
    Display the running time for this video.
    Add the running time to the accumulator.
Close the file.
Display the contents of the accumulator as the total running time.

Program 6-12 shows the code for the second program.

Program 6-12 (read_running_times.py)

```
# This program the values in the video_times.txt
# file and calculates their total.

def main():
    # Open the video_times.txt file for reading.
    video_file = open('video_times.txt', 'r')

    # Initialize an accumulator to 0.0.
    total = 0.0

    # Initialize a variable to keep count of the videos.
    count = 0

    print('Here are the running times for each video:')

    # Get the values from the file and total them.
    for line in video_file:
        # Convert a line to a float.
        run_time = float(line)
```

```
        # Add 1 to the count variable.
        count += 1

        # Display the time.
        print('Video #', count, ': ', run_time, sep='')

        # Add the time to total.
        total += run_time

    # Close the file.
    video_file.close()

    # Display the total of the running times.
    print('The total running time is', total, 'seconds.')

# Call the main function.
main()
```

Program Output

```
Here are the running times for each video:
Video #1: 24.5
Video #2: 12.2
Video #3: 14.6
Video #4: 20.4
Video #5: 22.5
Video #6: 19.3
The total running time is 113.5 seconds.
```

Checkpoint

6.12 Write a short program that uses a `for` loop to write the numbers 1 through 10 to a file.

6.13 What does it mean when the `readline` method returns an empty string?

6.14 Assume the file `data.txt` exists and contains several lines of text. Write a short program using the `while` loop that displays each line in the file.

6.15 Revise the program that you wrote for Checkpoint 6.14 to use the `for` loop instead of the `while` loop.

6.3 Processing Records

CONCEPT: The data that is stored in a file is frequently organized in records. A record is a complete set of data about an item, and a field is an individual piece of data within a record.

When data is written to a file, it is often organized into records and fields. A *record* is a complete set of data that describes one item, and a *field* is a single piece of data within a record. For example, suppose we want to store data about employees in a file. The file will contain a record for each employee. Each record will be a collection of fields, such as name, ID number, and department. This is illustrated in Figure 6-18.

Figure 6-18 Fields in a record

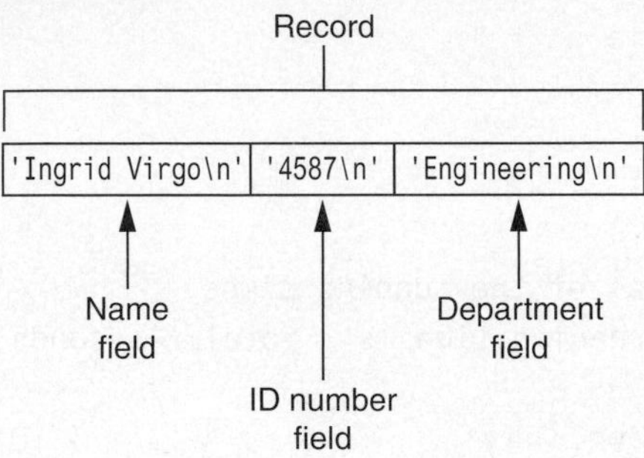

Each time you write a record to a sequential access file, you write the fields that make up the record, one after the other. For example, Figure 6-19 shows a file that contains three employee records. Each record consists of the employee's name, ID number, and department.

Figure 6-19 Records in a file

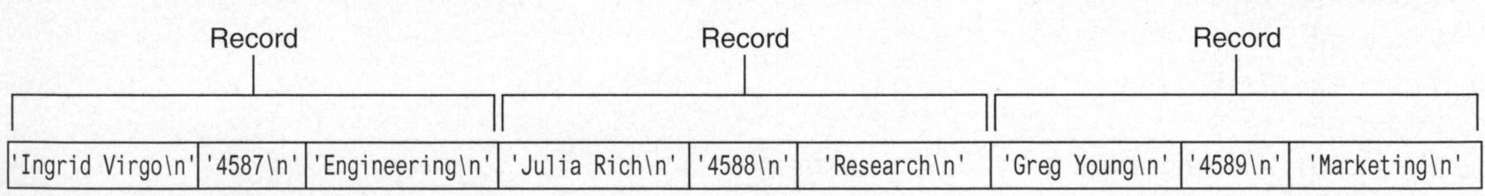

Program 6-13 shows a simple example of how employee records can be written to a file.

Program 6-13 (save_emp_records.py)

```
# This program gets employee data from the user and
# saves it as records in the employee.txt file.

def main():
    # Get the number of employee records to create.
    num_emps = int(input('How many employee records ' +
                         'do you want to create? '))

    # Open a file for writing.
    emp_file = open('employees.txt', 'w')

    # Get each employee's data and write it to
    # the file.
    for count in range(1, num_emps + 1):
```

```
15         # Get the data for an employee.
16         print('Enter data for employee #', count, sep='')
17         name = input('Name: ')
18         id_num = input('ID number: ')
19         dept = input('Department: ')
20 
21         # Write the data as a record to the file.
22         emp_file.write(name + '\n')
23         emp_file.write(id_num + '\n')
24         emp_file.write(dept + '\n')
25 
26         # Display a blank line.
27         print()
28 
29     # Close the file.
30     emp_file.close()
31     print('Employee records written to employees.txt.')
32 
33 # Call the main function.
34 main()
```

Program Output (with input shown in bold)

```
How many employee records do you want to create? 3 [Enter]
Enter the data for employee #1

Name: Ingrid Virgo [Enter]
ID number: 4587 [Enter]
Department: Engineering [Enter]
Enter the data for employee #2

Name: Julia Rich [Enter]
ID number: 4588 [Enter]
Department: Research [Enter]
Enter the data for employee #3

Name: Greg Young [Enter]
ID number: 4589 [Enter]
Department: Marketing [Enter]

Employee records written to employees.txt.
```

The statement in lines 6 and 7 prompts the user for the number of employee records that he or she wants to create. Inside the loop, in lines 17 through 19, the program gets an employee's name, ID number, and department. These three items, which together make an employee record, are written to the file in lines 22 through 24. The loop iterates once for each employee record.

When we read a record from a sequential access file, we read the data for each field, one after the other, until we have read the complete record. Program 6-14 demonstrates how we can read the employee records in the `employee.txt` file.

Program 6-14 (read_emp_records.py)

```
# This program displays the records that are
# in the employees.txt file.

def main():
    # Open the employees.txt file.
    emp_file = open('employees.txt', 'r')

    # Read the first line from the file, which is
    # the name field of the first record.
    name = emp_file.readline()

    # If a field was read, continue processing.
    while name != '':
        # Read the ID number field.
        id_num = emp_file.readline()

        # Read the department field.
        dept = emp_file.readline()

        # Strip the newlines from the fields.
        name = name.rstrip('\n')
        id_num = id_num.rstrip('\n')
        dept = dept.rstrip('\n')

        # Display the record.
        print('Name:', name)
        print('ID:', id_num)
        print('Dept:', dept)
        print()

        # Read the name field of the next record.
        name = emp_file.readline()

    # Close the file.
    emp_file.close()

# Call the main function.
main()
```

Program Output

```
Name: Ingrid Virgo
ID: 4587
Dept: Engineering
```

```
Name: Julia Rich
ID: 4588
Dept: Research

Name: Greg Young
ID: 4589
Dept: Marketing
```

This program opens the file in line 6, then in line 10 reads the first field of the first record. This will be the first employee's name. The `while` loop in line 13 tests the value to determine whether it is an empty string. If it is not, then the loop iterates. Inside the loop, the program reads the record's second and third fields (the employee's ID number and department), and displays them. Then, in line 32 the first field of the next record (the next employee's name) is read. The loop starts over and this process continues until there are no more records to read.

Programs that store records in a file typically require more capabilities than simply writing and reading records. In the following *In the Spotlight* sections, we will examine algorithms for adding records to a file, searching a file for specific records, modifying a record, and deleting a record.

In the Spotlight:
Adding and Displaying Records

Midnight Coffee Roasters, Inc. is a small company that imports raw coffee beans from around the world and roasts them to create a variety of gourmet coffees. Julie, the owner of the company, has asked you to write a series of programs that she can use to manage her inventory. After speaking with her, you have determined that a file is needed to keep inventory records. Each record should have two fields to hold the following data:

- Description. A string containing the name of the coffee
- Quantity in inventory. The number of pounds in inventory, as a floating-point number

Your first job is to write a program that can be used to add records to the file. Program 6-15 shows the code. Note the output file is opened in append mode. Each time the program is executed, the new records will be added to the file's existing contents.

Program 6-15 (add_coffee_record.py)

```
# This program adds coffee inventory records to
# the coffee.txt file.

def main():
    # Create a variable to control the loop.
    another = 'y'
```

(program continues)

Program 6-15 *(continued)*

```

    # Open the coffee.txt file in append mode.
    coffee_file = open('coffee.txt', 'a')

    # Add records to the file.
    while another == 'y' or another == 'Y':
        # Get the coffee record data.
        print('Enter the following coffee data:')
        descr = input('Description: ')
        qty = int(input('Quantity (in pounds): '))

        # Append the data to the file.
        coffee_file.write(descr + '\n')
        coffee_file.write(str(qty) + '\n')

        # Determine whether the user wants to add
        # another record to the file.
        print('Do you want to add another record?')
        another = input('Y = yes, anything else = no: ')

    # Close the file.
    coffee_file.close()
    print('Data appended to coffee.txt.')

# Call the main function.
main()
```

Program Output (with input shown in bold)

```
Enter the following coffee data:
Description: Brazilian Dark Roast Enter
Quantity (in pounds): 18 Enter
Do you want to enter another record?
Y = yes, anything else = no: y Enter
Description: Sumatra Medium Roast Enter
Quantity (in pounds): 25 Enter
Do you want to enter another record?
Y = yes, anything else = no: n Enter
Data appended to coffee.txt.
```

Your next job is to write a program that displays all of the records in the inventory file. Program 6-16 shows the code.

Program 6-16 (show_coffee_records.py)

```
# This program displays the records in the
# coffee.txt file.
```

```

def main():
    # Open the coffee.txt file.
    coffee_file = open('coffee.txt', 'r')

    # Read the first record's description field.
    descr = coffee_file.readline()

    # Read the rest of the file.
    while descr != '':
        # Read the quantity field.
        qty = float(coffee_file.readline())

        # Strip the \n from the description.
        descr = descr.rstrip('\n')

        # Display the record.
        print('Description:', descr)
        print('Quantity:', qty)

        # Read the next description.
        descr = coffee_file.readline()

    # Close the file.
    coffee_file.close()

# Call the main function.
main()
```

Program Output

```
Description: Brazilian Dark Roast
Quantity: 18.0
Description: Sumatra Medium Roast
Quantity: 25.0
```

In the Spotlight:
Searching for a Record

Julie has been using the first two programs that you wrote for her. She now has several records stored in the `coffee.txt` file and has asked you to write another program that she can use to search for records. She wants to be able to enter a description and see a list of all the records matching that description. Program 6-17 shows the code for the program.

Program 6-17 (search_coffee_records.py)

```
# This program allows the user to search the
# coffee.txt file for records matching a
# description.

def main():
    # Create a bool variable to use as a flag.
    found = False

    # Get the search value.
    search = input('Enter a description to search for: ')

    # Open the coffee.txt file.
    coffee_file = open('coffee.txt', 'r')

    # Read the first record's description field.
    descr = coffee_file.readline()

    # Read the rest of the file.
    while descr != '':
        # Read the quantity field.
        qty = float(coffee_file.readline())

        # Strip the \n from the description.
        descr = descr.rstrip('\n')

        # Determine whether this record matches
        # the search value.
        if descr == search:
            # Display the record.
            print('Description:', descr)
            print('Quantity:', qty)
            print()
            # Set the found flag to True.
            found = True

        # Read the next description.
        descr = coffee_file.readline()

    # Close the file.
    coffee_file.close()

    # If the search value was not found in the file
    # display a message.
    if not found:
        print('That item was not found in the file.')

```

```
# Call the main function.
main()
```

Program Output (with input shown in bold)

```
Enter a description to search for: Sumatra Medium Roast [Enter]
Description: Sumatra Medium Roast
Quantity: 25.0
```

Program Output (with input shown in bold)

```
Enter a description to search for: Mexican Altura [Enter]
That item was not found in the file.
```

In the Spotlight:

Modifying Records

Julie is very happy with the programs that you have written so far. Your next job is to write a program that she can use to modify the quantity field in an existing record. This will allow her to keep the records up to date as coffee is sold or more coffee of an existing type is added to inventory.

To modify a record in a sequential file, you must create a second temporary file. You copy all of the original file's records to the temporary file, but when you get to the record that is to be modified, you do not write its old contents to the temporary file. Instead, you write its new modified values to the temporary file. Then, you finish copying any remaining records from the original file to the temporary file.

The temporary file then takes the place of the original file. You delete the original file and rename the temporary file, giving it the name that the original file had on the computer's disk. Here is the general algorithm for your program.

Open the original file for input and create a temporary file for output.
Get the description of the record to be modified and the new value for the quantity.
Read the first description field from the original file.
While the description field is not empty:
    Read the quantity field.
    If this record's description field matches the description entered:
        Write the new data to the temporary file.
    Else:
        Write the existing record to the temporary file.
    Read the next description field.
Close the original file and the temporary file.
Delete the original file.
Rename the temporary file, giving it the name of the original file.

Notice at the end of the algorithm you delete the original file then rename the temporary file. The Python standard library's `os` module provides a function named `remove`, that deletes a file on the disk. You simply pass the name of the file as an argument to the function. Here is an example of how you would delete a file named `coffee.txt`:

```
remove('coffee.txt')
```

The `os` module also provides a function named rename, that renames a file. Here is an example of how you would use it to rename the file `temp.txt` to `coffee.txt`:

```
rename('temp.txt', 'coffee.txt')
```

Program 6-18 shows the code for the program.

Program 6-18 (`modify_coffee_records.py`)

```
# This program allows the user to modify the quantity
# in a record in the coffee.txt file.

import os # Needed for the remove and rename functions

def main():
    # Create a bool variable to use as a flag.
    found = False

    # Get the search value and the new quantity.
    search = input('Enter a description to search for: ')
    new_qty = int(input('Enter the new quantity: '))

    # Open the original coffee.txt file.
    coffee_file = open('coffee.txt', 'r')

    # Open the temporary file.
    temp_file = open('temp.txt', 'w')

    # Read the first record's description field.
    descr = coffee_file.readline()

    # Read the rest of the file.
    while descr != '':
        # Read the quantity field.
        qty = float(coffee_file.readline())

        # Strip the \n from the description.
        descr = descr.rstrip('\n')

        # Write either this record to the temporary file,
        # or the new record if this is the one that is
        # to be modified.
```

```
        if descr == search:
            # Write the modified record to the temp file.
            temp_file.write(descr + '\n')
            temp_file.write(str(new_qty) + '\n')

            # Set the found flag to True.
            found = True
        else:
            # Write the original record to the temp file.
            temp_file.write(descr + '\n')
            temp_file.write(str(qty) + '\n')

        # Read the next description.
        descr = coffee_file.readline()

    # Close the coffee file and the temporary file.
    coffee_file.close()
    temp_file.close()

    # Delete the original coffee.txt file.
    os.remove('coffee.txt')

    # Rename the temporary file.
    os.rename('temp.txt', 'coffee.txt')

    # If the search value was not found in the file
    # display a message.
    if found:
        print('The file has been updated.')
    else:
        print('That item was not found in the file.')

# Call the main function.
main()
```

Program Output (with input shown in bold)

Enter a description to search for: **Brazilian Dark Roast** [Enter]
Enter the new quantity: **10** [Enter]
The file has been updated.

NOTE: When working with a sequential access file, it is necessary to copy the entire file each time one item in the file is modified. As you can imagine, this approach is inefficient, especially if the file is large. Other, more advanced techniques are available, especially when working with direct access files, that are much more efficient. We do not cover those advanced techniques in this book, but you will probably study them in later courses.

In the Spotlight:
Deleting Records

Your last task is to write a program that Julie can use to delete records from the `coffee.txt` file. Like the process of modifying a record, the process of deleting a record from a sequential access file requires that you create a second temporary file. You copy all of the original file's records to the temporary file, except for the record that is to be deleted. The temporary file then takes the place of the original file. You delete the original file and rename the temporary file, giving it the name that the original file had on the computer's disk. Here is the general algorithm for your program.

Open the original file for input and create a temporary file for output.
Get the description of the record to be deleted.
Read the description field of the first record in the original file.
While the description is not empty:
    Read the quantity field.
    If this record's description field does not match the description entered:
        Write the record to the temporary file.
    Read the next description field.
Close the original file and the temporary file.
Delete the original file.
Rename the temporary file, giving it the name of the original file.

Program 6-19 shows the program's code.

Program 6-19 (delete_coffee_record.py)

```
# This program allows the user to delete
# a record in the coffee.txt file.

import os # Needed for the remove and rename functions

def main():
    # Create a bool variable to use as a flag.
    found = False

    # Get the coffee to delete.
    search = input('Which coffee do you want to delete? ')

    # Open the original coffee.txt file.
    coffee_file = open('coffee.txt', 'r')

    # Open the temporary file.
    temp_file = open('temp.txt', 'w')

    # Read the first record's description field.
    descr = coffee_file.readline()

```

```
    # Read the rest of the file.
    while descr != '':
        # Read the quantity field.
        qty = float(coffee_file.readline())

        # Strip the \n from the description.
        descr = descr.rstrip('\n')

        # If this is not the record to delete, then
        # write it to the temporary file.
        if descr != search:
            # Write the record to the temp file.
            temp_file.write(descr + '\n')
            temp_file.write(str(qty) + '\n')
        else:
            # Set the found flag to True.
            found = True

        # Read the next description.
        descr = coffee_file.readline()

    # Close the coffee file and the temporary file.
    coffee_file.close()
    temp_file.close()

    # Delete the original coffee.txt file.
    os.remove('coffee.txt')

    # Rename the temporary file.
    os.rename('temp.txt', 'coffee.txt')

    # If the search value was not found in the file
    # display a message.
    if found:
        print('The file has been updated.')
    else:
        print('That item was not found in the file.')

# Call the main function.
main()
```

Program Output (with input shown in bold)

Which coffee do you want to delete? **Brazilian Dark Roast** Enter
The file has been updated.

NOTE: When working with a sequential access file, it is necessary to copy the entire file each time one item in the file is deleted. As was previously mentioned, this approach is inefficient, especially if the file is large. Other, more advanced techniques are available, especially when working with direct access files, that are much more efficient. We do not cover those advanced techniques in this book, but you will probably study them in later courses.

Checkpoint

6.16 What is a record? What is a field?

6.17 Describe the way that you use a temporary file in a program that modifies a record in a sequential access file.

6.18 Describe the way that you use a temporary file in a program that deletes a record from a sequential file.

6.4 Exceptions

CONCEPT: An exception is an error that occurs while a program is running, causing the program to abruptly halt. You can use the `try/except` statement to gracefully handle exceptions.

An exception is an error that occurs while a program is running. In most cases, an exception causes a program to abruptly halt. For example, look at Program 6-20. This program gets two numbers from the user then divides the first number by the second number. In the sample running of the program, however, an exception occurred because the user entered 0 as the second number. (Division by 0 causes an exception because it is mathematically impossible.)

Program 6-20 (division.py)

```
# This program divides a number by another number.

def main():
    # Get two numbers.
    num1 = int(input('Enter a number: '))
    num2 = int(input('Enter another number: '))

    # Divide num1 by num2 and display the result.
    result = num1 / num2
    print(num1, 'divided by', num2, 'is', result)

# Call the main function.
main()
```

Program Output (with input shown in bold)

```
Enter a number: 10 [Enter]
Enter another number: 0 [Enter]
```

```
Traceback (most recent call last):
  File "C:\Python\division.py," line 13, in <module>
    main()
  File "C:\Python\division.py," line 9, in main
    result = num1 / num2
ZeroDivisionError: integer division or modulo by zero
```

The lengthy error message that is shown in the sample run is called a *traceback*. The traceback gives information regarding the line number(s) that caused the exception. (When an exception occurs, programmers say that an exception was raised.) The last line of the error message shows the name of the exception that was raised (`ZeroDivisionError`) and a brief description of the error that caused the exception to be raised (`integer division or modulo by zero`).

You can prevent many exceptions from being raised by carefully coding your program. For example, Program 6-21 shows how division by 0 can be prevented with a simple `if` statement. Rather than allowing the exception to be raised, the program tests the value of `num2`, and displays an error message if the value is 0. This is an example of gracefully avoiding an exception.

Program 6-21 (division.py)

```
# This program divides a number by another number.

def main():
    # Get two numbers.
    num1 = int(input('Enter a number: '))
    num2 = int(input('Enter another number: '))

    # If num2 is not 0, divide num1 by num2
    # and display the result.
    if num2 != 0:
        result = num1 / num2
        print(num1, 'divided by', num2, 'is', result)
    else:
        print('Cannot divide by zero.')

# Call the main function.
main()
```

Program Output (with input shown in bold)

```
Enter a number: 10 [Enter]
Enter another number: 0 [Enter]
Cannot divide by zero.
```

Some exceptions cannot be avoided regardless of how carefully you write your program. For example, look at Program 6-22. This program calculates gross pay. It prompts the user to enter the number of hours worked and the hourly pay rate. It gets the user's gross pay by multiplying these two numbers and displays that value on the screen.

Program 6-22 (gross_pay1.py)

```
1  # This program calculates gross pay.
2
3  def main():
4      # Get the number of hours worked.
5      hours = int(input('How many hours did you work? '))
6
7      # Get the hourly pay rate.
8      pay_rate = float(input('Enter your hourly pay rate: '))
9
10     # Calculate the gross pay.
11     gross_pay = hours * pay_rate
12
13     # Display the gross pay.
14     print('Gross pay: $', format(gross_pay, ',.2f'), sep='')
15
16 # Call the main function.
17 main()
```

Program Output (with input shown in bold)

```
How many hours did you work? forty [Enter]
Traceback (most recent call last):
  File "C:\Users\Tony\Documents\Python\Source
Code\Chapter 06\gross_pay1.py", line 17, in <module>
    main()
  File "C:\Users\Tony\Documents\Python\Source
Code\Chapter 06\gross_pay1.py", line 5, in main
    hours = int(input('How many hours did you work? '))
ValueError: invalid literal for int() with base 10: 'forty'
```

Look at the sample running of the program. An exception occurred because the user entered the string `'forty'` instead of the number 40 when prompted for the number of hours worked. Because the string `'forty'` cannot be converted to an integer, the `int()` function raised an exception in line 5, and the program halted. Look carefully at the last line of the traceback message, and you will see that the name of the exception is `ValueError`, and its description is: `invalid literal for int() with base 10: 'forty'`.

Python, like most modern programming languages, allows you to write code that responds to exceptions when they are raised, and prevents the program from abruptly crashing. Such code is called an *exception handler* and is written with the `try/except` statement. There are several ways to write a `try/except` statement, but the following general format shows the simplest variation:

```
try:
    statement
    statement
    etc.
```

```
except ExceptionName:
    statement
    statement
    etc.
```

First, the key word `try` appears, followed by a colon. Next, a code block appears which we will refer to as the *try suite*. The *try suite* is one or more statements that can potentially raise an exception.

After the try suite, an *`except` clause* appears. The `except` clause begins with the key word `except`, optionally followed by the name of an exception, and ending with a colon. Beginning on the next line is a block of statements that we will refer to as a *handler*.

When the `try/except` statement executes, the statements in the try suite begin to execute. The following describes what happens next:

- If a statement in the try suite raises an exception that is specified by the *`ExceptionName`* in an `except` clause, then the handler that immediately follows the `except` clause executes. Then, the program resumes execution with the statement immediately following the `try/except` statement.
- If a statement in the try suite raises an exception that is *not* specified by the `ExceptionName` in an `except` clause, then the program will halt with a traceback error message.
- If the statements in the try suite execute without raising an exception, then any `except` clauses and handlers in the statement are skipped, and the program resumes execution with the statement immediately following the `try/except` statement.

Program 6-23 shows how we can write a `try/except` statement to gracefully respond to a `ValueError` exception.

Program 6-23 (gross_pay2.py)

```
# This program calculates gross pay.

def main():
    try:
        # Get the number of hours worked.
        hours = int(input('How many hours did you work? '))

        # Get the hourly pay rate.
        pay_rate = float(input('Enter your hourly pay rate: '))

        # Calculate the gross pay.
        gross_pay = hours * pay_rate

        # Display the gross pay.
        print('Gross pay: $', format(gross_pay, ',.2f'), sep='')
    except ValueError:
        print('ERROR: Hours worked and hourly pay rate must')
        print('be valid numbers.')
```

(program continues)

Program 6-23 *(continued)*

```
19
20  # Call the main function.
21  main()
```

Program Output (with input shown in bold)

```
How many hours did you work? forty [Enter]
ERROR: Hours worked and hourly pay rate must
be valid numbers.
```

Let's look at what happened in the sample run. The statement in line 6 prompts the user to enter the number of hours worked, and the user enters the string `'forty'`. Because the string `'forty'` cannot be converted to an integer, the `int()` function raises a `ValueError` exception. As a result, the program jumps immediately out of the try suite to the `except ValueError` clause in line 16 and begins executing the handler block that begins in line 17. This is illustrated in Figure 6-20.

Figure 6-20 Handling an exception

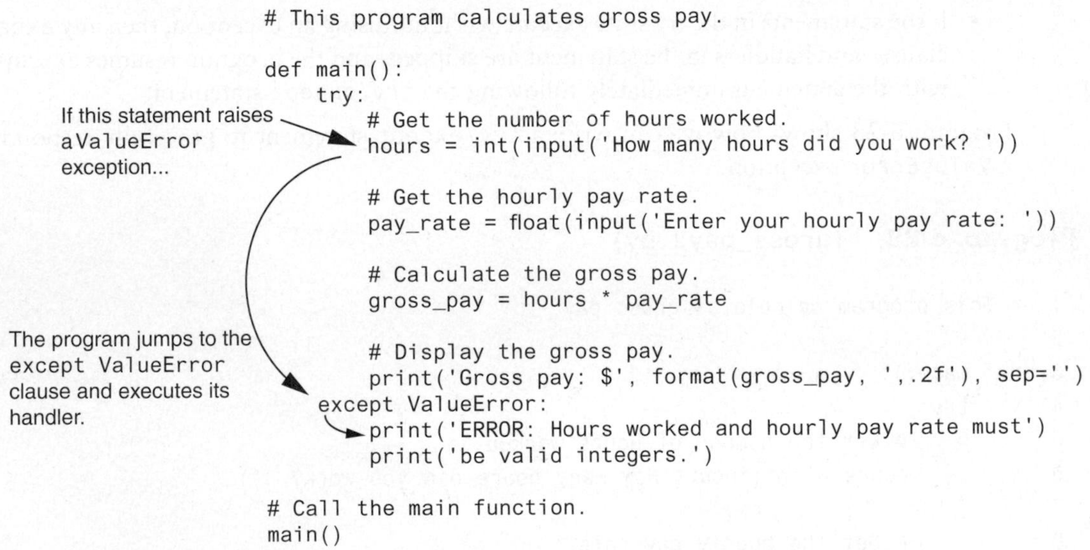

```
# This program calculates gross pay.

def main():
    try:
        # Get the number of hours worked.
        hours = int(input('How many hours did you work? '))

        # Get the hourly pay rate.
        pay_rate = float(input('Enter your hourly pay rate: '))

        # Calculate the gross pay.
        gross_pay = hours * pay_rate

        # Display the gross pay.
        print('Gross pay: $', format(gross_pay, ',.2f'), sep='')
    except ValueError:
        print('ERROR: Hours worked and hourly pay rate must')
        print('be valid integers.')

# Call the main function.
main()
```

If this statement raises a ValueError exception...

The program jumps to the except ValueError clause and executes its handler.

Let's look at another example in Program 6-24. This program, which does not use exception handling, gets the name of a file from the user then displays the contents of the file. The program works as long as the user enters the name of an existing file. An exception will be raised, however, if the file specified by the user does not exist. This is what happened in the sample run.

Program 6-24 (display_file.py)

```
# This program displays the contents
# of a file.

```

```
4  def main():
5      # Get the name of a file.
6      filename = input('Enter a filename: ')
7
8      # Open the file.
9      infile = open(filename, 'r')
10
11     # Read the file's contents.
12     contents = infile.read()
13
14     # Display the file's contents.
15     print(contents)
16
17     # Close the file.
18     infile.close()
19
20 # Call the main function.
21 main()
```

Program Output (with input shown in bold)

```
Enter a filename: bad_file.txt [Enter]
Traceback (most recent call last):
File "C:\Python\display_file.py," line 21, in <module>
main()
File "C:\Python\display_file.py," line 9, in main
infile = open(filename, 'r')
IOError: [Errno 2] No such file or directory: 'bad_file.txt'
```

The statement in line 9 raised the exception when it called the `open` function. Notice in the traceback error message that the name of the exception that occurred is `IOError`. This is an exception that is raised when a file I/O operation fails. You can see in the traceback message that the cause of the error was `No such file or directory: 'bad_file.txt'`.

Program 6-25 shows how we can modify Program 6-24 with a `try/except` statement that gracefully responds to an `IOError` exception. In the sample run, assume the file `bad_file.txt` does not exist.

Program 6-25 (display_file2.py)

```
# This program displays the contents
# of a file.

def main():
    # Get the name of a file.
    filename = input('Enter a filename: ')

```

(program continues)

Program 6-25 *(continued)*

```
 8      try:
 9          # Open the file.
10          infile = open(filename, 'r')
11
12          # Read the file's contents.
13          contents = infile.read()
14
15          # Display the file's contents.
16          print(contents)
17
18          # Close the file.
19          infile.close()
20      except IOError:
21          print('An error occurred trying to read')
22          print('the file', filename)
23
24  # Call the main function.
25  main()
```

Program Output (with input shown in bold)

```
Enter a filename: bad_file.txt [Enter]
An error occurred trying to read the file bad_file.txt
```

Let's look at what happened in the sample run. When line 6 executed, the user entered `bad_file.txt`, which was assigned to the `filename` variable. Inside the try suite, line 10 attempts to open the file `bad_file.txt`. Because this file does not exist, the statement raises an `IOError` exception. When this happens, the program exits the try suite, skipping lines 11 through 19. Because the `except` clause in line 20 specifies the `IOError` exception, the program jumps to the handler that begins in line 21.

Handling Multiple Exceptions

In many cases, the code in a try suite will be capable of throwing more than one type of exception. In such a case, you need to write an `except` clause for each type of exception that you want to handle. For example, Program 6-26 reads the contents of a file named `sales_data.txt`. Each line in the file contains the sales amount for one month, and the file has several lines. Here are the contents of the file:

```
24987.62
26978.97
32589.45
31978.47
22781.76
29871.44
```

Program 6-26 reads all of the numbers from the file and adds them to an accumulator variable.

Program 6-26 (sales_report1.py)

```
1  # This program displays the total of the
2  # amounts in the sales_data.txt file.
3
4  def main():
5      # Initialize an accumulator.
6      total = 0.0
7
8      try:
9          # Open the sales_data.txt file.
10         infile = open('sales_data.txt', 'r')
11
12         # Read the values from the file and
13         # accumulate them.
14         for line in infile:
15             amount = float(line)
16             total += amount
17
18         # Close the file.
19         infile.close()
20
21         # Print the total.
22         print(format(total, ',.2f'))
23
24     except IOError:
25         print('An error occured trying to read the file.')
26
27     except ValueError:
28         print('Non-numeric data found in the file.')
29
30     except:
31         print('An error occured.')
32
33 # Call the main function.
34 main()
```

The try suite contains code that can raise different types of exceptions. For example:

- The statement in line 10 can raise an `IOError` exception if the `sales_data.txt` file does not exist. The `for` loop in line 14 can also raise an `IOError` exception if it encounters a problem reading data from the file.
- The `float` function in line 15 can raise a `ValueError` exception if the `line` variable references a string that cannot be converted to a floating-point number (an alphabetic string, for example).

Notice the `try/except` statement has three `except` clauses:

- The `except` clause in line 24 specifies the `IOError` exception. Its handler in line 25 will execute if an `IOError` exception is raised.
- The `except` clause in line 27 specifies the `ValueError` exception. Its handler in line 28 will execute if a `ValueError` exception is raised.
- The `except` clause in line 30 does not list a specific exception. Its handler in line 31 will execute if an exception that is not handled by the other `except` clauses is raised.

If an exception occurs in the try suite, the Python interpreter examines each of the `except` clauses, from top to bottom, in the `try/except` statement. When it finds an `except` clause that specifies a type that matches the type of exception that occurred, it branches to that `except` clause. If none of the `except` clauses specifies a type that matches the exception, the interpreter branches to the `except` clause in line 30.

Using One `except` Clause to Catch All Exceptions

The previous example demonstrated how multiple types of exceptions can be handled individually in a `try/except` statement. Sometimes you might want to write a `try/except` statement that simply catches any exception that is raised in the try suite and, regardless of the exception's type, responds the same way. You can accomplish that in a `try/except` statement by writing one `except` clause that does not specify a particular type of exception. Program 6-27 shows an example.

Program 6-27 (sales_report2.py)

```
# This program displays the total of the
# amounts in the sales_data.txt file.

def main():
    # Initialize an accumulator.
    total = 0.0

    try:
        # Open the sales_data.txt file.
        infile = open('sales_data.txt', 'r')

        # Read the values from the file and
        # accumulate them.
        for line in infile:
            amount = float(line)
            total += amount

        # Close the file.
        infile.close()

        # Print the total.
        print(format(total, ',.2f'))
```

```
23     except:
24         print('An error occurred.')
25
26 # Call the main function.
27 main()
```

Notice the try/except statement in this program has only one except clause, in line 23. The except clause does not specify an exception type, so any exception that occurs in the try suite (lines 9 through 22) causes the program to branch to line 23 and execute the statement in line 24.

Displaying an Exception's Default Error Message

When an exception is thrown, an object known as an *exception object* is created in memory. The exception object usually contains a default error message pertaining to the exception. (In fact, it is the same error message that you see displayed at the end of a traceback when an exception goes unhandled.) When you write an except clause, you can optionally assign the exception object to a variable, as shown here:

```
except ValueError as err:
```

This except clause catches ValueError exceptions. The expression that appears after the except clause specifies that we are assigning the exception object to the variable err. (There is nothing special about the name err. That is simply the name that we have chosen for the examples. You can use any name that you wish.) After doing this, in the exception handler you can pass the err variable to the print function to display the default error message that Python provides for that type of error. Program 6-28 shows an example of how this is done.

Program 6-28 (gross_pay3.py)

```
# This program calculates gross pay.

def main():
    try:
        # Get the number of hours worked.
        hours = int(input('How many hours did you work? '))

        # Get the hourly pay rate.
        pay_rate = float(input('Enter your hourly pay rate: '))

        # Calculate the gross pay.
        gross_pay = hours * pay_rate

        # Display the gross pay.
        print('Gross pay: $', format(gross_pay, ',.2f'), sep='')
    except ValueError as err:
        print(err)

```

(program continues)

Program 6-28 *(continued)*

```
19 # Call the main function.
20 main()
```

Program Output (with input shown in bold)

```
How many hours did you work? forty [Enter]
invalid literal for int() with base 10: 'forty'
```

When a `ValueError` exception occurs inside the try suite (lines 5 through 15), the program branches to the `except` clause in line 16. The expression `ValueError as err` in line 16 causes the resulting exception object to be assigned to a variable named `err`. The statement in line 17 passes the `err` variable to the `print` function, which causes the exception's default error message to be displayed.

If you want to have just one `except` clause to catch all the exceptions that are raised in a try suite, you can specify `Exception` as the type. Program 6-29 shows an example.

Program 6-29 **(sales_report3.py)**

```
# This program displays the total of the
# amounts in the sales_data.txt file.

def main():
    # Initialize an accumulator.
    total = 0.0

    try:
        # Open the sales_data.txt file.
        infile = open('sales_data.txt', 'r')

        # Read the values from the file and
        # accumulate them.
        for line in infile:
            amount = float(line)
            total += amount

        # Close the file.
        infile.close()

        # Print the total.
        print(format(total, ',.2f'))
    except Exception as err:
        print(err)

# Call the main function.
main()
```

The `else` Clause

The `try/except` statement may have an optional `else` clause, which appears after all the `except` clauses. Here is the general format of a `try/except` statement with an `else` clause:

```
try:
    statement
    statement
    etc.
except ExceptionName:
    statement
    statement
    etc.
else:
    statement
    statement
    etc.
```

The block of statements that appears after the `else` clause is known as the *else suite*. The statements in the else suite are executed after the statements in the try suite, only if no exceptions were raised. If an exception is raised, the else suite is skipped. Program 6-30 shows an example.

Program 6-30 (sales_report4.py)

```
# This program displays the total of the
# amounts in the sales_data.txt file.

def main():
    # Initialize an accumulator.
    total = 0.0

    try:
        # Open the sales_data.txt file.
        infile = open('sales_data.txt', 'r')

        # Read the values from the file and
        # accumulate them.
        for line in infile:
            amount = float(line)
            total += amount

        # Close the file.
        infile.close()
    except Exception as err:
        print(err)
    else:
        # Print the total.
        print(format(total, ',.2f'))
```

(program continues)

Program 6-30 *(continued)*

```
25
26 # Call the main function.
27 main()
```

In Program 6-30, the statement in line 24 is executed only if the statements in the try suite (lines 9 through 19) execute without raising an exception.

The `finally` Clause

The `try/except` statement may have an optional `finally` clause, which must appear after all the `except` clauses. Here is the general format of a `try/except` statement with a `finally` clause:

```
try:
    statement
    statement
    etc.
except ExceptionName:
    statement
    statement
    etc.
finally:
    statement
    statement
    etc.
```

The block of statements that appears after the `finally` clause is known as the *finally suite*. The statements in the finally suite are always executed after the try suite has executed, and after any exception handlers have executed. The statements in the finally suite execute whether an exception occurs or not. The purpose of the finally suite is to perform cleanup operations, such as closing files or other resources. Any code that is written in the finally suite will always execute, even if the try suite raises an exception.

What If an Exception Is Not Handled?

Unless an exception is handled, it will cause the program to halt. There are two possible ways for a thrown exception to go unhandled. The first possibility is for the `try/except` statement to contain no `except` clauses specifying an exception of the right type. The second possibility is for the exception to be raised from outside a try suite. In either case, the exception will cause the program to halt.

In this section, you've seen examples of programs that can raise `ZeroDivisionError` exceptions, `IOError` exceptions, and `ValueError` exceptions. There are many different types of exceptions that can occur in a Python program. When you are designing `try/except` statements, one way you can learn about the exceptions that you need to handle is to consult the Python documentation. It gives detailed information about each possible exception and the types of errors that can cause them to occur.

Another way that you can learn about the exceptions that can occur in a program is through experimentation. You can run a program and deliberately perform actions that will cause errors. By watching the traceback error messages that are displayed, you will see the names of the exceptions that are raised. You can then write `except` clauses to handle these exceptions.

Checkpoint

6.19 Briefly describe what an exception is.

6.20 If an exception is raised and the program does not handle it with a `try/except` statement, what happens?

6.21 What type of exception does a program raise when it tries to open a nonexistent file?

6.22 What type of exception does a program raise when it uses the `float` function to convert a non-numeric string to a number?

Review Questions

Multiple Choice

1. A file that data is written to is known as a(n) ______________.
   a. input file
   b. output file
   c. sequential access file
   d. binary file
2. A file that data is read from is known as a(n) ______________.
   a. input file
   b. output file
   c. sequential access file
   d. binary file
3. Before a file can be used by a program, it must be ______________.
   a. formatted
   b. encrypted
   c. closed
   d. opened
4. When a program is finished using a file, it should do this.
   a. erase the file
   b. open the file
   c. close the file
   d. encrypt the file
5. The contents of this type of file can be viewed in an editor such as Notepad.
   a. text file
   b. binary file
   c. English file
   d. human-readable file

6. This type of file contains data that has not been converted to text.
   a. text file
   b. binary file
   c. Unicode file
   d. symbolic file
7. When working with this type of file, you access its data from the beginning of the file to the end of the file.
   a. ordered access
   b. binary access
   c. direct access
   d. sequential access
8. When working with this type of file, you can jump directly to any piece of data in the file without reading the data that comes before it.
   a. ordered access
   b. binary access
   c. direct access
   d. sequential access
9. This is a small "holding section" in memory that many systems write data to before writing the data to a file.
   a. buffer
   b. variable
   c. virtual file
   d. temporary file
10. This marks the location of the next item that will be read from a file.
    a. input position
    b. delimiter
    c. pointer
    d. read position
11. When a file is opened in this mode, data will be written at the end of the file's existing contents.
    a. output mode
    b. append mode
    c. backup mode
    d. read-only mode
12. This is a single piece of data within a record.
    a. field
    b. variable
    c. delimiter
    d. subrecord
13. When an exception is generated, it is said to have been __________.
    a. built
    b. raised
    c. caught
    d. killed

14. This is a section of code that gracefully responds to exceptions.
    a. exception generator
    b. exception manipulator
    c. exception handler
    d. exception monitor
15. You write this statement to respond to exceptions.
    a. `run/handle`
    b. `try/except`
    c. `try/handle`
    d. `attempt/except`

True or False

1. When working with a sequential access file, you can jump directly to any piece of data in the file without reading the data that comes before it.
2. When you open a file that file already exists on the disk using the `'w'` mode, the contents of the existing file will be erased.
3. The process of opening a file is only necessary with input files. Output files are automatically opened when data is written to them.
4. When an input file is opened, its read position is initially set to the first item in the file.
5. When a file that already exists is opened in append mode, the file's existing contents are erased.
6. If you do not handle an exception, it is ignored by the Python interpreter, and the program continues to execute.
7. You can have more than one `except` clause in a `try/except` statement.
8. The else suite in a `try/except` statement executes only if a statement in the try suite raises an exception.
9. The finally suite in a `try/except` statement executes only if no exceptions are raised by statements in the try suite.

Short Answer

1. Describe the three steps that must be taken when a file is used by a program.
2. Why should a program close a file when it's finished using it?
3. What is a file's read position? Where is the read position when a file is first opened for reading?
4. If an existing file is opened in append mode, what happens to the file's existing contents?
5. If a file does not exist and a program attempts to open it in append mode, what happens?

Algorithm Workbench

1. Write a program that opens an output file with the filename `my_name.txt`, writes your name to the file, then closes the file.
2. Write a program that opens the `my_name.txt` file that was created by the program in problem 1, reads your name from the file, displays the name on the screen, then closes the file.

3. Write code that does the following: opens an output file with the filename `number_list.txt`, uses a loop to write the numbers 1 through 100 to the file, then closes the file.
4. Write code that does the following: opens the `number_list.txt` file that was created by the code you wrote in question 3, reads all of the numbers from the file and displays them, then closes the file.
5. Modify the code that you wrote in problem 4 so it adds all of the numbers read from the file and displays their total.
6. Write code that opens an output file with the filename `number_list.txt`, but does not erase the file's contents if it already exists.
7. A file exists on the disk named `students.txt`. The file contains several records, and each record contains two fields: (1) the student's name, and (2) the student's score for the final exam. Write code that deletes the record containing "John Perz" as the student name.
8. A file exists on the disk named `students.txt`. The file contains several records, and each record contains two fields: (1) the student's name, and (2) the student's score for the final exam. Write code that changes Julie Milan's score to 100.
9. What will the following code display?

```
try:
  x = float('abc123')
  print('The conversion is complete.')
except IOError:
  print('This code caused an IOError.')
except ValueError:
  print('This code caused a ValueError.')
print('The end.')
```

10. What will the following code display?

```
try:
  x = float('abc123')
  print(x)
except IOError:
  print('This code caused an IOError.')
except ZeroDivisionError:
  print('This code caused a ZeroDivisionError.')
except:
  print('An error happened.')
print('The end.')
```

Programming Exercises

1. File Display

VideoNote
File Display

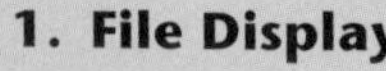

Assume a file containing a series of integers is named `numbers.txt` and exists on the computer's disk. Write a program that displays all of the numbers in the file.

2. File Head Display

Write a program that asks the user for the name of a file. The program should display only the first five lines of the file's contents. If the file contains less than five lines, it should display the file's entire contents.

3. Line Numbers

Write a program that asks the user for the name of a file. The program should display the contents of the file with each line preceded with a line number followed by a colon. The line numbering should start at 1.

4. Item Counter

Assume a file containing a series of names (as strings) is named `names.txt` and exists on the computer's disk. Write a program that displays the number of names that are stored in the file. *(Hint: Open the file and read every string stored in it. Use a variable to keep a count of the number of items that are read from the file.)*

5. Sum of Numbers

Assume a file containing a series of integers is named `numbers.txt` and exists on the computer's disk. Write a program that reads all of the numbers stored in the file and calculates their total.

6. Average of Numbers

Assume a file containing a series of integers is named `numbers.txt` and exists on the computer's disk. Write a program that calculates the average of all the numbers stored in the file.

7. Random Number File Writer

Write a program that writes a series of random numbers to a file. Each random number should be in the range of 1 through 500. The application should let the user specify how many random numbers the file will hold.

8. Random Number File Reader

This exercise assumes you have completed Programming Exercise 7, *Random Number File Writer*. Write another program that reads the random numbers from the file, displays the numbers, then displays the following data:

- The total of the numbers
- The number of random numbers read from the file

9. Exception Handing

Modify the program that you wrote for Exercise 6 so it handles the following exceptions:

- It should handle any `IOError` exceptions that are raised when the file is opened and data is read from it.
- It should handle any `ValueError` exceptions that are raised when the items that are read from the file are converted to a number.

10. Golf Scores

The Springfork Amateur Golf Club has a tournament every weekend. The club president has asked you to write two programs:

1. A program that will read each player's name and golf score as keyboard input, then save these as records in a file named `golf.txt`. (Each record will have a field for the player's name and a field for the player's score.)
2. A program that reads the records from the `golf.txt` file and displays them.

11. Personal Web Page Generator

Write a program that asks the user for his or her name, then asks the user to enter a sentence that describes himself or herself. Here is an example of the program's screen:

```
Enter your name: Julie Taylor [Enter]
Describe yourself: I am a computer science major, a member of the
Jazz club, and I hope to work as a mobile app developer after I
graduate. [Enter]
```

Once the user has entered the requested input, the program should create an HTML file, containing the input, for a simple Web page. Here is an example of the HTML content, using the sample input previously shown:

```
<html>
<head>
</head>
<body>
    <center>
        <h1>Julie Taylor</h1>
    </center>
    <hr />
    I am a computer science major, a member of the Jazz club,
    and I hope to work as a mobile app developer after I graduate.
    <hr />
</body>
</html>
```

12. Average Steps Taken

A Personal Fitness Tracker is a wearable device that tracks your physical activity, calories burned, heart rate, sleeping patterns, and so on. One common physical activity that most of these devices track is the number of steps you take each day.

If you have downloaded this book's source code from the Computer Science Portal, you will find a file named `steps.txt` in the Chapter 06 folder. (The Computer Science Portal can be found at www.pearsonhighered.com/gaddis.) The `steps.txt` file contains the number of steps a person has taken each day for a year. There are 365 lines in the file, and each line contains the number of steps taken during a day. (The first line is the number of steps taken on January 1st, the second line is the number of steps taken on January 2nd, and so forth.) Write a program that reads the file, then displays the average number of steps taken for each month. (The data is from a year that was not a leap year, so February has 28 days.)

CHAPTER

7 Lists and Tuples

TOPICS

7.1 Sequences

CONCEPT: A sequence is an object that holds multiple items of data, stored one after the other. You can perform operations on a sequence to examine and manipulate the items stored in it.

A *sequence* is an object that contains multiple items of data. The items that are in a sequence are stored one after the other. Python provides various ways to perform operations on the items that are stored in a sequence.

There are several different types of sequence objects in Python. In this chapter, we will look at two of the fundamental sequence types: lists and tuples. Both lists and tuples are sequences that can hold various types of data. The difference between lists and tuples is simple: a list is mutable, which means that a program can change its contents, but a tuple is immutable, which means that once it is created, its contents cannot be changed. We will explore some of the operations that you may perform on these sequences, including ways to access and manipulate their contents.

7.2 Introduction to Lists

CONCEPT: A list is an object that contains multiple data items. Lists are mutable, which means that their contents can be changed during a program's execution. Lists are dynamic data structures, meaning that items may be added to them or removed from them. You can use indexing, slicing, and various methods to work with lists in a program.

A *list* is an object that contains multiple data items. Each item that is stored in a list is called an *element*. Here is a statement that creates a list of integers:

```
even_numbers = [2, 4, 6, 8, 10]
```

The items that are enclosed in brackets and separated by commas are the list elements. After this statement executes, the variable even_numbers will reference the list, as shown in Figure 7-1.

Figure 7-1 A list of integers

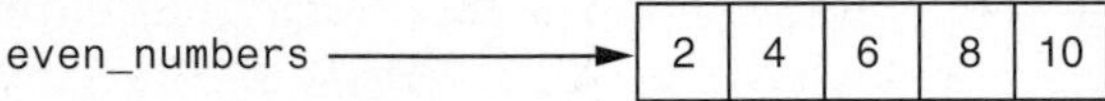

The following is another example:

```
names = ['Molly', 'Steven', 'Will', 'Alicia', 'Adriana']
```

This statement creates a list of five strings. After the statement executes, the name variable will reference the list as shown in Figure 7-2.

Figure 7-2 A list of strings

A list can hold items of different types, as shown in the following example:

```
info = ['Alicia', 27, 1550.87]
```

This statement creates a list containing a string, an integer, and a floating-point number. After the statement executes, the info variable will reference the list as shown in Figure 7-3.

Figure 7-3 A list holding different types

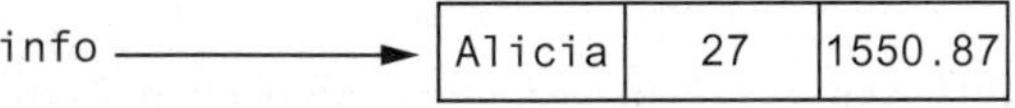

You can use the print function to display an entire list, as shown here:

```
numbers = [5, 10, 15, 20]
print(numbers)
```

In this example, the print function will display the elements of the list like this:

```
[5, 10, 15, 20]
```

Python also has a built-in list() function that can convert certain types of objects to lists. For example, recall from Chapter 4 that the range function returns an iterable, which is an object that holds a series of values that can be iterated over. You can use a statement such as the following to convert the range function's iterable object to a list:

```
numbers = list(range(5))
```

When this statement executes, the following things happen:

- The `range` function is called with 5 passed as an argument. The function returns an iterable containing the values 0, 1, 2, 3, 4.
- The `iterable` is passed as an argument to the `list()` function. The `list()` function returns the list `[0, 1, 2, 3, 4]`.
- The list `[0, 1, 2, 3, 4]` is assigned to the `numbers` variable.

Here is another example:

```
numbers = list(range(1, 10, 2))
```

Recall from Chapter 4 that when you pass three arguments to the `range` function, the first argument is the starting value, the second argument is the ending limit, and the third argument is the step value. This statement will assign the list `[1, 3, 5, 7, 9]` to the `numbers` variable.

The Repetition Operator

You learned in Chapter 2 that the `*` symbol multiplies two numbers. However, when the operand on the left side of the `*` symbol is a sequence (such as a list) and the operand on the right side is an integer, it becomes the *repetition operator*. The repetition operator makes multiple copies of a list and joins them all together. Here is the general format:

```
list * n
```

In the general format, *`list`* is a list, and *n* is the number of copies to make. The following interactive session demonstrates:

```
1 >>> numbers = [0] * 5 Enter
2 >>> print(numbers) Enter
3 [0, 0, 0, 0, 0]
4 >>>
```

Let's take a closer look at each statement:

- In line 1, the expression `[0] * 5` makes five copies of the list `[0]` and joins them all together in a single list. The resulting list is assigned to the `numbers` variable.
- In line 2, the `numbers` variable is passed to the `print` function. The function's output is shown in line 3.

Here is another interactive mode demonstration:

```
>>> numbers = [1, 2, 3] * 3 Enter
>>> print(numbers) Enter
[1, 2, 3, 1, 2, 3, 1, 2, 3]
>>>
```

NOTE: Most programming languages allow you to create sequence structures known as *arrays*, which are similar to lists, but are much more limited in their capabilities. You cannot create traditional arrays in Python because lists serve the same purpose and provide many more built-in capabilities.

Iterating over a List with the for Loop

In Section 7.1, we discussed techniques for accessing the individual characters in a string. Many of the same programming techniques also apply to lists. For example, you can iterate over a list with the `for` loop, as shown here:

```
numbers = [99, 100, 101, 102]
for n in numbers:
    print(n)
```

If we run this code, it will print:

```
99
100
101
102
```

Indexing

Another way that you can access the individual elements in a list is with an *index*. Each element in a list has an index that specifies its position in the list. Indexing starts at 0, so the index of the first element is 0, the index of the second element is 1, and so forth. The index of the last element in a list is 1 less than the number of elements in the list.

For example, the following statement creates a list with 4 elements:

```
my_list = [10, 20, 30, 40]
```

The indexes of the elements in this list are 0, 1, 2, and 3. We can print the elements of the list with the following statement:

```
print(my_list[0], my_list[1], my_list[2], my_list[3])
```

The following loop also prints the elements of the list:

```
index = 0
while index < 4:
    print(my_list[index])
    index += 1
```

You can also use negative indexes with lists to identify element positions relative to the end of the list. The Python interpreter adds negative indexes to the length of the list to determine the element position. The index −1 identifies the last element in a list, −2 identifies the next to last element, and so forth. The following code shows an example:

```
my_list = [10, 20, 30, 40]
print(my_list[-1], my_list[-2], my_list[-3], my_list[-4])
```

In this example, the `print` function will display:

```
40   30   20   10
```

An `IndexError` exception will be raised if you use an invalid index with a list. For example, look at the following code:

```
# This code will cause an IndexError exception.
my_list = [10, 20, 30, 40]
```

```
index = 0
while index < 5:
    print(my_list[index])
    index += 1
```

The last time that this loop begins an iteration, the `index` variable will be assigned the value 4, which is an invalid index for the list. As a result, the statement that calls the `print` function will cause an `IndexError` exception to be raised.

The `len` Function

Python has a built-in function named `len` that returns the length of a sequence, such as a list. The following code demonstrates:

```
my_list = [10, 20, 30, 40]
size = len(my_list)
```

The first statement assigns the list `[10, 20, 30, 40]` to the `my_list` variable. The second statement calls the `len` function, passing the `my_list` variable as an argument.

The function returns the value 4, which is the number of elements in the list. This value is assigned to the `size` variable.

The `len` function can be used to prevent an `IndexError` exception when iterating over a list with a loop. Here is an example:

```
my_list = [10, 20, 30, 40]
index = 0
while index < len(my_list):
    print(my_list[index])
    index += 1
```

Lists Are Mutable

Lists in Python are *mutable*, which means their elements can be changed. Consequently, an expression in the form `list[index]` can appear on the left side of an assignment operator. The following code shows an example:

```
1  numbers = [1, 2, 3, 4, 5]
2  print(numbers)
3  numbers[0] = 99
4  print(numbers)
```

The statement in line 2 will display

```
[1, 2, 3, 4, 5]
```

The statement in line 3 assigns 99 to `numbers[0]`. This changes the first value in the list to 99. When the statement in line 4 executes, it will display

```
[99, 2, 3, 4, 5]
```

When you use an indexing expression to assign a value to a list element, you must use a valid index for an existing element or an `IndexError` exception will occur. For example, look at the following code:

```
numbers = [1, 2, 3, 4, 5]     # Create a list with 5 elements.
numbers[5] = 99               # This raises an exception!
```

The numbers list that is created in the first statement has five elements, with the indexes 0 through 4. The second statement will raise an IndexError exception because the numbers list has no element at index 5.

If you want to use indexing expressions to fill a list with values, you have to create the list first, as shown here:

```
1  # Create a list with 5 elements.
2  numbers = [0] * 5
3
4  # Fill the list with the value 99.
5  index = 0
6  while index < len(numbers):
7      numbers[index] = 99
8      index += 1
```

The statement in line 2 creates a list with five elements, each element assigned the value 0. The loop in lines 6 through 8 then steps through the list elements, assigning 99 to each one.

Program 7-1 shows an example of how user input can be assigned to the elements of a list. This program gets sales amounts from the user and assigns them to a list.

Program 7-1 (sales_list.py)

```
# The NUM_DAYS constant holds the number of
# days that we will gather sales data for.
NUM_DAYS = 5

def main():
    # Create a list to hold the sales
    # for each day.
    sales = [0] * NUM_DAYS

    # Create a variable to hold an index.
    index = 0

    print('Enter the sales for each day.')

    # Get the sales for each day.
    while index < NUM_DAYS:
        print('Day #', index + 1, ': ', sep='', end='')
        sales[index] = float(input())
        index += 1

```

```
21     # Display the values entered.
22     print('Here are the values you entered:')
23     for value in sales:
24         print(value)
25
26 # Call the main function.
27 main()
```

Program Output (with input shown in bold)

```
Enter the sales for each day.
Day #1: 1000 Enter
Day #2: 2000 Enter
Day #3: 3000 Enter
Day #4: 4000 Enter
Day #5: 5000 Enter
Here are the values you entered:
1000.0
2000.0
3000.0
4000.0
5000.0
```

The statement in line 3 creates the variable `NUM_DAYS`, which is used as a constant for the number of days. The statement in line 8 creates a list with five elements, with each element assigned the value 0. Line 11 creates a variable named `index` and assigns the value 0 to it.

The loop in lines 16 through 19 iterates 5 times. The first time it iterates, `index` references the value 0, so the statement in line 18 assigns the user's input to `sales[0]`. The second time the loop iterates, index references the value 1, so the statement in line 18 assigns the user's input to `sales[1]`. This continues until input values have been assigned to all the elements in the list.

Concatenating Lists

To concatenate means to join two things together. You can use the + operator to concatenate two lists. Here is an example:

```
list1 = [1, 2, 3, 4]
list2 = [5, 6, 7, 8]
list3 = list1 + list2
```

After this code executes, `list1` and `list2` remain unchanged, and `list3` references the following list:

```
[1, 2, 3, 4, 5, 6, 7, 8]
```

The following interactive mode session also demonstrates list concatenation:

```
>>> girl_names = ['Joanne', 'Karen', 'Lori'] Enter
>>> boy_names = ['Chris', 'Jerry', 'Will'] Enter
>>> all_names = girl_names + boy_names Enter
```

```
>>> print(all_names) Enter
['Joanne', 'Karen', 'Lori', 'Chris', 'Jerry', 'Will']
```

You can also use the += augmented assignment operator to concatenate one list to another. Here is an example:

```
list1 = [1, 2, 3, 4]
list2 = [5, 6, 7, 8]
list1 += list2
```

The last statement appends `list2` to `list1`. After this code executes, `list2` remains unchanged, but `list1` references the following list:

```
[1, 2, 3, 4, 5, 6, 7, 8]
```

The following interactive mode session also demonstrates the += operator used for list concatenation:

```
>>> girl_names = ['Joanne', 'Karen', 'Lori'] Enter
>>> girl_names += ['Jenny', 'Kelly'] Enter
>>> print(girl_names) Enter
['Joanne', 'Karen', 'Lori', 'Jenny', 'Kelly']
>>>
```

NOTE: Keep in mind that you can concatenate lists only with other lists. If you try to concatenate a list with something that is not a list, an exception will be raised.

Checkpoint

7.1 What will the following code display?

```
numbers = [1, 2, 3, 4, 5]
numbers[2] = 99
print(numbers)
```

7.2 What will the following code display?

```
numbers = list(range(3))
print(numbers)
```

7.3 What will the following code display?

```
numbers = [10] * 5
print(numbers)
```

7.4 What will the following code display?

```
numbers = list(range(1, 10, 2))
for n in numbers:
    print(n)
```

7.5 What will the following code display?

```
numbers = [1, 2, 3, 4, 5]
print(numbers[-2])
```

7.6 How do you find the number of elements in a list?

7.7 What will the following code display?

```
numbers1 = [1, 2, 3]
numbers2 = [10, 20, 30]
numbers3 = numbers1 + numbers2
print(numbers1)
print(numbers2)
print(numbers3)
```

7.8 What will the following code display?

```
numbers1 = [1, 2, 3]
numbers2 = [10, 20, 30]
numbers2 += numbers1
print(numbers1)
print(numbers2)
```

7.3 List Slicing

CONCEPT: A slicing expression selects a range of elements from a sequence.

You have seen how indexing allows you to select a specific element in a sequence. Sometimes you want to select more than one element from a sequence. In Python, you can write expressions that select subsections of a sequence, known as slices.

VideoNote
List Slicing

A *slice* is a span of items that are taken from a sequence. When you take a slice from a list, you get a span of elements from within the list. To get a slice of a list, you write an expression in the following general format:

```
list_name[start : end]
```

In the general format, `start` is the index of the first element in the slice, and *end* is the index marking the end of the slice. The expression returns a list containing a copy of the elements from `start` up to (but not including) *end*. For example, suppose we create the following list:

```
days = ['Sunday', 'Monday', 'Tuesday', 'Wednesday',
        'Thursday', 'Friday', 'Saturday']
```

The following statement uses a slicing expression to get the elements from indexes 2 up to, but not including, 5:

```
mid_days = days[2:5]
```

After this statement executes, the `mid_days` variable references the following list:

```
['Tuesday', 'Wednesday', 'Thursday']
```

You can quickly use the interactive mode interpreter to see how slicing works. For example, look at the following session. (We have added line numbers for easier reference.)

```
1  >>> numbers = [1, 2, 3, 4, 5] [Enter]
2  >>> print(numbers) [Enter]
3  [1, 2, 3, 4, 5]
```

```
4 >>> print(numbers[1:3]) Enter
5 [2, 3]
6 >>>
```

Here is a summary of each line:

- In line 1, we created the list and `[1, 2, 3, 4, 5]` and assigned it to the `numbers` variable.
- In line 2, we passed `numbers` as an argument to the `print` function. The `print` function displayed the list in line 3.
- In line 4, we sent the slice `numbers[1:3]` as an argument to the `print` function. The `print` function displayed the slice in line 5.

If you leave out the *`start`* index in a slicing expression, Python uses 0 as the starting index. The following interactive mode session shows an example:

```
1 >>> numbers = [1, 2, 3, 4, 5] Enter
2 >>> print(numbers) Enter
3 [1, 2, 3, 4, 5]
4 >>> print(numbers[:3]) Enter
5 [1, 2, 3]
6 >>>
```

Notice line 4 sends the slice `numbers[:3]` as an argument to the `print` function. Because the starting index was omitted, the slice contains the elements from index 0 up to 3.

If you leave out the *end* index in a slicing expression, Python uses the length of the list as the *end* index. The following interactive mode session shows an example:

```
1 >>> numbers = [1, 2, 3, 4, 5] Enter
2 >>> print(numbers) Enter
3 [1, 2, 3, 4, 5]
4 >>> print(numbers[2:]) Enter
5 [3, 4, 5]
6 >>>
```

Notice line 4 sends the slice `numbers[2:]` as an argument to the `print` function. Because the ending index was omitted, the slice contains the elements from index 2 through the end of the list.

If you leave out both the *`start`* and *end* index in a slicing expression, you get a copy of the entire list. The following interactive mode session shows an example:

```
1 >>> numbers = [1, 2, 3, 4, 5] Enter
2 >>> print(numbers) Enter
3 [1, 2, 3, 4, 5]
4 >>> print(numbers[:])Enter
5 [1, 2, 3, 4, 5]
6 >>>
```

The slicing examples we have seen so far get slices of consecutive elements from lists. Slicing expressions can also have step value, which can cause elements to be skipped in the list. The following interactive mode session shows an example of a slicing expression with a step value:

```
1 >>> numbers = [1, 2, 3, 4, 5, 6, 7, 8, 9, 10] Enter
2 >>> print(numbers) Enter
3 [1, 2, 3, 4, 5, 6, 7, 8, 9, 10]
4 >>> print(numbers[1:8:2]) Enter
5 [2, 4, 6, 8]
6 >>>
```

In the slicing expression in line 4, the third number inside the brackets is the step value. A step value of 2, as used in this example, causes the slice to contain every second element from the specified range in the list.

You can also use negative numbers as indexes in slicing expressions to reference positions relative to the end of the list. Python adds a negative index to the length of a list to get the position referenced by that index. The following interactive mode session shows an example:

```
>>> numbers = [1, 2, 3, 4, 5, 6, 7, 8, 9, 10] Enter
>>> print(numbers) Enter
[1, 2, 3, 4, 5, 6, 7, 8, 9, 10]
>>> print(numbers[-5:]) Enter
[6, 7, 8, 9, 10]
>>>
```

NOTE: Invalid indexes do not cause slicing expressions to raise an exception. For example:

- If the *end* index specifies a position beyond the end of the list, Python will use the length of the list instead.
- If the *start* index specifies a position before the beginning of the list, Python will use 0 instead.
- If the *start* index is greater than the *end* index, the slicing expression will return an empty list.

Checkpoint

7.9 What will the following code display?

```
numbers = [1, 2, 3, 4, 5]
my_list = numbers[1:3]
print(my_list)
```

7.10 What will the following code display?

```
numbers = [1, 2, 3, 4, 5]
my_list = numbers[1:]
print(my_list)
```

7.11 What will the following code display?

```
numbers = [1, 2, 3, 4, 5]
my_list = numbers[:1]
print(my_list)
```

7.12 What will the following code display?

```
numbers = [1, 2, 3, 4, 5]
my_list = numbers[:]
print(my_list)
```

7.13 What will the following code display?

```
numbers = [1, 2, 3, 4, 5]
my_list = numbers[-3:]
print(my_list)
```

7.4 Finding Items in Lists with the `in` Operator

CONCEPT: You can search for an item in a list using the `in` operator.

In Python, you can use the `in` operator to determine whether an item is contained in a list. Here is the general format of an expression written with the `in` operator to search for an item in a list:

```
item in list
```

In the general format, *`item`* is the item for which you are searching, and *`list`* is a list. The expression returns true if *`item`* is found in the *`list`*, or false otherwise. Program 7-2 shows an example.

Program 7-2 (in_list.py)

```
# This program demonstrates the in operator
# used with a list.

def main():
    # Create a list of product numbers.
    prod_nums = ['V475', 'F987', 'Q143', 'R688']

    # Get a product number to search for.
    search = input('Enter a product number: ')

    # Determine whether the product number is in the list.
    if search in prod_nums:
        print(search, 'was found in the list.')
    else:
        print(search, 'was not found in the list.')

# Call the main function.
main()
```

Program Output (with input shown in bold)

```
Enter a product number: Q143 [Enter]
Q143 was found in the list.
```

Program Output (with input shown in bold)

```
Enter a product number: B000 [Enter]
B000 was not found in the list.
```

The program gets a product number from the user in line 9 and assigns it to the `search` variable. The `if` statement in line 12 determines whether `search` is in the `prod_nums` list.

You can use the `not in` operator to determine whether an item is *not* in a list. Here is an example:

```
if search not in prod_nums:
    print(search, 'was not found in the list.')
else:
    print(search, 'was found in the list.')
```

Checkpoint

7.14 What will the following code display?

```
names = ['Jim', 'Jill', 'John', 'Jasmine']
if 'Jasmine' not in names:
    print('Cannot find Jasmine.')
else:
    print("Jasmine's family:")
    print(names)
```

7.5 List Methods and Useful Built-in Functions

CONCEPT: Lists have numerous methods that allow you to work with the elements that they contain. Python also provides some built-in functions that are useful for working with lists.

Lists have numerous methods that allow you to add elements, remove elements, change the ordering of elements, and so forth. We will look at a few of these methods,[1] which are listed in Table 7-1.

The append Method

The `append` method is commonly used to add items to a list. The item that is passed as an argument is appended to the end of the list's existing elements. Program 7-3 shows an example.

[1] We do not cover all of the list methods in this book. For a description of all of the list methods, see the Python documentation at www.python.org.

Table 7-1 A few of the list methods

Method	Description
`append(item)`	Adds *item* to the end of the list.
`index(item)`	Returns the index of the first element whose value is equal to item. A `ValueError` exception is raised if item is not found in the list.
`insert(index, item)`	Inserts *item* into the list at the specified *index*. When an item is inserted into a list, the list is expanded in size to accommodate the new item. The item that was previously at the specified index, and all the items after it, are shifted by one position toward the end of the list. No exceptions will occur if you specify an invalid index. If you specify an index beyond the end of the list, the item will be added to the end of the list. If you use a negative index that specifies an invalid position, the item will be inserted at the beginning of the list.
`sort()`	Sorts the items in the list so they appear in ascending order (from the lowest value to the highest value).
`remove(item)`	Removes the first occurrence of *item* from the list. A `ValueError` exception is raised if item is not found in the list.
`reverse()`	Reverses the order of the items in the list.

Program 7-3 (list_append.py)

```
# This program demonstrates how the append
# method can be used to add items to a list.

def main():
    # First, create an empty list.
    name_list = []

    # Create a variable to control the loop.
    again = 'y'

    # Add some names to the list.
    while again == 'y':
        # Get a name from the user.
        name = input('Enter a name: ')

        # Append the name to the list.
        name_list.append(name)

        # Add another one?
        print('Do you want to add another name?')
        again = input('y = yes, anything else = no: ')
        print()

```

```
24     # Display the names that were entered.
25     print('Here are the names you entered.')
26
27     for name in name_list:
28         print(name)
29
30 # Call the main function.
31 main()
```

Program Output (with input shown in bold)

```
Enter a name: Kathryn [Enter]
Do you want to add another name?
y = yes, anything else = no: y [Enter]

Enter a name: Chris [Enter]
Do you want to add another name?
y = yes, anything else = no: y [Enter]

Enter a name: Kenny [Enter]
Do you want to add another name?
y = yes, anything else = no: y [Enter]

Enter a name: Renee [Enter]
Do you want to add another name?
y = yes, anything else = no: n [Enter]

Here are the names you entered.
Kathryn
Chris
Kenny
Renee
```

Notice the statement in line 6:

```
name_list = []
```

This statement creates an empty list (a list with no elements) and assigns it to the `name_list` variable. Inside the loop, the append method is called to build the list. The first time the method is called, the argument passed to it will become element 0. The second time the method is called, the argument passed to it will become element 1. This continues until the user exits the loop.

The `index` Method

Earlier, you saw how the `in` operator can be used to determine whether an item is in a list. Sometimes you need to know not only whether an item is in a list, but where it is located. The `index` method is useful in these cases. You pass an argument to the `index` method, and it returns the index of the first element in the list containing that item. If the item is not found in the list, the method raises a `ValueError` exception. Program 7-4 demonstrates the `index` method.

Program 7-4 (index_list.py)

```
1   # This program demonstrates how to get the
2   # index of an item in a list and then replace
3   # that item with a new item.
4
5   def main():
6       # Create a list with some items.
7       food = ['Pizza', 'Burgers', 'Chips']
8
9       # Display the list.
10      print('Here are the items in the food list:')
11      print(food)
12
13      # Get the item to change.
14      item = input('Which item should I change? ')
15
16      try:
17          # Get the item's index in the list.
18          item_index = food.index(item)
19
20          # Get the value to replace it with.
21          new_item = input('Enter the new value: ')
22
23          # Replace the old item with the new item.
24          food[item_index] = new_item
25
26          # Display the list.
27          print('Here is the revised list:')
28          print(food)
29      except ValueError:
30          print('That item was not found in the list.')
31
32  # Call the main function.
33  main()
```

Program Output (with input shown in bold)

```
Here are the items in the food list:
['Pizza', 'Burgers', 'Chips']
Which item should I change? Burgers Enter
Enter the new value: Pickles Enter
Here is the revised list:
['Pizza', 'Pickles', 'Chips']
```

The elements of the food list are displayed in line 11, and in line 14, the user is asked which item he or she wants to change. Line 18 calls the index method to get the index of the item.

Line 21 gets the new value from the user, and line 24 assigns the new value to the element holding the old value.

The `insert` Method

The `insert` method allows you to insert an item into a list at a specific position. You pass two arguments to the `insert` method: an index specifying where the item should be inserted and the item that you want to insert. Program 7-5 shows an example.

Program 7-5 (insert_list.py)

```
# This program demonstrates the insert method.

def main():
    # Create a list with some names.
    names = ['James', 'Kathryn', 'Bill']

    # Display the list.
    print('The list before the insert:')
    print(names)

    # Insert a new name at element 0.
    names.insert(0, 'Joe')

    # Display the list again.
    print('The list after the insert:')
    print(names)

# Call the main function.
main()
```

Program Output

```
The list before the insert:
['James', 'Kathryn', 'Bill']
The list after the insert:
['Joe', 'James', 'Kathryn', 'Bill']
```

The `sort` Method

The `sort` method rearranges the elements of a list so they appear in ascending order (from the lowest value to the highest value). Here is an example:

```
my_list = [9, 1, 0, 2, 8, 6, 7, 4, 5, 3]
print('Original order:', my_list)
my_list.sort()
print('Sorted order:', my_list)
```

When this code runs, it will display the following:

```
Original order: [9, 1, 0, 2, 8, 6, 7, 4, 5, 3]
Sorted order: [0, 1, 2, 3, 4, 5, 6, 7, 8, 9]
```

Here is another example:

```
my_list = ['beta', 'alpha', 'delta', 'gamma']
print('Original order:', my_list)
my_list.sort()
print('Sorted order:', my_list)
```

When this code runs, it will display the following:

```
Original order: ['beta', 'alpha', 'delta', 'gamma']
Sorted order: ['alpha', 'beta', 'delta', 'gamma']
```

The `remove` Method

The `remove` method removes an item from the list. You pass an item to the method as an argument, and the first element containing that item is removed. This reduces the size of the list by one element. All of the elements after the removed element are shifted one position toward the beginning of the list. A `ValueError` exception is raised if the item is not found in the list. Program 7-6 demonstrates the method.

Program 7-6 (remove_item.py)

```
# This program demonstrates how to use the remove
# method to remove an item from a list.

def main():
    # Create a list with some items.
    food = ['Pizza', 'Burgers', 'Chips']

    # Display the list.
    print('Here are the items in the food list:')
    print(food)

    # Get the item to change.
    item = input('Which item should I remove? ')

    try:
        # Remove the item.
        food.remove(item)

        # Display the list.
        print('Here is the revised list:')
        print(food)

    except ValueError:
```

```
            print('That item was not found in the list.')

# Call the main function.
main()
```

Program Output (with input shown in bold)

```
Here are the items in the food list:
['Pizza', 'Burgers', 'Chips']
Which item should I remove? Burgers [Enter]
Here is the revised list:
['Pizza', 'Chips']
```

The `reverse` Method

The `reverse` method simply reverses the order of the items in the list. Here is an example:

```
my_list = [1, 2, 3, 4, 5]
print('Original order:', my_list)
my_list.reverse()
print('Reversed:', my_list)
```

This code will display the following:

```
Original order: [1, 2, 3, 4, 5]
Reversed: [5, 4, 3, 2, 1]
```

The `del` Statement

The `remove` method you saw earlier removes a specific item from a list, if that item is in the list. Some situations might require you remove an element from a specific index, regardless of the item that is stored at that index. This can be accomplished with the `del` statement. Here is an example of how to use the `del` statement:

```
my_list = [1, 2, 3, 4, 5]
print('Before deletion:', my_list)
del my_list[2]
print('After deletion:', my_list)
```

This code will display the following:

```
Before deletion: [1, 2, 3, 4, 5]
After deletion: [1, 2, 4, 5]
```

The `min` and `max` Functions

Python has two built-in functions named `min` and `max` that work with sequences. The `min` function accepts a sequence, such as a list, as an argument and returns the item that has the lowest value in the sequence. Here is an example:

```
my_list = [5, 4, 3, 2, 50, 40, 30]
print('The lowest value is', min(my_list))
```

This code will display the following:

```
The lowest value is 2
```

The `max` function accepts a sequence, such as a list, as an argument and returns the item that has the highest value in the sequence. Here is an example:

```
my_list = [5, 4, 3, 2, 50, 40, 30]
print('The highest value is', max(my_list))
```

This code will display the following:

```
The highest value is 50
```

Checkpoint

7.15 What is the difference between calling a list's `remove` method and using the `del` statement to remove an element?

7.16 How do you find the lowest and highest values in a list?

7.17 Assume the following statement appears in a program:

```
names = []
```

Which of the following statements would you use to add the string 'Wendy' to the list at index 0? Why would you select this statement instead of the other?

a. `names[0] = 'Wendy'`
b. `names.append('Wendy')`

7.18 Describe the following list methods:

a. `index`
b. `insert`
c. `sort`
d. `reverse`

7.6 Copying Lists

CONCEPT: To make a copy of a list, you must copy the list's elements.

Recall that in Python, assigning one variable to another variable simply makes both variables reference the same object in memory. For example, look at the following code:

```
# Create a list.
list1 = [1, 2, 3, 4]
# Assign the list to the list2 variable.
list2 = list1
```

After this code executes, both variables `list1` and `list2` will reference the same list in memory. This is shown in Figure 7-4.

Figure 7-4 `list1` and `list2` reference the same list

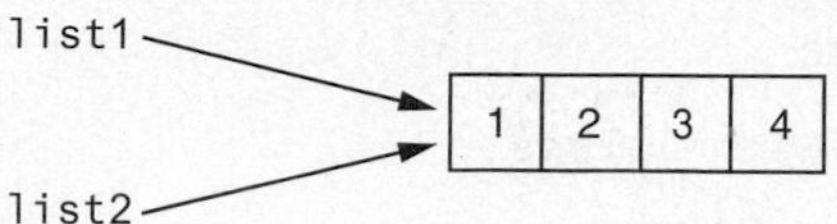

To demonstrate this, look at the following interactive session:

```
1  >>> list1 = [1, 2, 3, 4] Enter
2  >>> list2 = list1 Enter
3  >>> print(list1) Enter
4  [1, 2, 3, 4]
5  >>> print(list2) Enter
6  [1, 2, 3, 4]
7  >>> list1[0] = 99 Enter
8  >>> print(list1) Enter
9  [99, 2, 3, 4]
10 >>> print(list2) Enter
11 [99, 2, 3, 4]
12 >>>
```

Let's take a closer look at each line:

- In line 1, we create a list of integers and assign the list to the `list1` variable.
- In line 2, we assign `list1` to `list2`. After this, both `list1` and `list2` reference the same list in memory.
- In line 3, we print the list referenced by `list1`. The output of the `print` function is shown in line 4.
- In line 5, we print the list referenced by `list2`. The output of the `print` function is shown in line 6. Notice it is the same as the output shown in line 4.
- In line 7, we change the value of `list[0]` to 99.
- In line 8, we print the list referenced by `list1`. The output of the `print` function is shown in line 9. Notice the first element is now 99.
- In line 10, we print the list referenced by `list2`. The output of the `print` function is shown in line 11. Notice the first element is 99.

In this interactive session, the `list1` and `list2` variables reference the same list in memory.

Suppose you wish to make a copy of the list, so `list1` and `list2` reference two separate but identical lists. One way to do this is with a loop that copies each element of the list. Here is an example:

```
# Create a list with values.
list1 = [1, 2, 3, 4]
# Create an empty list.
list2 = []
# Copy the elements of list1 to list2.
for item in list1:
    list2.append(item)
```

After this code executes, `list1` and `list2` will reference two separate but identical lists. A simpler and more elegant way to accomplish the same task is to use the concatenation operator, as shown here:

```
# Create a list with values.
list1 = [1, 2, 3, 4]
# Create a copy of list1.
list2 = [] + list1
```

The last statement in this code concatenates an empty list with `list1` and assigns the resulting list to `list2`. As a result, `list1` and `list2` will reference two separate but identical lists.

7.7 Processing Lists

So far, you've learned a wide variety of techniques for working with lists. Now we will look at a number of ways that programs can process the data held in a list. For example, the following *In the Spotlight* section shows how list elements can be used in calculations.

In the Spotlight:
Using List Elements in a Math Expression

Megan owns a small neighborhood coffee shop, and she has six employees who work as baristas (coffee bartenders). All of the employees have the same hourly pay rate. Megan has asked you to design a program that will allow her to enter the number of hours worked by each employee, then display the amounts of all the employees' gross pay. You determine the program should perform the following steps:

1. For each employee: get the number of hours worked and store it in a list element.
2. For each list element: use the value stored in the element to calculate an employee's gross pay. Display the amount of the gross pay.

Program 7-7 shows the code for the program.

Program 7-7 (barista_pay.py)

```
# This program calculates the gross pay for
# each of Megan's baristas.

# NUM_EMPLOYEES is used as a constant for the
# size of the list.
NUM_EMPLOYEES = 6

```

```
8  def main():
9      # Create a list to hold employee hours.
10     hours = [0] * NUM_EMPLOYEES
11
12     # Get each employee's hours worked.
13     for index in range(NUM_EMPLOYEES):
14         print('Enter the hours worked by employee ',
15               index + 1, ': ', sep='', end='')
16         hours[index] = float(input())
17
18     # Get the hourly pay rate.
19     pay_rate = float(input('Enter the hourly pay rate: '))
20
21     # Display each employee's gross pay.
22     for index in range(NUM_EMPLOYEES):
23         gross_pay = hours[index] * pay_rate
24         print('Gross pay for employee ', index + 1, ': $',
25               format(gross_pay, ',.2f'), sep='')
26
27 # Call the main function.
28 main()
```

Program Output (with input shown in bold)

```
Enter the hours worked by employee 1: 10 Enter
Enter the hours worked by employee 2: 20 Enter
Enter the hours worked by employee 3: 15 Enter
Enter the hours worked by employee 4: 40 Enter
Enter the hours worked by employee 5: 20 Enter
Enter the hours worked by employee 6: 18 Enter
Enter the hourly pay rate: 12.75 Enter
Gross pay for employee 1: $127.50
Gross pay for employee 2: $255.00
Gross pay for employee 3: $191.25
Gross pay for employee 4: $510.00
Gross pay for employee 5: $255.00
Gross pay for employee 6: $229.50
```

NOTE: Suppose Megan's business increases and she hires two additional baristas. This would require you to change the program so it processes eight employees instead of six. Because you used a constant for the list size, this is a simple modification—you just change the statement in line 6 to read:

```
NUM_EMPLOYEES = 8
```

(continued)

Because the NUM_EMPLOYEES constant is used in line 10 to create the list, the size of the hours list will automatically become eight. Also, because you used the NUM_EMPLOYEES constant to control the loop iterations in lines 13 and 22, the loops will automatically iterate eight times, once for each employee.

Imagine how much more difficult this modification would be if you had not used a constant to determine the list size. You would have to change each individual statement in the program that refers to the list size. Not only would this require more work, but it would open the possibility for errors. If you overlooked any one of the statements that refer to the list size, a bug would occur.

Totaling the Values in a List

Assuming a list contains numeric values, to calculate the total of those values, you use a loop with an accumulator variable. The loop steps through the list, adding the value of each element to the accumulator. Program 7-8 demonstrates the algorithm with a list named numbers.

Program 7-8 (total_list.py)

```
# This program calculates the total of the values
# in a list.

def main():
    # Create a list.
    numbers = [2, 4, 6, 8, 10]

    # Create a variable to use as an accumulator.
    total = 0

    # Calculate the total of the list elements.
    for value in numbers:
        total += value

    # Display the total of the list elements.
    print('The total of the elements is', total)

# Call the main function.
main()
```

Program Output

```
The total of the elements is 30
```

Averaging the Values in a List

The first step in calculating the average of the values in a list is to get the total of the values. You saw how to do that with a loop in the preceding section. The second step is to divide the total by the number of elements in the list. Program 7-9 demonstrates the algorithm.

Program 7-9 (average_list.py)

```
# This program calculates the average of the values
# in a list.

def main():
    # Create a list.
    scores = [2.5, 7.3, 6.5, 4.0, 5.2]

    # Create a variable to use as an accumulator.
    total = 0.0

    # Calculate the total of the list elements.
    for value in scores:
        total += value

    # Calculate the average of the elements.
    average = total / len(scores)

    # Display the total of the list elements.
    print('The average of the elements is', average)

# Call the main function.
main()
```

Program Output

```
The average of the elements is 5.3
```

Passing a List as an Argument to a Function

Recall from Chapter 5 that as a program grows larger and more complex, it should be broken down into functions that each performs a specific task. This makes the program easier to understand and to maintain.

You can easily pass a list as an argument to a function. This gives you the ability to put many of the operations that you perform on a list in their own functions. When you need to call these functions, you can pass the list as an argument.

Program 7-10 shows an example of a program that uses such a function. The function in this program accepts a list as an argument and returns the total of the list's elements.

Program 7-10 (total_function.py)

```
# This program uses a function to calculate the
# total of the values in a list.

def main():
    # Create a list.
    numbers = [2, 4, 6, 8, 10]

    # Display the total of the list elements.
    print('The total is', get_total(numbers))

# The get_total function accepts a list as an
# argument returns the total of the values in
# the list.
def get_total(value_list):
    # Create a variable to use as an accumulator.
    total = 0

    # Calculate the total of the list elements.
    for num in value_list:
        total += num

    # Return the total.
    return total

# Call the main function.
main()
```

Program Output

```
The total is 30
```

Returning a List from a Function

A function can return a reference to a list. This gives you the ability to write a function that creates a list and adds elements to it, then returns a reference to the list so other parts of the program can work with it. The code in Program 7-11 shows an example. It uses a function named `get_values` that gets a series of values from the user, stores them in a list, then returns a reference to the list.

Program 7-11 (return_list.py)

```
# This program uses a function to create a list.
# The function returns a reference to the list.

```

```
def main():
    # Get a list with values stored in it.
    numbers = get_values()

    # Display the values in the list.
    print('The numbers in the list are:')
    print(numbers)

# The get_values function gets a series of numbers
# from the user and stores them in a list. The
# function returns a reference to the list.
def get_values():
    # Create an empty list.
    values = []

    # Create a variable to control the loop.
    again = 'y'

    # Get values from the user and add them to
    # the list.
    while again == 'y':
        # Get a number and add it to the list.
        num = int(input('Enter a number: '))
        values.append(num)

        # Want to do this again?
        print('Do you want to add another number?')
        again = input('y = yes, anything else = no: ')
        print()

    # Return the list.
    return values

# Call the main function.
main()
```

Program Output (with input shown in bold)

Enter a number: **1** Enter
Do you want to add another number?
y = yes, anything else = no: **y** Enter

Enter a number: **2** Enter
Do you want to add another number?
y = yes, anything else = no: **y** Enter

Enter a number: **3** Enter
Do you want to add another number?
y = yes, anything else = no: **y** Enter

(program output continues)

Program Output *(continued)*

```
Enter a number: 4 Enter
Do you want to add another number?
y = yes, anything else = no: y Enter
Enter a number: 5 Enter
Do you want to add another number?
y = yes, anything else = no: n Enter
The numbers in the list are:
[1, 2, 3, 4, 5]
```

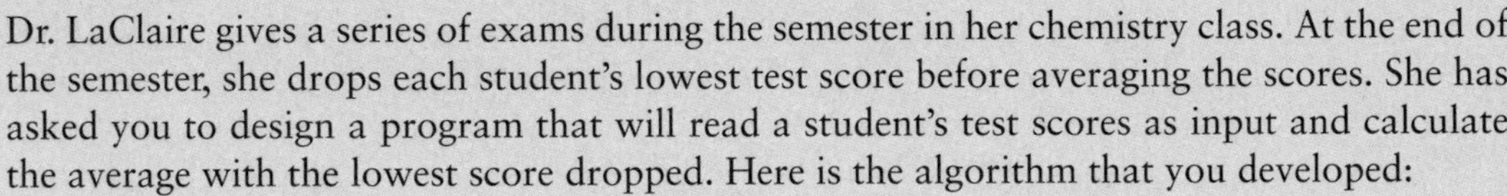

In the Spotlight:
Processing a List

Dr. LaClaire gives a series of exams during the semester in her chemistry class. At the end of the semester, she drops each student's lowest test score before averaging the scores. She has asked you to design a program that will read a student's test scores as input and calculate the average with the lowest score dropped. Here is the algorithm that you developed:

Get the student's test scores.
Calculate the total of the scores.
Find the lowest score.
Subtract the lowest score from the total. This gives the adjusted total.
Divide the adjusted total by 1 less than the number of test scores. This is the average.
Display the average.

Program 7-12 shows the code for the program, which is divided into three functions. Rather than presenting the entire program at once, let's first examine the `main` function, then each additional function separately. Here is the `main` function:

Program 7-12 **`drop_lowest_score.py: main function`**

```
# This program gets a series of test scores and
# calculates the average of the scores with the
# lowest score dropped.

def main():
    # Get the test scores from the user.
    scores = get_scores()

    # Get the total of the test scores.
    total = get_total(scores)

    # Get the lowest test score.
```

```
13        lowest = min(scores)
14
15        # Subtract the lowest score from the total.
16        total -= lowest
17
18        # Calculate the average. Note that we divide
19        # by 1 less than the number of scores because
20        # the lowest score was dropped.
21        average = total / (len(scores) - 1)
22
23        # Display the average.
24        print('The average, with the lowest score dropped',
25              'is:', average)
26
```

Line 7 calls the `get_scores` function. The function gets the test scores from the user and returns a reference to a list containing those scores. The list is assigned to the scores variable.

Line 10 calls the `get_total` function, passing the `scores` list as an argument. The function returns the total of the values in the list. This value is assigned to the `total` variable.

Line 13 calls the built-in `min` function, passing the `scores` list as an argument. The function returns the lowest value in the list. This value is assigned to the `lowest` variable.

Line 16 subtracts the lowest test score from the `total` variable. Then, line 21 calculates the average by dividing `total` by `len(scores) − 1`. (The program divides by `len (scores) − 1` because the lowest test score was dropped.) Lines 24 and 25 display the average.

Next is the `get_scores` function.

Program 7-12 **`drop_lowest_score.py: get_scores function`**

```
27  # The get_scores function gets a series of test
28  # scores from the user and stores them in a list.
29  # A reference to the list is returned.
30  def get_scores():
31      # Create an empty list.
32      test_scores = []
33
34      # Create a variable to control the loop.
35      again = 'y'
36
37      # Get the scores from the user and add them to
38      # the list.
39      while again == 'y':
40          # Get a score and add it to the list.
```

(program continues)

Program 7-12 *(continued)*

```
41          value = float(input('Enter a test score: '))
42          test_scores.append(value)
43
44          # Want to do this again?
45          print('Do you want to add another score?')
46          again = input('y = yes, anything else = no: ')
47          print()
48
49      # Return the list.
50      return test_scores
51
```

The get_scores function prompts the user to enter a series of test scores. As each score is entered, it is appended to a list. The list is returned in line 50. Next is the get_total function.

Program 7-12 **drop_lowest_score.py: get_total function**

```
52  # The get_total function accepts a list as an
53  # argument returns the total of the values in
54  # the list.
55  def get_total(value_list):
56      # Create a variable to use as an accumulator.
57      total = 0.0
58
59      # Calculate the total of the list elements.
60      for num in value_list:
61          total += num
62
63      # Return the total.
64      return total
65
66  # Call the main function.
67  main()
```

This function accepts a list as an argument. It uses an accumulator and a loop to calculate the total of the values in the list. Line 64 returns the total.

Program Output (with input shown in bold)

```
Enter a test score: 92 [Enter]
Do you want to add another score?
Y = yes, anything else = no: y [Enter]

Enter a test score: 67 [Enter]
Do you want to add another score?
Y = yes, anything else = no: y [Enter]
```

```
Enter a test score: 75 Enter
Do you want to add another score?
Y = yes, anything else = no: y Enter
Enter a test score: 88 Enter
Do you want to add another score?
Y = yes, anything else = no: n Enter
The average, with the lowest score dropped is: 85.0
```

Working with Lists and Files

Some tasks may require you to save the contents of a list to a file, so the data can be used at a later time. Likewise, some situations may require you to read the data from a file into a list. For example, suppose you have a file that contains a set of values that appear in random order, and you want to sort the values. One technique for sorting the values in the file would be to read them into a list, call the list's `sort` method, then write the values in the list back to the file.

Saving the contents of a list to a file is a straightforward procedure. In fact, Python file objects have a method named `writelines` that writes an entire list to a file. A drawback to the `writelines` method, however, is that it does not automatically write a newline (`'\n'`) at the end of each item. Consequently, each item is written to one long line in the file. Program 7-13 demonstrates the method.

Program 7-13 (`writelines.py`)

```
# This program uses the writelines method to save
# a list of strings to a file.

def main():
    # Create a list of strings.
    cities = ['New York', 'Boston', 'Atlanta', 'Dallas']

    # Open a file for writing.
    outfile = open('cities.txt', 'w')

    # Write the list to the file.
    outfile.writelines(cities)

    # Close the file.
    outfile.close()

# Call the main function.
main()
```

After this program executes, the `cities.txt` file will contain the following line:

```
New YorkBostonAtlantaDallas
```

An alternative approach is to use the `for` loop to iterate through the list, writing each element with a terminating newline character. Program 7-14 shows an example.

Program 7-14 (write_list.py)

```
# This program saves a list of strings to a file.

def main():
    # Create a list of strings.
    cities = ['New York', 'Boston', 'Atlanta', 'Dallas']

    # Open a file for writing.
    outfile = open('cities.txt', 'w')

    # Write the list to the file.
    for item in cities:
        outfile.write(item + '\n')

    # Close the file.
    outfile.close()

# Call the main function.
main()
```

After this program executes, the `cities.txt` file will contain the following lines:

```
New York
Boston
Atlanta
Dallas
```

File objects in Python have a method named `readlines` that returns a file's contents as a list of strings. Each line in the file will be an item in the list. The items in the list will include their terminating newline character, which in many cases you will want to strip. Program 7-15 shows an example. The statement in line 8 reads the files contents into a list, and the loop in lines 15 through 17 steps through the list, stripping the `'\n'` character from each element.

Program 7-15 (read_list.py)

```
1  # This program reads a file's contents into a list.
2
3  def main():
4      # Open a file for reading.
```

```
    infile = open('cities.txt', 'r')

    # Read the contents of the file into a list.
    cities = infile.readlines()

    # Close the file.
    infile.close()

    # Strip the \n from each element.
    index = 0
    while index < len(cities):
        cities[index] = cities[index].rstrip('\n')
        index += 1

    # Print the contents of the list.
    print(cities)

# Call the main function.
main()
```

Program Output

```
['New York', 'Boston', 'Atlanta', 'Dallas']
```

Program 7-16 shows another example of how a list can be written to a file. In this example, a list of numbers is written. Notice in line 12, each item is converted to a string with the `str` function, then a `'\n'` is concatenated to it.

Program 7-16 (write_number_list.py)

```
1  # This program saves a list of numbers to a file.
2
3  def main():
4      # Create a list of numbers.
5      numbers = [1, 2, 3, 4, 5, 6, 7]
6
7      # Open a file for writing.
8      outfile = open('numberlist.txt', 'w')
9
10     # Write the list to the file.
11     for item in numbers:
12         outfile.write(str(item) + '\n')
13
14     # Close the file.
15     outfile.close()
16
17 # Call the main function.
18 main()
```

When you read numbers from a file into a list, the numbers will have to be converted from strings to a numeric type. Program 7-17 shows an example.

Program 7-17 (read_number_list.py)

```
# This program reads numbers from a file into a list.

def main():
    # Open a file for reading.
    infile = open('numberlist.txt', 'r')

    # Read the contents of the file into a list.
    numbers = infile.readlines()

    # Close the file.
    infile.close()

    # Convert each element to an int.
    index = 0
    while index < len(numbers):
        numbers[index] = int(numbers[index])
        index += 1

    # Print the contents of the list.
    print(numbers)

# Call the main function.
main()
```

Program Output

```
[1, 2, 3, 4, 5, 6, 7]
```

7.8 Two-Dimensional Lists

CONCEPT: A two-dimensional list is a list that has other lists as its elements.

The elements of a list can be virtually anything, including other lists. To demonstrate, look at the following interactive session:

```
>>> students = [['Joe', 'Kim'], ['Sam', 'Sue'], ['Kelly', 'Chris']] [Enter]
>>> print(students) [Enter]
[['Joe', 'Kim'], ['Sam', 'Sue'], ['Kelly', 'Chris']]
>>> print(students[0]) [Enter]
['Joe', 'Kim']
>>> print(students[1]) [Enter]
```

```
7  ['Sam', 'Sue']
8  >>> print(students[2]) Enter
9  ['Kelly', 'Chris']
10 >>>
```

Let's take a closer look at each line.

- Line 1 creates a list and assigns it to the students variable. The list has three elements, and each element is also a list. The element at students[0] is
  ['Joe', 'Kim']

  The element at students[1] is
  ['Sam', 'Sue']

  The element at students[2] is
  ['Kelly', 'Chris']
- Line 2 prints the entire students list. The output of the print function is shown in line 3.
- Line 4 prints the students[0] element. The output of the print function is shown in line 5.
- Line 6 prints the students[1] element. The output of the print function is shown in line 7.
- Line 8 prints the students[2] element. The output of the print function is shown in line 9.

Lists of lists are also known as *nested lists*, or *two-dimensional lists*. It is common to think of a two-dimensional list as having rows and columns of elements, as shown in Figure 7-5. This figure shows the two-dimensional list that was created in the previous interactive session as having three rows and two columns. Notice the rows are numbered 0, 1, and 2, and the columns are numbered 0 and 1. There is a total of six elements in the list.

Figure 7-5 A two-dimensional list

	Column 0	Column 1
Row 0	'Joe'	'Kim'
Row 1	'Sam'	'Sue'
Row 2	'Kelly'	'Chris'

Two-dimensional lists are useful for working with multiple sets of data. For example, suppose you are writing a grade-averaging program for a teacher. The teacher has three students, and each student takes three exams during the semester. One approach would be to create three separate lists, one for each student. Each of these lists would have three elements, one for each exam score. This approach would be cumbersome, however, because you would have to separately process each of the lists. A better approach would be to use a two-dimensional list with three rows (one for each student) and three columns (one for each exam score), as shown in Figure 7-6.

Figure 7-6 Two-dimensional list with three rows and three columns

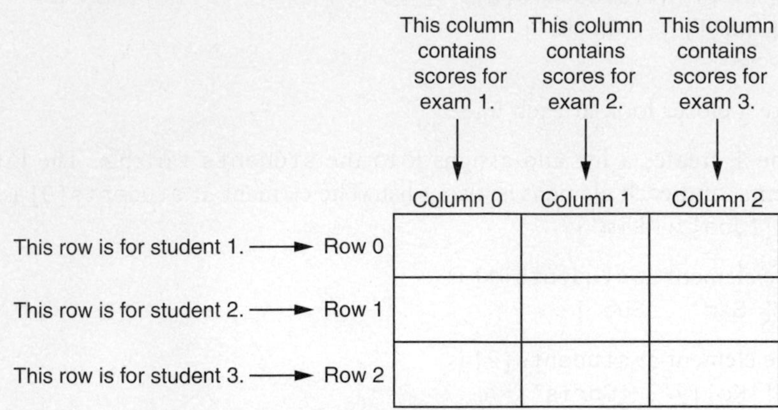

When processing the data in a two-dimensional list, you need two subscripts: one for the rows, and one for the columns. For example, suppose we create a two-dimensional list with the following statement:

```
scores = [[0, 0, 0],
          [0, 0, 0],
          [0, 0, 0]]
```

The elements in row 0 are referenced as follows:

```
scores[0][0]
scores[0][1]
scores[0][2]
```

The elements in row 1 are referenced as follows:

```
scores[1][0]
scores[1][1]
scores[1][2]
```

And, the elements in row 2 are referenced as follows:

```
scores[2][0]
scores[2][1]
scores[2][2]
```

Figure 7-7 illustrates the two-dimensional list, with the subscripts shown for each element.

Figure 7-7 Subscripts for each element of the `scores` list

	Column 0	Column 1	Column 2
Row 0	scores[0][0]	scores[0][1]	scores[0][2]
Row 1	scores[1][0]	scores[1][1]	scores[1][2]
Row 2	scores[2][0]	scores[2][1]	scores[2][2]

Programs that process two-dimensional lists typically do so with nested loops. Let's look at an example. Program 7-18 creates a two-dimensional list and assigns random numbers to each of its elements.

Program 7-18 (random_numbers.py)

```
 1 # This program assigns random numbers to
 2 # a two-dimensional list.
 3 import random
 4
 5 # Constants for rows and columns
 6 ROWS = 3
 7 COLS = 4
 8
 9 def main():
10     # Create a two-dimensional list.
11     values = [[0, 0, 0, 0],
12               [0, 0, 0, 0],
13               [0, 0, 0, 0]]
14
15     # Fill the list with random numbers.
16     for r in range(ROWS):
17         for c in range(COLS):
18             values[r][c] = random.randint(1, 100)
19
20     # Display the random numbers.
21     print(values)
22
23 # Call the main function.
24 main()
```

Program Output

```
[[4, 17, 34, 24], [46, 21, 54, 10], [54, 92, 20, 100]]
```

Let's take a closer look at the program:

- Lines 6 and 7 create global constants for the number of rows and columns.
- Lines 11 through 13 create a two-dimensional list and assign it to the `values` variable. We can think of the list as having three rows and four columns. Each element is assigned the value 0.
- Lines 16 through 18 are a set of nested `for` loops. The outer loop iterates once for each row, and it assigns the variable `r` the values 0 through 2. The inner loop iterates once for each column, and it assigns the variable `c` the values 0 through 3. The statement in line 18 executes once for each element of the list, assigning it a random integer in the range of 1 through 100.
- Line 21 displays the list's contents.

Notice the statement in line 21 passes the values list as an argument to the print function; as a result, the entire list is displayed on the screen. Suppose we do not like the way that the print function displays the list enclosed in brackets, with each nested list also enclosed in brackets. For example, suppose we want to display each list element on a line by itself, like this:

```
4
17
34
24
46
```
and so forth.

To accomplish that, we can write a set of nested loops, such as

```
for r in range(ROWS):
    for c in range(COLS):
        print(values[r][c])
```

Checkpoint

7.19 Look at the following interactive session, in which a two-dimensional list is created. How many rows and how many columns are in the list?

```
numbers = [[1, 2], [10, 20], [100, 200], [1000, 2000]]
```

7.20 Write a statement that creates a two-dimensional list with three rows and four columns. Each element should be assigned the value 0.

7.21 Write a set of nested loops that display the contents of the numbers list shown in Checkpoint question 7.19.

7.9 Tuples

CONCEPT: A tuple is an immutable sequence, which means that its contents cannot be changed.

A *tuple* is a sequence, very much like a list. The primary difference between tuples and lists is that tuples are immutable. That means once a tuple is created, it cannot be changed. When you create a tuple, you enclose its elements in a set of parentheses, as shown in the following interactive session:

```
>>> my_tuple = (1, 2, 3, 4, 5) Enter
>>> print(my_tuple) Enter
(1, 2, 3, 4, 5)
>>>
```

The first statement creates a tuple containing the elements 1, 2, 3, 4, and 5 and assigns it to the variable `my_tuple`. The second statement sends `my_tuple` as an argument to the `print` function, which displays its elements. The following session shows how a `for` loop can iterate over the elements in a tuple:

```
>>> names = ('Holly', 'Warren', 'Ashley') Enter
>>> for n in names: Enter
        print(n) Enter Enter
Holly
Warren
Ashley
>>>
```

Like lists, tuples support indexing, as shown in the following session:

```
>>> names = ('Holly', 'Warren', 'Ashley') Enter
>>> for i in range(len(names)): Enter
        print(names[i]) Enter Enter

Holly
Warren
Ashley
>>>
```

In fact, tuples support all the same operations as lists, except those that change the contents of the list. Tuples support the following:

- Subscript indexing (for retrieving element values only)
- Methods such as `index`
- Built-in functions such as `len`, `min`, and `max`
- Slicing expressions
- The `in` operator
- The `+` and `*` operators

Tuples do not support methods such as `append`, `remove`, `insert`, `reverse`, and `sort`.

NOTE: If you want to create a tuple with just one element, you must write a trailing comma after the element's value, as shown here:

```
my_tuple = (1,)     # Creates a tuple with one element.
```

If you omit the comma, you will not create a tuple. For example, the following statement simply assigns the integer value 1 to the `value` variable:

```
value = (1)         # Creates an integer.
```

What's the Point?

If the only difference between lists and tuples is immutability, you might wonder why tuples exist. One reason that tuples exist is performance. Processing a tuple is faster than processing a list, so tuples are good choices when you are processing lots of data, and that data will not be modified. Another reason is that tuples are safe. Because you are not allowed to change the contents of a tuple, you can store data in one and rest assured that it will not be modified (accidentally or otherwise) by any code in your program.

Additionally, there are certain operations in Python that require the use of a tuple. As you learn more about Python, you will encounter tuples more frequently.

Converting Between Lists and Tuples

You can use the built-in `list()` function to convert a tuple to a list, and the built-in `tuple()` function to convert a list to a tuple. The following interactive session demonstrates:

```
1 >>> number_tuple = (1, 2, 3) Enter
2 >>> number_list = list(number_tuple) Enter
3 >>> print(number_list) Enter
4 [1, 2, 3]
5 >>> str_list = ['one', 'two', 'three'] Enter
6 >>> str_tuple = tuple(str_list) Enter
7 >>> print(str_tuple) Enter
8 ('one', 'two', 'three')
9 >>>
```

Here's a summary of the statements:

- Line 1 creates a tuple and assigns it to the `number_tuple` variable.
- Line 2 passes `number_tuple` to the `list()` function. The function returns a list containing the same values as `number_tuple`, and it is assigned to the `number_list` variable.
- Line 3 passes `number_list` to the `print` function. The function's output is shown in line 4.
- Line 5 creates a list of strings and assigns it to the `str_list` variable.
- Line 6 passes `str_list` to the `tuple()` function. The function returns a tuple containing the same values as `str_list`, and it is assigned to `str_tuple`.
- Line 7 passes `str_tuple` to the `print` function. The function's output is shown in line 8.

Checkpoint

7.22 What is the primary difference between a list and a tuple?

7.23 Give two reasons why tuples exist.

7.24 Assume `my_list` references a list. Write a statement that converts it to a tuple.

7.25 Assume `my_tuple` references a tuple. Write a statement that converts it to a list.

7.10 Plotting List Data with the matplotlib Package

The matplotlib package is a library for creating two-dimensional charts and graphs. It is not part of the standard Python library, so you will have to install it separately, after you have installed Python on your system. To install matplotlib on a Windows system, open a command prompt window and enter the following command:

```
pip install matplotlib
```

On a Mac or a Linux system, open a Terminal window and enter the following command:

```
sudo pip3 install matplotlib
```

TIP: See Appendix F for more information about packages and the pip utility.

Once you enter the command, the pip utility will start downloading and installing the package. Once the process is finished, you can verify that the package was correctly installed by starting IDLE and entering the command

```
>>> import matplotlib
```

If you do not see an error message, you can assume the package was successfully installed.

Importing the pyplot Module

The matplotlib package contains a module named pyplot that you will need to import in order to create all of the graphs that we will demonstrate in this chapter. There are several different techniques for importing the module. Perhaps the most straightforward technique is like this:

```
import matplotlib.pyplot
```

Within the pyplot module, there are several functions that you will call to build and display graphs. When you use this form of the import statement, you have to prefix each function call with matplotlib.pyplot. For example, there is a function named plot that you will call to create line graphs, and you would call the plot function like this:

```
matplotlib.pyplot.plot(arguments...)
```

Having to type matplotlib.pyplot before the name of each function call can become tiresome, so we will use a slightly different technique to import the module. We will use the following import statement, which creates an *alias* for the matplotlib.pyplot module:

```
import matplotlib.pyplot as plt
```

This statement imports the matplotlib.pyplot module, and it creates an alias for the module named plt. This allows us to use the plt prefix to call any function in the matplotlib.pyplot module. For example, we can call the plot function like this:

```
plt.plot(arguments...)
```

TIP: For more information about the `import` statement, see Appendix E.

Plotting a Line Graph

You can use the `plot` function to create a line graph that connects a series of data points with straight lines. The line graph has a horizontal *X* axis and a vertical *Y* axis. Each data point in the graph is located at a (*X*, *Y*) coordinate.

To create a line graph, you first create two lists: one containing the *X* coordinates of each data point, and another containing the *Y* coordinates of each data point. For example, suppose we have five data points, located at the following coordinates:

(0, 0)
(1, 3)
(2, 1)
(3, 5)
(4, 2)

We would create two lists to hold the coordinates, such as the following:

```
x_coords = [0, 1, 2, 3, 4]
y_coords = [0, 3, 1, 5, 2]
```

Next, we call the `plot` function to create the graph, passing the lists as arguments. Here is an example:

```
plt.plot(x_coords, y_coords)
```

The `plot` function builds the line graph in memory, but does not display it. To display the graph, you call the `show` function, as shown here:

```
plt.show()
```

Program 7-19 shows a complete example. When you run the program, the graphics window shown in Figure 7-8 is displayed.

Program 7-19 (line_graph1.py)

```
# This program displays a simple line graph.
import matplotlib.pyplot as plt

def main():
    # Create lists with the X and Y coordinates of each data point.
    x_coords = [0, 1, 2, 3, 4]
    y_coords = [0, 3, 1, 5, 2]

    # Build the line graph.
    plt.plot(x_coords, y_coords)
```

```
    # Display the line graph.
    plt.show()

# Call the main function.
main()
```

Figure 7-8 Output of Program 7-19

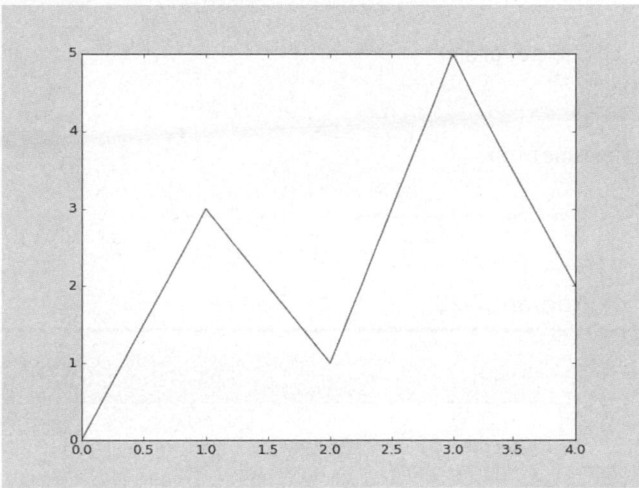

Adding a Title, Axis Labels, and a Grid

You can add a title to your graph with the `title` function. You simply call the function, passing the string that you want displayed as a title. The title will be displayed just above the graph. You can also add descriptive labels to the *X* and *Y* axes with the `xlabel` and `ylabel` functions. You call these functions, passing a string that you want displayed along the axis. You can also add a grid to the graph by calling the `grid` function, passing `True` as an argument. Program 7-20 shows an example.

Program 7-20 (`line_graph2.py`)

```
# This program displays a simple line graph.
import matplotlib.pyplot as plt

def main():
    # Create lists with the X and Y coordinates of each data point.
    x_coords = [0, 1, 2, 3, 4]
    y_coords = [0, 3, 1, 5, 2]

    # Build the line graph.
    plt.plot(x_coords, y_coords)

    # Add a title.
    plt.title('Sample Data')

```

(program continues)

Program 7-20 *(continued)*

```
    # Add labels to the axes.
    plt.xlabel('This is the X axis')
    plt.ylabel('This is the Y axis')

    # Add a grid.
    plt.grid(True)

    # Display the line graph.
    plt.show()

# Call the main function.
main()
```

Figure 7-9 Output of Program 7-20

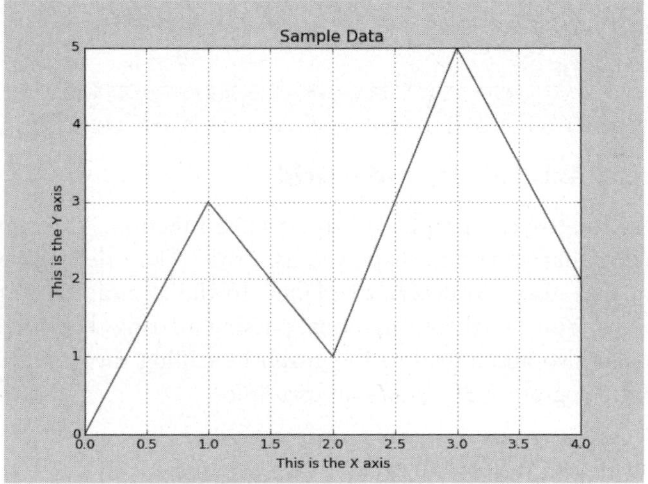

Customizing the *X* and *Y* Axes

By default, the *X* axis begins at the lowest *X* coordinate in your set of data points, and it ends at the highest *X* coordinate in your set of data points. For example, notice in Program 7-20, the lowest *X* coordinate is 0, and the highest *X* coordinate is 4. Now look at the program's output in Figure 7-9, and notice the *X* axis begins at 0 and ends at 4.

The *Y* axis, by default, is configured in the same way. It begins at the lowest *Y* coordinate in your set of data points, and it ends at the highest *Y* coordinate in your set of data points. Once again, look at Program 7-20, and notice the lowest *Y* coordinate is 0, and the highest *Y* coordinate is 5. In the program's output, the *Y* axis begins at 0 and ends at 5.

You can change the lower and upper limits of the *X* and *Y* axes by calling the `xlim` and `ylim` functions. Here is an example of calling the `xlim` function, using keyword arguments to set the lower and upper limits of the *X* axis:

```
plt.xlim(xmin=1, xmax=100)
```

This statement configures the *X* axis to begin at the value 1 and end at the value 100. Here is an example of calling the `ylim` function, using keyword arguments to set the lower and upper limits of the *Y* axis:

```
plt.ylim(ymin=10, ymax=50)
```

This statement configures the *Y* axis to begin at the value 10 and end at the value 50. Program 7-21 shows a complete example. In line 20, the *X* axis is configured to begin at −1 and end at 10. In line 21, the *Y* axis is configured to begin at −1 and end at 6. The program's output is shown in Figure 7-10.

Program 7-21 (`line_graph3.py`)

```
1   # This program displays a simple line graph.
2   import matplotlib.pyplot as plt
3
4   def main():
5       # Create lists with the X and Y coordinates of each data point.
6       x_coords = [0, 1, 2, 3, 4]
7       y_coords = [0, 3, 1, 5, 2]
8
9       # Build the line graph.
10      plt.plot(x_coords, y_coords)
11
12      # Add a title.
13      plt.title('Sample Data')
14
15      # Add labels to the axes.
16      plt.xlabel('This is the X axis')
17      plt.ylabel('This is the Y axis')
18
19      # Set the axis limits.
20      plt.xlim(xmin=-1, xmax=10)
21      plt.ylim(ymin=-1, ymax=6)
22
23      # Add a grid.
24      plt.grid(True)
25
26      # Display the line graph.
27      plt.show()
28
29  # Call the main function.
30  main()
```

Figure 7-10 Output of Program 7-21

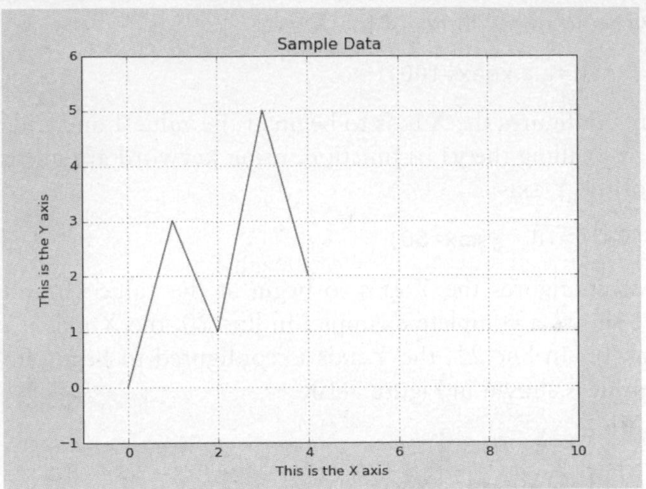

You can customize each tick mark's label with the `xticks` and `yticks` functions. These functions each take two lists as arguments. The first argument is a list of tick mark locations, and the second argument is a list of labels to display at the specified locations. Here is an example, using the `xticks` function:

```
plt.xticks([0, 1, 2], ['Baseball', 'Basketball', 'Football'])
```

In this example, `'Baseball'` will be displayed at tick mark 0, `'Basketball'` will be displayed at tick mark 1, and `'Football'` will be displayed at tick mark 2. Here is an example, using the `yticks` function:

```
plt.yticks([0, 1, 2, 3], ['Zero', 'Quarter', 'Half', 'Three Quarters'])
```

In this example, `'Zero'` will be displayed at tick mark 0, `'Quarter'` will be displayed at tick mark 1, `'Half'` will be displayed at tick mark 2, and `'Three Quarters'` will be displayed at tick mark 3.

Program 7-22 shows a complete example. In the program's output, the tick mark labels on the *X* axis display years, and the tick mark labels on the *Y* axis display sales in millions of dollars. The statement in lines 20 and 21 calls the `xticks` function to customize the *X* axis in the following manner:

- `'2016'` will be displayed at tick mark 0
- `'2017'` will be displayed at tick mark 1
- `'2018'` will be displayed at tick mark 2
- `'2019'` will be displayed at tick mark 3
- `'2020'` will be displayed at tick mark 4

Then, the statement in lines 22 and 23 calls the `yticks` function to customize the *Y* axis in the following manner:

- `'$0m'` will be displayed at tick mark 0
- `'$1m'` will be displayed at tick mark 1

- '$2m' will be displayed at tick mark 2
- '$3m' will be displayed at tick mark 3
- '$4m' will be displayed at tick mark 4
- '$5m' will be displayed at tick mark 5

The program's output is shown in Figure 7-11.

Program 7-22 (line_graph4.py)

```
# This program displays a simple line graph.
import matplotlib.pyplot as plt

def main():
    # Create lists with the X and Y coordinates of each data point.
    x_coords = [0, 1, 2, 3, 4]
    y_coords = [0, 3, 1, 5, 2]

    # Build the line graph.
    plt.plot(x_coords, y_coords)

    # Add a title.
    plt.title('Sales by Year')

    # Add labels to the axes.
    plt.xlabel('Year')
    plt.ylabel('Sales')

    # Customize the tick marks.
    plt.xticks([0, 1, 2, 3, 4],
               ['2016', '2017', '2018', '2019', '2020'])
    plt.yticks([0, 1, 2, 3, 4, 5],
               ['$0m', '$1m', '$2m', '$3m', '$4m', '$5m'])

    # Add a grid.
    plt.grid(True)

    # Display the line graph.
    plt.show()

# Call the main function.
main()
```

Figure 7-11 Output of Program 7-22

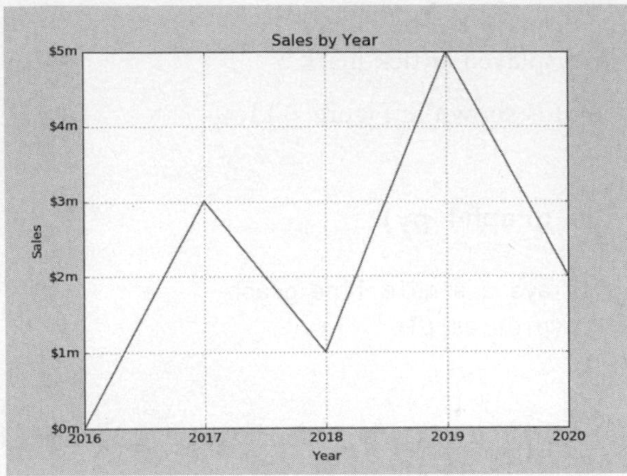

Displaying Markers at the Data Points

You can display a round dot as a marker at each data point in your line graph by using the keyword argument `marker='o'` with the `plot` function. Program 7-23 shows an example. The program's output is shown in Figure 7-12.

Program 7-23 (line_graph5.py)

```
# This program displays a simple line graph.
import matplotlib.pyplot as plt

def main():
    # Create lists with the X and Y coordinates of each data point.
    x_coords = [0, 1, 2, 3, 4]
    y_coords = [0, 3, 1, 5, 2]

    # Build the line graph.
    plt.plot(x_coords, y_coords, marker='o')

    # Add a title.
    plt.title('Sales by Year')

    # Add labels to the axes.
    plt.xlabel('Year')
    plt.ylabel('Sales')

    # Customize the tick marks.
    plt.xticks([0, 1, 2, 3, 4],
               ['2016', '2017', '2018', '2019', '2020'])
    plt.yticks([0, 1, 2, 3, 4, 5],
               ['$0m', '$1m', '$2m', '$3m', '$4m', '$5m'])
```

```

    # Add a grid.
    plt.grid(True)

    # Display the line graph.
    plt.show()

# Call the main function.
main()
```

Figure 7-12 Output of Program 7-23

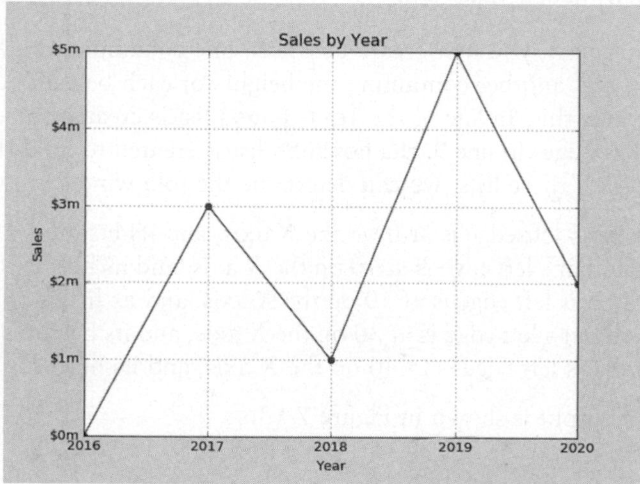

In addition to round dots, you can display other types of marker symbols. Table 7-2 shows a few of the accepted `marker=` arguments and describes the type of marker symbol each displays.

Table 7-2 Some of the marker symbols

`marker=` Argument	Result
`marker='o'`	Displays round dots as markers
`marker='s'`	Displays squares as markers
`marker='*'`	Displays small stars as markers
`marker='D'`	Displays small diamonds as markers
`marker='^'`	Displays upward triangles as markers
`marker='v'`	Displays downward triangles as markers
`marker='>'`	Displays right-pointing triangles as markers
`marker='<'`	Displays left-pointing triangles as markers

NOTE: If you pass the marker character as a positional argument (instead of passing it as a keyword argument), the `plot` function will draw markers at the data points, but it will not connect them with lines. Here is an example:

```
plt.plot(x_coords, y_coords, 'o')
```

Plotting a Bar Chart

You can use the `bar` function in the `matplotlib.pyplot` module to create a bar chart. A bar chart has a horizontal *X* axis, a vertical *Y* axis, and a series of bars that typically originate from the *X* axis. Each bar represents a value, and the bar's height is proportional to the value that the bar represents.

To create a bar chart, you first create two lists: one containing the *X* coordinates of each bar's left edge, and another containing the heights of each bar, along the *Y* axis. Program 7-24 demonstrates this. In line 6, the `left_edges` list is created to hold the *X* coordinates of each bar's left edge. In line 9, the `heights` list is created to hold the height of each bar. Looking at both of these lists, we can determine the following:

- The first bar's left edge is at 0 on the *X* axis, and its height is 100 along the *Y* axis.
- The second bar's left edge is at 10 on the *X* axis, and its height is 200 along the *Y* axis.
- The third bar's left edge is at 20 on the *X* axis, and its height is 300 along the *Y* axis.
- The fourth bar's left edge is at 30 on the *X* axis, and its height is 400 along the *Y* axis.
- The fifth bar's left edge is at 40 on the *X* axis, and its height is 500 along the *Y* axis.

The program's output is shown in Figure 7-13.

Program 7-24 (bar_chart1.py)

```
1  # This program displays a simple bar chart.
2  import matplotlib.pyplot as plt
3
4  def main():
5      # Create a list with the X coordinates of each bar's left edge.
6      left_edges = [0, 10, 20, 30, 40]
7
8      # Create a list with the heights of each bar.
9      heights = [100, 200, 300, 400, 500]
10
11     # Build the bar chart.
12     plt.bar(left_edges, heights)
13
14     # Display the bar chart.
15     plt.show()
16
17 # Call the main function.
18 main()
```

Figure 7-13 Output of Program 7-24

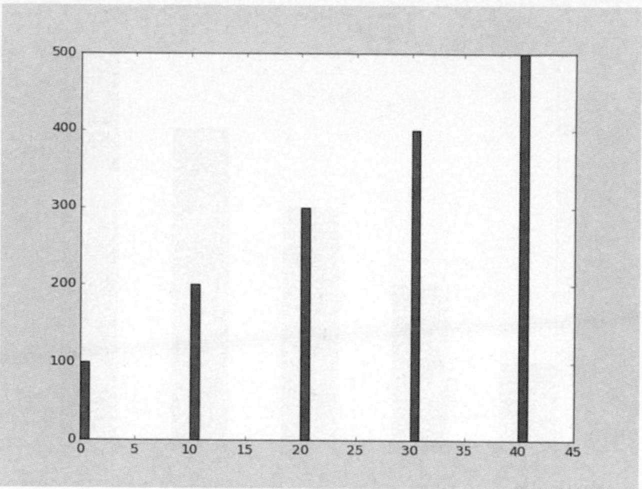

Customizing the Bar Width

The default width of each bar in a bar graph is 0.8 along the *X* axis. You can change the bar width by passing a third argument to the `bar` function. Program 7-25 demonstrates this by setting the bar width to 5. The program's output is shown in Figure 7-14.

Program 7-25 (bar_chart2.py)

```
# This program displays a simple bar chart.
import matplotlib.pyplot as plt

def main():
    # Create a list with the X coordinates of each bar's left edge.
    left_edges = [0, 10, 20, 30, 40]

    # Create a list with the heights of each bar.
    heights = [100, 200, 300, 400, 500]

    # Create a variable for the bar width.
    bar_width = 5

    # Build the bar chart.
    plt.bar(left_edges, heights, bar_width)

    # Display the bar chart.
    plt.show()

# Call the main function.
main()
```

Figure 7-14 Output of Program 7-25

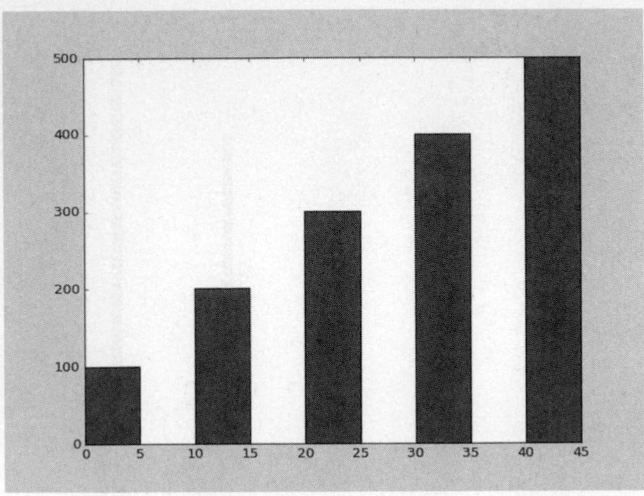

Changing the Colors of the Bars

The `bar` function has a `color` parameter that you can use to change the colors of the bars in a bar chart. The argument that you pass into this parameter is a tuple containing a series of color codes. Table 7-3 shows the basic color codes.

Table 7-3 Color codes

Color Code	Corresponding Color
`'b'`	Blue
`'g'`	Green
`'r'`	Red
`'c'`	Cyan
`'m'`	Magenta
`'y'`	Yellow
`'k'`	Black
`'w'`	White

The following statement shows an example of how to pass a tuple of color codes as a keyword argument:

```
plt.bar(left_edges, heights, color=('r', 'g', 'b', 'w', 'k'))
```

When this statement executes, the colors of the bars in the resulting bar chart will be as follows:

- The first bar will be red.
- The second bar will be green.
- The third bar will be blue.
- The fourth bar will be white.
- The fifth bar will be black.

Adding a Title, Axis Labels, and Customizing the Tick Mark Labels

You can use the same functions described in the section on line graphs to add a title and axis labels to your bar chart, as well as to customize the *X* and *Y* axes. For example, look at Program 7-26. Line 18 calls the `title` function to add a title to chart, and lines 21 and 22 call the `xlabel` and `ylabel` functions to add labels to the *X* and *Y* axes. Lines 25 and 26 call the `xticks` function to display custom tick mark labels along the *X* axis, and lines 27 and 28 call the `yticks` function to display custom tick mark labels along the *Y* axis. The program's output is shown in Figure 7-15.

Program 7-26 (bar_chart3.py)

```
 1  # This program displays a sales chart.
 2  import matplotlib.pyplot as plt
 3
 4  def main():
 5      # Create a list with the X coordinates of each bar's left edge.
 6      left_edges = [0, 10, 20, 30, 40]
 7
 8      # Create a list with the heights of each bar.
 9      heights = [100, 200, 300, 400, 500]
10
11      # Create a variable for the bar width.
12      bar_width = 10
13
14      # Build the bar chart.
15      plt.bar(left_edges, heights, bar_width, color=('r', 'g', 'b', 'w', 'k'))
16
17      # Add a title.
18      plt.title('Sales by Year')
19
20      # Add labels to the axes.
21      plt.xlabel('Year')
22      plt.ylabel('Sales')
23
24      # Customize the tick marks.
25      plt.xticks([5, 15, 25, 35, 45],
26                 ['2016', '2017', '2018', '2019', '2020'])
27      plt.yticks([0, 100, 200, 300, 400, 500],
28                 ['$0m', '$1m', '$2m', '$3m', '$4m', '$5m'])
29
30      # Display the bar chart.
31      plt.show()
32
33  # Call the main function.
34  main()
```

Figure 7-15 Output of Program 7-26

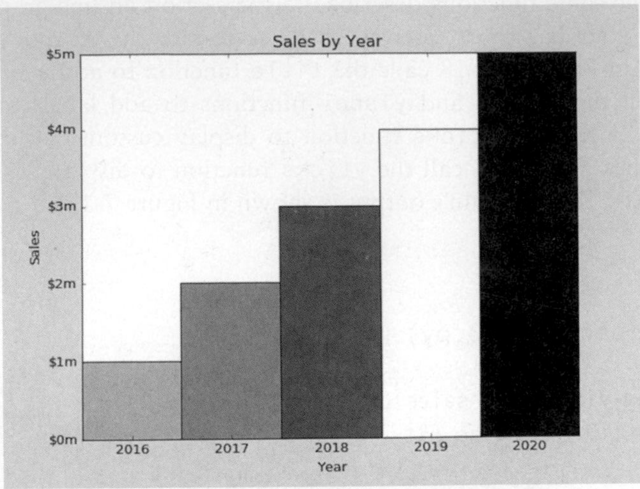

Plotting a Pie Chart

A pie chart is a graph that shows a circle that is divided into slices. The circle represents the whole, and the slices represent percentages of the whole. You use the `pie` function in the `matplotlib.pyplot` module to create a pie chart.

When you call the `pie` function, you pass a list of values as an argument. The `pie` function will calculate the sum of the values in the list, then use that sum as the value of the whole. Then, each element in the list will become a slice in the pie chart. The size of a slice represents that element's value as a percentage of the whole.

Program 7-27 shows an example. Line 6 creates a list containing the values 10, 30, 40, and 20. Then, line 9 passes the list as an argument to the `pie` function. We can make the following observations about the resulting pie chart:

- The sum of the list elements is 200, so the pie chart's whole will be 200.
- There are four elements in the list, so the pie chart will be divided into four slices.
- The first slice represents the value 20, so its size will be 10 percent of the whole.
- The second slice represents the value 60, so its size will be 30 percent of the whole.
- The third slice represents the value 80, so its size will be 40 percent of the whole.
- The fourth slice represents the value 40, so its size will be 20 percent of the whole.

The program's output is shown in Figure 7-16.

Program 7-27 (pie_chart1.py)

```
1  # This program displays a simple pie chart.
2  import matplotlib.pyplot as plt
3
4  def main():
5      # Create a list of values
6      values = [20, 60, 80, 40]
```

```

    # Create a pie chart from the values.
    plt.pie(values)

    # Display the pie chart.
    plt.show()

# Call the main function.
main()
```

Figure 7-16 Output of Program 7-27

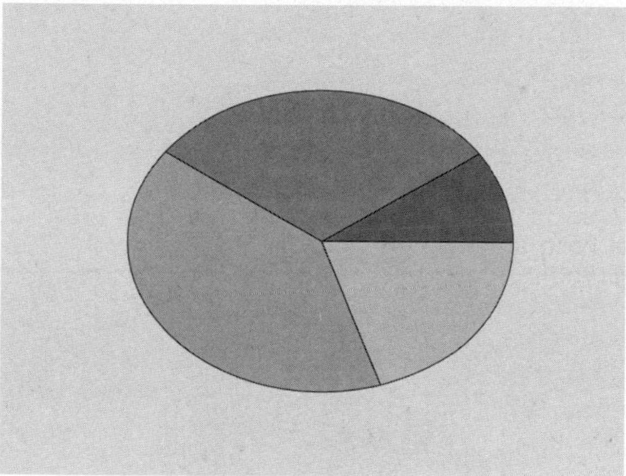

Displaying Slice Labels and a Chart Title

The `pie` function has a `labels` parameter that you can use to display labels for the slices in the pie chart. The argument that you pass into this parameter is a list containing the desired labels, as strings. Program 7-28 shows an example. Line 9 creates a list named `slice_labels`. Then, in line 12, the keyword argument `labels=slice_labels` is passed to the `pie` function. As a result, the string `'1st Qtr'` will be displayed as a label for the first slice, `'2nd Qtr'` will be displayed as a label for the second slice, and so forth. Line 15 uses the `title` function to display the title `'Sales by Quarter'`. The program's output is shown in Figure 7-17.

Program 7-28 (pie_chart2.py)

```
1  # This program displays a simple pie chart.
2  import matplotlib.pyplot as plt
3
4  def main():
5      # Create a list of sales amounts.
6      sales = [100, 400, 300, 600]
7
```

(program continues)

Program 7-28 *(continued)*

```
    # Create a list of labels for the slices.
    slice_labels = ['1st Qtr', '2nd Qtr', '3rd Qtr', '4th Qtr']

    # Create a pie chart from the values.
    plt.pie(sales, labels=slice_labels)

    # Add a title.
    plt.title('Sales by Quarter')

    # Display the pie chart.
    plt.show()

# Call the main function.
main()
```

Figure 7-17 Output of Program 7-28

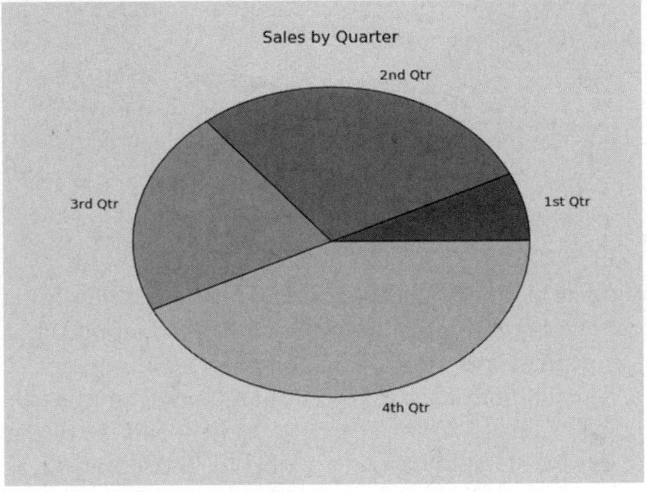

Changing the Colors of the Slices

The `pie` function automatically changes the color of the slices, in the following order: blue, green, red, cyan, magenta, yellow, black, and white. You can specify a different set of colors, however, by passing a tuple of color codes as an argument to the `pie` function's `colors` parameter. The color codes for the basic colors were previously shown in Table 7-3. The following statement shows an example of how to pass a tuple of color codes as a keyword argument:

```
plt.pie(values, colors=('r', 'g', 'b', 'w', 'k'))
```

When this statement executes, the colors of the slices in the resulting pie chart will be red, green, blue, white, and black.

Checkpoint

7.26 To create a graph with the `plot` function, what two arguments you must pass?

7.27 What sort of graph does the `plot` function produce?

7.28 What functions do you use to add labels to the *X* and *Y* axes in a graph?

7.29 How do you change the lower and upper limits of the *X* and *Y* axes in a graph?

7.30 How do you customize the tick marks along the *X* and *Y* axes in a graph?

7.31 To create a bar chart with the `bar` function, what two arguments you must pass?

7.32 Assume the following statement calls the `bar` function to construct a bar chart with four bars. What color will the bars be?

```
plt.bar(left_edges, heights, color=('r', 'b', 'r', 'b'))
```

7.33 To create a pie chart with the `pie` function, what argument you must pass?

Review Questions

Multiple Choice

1. This term refers to an individual item in a list.
   a. element
   b. bin
   c. cubbyhole
   d. slot
2. This is a number that identifies an item in a list.
   a. element
   b. index
   c. bookmark
   d. identifier
3. This is the first index in a list.
   a. −1
   b. 1
   c. 0
   d. The size of the list minus one
4. This is the last index in a list.
   a. 1
   b. 99
   c. 0
   d. The size of the list minus one
5. This will happen if you try to use an index that is out of range for a list.
   a. A `ValueError` exception will occur.
   b. An `IndexError` exception will occur.
   c. The list will be erased and the program will continue to run.
   d. Nothing—the invalid index will be ignored.

6. This function returns the length of a list.
   a. `length`
   b. `size`
   c. `len`
   d. `lengthof`
7. When the `*` operator's left operand is a list and its right operand is an integer, the operator becomes this.
   a. The multiplication operator
   b. The repetition operator
   c. The initialization operator
   d. Nothing—the operator does not support those types of operands.
8. This list method adds an item to the end of an existing list.
   a. `add`
   b. `add_to`
   c. `increase`
   d. `append`
9. This removes an item at a specific index in a list.
   a. the `remove` method
   b. the `delete` method
   c. the `del` statement
   d. the `kill` method
10. Assume the following statement appears in a program:

    `mylist = []`

    Which of the following statements would you use to add the string `'Labrador'` to the list at index 0?
    a. `mylist[0] = 'Labrador'`
    b. `mylist.insert(0, 'Labrador')`
    c. `mylist.append('Labrador')`
    d. `mylist.insert('Labrador', 0)`
11. If you call the `index` method to locate an item in a list and the item is not found, this happens.
    a. A `ValueError` exception is raised.
    b. An `InvalidIndex` exception is raised.
    c. The method returns −1.
    d. Nothing happens. The program continues running at the next statement.
12. This built-in function returns the highest value in a list.
    a. `highest`
    b. `max`
    c. `greatest`
    d. `best_of`
13. This file object method returns a list containing the file's contents.
    a. `to_list`
    b. `getlist`
    c. `readline`
    d. `readlines`

14. Which of the following statements creates a tuple?
    a. `values = [1, 2, 3, 4]`
    b. `values = {1, 2, 3, 4}`
    c. `values = (1)`
    d. `values = (1,)`

True or False

1. Lists in Python are immutable.
2. Tuples in Python are immutable.
3. The `del` statement deletes an item at a specified index in a list.
4. Assume `list1` references a list. After the following statement executes, `list1` and `list2` will reference two identical but separate lists in memory:

   ```
   list2 = list1
   ```
5. A file object's `writelines` method automatically writes a newline (`'\n'`) after writing each list item to the file.
6. You can use the + operator to concatenate two lists.
7. A list can be an element in another list.
8. You can remove an element from a tuple by calling the tuple's remove method.

Short Answer

1. Look at the following statement:

   ```
   numbers = [10, 20, 30, 40, 50]
   ```
   a. How many elements does the list have?
   b. What is the index of the first element in the list?
   c. What is the index of the last element in the list?
2. Look at the following statement:

   ```
   numbers = [1, 2, 3]
   ```
   a. What value is stored in `numbers[2]`?
   b. What value is stored in `numbers[0]`?
   c. What value is stored in `numbers[-1]`?
3. What will the following code display?

   ```
   values = [2, 4, 6, 8, 10]
   print(values[1:3])
   ```
4. What does the following code display?

   ```
   numbers = [1, 2, 3, 4, 5, 6, 7]
   print(numbers[5:])
   ```
5. What does the following code display?

   ```
   numbers = [1, 2, 3, 4, 5, 6, 7, 8]
   print(numbers[-4:])
   ```
6. What does the following code display?

   ```
   values = [2] * 5
   print(values)
   ```

Algorithm Workbench

1. Write a statement that creates a list with the following strings: `'Einstein'`, `'Newton'`, `'Copernicus'`, and `'Kepler'`.
2. Assume `names` references a list. Write a `for` loop that displays each element of the list.
3. Assume the list `numbers1` has 100 elements, and `numbers2` is an empty list. Write code that copies the values in `numbers1` to `numbers2`.
4. Draw a flowchart showing the general logic for totaling the values in a list.
5. Write a function that accepts a list as an argument (assume the list contains integers) and returns the total of the values in the list.
6. Assume the `names` variable references a list of strings. Write code that determines whether `'Ruby'` is in the names list. If it is, display the message `'Hello Ruby'`. Otherwise, display the message `'No Ruby'`.
7. What will the following code print?

```
list1 = [40, 50, 60]
list2 = [10, 20, 30]
list3 = list1 + list2
print(list3)
```

8. Write a statement that creates a two-dimensional list with 5 rows and 3 columns. Then write nested loops that get an integer value from the user for each element in the list.

Programming Exercises

1. Total Sales

Design a program that asks the user to enter a store's sales for each day of the week. The amounts should be stored in a list. Use a loop to calculate the total sales for the week and display the result.

2. Lottery Number Generator

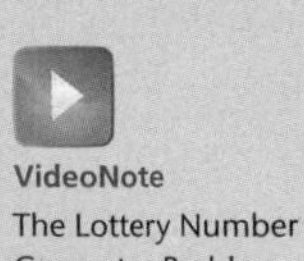

VideoNote
The Lottery Number Generator Problem

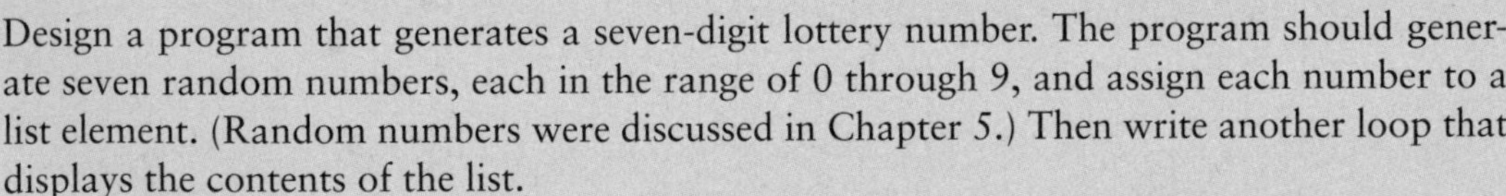

Design a program that generates a seven-digit lottery number. The program should generate seven random numbers, each in the range of 0 through 9, and assign each number to a list element. (Random numbers were discussed in Chapter 5.) Then write another loop that displays the contents of the list.

3. Rainfall Statistics

Design a program that lets the user enter the total rainfall for each of 12 months into a list. The program should calculate and display the total rainfall for the year, the average monthly rainfall, the months with the highest and lowest amounts.

4. Number Analysis Program

Design a program that asks the user to enter a series of 20 numbers. The program should store the numbers in a list then display the following data:

- The lowest number in the list
- The highest number in the list
- The total of the numbers in the list
- The average of the numbers in the list

5. Charge Account Validation

If you have downloaded the source code from the Computer Science Portal you will find a file named `charge_accounts.txt` in the *Chapter 07* folder. This file has a list of a company's valid charge account numbers. Each account number is a seven-digit number, such as `5658845`.

Write a program that reads the contents of the file into a list. The program should then ask the user to enter a charge account number. The program should determine whether the number is valid by searching for it in the list. If the number is in the list, the program should display a message indicating the number is valid. If the number is not in the list, the program should display a message indicating the number is invalid.

(You can access the Computer Science Portal at www.pearsonhighered.com/gaddis.)

6. Larger Than *n*

In a program, write a function that accepts two arguments: a list, and a number *n*. Assume that the list contains numbers. The function should display all of the numbers in the list that are greater than the number *n*.

7. Driver's License Exam

The local driver's license office has asked you to create an application that grades the written portion of the driver's license exam. The exam has 20 multiple-choice questions. Here are the correct answers:

1. A	6. B	11. A	16. C
2. C	7. C	12. D	17. B
3. A	8. A	13. C	18. B
4. A	9. C	14. A	19. D
5. D	10. B	15. D	20. A

Your program should store these correct answers in a list. The program should read the student's answers for each of the 20 questions from a text file and store the answers in another list. (Create your own text file to test the application.) After the student's answers have been read from the file, the program should display a message indicating whether the student passed or failed the exam. (A student must correctly answer 15 of the 20 questions to pass the exam.) It should then display the total number of correctly answered questions, the total number of incorrectly answered questions, and a list showing the question numbers of the incorrectly answered questions.

8. Name Search

If you have downloaded the source code you will find the following files in the *Chapter 07* folder:

- `GirlNames.txt` This file contains a list of the 200 most popular names given to girls born in the United States from the year 2000 through 2009.
- `BoyNames.txt` This file contains a list of the 200 most popular names given to boys born in the United States from the year 2000 through 2009.

Write a program that reads the contents of the two files into two separate lists. The user should be able to enter a boy's name, a girl's name, or both, and the application will display messages indicating whether the names were among the most popular.

(You can access the Computer Science Portal at www.pearsonhighered.com/gaddis.)

9. Population Data

If you have downloaded the source code you will find a file named `USPopulation.txt` in the *Chapter 07* folder. The file contains the midyear population of the United States, in thousands, during the years 1950 through 1990. The first line in the file contains the population for 1950, the second line contains the population for 1951, and so forth.

Write a program that reads the file's contents into a list. The program should display the following data:

- The average annual change in population during the time period
- The year with the greatest increase in population during the time period
- The year with the smallest increase in population during the time period

10. World Series Champions

If you have downloaded the source code you will find a file named `WorldSeriesWinners.txt` in the *Chapter 07* folder. This file contains a chronological list of the World Series winning teams from 1903 through 2009. (The first line in the file is the name of the team that won in 1903, and the last line is the name of the team that won in 2009. Note the World Series was not played in 1904 or 1994.)

Write a program that lets the user enter the name of a team, then displays the number of times that team has won the World Series in the time period from 1903 through 2009.

TIP: Read the contents of the `WorldSeriesWinners.txt` file into a list. When the user enters the name of a team, the program should step through the list, counting the number of times the selected team appears.

11. Lo Shu Magic Square

The Lo Shu Magic Square is a grid with 3 rows and 3 columns, shown in Figure 7-18. The Lo Shu Magic Square has the following properties:

- The grid contains the numbers 1 through 9 exactly.
- The sum of each row, each column, and each diagonal all add up to the same number. This is shown in Figure 7-19.

In a program you can simulate a magic square using a two-dimensional list. Write a function that accepts a two-dimensional list as an argument and determines whether the list is a Lo Shu Magic Square. Test the function in a program.

Figure 7-18 The Lo Shu Magic Square

4	9	2
3	5	7
8	1	6

Figure 7-19 The sum of the rows, columns, and diagonals

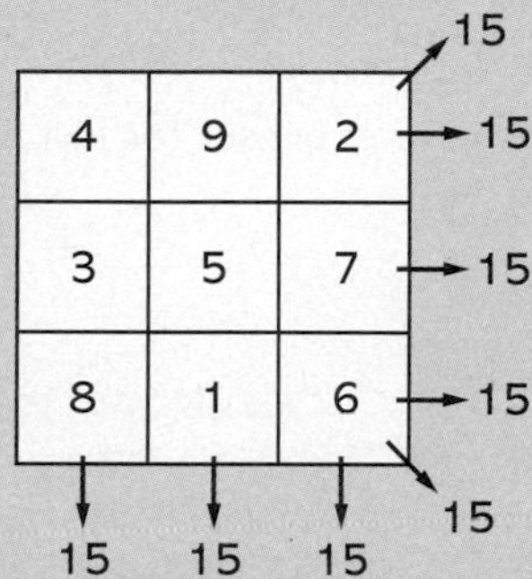

12. Prime Number Generation

A positive integer greater than 1 is said to be *prime* if it has no divisors other than 1 and itself. A positive integer greater than 1 is *composite* if it is not prime. Write a program that asks the user to enter an integer greater than 1, then displays all of the prime numbers that are less than or equal to the number entered. The program should work as follows:

- Once the user has entered a number, the program should populate a list with all of the integers from 2 up through the value entered.
- The program should then use a loop to step through the list. The loop should pass each element to a function that displays the element whether it is a prime number.

13. Magic 8 Ball

Write a program that simulates a Magic 8 Ball, which is a fortune-telling toy that displays a random response to a yes or no question. In the student sample programs for this book, you will find a text file named `8_ball_responses.txt`. The file contains 12 responses, such as "I don't think so", "Yes, of course!", "I'm not sure", and so forth. The program should read the responses from the file into a list. It should prompt the user to ask a question, then display one of the responses, randomly selected from the list. The program should repeat until the user is ready to quit.

Contents of 8_ball_responses.txt:

```
Yes, of course!
Without a doubt, yes.
You can count on it.
For sure!
Ask me later.
I'm not sure.
I can't tell you right now.
I'll tell you after my nap.
No way!
I don't think so.
Without a doubt, no.
The answer is clearly NO.
```

14. Expense Pie Chart

Create a text file that contains your expenses for last month in the following categories:

- Rent
- Gas
- Food
- Clothing
- Car payment
- Misc

Write a Python program that reads the data from the file and uses `matplotlib` to plot a pie chart showing how you spend your money.

15. 1994 Weekly Gas Graph

In the student sample programs for this book, you will find a text file named `1994_Weekly_Gas_Averages.txt`. The file contains the average gas price for each week in the year 1994. (There are 52 lines in the file.) Using `matplotlib`, write a Python program that reads the contents of the file then plots the data as either a line graph or a bar chart. Be sure to display meaningful labels along the *X* and *Y* axes, as well as the tick marks.

CHAPTER 8 More About Strings

TOPICS

8.1 Basic String Operations

CONCEPT: Python provides several ways to access the individual characters in a string. Strings also have methods that allow you to perform operations on them.

Many of the programs that you have written so far have worked with strings, but only in a limited way. The operations that you have performed with strings so far have primarily involved only input and output. For example, you have read strings as input from the keyboard and from files, and sent strings as output to the screen and to files.

There are many types of programs that not only read strings as input and write strings as output, but also perform operations on strings. Word processing programs, for example, manipulate large amounts of text, and thus work extensively with strings. Email programs and search engines are other examples of programs that perform operations on strings.

Python provides a wide variety of tools and programming techniques that you can use to examine and manipulate strings. In fact, strings are a type of sequence, so many of the concepts that you learned about sequences in Chapter 7 apply to strings as well. We will look at many of these in this chapter.

Accessing the Individual Characters in a String

Some programming tasks require that you access the individual characters in a string. For example, you are probably familiar with websites that require you to set up a password. For security reasons, many sites require that your password have at least one uppercase letter, at least one lowercase letter, and at least one digit. When you set up your password, a program examines each character to ensure that the password meets these qualifications. (Later in this chapter, you will see an example of a program that does this sort of thing.) In this section, we will look at two techniques that you can use in Python to access the individual characters in a string: using the `for` loop, and indexing.

Iterating over a String with the `for` Loop

One of the easiest ways to access the individual characters in a string is to use the `for` loop. Here is the general format:

```
for variable in string:
    statement
    statement
    etc.
```

In the general format, *variable* is the name of a variable, and *string* is either a string literal or a variable that references a string. Each time the loop iterates, *variable* will reference a copy of a character in *string*, beginning with the first character. We say that the loop iterates over the characters in the string. Here is an example:

```
name = 'Juliet'
for ch in name:
    print(ch)
```

The `name` variable references a string with six characters, so this loop will iterate six times. The first time the loop iterates, the `ch` variable will reference `'J'`, the second time the loop iterates the `ch` variable will reference `'u'`, and so forth. This is illustrated in Figure 8-1. When the code executes, it will display the following:

```
J
u
l
i
e
t
```

Figure 8-1 Iterating over the string `'Juliet'`

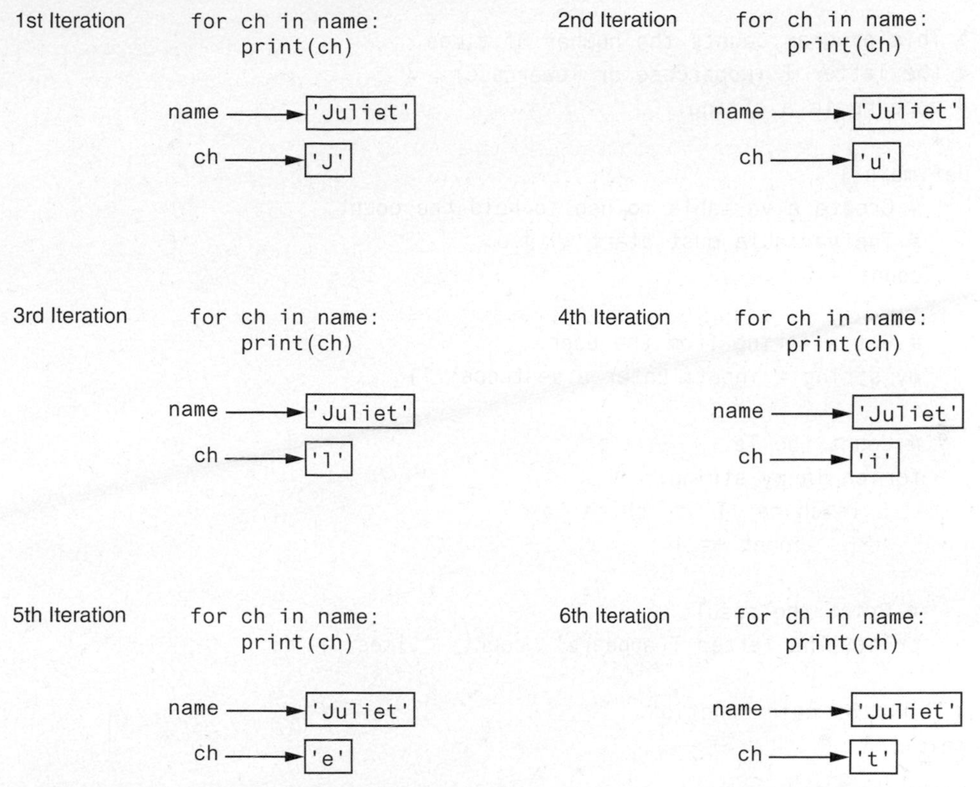

NOTE: Figure 8-1 illustrates how the `ch` variable references a copy of a character from the string as the loop iterates. If we change the value that `ch` references in the loop, it has no effect on the string referenced by `name`. To demonstrate, look at the following:

```
1 name = 'Juliet'
2 for ch in name:
3     ch = 'X'
4 print(name)
```

The statement in line 3 merely reassigns the `ch` variable to a different value each time the loop iterates. It has no effect on the string `'Juliet'` that is referenced by `name`, and it has no effect on the number of times the loop iterates. When this code executes, the statement in line 4 will print:

```
Juliet
```

Program 8-1 shows another example. This program asks the user to enter a string. It then uses a `for` loop to iterate over the string, counting the number of times that the letter T (uppercase or lowercase) appears.

Program 8-1 (count_Ts.py)

```
# This program counts the number of times
# the letter T (uppercase or lowercase)
# appears in a string.

def main():
    # Create a variable to use to hold the count.
    # The variable must start with 0.
    count = 0

    # Get a string from the user.
    my_string = input('Enter a sentence: ')

    # Count the Ts.
    for ch in my_string:
        if ch == 'T' or ch == 't':
            count += 1

    # Print the result.
    print('The letter T appears', count, 'times.')

# Call the main function.
main()
```

Program Output (with input shown in bold)

```
Enter a sentence: Today we sold twenty-two toys. [Enter]
The letter T appears 5 times.
```

Indexing

Another way that you can access the individual characters in a string is with an index. Each character in a string has an index that specifies its position in the string. Indexing starts at 0, so the index of the first character is 0, the index of the second character is 1, and so forth. The index of the last character in a string is 1 less than the number of characters in the string. Figure 8-2 shows the indexes for each character in the string `'Roses are red'`. The string has 13 characters, so the character indexes range from 0 through 12.

Figure 8-2 String indexes

You can use an index to retrieve a copy of an individual character in a string, as shown here:

```
my_string = 'Roses are red'
ch = my_string[6]
```

The expression `my_string[6]` in the second statement returns a copy of the character at index 6 in `my_string`. After this statement executes, `ch` will reference `'a'` as shown in Figure 8-3.

Figure 8-3 Getting a copy of a character from a string

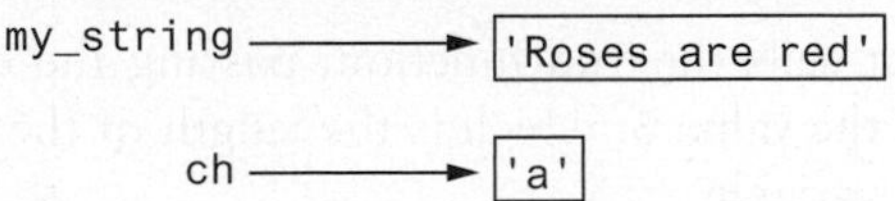

Here is another example:

```
my_string = 'Roses are red'
print(my_string[0], my_string[6], my_string[10])
```

This code will print the following:

```
R a r
```

You can also use negative numbers as indexes, to identify character positions relative to the end of the string. The Python interpreter adds negative indexes to the length of the string to determine the character position. The index –1 identifies the last character in a string, –2 identifies the next to last character, and so forth. The following code shows an example:

```
my_string = 'Roses are red'
print(my_string[-1], my_string[-2], my_string[-13])
```

This code will print the following:

```
d e R
```

`IndexError` Exceptions

An `IndexError` exception will occur if you try to use an index that is out of range for a particular string. For example, the string `'Boston'` has 6 characters, so the valid indexes are 0 through 5. (The valid negative indexes are –1 through –6.) The following is an example of code that causes an `IndexError` exception:

```
city = 'Boston'
print(city[6])
```

This type of error is most likely to happen when a loop incorrectly iterates beyond the end of a string, as shown here:

```
city = 'Boston'
index = 0
while index < 7:
    print(city[index])
    index += 1
```

The last time that this loop iterates, the `index` variable will be assigned the value 6, which is an invalid index for the string `'Boston'`. As a result, the `print` function will cause an `IndexError` exception to be raised.

The `len` Function

In Chapter 7, you learned about the `len` function, which returns the length of a sequence. The `len` function can also be used to get the length of a string. The following code demonstrates:

```
city = 'Boston'
size = len(city)
```

The second statement calls the `len` function, passing the `city` variable as an argument. The function returns the value 6, which is the length of the string `'Boston'`. This value is assigned to the `size` variable.

The `len` function is especially useful to prevent loops from iterating beyond the end of a string, as shown here:

```
city = 'Boston'
index = 0
while index < len(city):
    print(city[index])
    index += 1
```

Notice the loop iterates as long as `index` is *less than* the length of the string. This is because the index of the last character in a string is always 1 less than the length of the string.

String Concatenation

A common operation that performed on strings is *concatenation*, or appending one string to the end of another string. You have seen examples in earlier chapters that use the + operator to concatenate strings. The + operator produces a string that is the combination of the two strings used as its operands. The following interactive session demonstrates:

```
1  >>> message = 'Hello ' + 'world' Enter
2  >>> print(message) Enter
3  Hello world
4  >>>
```

Line 1 concatenates the strings `'Hello'` and `'world'` to produce the string `'Hello world'`. The string `'Hello world'` is then assigned to the `message` variable. Line 2 prints the string that is referenced by the `message` variable. The output is shown in line 3.

Here is another interactive session that demonstrates concatenation:

```
1  >>> first_name = 'Emily' Enter
2  >>> last_name = 'Yeager' Enter
3  >>> full_name = first_name + ' ' + last_name Enter
4  >>> print(full_name) Enter
5  Emily Yeager
6  >>>
```

Line 1 assigns the string `'Emily'` to the `first_name` variable. Line 2 assigns the string `'Yeager'` to the `last_name` variable. Line 3 produces a string that is the concatenation of `first_name`, followed by a space, followed by `last_name`. The resulting string is assigned to the `full_name` variable. Line 4 prints the string referenced by `full_name`. The output is shown in line 5.

You can also use the += operator to perform concatenation. The following interactive session demonstrates:

```
1  >>> letters = 'abc' Enter
2  >>> letters += 'def' Enter
3  >>> print(letters) Enter
4  abcdef
5  >>>
```

The statement in line 2 performs string concatenation. It works the same as

```
letters = letters + 'def'
```

After the statement in line 2 executes, the `letters` variable will reference the string `'abcdef'`. Here is another example:

```
>>> name = 'Kelly' Enter              # name is 'Kelly'
>>> name += ' ' Enter                 # name is 'Kelly '
>>> name += 'Yvonne' Enter            # name is 'Kelly Yvonne'
>>> name += ' ' Enter                 # name is 'Kelly Yvonne '
>>> name += 'Smith' Enter             # name is 'Kelly Yvonne Smith'
>>> print(name) e
Kelly Yvonne Smith
>>>
```

Keep in mind that the operand on the left side of the += operator must be an existing variable. If you specify a nonexistent variable, an exception is raised.

Strings Are Immutable

In Python, strings are immutable, which means once they are created, they cannot be changed. Some operations, such as concatenation, give the impression that they modify strings, but in reality they do not. For example, look at Program 8-2.

Program 8-2 (concatenate.py)

```
# This program concatenates strings.

def main():
    name = 'Carmen'
    print('The name is', name)
    name = name + ' Brown'
    print('Now the name is', name)

# Call the main function.
main()
```

Program Output

```
The name is Carmen
Now the name is Carmen Brown
```

The statement in line 4 assigns the string `'Carmen'` to the `name` variable, as shown in Figure 8-4. The statement in line 6 concatenates the string `' Brown'` to the string `'Carmen'` and assigns the result to the `name` variable, as shown in Figure 8-5. As you can see from the figure, the original string `'Carmen'` is not modified. Instead, a new string containing `'Carmen Brown'` is created and assigned to the `name` variable. (The original string, `'Carmen'` is no longer usable because no variable references it. The Python interpreter will eventually remove the unusable string from memory.)

Figure 8-4 The string 'Carmen' assigned to name

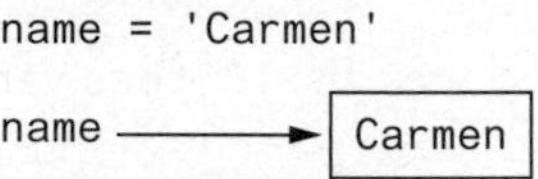

Figure 8-5 The string 'Carmen Brown' assigned to name

name = name + ' Brown'

name

Carmen

Carmen Brown

Because strings are immutable, you cannot use an expression in the form *`string[index]`* on the left side of an assignment operator. For example, the following code will cause an error:

```
# Assign 'Bill' to friend.
friend = 'Bill'
# Can we change the first character to 'J'?
friend[0] = 'J'      # No, this will cause an error!
```

The last statement in this code will raise an exception because it attempts to change the value of the first character in the string `'Bill'`.

Checkpoint

8.1 Assume the variable `name` references a string. Write a `for` loop that prints each character in the string.

8.2 What is the index of the first character in a string?

8.3 If a string has 10 characters, what is the index of the last character?

8.4 What happens if you try to use an invalid index to access a character in a string?

8.5 How do you find the length of a string?

8.6 What is wrong with the following code?

```
animal = 'Tiger'
animal[0] = 'L'
```

8.2 String Slicing

CONCEPT: You can use slicing expressions to select a range of characters from a string

You learned in Chapter 7 that a slice is a span of items that are taken from a sequence. When you take a slice from a string, you get a span of characters from within the string. String slices are also called *substrings*.

To get a slice of a string, you write an expression in the following general format:

```
string[start : end]
```

In the general format, `start` is the index of the first character in the slice, and *end* is the index marking the end of the slice. The expression will return a string containing a copy of the characters from `start` up to (but not including) *end*. For example, suppose we have the following:

```
full_name = 'Patty Lynn Smith'
middle_name = full_name[6:10]
```

The second statement assigns the string `'Lynn'` to the `middle_name` variable. If you leave out the `start` index in a slicing expression, Python uses 0 as the starting index. Here is an example:

```
full_name = 'Patty Lynn Smith'
first_name = full_name[:5]
```

The second statement assigns the string `'Patty'` to `first_name`. If you leave out the *end* index in a slicing expression, Python uses the length of the string as the *end* index. Here is an example:

```
full_name = 'Patty Lynn Smith'
last_name = full_name[11:]
```

The second statement assigns the string `'Smith'` to `last_name`. What do you think the following code will assign to the `my_string` variable?

```
full_name = 'Patty Lynn Smith'
my_string = full_name[:]
```

The second statement assigns the entire string `'Patty Lynn Smith'` to `my_string`. The statement is equivalent to:

```
my_string = full_name[0 : len(full_name)]
```

The slicing examples we have seen so far get slices of consecutive characters from strings. Slicing expressions can also have step value, which can cause characters to be skipped in the string. Here is an example of code that uses a slicing expression with a step value:

```
letters = 'ABCDEFGHIJKLMNOPQRSTUVWXYZ'
print(letters[0:26:2])
```

The third number inside the brackets is the step value. A step value of 2, as used in this example, causes the slice to contain every second character from the specified range in the string. The code will print the following:

```
ACEGIKMOQSUWY
```

You can also use negative numbers as indexes in slicing expressions to reference positions relative to the end of the string. Here is an example:

```
full_name = 'Patty Lynn Smith'
last_name = full_name[-5:]
```

Recall that Python adds a negative index to the length of a string to get the position referenced by that index. The second statement in this code assigns the string `'Smith'` to the `last_name` variable.

NOTE: Invalid indexes do not cause slicing expressions to raise an exception. For example:

- If the *end* index specifies a position beyond the end of the string, Python will use the length of the string instead.
- If the *start* index specifies a position before the beginning of the string, Python will use 0 instead.
- If the *start* index is greater than the *end* index, the slicing expression will return an empty string.

In the Spotlight:

Extracting Characters from a String

At a university, each student is assigned a system login name, which the student uses to log into the campus computer system. As part of your internship with the university's Information Technology department, you have been asked to write the code that generates system login names for students. You will use the following algorithm to generate a login name:

1. *Get the first three characters of the student's first name. (If the first name is less than three characters in length, use the entire first name.)*
2. *Get the first three characters of the student's last name. (If the last name is less than three characters in length, use the entire last name.)*
3. *Get the last three characters of the student's ID number. (If the ID number is less than three characters in length, use the entire ID number.)*
4. *Concatenate the three sets of characters to generate the login name.*

For example, if a student's name is Amanda Spencer, and her ID number is ENG6721, her login name would be AmaSpe721. You decide to write a function named `get_login_name` that accepts a student's first name, last name, and ID number as arguments, and returns the student's login name as a string. You will save the function in a module named `login.py`. This module can then be imported into any Python program that needs to generate a login name. Program 8-3 shows the code for the `login.py` module.

Program 8-3 (`login.py`)

```
# The get_login_name function accepts a first name,
# last name, and ID number as arguments. It returns
# a system login name.

```

```
5  def get_login_name(first, last, idnumber):
6      # Get the first three letters of the first name.
7      # If the name is less than 3 characters, the
8      # slice will return the entire first name.
9      set1 = first[0 : 3]
10 
11     # Get the first three letters of the last name.
12     # If the name is less than 3 characters, the
13     # slice will return the entire last name.
14     set2 = last[0 : 3]
15 
16     # Get the last three characters of the student ID.
17     # If the ID number is less than 3 characters, the
18     # slice will return the entire ID number.
19     set3 = idnumber[-3 :]
20 
21     # Put the sets of characters together.
22     login_name = set1 + set2 + set3
23 
24     # Return the login name.
25     return login_name
```

The `get_login_name` function accepts three string arguments: a first name, a last name, and an ID number. The statement in line 9 uses a slicing expression to get the first three characters of the string referenced by `first` and assigns those characters, as a string, to the `set1` variable. If the string referenced by `first` is less than three characters long, then the value 3 will be an invalid ending index. If this is the case, Python will use the length of the string as the ending index, and the slicing expression will return the entire string.

The statement in line 14 uses a slicing expression to get the first three characters of the string referenced by `last`, and assigns those characters, as a string, to the `set2` variable. The entire string referenced by `last` will be returned if it is less than three characters.

The statement in line 19 uses a slicing expression to get the last three characters of the string referenced by `idnumber` and assigns those characters, as a string, to the `set3` variable. If the string referenced by `idnumber` is less than three characters, then the value −3 will be an invalid starting index. If this is the case, Python will use 0 as the starting index.

The statement in line 22 assigns the concatenation of `set1`, `set2`, and `set3` to the `login_name` variable. The variable is returned in line 25. Program 8-4 shows a demonstration of the function.

Program 8-4 (`generate_login.py`)

```
# This program gets the user's first name, last name, and
# student ID number. Using this data it generates a
# system login name.

```

(program continues)

Program 8-4 *(continued)*

```
import login

def main():
    # Get the user's first name, last name, and ID number.
    first = input('Enter your first name: ')
    last = input('Enter your last name: ')
    idnumber = input('Enter your student ID number: ')

    # Get the login name.
    print('Your system login name is:')
    print(login.get_login_name(first, last, idnumber))

# Call the main function.
main()
```

Program Output (with input shown in bold)

```
Enter your first name: Holly [Enter]
Enter your last name: Gaddis [Enter]
Enter your student ID number: CSC34899 [Enter]
Your system login name is:
HolGad899
```

Program Output (with input shown in bold)

```
Enter your first name: Jo [Enter]
Enter your last name: Cusimano [Enter]
Enter your student ID number: BIO4497 [Enter]
Your system login name is:
JoCus497
```

Checkpoint

8.7 What will the following code display?

```
mystring = 'abcdefg'
print(mystring[2:5])
```

8.8 What will the following code display?

```
mystring = 'abcdefg'
print(mystring[3:])
```

8.9 What will the following code display?

```
mystring = 'abcdefg'
print(mystring[:3])
```

8.10 What will the following code display?

```
mystring = 'abcdefg'
print(mystring[:])
```

8.3 Testing, Searching, and Manipulating Strings

CONCEPT: Python provides operators and methods for testing strings, searching the contents of strings, and getting modified copies of strings.

Testing Strings with `in` and `not in`

In Python, you can use the `in` operator to determine whether one string is contained in another string. Here is the general format of an expression using the `in` operator with two strings:

```
string1 in string2
```

`string1` and *`string2`* can be either string literals or variables referencing strings. The expression returns true if *`string1`* is found in *`string2`*. For example, look at the following code:

```
text = 'Four score and seven years ago'
if 'seven' in text:
    print('The string "seven" was found.')
else:
    print('The string "seven" was not found.')
```

This code determines whether the string `'Four score and seven years ago'` contains the string `'seven'`. If we run this code, it will display:

```
The string "seven" was found.
```

You can use the `not in` operator to determine whether one string is *not* contained in another string. Here is an example:

```
names = 'Bill Joanne Susan Chris Juan Katie'
if 'Pierre' not in names:
    print('Pierre was not found.')
else:
    print('Pierre was found.')
```

If we run this code, it will display:

```
Pierre was not found.
```

String Methods

Recall from Chapter 6 that a method is a function that belongs to an object and performs some operation on that object. Strings in Python have numerous methods.[1] In this section, we will discuss several string methods for performing the following types of operations:

- Testing the values of strings
- Performing various modifications
- Searching for substrings and replacing sequences of characters

[1] We do not cover all of the string methods in this book. For a comprehensive list of string methods, see the Python documentation at www.python.org.

Here is the general format of a string method call:

```
stringvar.method(arguments)
```

In the general format, `stringvar` is a variable that references a string, `method` is the name of the method that is being called, and `arguments` is one or more arguments being passed to the method. Let's look at some examples.

String Testing Methods

The string methods shown in Table 8-1 test a string for specific characteristics. For example, the `isdigit` method returns true if the string contains only numeric digits. Otherwise, it returns false. Here is an example:

```
string1 = '1200'
if string1.isdigit():
    print(string1, 'contains only digits.')
else:
    print(string1, 'contains characters other than digits.')
```

This code will display

```
1200 contains only digits.
```

Here is another example:

```
string2 = '123abc'
if string2.isdigit():
    print(string2, 'contains only digits.')
else:
    print(string2, 'contains characters other than digits.')
```

This code will display

```
123abc contains characters other than digits.
```

Table 8-1 Some string testing methods

Method	Description
`isalnum()`	Returns true if the string contains only alphabetic letters or digits and is at least one character in length. Returns false otherwise.
`isalpha()`	Returns true if the string contains only alphabetic letters and is at least one character in length. Returns false otherwise.
`isdigit()`	Returns true if the string contains only numeric digits and is at least one character in length. Returns false otherwise.
`islower()`	Returns truc if all of the alphabetic letters in the string are lowercase, and the string contains at least one alphabetic letter. Returns false otherwise.
`isspace()`	Returns true if the string contains only whitespace characters and is at least one character in length. Returns false otherwise. (Whitespace characters are spaces, newlines (`\n`), and tabs (`\t`).
`isupper()`	Returns true if all of the alphabetic letters in the string are uppercase, and the string contains at least one alphabetic letter. Returns false otherwise.

Program 8-5 demonstrates several of the string testing methods. It asks the user to enter a string then displays various messages about the string, depending on the return value of the methods.

Program 8-5 (string_test.py)

```
# This program demonstrates several string testing methods.

def main():
    # Get a string from the user.
    user_string = input('Enter a string: ')

    print('This is what I found about that string:')

    # Test the string.
    if user_string.isalnum():
        print('The string is alphanumeric.')
    if user_string.isdigit():
        print('The string contains only digits.')
    if user_string.isalpha():
        print('The string contains only alphabetic characters.')
    if user_string.isspace():
        print('The string contains only whitespace characters.')
    if user_string.islower():
        print('The letters in the string are all lowercase.')
    if user_string.isupper():
        print('The letters in the string are all uppercase.')

# Call the string.
main()
```

Program Output (with input shown in bold)

```
Enter a string: abc [Enter]
This is what I found about that string:
The string is alphanumeric.
The string contains only alphabetic characters.
The letters in the string are all lowercase.
```

Program Output (with input shown in bold)

```
Enter a string: 123 [Enter]
This is what I found about that string:
The string is alphanumeric.
The string contains only digits.
```

Program Output (with input shown in bold)

```
Enter a string: 123ABC [Enter]
This is what I found about that string:
The string is alphanumeric.
The letters in the string are all uppercase.
```

Modification Methods

Although strings are immutable, meaning they cannot be modified, they do have a number of methods that return modified versions of themselves. Table 8-2 lists several of these methods.

Table 8-2 String Modification Methods

Method	Description
`lower()`	Returns a copy of the string with all alphabetic letters converted to lowercase. Any character that is already lowercase, or is not an alphabetic letter, is unchanged.
`lstrip()`	Returns a copy of the string with all leading whitespace characters removed. Leading whitespace characters are spaces, newlines (`\n`), and tabs (`\t`) that appear at the beginning of the string.
`lstrip(char)`	The *char* argument is a string containing a character. Returns a copy of the string with all instances of *char* that appear at the beginning of the string removed.
`rstrip()`	Returns a copy of the string with all trailing whitespace characters removed. Trailing whitespace characters are spaces, newlines (`\n`), and tabs (`\t`) that appear at the end of the string.
`rstrip(char)`	The *char* argument is a string containing a character. The method returns a copy of the string with all instances of *char* that appear at the end of the string removed.
`strip()`	Returns a copy of the string with all leading and trailing whitespace characters removed.
`strip(char)`	Returns a copy of the string with all instances of *char* that appear at the beginning and the end of the string removed.
`upper()`	Returns a copy of the string with all alphabetic letters converted to uppercase. Any character that is already uppercase, or is not an alphabetic letter, is unchanged.

For example, the `lower` method returns a copy of a string with all of its alphabetic letters converted to lowercase. Here is an example:

```
letters = 'WXYZ'
print(letters, letters.lower())
```

This code will print

```
WXYZ wxyz
```

The `upper` method returns a copy of a string with all of its alphabetic letters converted to uppercase. Here is an example:

```
letters = 'abcd'
print(letters, letters.upper())
```

This code will print

```
abcd ABCD
```

The `lower` and `upper` methods are useful for making case-insensitive string comparisons. String comparisons are case-sensitive, which means the uppercase characters are distinguished from the lowercase characters. For example, in a case-sensitive comparison, the string `'abc'` is not considered the same as the string `'ABC'` or the string `'Abc'` because the case of the characters are different. Sometimes it is more convenient to perform a *case-insensitive* comparison, in which the case of the characters is ignored. In a case-insensitive comparison, the string `'abc'` is considered the same as `'ABC'` and `'Abc'`.

For example, look at the following code:

```
again = 'y'
while again.lower() == 'y':
    print('Hello')
    print('Do you want to see that again?')
    again = input('y = yes, anything else = no: ')
```

Notice the last statement in the loop asks the user to enter `y` to see the message displayed again. The loop iterates as long as the expression `again.lower() =='y'` is true. The expression will be true if the `again` variable references either `'y'` or `'Y'`.

Similar results can be achieved by using the `upper` method, as shown here:

```
again = 'y'
while again.upper() == 'Y':
    print('Hello')
    print('Do you want to see that again?')
    again = input('y = yes, anything else = no: ')
```

Searching and Replacing

Programs commonly need to search for substrings, or strings that appear within other strings. For example, suppose you have a document opened in your word processor, and you need to search for a word that appears somewhere in it. The word that you are searching for is a substring that appears inside a larger string, the document.

Table 8-3 lists some of the Python string methods that search for substrings, as well as a method that replaces the occurrences of a substring with another string.

Table 8-3 Search and replace methods

Method	Description
`endswith(`*`substring`*`)`	The *`substring`* argument is a string. The method returns true if the string ends with *`substring`*.
`find(`*`substring`*`)`	The *`substring`* argument is a string. The method returns the lowest index in the string where *`substring`* is found. If *`substring`* is not found, the method returns −1.
`replace(`*`old, new`*`)`	The *`old`* and *`new`* arguments are both strings. The method returns a copy of the string with all instances of *`old`* replaced by *`new`*.
`startswith(`*`substring`*`)`	The *`substring`* argument is a string. The method returns true if the string starts with *`substring`*.

The `endswith` method determines whether a string ends with a specified substring. Here is an example:

```
filename = input('Enter the filename: ')
if filename.endswith('.txt'):
    print('That is the name of a text file.')
elif filename.endswith('.py'):
    print('That is the name of a Python source file.')
elif filename.endswith('.doc'):
    print('That is the name of a word processing document.')
else:
    print('Unknown file type.')
```

The `startswith` method works like the `endswith` method, but determines whether a string begins with a specified substring.

The `find` method searches for a specified substring within a string. The method returns the lowest index of the substring, if it is found. If the substring is not found, the method returns −1. Here is an example:

```
string = 'Four score and seven years ago'
position = string.find('seven')
if position != -1:
    print('The word "seven" was found at index', position)
else:
    print('The word "seven" was not found.')
```

This code will display

```
The word "seven" was found at index 15
```

The `replace` method returns a copy of a string, where every occurrence of a specified substring has been replaced with another string. For example, look at the following code:

```
string = 'Four score and seven years ago'
new_string = string.replace('years', 'days')
print(new_string)
```

This code will display

```
Four score and seven days ago
```

In the Spotlight:

Validating the Characters in a Password

At the university, passwords for the campus computer system must meet the following requirements:

- The password must be at least seven characters long.
- It must contain at least one uppercase letter.

- It must contain at least one lowercase letter.
- It must contain at least one numeric digit.

When a student sets up his or her password, the password must be validated to ensure it meets these requirements. You have been asked to write the code that performs this validation. You decide to write a function named `valid_password` that accepts the password as an argument and returns either true or false, to indicate whether it is valid. Here is the algorithm for the function, in pseudocode:

```
valid_password function:
   Set the correct_length variable to false
   Set the has_uppercase variable to false
   Set the has_lowercase variable to false
   Set the has_digit variable to false
   If the password's length is seven characters or greater:
      Set the correct_length variable to true
      for each character in the password:
         if the character is an uppercase letter:
            Set the has_uppercase variable to true
         if the character is a lowercase letter:
            Set the has_lowercase variable to true
         if the character isa digit:
            Set the has_digit variable to true
   If correct_length and has_uppercase and has_lowercase and has_digit:
      Set the is_valid variable to true
   else:
      Set the is_valid variable to false
   Return the is_valid variable
```

Earlier (in the previous *In the Spotlight* section) you created a function named `get_login_name` and stored that function in the `login` module. Because the `valid_password` function's purpose is related to the task of creating a student's login account, you decide to store the `valid_password` function in the `login` module as well. Program 8-6 shows the login module with the `valid_password` function added to it. The function begins at line 34.

Program 8-6 (`login.py`)

```
1  # The get_login_name function accepts a first name,
2  # last name, and ID number as arguments. It returns
3  # a system login name.
4
5  def get_login_name(first, last, idnumber):
6      # Get the first three letters of the first name.
7      # If the name is less than 3 characters, the
8      # slice will return the entire first name.
9      set1 = first[0 : 3]
10
```

(program continues)

Program 8-6 *(continued)*

```
    # Get the first three letters of the last name.
    # If the name is less than 3 characters, the
    # slice will return the entire last name.
    set2 = last[0 : 3]

    # Get the last three characters of the student ID.
    # If the ID number is less than 3 characters, the
    # slice will return the entire ID number.
    set3 = idnumber[-3 :]

    # Put the sets of characters together.
    login_name = set1  + set2 + set3

    # Return the login name.
    return login_name

# The valid_password function accepts a password as
# an argument and returns either true or false to
# indicate whether the password is valid. A valid
# password must be at least 7 characters in length,
# have at least one uppercase letter, one lowercase
# letter, and one digit.

def valid_password(password):
    # Set the Boolean variables to false.
    correct_length = False
    has_uppercase = False
    has_lowercase = False
    has_digit = False

    # Begin the validation. Start by testing the
    # password's length.
    if len(password) >= 7:
        correct_length = True

        # Test each character and set the
        # appropriate flag when a required
        # character is found.
        for ch in password:
            if ch.isupper():
                has_uppercase = True
            if ch.islower():
                has_lowercase = True
            if ch.isdigit():
                has_digit = True
```

```
    # Determine whether all of the requirements
    # are met. If they are, set is_valid to true.
    # Otherwise, set is_valid to false.
    if correct_length and has_uppercase and \
        has_lowercase and has_digit:
        is_valid = True
    else:
        is_valid = False

    # Return the is_valid variable.
    return is_valid
```

Program 8-7 imports the login module and demonstrates the `valid_password` function.

Program 8-7 (validate_password.py)

```
# This program gets a password from the user and
# validates it.

import login

def main():
    # Get a password from the user.
    password = input('Enter your password: ')

    # Validate the password.
    while not login.valid_password(password):
        print('That password is not valid.')
        password = input('Enter your password: ')

    print('That is a valid password.')

# Call the main function.
main()
```

Program Output (with input shown in bold)

```
Enter your password: bozo [Enter]
That password is not valid.
Enter your password: kangaroo [Enter]
That password is not valid.
Enter your password: Tiger9 [Enter]
That password is not valid.
Enter your password: Leopard6 [Enter]
That is a valid password.
```

The Repetition Operator

In Chapter 7, you learned how to duplicate a list with the repetition operator (*). The repetition operator works with strings as well. Here is the general format:

```
string_to_copy * n
```

The repetition operator creates a string that contains *n* repeated copies of `string_to_copy`. Here is an example:

```
my_string = 'w' * 5
```

After this statement executes, `my_string` will reference the string `'wwwww'`. Here is another example:

```
print('Hello' * 5)
```

This statement will print:

```
HelloHelloHelloHelloHello
```

Program 8-8 demonstrates the repetition operator.

Program 8-8 **(repetition_operator.py)**

```
# This program demonstrates the repetition operator.

def main():
    # Print nine rows increasing in length.
    for count in range(1, 10):
        print('Z' * count)

    # Print nine rows decreasing in length.
    for count in range(8, 0, -1):
        print('Z' * count)

# Call the main function.
main()
```

Program Output

```
Z
ZZ
ZZZ
ZZZZ
ZZZZZ
ZZZZZZ
ZZZZZZZ
ZZZZZZZZ
ZZZZZZZZZ
ZZZZZZZZ
```

```
ZZZZZZZ
ZZZZZZ
ZZZZZ
ZZZZ
ZZZ
ZZ
Z
```

Splitting a String

Strings in Python have a method named `split` that returns a list containing the words in the string. Program 8-9 shows an example.

Program 8-9 (string_split.py)

```
# This program demonstrates the split method.

def main():
    # Create a string with multiple words.
    my_string = 'One two three four'

    # Split the string.
    word_list = my_string.split()

    # Print the list of words.
    print(word_list)

# Call the main function.
main()
```

Program Output

```
['One', 'two', 'three', 'four']
```

By default, the split method uses spaces as separators (that is, it returns a list of the words in the string that are separated by spaces). You can specify a different separator by passing it as an argument to the split method. For example, suppose a string contains a date, as shown here:

```
date_string = '11/26/2018'
```

If you want to break out the month, day, and year as items in a list, you can call the `split` method using the `'/'` character as a separator, as shown here:

```
date_list = date_string.split('/')
```

After this statement executes, the `date_list` variable will reference this list:

```
['11', '26', '2018']
```

Program 8-10 demonstrates this.

Program 8-10 (split_date.py)

```
# This program calls the split method, using the
# '/' character as a separator.

def main():
    # Create a string with a date.
    date_string = '11/26/2018'

    # Split the date.
    date_list = date_string.split('/')

    # Display each piece of the date.
    print('Month:', date_list[0])
    print('Day:', date_list[1])
    print('Year:', date_list[2])

# Call the main function.
main()
```

Program Output

```
Month: 11
Day: 26
Year: 2018
```

Checkpoint

8.11 Write code using the `in` operator that determines whether `'d'` is in `mystring`.

8.12 Assume the variable `big` references a string. Write a statement that converts the string it references to lowercase and assigns the converted string to the variable `little`.

8.13 Write an `if` statement that displays "Digit" if the string referenced by the variable `ch` contains a numeric digit. Otherwise, it should display "No digit."

8.14 What is the output of the following code?

```
ch = 'a'
ch2 = ch.upper()
print(ch, ch2)
```

8.15 Write a loop that asks the user "Do you want to repeat the program or quit? (R/Q)". The loop should repeat until the user has entered an R or Q (either uppercase or lowercase).

8.16 What will the following code display?

```
var = '$'
print(var.upper())
```

8.17 Write a loop that counts the number of uppercase characters that appear in the string referenced by the variable `mystring`.

8.18 Assume the following statement appears in a program:

```
days = 'Monday Tuesday Wednesday'
```

Write a statement that splits the string, creating the following list:

```
['Monday', 'Tuesday', 'Wednesday']
```

8.19 Assume the following statement appears in a program:

```
values = 'one$two$three$four'
```

Write a statement that splits the string, creating the following list:

```
['one', 'two', 'three', 'four']
```

Review Questions

Multiple Choice

1. This is the first index in a string.
   a. -1
   b. 1
   c. 0
   d. The size of the string minus one
2. This is the last index in a string.
   a. 1
   b. 99
   c. 0
   d. The size of the string minus one
3. This will happen if you try to use an index that is out of range for a string.
   a. A `ValueError` exception will occur.
   b. An `IndexError` exception will occur.
   c. The string will be erased and the program will continue to run.
   d. Nothing—the invalid index will be ignored.
4. This function returns the length of a string.
   a. `length`
   b. `size`
   c. `len`
   d. `lengthof`
5. This string method returns a copy of the string with all leading whitespace characters removed.
   a. `lstrip`
   b. `rstrip`
   c. `remove`
   d. `strip_leading`

6. This string method returns the lowest index in the string where a specified substring is found.
   a. `first_index_of`
   b. `locate`
   c. `find`
   d. `index_of`
7. This operator determines whether one string is contained inside another string.
   a. `contains`
   b. `is_in`
   c. `==`
   d. `in`
8. This string method returns true if a string contains only alphabetic characters and is at least one character in length.
   a. the `isalpha` method
   b. the `alpha` method
   c. the `alphabetic` method
   d. the `isletters` method
9. This string method returns true if a string contains only numeric digits and is at least one character in length.
   a. the `digit` method
   b. the `isdigit` method
   c. the `numeric` method
   d. the `isnumber` method
10. This string method returns a copy of the string with all leading and trailing whitespace characters removed.
    a. `clean`
    b. `strip`
    c. `remove_whitespace`
    d. `rstrip`

True or False

1. Once a string is created, it cannot be changed.
2. You can use the `for` loop to iterate over the individual characters in a string.
3. The `isupper` method converts a string to all uppercase characters.
4. The repetition operator (`*`) works with strings as well as with lists.
5. When you call a string's `split` method, the method divides the string into two substrings.

Short Answer

1. What does the following code display?

```
mystr = 'yes'
mystr += 'no'
mystr += 'yes'
print(mystr)
```

2. What does the following code display?
```
mystr = 'abc' * 3
print(mystr)
```
3. What will the following code display?
```
mystring = 'abcdefg'
print(mystring[2:5])
```
4. What does the following code display?
```
numbers = [1, 2, 3, 4, 5, 6, 7]
print(numbers[4:6])
```
5. What does the following code display?
```
name = 'joe'
print(name.lower())
print(name.upper())
print(name)
```

Algorithm Workbench

1. Assume `choice` references a string. The following `if` statement determines whether `choice` is equal to 'Y' or 'y':
```
if choice == 'Y' or choice == 'y':
```
Rewrite this statement so it only makes one comparison, and does not use the `or` operator. (*Hint: use either the* `upper` *or* `lower` *methods.*)
2. Write a loop that counts the number of space characters that appear in the string referenced by `mystring`.
3. Write a loop that counts the number of digits that appear in the string referenced by `mystring`.
4. Write a loop that counts the number of lowercase characters that appear in the string referenced by `mystring`.
5. Write a function that accepts a string as an argument and returns true if the argument ends with the substring `'.com'`. Otherwise, the function should return false.
6. Write code that makes a copy of a string with all occurrences of the lowercase letter `'t'` converted to uppercase.
7. Write a function that accepts a string as an argument and displays the string backwards.
8. Assume `mystring` references a string. Write a statement that uses a slicing expression and displays the first 3 characters in the string.
9. Assume `mystring` references a string. Write a statement that uses a slicing expression and displays the last 3 characters in the string.
10. Look at the following statement:
```
mystring = 'cookies>milk>fudge>cake>ice cream'
```
Write a statement that splits this string, creating the following list:
```
['cookies', 'milk', 'fudge', 'cake', 'ice cream']
```

Programming Exercises

1. Initials

Write a program that gets a string containing a person's first, middle, and last names, and displays their first, middle, and last initials. For example, if the user enters John William Smith, the program should display J. W. S.

2. Sum of Digits in a String

Write a program that asks the user to enter a series of single-digit numbers with nothing separating them. The program should display the sum of all the single digit numbers in the string. For example, if the user enters 2514, the method should return 12, which is the sum of 2, 5, 1, and 4.

3. Date Printer

Write a program that reads a string from the user containing a date in the form mm/dd/yyyy. It should print the date in the format March 12, 2018.

4. Morse Code Converter

Morse code is a code where each letter of the English alphabet, each digit, and various punctuation characters are represented by a series of dots and dashes. Table 8-4 shows part of the code.

Write a program that asks the user to enter a string, then converts that string to Morse code.

Table 8-4 Morse code

Character	Code	Character	Code	Character	Code	Character	Code
space	*space*	6	–....	G	––.	Q	––.–
comma	––..––	7	––...	H	....	R	.–.
period	.–.–.–	8	–––..	I	..	S	...
question mark	..––..	9	––––.	J	.–––	T	–
0	–––––	A	.–	K	–.–	U	..–
1	.––––	B	–...	L	.–..	V	...–
2	..–––	C	–.–.	M	––	W	.––
3	...––	D	–..	N	–.	X	–..–
4	....–	E	.	O	–––	Y	–.––
5	.....	F	..–.	P	.––.	Z	––..

5. Alphabetic Telephone Number Translator

Many companies use telephone numbers like 555-GET-FOOD so the number is easier for their customers to remember. On a standard telephone, the alphabetic letters are mapped to numbers in the following fashion:

A, B, and C = 2
D, E, and F = 3
G, H, and I = 4
J, K, and L = 5
M, N, and O = 6
P, Q, R, and S = 7
T, U, and V = 8
W, X, Y, and Z = 9

Write a program that asks the user to enter a 10-character telephone number in the format XXX-XXX-XXXX. The application should display the telephone number with any alphabetic characters that appeared in the original translated to their numeric equivalent. For example, if the user enters 555-GET-FOOD, the application should display `555-438-3663`.

6. Average Number of Words

If you have downloaded the source code from the Computer Science Portal you will find a file named `text.txt` in the *Chapter 08* folder. The text that is in the file is stored as one sentence per line. Write a program that reads the file's contents and calculates the average number of words per sentence.

(You can access the Computer Science Portal at www.pearsonhighered.com/gaddis.)

7. Character Analysis

If you have downloaded the source code you will find a file named `text.txt` in the *Chapter 08* folder. Write a program that reads the file's contents and determines the following:

- The number of uppercase letters in the file
- The number of lowercase letters in the file
- The number of digits in the file
- The number of whitespace characters in the file

8. Sentence Capitalizer

Write a program with a function that accepts a string as an argument and returns a copy of the string with the first character of each sentence capitalized. For instance, if the argument is "hello. my name is Joe. what is your name?" the function should return the string "`Hello. My name is Joe. What is your name?`" The program should let the user enter a string and then pass it to the function. The modified string should be displayed.

VideoNote
The Vowels and Consonants problem

9. Vowels and Consonants

Write a program with a function that accepts a string as an argument and returns the number of vowels that the string contains. The application should have another function that accepts a string as an argument and returns the number of consonants that the string contains. The application should let the user enter a string, and should display the number of vowels and the number of consonants it contains.

10. Most Frequent Character

Write a program that lets the user enter a string and displays the character that appears most frequently in the string.

11. Word Separator

Write a program that accepts as input a sentence in which all of the words are run together, but the first character of each word is uppercase. Convert the sentence to a string in which the words are separated by spaces, and only the first word starts with an uppercase letter. For example the string "`StopAndSmellTheRoses.`" would be converted to "`Stop and smell the roses.`"

12. Pig Latin

Write a program that accepts a sentence as input and converts each word to "Pig Latin." In one version, to convert a word to Pig Latin, you remove the first letter and place that letter at the end of the word. Then, you append the string "ay" to the word. Here is an example:

English:	I SLEPT MOST OF THE NIGHT
Pig Latin:	IAY LEPTSAY OSTMAY FOAY HETAY IGHTNAY

13. PowerBall Lottery

To play the PowerBall lottery, you buy a ticket that has five numbers in the range of 1–69, and a "PowerBall" number in the range of 1–26. (You can pick the numbers yourself, or you can let the ticket machine randomly pick them for you.) Then, on a specified date, a winning set of numbers is randomly selected by a machine. If your first five numbers match the first five winning numbers in any order, and your PowerBall number matches the winning PowerBall number, then you win the jackpot, which is a very large amount of money. If your numbers match only some of the winning numbers, you win a lesser amount, depending on how many of the winning numbers you have matched.

In the student sample programs for this book, you will find a file named `pbnumbers.txt`, containing the winning PowerBall numbers that were selected between February 3, 2010 and May 11, 2016 (the file contains 654 sets of winning numbers). Figure 8-6 shows an example of the first few lines of the file's contents. Each line in the file contains the set of six numbers that were selected on a given date. The numbers are separated by a space, and the last number in each line is the PowerBall number for that day. For example, the first line in the file shows the numbers for February 3, 2010, which were 17, 22, 36, 37, 52, and the PowerBall number 24.

Figure 8-6 The pbnumbers.txt file

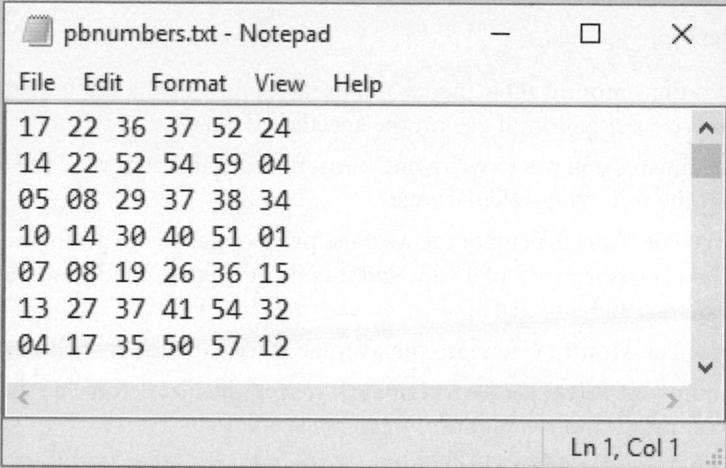

Write one or more programs that work with this file to perform the following:

- Display the 10 most common numbers, ordered by frequency
- Display the 10 least common numbers, ordered by frequency
- Display the 10 most overdue numbers (numbers that haven't been drawn in a long time), ordered from most overdue to least overdue
- Display the frequency of each number 1–69, and the frequency of each Powerball number 1–26

14. Gas Prices

In the student sample program files for this chapter, you will find a text file named `GasPrices.txt`. The file contains the weekly average prices for a gallon of gas in the United States, beginning on April 5th, 1993, and ending on August 26th, 2013. Figure 8-7 shows an example of the first few lines of the file's contents:

Figure 8-7 The GasPrices.txt file

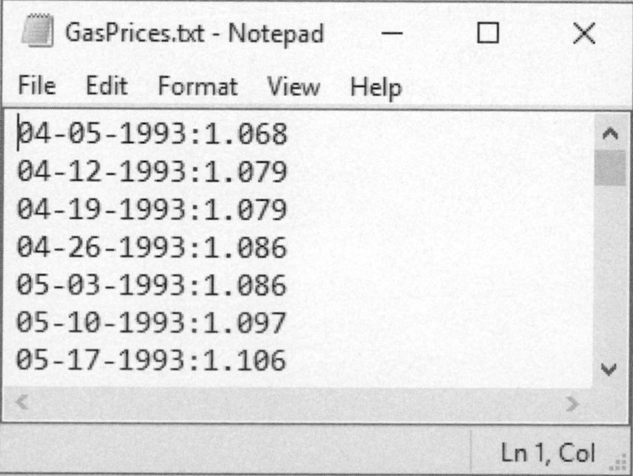

Each line in the file contains the average price for a gallon of gas on a specific date. Each line is formatted in the following way:

```
MM-DD-YYYY:Price
```

MM is the two-digit month, *DD* is the two-digit day, and *YYYY* is the four-digit year. `Price` is the average price per gallon of gas on the specified date.

For this assignment, you are to write one or more programs that read the contents of the file and perform the following calculations:

Average Price Per Year: Calculate the average price of gas per year, for each year in the file. (The file's data starts in April of 1993, and it ends in August 2013. Use the data that is present for the years 1993 and 2013.)

Average Price Per Month: Calculate the average price for each month in the file.

Highest and Lowest Prices Per Year: For each year in the file, determine the date and amount for the lowest price, and the highest price.

List of Prices, Lowest to Highest: Generate a text file that lists the dates and prices, sorted from the lowest price to the highest.

List of Prices, Highest to lowest: Generate a text file that lists the dates and prices, sorted from the highest price to the lowest.

You can write one program to perform all of these calculations, or you can write different programs, one for each calculation.

CHAPTER

9 Dictionaries and Sets

TOPICS

9.1 Dictionaries

CONCEPT: A dictionary is an object that stores a collection of data. Each element in a dictionary has two parts: a key and a value. You use a key to locate a specific value.

VideoNote Introduction to Dictionaries

When you hear the word "dictionary," you probably think about a large book such as the Merriam-Webster dictionary, containing words and their definitions. If you want to know the meaning of a particular word, you locate it in the dictionary to find its definition.

In Python, a *dictionary* is an object that stores a collection of data. Each element that is stored in a dictionary has two parts: a *key* and a *value*. In fact, dictionary elements are commonly referred to as *key-value pairs*. When you want to retrieve a specific value from a dictionary, you use the key that is associated with that value. This is similar to the process of looking up a word in the Merriam-Webster dictionary, where the words are keys and the definitions are values.

For example, suppose each employee in a company has an ID number, and we want to write a program that lets us look up an employee's name by entering that employee's ID number. We could create a dictionary in which each element contains an employee ID number as the key, and that employee's name as the value. If we know an employee's ID number, then we can retrieve that employee's name.

Another example would be a program that lets us enter a person's name and gives us that person's phone number. The program could use a dictionary in which each element contains a person's name as the key, and that person's phone number as the value. If we know a person's name, then we can retrieve that person's phone number.

NOTE: Key-value pairs are often referred to as *mappings* because each key is mapped to a value.

Creating a Dictionary

You can create a dictionary by enclosing the elements inside a set of curly braces ({}). An element consists of a key, followed by a colon, followed by a value. The elements are separated by commas. The following statement shows an example:

```
phonebook = {'Chris':'555-1111', 'Katie':'555-2222', 'Joanne':'555-3333'}
```

This statement creates a dictionary and assigns it to the phonebook variable. The dictionary contains the following three elements:

- The first element is 'Chris':'555-1111'. In this element, the key is 'Chris' and the value is '555-1111'.
- The second element is 'Katie':'555-2222'. In this element, the key is 'Katie' and the value is '555-2222'.
- The third element is 'Joanne':'555-3333'. In this element, the key is 'Joanne' and the value is '555-3333'.

In this example, the keys and the values are strings. The values in a dictionary can be objects of any type, but the keys must be immutable objects. For example, keys can be strings, integers, floating-point values, or tuples. Keys cannot be lists or any other type of immutable object.

Retrieving a Value from a Dictionary

The elements in a dictionary are not stored in any particular order. For example, look at the following interactive session in which a dictionary is created and its elements are displayed:

```
>>> phonebook = {'Chris':'555-1111', 'Katie':'555-2222',
'Joanne':'555-3333'} Enter
>>> phonebook Enter
{'Chris': '555-1111', 'Joanne': '555-3333', 'Katie': '555-2222'}
>>>
```

Notice the order in which the elements are displayed is different than the order in which they were created. This illustrates how dictionaries are not sequences, like lists, tuples, and strings. As a result, you cannot use a numeric index to retrieve a value by its position from a dictionary. Instead, you use a key to retrieve a value.

To retrieve a value from a dictionary, you simply write an expression in the following general format:

```
dictionary_name[key]
```

In the general format, *dictionary_name* is the variable that references the dictionary, and *key* is a key. If the key exists in the dictionary, the expression returns the value that is associated with the key. If the key does not exist, a KeyError exception is raised. The following interactive session demonstrates:

```
1 >>> phonebook = {'Chris':'555-1111', 'Katie':'555-2222',
  'Joanne':'555-3333'} Enter
2 >>> phonebook['Chris'] Enter
3 '555-1111'
4 >>> phonebook['Joanne'] Enter
5 '555-3333'
6 >>> phonebook['Katie'] Enter
7 '555-2222'
8 >>> phonebook['Kathryn'] Enter
Traceback (most recent call last):
  File "<pyshell#5>", line 1, in <module>
    phonebook['Kathryn']
KeyError: 'Kathryn'
>>>
```

Let's take a closer look at the session:

- Line 1 creates a dictionary containing names (as keys) and phone numbers (as values).
- In line 2, the expression phonebook['Chris'] returns the value from the phonebook dictionary that is associated with the key 'Chris'. The value is displayed in line 3.
- In line 4, the expression phonebook['Joanne'] returns the value from the phonebook dictionary that is associated with the key 'Joanne'. The value is displayed in line 5.
- In line 6, the expression phonebook['Katie'] returns the value from the phonebook dictionary that is associated with the key 'Katie'. The value is displayed in line 7.
- In line 8, the expression phonebook['Kathryn'] is entered. There is no such key as 'Kathryn' in the phonebook dictionary, so a KeyError exception is raised.

NOTE: Remember that string comparisons are case sensitive. The expression phonebook['katie'] will not locate the key 'Katie' in the dictionary.

Using the in and not in Operators to Test for a Value in a Dictionary

As previously demonstrated, a KeyError exception is raised if you try to retrieve a value from a dictionary using a nonexistent key. To prevent such an exception, you can use the in operator to determine whether a key exists before you try to use it to retrieve a value. The following interactive session demonstrates:

```
>>> phonebook = {'Chris':'555-1111', 'Katie':'555-2222',
'Joanne':'555-3333'} Enter
>>> if 'Chris' in phonebook: Enter
        print(phonebook['Chris']) Enter Enter

555-1111
>>>
```

The `if` statement in line 2 determines whether the key `'Chris'` is in the `phonebook` dictionary. If it is, the statement in line 3 displays the value that is associated with that key.

You can also use the `not in` operator to determine whether a key does not exist, as demonstrated in the following session:

```
>>> phonebook = {'Chris':'555-1111', 'Katie':'555-2222'} Enter
>>> if 'Joanne' not in phonebook: Enter
        print('Joanne is not found.') Enter Enter

Joanne is not found.
>>>
```

NOTE: Keep in mind that string comparisons with the `in` and `not in` operators are case sensitive.

Adding Elements to an Existing Dictionary

Dictionaries are mutable objects. You can add new key-value pairs to a dictionary with an assignment statement in the following general format:

```
dictionary_name[key] = value
```

In the general format, *`dictionary_name`* is the variable that references the dictionary, and *`key`* is a key. If *`key`* already exists in the dictionary, its associated value will be changed to *`value`*. If the *`key`* does not exist, it will be added to the dictionary, along with *`value`* as its associated value. The following interactive session demonstrates:

```
1 >>> phonebook = {'Chris':'555-1111', 'Katie':'555-2222',
  'Joanne':'555-3333'} Enter
2 >>> phonebook['Joe'] = '555-0123' Enter
3 >>> phonebook['Chris'] = '555-4444' Enter
4 >>> phonebook Enter
5 {'Chris': '555-4444', 'Joanne': '555-3333', 'Joe': '555-0123',
   'Katie': '555-2222'}
6 >>>
```

Let's take a closer look at the session:

- Line 1 creates a dictionary containing names (as keys) and phone numbers (as values).
- The statement in line 2 adds a new key-value pair to the `phonebook` dictionary. Because there is no key `'Joe'` in the dictionary, this statement adds the key `'Joe'`, along with its associated value `'555-0123'`.
- The statement in line 3 changes the value that is associated with an existing key. Because the key `'Chris'` already exists in the `phonebook` dictionary, this statement changes its associated value to `'555-4444'`.
- Line 4 displays the contents of the `phonebook` dictionary. The output is shown in line 5.

NOTE: You cannot have duplicate keys in a dictionary. When you assign a value to an existing key, the new value replaces the existing value.

Deleting Elements

You can delete an existing key-value pair from a dictionary with the `del` statement. Here is the general format:

```
del dictionary_name[key]
```

In the general format, *`dictionary_name`* is the variable that references the dictionary, and *`key`* is a key. After the statement executes, the *`key`* and its associated value will be deleted from the dictionary. If the *`key`* does not exist, a `KeyError` exception is raised. The following interactive session demonstrates:

```
1   >>> phonebook = {'Chris':'555-1111', 'Katie':'555-2222',
    'Joanne':'555-3333'} [Enter]
2   >>> phonebook [Enter]
3   {'Chris': '555-1111', 'Joanne': '555-3333', 'Katie': '555-2222'}
4   >>> del phonebook['Chris'] [Enter]
5   >>> phonebook [Enter]
6   {'Joanne': '555-3333', 'Katie': '555-2222'}
7   >>> del phonebook['Chris'] [Enter]
8   Traceback (most recent call last):
9       File "<pyshell#5>", line 1, in <module>
10          del phonebook['Chris']
11  KeyError: 'Chris'
12  >>>
```

Let's take a closer look at the session:

- Line 1 creates a dictionary, and line 2 displays its contents.
- Line 4 deletes the element with the key `'Chris'`, and line 5 displays the contents of the dictionary. You can see in the output in line 6 that the element no longer exists in the dictionary.
- Line 7 tries to delete the element with the key `'Chris'` again. Because the element no longer exists, a `KeyError` exception is raised.

To prevent a `KeyError` exception from being raised, you should use the `in` operator to determine whether a key exists before you try to delete it and its associated value. The following interactive session demonstrates:

```
>>> phonebook = {'Chris':'555-1111', 'Katie':'555-2222',
'Joanne':'555-3333'} [Enter]
>>> if 'Chris' in phonebook: [Enter]
        del phonebook['Chris'] [Enter] [Enter]

>>> phonebook [Enter]
{'Joanne': '555-3333', 'Katie': '555-2222'}
>>>
```

Getting the Number of Elements in a Dictionary

You can use the built-in `len` function to get the number of elements in a dictionary. The following interactive session demonstrates:

```
>>> phonebook = {'Chris':'555-1111', 'Katie':'555-2222'} [Enter]
>>> num_items = len(phonebook) [Enter]
```

```
3  >>> print(num_items) Enter
4  2
5  >>>
```

Here is a summary of the statements in the session:

- Line 1 creates a dictionary with two elements and assigns it to the `phonebook` variable.
- Line 2 calls the `len` function passing the `phonebook` variable as an argument. The function returns the value 2, which is assigned to the `num_items` variable.
- Line 3 passes `num_items` to the `print` function. The function's output is shown in line 4.

Mixing Data Types in a Dictionary

As previously mentioned, the keys in a dictionary must be immutable objects, but their associated values can be any type of object. For example, the values can be lists, as demonstrated in the following interactive session. In this session, we create a dictionary in which the keys are student names, and the values are lists of test scores.

```
1   >>> test_scores = { 'Kayla' : [88, 92, 100], Enter
2                       'Luis' : [95, 74, 81], Enter
3                       'Sophie' : [72, 88, 91], Enter
4                       'Ethan' : [70, 75, 78] } Enter
5   >>> test_scores Enter
6   {'Kayla': [88, 92, 100], 'Sophie': [72, 88, 91], 'Ethan': [70, 75, 78],
7   'Luis': [95, 74, 81]}
8   >>> test_scores['Sophie'] Enter
9   [72, 88, 91]
10  >>> kayla_scores = test_scores['Kayla'] Enter
11  >>> print(kayla_scores) Enter
12  [88, 92, 100]
13  >>>
```

Let's take a closer look at the session. This statement in lines 1 through 4 creates a dictionary and assigns it to the `test_scores` variable. The dictionary contains the following four elements:

- The first element is `'Kayla' : [88, 92, 100]`. In this element, the key is `'Kayla'` and the value is the list `[88, 92, 100]`.
- The second element is `'Luis' : [95, 74, 81]`. In this element, the key is `'Luis'` and the value is the list `[95, 74, 81]`.
- The third element is `'Sophie' : [72, 88, 91]`. In this element, the key is `'Sophie'` and the value is the list `[72, 88, 91]`.
- The fourth element is `'Ethan' : [70, 75, 78]`. In this element, the key is `'Ethan'` and the value is the list `[70, 75, 78]`.

Here is a summary of the rest of the session:

- Line 5 displays the contents of the dictionary, as shown in lines 6 through 7.
- Line 8 retrieves the value that is associated with the key `'Sophie'`. The value is displayed in line 9.

- Line 10 retrieves the value that is associated with the key `'Kayla'` and assigns it to the `kayla_scores` variable. After this statement executes, the `kayla_scores` variable references the list `[88, 92, 100]`.
- Line 11 passes the `kayla_scores` variable to the `print` function. The function's output is shown in line 12.

The values that are stored in a single dictionary can be of different types. For example, one element's value might be a string, another element's value might be a list, and yet another element's value might be an integer. The keys can be of different types, too, as long as they are immutable. The following interactive session demonstrates how different types can be mixed in a dictionary:

```
1  >>> mixed_up = {'abc':1, 999:'yada yada', (3, 6, 9):[3, 6, 9]} Enter
2  >>> mixed_up Enter
3  {(3, 6, 9): [3, 6, 9], 'abc': 1, 999: 'yada yada'}
4  >>>
```

This statement in line 1 creates a dictionary and assigns it to the `mixed_up` variable. The dictionary contains the following elements:

- The first element is `'abc':1`. In this element, the key is the string `'abc'` and the value is the integer 1.
- The second element is `999:'yada yada'`. In this element, the key is the integer 999 and the value is the string `'yada yada'`.
- The third element is `(3, 6, 9):[3, 6, 9]`. In this element, the key is the tuple `(3, 6, 9)` and the value is the list `[3, 6, 9]`.

The following interactive session gives a more practical example. It creates a dictionary that contains various pieces of data about an employee:

```
1  >>> employee = {'name' : 'Kevin Smith', 'id' : 12345, 'payrate' :
   25.75 } Enter
2  >>> employee Enter
3  {'payrate': 25.75, 'name': 'Kevin Smith', 'id': 12345}
4  >>>
```

This statement in line 1 creates a dictionary and assigns it to the `employee` variable. The dictionary contains the following elements:

- The first element is `'name' : 'Kevin Smith'`. In this element, the key is the string `'name'` and the value is the string `'Kevin Smith'`.
- The second element is `'id' : 12345`. In this element, the key is the string `'id'` and the value is the integer 12345.
- The third element is `'payrate' : 25.75`. In this element, the key is the string `'payrate'` and the value is the floating-point number 25.75.

Creating an Empty Dictionary

Sometimes, you need to create an empty dictionary and then add elements to it as the program executes. You can use an empty set of curly braces to create an empty dictionary, as demonstrated in the following interactive session:

```
1  >>> phonebook = {} Enter
2  >>> phonebook['Chris'] = '555-1111' Enter
```

```
3  >>> phonebook['Katie'] = '555-2222' Enter
4  >>> phonebook['Joanne'] = '555-3333' Enter
5  >>> phonebook Enter
6  {'Chris': '555-1111', 'Joanne': '555-3333', 'Katie': '555-2222'}
7  >>>
```

The statement in line 1 creates an empty dictionary and assigns it to the phonebook variable. Lines 2 through 4 add key-value pairs to the dictionary, and the statement in line 5 displays the dictionary's contents.

You can also use the built-in dict() method to create an empty dictionary, as shown in the following statement:

```
phonebook = dict()
```

After this statement executes, the phonebook variable will reference an empty dictionary.

Using the for Loop to Iterate over a Dictionary

You can use the for loop in the following general format to iterate over all the keys in a dictionary:

```
for var in dictionary:
    statement
    statement
    etc.
```

In the general format, *var* is the name of a variable and *dictionary* is the name of a dictionary. This loop iterates once for each element in the dictionary. Each time the loop iterates, *var* is assigned a key. The following interactive session demonstrates:

```
1  >>> phonebook = {'Chris':'555-1111', Enter
2                   'Katie':'555-2222', Enter
3                   'Joanne':'555-3333'} Enter
4  >>> for key in phonebook: Enter
5          print(key) Enter Enter
6
7
8  Chris
9  Joanne
10 Katie
11 >>> for key in phonebook: Enter
12         print(key, phonebook[key]) Enter Enter
13
14
15 Chris 555-1111
16 Joanne 555-3333
17 Katie 555-2222
18 >>>
```

Here is a summary of the statements in the session:

- Lines 1 through 3 create a dictionary with three elements and assign it to the phonebook variable.

- Lines 4 through 5 contain a `for` loop that iterates once for each element of the `phonebook` dictionary. Each time the loop iterates, the `key` variable is assigned a key. Line 5 prints the value of the `key` variable. Lines 8 through 9 show the output of the loop.
- Lines 11 through 12 contain another `for` loop that iterates once for each element of the `phonebook` dictionary, assigning a key to the `key` variable. Line 5 prints the `key` variable, followed by the value that is associated with that key. Lines 15 through 17 show the output of the loop.

Some Dictionary Methods

Dictionary objects have several methods. In this section, we look at some of the more useful ones, which are summarized in Table 9-1.

Table 9-1 Some of the dictionary methods

Method	Description
`clear`	Clears the contents of a dictionary.
`get`	Gets the value associated with a specified key. If the key is not found, the method does not raise an exception. Instead, it returns a default value.
`items`	Returns all the keys in a dictionary and their associated values as a sequence of tuples.
`keys`	Returns all the keys in a dictionary as a sequence of tuples.
`pop`	Returns the value associated with a specified key and removes that key-value pair from the dictionary. If the key is not found, the method returns a default value.
`popitem`	Returns a randomly selected key-value pair as a tuple from the dictionary and removes that key-value pair from the dictionary.
`values`	Returns all the values in the dictionary as a sequence of tuples.

The `clear` Method

The `clear` method deletes all the elements in a dictionary, leaving the dictionary empty. The method's general format is

```
dictionary.clear()
```

The following interactive session demonstrates the method:

```
>>> phonebook = {'Chris':'555-1111', 'Katie':'555-2222'} Enter
>>> phonebook Enter
{'Chris': '555-1111', 'Katie': '555-2222'}
>>> phonebook.clear() Enter
>>> phonebook Enter
{}
>>>
```

Notice after the statement in line 4 executes, the `phonebook` dictionary contains no elements.

The `get` Method

You can use the `get` method as an alternative to the `[]` operator for getting a value from a dictionary. The `get` method does not raise an exception if the specified key is not found. Here is the method's general format:

```
dictionary.get(key, default)
```

In the general format, *`dictionary`* is the name of a dictionary, *`key`* is a key to search for in the dictionary, and *`default`* is a default value to return if the *`key`* is not found. When the method is called, it returns the value that is associated with the specified *`key`*. If the specified *`key`* is not found in the dictionary, the method returns *`default`*. The following interactive session demonstrates:

```
1 >>> phonebook = {'Chris':'555-1111', 'Katie':'555-2222'} Enter
2 >>> value = phonebook.get('Katie', 'Entry not found') Enter
3 >>> print(value) Enter
4 555-2222
5 >>> value = phonebook.get('Andy', 'Entry not found') Enter
6 >>> print(value) Enter
7 Entry not found
8 >>>
```

Let's take a closer look at the session:

- The statement in line 2 searches for the key `'Katie'` in the `phonebook` dictionary. The key is found, so its associated value is returned and assigned to the `value` variable.
- Line 3 passes the `value` variable to the `print` function. The function's output is shown in line 4.
- The statement in line 5 searches for the key `'Andy'` in the `phonebook` dictionary. The key is not found, so the string `'Entry not found'` is assigned to the `value` variable.
- Line 6 passes the `value` variable to the `print` function. The function's output is shown in line 7.

The `items` Method

The `items` method returns all of a dictionary's keys and their associated values. They are returned as a special type of sequence known as a *dictionary view*. Each element in the dictionary view is a tuple, and each tuple contains a key and its associated value. For example, suppose we have created the following dictionary:

```
phonebook = {'Chris':'555-1111', 'Katie':'555-2222', 'Joanne':'555-3333'}
```

If we call the `phonebook.items()` method, it returns the following sequence:

```
[('Chris', '555-1111'), ('Joanne', '555-3333'), ('Katie', '555-2222')]
```

Notice the following:

- The first element in the sequence is the tuple `('Chris', '555-1111')`.
- The second element in the sequence is the tuple `('Joanne', '555-3333')`.
- The third element in the sequence is the tuple `('Katie', '555-2222')`.

You can use the for loop to iterate over the tuples in the sequence. The following interactive session demonstrates:

```
1  >>> phonebook = {'Chris':'555-1111', Enter
2                   'Katie':'555-2222', Enter
3                   'Joanne':'555-3333'} Enter
4  >>> for key, value in phonebook.items(): Enter
5           print(key, value) Enter Enter
6
7
8  Chris 555-1111
9  Joanne 555-3333
10 Katie 555-2222
11 >>>
```

Here is a summary of the statements in the session:

- Lines 1 through 3 create a dictionary with three elements and assign it to the phonebook variable.
- The for loop in lines 4 through 5 calls the phonebook.items() method, which returns a sequence of tuples containing the key-value pairs in the dictionary. The loop iterates once for each tuple in the sequence. Each time the loop iterates, the values of a tuple are assigned to the key and value variables. Line 5 prints the value of the key variable, followed by the value of the value variable. Lines 8 through 10 show the output of the loop.

The keys Method

The keys method returns all of a dictionary's keys as a dictionary view, which is a type of sequence. Each element in the dictionary view is a key from the dictionary. For example, suppose we have created the following dictionary:

```
phonebook = {'Chris':'555-1111', 'Katie':'555-2222', 'Joanne':'555-3333'}
```

If we call the phonebook.keys() method, it will return the following sequence:

```
['Chris', 'Joanne', 'Katie']
```

The following interactive session shows how you can use a for loop to iterate over the sequence that is returned from the keys method:

```
>>> phonebook = {'Chris':'555-1111', Enter
                 'Katie':'555-2222', Enter
                 'Joanne':'555-3333'} Enter
>>> for key in phonebook.keys(): Enter
        print(key) Enter Enter


Chris
Joanne
Katie
>>>
```

The pop Method

The pop method returns the value associated with a specified key and removes that key-value pair from the dictionary. If the key is not found, the method returns a default value. Here is the method's general format:

```
dictionary.pop(key, default)
```

In the general format, *dictionary* is the name of a dictionary, *key* is a key to search for in the dictionary, and *default* is a default value to return if the *key* is not found. When the method is called, it returns the value that is associated with the specified *key*, and it removes that key-value pair from the dictionary. If the specified *key* is not found in the dictionary, the method returns *default*. The following interactive session demonstrates:

```
1  >>> phonebook = {'Chris':'555-1111', Enter
2                   'Katie':'555-2222', Enter
3                   'Joanne':'555-3333'} Enter
4  >>> phone_num = phonebook.pop('Chris', 'Entry not found') Enter
5  >>> phone_num Enter
6  '555-1111'
7  >>> phonebook Enter
8  {'Joanne': '555-3333', 'Katie': '555-2222'}
9  >>> phone_num = phonebook.pop('Andy', 'Element not found') Enter
10 >>> phone_num Enter
11 'Element not found'
12 >>> phonebook Enter
13 {'Joanne': '555-3333', 'Katie': '555-2222'}
14 >>>
```

Here is a summary of the statements in the session:

- Lines 1 through 3 create a dictionary with three elements and assign it to the phonebook variable.
- Line 4 calls the phonebook.pop() method, passing 'Chris' as the key to search for. The value that is associated with the key 'Chris' is returned and assigned to the phone_num variable. The key-value pair containing the key 'Chris' is removed from the dictionary.
- Line 5 displays the value assigned to the phone_num variable. The output is displayed in line 6. Notice this is the value that was associated with the key 'Chris'.
- Line 7 displays the contents of the phonebook dictionary. The output is shown in line 8. Notice the key-value pair that contained the key 'Chris' is no longer in the dictionary.
- Line 9 calls the phonebook.pop() method, passing 'Andy' as the key to search for. The key is not found, so the string 'Entry not found' is assigned to the phone_num variable.
- Line 10 displays the value assigned to the phone_num variable. The output is displayed in line 11.
- Line 12 displays the contents of the phonebook dictionary. The output is shown in line 13.

The `popitem` Method

The `popitem` method returns a randomly selected key-value pair, and it removes that key-value pair from the dictionary. The key-value pair is returned as a tuple. Here is the method's general format:

```
dictionary.popitem()
```

You can use an assignment statement in the following general format to assign the returned key and value to individual variables:

```
k, v = dictionary.popitem()
```

This type of assignment is known as a *multiple assignment* because multiple variables are being assigned at once. In the general format, *k* and *v* are variables. After the statement executes, *k* is assigned a randomly selected key from the *dictionary*, and *v* is assigned the value associated with that key. The key-value pair is removed from the *dictionary*.

The following interactive session demonstrates:

```
1  >>> phonebook = {'Chris':'555-1111', Enter
2                  'Katie':'555-2222', Enter
3                  'Joanne':'555-3333'} Enter
4  >>> phonebook Enter
5  {'Chris': '555-1111', 'Joanne': '555-3333', 'Katie': '555-2222'}
6  >>> key, value = phonebook.popitem() Enter
7  >>> print(key, value) Enter
8  Chris 555-1111
9  >>> phonebook Enter
10 {'Joanne': '555-3333', 'Katie': '555-2222'}
11 >>>
```

Here is a summary of the statements in the session:

- Lines 1 through 3 create a dictionary with three elements and assign it to the `phonebook` variable.
- Line 4 displays the dictionary's contents, shown in line 5.
- Line 6 calls the `phonebook.popitem()` method. The key and value that are returned from the method are assigned to the variables `key` and `value`. The key-value pair is removed from the dictionary.
- Line 7 displays the values assigned to the `key` and `value` variables. The output is shown in line 8.
- Line 9 displays the contents of the dictionary. The output is shown in line 10. Notice that the key-value pair that was returned from the `popitem` method in line 6 has been removed.

Keep in mind that the `popitem` method raises a `KeyError` exception if it is called on an empty dictionary.

The `values` Method

The `values` method returns all a dictionary's values (without their keys) as a dictionary view, which is a type of sequence. Each element in the dictionary view is a value from the dictionary. For example, suppose we have created the following dictionary:

```
phonebook = {'Chris':'555-1111', 'Katie':'555-2222', 'Joanne':'555-3333'}
```

If we call the phonebook.values() method, it returns the following sequence:

```
['555-1111', '555-2222', '555-3333']
```

The following interactive session shows how you can use a for loop to iterate over the sequence that is returned from the values method:

```
>>> phonebook = {'Chris':'555-1111', [Enter]
                 'Katie':'555-2222', [Enter]
                 'Joanne':'555-3333'} [Enter]
>>> for val in phonebook.values(): [Enter]
        print(val) [Enter] [Enter]
555-1111
555-3333
555-2222
>>>
```

In the Spotlight:

Using a Dictionary to Simulate a Deck of Cards

In some games involving poker cards, the cards are assigned numeric values. For example, in the game of Blackjack, the cards are given the following numeric values:

- Numeric cards are assigned the value they have printed on them. For example, the value of the 2 of spades is 2, and the value of the 5 of diamonds is 5.
- Jacks, queens, and kings are valued at 10.
- Aces are valued at either 1 or 11, depending on the player's choice.

In this section, we look at a program that uses a dictionary to simulate a standard deck of poker cards, where the cards are assigned numeric values similar to those used in Blackjack. (In the program, we assign the value 1 to all aces.) The key-value pairs use the name of the card as the key, and the card's numeric value as the value. For example, the key-value pair for the queen of hearts is

```
'Queen of Hearts':10
```

And the key-value pair for the 8 of diamonds is

```
'8 of Diamonds':8
```

The program prompts the user for the number of cards to deal, and it randomly deals a hand of that many cards from the deck. The names of the cards are displayed, as well as the total numeric value of the hand. Program 9-1 shows the program code. The program is divided into three functions: main, create_deck, and deal_cards. Rather than presenting the entire program at once, let's first examine the main function.

Program 9-1 (`card_dealer.py`: **main function**)

```
1  # This program uses a dictionary as a deck of cards.
2
3  def main():
4      # Create a deck of cards.
5      deck = create_deck()
6
7      # Get the number of cards to deal.
8      num_cards = int(input('How many cards should I deal? '))
9
10     # Deal the cards.
11     deal_cards(deck, num_cards)
12
```

Line 5 calls the `create_deck` function. The function creates a dictionary containing the key-value pairs for a deck of cards, and it returns a reference to the dictionary. The reference is assigned to the `deck` variable.

Line 8 prompts the user to enter the number of cards to deal. The input is converted to an `int` and assigned to the `num_cards` variable.

Line 11 calls the `deal_cards` function passing the `deck` and `num_cards` variables as arguments. The `deal_cards` function deals the specified number of cards from the deck.

Next is the `create_deck` function.

Program 9-1 (`card_dealer.py`: **create_deck function**)

```
13 # The create_deck function returns a dictionary
14 # representing a deck of cards.
15 def create_deck():
16     # Create a dictionary with each card and its value
17     # stored as key-value pairs.
18     deck = {'Ace of Spades':1, '2 of Spades':2, '3 of Spades':3,
19             '4 of Spades':4, '5 of Spades':5, '6 of Spades':6,
20             '7 of Spades':7, '8 of Spades':8, '9 of Spades':9,
21             '10 of Spades':10, 'Jack of Spades':10,
22             'Queen of Spades':10, 'King of Spades': 10,
23
24             'Ace of Hearts':1, '2 of Hearts':2, '3 of Hearts':3,
25             '4 of Hearts':4, '5 of Hearts':5, '6 of Hearts':6,
26             '7 of Hearts':7, '8 of Hearts':8, '9 of Hearts':9,
27             '10 of Hearts':10, 'Jack of Hearts':10,
28             'Queen of Hearts':10, 'King of Hearts': 10,
29
30             'Ace of Clubs':1, '2 of Clubs':2, '3 of Clubs':3,
31             '4 of Clubs':4, '5 of Clubs':5, '6 of Clubs':6,
```

(program continues)

Program 9-1 *(continued)*

```
32              '7 of Clubs':7, '8 of Clubs':8, '9 of Clubs':9,
33              '10 of Clubs':10, 'Jack of Clubs':10,
34              'Queen of Clubs':10, 'King of Clubs': 10,
35
36              'Ace of Diamonds':1, '2 of Diamonds':2, '3 of Diamonds':3,
37              '4 of Diamonds':4, '5 of Diamonds':5, '6 of Diamonds':6,
38              '7 of Diamonds':7, '8 of Diamonds':8, '9 of Diamonds':9,
39              '10 of Diamonds':10, 'Jack of Diamonds':10,
40              'Queen of Diamonds':10, 'King of Diamonds': 10}
41
42      # Return the deck.
43      return deck
44
```

The code in lines 18 through 40 creates a dictionary with key-value pairs representing the cards in a standard poker deck. (The blank lines that appear in lines 22, 29, and 35 were inserted to make the code easier to read.)

Line 43 returns a reference to the dictionary.

Next is the `deal_cards` function.

Program 9-1 **(`card_dealer.py`: `deal_cards` function)**

```
45  # The deal_cards function deals a specified number of cards
46  # from the deck.
47
48  def deal_cards(deck, number):
49      # Initialize an accumulator for the hand value.
50      hand_value = 0
51
52      # Make sure the number of cards to deal is not
53      # greater than the number of cards in the deck.
54      if number > len(deck):
55          number = len(deck)
56
57      # Deal the cards and accumulate their values.
58      for count in range(number):
59          card, value = deck.popitem()
60          print(card)
61          hand_value += value
62
63      # Display the value of the hand.
64      print('Value of this hand:', hand_value)
65
66  # Call the main function.
67  main()
```

The deal_cards function accepts two arguments: the number of cards to deal and the deck from which deal them. Line 50 initializes an accumulator variable named hand_value to 0. The if statement in line 54 determines whether the number of cards to deal is greater than the number of cards in the deck. If so, line 55 sets the number of cards to deal to the number of cards in the deck.

The for loop that begins in line 58 iterates once for each card that is to be dealt. Inside the loop, the statement in line 59 calls the popitem method to randomly return a key-value pair from the deck dictionary. The key is assigned to the card variable, and the value is assigned to the value variable. Line 60 displays the name of the card, and line 61 adds the card's value to the hand_value accumulator.

After the loop has finished, line 64 displays the total value of the hand.

Program Output (with input shown in bold)

```
How many cards should I deal? 5 [Enter]
8 of Hearts
5 of Diamonds
5 of Hearts
Queen of Clubs
10 of Spades
Value of this hand: 38
```

In the Spotlight:
Storing Names and Birthdays in a Dictionary

In this section, we look at a program that keeps your friends' names and birthdays in a dictionary. Each entry in the dictionary uses a friend's name as the key, and that friend's birthday as the value. You can use the program to look up your friends' birthdays by entering their names.

The program displays a menu that allows the user to make one of the following choices:

1. Look up a birthday
2. Add a new birthday
3. Change a birthday
4. Delete a birthday
5. Quit the program

The program initially starts with an empty dictionary, so you have to choose item 2 from the menu to add a new entry. Once you have added a few entries, you can choose item 1 to look up a specific person's birthday, item 3 to change an existing birthday in the dictionary, item 4 to delete a birthday from the dictionary, or item 5 to quit the program.

Program 9-2 shows the program code. The program is divided into six functions: `main`, `get_menu_choice`, `look_up`, `add`, `change`, and `delete`. Rather than presenting the entire program at once, let's first examine the global constants and the `main` function.

Program 9-2 (birthdays.py: main function)

```
1  # This program uses a dictionary to keep friends'
2  # names and birthdays.
3
4  # Global constants for menu choices
5  LOOK_UP = 1
6  ADD = 2
7  CHANGE = 3
8  DELETE = 4
9  QUIT = 5
10
11 # main function
12 def main():
13     # Create an empty dictionary.
14     birthdays = {}
15
16     # Initialize a variable for the user's choice.
17     choice = 0
18
19     while choice != QUIT:
20         # Get the user's menu choice.
21         choice = get_menu_choice()
22
23         # Process the choice.
24         if choice == LOOK_UP:
25             look_up(birthdays)
26         elif choice == ADD:
27             add(birthdays)
28         elif choice == CHANGE:
29             change(birthdays)
30         elif choice == DELETE:
31             delete(birthdays)
32
```

The global constants that are declared in lines 5 through 9 are used to test the user's menu selection. Inside the `main` function, line 14 creates an empty dictionary referenced by the `birthdays` variable. Line 17 initializes the `choice` variable with the value 0. This variable holds the user's menu selection.

The `while` loop that begins in line 19 repeats until the user chooses to quit the program. Inside the loop, line 21 calls the `get_menu_choice` function. The `get_menu_choice` function displays the menu and returns the user's selection. The value that is returned is assigned to the `choice` variable.

The if-elif statement in lines 24 through 31 processes the user's menu choice. If the user selects item 1, line 25 calls the look_up function. If the user selects item 2, line 27 calls the add function. If the user selects item 3, line 29 calls the change function. If the user selects item 4, line 31 calls the delete function.

The get_menu_choice function is next.

Program 9-2 (birthdays.py: get_menu_choice function)

```
33  # The get_menu_choice function displays the menu
34  # and gets a validated choice from the user.
35  def get_menu_choice():
36      print()
37      print('Friends and Their Birthdays')
38      print('--------------------------')
39      print('1. Look up a birthday')
40      print('2. Add a new birthday')
41      print('3. Change a birthday')
42      print('4. Delete a birthday')
43      print('5. Quit the program')
44      print()
45
46      # Get the user's choice.
47      choice = int(input('Enter your choice: '))
48
49      # Validate the choice.
50      while choice < LOOK_UP or choice > QUIT:
51          choice = int(input('Enter a valid choice: '))
52
53      # return the user's choice.
54      return choice
55
```

The statements in lines 36 through 44 display the menu on the screen. Line 47 prompts the user to enter his or her choice. The input is converted to an int and assigned to the choice variable. The while loop in lines 50 through 51 validates the user's input and, if necessary, prompts the user to reenter his or her choice. Once a valid choice is entered, it is returned from the function in line 54.

The look_up function is next.

Program 9-2 (birthdays.py: look_up function)

```
# The look_up function looks up a name in the
# birthdays dictionary.
def look_up(birthdays):
    # Get a name to look up.
    name = input('Enter a name: ')
```

(program continues)

Program 9-2 *(continued)*

```
61
62      # Look it up in the dictionary.
63      print(birthdays.get(name, 'Not found.'))
64
```

The purpose of the `look_up` function is to allow the user to look up a friend's birthday. It accepts the dictionary as an argument. Line 60 prompts the user to enter a name, and line 63 passes that name as an argument to the dictionary's `get` function. If the name is found, its associated value (the friend's birthday) is returned and displayed. If the name is not found, the string '`Not found.`' is displayed.

The add function is next.

Program 9-2 **(`birthdays.py`: add function)**

```
65  # The add function adds a new entry into the
66  # birthdays dictionary.
67  def add(birthdays):
68      # Get a name and birthday.
69      name = input('Enter a name: ')
70      bday = input('Enter a birthday: ')
71
72      # If the name does not exist, add it.
73      if name not in birthdays:
74          birthdays[name] = bday
75      else:
76          print('That entry already exists.')
77
```

The purpose of the add function is to allow the user to add a new birthday to the dictionary. It accepts the dictionary as an argument. Lines 69 and 70 prompt the user to enter a name and a birthday. The `if` statement in line 73 determines whether the name is not already in the dictionary. If not, line 74 adds the new name and birthday to the dictionary. Otherwise, a message indicating that the entry already exists is printed in line 76.

The change function is next.

Program 9-2 **(`birthdays.py`: change function)**

```
78  # The change function changes an existing
79  # entry in the birthdays dictionary.
80  def change(birthdays):
81      # Get a name to look up.
82      name = input('Enter a name: ')
```

```
83
84      if name in birthdays:
85          # Get a new birthday.
86          bday = input('Enter the new birthday: ')
87
88          # Update the entry.
89          birthdays[name] = bday
90      else:
91          print('That name is not found.')
92
```

The purpose of the `change` function is to allow the user to change an existing birthday in the dictionary. It accepts the dictionary as an argument. Line 82 gets a name from the user. The `if` statement in line 84 determines whether the name is in the dictionary. If so, line 86 gets the new birthday, and line 89 stores that birthday in the dictionary. If the name is not in the dictionary, line 91 prints a message indicating so.

The `delete` function is next.

Program 9-2 **(`birthdays.py: change function`)**

```
93  # The delete function deletes an entry from the
94  # birthdays dictionary.
95  def delete(birthdays):
96      # Get a name to look up.
97      name = input('Enter a name: ')
98
99      # If the name is found, delete the entry.
100     if name in birthdays:
101         del birthdays[name]
102     else:
103         print('That name is not found.')
104
105 # Call the main function.
106 main()
```

The purpose of the `delete` function is to allow the user to delete an existing birthday from the dictionary. It accepts the dictionary as an argument. Line 97 gets a name from the user. The `if` statement in line 100 determines whether the name is in the dictionary. If so, line 101 deletes it. If the name is not in the dictionary, line 103 prints a message indicating so.

Program Output (with input shown in bold)

```
Friends and Their Birthdays
--------------------------
1. Look up a birthday
2. Add a new birthday
3. Change a birthday
```

(program output continues)

Program Output *(continued)*

```
4. Delete a birthday
5. Quit the program

Enter your choice: 2 Enter
Enter a name: Cameron Enter
Enter a birthday: 10/12/1990 Enter

Friends and Their Birthdays
---------------------------
1. Look up a birthday
2. Add a new birthday
3. Change a birthday
4. Delete a birthday
5. Quit the program

Enter your choice: 2 Enter
Enter a name: Kathryn Enter
Enter a birthday: 5/7/1989 Enter

Friends and Their Birthdays
---------------------------
1. Look up a birthday
2. Add a new birthday
3. Change a birthday
4. Delete a birthday
5. Quit the program

Enter your choice: 1 Enter
Enter a name: Cameron Enter
10/12/1990

Friends and Their Birthdays
---------------------------
1. Look up a birthday
2. Add a new birthday
3. Change a birthday
4. Delete a birthday
5. Quit the program

Enter your choice: 1 Enter
Enter a name: Kathryn Enter
5/7/1989

Friends and Their Birthdays
---------------------------
1. Look up a birthday
2. Add a new birthday
3. Change a birthday
```

```
4. Delete a birthday
5. Quit the program

Enter your choice: 3 Enter
Enter a name: Kathryn Enter
Enter the new birthday: 5/7/1988 Enter

Friends and Their Birthdays
--------------------------
1. Look up a birthday
2. Add a new birthday
3. Change a birthday
4. Delete a birthday
5. Quit the program

Enter your choice: 1 Enter
Enter a name: Kathryn Enter
5/7/1988

Friends and Their Birthdays
--------------------------
1. Look up a birthday
2. Add a new birthday
3. Change a birthday
4. Delete a birthday
5. Quit the program

Enter your choice: 4 Enter
Enter a name: Cameron Enter

Friends and Their Birthdays
--------------------------
1. Look up a birthday
2. Add a new birthday
3. Change a birthday
4. Delete a birthday
5. Quit the program

Enter your choice: 1 Enter
Enter a name: Cameron Enter
Not found.

Friends and Their Birthdays
--------------------------
1. Look up a birthday
2. Add a new birthday
3. Change a birthday
4. Delete a birthday
5. Quit the program

Enter your choice: 5 Enter
```

Checkpoint

9.1 An element in a dictionary has two parts. What are they called?

9.2 Which part of a dictionary element must be immutable?

9.3 Suppose `'start' : 1472` is an element in a dictionary. What is the key? What is the value?

9.4 Suppose a dictionary named `employee` has been created. What does the following statement do?

```
employee['id'] = 54321
```

9.5 What will the following code display?

```
stuff = {1 : 'aaa', 2 : 'bbb', 3 : 'ccc'}
print(stuff[3])
```

9.6 How can you determine whether a key-value pair exists in a dictionary?

9.7 Suppose a dictionary named `inventory` exists. What does the following statement do?

```
del inventory[654]
```

9.8 What will the following code display?

```
stuff = {1 : 'aaa', 2 : 'bbb', 3 : 'ccc'}
print(len(stuff))
```

9.9 What will the following code display?

```
stuff = {1 : 'aaa', 2 : 'bbb', 3 : 'ccc'}
for k in stuff:
    print(k)
```

9.10 What is the difference between the dictionary methods `pop` and `popitem`?

9.11 What does the `items` method return?

9.12 What does the `keys` method return?

9.13 What does the `values` method return?

9.2 Sets

CONCEPT: A set contains a collection of unique values and works like a mathematical set.

VideoNote Introduction to Sets

A *set* is an object that stores a collection of data in the same way as mathematical sets. Here are some important things to know about sets:

- All the elements in a set must be unique. No two elements can have the same value.
- Sets are unordered, which means that the elements in a set are not stored in any particular order.
- The elements that are stored in a set can be of different data types.

Creating a Set

To create a set, you have to call the built-in `set` function. Here is an example of how you create an empty set:

```
myset = set()
```

After this statement executes, the `myset` variable will reference an empty set. You can also pass one argument to the `set` function. The argument that you pass must be an object that contains iterable elements, such as a list, a tuple, or a string. The individual elements of the object that you pass as an argument become elements of the set. Here is an example:

```
myset = set(['a', 'b', 'c'])
```

In this example, we are passing a list as an argument to the `set` function. After this statement executes, the `myset` variable references a set containing the elements `'a'`, `'b'`, and `'c'`.

If you pass a string as an argument to the `set` function, each individual character in the string becomes a member of the set. Here is an example:

```
myset = set('abc')
```

After this statement executes, the `myset` variable will reference a set containing the elements `'a'`, `'b'`, and `'c'`.

Sets cannot contain duplicate elements. If you pass an argument containing duplicate elements to the `set` function, only one of the duplicated elements will appear in the set. Here is an example:

```
myset = set('aaabc')
```

The character `'a'` appears multiple times in the string, but it will appear only once in the set. After this statement executes, the `myset` variable will reference a set containing the elements `'a'`, `'b'`, and `'c'`.

What if you want to create a set in which each element is a string containing more than one character? For example, how would you create a set containing the elements `'one'`, `'two'`, and `'three'`? The following code does not accomplish the task, because you can pass no more than one argument to the `set` function:

```
# This is an ERROR!
myset = set('one', 'two', 'three')
```

The following does not accomplish the task either:

```
# This does not do what we intend.
myset = set('one two three')
```

After this statement executes, the `myset` variable will reference a set containing the elements `'o'`, `'n'`, `'e'`, `' '`, `'t'`, `'w'`, `'h'`, and `'r'`. To create the set that we want, we have to pass a list containing the strings 'one', 'two', and 'three' as an argument to the `set` function. Here is an example:

```
# OK, this works.
myset = set(['one', 'two', 'three'])
```

After this statement executes, the `myset` variable will reference a set containing the elements `'one'`, `'two'`, and `'three'`.

Getting the Number of Elements in a Set

As with lists, tuples, and dictionaries, you can use the `len` function to get the number of elements in a set. The following interactive session demonstrates:

```
>>> myset = set([1, 2, 3, 4, 5]) Enter
>>> len(myset) Enter
5
>>>
```

Adding and Removing Elements

Sets are mutable objects, so you can add items to them and remove items from them. You use the `add` method to add an element to a set. The following interactive session demonstrates:

```
1 >>> myset = set() Enter
2 >>> myset.add(1) Enter
3 >>> myset.add(2) Enter
4 >>> myset.add(3) Enter
5 >>> myset Enter
6 {1, 2, 3}
7 >>> myset.add(2) Enter
8 >>> myset
9 {1, 2, 3}
```

The statement in line 1 creates an empty set and assigns it to the `myset` variable. The statements in lines 2 through 4 add the values 1, 2, and 3 to the set. Line 5 displays the contents of the set, which is shown in line 6.

The statement in line 7 attempts to add the value 2 to the set. The value 2 is already in the set, however. If you try to add a duplicate item to a set with the `add` method, the method does not raise an exception. It simply does not add the item.

You can add a group of elements to a set all at one time with the `update` method. When you call the `update` method as an argument, you pass an object that contains iterable elements, such as a list, a tuple, string, or another set. The individual elements of the object that you pass as an argument become elements of the set. The following interactive session demonstrates:

```
1 >>> myset = set([1, 2, 3]) Enter
2 >>> myset.update([4, 5, 6]) Enter
3 >>> myset Enter
4 {1, 2, 3, 4, 5, 6}
5 >>>
```

The statement in line 1 creates a set containing the values 1, 2, and 3. Line 2 adds the values 4, 5, and 6. The following session shows another example:

```
>>> set1 = set([1, 2, 3]) Enter
>>> set2 = set([8, 9, 10]) Enter
>>> set1.update(set2) Enter
```

```
4   >>> set1
5   {1, 2, 3, 8, 9, 10}
6   >>> set2 Enter
7   {8, 9, 10}
8   >>>
```

Line 1 creates a set containing the values 1, 2, and 3 and assigns it to the `set1` variable. Line 2 creates a set containing the values 8, 9, and 10 and assigns it to the `set2` variable. Line 3 calls the `set1.update` method, passing `set2` as an argument. This causes the element of `set2` to be added to `set1`. Notice `set2` remains unchanged. The following session shows another example:

```
1   >>> myset = set([1, 2, 3]) Enter
2   >>> myset.update('abc') Enter
3   >>> myset Enter
4   {'a', 1, 2, 3, 'c', 'b'}
5   >>>
```

The statement in line 1 creates a set containing the values 1, 2, and 3. Line 2 calls the `myset.update` method, passing the string `'abc'` as an argument. This causes the each character of the string to be added as an element to `myset`.

You can remove an item from a set with either the `remove` method or the `discard` method. You pass the item that you want to remove as an argument to either method, and that item is removed from the set. The only difference between the two methods is how they behave when the specified item is not found in the set. The `remove` method raises a `KeyError` exception, but the `discard` method does not raise an exception. The following interactive session demonstrates:

```
1   >>> myset = set([1, 2, 3, 4, 5]) Enter
2   >>> myset Enter
3   {1, 2, 3, 4, 5}
4   >>> myset.remove(1) Enter
5   >>> myset Enter
6   {2, 3, 4, 5}
7   >>> myset.discard(5) Enter
8   >>> myset Enter
9   {2, 3, 4}
10  >>> myset.discard(99) Enter
11  >>> myset.remove(99) Enter
12  Traceback (most recent call last):
13    File "<pyshell#12>", line 1, in <module>
14      myset.remove(99)
15  KeyError: 99
16  >>>
```

Line 1 creates a set with the elements 1, 2, 3, 4, and 5. Line 2 displays the contents of the set, which is shown in line 3. Line 4 calls the `remove` method to remove the value 1 from the set. You can see in the output shown in line 6 that the value 1 is no longer in the set. Line 7 calls the `discard` method to remove the value 5 from the set. You can see in the output in line 9 that the value 5 is no longer in the set. Line 10 calls the `discard` method to remove the value 99 from the set. The value is not found in the set, but the `discard` method does not raise an exception. Line 11 calls the `remove` method to remove the value 99 from the set. Because the value is not in the set, a `KeyError` exception is raised, as shown in lines 12 through 15.

You can clear all the elements of a set by calling the `clear` method. The following interactive session demonstrates:

```
1 >>> myset = set([1, 2, 3, 4, 5]) Enter
2 >>> myset Enter
3 {1, 2, 3, 4, 5}
4 >>> myset.clear() Enter
5 >>> myset Enter
6 set()
7 >>>
```

The statement in line 4 calls the `clear` method to clear the set. Notice in line 6 that when we display the contents of an empty set, the interpreter displays `set()`.

Using the `for` Loop to Iterate over a Set

You can use the `for` loop in the following general format to iterate over all the elements in a set:

```
for var in set:
    statement
    statement
    etc.
```

In the general format, *`var`* is the name of a variable and *`set`* is the name of a set. This loop iterates once for each element in the set. Each time the loop iterates, *`var`* is assigned an element. The following interactive session demonstrates:

```
1 >>> myset = set(['a', 'b', 'c']) Enter
2 >>> for val in myset: Enter
3         print(val) Enter Enter
4
5 a
6 c
7 b
8 >>>
```

Lines 2 through 3 contain a `for` loop that iterates once for each element of the `myset` set. Each time the loop iterates, an element of the set is assigned to the `val` variable. Line 3 prints the value of the `val` variable. Lines 5 through 7 show the output of the loop.

Using the `in` and `not in` Operators to Test for a Value in a Set

You can use the `in` operator to determine whether a value exists in a set. The following interactive session demonstrates:

```
1 >>> myset = set([1, 2, 3]) [Enter]
2 >>> if 1 in myset: [Enter]
3         print('The value 1 is in the set.') [Enter] [Enter]
4
5 The value 1 is in the set.
6 >>>
```

The `if` statement in line 2 determines whether the value 1 is in the `myset` set. If it is, the statement in line 3 displays a message.

You can also use the `not in` operator to determine if a value does not exist in a set, as demonstrated in the following session:

```
>>> myset = set([1, 2, 3]) [Enter]
>>> if 99 not in myset: [Enter]
        print('The value 99 is not in the set.') [Enter] [Enter]

The value 99 is not in the set.
>>>
```

Finding the Union of Sets

The union of two sets is a set that contains all the elements of both sets. In Python, you can call the `union` method to get the union of two sets. Here is the general format:

`set1``.union(`*`set2`*`)`

In the general format, *`set1`* and *`set2`* are sets. The method returns a set that contains the elements of both *`set1`* and *`set2`*. The following interactive session demonstrates:

```
1 >>> set1 = set([1, 2, 3, 4]) [Enter]
2 >>> set2 = set([3, 4, 5, 6]) [Enter]
3 >>> set3 = set1.union(set2) [Enter]
4 >>> set3 [Enter]
5 {1, 2, 3, 4, 5, 6}
6 >>>
```

The statement in line 3 calls the `set1` object's `union` method, passing `set2` as an argument. The method returns a set that contains all the elements of `set1` and `set2` (without duplicates, of course). The resulting set is assigned to the `set3` variable.

You can also use the `|` operator to find the union of two sets. Here is the general format of an expression using the `|` operator with two sets:

`set1`` | `*`set2`*

In the general format, *`set1`* and *`set2`* are sets. The expression returns a set that contains the elements of both *`set1`* and *`set2`*. The following interactive session demonstrates:

```
>>> set1 = set([1, 2, 3, 4]) [Enter]
>>> set2 = set([3, 4, 5, 6]) [Enter]
>>> set3 = set1 | set2 [Enter]
>>> set3 [Enter]
{1, 2, 3, 4, 5, 6}
>>>
```

Finding the Intersection of Sets

The intersection of two sets is a set that contains only the elements that are found in both sets. In Python, you can call the `intersection` method to get the intersection of two sets. Here is the general format:

```
set1.intersection(set2)
```

In the general format, *set1* and *set2* are sets. The method returns a set that contains the elements that are found in both *set1* and *set2*. The following interactive session demonstrates:

```
1 >>> set1 = set([1, 2, 3, 4]) Enter
2 >>> set2 = set([3, 4, 5, 6]) Enter
3 >>> set3 = set1.intersection(set2) Enter
4 >>> set3 Enter
5 {3, 4}
6 >>>
```

The statement in line 3 calls the `set1` object's `intersection` method, passing `set2` as an argument. The method returns a set that contains the elements that are found in both `set1` and `set2`. The resulting set is assigned to the `set3` variable.

You can also use the `&` operator to find the intersection of two sets. Here is the general format of an expression using the `&` operator with two sets:

```
set1 & set2
```

In the general format, *set1* and *set2* are sets. The expression returns a set that contains the elements that are found in both *set1* and *set2*. The following interactive session demonstrates:

```
>>> set1 = set([1, 2, 3, 4]) Enter
>>> set2 = set([3, 4, 5, 6]) Enter
>>> set3 = set1 & set2 Enter
>>> set3 Enter
{3, 4}
>>>
```

Finding the Difference of Sets

The difference of `set1` and `set2` is the elements that appear in `set1` but do not appear in `set2`. In Python, you can call the `difference` method to get the difference of two sets. Here is the general format:

```
set1.difference(set2)
```

In the general format, *set1* and *set2* are sets. The method returns a set that contains the elements that are found in *set1* but not in *set2*. The following interactive session demonstrates:

```
>>> set1 = set([1, 2, 3, 4]) Enter
>>> set2 = set([3, 4, 5, 6]) Enter
>>> set3 = set1.difference(set2) Enter
>>> set3 Enter
{1, 2}
>>>
```

You can also use the - operator to find the difference of two sets. Here is the general format of an expression using the - operator with two sets:

```
set1 - set2
```

In the general format, *set1* and *set2* are sets. The expression returns a set that contains the elements that are found in *set1* but not in *set2*. The following interactive session demonstrates:

```
>>> set1 = set([1, 2, 3, 4]) Enter
>>> set2 = set([3, 4, 5, 6]) Enter
>>> set3 = set1 - set2 Enter
>>> set3 Enter
{1, 2}
>>>
```

Finding the Symmetric Difference of Sets

The symmetric difference of two sets is a set that contains the elements that are not shared by the sets. In other words, it is the elements that are in one set but not in both. In Python, you can call the `symmetric_difference` method to get the symmetric difference of two sets. Here is the general format:

```
set1.symmetric_difference(set2)
```

In the general format, *set1* and *set2* are sets. The method returns a set that contains the elements that are found in either *set1* or *set2* but not both sets. The following interactive session demonstrates:

```
>>> set1 = set([1, 2, 3, 4]) Enter
>>> set2 = set([3, 4, 5, 6]) Enter
>>> set3 = set1.symmetric_difference(set2) Enter
>>> set3 Enter
{1, 2, 5, 6}
>>>
```

You can also use the ^ operator to find the symmetric difference of two sets. Here is the general format of an expression using the ^ operator with two sets:

```
set1 ^ set2
```

In the general format, *set1* and *set2* are sets. The expression returns a set that contains the elements that are found in either *set1* or *set2*, but not both sets. The following interactive session demonstrates:

```
>>> set1 = set([1, 2, 3, 4]) Enter
>>> set2 = set([3, 4, 5, 6]) Enter
>>> set3 = set1 ^ set2 Enter
>>> set3 Enter
{1, 2, 5, 6}
>>>
```

Finding Subsets and Supersets

Suppose you have two sets, and one of those sets contains all of the elements of the other set. Here is an example:

```
set1 = set([1, 2, 3, 4])
set2 = set([2, 3])
```

In this example, `set1` contains all the elements of `set2`, which means that `set2` is a *subset* of `set1`. It also means that `set1` is a *superset* of `set2`. In Python, you can call the `issubset` method to determine whether one set is a subset of another. Here is the general format:

```
set2.issubset(set1)
```

In the general format, *`set1`* and *`set2`* are sets. The method returns `True` if `set2` is a subset of `set1`. Otherwise, it returns `False`. You can call the `issuperset` method to determine whether one set is a superset of another. Here is the general format:

```
set1.issuperset(set2)
```

In the general format, *`set1`* and *`set2`* are sets. The method returns `True` if `set1` is a superset of `set2`. Otherwise, it returns `False`. The following interactive session demonstrates:

```
>>> set1 = set([1, 2, 3, 4]) Enter
>>> set2 = set([2, 3]) Enter
>>> set2.issubset(set1) Enter
True
>>> set1.issuperset(set2) Enter
True
>>>
```

You can also use the <= operator to determine whether one set is a subset of another and the >= operator to determine whether one set is a superset of another. Here is the general format of an expression using the <= operator with two sets:

```
set2 <= set1
```

In the general format, *`set1`* and *`set2`* are sets. The expression returns `True` if `set2` is a subset of `set1`. Otherwise, it returns `False`. Here is the general format of an expression using the >= operator with two sets:

```
set1 >= set2
```

In the general format, *`set1`* and *`set2`* are sets. The expression returns `True` if `set1` is a subset of `set2`. Otherwise, it returns `False`. The following interactive session demonstrates:

```
>>> set1 = set([1, 2, 3, 4]) Enter
>>> set2 = set([2, 3]) Enter
>>> set2 <= set1 Enter
True
>>> set1 >= set2 Enter
True
>>> set1 <= set2 Enter
False
```

In the Spotlight:
Set Operations

In this section, you will look at Program 9-3, which demonstrates various set operations. The program creates two sets: one that holds the names of students on the baseball team, and another that holds the names of students on the basketball team. The program then performs the following operations:

- It finds the intersection of the sets to display the names of students who play both sports.
- It finds the union of the sets to display the names of students who play either sport.
- It finds the difference of the baseball and basketball sets to display the names of students who play baseball but not basketball.
- It finds the difference of the basketball and baseball (*basketball – baseball*) sets to display the names of students who play basketball but not baseball. It also finds the difference of the baseball and basketball (*baseball – basketball*) sets to display the names of students who play baseball but not basketball.
- It finds the symmetric difference of the basketball and baseball sets to display the names of students who play one sport but not both.

Program 9-3 (sets.py)

```
# This program demonstrates various set operations.
baseball = set(['Jodi', 'Carmen', 'Aida', 'Alicia'])
basketball = set(['Eva', 'Carmen', 'Alicia', 'Sarah'])

# Display members of the baseball set.
print('The following students are on the baseball team:')
for name in baseball:
    print(name)

# Display members of the basketball set.
print()
print('The following students are on the basketball team:')
for name in basketball:
    print(name)

# Demonstrate intersection
print()
print('The following students play both baseball and basketball:')
for name in baseball.intersection(basketball):
    print(name)

# Demonstrate union
print()
print('The following students play either baseball or basketball:')
```

(program continues)

Program 9-3 *(continued)*

```
for name in baseball.union(basketball):
    print(name)

# Demonstrate difference of baseball and basketball
print()
print('The following students play baseball, but not basketball:')
for name in baseball.difference(basketball):
    print(name)

# Demonstrate difference of basketball and baseball
print()
print('The following students play basketball, but not baseball:')
for name in basketball.difference(baseball):
    print(name)

# Demonstrate symmetric difference
print()
print('The following students play one sport, but not both:')
for name in baseball.symmetric_difference(basketball):
    print(name)
```

Program Output

```
The following students are on the baseball team:
Jodi
Aida
Carmen
Alicia

The following students are on the basketball team:
Sarah
Eva
Alicia
Carmen

The following students play both baseball and basketball:
Alicia
Carmen

The following students play either baseball or basketball:
Sarah
Alicia
Jodi
Eva
Aida
Carmen

The following students play baseball but not basketball:
Jodi
Aida
```

```
The following students play basketball but not baseball:
Sarah
Eva

The following students play one sport but not both:
Sarah
Aida
Jodi
Eva
```

Checkpoint

9.14 Are the elements of a set ordered or unordered?

9.15 Does a set allow you to store duplicate elements?

9.16 How do you create an empty set?

9.17 After the following statement executes, what elements will be stored in the `myset` set?

```
myset = set('Jupiter')
```

9.18 After the following statement executes, what elements will be stored in the `myset` set?

```
myset = set(25)
```

9.19 After the following statement executes, what elements will be stored in the `myset` set?

```
myset = set('www xxx yyy zzz')
```

9.20 After the following statement executes, what elements will be stored in the `myset` set?

```
myset = set([1, 2, 2, 3, 4, 4, 4])
```

9.21 After the following statement executes, what elements will be stored in the `myset` set?

```
myset = set(['www', 'xxx', 'yyy', 'zzz'])
```

9.22 How do you determine the number of elements in a set?

9.23 After the following statement executes, what elements will be stored in the `myset` set?

```
myset = set([10, 9, 8])
myset.update([1, 2, 3])
```

9.24 After the following statement executes, what elements will be stored in the `myset` set?

```
myset = set([10, 9, 8])
myset.update('abc')
```

9.25 What is the difference between the `remove` and `discard` methods?

9.26 How can you determine whether a specific element exists in a set?

9.27 After the following code executes, what elements will be members of `set3`?

```
set1 = set([10, 20, 30])
set2 = set([100, 200, 300])
set3 = set1.union(set2)
```

9.28 After the following code executes, what elements will be members of `set3`?

```
set1 = set([1, 2, 3, 4])
set2 = set([3, 4, 5, 6])
set3 = set1.intersection(set2)
```

9.29 After the following code executes, what elements will be members of `set3`?

```
set1 = set([1, 2, 3, 4])
set2 = set([3, 4, 5, 6])
set3 = set1.difference(set2)
```

9.30 After the following code executes, what elements will be members of `set3`?

```
set1 = set([1, 2, 3, 4])
set2 = set([3, 4, 5, 6])
set3 = set2.difference(set1)
```

9.31 After the following code executes, what elements will be members of `set3`?

```
set1 = set(['a', 'b', 'c'])
set2 = set(['b', 'c', 'd'])
set3 = set1.symmetric_difference(set2)
```

9.32 Look at the following code:

```
set1 = set([1, 2, 3, 4])
set2 = set([2, 3])
```

Which of the sets is a subset of the other?

Which of the sets is a superset of the other?

9.3 Serializing Objects

CONCEPT: Serializing a object is the process of converting the object to a stream of bytes that can be saved to a file for later retrieval. In Python, object serialization is called pickling.

In Chapter 6, you learned how to store data in a text file. Sometimes you need to store the contents of a complex object, such as a dictionary or a set, to a file. The easiest way to save an object to a file is to serialize the object. When an object is *serialized*, it is converted to a stream of bytes that can be easily stored in a file for later retrieval.

In Python, the process of serializing an object is referred to as *pickling*. The Python standard library provides a module named `pickle` that has various functions for serializing, or pickling, objects.

Once you import the `pickle` module, you perform the following steps to pickle an object:

- You open a file for binary writing.
- You call the `pickle` module's `dump` method to pickle the object and write it to the specified file.
- After you have pickled all the objects that you want to save to the file, you close the file.

Let's take a more detailed look at these steps. To open a file for binary writing, you use `'wb'` as the mode when you call the `open` function. For example, the following statement opens a file named `mydata.dat` for binary writing:

```
outputfile = open('mydata.dat', 'wb')
```

Once you have opened a file for binary writing, you call the `pickle` module's `dump` function. Here is the general format of the `dump` method:

```
pickle.dump(object, file)
```

In the general format, *`object`* is a variable that references the object you want to pickle, and *`file`* is a variable that references a file object. After the function executes, the object referenced by *`object`* will be serialized and written to the file. (You can pickle just about any type of object, including lists, tuples, dictionaries, sets, strings, integers, and floating-point numbers.)

You can save as many pickled objects as you want to a file. When you are finished, you call the file object's `close` method to close the file. The following interactive session provides a simple demonstration of pickling a dictionary:

```
1 >>> import pickle Enter
2 >>> phonebook = {'Chris' : '555-1111', Enter
3                  'Katie' : '555-2222', Enter
4                  'Joanne' : '555-3333'} Enter
5 >>> output_file = open('phonebook.dat', 'wb') Enter
6 >>> pickle.dump(phonebook, output_file) Enter
7 >>> output_file.close() Enter
8 >>>
```

Let's take a closer look at the session:

- Line 1 imports the `pickle` module.
- Lines 2 through 4 create a dictionary containing names (as keys) and phone numbers (as values).
- Line 5 opens a file named `phonebook.dat` for binary writing.
- Line 6 calls the `pickle` module's `dump` function to serialize the `phonebook` dictionary and write it to the `phonebook.dat` file.
- Line 7 closes the `phonebook.dat` file.

At some point, you will need to retrieve, or unpickle, the objects that you have pickled. Here are the steps that you perform:

- You open a file for binary reading.
- You call the `pickle` module's `load` function to retrieve an object from the file and unpickle it.
- After you have unpickled all the objects that you want from the file, you close the file.

Let's take a more detailed look at these steps. To open a file for binary reading, you use `'rb'` as the mode when you call the `open` function. For example, the following statement opens a file named `mydata.dat` for binary reading:

```
inputfile = open('mydata.dat', 'rb')
```

Once you have opened a file for binary reading, you call the `pickle` module's `load` function. Here is the general format of a statement that calls the `load` function:

```
object = pickle.load(file)
```

In the general format, *`object`* is a variable, and *`file`* is a variable that references a file object. After the function executes, the *`object`* variable will reference an object that was retrieved from the file and unpickled.

You can unpickle as many objects as necessary from the file. (If you try to read past the end of the file, the load function will raise an `EOFError` exception.) When you are finished, you call the file object's `close` method to close the file. The following interactive session provides a simple demonstration of unpickling the `phonebook` dictionary that was pickled in the previous session:

```
1 >>> import pickle Enter
2 >>> input_file = open('phonebook.dat', 'rb') Enter
3 >>> pb = pickle.load(inputfile) Enter
4 >>> pb Enter
5 {'Chris': '555-1111', 'Joanne': '555-3333', 'Katie': '555-2222'}
6 >>> input_file.close() Enter
7 >>>
```

Let's take a closer look at the session:

- Line 1 imports the `pickle` module.
- Line 2 opens a file named `phonebook.dat` for binary reading.
- Line 3 calls the `pickle` module's `load` function to retrieve and unpickle an object from the `phonebook.dat` file. The resulting object is assigned to the `pb` variable.
- Line 4 displays the dictionary referenced by the `pb` variable. The output is shown in line 5.
- Line 6 closes the `phonebook.dat` file.

Program 9-4 shows an example program that demonstrates object pickling. It prompts the user to enter personal information (name, age, and weight) about as many people as he or she wishes. Each time the user enters information about a person, the information is stored in a dictionary, then the dictionary is pickled and saved to a file named `info.dat`. After the program has finished, the `info.dat` file will hold one pickled dictionary object for every person about whom the user entered information.

Program 9-4 **(pickle_objects.py)**

```
# This program demonstrates object pickling.
import pickle

# main function
```

```
def main():
    again = 'y' # To control loop repetition

    # Open a file for binary writing.
    output_file = open('info.dat', 'wb')

    # Get data until the user wants to stop.
    while again.lower() == 'y':
        # Get data about a person and save it.
        save_data(output_file)

        # Does the user want to enter more data?
        again = input('Enter more data? (y/n): ')

    # Close the file.
    output_file.close()

# The save_data function gets data about a person,
# stores it in a dictionary, and then pickles the
# dictionary to the specified file.
def save_data(file):
    # Create an empty dictionary.
    person = {}

    # Get data for a person and store
    # it in the dictionary.
    person['name'] = input('Name: ')
    person['age'] = int(input('Age: '))
    person['weight'] = float(input('Weight: '))

    # Pickle the dictionary.
    pickle.dump(person, file)

# Call the main function.
main()
```

Program Output (with input shown in bold)

Name: **Angie** Enter
Age: **25** Enter
Weight: **122** Enter
Enter more data? (y/n): **y** Enter
Name: **Carl** Enter
Age: **28** Enter
Weight: **175** Enter
Enter more data? (y/n): **n** Enter

Let's take a closer look at the main function:

- The again variable that is initialized in line 6 is used to control loop repetitions.
- Line 9 opens the file info.dat for binary writing. The file object is assigned to the output_file variable.
- The while loop that begins in line 12 repeats as long as the again variable references 'y' or 'Y'.
- Inside the while loop, line 14 calls the save_data function, passing the output_file variable as an argument. The purpose of the save_data function is to get data about a person and save it to the file as a pickled dictionary object.
- Line 17 prompts the user to enter y or n to indicate whether he or she wants to enter more data. The input is assigned to the again variable.
- Outside the loop, line 20 closes the file.

Now, let's look at the save_data function:

- Line 27 creates an empty dictionary, referenced by the person variable.
- Line 31 prompts the user to enter the person's name and stores the input in the person dictionary. After this statement executes, the dictionary will contain a key-value pair that has the string 'name' as the key and the user's input as the value.
- Line 32 prompts the user to enter the person's age and stores the input in the person dictionary. After this statement executes, the dictionary will contain a key-value pair that has the string 'age' as the key and the user's input, as an int, as the value.
- Line 33 prompts the user to enter the person's weight and stores the input in the person dictionary. After this statement executes, the dictionary will contain a key-value pair that has the string 'weight' as the key and the user's input, as a float, as the value.
- Line 36 pickles the person dictionary and writes it to the file.

Program 9-5 demonstrates how the dictionary objects that have been pickled and saved to the info.dat file can be retrieved and unpickled.

Program 9-5 (unpickle_objects.py)

```
# This program demonstrates object unpickling.
import pickle

# main function
def main():
    end_of_file = False # To indicate end of file

    # Open a file for binary reading.
    input_file = open('info.dat', 'rb')

    # Read to the end of the file.
    while not end_of_file:
        try:
            # Unpickle the next object.
            person = pickle.load(input_file)

```

```
17                 # Display the object.
18                 display_data(person)
19             except EOFError:
20                 # Set the flag to indicate the end
21                 # of the file has been reached.
22                 end_of_file = True
23 
24         # Close the file.
25         input_file.close()
26 
27     # The display_data function displays the person data
28     # in the dictionary that is passed as an argument.
29     def display_data(person):
30         print('Name:', person['name'])
31         print('Age:', person['age'])
32         print('Weight:', person['weight'])
33         print()
34 
35     # Call the main function.
36     main()
```

Program Output

```
Name: Angie
Age: 25
Weight: 122.0

Name: Carl
Age: 28
Weight: 175.0
```

Let's take a closer look at the main function:

- The `end_of_file` variable that is initialized in line 6 is used to indicate when the program has reached the end of the `info.dat` file. Notice the variable is initialized with the Boolean value `False`.
- Line 9 opens the file `info.dat` for binary reading. The file object is assigned to the `input_file` variable.
- The `while` loop that begins in line 12 repeats as long as `end_of_file` is `False`.
- Inside the `while` loop, a `try/except` statement appears in lines 13 through 22.
- Inside the try suite, line 15 reads an object from the file, unpickles it, and assigns it to the `person` variable. If the end of the file has already been reached, this statement raises an `EOFError` exception, and the program jumps to the `except` clause in 19. Otherwise, line 18 calls the `display_data` function, passing the `person` variable as an argument.
- When an `EOFError` exception occurs, line 22 sets the `end_of_file` variable to `True`. This causes the `while` loop to stop iterating.

Now, let's look at the `display_data` function:

- When the function is called, the `person` parameter references a dictionary that was passed as an argument.
- Line 30 prints the value that is associated with the key `'name'` in the `person` dictionary.
- Line 31 prints the value that is associated with the key `'age'` in the `person` dictionary.
- Line 32 prints the value that is associated with the key `'weight'` in the `person` dictionary.
- Line 33 prints a blank line.

Checkpoint

9.33 What is object serialization?

9.34 When you open a file for the purpose of saving a pickled object to it, what file access mode do you use?

9.35 When you open a file for the purpose of retrieving a pickled object from it, what file access mode do you use?

9.36 What module do you import if you want to pickle objects?

9.37 What function do you call to pickle an object?

9.38 What function do you call to retrieve and unpickle an object?

Review Questions

Multiple Choice

1. You can use the _________ operator to determine whether a key exists in a dictionary.
   a. `&`
   b. `in`
   c. `^`
   d. `?`
2. You use _________ to delete an element from a dictionary.
   a. the `remove` method
   b. the `erase` method
   c. the `delete` method
   d. the `del` statement
3. The _________ function returns the number of elements in a dictionary:
   a. `size()`
   b. `len()`
   c. `elements()`
   d. `count()`
4. You can use _________ to create an empty dictionary.
   a. `{}`
   b. `()`
   c. `[]`
   d. `empty()`

5. The ________ method returns a randomly selected key-value pair from a dictionary.
   a. `pop()`
   b. `random()`
   c. `popitem()`
   d. `rand_pop()`
6. The ________ method returns the value associated with a specified key and removes that key-value pair from the dictionary.
   a. `pop()`
   b. `random()`
   c. `popitem()`
   d. `rand_pop()`
7. The ________ dictionary method returns the value associated with a specified key. If the key is not found, it returns a default value.
   a. `pop()`
   b. `key()`
   c. `value()`
   d. `get()`
8. The ________ method returns all of a dictionary's keys and their associated values as a sequence of tuples.
   a. `keys_values()`
   b. `values()`
   c. `items()`
   d. `get()`
9. The following function returns the number of elements in a set:
   a. `size()`
   b. `len()`
   c. `elements()`
   d. `count()`
10. You can add one element to a set with this method.
    a. `append`
    b. `add`
    c. `update`
    d. `merge`
11. You can add a group of elements to a set with this method.
    a. `append`
    b. `add`
    c. `update`
    d. `merge`
12. This set method removes an element, but does not raise an exception if the element is not found.
    a. `remove`
    b. `discard`
    c. `delete`
    d. `erase`

13. This `set` method removes an element and raises an exception if the element is not found.
    a. `remove`
    b. `discard`
    c. `delete`
    d. `erase`
14. This operator can be used to find the union of two sets.
    a. `|`
    b. `&`
    c. `-`
    d. `^`
15. This operator can be used to find the difference of two sets.
    a. `|`
    b. `&`
    c. `-`
    d. `^`
16. This operator can be used to find the intersection of two sets.
    a. `|`
    b. `&`
    c. `-`
    d. `^`
17. This operator can be used to find the symmetric difference of two sets.
    a. `|`
    b. `&`
    c. `-`
    d. `^`

True or False

1. The keys in a dictionary must be mutable objects.
2. Dictionaries are not sequences.
3. A tuple can be a dictionary key.
4. A list can be a dictionary key.
5. The dictionary method `popitem` does not raise an exception if it is called on an empty dictionary.
6. The following statement creates an empty dictionary:
   ```
   mydct = {}
   ```
7. The following statement creates an empty set:
   ```
   myset = ()
   ```
8. Sets store their elements in an unordered fashion.
9. You can store duplicate elements in a set.
10. The `remove` method raises an exception if the specified element is not found in the set.

Short Answer

1. What will the following code display?

```
dct = {'Monday':1, 'Tuesday':2, 'Wednesday':3}
print(dct['Tuesday'])
```

2. What will the following code display?

```
dct = {'Monday':1, 'Tuesday':2, 'Wednesday':3}
print(dct.get('Monday', 'Not found'))
```

3. What will the following code display?

```
dct = {'Monday':1, 'Tuesday':2, 'Wednesday':3}
print(dct.get('Friday', 'Not found'))
```

4. What will the following code display?

```
stuff = {'aaa' : 111, 'bbb' : 222, 'ccc' : 333}
print(stuff['bbb'])
```

5. How do you delete an element from a dictionary?
6. How do you determine the number of elements that are stored in a dictionary?
7. What will the following code display?

```
dct = {1:[0, 1], 2:[2, 3], 3:[4, 5]}
print(dct[3])
```

8. What values will the following code display? (Don't worry about the order in which they will be displayed.)

```
dct = {1:[0, 1], 2:[2, 3], 3:[4, 5]}
for k in dct:
    print(k)
```

9. After the following statement executes, what elements will be stored in the `myset` set?

```
myset = set('Saturn')
```

10. After the following statement executes, what elements will be stored in the `myset` set?

```
myset = set(10)
```

11. After the following statement executes, what elements will be stored in the `myset` set?

```
myset = set('a bb ccc dddd')
```

12. After the following statement executes, what elements will be stored in the `myset` set?

```
myset = set([2, 4, 4, 6, 6, 6, 6])
```

13. After the following statement executes, what elements will be stored in the `myset` set?

```
myset = set(['a', 'bb', 'ccc', 'dddd'])
```

14. What will the following code display?

```
myset = set('1 2 3')
print(len(myset))
```

15. After the following code executes, what elements will be members of `set3`?

```
set1 = set([10, 20, 30, 40])
set2 = set([40, 50, 60])
set3 = set1.union(set2)
```

16. After the following code executes, what elements will be members of set3?

```
set1 = set(['o', 'p', 's', 'v'])
set2 = set(['a', 'p', 'r', 's'])
set3 = set1.intersection(set2)
```

17. After the following code executes, what elements will be members of set3?

```
set1 = set(['d', 'e', 'f'])
set2 = set(['a', 'b', 'c', 'd', 'e'])
set3 = set1.difference(set2)
```

18. After the following code executes, what elements will be members of set3?

```
set1 = set(['d', 'e', 'f'])
set2 = set(['a', 'b', 'c', 'd', 'e'])
set3 = set2.difference(set1)
```

19. After the following code executes, what elements will be members of set3?

```
set1 = set([1, 2, 3])
set2 = set([2, 3, 4])
set3 = set1.symmetric_difference(set2)
```

20. Look at the following code:

```
set1 = set([100, 200, 300, 400, 500])
set2 = set([200, 400, 500])
```

Which of the sets is a subset of the other?

Which of the sets is a superset of the other?

Algorithm Workbench

1. Write a statement that creates a dictionary containing the following key-value pairs:

```
'a' : 1
'b' : 2
'c' : 3
```

2. Write a statement that creates an empty dictionary.
3. Assume the variable `dct` references a dictionary. Write an `if` statement that determines whether the key `'James'` exists in the dictionary. If so, display the value that is associated with that key. If the key is not in the dictionary, display a message indicating so.
4. Assume the variable `dct` references a dictionary. Write an `if` statement that determines whether the key `'Jim'` exists in the dictionary. If so, delete `'Jim'` and its associated value.
5. Write code to create a set with the following integers as members: 10, 20, 30, and 40.
6. Assume each of the variables `set1` and `set2` references a set. Write code that creates another set containing all the elements of `set1` and `set2`, and assigns the resulting set to the variable `set3`.
7. Assume each of the variables `set1` and `set2` references a set. Write code that creates another set containing only the elements that are found in both `set1` and `set2`, and assigns the resulting set to the variable `set3`.

8. Assume each of the variables `set1` and `set2` references a set. Write code that creates another set containing the elements that appear in `set1` but not in `set2`, and assigns the resulting set to the variable `set3`.
9. Assume each of the variables `set1` and `set2` references a set. Write code that creates another set containing the elements that appear in `set2` but not in `set1`, and assigns the resulting set to the variable `set3`.
10. Assume each of the variables `set1` and `set2` references a set. Write code that creates another set containing the elements that are not shared by `set1` and `set2`, and assigns the resulting set to the variable `set3`.
11. Assume the variable `dct` references a dictionary. Write code that pickles the dictionary and saves it to a file named `mydata.dat`.
12. Write code that retrieves and unpickles the dictionary that you pickled in Algorithm Workbench 11.

Programming Exercises

1. Course information

Write a program that creates a dictionary containing course numbers and the room numbers of the rooms where the courses meet. The dictionary should have the following key-value pairs:

Course Number (key)	Room Number (value)
CS101	3004
CS102	4501
CS103	6755
NT110	1244
CM241	1411

The program should also create a dictionary containing course numbers and the names of the instructors that teach each course. The dictionary should have the following key-value pairs:

Course Number (key)	Instructor (value)
CS101	Haynes
CS102	Alvarado
CS103	Rich
NT110	Burke
CM241	Lee

The program should also create a dictionary containing course numbers and the meeting times of each course. The dictionary should have the following key-value pairs:

Course Number (key)	Meeting Time (value)
CS101	8:00 a.m.
CS102	9:00 a.m.
CS103	10:00 a.m.
NT110	11:00 a.m.
CM241	1:00 p.m.

The program should let the user enter a course number, then it should display the course's room number, instructor, and meeting time.

2. Capital Quiz

VideoNote
The Capital Quiz Problem

Write a program that creates a dictionary containing the U.S. states as keys, and their capitals as values. (Use the Internet to get a list of the states and their capitals.) The program should then randomly quiz the user by displaying the name of a state and asking the user to enter that state's capital. The program should keep a count of the number of correct and incorrect responses. (As an alternative to the U.S. states, the program can use the names of countries and their capitals.)

3. File Encryption and Decryption

Write a program that uses a dictionary to assign "codes" to each letter of the alphabet. For example:

```
codes = { 'A' : '%', 'a' : '9', 'B' : '@', 'b' : '#', etc...}
```

Using this example, the letter `A` would be assigned the symbol `%`, the letter `a` would be assigned the number 9, the letter `B` would be assigned the symbol `@`, and so forth.

The program should open a specified text file, read its contents, then use the dictionary to write an encrypted version of the file's contents to a second file. Each character in the second file should contain the code for the corresponding character in the first file.

Write a second program that opens an encrypted file and displays its decrypted contents on the screen.

4. Unique Words

Write a program that opens a specified text file then displays a list of all the unique words found in the file.

Hint: Store each word as an element of a set.

5. Word Frequency

Write a program that reads the contents of a text file. The program should create a dictionary in which the keys are the individual words found in the file and the values are the number of times each word appears. For example, if the word "the" appears 128 times, the dictionary would contain an element with `'the'` as the key and 128 as the value. The program should either display the frequency of each word or create a second file containing a list of each word and its frequency.

6. File Analysis

Write a program that reads the contents of two text files and compares them in the following ways:

- It should display a list of all the unique words contained in both files.
- It should display a list of the words that appear in both files.
- It should display a list of the words that appear in the first file but not the second.
- It should display a list of the words that appear in the second file but not the first.
- It should display a list of the words that appear in either the first or second file, but not both.

Hint: Use set operations to perform these analyses.

7. World Series Winners

In this chapter's source code folder (available on the Computer Science Portal at www.pearsonhighered.com/gaddis), you will find a text file named `WorldSeriesWinners.txt`. This file contains a chronological list of the World Series' winning teams from 1903 through 2009. The first line in the file is the name of the team that won in 1903, and the last line is the name of the team that won in 2009. (Note the World Series was not played in 1904 or 1994. There are entries in the file indicating this.)

Write a program that reads this file and creates a dictionary in which the keys are the names of the teams, and each key's associated value is the number of times the team has won the World Series. The program should also create a dictionary in which the keys are the years, and each key's associated value is the name of the team that won that year.

The program should prompt the user for a year in the range of 1903 through 2009. It should then display the name of the team that won the World Series that year, and the number of times that team has won the World Series.

8. Name and Email Addresses

Write a program that keeps names and email addresses in a dictionary as key-value pairs. The program should display a menu that lets the user look up a person's email address, add a new name and email address, change an existing email address, and delete an existing name and email address. The program should pickle the dictionary and save it to a file when the user exits the program. Each time the program starts, it should retrieve the dictionary from the file and unpickle it.

9. Blackjack Simulation

Previously in this chapter you saw the `card_dealer.py` program that simulates cards being dealt from a deck. Enhance the program so it simulates a simplified version of the game of Blackjack between two virtual players. The cards have the following values:

- Numeric cards are assigned the value they have printed on them. For example, the value of the 2 of spades is 2, and the value of the 5 of diamonds is 5.
- Jacks, queens, and kings are valued at 10.
- Aces are valued at 1 or 11, depending on the player's choice.

The program should deal cards to each player until one player's hand is worth more than 21 points. When that happens, the other player is the winner. (It is possible that both players' hands will simultaneously exceed 21 points, in which case neither player wins.) The program should repeat until all the cards have been dealt from the deck.

If a player is dealt an ace, the program should decide the value of the card according to the following rule: The ace will be worth 11 points, unless that makes the player's hand exceed 21 points. In that case, the ace will be worth 1 point.

10. Word Index

Write a program that reads the contents of a text file. The program should create a dictionary in which the key-value pairs are described as follows:

- Key. The keys are the individual words found in the file.
- Values. Each value is a list that contains the line numbers in the file where the word (the key) is found.

For example, suppose the word "robot" is found in lines 7, 18, 94, and 138. The dictionary would contain an element in which the key was the string "robot", and the value was a list containing the numbers 7, 18, 94, and 138.

Once the dictionary is built, the program should create another text file, known as a word index, listing the contents of the dictionary. The word index file should contain an alphabetical listing of the words that are stored as keys in the dictionary, along with the line numbers where the words appear in the original file. Figure 9-1 shows an example of an original text file (`Kennedy.txt`) and its index file (`index.txt`).

Figure 9-1 Example of original file and index file

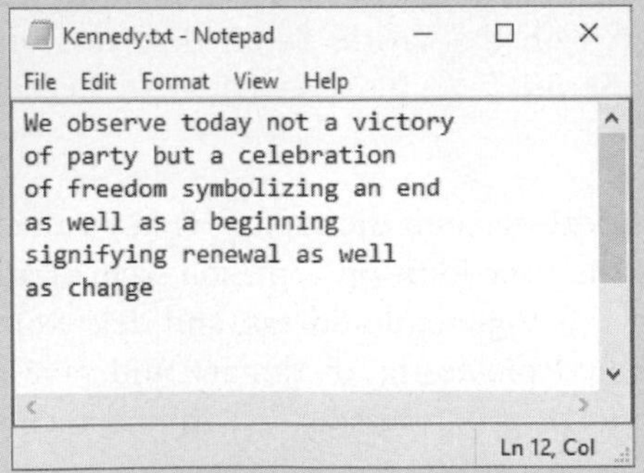
Kennedy.txt - Notepad

File Edit Format View Help

```
We observe today not a victory
of party but a celebration
of freedom symbolizing an end
as well as a beginning
signifying renewal as well
as change
```

Ln 12, Col

index.txt - Notepad

File Edit Format View Help

```
We: 1
a: 1 2 4
an: 3
as: 4 5 6
beginning: 4
but: 2
celebration: 2
change: 6
end: 3
freedom: 3
not: 1
observe: 1
of: 2 3
party: 2
renewal: 5
signifying: 5
symbolizing: 3
today: 1
victory: 1
well: 4 5
```

Ln 21, Col 1

CHAPTER 10

Classes and Object-Oriented Programming

TOPICS

10.1 Procedural and Object-Oriented Programming

CONCEPT: Procedural programming is a method of writing software. It is a programming practice centered on the procedures or actions that take place in a program. Object-oriented programming is centered on objects. Objects are created from abstract data types that encapsulate data and functions together.

There are primarily two methods of programming in use today: procedural and object-oriented. The earliest programming languages were procedural, meaning a program was made of one or more procedures. You can think of a *procedure* simply as a function that performs a specific task such as gathering input from the user, performing calculations, reading or writing files, displaying output, and so on. The programs that you have written so far have been procedural in nature.

Typically, procedures operate on data items that are separate from the procedures. In a procedural program, the data items are commonly passed from one procedure to another. As you might imagine, the focus of procedural programming is on the creation of procedures that operate on the program's data. The separation of data and the code that operates on the data can lead to problems, however, as the program becomes larger and more complex.

For example, suppose you are part of a programming team that has written an extensive customer database program. The program was initially designed so a customer's name, address, and phone number were referenced by three variables. Your job was to design several functions that accept those three variables as arguments and perform operations on them. The software has been operating successfully for some time, but your team has been asked to update it by adding several new features. During the revision process, the senior programmer informs you that the customer's name, address, and phone number will no longer be stored in variables. Instead, they will be stored in a list. This means you will have to modify all of the functions that you have designed so they accept and work with a list instead of the three variables. Making these extensive modifications not only is a great deal of work, but also opens the opportunity for errors to appear in your code.

Whereas procedural programming is centered on creating procedures (functions), *object-oriented programming* (OOP) is centered on creating objects. An *object* is a software entity that contains both data and procedures. The data contained in an object is known as the object's *data attributes*. An object's data attributes are simply variables that reference data. The procedures that an object performs are known as *methods*. An object's methods are functions that perform operations on the object's data attributes. The object is, conceptually, a self-contained unit that consists of data attributes and methods that operate on the data attributes. This is illustrated in Figure 10-1.

Figure 10-1 An object contains data attributes and methods

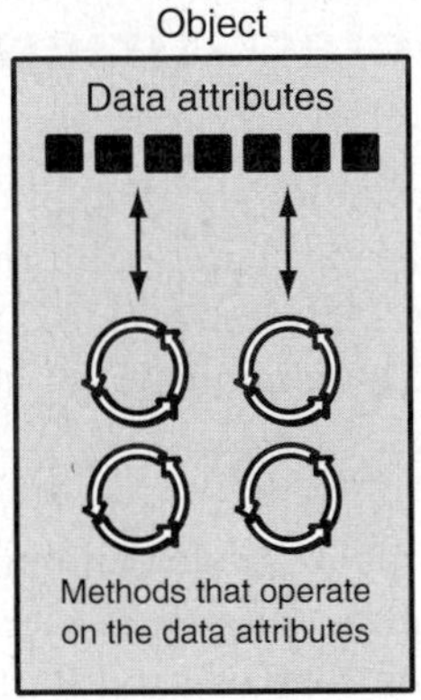

OOP addresses the problem of code and data separation through encapsulation and data hiding. *Encapsulation* refers to the combining of data and code into a single object. *Data hiding* refers to an object's ability to hide its data attributes from code that is outside the object. Only the object's methods may directly access and make changes to the object's data attributes.

An object typically hides its data, but allows outside code to access its methods. As shown in Figure 10-2, the object's methods provide programming statements outside the object with indirect access to the object's data attributes.

Figure 10-2 Code outside the object interacts with the object's methods

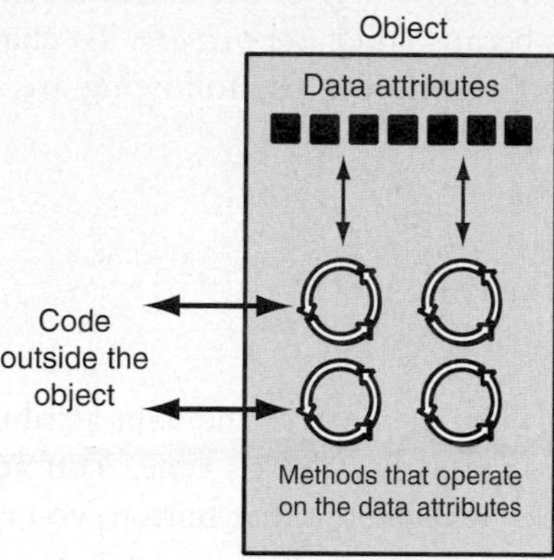

When an object's data attributes are hidden from outside code, and access to the data attributes is restricted to the object's methods, the data attributes are protected from accidental corruption. In addition, the code outside the object does not need to know about the format or internal structure of the object's data. The code only needs to interact with the object's methods. When a programmer changes the structure of an object's internal data attributes, he or she also modifies the object's methods so they may properly operate on the data. The way in which outside code interacts with the methods, however, does not change.

Object Reusability

In addition to solving the problems of code and data separation, the use of OOP has also been encouraged by the trend of *object reusability*. An object is not a stand-alone program, but is used by programs that need its services. For example, Sharon is a programmer who has developed a set of objects for rendering 3D images. She is a math whiz and knows a lot about computer graphics, so her objects are coded to perform all of the necessary 3D mathematical operations and handle the computer's video hardware. Tom, who is writing a program for an architectural firm, needs his application to display 3D images of buildings. Because he is working under a tight deadline and does not possess a great deal of knowledge about computer graphics, he can use Sharon's objects to perform the 3D rendering (for a small fee, of course!).

An Everyday Example of an Object

Imagine that your alarm clock is actually a software object. If it were, it would have the following data attributes:

- `current_second` (a value in the range of 0–59)
- `current_minute` (a value in the range of 0–59)
- `current_hour` (a value in the range of 1–12)
- `alarm_time` (a valid hour and minute)
- `alarm_is_set` (True or False)

As you can see, the data attributes are merely values that define the *state* in which the alarm clock is currently. You, the user of the alarm clock object, cannot directly manipulate these data attributes because they are *private*. To change a data attribute's value, you must use one of the object's methods. The following are some of the alarm clock object's methods:

- set_time
- set_alarm_time
- set_alarm_on
- set_alarm_off

Each method manipulates one or more of the data attributes. For example, the set_time method allows you to set the alarm clock's time. You activate the method by pressing a button on top of the clock. By using another button, you can activate the set_alarm_time method.

In addition, another button allows you to execute the set_alarm_on and set_alarm_off methods. Notice all of these methods can be activated by you, who are outside the alarm clock. Methods that can be accessed by entities outside the object are known as *public methods*.

The alarm clock also has *private methods,* which are part of the object's private, internal workings. External entities (such as you, the user of the alarm clock) do not have direct access to the alarm clock's private methods. The object is designed to execute these methods automatically and hide the details from you. The following are the alarm clock object's private methods:

- increment_current_second
- increment_current_minute
- increment_current_hour
- sound_alarm

Every second the increment_current_second method executes. This changes the value of the current_second data attribute. If the current_second data attribute is set to 59 when this method executes, the method is programmed to reset current_second to 0, and then cause the increment_current_minute method to execute. This method adds 1 to the current_minute data attribute, unless it is set to 59. In that case, it resets current_minute to 0 and causes the increment_current_hour method to execute. The increment_current_minute method compares the new time to the alarm_time. If the two times match and the alarm is turned on, the sound_alarm method is executed.

Checkpoint

10.1 What is an object?

10.2 What is encapsulation?

10.3 Why is an object's internal data usually hidden from outside code?

10.4 What are public methods? What are private methods?

10.2 Classes

CONCEPT: A class is code that specifies the data attributes and methods for a particular type of object.

VideoNote Classes and Objects

Now, let's discuss how objects are created in software. Before an object can be created, it must be designed by a programmer. The programmer determines the data attributes and methods that are necessary, then creates a *class*. A class is code that specifies the data attributes and methods of a particular type of object. Think of a class as a "blueprint" from which objects may be created. It serves a similar purpose as the blueprint for a house. The blueprint itself is not a house, but is a detailed description of a house. When we use the blueprint to build an actual house, we could say we are building an *instance* of the house described by the blueprint. If we so desire, we can build several identical houses from the same blueprint. Each house is a separate instance of the house described by the blueprint. This idea is illustrated in Figure 10-3.

Figure 10-3 A blueprint and houses built from the blueprint

Blueprint that describes a house

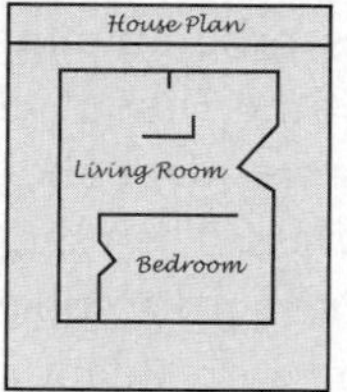

Instances of the house described by the blueprint

Another way of thinking about the difference between a class and an object is to think of the difference between a cookie cutter and a cookie. While a cookie cutter itself is not a cookie, it describes a cookie. The cookie cutter can be used to make several cookies, as shown in Figure 10-4. Think of a class as a cookie cutter, and the objects created from the class as cookies.

So, a class is a description of an object's characteristics. When the program is running, it can use the class to create, in memory, as many objects of a specific type as needed. Each object that is created from a class is called an *instance* of the class.

Figure 10-4 The cookie cutter metaphor

For example, Jessica is an entomologist (someone who studies insects), and she also enjoys writing computer programs. She designs a program to catalog different types of insects. As part of the program, she creates a class named `Insect`, which specifies characteristics that are common to all types of insects. The `Insect` class is a specification from which objects may be created. Next, she writes programming statements that create an object named `housefly`, which is an instance of the `Insect` class. The `housefly` object is an entity that occupies computer memory and stores data about a housefly. It has the data attributes and methods specified by the `Insect` class. Then she writes programming statements that create an object named `mosquito`. The `mosquito` object is also an instance of the `Insect` class. It has its own area in memory and stores data about a mosquito. Although the `housefly` and `mosquito` objects are separate entities in the computer's memory, they were both created from the `Insect` class. This means that each of the objects has the data attributes and methods described by the `Insect` class. This is illustrated in Figure 10-5.

Figure 10-5 The `housefly` and `mosquito` objects are instances of the `Insect` class

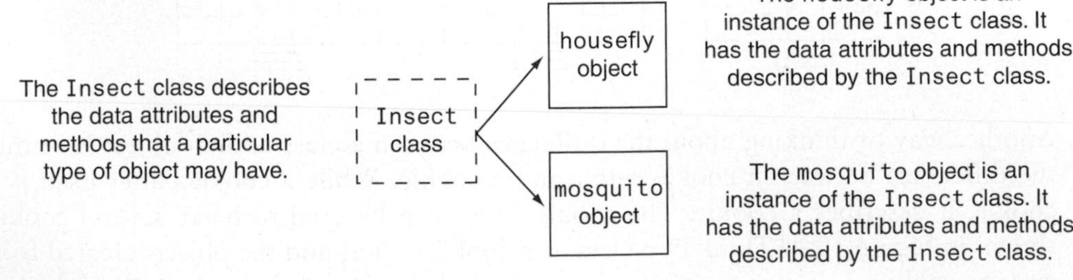

Class Definitions

To create a class, you write a *class definition*. A class definition is a set of statements that define a class's methods and data attributes. Let's look at a simple example. Suppose we are writing a program to simulate the tossing of a coin. In the program, we need to repeatedly toss the coin and each time determine whether it landed heads up or tails up. Taking an object-oriented approach, we will write a class named `Coin` that can perform the behaviors of the coin.

Program 10-1 shows the class definition, which we will explain shortly. Note this is not a complete program. We will add to it as we go along.

Program 10-1 (`Coin` **class, not a complete program**)

```
1  import random
2
3  # The Coin class simulates a coin that can
4  # be flipped.
5
6  class Coin:
7
8      # The __init__ method initializes the
9      # sideup data attribute with 'Heads'.
10
11     def __init__(self):
12         self.sideup = 'Heads'
13
14     # The toss method generates a random number
15     # in the range of 0 through 1. If the number
16     # is 0, then sideup is set to 'Heads'.
17     # Otherwise, sideup is set to 'Tails'.
18
19     def toss(self):
20         if random.randint(0, 1) == 0:
21             self.sideup = 'Heads'
22         else:
23             self.sideup = 'Tails'
24
25     # The get_sideup method returns the value
26     # referenced by sideup.
27
28     def get_sideup(self):
29         return self.sideup
```

In line 1, we import the `random` module. This is necessary because we use the `randint` function to generate a random number. Line 6 is the beginning of the class definition. It begins with the keyword `class`, followed by the class name, which is `Coin`, followed by a colon.

The same rules that apply to variable names also apply to class names. However, notice that we started the class name, `Coin`, with an uppercase letter. This is not a requirement, but it is a widely used convention among programmers. This helps to easily distinguish class names from variable names when reading code.

The `Coin` class has three methods:

- The `__init__` method appears in lines 11 through 12.
- The `toss` method appears in lines 19 through 23.
- The `get_sideup` method appears in lines 28 through 29.

Except for the fact that they appear inside a class, notice these method definitions look like any other function definition in Python. They start with a header line, which is followed by an indented block of statements.

Take a closer look at the header for each of the method definitions (lines 11, 19, and 28) and notice each method has a parameter variable named `self`:

Line 11: `def __init__(self):`
Line 19: `def toss(self):`
Line 28: `def get_sideup(self):`

The `self` parameter[1] is required in every method of a class. Recall from our earlier discussion on object-oriented programming that a method operates on a specific object's data attributes. When a method executes, it must have a way of knowing which object's data attributes it is supposed to operate on. That's where the `self` parameter comes in. When a method is called, Python makes the `self` parameter reference the specific object that the method is supposed to operate on.

Let's look at each of the methods. The first method, which is named `__init__`, is defined in lines 11 through 12:

```
def __init__(self):
    self.sideup = 'Heads'
```

Most Python classes have a special method named `__init__`, which is automatically executed when an instance of the class is created in memory. The `__init__` method is commonly known as an *initializer method* because it initializes the object's data attributes. (The name of the method starts with two underscore characters, followed by the word `init`, followed by two more underscore characters.)

Immediately after an object is created in memory, the `__init__` method executes, and the `self` parameter is automatically assigned the object that was just created. Inside the method, the statement in line 12 executes:

```
self.sideup = 'Heads'
```

This statement assigns the string `'Heads'` to the `sideup` data attribute belonging to the object that was just created. As a result of this `__init__` method, each object we create from the `Coin` class will initially have a `sideup` attribute that is set to `'Heads'`.

NOTE: The `__init__` method is usually the first method inside a class definition.

[1] The parameter must be present in a method. You are not required to name it `self`, but this is strongly recommended to conform with standard practice.

The `toss` method appears in lines 19 through 23:

```
def toss(self):
    if random.randint(0, 1) == 0:
        self.sideup = 'Heads'
    else:
        self.sideup = 'Tails'
```

This method also has the required `self` parameter variable. When the `toss` method is called, `self` will automatically reference the object on which the method is to operate.

The `toss` method simulates the tossing of the coin. When the method is called, the `if` statement in line 20 calls the `random.randint` function to get a random integer in the range of 0 through 1. If the number is 0, then the statement in line 21 assigns `'Heads'` to `self.sideup`. Otherwise, the statement in line 23 assigns `'Tails'` to `self.sideup`.

The `get_sideup` method appears in lines 28 through 29:

```
def get_sideup(self):
    return self.sideup
```

Once again, the method has the required `self` parameter variable. This method simply returns the value of `self.sideup`. We call this method any time we want to know which side of the coin is facing up.

To demonstrate the `Coin` class, we need to write a complete program that uses it to create an object. Program 10-2 shows an example. The `Coin` class definition appears in lines 6 through 29. The program has a `main` function, which appears in lines 32 through 44.

Program 10-2 (coin_demo1.py)

```
1   import random
2
3   # The Coin class simulates a coin that can
4   # be flipped.
5
6   class Coin:
7
8       # The __init__ method initializes the
9       # sideup data attribute with 'Heads'.
10
11      def __init__(self):
12          self.sideup = 'Heads'
13
14      # The toss method generates a random number
15      # in the range of 0 through 1. If the number
16      # is 0, then sideup is set to 'Heads'.
17      # Otherwise, sideup is set to 'Tails'.
18
19      def toss(self):
20          if random.randint(0, 1) == 0:
```

(program continues)

Program 10-2 *(continued)*

```
21                 self.sideup = 'Heads'
22             else:
23                 self.sideup = 'Tails'
24
25         # The get_sideup method returns the value
26         # referenced by sideup.
27
28         def get_sideup(self):
29             return self.sideup
30
31     # The main function.
32     def main():
33         # Create an object from the Coin class.
34         my_coin = Coin()
35
36         # Display the side of the coin that is facing up.
37         print('This side is up:', my_coin.get_sideup())
38
39         # Toss the coin.
40         print('I am tossing the coin ...')
41         my_coin.toss()
42
43         # Display the side of the coin that is facing up.
44         print('This side is up:', my_coin.get_sideup())
45
46     # Call the main function.
47     main()
```

Program Output

```
This side is up: Heads
I am tossing the coin ...
This side is up: Tails
```

Program Output

```
This side is up: Heads
I am tossing the coin ...
This side is up: Heads
```

Program Output

```
This side is up: Heads
I am tossing the coin ...
This side is up: Tails
```

Take a closer look at the statement in line 34:

```
my_coin = Coin()
```

The expression `Coin()` that appears on the right side of the = operator causes two things to happen:

1. An object is created in memory from the `Coin` class.
2. The `Coin` class's `__init__` method is executed, and the `self` parameter is automatically set to the object that was just created. As a result, that object's `sideup` attribute is assigned the string `'Heads'`.

Figure 10-6 illustrates these steps.

Figure 10-6 Actions caused by the `Coin()` expression

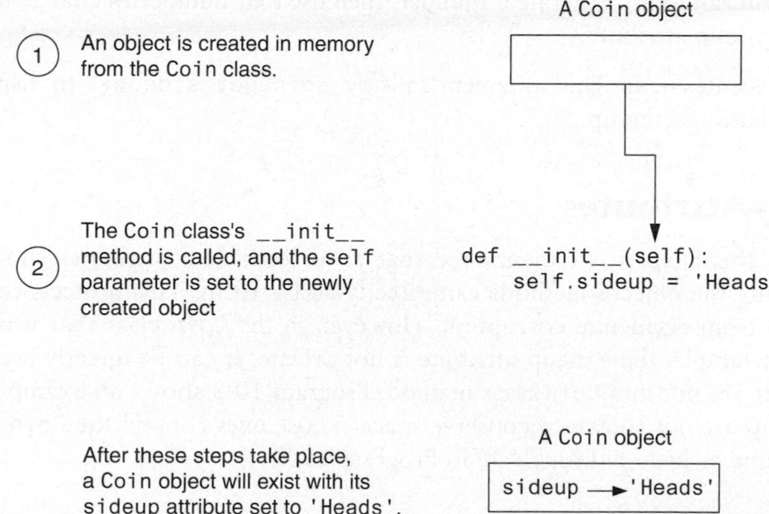

After this, the = operator assigns the `Coin` object that was just created to the `my_coin` variable. Figure 10-7 shows that after the statement in line 12 executes, the `my_coin` variable will reference a `Coin` object, and that object's `sideup` attribute will be assigned the string `'Heads'`.

Figure 10-7 The `my_coin` variable references a `Coin` object

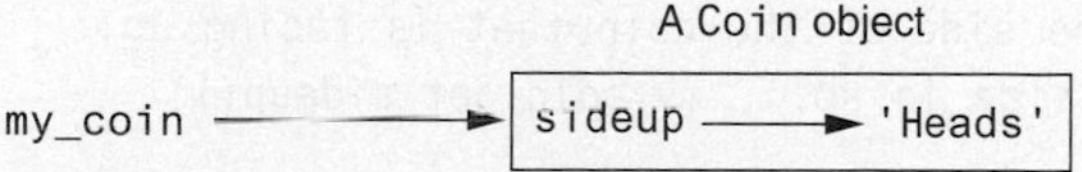

The next statement to execute is line 37:

```
print('This side is up:', my_coin.get_sideup())
```

This statement prints a message indicating the side of the coin that is facing up. Notice the following expression appears in the statement:

```
my_coin.get_sideup()
```

This expression uses the object referenced by `my_coin` to call the `get_sideup` method. When the method executes, the `self` parameter will reference the `my_coin` object. As a result, the method returns the string `'Heads'`.

Notice we did not have to pass an argument to the `sideup` method, despite the fact that it has the `self` parameter variable. When a method is called, Python automatically passes a reference to the calling object into the method's first parameter. As a result, the `self` parameter will automatically reference the object on which the method is to operate.

Lines 40 and 41 are the next statements to execute:

```
print('I am tossing the coin ...')
my_coin.toss()
```

The statement in line 41 uses the object referenced by `my_coin` to call the `toss` method. When the method executes, the `self` parameter will reference the `my_coin` object. The method will randomly generate a number, then use that number to change the value of the object's `sideup` attribute.

Line 44 executes next. This statement calls `my_coin.get_sideup()` to display the side of the coin that is facing up.

Hiding Attributes

Earlier in this chapter, we mentioned that an object's data attributes should be private, so that only the object's methods can directly access them. This protects the object's data attributes from accidental corruption. However, in the `Coin` class that was shown in the previous example, the `sideup` attribute is not private. It can be directly accessed by statements that are not in a `Coin` class method. Program 10-3 shows an example. Note lines 1 through 30 are not shown to conserve space. Those lines contain the `Coin` class, and they are the same as lines 1 through 30 in Program 10-2.

Program 10-3 (coin_demo2.py)

Lines 1 through 30 are omitted. These lines are the same as lines 1 through 30 in Program 10-2.

```
31  # The main function.
32  def main():
33      # Create an object from the Coin class.
34      my_coin = Coin()
35
36      # Display the side of the coin that is facing up.
37      print('This side is up:', my_coin.get_sideup())
38
39      # Toss the coin.
40      print('I am tossing the coin ...')
41      my_coin.toss()
42
43      # But now I'm going to cheat! I'm going to
44      # directly change the value of the object's
45      # sideup attribute to 'Heads'.
46      my_coin.sideup = 'Heads'
47
48      # Display the side of the coin that is facing up.
49      print('This side is up:', my_coin.get_sideup())
```

```
50
51  # Call the main function.
52  main()
```

Program Output

```
This side is up: Heads
I am tossing the coin ...
This side is up: Heads
```

Program Output

```
This side is up: Heads
I am tossing the coin ...
This side is up: Heads
```

Program Output

```
This side is up: Heads
I am tossing the coin ...
This side is up: Heads
```

Line 34 creates a `Coin` object in memory and assigns it to the `my_coin` variable. The statement in line 37 displays the side of the coin that is facing up, then line 41 calls the object's `toss` method. Then, the statement in line 46 directly assigns the string `'Heads'` to the object's `sideup` attribute:

```
my_coin.sideup = 'Heads'
```

Regardless of the outcome of the `toss` method, this statement will change the `my_coin` object's `sideup` attribute to `'Heads'`. As you can see from the three sample runs of the program, the coin always lands heads up!

If we truly want to simulate a coin that is being tossed, then we don't want code outside the class to be able to change the result of the `toss` method. To prevent this from happening, we need to make the `sideup` attribute private. In Python, you can hide an attribute by starting its name with two underscore characters. If we change the name of the `sideup` attribute to `__sideup`, then code outside the `Coin` class will not be able to access it. Program 10-4 shows a new version of the `Coin` class, with this change made.

Program 10-4 (coin_demo3.py)

```
import random

# The Coin class simulates a coin that can
# be flipped.

class Coin:

    # The __init__ method initializes the
    # __sideup data attribute with 'Heads'.
```

(program continues)

Program 10-4 *(continued)*

```

    def __init__(self):
    self.__sideup = 'Heads'

    # The toss method generates a random number
    # in the range of 0 through 1. If the number
    # is 0, then sideup is set to 'Heads'.
    # Otherwise, sideup is set to 'Tails'.

    def toss(self):
        if random.randint(0, 1) == 0:
            self.__sideup = 'Heads'
        else:
            self.__sideup = 'Tails'

    # The get_sideup method returns the value
    # referenced by sideup.

    def get_sideup(self):
        return self.__sideup

# The main function.
def main():
    # Create an object from the Coin class.
    my_coin = Coin()

    # Display the side of the coin that is facing up.
    print('This side is up:', my_coin.get_sideup())

    # Toss the coin.
    print('I am going to toss the coin ten times:')
    for count in range(10):
        my_coin.toss()
        print(my_coin.get_sideup())

# Call the main function.
main()
```

Program Output

```
This side is up: Heads
I am going to toss the coin ten times:
Tails
Heads
Heads
```

```
Tails
Tails
Tails
Tails
Tails
Heads
Heads
```

Storing Classes in Modules

The programs you have seen so far in this chapter have the Coin class definition in the same file as the programming statements that use the Coin class. This approach works fine with small programs that use only one or two classes. As programs use more classes, however, the need to organize those classes becomes greater.

Programmers commonly organize their class definitions by storing them in modules. Then the modules can be imported into any programs that need to use the classes they contain. For example, suppose we decide to store the Coin class in a module named coin. Program 10-5 shows the contents of the coin.py file. Then, when we need to use the Coin class in a program, we can import the coin module. This is demonstrated in Program 10-6.

Program 10-5 (coin.py)

```
import random

# The Coin class simulates a coin that can
# be flipped.

class Coin:

    # The __init__ method initializes the
    # __sideup data attribute with 'Heads'.

    def __init__(self):
        self.__sideup = 'Heads'

    # The toss method generates a random number
    # in the range of 0 through 1. If the number
    # is 0, then sideup is set to 'Heads'.
    # Otherwise, sideup is set to 'Tails'.

    def toss(self):
        if random.randint(0, 1) == 0:
            self.__sideup = 'Heads'
        else:
            self.__sideup = 'Tails'
```

(program continues)

Program 10-5 *(continued)*

```

    # The get_sideup method returns the value
    # referenced by sideup.

    def get_sideup(self):
        return self.__sideup
```

Program 10-6 (coin_demo4.py)

```
# This program imports the coin module and
# creates an instance of the Coin class.

import coin

def main():
    # Create an object from the Coin class.
    my_coin = coin.Coin()

    # Display the side of the coin that is facing up.
    print('This side is up:', my_coin.get_sideup())

    # Toss the coin.
    print('I am going to toss the coin ten times:')
    for count in range(10):
        my_coin.toss()
        print(my_coin.get_sideup())

# Call the main function.
main()
```

Program Output

```
This side is up: Heads
I am going to toss the coin ten times:
Tails
Tails
Heads
Tails
Heads
Heads
Tails
Heads
Tails
Tails
```

Line 4 imports the `coin` module. Notice in line 8, we had to qualify the name of the `Coin` class by prefixing it with the name of the module, followed by a dot:

```
my_coin = coin.Coin()
```

The BankAccount Class

Let's look at another example. Program 10-7 shows a `BankAccount` class, stored in a module named `bankaccount`. Objects that are created from this class will simulate bank accounts, allowing us to have a starting balance, make deposits, make withdrawals, and get the current balance.

Program 10-7 (bankaccount.py)

```
1  # The BankAccount class simulates a bank account.
2
3  class BankAccount:
4
5      # The __init__ method accepts an argument for
6      # the account's balance. It is assigned to
7      # the __balance attribute.
8
9      def __init__(self, bal):
10         self.__balance = bal
11
12     # The deposit method makes a deposit into the
13     # account.
14
15     def deposit(self, amount):
16         self.__balance += amount
17
18     # The withdraw method withdraws an amount
19     # from the account.
20
21     def withdraw(self, amount):
22         if self.__balance >= amount:
23             self.__balance -= amount
24         else:
25             print('Error: Insufficient funds')
26
27     # The get_balance method returns the
28     # account balance.
29
30     def get_balance(self):
31         return self.__balance
```

Notice the `__init__` method has two parameter variables: `self` and `bal`. The `bal` parameter will accept the account's starting balance as an argument. In line 10, the `bal` parameter amount is assigned to the object's `__balance` attribute.

The deposit method is in lines 15 through 16. This method has two parameter variables: self and amount. When the method is called, the amount that is to be deposited into the account is passed into the amount parameter. The value of the parameter is then added to the __balance attribute in line 16.

The withdraw method is in lines 21 through 25. This method has two parameter variables: self and amount. When the method is called, the amount that is to be withdrawn from the account is passed into the amount parameter. The if statement that begins in line 22 determines whether there is enough in the account balance to make the withdrawal. If so, amount is subtracted from __balance in line 23. Otherwise, line 25 displays the message 'Error: Insufficient funds'.

The get_balance method is in lines 30 through 31. This method returns the value of the __balance attribute.

Program 10-8 demonstrates how to use the class.

Program 10-8 (account_test.py)

```
# This program demonstrates the BankAccount class.

import bankaccount

def main():
    # Get the starting balance.
    start_bal = float(input('Enter your starting balance: '))

    # Create a BankAccount object.
    savings = bankaccount.BankAccount(start_bal)

    # Deposit the user's paycheck.
    pay = float(input('How much were you paid this week? '))
    print('I will deposit that into your account.')
    savings.deposit(pay)

    # Display the balance.
    print('Your account balance is $',
          format(savings.get_balance(), ',.2f'),
          sep='')

    # Get the amount to withdraw.
    cash = float(input('How much would you like to withdraw? '))
    print('I will withdraw that from your account.')
    savings.withdraw(cash)

    # Display the balance.
    print('Your account balance is $',
          format(savings.get_balance(), ',.2f'),
          sep='')
```

```
31
32    # Call the main function.
33    main()
```

Program Output (with input shown in bold)

```
Enter your starting balance: 1000.00 [Enter]
How much were you paid this week? 500.00 [Enter]
I will deposit that into your account.
Your account balance is $1,500.00
How much would you like to withdraw? 1200.00 [Enter]
I will withdraw that from your account.
Your account balance is $300.00
```

Program Output (with input shown in bold)

```
Enter your starting balance: 1000.00 [Enter]
How much were you paid this week? 500.00 [Enter]
I will deposit that into your account.
Your account balance is $1,500.00
How much would you like to withdraw? 2000.00 [Enter]
I will withdraw that from your account.
Error: Insufficient funds
Your account balance is $1,500.00
```

Line 7 gets the starting account balance from the user and assigns it to the `start_bal` variable. Line 10 creates an instance of the `BankAccount` class and assigns it to the `savings` variable. Take a closer look at the statement:

```
savings = bankaccount.BankAccount(start_bal)
```

Notice the `start_bal` variable is listed inside the parentheses. This causes the `start_bal` variable to be passed as an argument to the `__init__` method. In the `__init__` method, it will be passed into the `bal` parameter.

Line 13 gets the amount of the user's pay and assigns it to the `pay` variable. In line 15, the `savings.deposit` method is called, passing the `pay` variable as an argument. In the `deposit` method, it will be passed into the `amount` parameter.

The statement in lines 18 through 20 displays the account balance. It displays the value returned from the `savings.get_balance` method.

Line 23 gets the amount that the user wants to withdraw and assigns it to the `cash` variable. In line 25 the `savings.withdraw` method is called, passing the `cash` variable as an argument. In the `withdraw` method, it will be passed into the `amount` parameter. The statement in lines 28 through 30 displays the ending account balance.

The `__str__` Method

Quite often, we need to display a message that indicates an object's state. An object's *state* is simply the values of the object's attributes at any given moment. For example, recall the `BankAccount` class has one data attribute: `__balance`. At any given moment, a `BankAccount` object's `__balance` attribute will reference some value. The value of the __balance attribute represents the object's state at that moment. The following might be an example of code that displays a BankAccount object's state:

```
account = bankaccount.BankAccount(1500.0)
print('The balance is $', format(savings.get_balance(), ',.2f'), sep='')
```

The first statement creates a BankAccount object, passing the value 1500.0 to the __init__ method. After this statement executes, the account variable will reference the BankAccount object. The second line displays a string showing the value of the object's __balance attribute. The output of this statement will look like this:

```
The balance is $1,500.00
```

Displaying an object's state is a common task. It is so common that many programmers equip their classes with a method that returns a string containing the object's state. In Python, you give this method the special name __str__. Program 10-9 shows the BankAccount class with a __str__ method added to it. The __str__ method appears in lines 36 through 37. It returns a string indicating the account balance.

Program 10-9 (bankaccount2.py)

```
1  # The BankAccount class simulates a bank account.
2
3  class BankAccount:
4
5      # The __init__ method accepts an argument for
6      # the account's balance. It is assigned to
7      # the __balance attribute.
8
9      def __init__(self, bal):
10         self.__balance = bal
11
12     # The deposit method makes a deposit into the
13     # account.
14
15     def deposit(self, amount):
16         self.__balance += amount
17
18     # The withdraw method withdraws an amount
19     # from the account.
20
21     def withdraw(self, amount):
22         if self.__balance >= amount:
23             self.__balance -= amount
24         else:
25             print('Error: Insufficient funds')
26
27     # The get_balance method returns the
28     # account balance.
29
30     def get_balance(self):
```

```
        return self.__balance

    # The __str__ method returns a string
    # indicating the object's state.

    def __str__(self):
        return 'The balance is $' + format(self.__balance, ',.2f')
```

You do not directly call the `__str__` method. Instead, it is automatically called when you pass an object as an argument to the `print` function. Program 10-10 shows an example.

Program 10-10 (account_test2.py)

```
# This program demonstrates the BankAccount class
# with the __str__ method added to it.

import bankaccount2

def main():
    # Get the starting balance.
    start_bal = float(input('Enter your starting balance: '))

    # Create a BankAccount object.
    savings = bankaccount2.BankAccount(start_bal)

    # Deposit the user's paycheck.
    pay = float(input('How much were you paid this week? '))
    print('I will deposit that into your account.')
    savings.deposit(pay)

    # Display the balance.
    print(savings)

    # Get the amount to withdraw.
    cash = float(input('How much would you like to withdraw? '))
    print('I will withdraw that from your account.')
    savings.withdraw(cash)

    # Display the balance.
    print(savings)

# Call the main function.
main()
```

Program Output (with input shown in bold)

```
Enter your starting balance: 1000.00 Enter
How much were you paid this week? 500.00 Enter
I will deposit that into your account.
```

(program output continues)

Program Output *(continued)*

```
The account balance is $1,500.00
How much would you like to withdraw? 1200.00 [Enter]
I will withdraw that from your account.
The account balance is $300.00
```

The name of the object, `savings`, is passed to the `print` function in lines 19 and 27. This causes the `BankAccount` class's `__str__` method to be called. The string that is returned from the `__str__` method is then displayed.

The `__str__` method is also called automatically when an object is passed as an argument to the built-in `str` function. Here is an example:

```
account = bankaccount2.BankAccount(1500.0)
message = str(account)
print(message)
```

In the second statement, the `account` object is passed as an argument to the `str` function. This causes the `BankAccount` class's `__str__` method to be called. The string that is returned is assigned to the `message` variable then displayed by the `print` function in the third line.

Checkpoint

10.5 You hear someone make the following comment: "A blueprint is a design for a house. A carpenter can use the blueprint to build the house. If the carpenter wishes, he or she can build several identical houses from the same blueprint." Think of this as a metaphor for classes and objects. Does the blueprint represent a class, or does it represent an object?

10.6 In this chapter, we use the metaphor of a cookie cutter and cookies that are made from the cookie cutter to describe classes and objects. In this metaphor, are objects the cookie cutter, or the cookies?

10.7 What is the purpose of the `__init__` method? When does it execute?

10.8 What is the purpose of the `self` parameter in a method?

10.9 In a Python class, how do you hide an attribute from code outside the class?

10.10 What is the purpose of the `__str__` method?

10.11 How do you call the `__str__` method?

10.3 Working with Instances

CONCEPT: Each instance of a class has its own set of data attributes.

When a method uses the `self` parameter to create an attribute, the attribute belongs to the specific object that `self` references. We call these attributes *instance attributes* because they belong to a specific instance of the class.

It is possible to create many instances of the same class in a program. Each instance will then have its own set of attributes. For example, look at Program 10-11. This program creates three instances of the `Coin` class. Each instance has its own `__sideup` attribute.

Program 10-11 (coin_demo5.py)

```
# This program imports the simulation module and
# creates three instances of the Coin class.

import coin

def main():
    # Create three objects from the Coin class.
    coin1 = coin.Coin()
    coin2 = coin.Coin()
    coin3 = coin.Coin()

    # Display the side of each coin that is facing up.
    print('I have three coins with these sides up:')
    print(coin1.get_sideup())
    print(coin2.get_sideup())
    print(coin3.get_sideup())
    print()

    # Toss the coin.
    print('I am tossing all three coins ...')
    print()
    coin1.toss()
    coin2.toss()
    coin3.toss()

    # Display the side of each coin that is facing up.
    print('Now here are the sides that are up:')
    print(coin1.get_sideup())
    print(coin2.get_sideup())
    print(coin3.get_sideup())
    print()

# Call the main function.
main()
```

Program Output

```
I have three coins with these sides up:
Heads
Heads
Heads

I am tossing all three coins ...

Now here are the sides that are up:
Tails
Tails
Heads
```

In lines 8 through 10, the following statements create three objects, each an instance of the `Coin` class:

```
coin1 = coin.Coin()
coin2 = coin.Coin()
coin3 = coin.Coin()
```

Figure 10-8 illustrates how the `coin1`, `coin2`, and `coin3` variables reference the three objects after these statements execute. Notice each object has its own `__sideup` attribute. Lines 14 through 16 display the values returned from each object's `get_sideup` method.

Figure 10-8 The `coin1`, `coin2`, and `coin3` variables reference three `Coin` objects

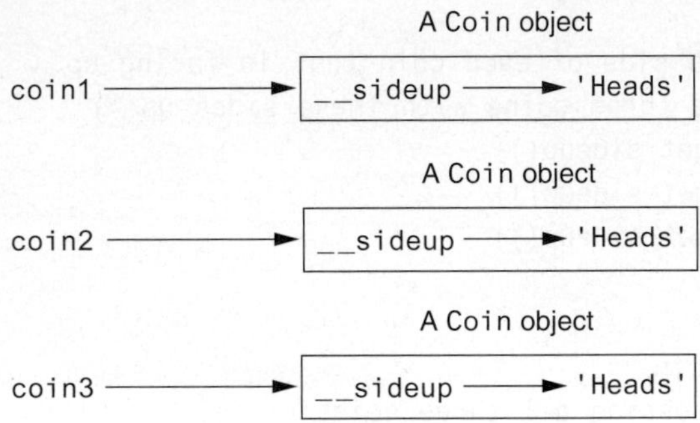

Then, the statements in lines 22 through 24 call each object's `toss` method:

```
coin1.toss()
coin2.toss()
coin3.toss()
```

Figure 10-9 shows how these statements changed each object's `__sideup` attribute in the program's sample run.

Figure 10-9 The objects after the `toss` method

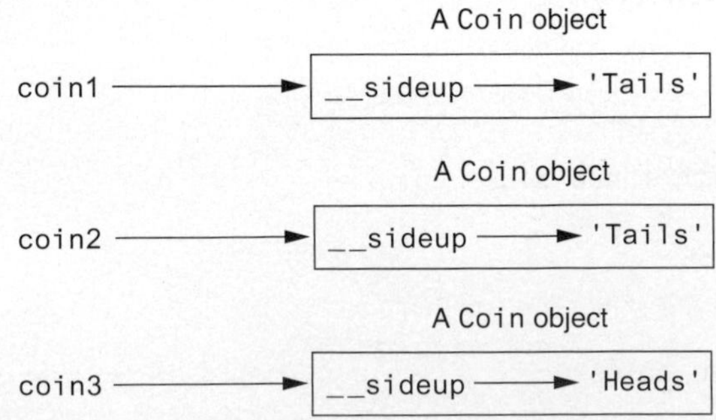

In the Spotlight:
Creating the CellPhone Class

Wireless Solutions, Inc. is a business that sells cell phones and wireless service. You are a programmer in the company's IT department, and your team is designing a program to manage all of the cell phones that are in inventory. You have been asked to design a class that represents a cell phone. The data that should be kept as attributes in the class are as follows:

- The name of the phone's manufacturer will be assigned to the `__manufact` attribute.
- The phone's model number will be assigned to the `__model` attribute.
- The phone's retail price will be assigned to the `__retail_price` attribute.

The class will also have the following methods:

- An `__init__` method that accepts arguments for the manufacturer, model number, and retail price.
- A `set_manufact` method that accepts an argument for the manufacturer. This method will allow us to change the value of the `__manufact` attribute after the object has been created, if necessary.
- A `set_model` method that accepts an argument for the model. This method will allow us to change the value of the `__model` attribute after the object has been created, if necessary.
- A `set_retail_price` method that accepts an argument for the retail price. This method will allow us to change the value of the `__retail_price` attribute after the object has been created, if necessary.
- A `get_manufact` method that returns the phone's manufacturer.
- A `get_model` method that returns the phone's model number.
- A `get_retail_price` method that returns the phone's retail price.

Program 10-12 shows the class definition. The class is stored in a module named `cellphone`.

Program 10-12 (`cellphone.py`)

```
# The CellPhone class holds data about a cell phone.

class CellPhone:

    # The __init__ method initializes the attributes.

    def __init__(self, manufact, model, price):
        self.__manufact = manufact
        self.__model = model
        self.__retail_price = price

    # The set_manufact method accepts an argument for
    # the phone's manufacturer.

    def set_manufact(self, manufact):
        self.__manufact = manufact
```

(program continues)

Program 10-12 *(continued)*

```

    # The set_model method accepts an argument for
    # the phone's model number.

    def set_model(self, model):
        self.__model = model

    # The set_retail_price method accepts an argument
    # for the phone's retail price.

    def set_retail_price(self, price):
        self.__retail_price = price

    # The get_manufact method returns the
    # phone's manufacturer.

    def get_manufact(self):
        return self.__manufact

    # The get_model method returns the
    # phone's model number.

    def get_model(self):
        return self.__model

    # The get_retail_price method returns the
    # phone's retail price.

    def get_retail_price(self):
        return self.__retail_price
```

The `CellPhone` class will be imported into several programs that your team is developing. To test the class, you write the code in Program 10-13. This is a simple program that prompts the user for the phone's manufacturer, model number, and retail price. An instance of the `CellPhone` class is created, and the data is assigned to its attributes.

Program 10-13 **(`cell_phone_test.py`)**

```
# This program tests the CellPhone class.

import cellphone

def main():
    # Get the phone data.
    man = input('Enter the manufacturer: ')
```

```
    mod = input('Enter the model number: ')
    retail = float(input('Enter the retail price: '))

    # Create an instance of the CellPhone class.
    phone = cellphone.CellPhone(man, mod, retail)

    # Display the data that was entered.
    print('Here is the data that you entered:')
    print('Manufacturer:', phone.get_manufact())
    print('Model Number:', phone.get_model())
    print('Retail Price: $', format(phone.get_retail_price(), ',.2f'), sep='')

# Call the main function.
main()
```

Program Output (with input shown in bold)

```
Enter the manufacturer: Acme Electronics [Enter]
Enter the model number: M1000 [Enter]
Enter the retail price: 199.99 [Enter]
Here is the data that you entered:
Manufacturer: Acme Electronics
Model Number: M1000
Retail Price: $199.99
```

Accessor and Mutator Methods

As mentioned earlier, it is a common practice to make all of a class's data attributes private, and to provide public methods for accessing and changing those attributes. This ensures that the object owning those attributes is in control of all the changes being made to them.

A method that returns a value from a class's attribute but does not change it is known as an *accessor method*. Accessor methods provide a safe way for code outside the class to retrieve the values of attributes, without exposing the attributes in a way that they could be changed by the code outside the method. In the `CellPhone` class that you saw in Program 10-12 (in the previous *In the Spotlight* section), the `get_manufact`, `get_model`, and `get_retail_price` methods are accessor methods.

A method that stores a value in a data attribute or changes the value of a data attribute in some other way is known as a *mutator method*. Mutator methods can control the way that a class's data attributes are modified. When code outside the class needs to change the value of an object's data attribute, it typically calls a mutator and passes the new value as an argument. If necessary, the mutator can validate the value before it assigns it to the data attribute. In Program 10-12, the `set_manufact`, `set_model`, and `set_retail_price` methods are mutator methods.

NOTE: Mutator methods are sometimes called "setters," and accessor methods are sometimes called "getters."

In the Spotlight:
Storing Objects in a List

The `CellPhone` class you created in the previous *In the Spotlight* section will be used in a variety of programs. Many of these programs will store `CellPhone` objects in lists. To test the ability to store `CellPhone` objects in a list, you write the code in Program 10-14. This program gets the data for five phones from the user, creates five `CellPhone` objects holding that data, and stores those objects in a list. It then iterates over the list displaying the attributes of each object.

Program 10-14 (cell_phone_list.py)

```
# This program creates five CellPhone objects and
# stores them in a list.

import cellphone

def main():
    # Get a list of CellPhone objects.
    phones = make_list()

    # Display the data in the list.
    print('Here is the data you entered:')
    display_list(phones)

# The make_list function gets data from the user
# for five phones. The function returns a list
# of CellPhone objects containing the data.

def make_list():
    # Create an empty list.
    phone_list = []

    # Add five CellPhone objects to the list.
    print('Enter data for five phones.')
    for count in range(1, 6):
        # Get the phone data.
        print('Phone number ' + str(count) + ':')
        man = input('Enter the manufacturer: ')
        mod = input('Enter the model number: ')
        retail = float(input('Enter the retail price: '))
        print()

        # Create a new CellPhone object in memory and
        # assign it to the phone variable.
        phone = cellphone.CellPhone(man, mod, retail)

        # Add the object to the list.
        phone_list.append(phone)
```

```

    # Return the list.
    return phone_list

# The display_list function accepts a list containing
# CellPhone objects as an argument and displays the
# data stored in each object.

def display_list(phone_list):
    for item in phone_list:
        print(item.get_manufact())
        print(item.get_model())
        print(item.get_retail_price())
        print()

# Call the main function.
main()
```

Program Output (with input shown in bold)

```
Enter data for five phones.

Phone number 1:
Enter the manufacturer: Acme Electronics [Enter]
Enter the model number: M1000 [Enter]
Enter the retail price: 199.99 [Enter]

Phone number 2:
Enter the manufacturer: Atlantic Communications [Enter]
Enter the model number: S2 [Enter]
Enter the retail price: 149.99 [Enter]

Phone number 3:
Enter the manufacturer: Wavelength Electronics [Enter]
Enter the model number: N477 [Enter]
Enter the retail price: 249.99 [Enter]

Phone number 4:
Enter the manufacturer: Edison Wireless [Enter]
Enter the model number: SLX88 [Enter]
Enter the retail price: 169.99 [Enter]

Phone number 5:
Enter the manufacturer: Sonic Systems [Enter]
Enter the model number: X99 [Enter]
Enter the retail price: 299.99 [Enter]

Here is the data you entered:
Acme Electronics
M1000
199.99
```

(program output continues)

Program Output *(continued)*

```
Atlantic Communications
S2
149.99

Wavelength Electronics
N477
249.99

Edison Wireless
SLX88
169.99

Sonic Systems
X99
299.99
```

The `make_list` function appears in lines 18 through 40. In line 20, an empty list named `phone_list` is created. The `for` loop, which begins in line 24, iterates five times. Each time the loop iterates, it gets the data for a cell phone from the user (lines 27 through 29), it creates an instance of the `CellPhone` class that is initialized with the data (line 34), and it appends the object to the `phone_list` list (line 37). Line 40 returns the list.

The `display_list` function in lines 46 through 51 accepts a list of `CellPhone` objects as an argument. The `for` loop that begins in line 47 iterates over the objects in the list, and displays the values of each object's attributes.

Passing Objects as Arguments

When you are developing applications that work with objects, you often need to write functions and methods that accept objects as arguments. For example, the following code shows a function named `show_coin_status` that accepts a `Coin` object as an argument:

```
def show_coin_status(coin_obj):
    print('This side of the coin is up:', coin_obj.get_sideup())
```

The following code sample shows how we might create a `Coin` object, then pass it as an argument to the `show_coin_status` function:

```
my_coin = coin.Coin()
show_coin_status(my_coin)
```

When you pass a object as an argument, the thing that is passed into the parameter variable is a reference to the object. As a result, the function or method that receives the object as an argument has access to the actual object. For example, look at the following `flip` method:

```
def flip(coin_obj):
    coin_obj.toss()
```

This method accepts a `Coin` object as an argument, and it calls the object's `toss` method. Program 10-15 demonstrates the method.

Program 10-15 (coin_argument.py)

```
 1  # This program passes a Coin object as
 2  # an argument to a function.
 3  import coin
 4
 5  # main function
 6  def main():
 7      # Create a Coin object.
 8      my_coin = coin.Coin()
 9
10      # This will display 'Heads'.
11      print(my_coin.get_sideup())
12
13      # Pass the object to the flip function.
14      flip(my_coin)
15
16      # This might display 'Heads', or it might
17      # display 'Tails'.
18      print(my_coin.get_sideup())
19
20  # The flip function flips a coin.
21  def flip(coin_obj):
22      coin_obj.toss()
23
24  # Call the main function.
25  main()
```

Program Output

```
Heads
Tails
```

Program Output

```
Heads
Heads
```

Program Output

```
Heads
Tails
```

The statement in line 8 creates a `Coin` object, referenced by the variable `my_coin`. Line 11 displays the value of the `my_coin` object's `__sideup` attribute. Because the object's `__init__` method set the `__sideup` attribute to `'Heads'`, we know that line 11 will display the string `'Heads'`. Line 14 calls the `flip` function, passing the `my_coin` object as an argument. Inside the `flip` function, the `my_coin` object's `toss` method is called. Then, line 18 displays the value of the `my_coin` object's `__sideup` attribute again. This time, we cannot predict whether `'Heads'` or `'Tails'` will be displayed because the `my_coin` object's `toss` method has been called.

In the Spotlight:
Pickling Your Own Objects

Recall from Chapter 9 that the `pickle` module provides functions for serializing objects. Serializing an object means converting it to a stream of bytes that can be saved to a file for later retrieval. The `pickle` module's `dump` function serializes (pickles) an object and writes it to a file, and the load function retrieves an object from a file and deserializes (unpickles) it.

In Chapter 9, you saw examples in which dictionary objects were pickled and unpickled. You can also pickle and unpickle objects of your own classes. Program 10-16 shows an example that pickles three `CellPhone` objects and saves them to a file. Program 10-17 retrieves those objects from the file and unpickles them.

Program 10-16 (pickle_cellphone.py)

```
# This program pickles CellPhone objects.
import pickle
import cellphone

# Constant for the filename.
FILENAME = 'cellphones.dat'

def main():
    # Initialize a variable to control the loop.
    again = 'y'

    # Open a file.
    output_file = open(FILENAME, 'wb')

    # Get data from the user.
    while again.lower() == 'y':
        # Get cell phone data.
        man = input('Enter the manufacturer: ')
        mod = input('Enter the model number: ')
        retail = float(input('Enter the retail price: '))

        # Create a CellPhone object.
        phone = cellphone.CellPhone(man, mod, retail)

        # Pickle the object and write it to the file.
        pickle.dump(phone, output_file)

        # Get more cell phone data?
        again = input('Enter more phone data? (y/n): ')

    # Close the file.
    output_file.close()
    print('The data was written to', FILENAME)
```

```

# Call the main function.
main()
```

Program Output (with input shown in bold)

```
Enter the manufacturer: ACME Electronics [Enter]
Enter the model number: M1000 [Enter]
Enter the retail price: 199.99 [Enter]
Enter more phone data? (y/n): y [Enter]
Enter the manufacturer: Sonic Systems [Enter]
Enter the model number: X99 [Enter]
Enter the retail price: 299.99 [Enter]
Enter more phone data? (y/n): n [Enter]
The data was written to cellphones.dat
```

Program 10-17 (unpickle_cellphone.py)

```
# This program unpickles CellPhone objects.
import pickle
import cellphone

# Constant for the filename.
FILENAME = 'cellphones.dat'

def main():
    end_of_file = False    # To indicate end of file

    # Open the file.
    input_file = open(FILENAME, 'rb')

    # Read to the end of the file.
    while not end_of_file:
        try:
            # Unpickle the next object.
            phone = pickle.load(input_file)

            # Display the cell phone data.
            display_data(phone)
        except EOFError:
            # Set the flag to indicate the end
            # of the file has been reached.
            end_of_file = True

    # Close the file.
    input_file.close()

```

(program continues)

Program 10-17 *(continued)*

```
# The display_data function displays the data
# from the CellPhone object passed as an argument.
def display_data(phone):
    print('Manufacturer:', phone.get_manufact())
    print('Model Number:', phone.get_model())
    print('Retail Price: $',
          format(phone.get_retail_price(), ',.2f'),
          sep='')
    print()

# Call the main function.
main()
```

Program Output

```
Manufacturer: ACME Electronics
Model Number: M1000
Retail Price: $199.99

Manufacturer: Sonic Systems
Model Number: X99
Retail Price: $299.99
```

In the Spotlight:
Storing Objects in a Dictionary

Recall from Chapter 9 that dictionaries are objects that store elements as key-value pairs. Each element in a dictionary has a key and a value. If you want to retrieve a specific value from the dictionary, you do so by specifying its key. In Chapter 9, you saw examples that stored values such as strings, integers, floating-point numbers, lists, and tuples in dictionaries. Dictionaries are also useful for storing objects that you create from your own classes.

Let's look at an example. Suppose you want to create a program that keeps contact information, such as names, phone numbers, and email addresses. You could start by writing a class such as the `Contact` class, shown in Program 10-18. An instance of the `Contact` class keeps the following data:

- A person's name is stored in the `__name` attribute.
- A person's phone number is stored in the `__phone` attribute.
- A person's email address is stored in the `__email` attribute.

The class has the following methods:

- An `__init__` method that accepts arguments for a person's name, phone number, and email address
- A `set_name` method that sets the `__name` attribute

- A set_phone method that sets the __phone attribute
- A set_email method that sets the __email attribute
- A get_name method that returns the __name attribute
- A get_phone method that returns the __phone attribute
- A get_email method that returns the __email attribute
- A __str__ method that returns the object's state as a string

Program 10-18 (contact.py)

```
# The Contact class holds contact information.

class Contact:
    # The __init__ method initializes the attributes.
    def __init__(self, name, phone, email):
        self.__name = name
        self.__phone = phone
        self.__email = email

    # The set_name method sets the name attribute.
    def set_name(self, name):
        self.__name = name

    # The set_phone method sets the phone attribute.
    def set_phone(self, phone):
        self.__phone = phone

    # The set_email method sets the email attribute.
    def set_email(self, email):
        self.__email = email

    # The get_name method returns the name attribute.
    def get_name(self):
        return self.__name

    # The get_phone method returns the phone attribute.
    def get_phone(self):
        return self.__phone

    # The get_email method returns the email attribute.
    def get_email(self):
        return self.__email

    # The __str__ method returns the object's state
    # as a string.
    def __str__(self):
        return "Name: " + self.__name + \
               "\nPhone: " + self.__phone + \
               "\nEmail: " + self.__email
```

Next, you could write a program that keeps `Contact` objects in a dictionary. Each time the program creates a `Contact` object holding a specific person's data, that object would be stored as a value in the dictionary, using the person's name as the key. Then, any time you need to retrieve a specific person's data, you would use that person's name as a key to retrieve the `Contact` object from the dictionary.

Program 10-19 shows an example. The program displays a menu that allows the user to perform any of the following operations:

- Look up a contact in the dictionary
- Add a new contact to the dictionary
- Change an existing contact in the dictionary
- Delete a contact from the dictionary
- Quit the program

Additionally, the program automatically pickles the dictionary and saves it to a file when the user quits the program. When the program starts, it automatically retrieves and unpickles the dictionary from the file. (Recall from Chapter 10 that pickling an object saves it to a file, and unpickling an object retrieves it from a file.) If the file does not exist, the program starts with an empty dictionary.

The program is divided into eight functions: `main`, `load_contacts`, `get_menu_choice`, `look_up`, `add`, `change`, `delete`, and `save_contacts`. Rather than presenting the entire program at once, let's first examine the beginning part, which includes the `import` statements, global constants, and the `main` function.

Program 10-19 (`contact_manager.py`: `main` **function**)

```
# This program manages contacts.
import contact
import pickle

# Global constants for menu choices
LOOK_UP = 1
ADD = 2
CHANGE = 3
DELETE = 4
QUIT = 5

# Global constant for the filename
FILENAME = 'contacts.dat'

# main function
def main():
    # Load the existing contact dictionary and
    # assign it to mycontacts.
    mycontacts = load_contacts()

    # Initialize a variable for the user's choice.
    choice = 0
```

```
23
24      # Process menu selections until the user
25      # wants to quit the program.
26      while choice != QUIT:
27          # Get the user's menu choice.
28          choice = get_menu_choice()
29
30          # Process the choice.
31          if choice == LOOK_UP:
32              look_up(mycontacts)
33          elif choice == ADD:
34              add(mycontacts)
35          elif choice == CHANGE:
36              change(mycontacts)
37          elif choice == DELETE:
38              delete(mycontacts)
39
40      # Save the mycontacts dictionary to a file.
41      save_contacts(mycontacts)
42
```

Line 2 imports the `contact` module, which contains the `Contact` class. Line 3 imports the `pickle` module. The global constants that are initialized in lines 6 through 10 are used to test the user's menu selection. The `FILENAME` constant that is initialized in line 13 holds the name of the file that will contain the pickled copy of the dictionary, which is `contacts.dat`.

Inside the `main` function, line 19 calls the `load_contacts` function. Keep in mind that if the program has been run before and names were added to the dictionary, those names have been saved to the `contacts.dat` file. The `load_contacts` function opens the file, gets the dictionary from it, and returns a reference to the dictionary. If the program has not been run before, the `contacts.dat` file does not exist. In that case, the `load_contacts` function creates an empty dictionary and returns a reference to it. So, after the statement in line 19 executes, the `mycontacts` variable references a dictionary. If the program has been run before, `mycontacts` references a dictionary containing `Contact` objects. If this is the first time the program has run, `mycontacts` references an empty dictionary.

Line 22 initializes the `choice` variable with the value 0. This variable will hold the user's menu selection.

The `while` loop that begins in line 26 repeats until the user chooses to quit the program. Inside the loop, line 28 calls the `get_menu_choice` function. The `get_menu_choice` function displays the following menu:

1. Look up a contact
2. Add a new contact
3. Change an existing contact
4. Delete a contact
5. Quit the program

The user's selection is returned from the `get_menu_choice` function and is assigned to the `choice` variable.

The `if-elif` statement in lines 31 through 38 processes the user's menu choice. If the user selects item 1, line 32 calls the `look_up` function. If the user selects item 2, line 34 calls the `add` function. If the user selects item 3, line 36 calls the `change` function. If the user selects item 4, line 38 calls the `delete` function.

When the user selects item 5 from the menu, the `while` loop stops repeating, and the statement in line 41 executes. This statement calls the `save_contacts` function, passing `mycontacts` as an argument. The `save_contacts` function saves the `mycontacts` dictionary to the `contacts.dat` file.

The `load_contacts` function is next.

Program 10-19 (`contact_manager.py`: `load_contacts` **function**)

```
43  def load_contacts():
44      try:
45          # Open the contacts.dat file.
46          input_file = open(FILENAME, 'rb')
47
48          # Unpickle the dictionary.
49          contact_dct = pickle.load(input_file)
50
51          # Close the phone_inventory.dat file.
52          input_file.close()
53      except IOError:
54          # Could not open the file, so create
55          # an empty dictionary.
56          contact_dct = {}
57
58      # Return the dictionary.
59      return contact_dct
60
```

Inside the try suite, line 46 attempts to open the `contacts.dat` file. If the file is successfully opened, line 49 loads the dictionary object from it, unpickles it, and assigns it to the `contact_dct` variable. Line 52 closes the file.

If the `contacts.dat` file does not exist (this will be the case the first time the program runs), the statement in line 46 raises an `IOError` exception. That causes the program to jump to the `except` clause in line 53. Then, the statement in line 56 creates an empty dictionary and assigns it to the `contact_dct` variable.

The statement in line 59 returns the `contact_dct` variable.

The `get_menu_choice` function is next.

Program 10-19 (`contact_manager.py`: `get_menu_choice` **function**)

```
61  # The get_menu_choice function displays the menu
62  # and gets a validated choice from the user.
63  def get_menu_choice():
64      print()
65      print('Menu')
66      print('---------------------------')
67      print('1. Look up a contact')
68      print('2. Add a new contact')
69      print('3. Change an existing contact')
70      print('4. Delete a contact')
71      print('5. Quit the program')
72      print()
73
74      # Get the user's choice.
75      choice = int(input('Enter your choice: '))
76
77      # Validate the choice.
78      while choice < LOOK_UP or choice > QUIT:
79          choice = int(input('Enter a valid choice: '))
80
81      # return the user's choice.
82      return choice
83
```

The statements in lines 64 through 72 display the menu on the screen. Line 75 prompts the user to enter his or her choice. The input is converted to an `int` and assigned to the `choice` variable. The `while` loop in lines 78 through 79 validates the user's input and, if necessary, prompts the user to reenter his or her choice. Once a valid choice is entered, it is returned from the function in line 82.

The `look_up` function is next.

Program 10-19 (`contact_manager.py`: `look_up` **function**)

```
# The look_up function looks up an item in the
# specified dictionary.
def look_up(mycontacts):
    # Get a name to look up.
    name = input('Enter a name: ')

    # Look it up in the dictionary.
    print(mycontacts.get(name, 'That name is not found.'))

```

The purpose of the `look_up` function is to allow the user to look up a specified contact. It accepts the `mycontacts` dictionary as an argument. Line 88 prompts the user to enter a name, and line 91 passes that name as an argument to the dictionary's `get` function. One of the following actions will happen as a result of line 91:

- If the specified name is found as a key in the dictionary, the `get` method returns a reference to the `Contact` object that is associated with that name. The `Contact` object is then passed as an argument to the `print` function. The `print` function displays the string that is returned from the `Contact` object's `__str__` method.
- If the specified name is not found as a key in the dictionary, the `get` method returns the string `'That name is not found.'`, which is displayed by the `print` function.

The add function is next.

Program 10-19 (`contact_manager.py`: add **function**)

```
93  # The add function adds a new entry into the
94  # specified dictionary.
95  def add(mycontacts):
96      # Get the contact info.
97      name = input('Name: ')
98      phone = input('Phone: ')
99      email = input('Email: ')
100
101     # Create a Contact object named entry.
102     entry = contact.Contact(name, phone, email)
103
104     # If the name does not exist in the dictionary,
105     # add it as a key with the entry object as the
106     # associated value.
107     if name not in mycontacts:
108         mycontacts[name] = entry
109         print('The entry has been added.')
110     else:
111         print('That name already exists.')
112
```

The purpose of the add function is to allow the user to add a new contact to the dictionary. It accepts the `mycontacts` dictionary as an argument. Lines 97 through 99 prompt the user to enter a name, a phone number, and an email address. Line 102 creates a new `Contact` object, initialized with the data entered by the user.

The `if` statement in line 107 determines whether the name is already in the dictionary. If not, line 108 adds the newly created `Contact` object to the dictionary, and line 109 prints a message indicating that the new data is added. Otherwise, a message indicating that the entry already exists is printed in line 111.

The change function is next.

Program 10-19 (`contact_manager.py`: `change` **function**)

```
113 # The change function changes an existing
114 # entry in the specified dictionary.
115 def change(mycontacts):
116     # Get a name to look up.
117     name = input('Enter a name: ')
118 
119     if name in mycontacts:
120         # Get a new phone number.
121         phone = input('Enter the new phone number: ')
122 
123         # Get a new email address.
124         email = input('Enter the new email address: ')
125 
126         # Create a contact object named entry.
127         entry = contact.Contact(name, phone, email)
128 
129         # Update the entry.
130         mycontacts[name] = entry
131         print('Information updated.')
132     else:
133         print('That name is not found.')
134 
```

The purpose of the `change` function is to allow the user to change an existing contact in the dictionary. It accepts the `mycontacts` dictionary as an argument. Line 117 gets a name from the user. The `if` statement in line 119 determines whether the name is in the dictionary. If so, line 121 gets the new phone number, and line 124 gets the new email address. Line 127 creates a new `Contact` object initialized with the existing name and the new phone number and email address. Line 130 stores the new `Contact` object in the dictionary, using the existing name as the key.

If the specified name is not in the dictionary, line 133 prints a message indicating so.

The `delete` function is next.

Program 10-19 (`contact_manager.py`: `delete` **function**)

```
135 # The delete function deletes an entry from the
136 # specified dictionary.
137 def delete(mycontacts):
138     # Get a name to look up.
139     name = input('Enter a name: ')
140 
141     # If the name is found, delete the entry.
142     if name in mycontacts:
143         del mycontacts[name]
```

(program continues)

Program 10-19 *(continued)*

```
144         print('Entry deleted.')
145     else:
146         print('That name is not found.')
147
```

The purpose of the `delete` function is to allow the user to delete an existing contact from the dictionary. It accepts the `mycontacts` dictionary as an argument. Line 139 gets a name from the user. The `if` statement in line 142 determines whether the name is in the dictionary. If so, line 143 deletes it, and line 144 prints a message indicating that the entry was deleted. If the name is not in the dictionary, line 146 prints a message indicating so.

The `save_contacts` function is next.

Program 10-19 **(`contact_manager.py`: `save_contacts` function)**

```
148 # The save_contacts funtion pickles the specified
149 # object and saves it to the contacts file.
150 def save_contacts(mycontacts):
151     # Open the file for writing.
152     output_file = open(FILENAME, 'wb')
153
154     # Pickle the dictionary and save it.
155     pickle.dump(mycontacts, output_file)
156
157     # Close the file.
158     output_file.close()
159
160 # Call the main function.
161 main()
```

The `save_contacts` function is called just before the program stops running. It accepts the `mycontacts` dictionary as an argument. Line 152 opens the `contacts.dat` file for writing. Line 155 pickles the `mycontacts` dictionary and saves it to the file. Line 158 closes the file.

The following program output shows two sessions with the program. The sample output does not demonstrate everything the program can do, but it does demonstrate how contacts are saved when the program ends and then loaded when the program runs again.

Program Output (with input shown in bold)

```
Menu
---------------------------
1. Look up a contact
2. Add a new contact
```

```
3. Change an existing contact
4. Delete a contact
5. Quit the program

Enter your choice: 2 [Enter]
Name: Matt Goldstein [Enter]
Phone: 617-555-1234 [Enter]
Email: matt@fakecompany.com [Enter]
The entry has been added.

Menu
---------------------------
1. Look up a contact
2. Add a new contact
3. Change an existing contact
4. Delete a contact
5. Quit the program

Enter your choice: 2 [Enter]
Name: Jorge Ruiz [Enter]
Phone: 919-555-1212 [Enter]
Email: jorge@myschool.edu [Enter]
The entry has been added.

Menu
---------------------------
1. Look up a contact
2. Add a new contact
3. Change an existing contact
4. Delete a contact
5. Quit the program

Enter your choice: 5 [Enter]
```

Program Output (with input shown in bold)

```
Menu
---------------------------
1. Look up a contact
2. Add a new contact
3. Change an existing contact
4. Delete a contact
5. Quit the program

Enter your choice: 1 [Enter]
Enter a name: Matt Goldstein [Enter]
Name: Matt Goldstein
Phone: 617-555-1234
Email: matt@fakecompany.com
```

(program output continues)

Program Output *(continued)*

```
Menu
--------------------------
1. Look up a contact
2. Add a new contact
3. Change an existing contact
4. Delete a contact
5. Quit the program
Enter your choice: 1 Enter
Enter a name: Jorge Ruiz Enter
Name: Jorge Ruiz
Phone: 919-555-1212
Email: jorge@myschool.edu
Menu
--------------------------
1. Look up a contact
2. Add a new contact
3. Change an existing contact
4. Delete a contact
5. Quit the program
Enter your choice: 5 Enter
```

Checkpoint

10.12 What is an instance attribute?

10.13 A program creates 10 instances of the `Coin` class. How many `__sideup` attributes exist in memory?

10.14 What is an accessor method? What is a mutator method?

10.4 Techniques for Designing Classes

The Unified Modeling Language

When designing a class, it is often helpful to draw a UML diagram. UML stands for Unified Modeling Language. It provides a set of standard diagrams for graphically depicting object-oriented systems. Figure 10-10 shows the general layout of a UML diagram for a class. Notice the diagram is a box that is divided into three sections. The top section is where you write the name of the class. The middle section holds a list of the class's data attributes. The bottom section holds a list of the class's methods.

Figure 10-10 General layout of a UML diagram for a class

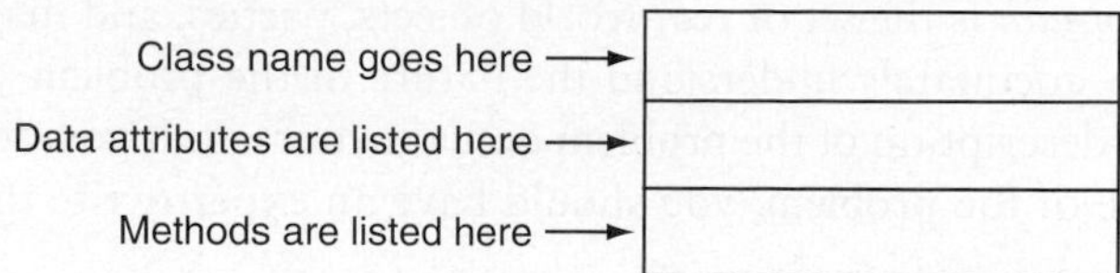

Following this layout, Figure 10-11 and 10-12 show UML diagrams for the `Coin` class and the `CellPhone` class that you saw previously in this chapter. Notice we did not show the `self` parameter in any of the methods, since it is understood that the `self` parameter is required.

Figure 10-11 UML diagram for the `Coin` class

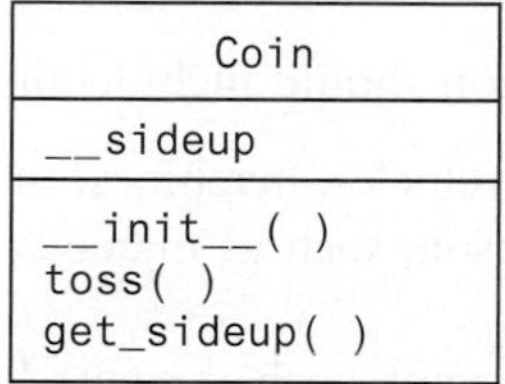

Figure 10-12 UML diagram for the `CellPhone` class

```
CellPhone
---------------------------------
__manufact
__model
__retail_price
---------------------------------
__init__(manufact, model, price)
set_manufact(manufact)
set_model(model)
set_retail_price(price)
get_manufact()
get_model()
get_retail_price()
```

Finding the Classes in a Problem

When developing an object-oriented program, one of your first tasks is to identify the classes that you will need to create. Typically, your goal is to identify the different types of real-world objects that are present in the problem, then create classes for those types of objects within your application.

Over the years, software professionals have developed numerous techniques for finding the classes in a given problem. One simple and popular technique involves the following steps:

1. Get a written description of the problem domain.
2. Identify all the nouns (including pronouns and noun phrases) in the description. Each of these is a potential class.
3. Refine the list to include only the classes that are relevant to the problem.

Let's take a closer look at each of these steps.

Writing a Description of the Problem Domain

The *problem domain* is the set of real-world objects, parties, and major events related to the problem. If you adequately understand the nature of the problem you are trying to solve, you can write a description of the problem domain yourself. If you do not thoroughly understand the nature of the problem, you should have an expert write the description for you.

For example, suppose we are writing a program that the manager of Joe's Automotive Shop will use to print service quotes for customers. Here is a description that an expert, perhaps Joe himself, might have written:

> Joe's Automotive Shop services foreign cars and specializes in servicing cars made by Mercedes, Porsche, and BMW. When a customer brings a car to the shop, the manager gets the customer's name, address, and telephone number. The manager then determines the make, model, and year of the car and gives the customer a service quote. The service quote shows the estimated parts charges, estimated labor charges, sales tax, and total estimated charges.

The problem domain description should include any of the following:

- Physical objects such as vehicles, machines, or products
- Any role played by a person, such as manager, employee, customer, teacher, student, etc.
- The results of a business event, such as a customer order, or in this case a service quote
- Recordkeeping items, such as customer histories and payroll records

Identify All of the Nouns

The next step is to identify all of the nouns and noun phrases. (If the description contains pronouns, include them too.) Here's another look at the previous problem domain description.

This time the nouns and noun phrases appear in bold.

> **Joe's Automotive Shop** services **foreign cars** and specializes in servicing **cars** made by **Mercedes**, **Porsche**, and **BMW**. When a **customer** brings a **car** to the **shop**, the **manager** gets the **customer's name**, **address**, and **telephone number**. The **manager** then determines the **make**, **model**, and **year** of the **car** and gives the **customer** a **service quote**. The **service quote** shows the **estimated parts charges**, **estimated labor charges**, **sales tax**, and **total estimated charges**.

Notice some of the nouns are repeated. The following list shows all of the nouns without duplicating any of them:

address
BMW
car
cars
customer
estimated labor charges
estimated parts charges
foreign cars
Joe's Automotive Shop
make
manager
Mercedes
model

name
Porsche
sales tax
service quote
shop
telephone number
total estimated charges
year

Refining the List of Nouns

The nouns that appear in the problem description are merely candidates to become classes. It might not be necessary to make classes for them all. The next step is to refine the list to include only the classes that are necessary to solve the particular problem at hand. We will look at the common reasons that a noun can be eliminated from the list of potential classes.

1. **Some of the nouns really mean the same thing.**

In this example, the following sets of nouns refer to the same thing:

- **car, cars,** and **foreign cars**
  These all refer to the general concept of a car.
- **Joe's Automotive Shop** and **shop**
  Both of these refer to the company "Joe's Automotive Shop."

We can settle on a single class for each of these. In this example, we will arbitrarily eliminate **cars** and **foreign cars** from the list and use the word **car**. Likewise, we will eliminate **Joe's Automotive Shop** from the list and use the word **shop**. The updated list of potential classes is:

---

address
BMW
car
~~cars~~
customer
estimated labor charges
estimated parts charges
~~foreign cars~~
~~Joe's Automotive Shop~~
make
manager
Mercedes
model
name
Porsche
sales tax
service quote

Because **car, cars,** and **foreign cars** mean the same thing in this problem, we have eliminated **cars** and **foreign cars**. Also, because **Joe's Automotive Shop** and **shop** mean the same thing, we have eliminated **Joe's Automotive Shop.**

(continued)

shop
telephone number
total estimated charges
year

---

2. **Some nouns might represent items that we do not need to be concerned with in order to solve the problem.**

A quick review of the problem description reminds us of what our application should do: print a service quote. In this example, we can eliminate two unnecessary classes from the list:

- We can cross **shop** off the list because our application only needs to be concerned with individual service quotes. It doesn't need to work with or determine any company-wide information. If the problem description asked us to keep a total of all the service quotes, then it would make sense to have a class for the shop.
- We will not need a class for the **manager** because the problem statement does not direct us to process any information about the manager. If there were multiple shop managers, and the problem description had asked us to record which manager generated each service quote, then it would make sense to have a class for the manager.

The updated list of potential classes at this point is:

---

address
BMW
car
~~cars~~
customer
estimated labor charges
estimated parts charges
~~foreign cars~~
~~Joe's Automotive Shop~~
make
~~manager~~
Mercedes
model
name
Porsche
sales tax
service quote
~~shop~~
telephone number
total estimated charges
year

Our problem description does not direct us to process any information about the **shop,** or any information about the **manager,** so we have eliminated those from the list.

---

3. **Some of the nouns might represent objects, not classes.**

We can eliminate **Mercedes, Porsche,** and **BMW** as classes because, in this example, they all represent specific cars and can be considered instances of a **car** class. At this point, the updated list of potential classes is:

address
~~BMW~~
car
~~cars~~
customer
estimated labor charges
estimated parts charges
~~foreign cars~~
~~Joe's Automotive Shop~~
~~manager~~
make
~~Mercedes~~
model
name
~~Porsche~~
sales tax
service quote
~~shop~~
telephone number
total estimated charges
year

We have eliminated **Mercedes, Porsche,** and **BMW** because they are all instances of a **car** class. That means that these nouns identify objects, not classes.

NOTE: Some object-oriented designers take note of whether a noun is plural or singular. Sometimes a plural noun will indicate a class, and a singular noun will indicate an object.

4. **Some of the nouns might represent simple values that can be assigned to a variable and do not require a class.**

Remember, a class contains data attributes and methods. Data attributes are related items that are stored in an object of the class and define the object's state. Methods are actions or behaviors that can be performed by an object of the class. If a noun represents a type of item that would not have any identifiable data attributes or methods, then it can probably be eliminated from the list. To help determine whether a noun represents an item that would have data attributes and methods, ask the following questions about it:

- Would you use a group of related values to represent the item's state?
- Are there any obvious actions to be performed by the item?

If the answers to both of these questions are no, then the noun probably represents a value that can be stored in a simple variable. If we apply this test to each of the nouns that remain in our list, we can conclude that the following are probably not classes: **address, estimated labor charges, estimated parts charges, make, model, name, sales tax, telephone number, total estimated charges,** and **year**. These are all simple string or numeric values that can be stored in variables. Here is the updated list of potential classes:

~~Address~~
~~BMW~~
car
~~cars~~
customer
~~estimated labor charges~~
~~estimated parts charges~~
~~foreign cars~~
~~Joe's Automotive Shop~~
~~make~~
~~manager~~
~~Mercedes~~
~~model~~
~~name~~
~~Porsche~~
~~sales tax~~
service quote
~~shop~~
~~telephone number~~
~~total estimated charges~~
~~year~~

We have eliminated **address, estimated labor charges, estimated parts charges, make, model, name, sales tax, telephone number, total estimated charges,** and **year** as classes because they represent simple values that can be stored in variables.

As you can see from the list, we have eliminated everything except **car, customer**, and **service quote**. This means that in our application, we will need classes to represent cars, customers, and service quotes. Ultimately, we will write a `Car` class, a `Customer` class, and a `ServiceQuote` class.

Identifying a Class's Responsibilities

Once the classes have been identified, the next task is to identify each class's responsibilities. A class's *responsibilities* are:

- the things that the class is responsible for knowing.
- the actions that the class is responsible for doing.

When you have identified the things that a class is responsible for knowing, then you have identified the class's data attributes. Likewise, when you have identified the actions that a class is responsible for doing, you have identified its methods.

It is often helpful to ask the questions "In the context of this problem, what must the class know? What must the class do?" The first place to look for the answers is in the description of the problem domain. Many of the things that a class must know and do will be mentioned. Some class responsibilities, however, might not be directly mentioned in the problem domain, so further consideration is often required. Let's apply this methodology to the classes we previously identified from our problem domain.

The `Customer` Class

In the context of our problem domain, what must the `Customer` class know? The description directly mentions the following items, which are all data attributes of a customer:

- the customer's name
- the customer's address
- the customer's telephone number

These are all values that can be represented as strings and stored as data attributes. The `Customer` class can potentially know many other things. One mistake that can be made at this point is to identify too many things that an object is responsible for knowing. In some applications, a `Customer` class might know the customer's email address. This particular problem domain does not mention that the customer's email address is used for any purpose, so we should not include it as a responsibility.

Now, let's identify the class's methods. In the context of our problem domain, what must the `Customer` class do? The only obvious actions are:

- initialize an object of the `Customer` class.
- set and return the customer's name.
- set and return the customer's address.
- set and return the customer's telephone number.

From this list we can see that the `Customer` class will have an `__init__` method, as well as accessors and mutators for the data attributes. Figure 10-13 shows a UML diagram for the `Customer` class. The Python code for the class is shown in Program 10-20.

Figure 10-13 UML diagram for the `Customer` class

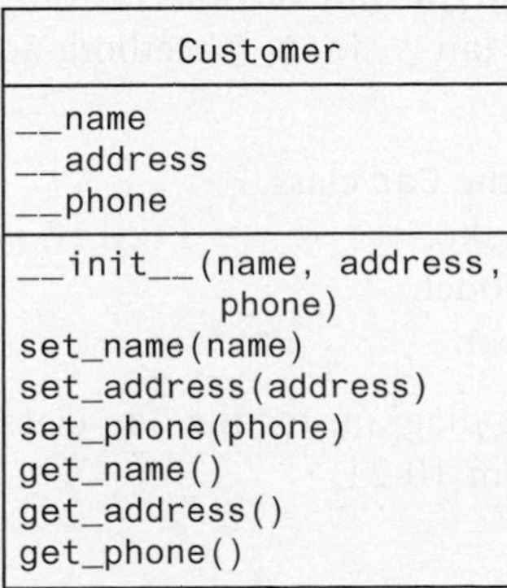

Program 10-20 (customer.py)

```
# Customer class
class Customer:
    def __init__(self, name, address, phone):
        self.__name = name
        self.__address = address
        self.__phone = phone

    def set_name(self, name):
        self.__name = name

    def set_address(self, address):
        self.__address = address

    def set_phone(self, phone):
        self.__phone = phone

    def get_name(self):
        return self.__name

    def get_address(self):
        return self.__address

    def get_phone(self):
        return self.__phone
```

The Car Class

In the context of our problem domain, what must an object of the `Car` class know? The following items are all data attributes of a car and are mentioned in the problem domain:

- the car's make
- the car's model
- the car's year

Now let's identify the class's methods. In the context of our problem domain, what must the `Car` class do? Once again, the only obvious actions are the standard set of methods that we will find in most classes (an `__init__` method, accessors, and mutators). Specifically, the actions are:

- initialize an object of the `Car` class.
- set and get the car's make.
- set and get the car's model.
- set and get the car's year.

Figure 10-14 shows a UML diagram for the `Car` class at this point. The Python code for the class is shown in Program 10-21.

Figure 10-14 UML diagram for the Car class

```
Car
-----------------------------
__make
__model
__year
-----------------------------
__init__(make, model,
         year)
set_make(make)
set_model(make)
set_year(y)
get_make( )
get_model( )
get_year( )
```

Program 10-21 (car.py)

```
# Car class
class Car:
    def __init__(self, make, model, year):
        self.__make = make
        self.__model = model
        self.__year = year

    def set_make(self, make):
        self.__make = make

    def set_model(self, model):
        self.__model = model

    def set_year(self, year):
        self.__year = year

    def get_make(self):
        return self.__make

    def get_model(self):
        return self.__model

    def get_year(self):
        return self.__year
```

The ServiceQuote Class

In the context of our problem domain, what must an object of the ServiceQuote class know? The problem domain mentions the following items:

- the estimated parts charges
- the estimated labor charges

- the sales tax
- the total estimated charges

The methods that we will need for this class are an `__init__` method and the accessors and mutators for the estimated parts charges and estimated labor charges attributes. In addition, the class will need methods that calculate and return the sales tax and the total estimated charges. Figure 10-15 shows a UML diagram for the `ServiceQuote` class. Program 10-22 shows an example of the class in Python code.

Figure 10-15 UML diagram for the `ServiceQuote` class

ServiceQuote
__parts_charges __labor_charges
__init__(pcharge, lcharge) set_parts_charges(pcharge) set_labor_charges(lcharge) get_parts_charges( ) get_labor_charges( ) get_sales_tax( ) get_total_charges( )

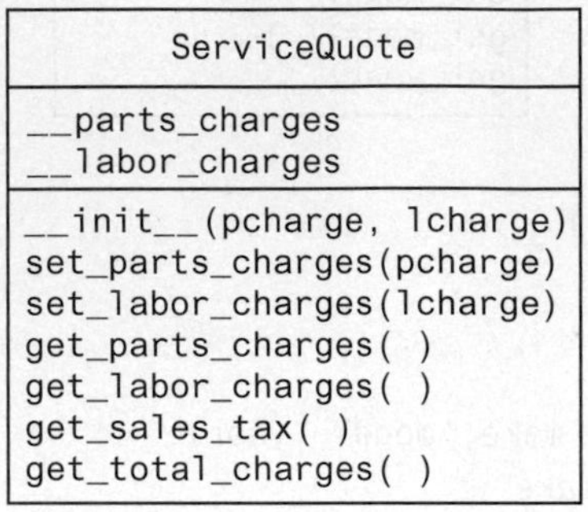

Program 10-22 (servicequote.py)

```
# Constant for the sales tax rate
TAX_RATE = 0.05

# ServiceQuote class
class ServiceQuote:
    def __init__(self, pcharge, lcharge):
        self.__parts_charges = pcharge
        self.__labor_charges = lcharge

    def set_parts_charges(self, pcharge):
        self.__parts_charges = pcharge

    def set_labor_charges(self, lcharge):
        self.__labor_charges = lcharge

    def get_parts_charges(self):
        return self.__parts_charges

    def get_labor_charges(self):
        return self.__labor_charges

    def get_sales_tax(self):
        return __parts_charges * TAX_RATE

```

```
    def get_total_charges(self):
        return __parts_charges + __labor_charges + \
               (__parts_charges * TAX_RATE)
```

This Is only the Beginning

You should look at the process that we have discussed in this section merely as a starting point. It's important to realize that designing an object-oriented application is an iterative process. It may take you several attempts to identify all of the classes that you will need and determine all of their responsibilities. As the design process unfolds, you will gain a deeper understanding of the problem, and consequently you will see ways to improve the design.

Checkpoint

10.15 The typical UML diagram for a class has three sections. What appears in these three sections?

10.16 What is a problem domain?

10.17 When designing an object-oriented application, who should write a description of the problem domain?

10.18 How do you identify the potential classes in a problem domain description?

10.19 What are a class's responsibilities?

10.20 What two questions should you ask to determine a class's responsibilities?

10.21 Will all of a class's actions always be directly mentioned in the problem domain description?

Review Questions

Multiple Choice

1. The ______________ programming practice is centered on creating functions that are separate from the data that they work on.
   a. modular
   b. procedural
   c. functional
   d. object-oriented
2. The ______________ programming practice is centered on creating objects.
   a. object-centric
   b. objective
   c. procedural
   d. object-oriented

3. A(n) ______________ is a component of a class that references data.
   a. method
   b. instance
   c. data attribute
   d. module
4. An object is a(n) ______________.
   a. blueprint
   b. cookie cutter
   c. variable
   d. instance
5. By doing this, you can hide a class's attribute from code outside the class.
   a. avoid using the `self` parameter to create the attribute
   b. begin the attribute's name with two underscores
   c. begin the name of the attribute with `private__`
   d. begin the name of the attribute with the `@` symbol
6. A(n) ______________ method gets the value of a data attribute but does not change it.
   a. retriever
   b. constructor
   c. mutator
   d. accessor
7. A(n) ______________ method stores a value in a data attribute or changes its value in some other way.
   a. modifier
   b. constructor
   c. mutator
   d. accessor
8. The ______________ method is automatically called when an object is created.
   a. `__init__`
   b. `init`
   c. `__str__`
   d. `__object__`
9. If a class has a method named `__str__`, which of these is a way to call the method?
   a. you call it like any other method: *`object`*`.__str__()`
   b. by passing an instance of the class to the built in `str` function
   c. the method is automatically called when the object is created
   d. by passing an instance of the class to the built-in `state` function
10. A set of standard diagrams for graphically depicting object-oriented systems is provided by ______________.
    a. the Unified Modeling Language
    b. flowcharts
    c. pseudocode
    d. the Object Hierarchy System

11. In one approach to identifying the classes in a problem, the programmer identifies the _______________ in a description of the problem domain.
    a. verbs
    b. adjectives
    c. adverbs
    d. nouns
12. In one approach to identifying a class's data attributes and methods, the programmer identifies the class's _______________.
    a. responsibilities
    b. name
    c. synonyms
    d. nouns

True or False

1. The practice of procedural programming is centered on the creation of objects.
2. Object reusability has been a factor in the increased use of object-oriented programming.
3. It is a common practice in object-oriented programming to make all of a class's data attributes accessible to statements outside the class.
4. A class method does not have to have a `self` parameter.
5. Starting an attribute name with two underscores will hide the attribute from code outside the class.
6. You cannot directly call the `__str__` method.
7. One way to find the classes needed for an object-oriented program is to identify all of the verbs in a description of the problem domain.

Short Answer

1. What is encapsulation?
2. Why should an object's data attributes be hidden from code outside the class?
3. What is the difference between a class and an instance of a class?
4. The following statement calls an object's method. What is the name of the method? What is the name of the variable that references the object?

   ```
   wallet.get_dollar()
   ```
5. When the `__init__` method executes, what does the `self` parameter reference?
6. In a Python class, how do you hide an attribute from code outside the class?
7. How do you call the `__str__` method?

Algorithm Workbench

1. Suppose `my_car` is the name of a variable that references an object, and `go` is the name of a method. Write a statement that uses the `my_car` variable to call the `go` method. (You do not have to pass any arguments to the `go` method.)

2. Write a class definition named Book. The Book class should have data attributes for a book's title, the author's name, and the publisher's name. The class should also have the following:
   a. An __init__ method for the class. The method should accept an argument for each of the data attributes.
   b. Accessor and mutator methods for each data attribute.
   c. An __str__ method that returns a string indicating the state of the object.
3. Look at the following description of a problem domain:

   The bank offers the following types of accounts to its customers: savings accounts, checking accounts, and money market accounts. Customers are allowed to deposit money into an account (thereby increasing its balance), withdraw money from an account (thereby decreasing its balance), and earn interest on the account. Each account has an interest rate.

   Assume that you are writing a program that will calculate the amount of interest earned for a bank account.
   a. Identify the potential classes in this problem domain.
   b. Refine the list to include only the necessary class or classes for this problem.
   c. Identify the responsibilities of the class or classes.

Programming Exercises

1. Pet Class

VideoNote
The Pet class

Write a class named Pet, which should have the following data attributes:

- __name (for the name of a pet)
- __animal_type (for the type of animal that a pet is. Example values are 'Dog', 'Cat', and 'Bird')
- __age (for the pet's age)

The Pet class should have an __init__ method that creates these attributes. It should also have the following methods:

- set_name
  This method assigns a value to the __name field.
- set_animal_type
  This method assigns a value to the __animal_type field.
- set_age
  This method assigns a value to the __age field.
- get_name
  This method returns the value of the __ name field.
- get_animal_type
  This method returns the value of the __animal_type field.
- get_age
  This method returns the value of the __age field.

Once you have written the class, write a program that creates an object of the class and prompts the user to enter the name, type, and age of his or her pet. This data should be stored as the object's attributes. Use the object's accessor methods to retrieve the pet's name, type, and age and display this data on the screen.

2. `Car` Class

Write a class named `Car` that has the following data attributes:

- `__year_model` (for the car's year model)
- `__make` (for the make of the car)
- `__speed` (for the car's current speed)

The `Car` class should have an `__init__` method that accepts the car's year model and make as arguments. These values should be assigned to the object's `__year_model` and `__make` data attributes. It should also assign 0 to the `__speed` data attribute.

The class should also have the following methods:

- `accelerate`
  The `accelerate` method should add 5 to the speed data attribute each time it is called.
- `brake`
  The `brake` method should subtract 5 from the speed data attribute each time it is called.
- `get_speed`
  The `get_speed` method should return the current speed.

Next, design a program that creates a `Car` object then calls the `accelerate` method five times. After each call to the `accelerate` method, get the current speed of the car and display it. Then call the `brake` method five times. After each call to the `brake` method, get the current speed of the car and display it.

3. Personal `Information` Class

Design a class that holds the following personal data: name, address, age, and phone number. Write appropriate accessor and mutator methods. Also, write a program that creates three instances of the class. One instance should hold your information, and the other two should hold your friends' or family members' information.

4. `Employee` Class

Write a class named `Employee` that holds the following data about an employee in attributes: name, ID number, department, and job title.

Once you have written the class, write a program that creates three `Employee` objects to hold the following data:

Name	ID Number	Department	Job Title
Susan Meyers	47899	Accounting	Vice President
Mark Jones	39119	IT	Programmer
Joy Rogers	81774	Manufacturing	Engineer

The program should store this data in the three objects, then display the data for each employee on the screen.

5. RetailItem Class

Write a class named RetailItem that holds data about an item in a retail store. The class should store the following data in attributes: item description, units in inventory, and price.

Once you have written the class, write a program that creates three RetailItem objects and stores the following data in them:

	Description	Units in Inventory	Price
Item #1	Jacket	12	59.95
Item #2	Designer Jeans	40	34.95
Item #3	Shirt	20	24.95

6. Patient Charges

Write a class named Patient that has attributes for the following data:

- First name, middle name, and last name
- Address, city, state, and ZIP code
- Phone number
- Name and phone number of emergency contact

The Patient class's __init__ method should accept an argument for each attribute. The Patient class should also have accessor and mutator methods for each attribute.

Next, write a class named Procedure that represents a medical procedure that has been performed on a patient. The Procedure class should have attributes for the following data:

- Name of the procedure
- Date of the procedure
- Name of the practitioner who performed the procedure
- Charges for the procedure

The Procedure class's __init__ method should accept an argument for each attribute. The Procedure class should also have accessor and mutator methods for each attribute.

Next, write a program that creates an instance of the Patient class, initialized with sample data. Then, create three instances of the Procedure class, initialized with the following data:

Procedure #1:	Procedure #2:	Procedure #3:
Procedure name: Physical Exam	Procedure name: X-ray	Procedure name: Blood test
Date: Today's date	Date: Today's date	Date: Today's date
Practitioner: Dr. Irvine	Practitioner: Dr. Jamison	Practitioner: Dr. Smith
Charge: 250.00	Charge: 500.00	Charge: 200.00

The program should display the patient's information, information about all three of the procedures, and the total charges of the three procedures.

7. Employee Management System

This exercise assumes you have created the `Employee` class for Programming Exercise 4. Create a program that stores `Employee` objects in a dictionary. Use the employee ID number as the key. The program should present a menu that lets the user perform the following actions:

- Look up an employee in the dictionary
- Add a new employee to the dictionary
- Change an existing employee's name, department, and job title in the dictionary
- Delete an employee from the dictionary
- Quit the program

When the program ends, it should pickle the dictionary and save it to a file. Each time the program starts, it should try to load the pickled dictionary from the file. If the file does not exist, the program should start with an empty dictionary.

8. Cash Register

This exercise assumes you have created the `RetailItem` class for Programming Exercise 5. Create a `CashRegister` class that can be used with the `RetailItem` class. The `CashRegister` class should be able to internally keep a list of `RetailItem` objects. The class should have the following methods:

- A method named `purchase_item` that accepts a `RetailItem` object as an argument. Each time the `purchase_item` method is called, the `RetailItem` object that is passed as an argument should be added to the list.
- A method named `get_total` that returns the total price of all the `RetailItem` objects stored in the `CashRegister` object's internal list.
- A method named `show_items` that displays data about the `RetailItem` objects stored in the `CashRegister` object's internal list.
- A method named clear that should clear the `CashRegister` object's internal list.

Demonstrate the `CashRegister` class in a program that allows the user to select several items for purchase. When the user is ready to check out, the program should display a list of all the items he or she has selected for purchase, as well as the total price.

9. Trivia Game

In this programming exercise, you will create a simple trivia game for two players. The program will work like this:

- Starting with player 1, each player gets a turn at answering 5 trivia questions. (There should be a total of 10 questions.) When a question is displayed, 4 possible answers are also displayed. Only one of the answers is correct, and if the player selects the correct answer, he or she earns a point.
- After answers have been selected for all the questions, the program displays the number of points earned by each player and declares the player with the highest number of points the winner.

To create this program, write a `Question` class to hold the data for a trivia question. The `Question` class should have attributes for the following data:

- A trivia question
- Possible answer 1
- Possible answer 2
- Possible answer 3
- Possible answer 4
- The number of the correct answer (1, 2, 3, or 4)

The `Question` class also should have an appropriate `__init__` method, accessors, and mutators.

The program should have a list or a dictionary containing 10 `Question` objects, one for each trivia question. Make up your own trivia questions on the subject or subjects of your choice for the objects.

CHAPTER

11 Inheritance

TOPICS

11.1 Introduction to Inheritance

CONCEPT: Inheritance allows a new class to extend an existing class. The new class inherits the members of the class it extends.

Generalization and Specialization

In the real world, you can find many objects that are specialized versions of other more general objects. For example, the term "insect" describes a general type of creature with various characteristics. Because grasshoppers and bumblebees are insects, they have all the general characteristics of an insect. In addition, they have special characteristics of their own. For example, the grasshopper has its jumping ability, and the bumblebee has its stinger. Grasshoppers and bumblebees are specialized versions of an insect. This is illustrated in Figure 11-1.

Figure 11-1 Bumblebees and grasshoppers are specialized versions of an insect

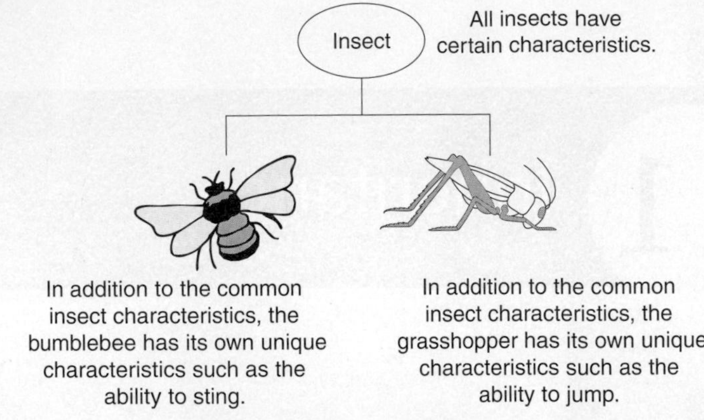

Inheritance and the "Is a" Relationship

When one object is a specialized version of another object, there is an "is a" relationship between them. For example, a grasshopper is an insect. Here are a few other examples of the "is a" relationship:

- A poodle is a dog.
- A car is a vehicle.
- A flower is a plant.
- A rectangle is a shape.
- A football player is an athlete.

When an "is a" relationship exists between objects, it means that the specialized object has all of the characteristics of the general object, plus additional characteristics that make it special. In object-oriented programming, inheritance is used to create an "is a" relationship among classes. This allows you to extend the capabilities of a class by creating another class that is a specialized version of it.

Inheritance involves a superclass and a subclass. The *superclass* is the general class and the *subclass* is the specialized class. You can think of the subclass as an extended version of the superclass. The subclass inherits attributes and methods from the superclass without any of them having to be rewritten. Furthermore, new attributes and methods may be added to the subclass, and that is what makes it a specialized version of the superclass.

NOTE: Superclasses are also called *base classes,* and subclasses are also called *derived classes.* Either set of terms is correct. For consistency, this text will use the terms superclass and subclass.

Let's look at an example of how inheritance can be used. Suppose we are developing a program that a car dealership can use to manage its inventory of used cars. The dealership's inventory includes three types of automobiles: cars, pickup trucks, and sport-utility vehicles (SUVs). Regardless of the type, the dealership keeps the following data about each automobile:

- Make
- Year model
- Mileage
- Price

Each type of vehicle that is kept in inventory has these general characteristics, plus its own specialized characteristics. For cars, the dealership keeps the following additional data:

- Number of doors (2 or 4)

For pickup trucks, the dealership keeps the following additional data:

- Drive type (two-wheel drive or four-wheel drive)

And for SUVs, the dealership keeps the following additional data:

- Passenger capacity

In designing this program, one approach would be to write the following three classes:

- A `Car` class with data attributes for the make, year model, mileage, price, and the number of doors.
- A `Truck` class with data attributes for the make, year model, mileage, price, and the drive type.
- An `SUV` class with data attributes for the make, year model, mileage, price, and the passenger capacity.

This would be an inefficient approach, however, because all three of the classes have a large number of common data attributes. As a result, the classes would contain a lot of duplicated code. In addition, if we discover later that we need to add more common attributes, we would have to modify all three classes.

A better approach would be to write an `Automobile` superclass to hold all the general data about an automobile, then write subclasses for each specific type of automobile. Program 11-1 shows the `Automobile` class's code, which appears in a module named `vehicles`.

Program 11-1 (Lines 1 through 44 of `vehicles.py`)

```
# The Automobile class holds general data
# about an automobile in inventory.

class Automobile:
    # The __init__method accepts arguments for the
    # make, model, mileage, and price. It initializes
    # the data attributes with these values.

    def __init__(self, make, model, mileage, price):
        self.__make = make
```

(program continues)

Program 11-1 *(continued)*

```
11          self.__model = model
12          self.__mileage = mileage
13          self.__price = price
14
15      # The following methods are mutators for the
16      # class's data attributes.
17
18      def set_make(self, make):
19          self.__make = make
20
21      def set_model(self, model):
22          self.__model = model
23
24      def set_mileage(self, mileage):
25          self.__mileage = mileage
26
27      def set_price(self, price):
28          self.__price = price
29
30      # The following methods are the accessors
31      # for the class's data attributes.
32
33      def get_make(self):
34          return self.__make
35
36      def get_model(self):
37          return self.__model
38
39      def get_mileage(self):
40          return self.__mileage
41
42      def get_price(self):
43          return self.__price
44
```

The `Automobile` class's `__init__` method accepts arguments for the vehicle's make, model, mileage, and price. It uses those values to initialize the following data attributes:

- `__make`
- `__model`
- `__mileage`
- `__price`

(Recall from Chapter 10 that a data attribute becomes hidden when its name begins with two underscores.) The methods that appear in lines 18 through 28 are mutators for each of the data attributes, and the methods in lines 33 through 43 are the accessors.

The Automobile class is a complete class from which we can create objects. If we wish, we can write a program that imports the vehicle module and creates instances of the Automobile class. However, the Automobile class holds only general data about an automobile. It does not hold any of the specific pieces of data that the dealership wants to keep about cars, pickup trucks, and SUVs. To hold data about those specific types of automobiles, we will write subclasses that inherit from the Automobile class. Program 11-2 shows the code for the Car class, which is also in the vehicles module.

Program 11-2 **(Lines 45 through 72 of vehicles.py)**

```
45 # The Car class represents a car. It is a subclass
46 # of the Automobile class.
47
48 class Car(Automobile):
49     # The __init__ method accepts arguments for the
50     # car's make, model, mileage, price, and doors.
51
52     def __init__(self, make, model, mileage, price, doors):
53         # Call the superclass's __init__ method and pass
54         # the required arguments. Note that we also have
55         # to pass self as an argument.
56         Automobile.__init__(self, make, model, mileage, price)
57
58         # Initialize the __doors attribute.
59         self.__doors = doors
60
61     # The set_doors method is the mutator for the
62     # __doors attribute.
63
64     def set_doors(self, doors):
65         self.__doors = doors
66
67     # The get_doors method is the accessor for the
68     # __doors attribute.
69
70     def get_doors(self):
71         return self.__doors
72
```

Take a closer look at the first line of the class declaration, in line 48:

```
class Car(Automobile):
```

This line indicates that we are defining a class named Car, and it inherits from the Automobile class. The Car class is the subclass, and the Automobile class is the superclass. If we want to express the relationship between the Car class and the Automobile class, we can say that a Car is an Automobile. Because the Car class extends the Automobile class, it inherits all of the methods and data attributes of the Automobile class.

Look at the header for the `__init__` method in line 52:

```
def __init__(self, make, model, mileage, price, doors):
```

Notice in addition to the required `self` parameter, the method has parameters named `make`, `model`, `mileage`, `price`, and `doors`. This makes sense because a `Car` object will have data attributes for the car's make, model, mileage, price, and number of doors. Some of these attributes are created by the `Automobile` class, however, so we need to call the `Automobile` class's `__init__` method and pass those values to it. That happens in line 56:

```
Automobile.__init__(self, make, model, mileage, price)
```

This statement calls the `Automobile` class's `__init__` method. Notice the statement passes the `self` variable, as well as the `make`, `model`, `mileage`, and `price` variables as arguments. When that method executes, it initializes the `__make`, `__model`, `__mileage`, and `__price` data attributes. Then, in line 59, the `__doors` attribute is initialized with the value passed into the `doors` parameter:

```
self.__doors = doors
```

The `set_doors` method, in lines 64 through 65, is the mutator for the `__doors` attribute, and the `get_doors` method, in lines 70 through 71, is the accessor for the `__doors` attribute. Before going any further, let's demonstrate the `Car` class, as shown in Program 11-3.

Program 11-3 (car_demo.py)

```
# This program demonstrates the Car class.

import vehicles

def main():
    # Create an object from the Car class.
    # The car is a 2007 Audi with 12,500 miles, priced
    # at $21,500.00, and has 4 doors.
    used_car = vehicles.Car('Audi', 2007, 12500, 21500.0, 4)

    # Display the car's data.
    print('Make:', used_car.get_make())
    print('Model:', used_car.get_model())
    print('Mileage:', used_car.get_mileage())
    print('Price:', used_car.get_price())
    print('Number of doors:', used_car.get_doors())

# Call the main function.
main()
```

Program Output

```
Make: Audi
Model: 2007
```

```
Mileage: 12500
Price: 21500.0
Number of doors: 4
```

Line 3 imports the `vehicles` module, which contains the class definitions for the `Automobile` and `Car` classes. Line 9 creates an instance of the `Car` class, passing `'Audi'` as the car's make, `2007` as the car's model, `12,500` as the mileage, `21,500.0` as the car's price, and 4 as the number of doors. The resulting object is assigned to the `used_car` variable.

The statements in lines 12 through 15 call the object's `get_make`, `get_model`, `get_mileage`, and `get_price` methods. Even though the `Car` class does not have any of these methods, it inherits them from the `Automobile` class. Line 16 calls the `get_doors` method, which is defined in the `Car` class.

Now let's look at the `Truck` class, which also inherits from the `Automobile` class. The code for the `Truck` class, which is also in the `vehicles` module, is shown in Program 11-4.

Program 11-4 **(Lines 73 through 100 of `vehicles.py`)**

```
# The Truck class represents a pickup truck. It is a
# subclass of the Automobile class.

class Truck(Automobile):
    # The __init__ method accepts arguments for the
    # Truck's make, model, mileage, price, and drive type.

    def __init__(self, make, model, mileage, price, drive_type):
        # Call the superclass's __init__ method and pass
        # the required arguments. Note that we also have
        # to pass self as an argument.
        Automobile.__init__(self, make, model, mileage, price)

        # Initialize the __drive_type attribute.
        self.__drive_type = drive_type

    # The set_drive_type method is the mutator for the
    # __drive_type attribute.

    def set_drive_type(self, drive_type):
        self.__drive = drive_type

    # The get_drive_type method is the accessor for the
    # __drive_type attribute.

    def get_drive_type(self):
        return self.__drive_type

```

The Truck class's __init__ method begins in line 80. Notice it takes arguments for the truck's make, model, mileage, price, and drive type. Just as the Car class did, the Truck class calls the Automobile class's __init__ method (in line 84) passing the make, model, mileage, and price as arguments. Line 87 creates the __drive_type attribute, initializing it to the value of the drive_type parameter.

The set_drive_type method in lines 92 through 93 is the mutator for the __drive_type attribute, and the get_drive_type method in lines 98 through 99 is the accessor for the attribute.

Now let's look at the SUV class, which also inherits from the Automobile class. The code for the SUV class, which is also in the vehicles module, is shown in Program 11-5.

Program 11-5 **(Lines 101 through 128 of vehicles.py)**

```
101 # The SUV class represents a sport utility vehicle. It
102 # is a subclass of the Automobile class.
103
104 class SUV(Automobile):
105     # The __init__ method accepts arguments for the
106     # SUV's make, model, mileage, price, and passenger
107     # capacity.
108
109     def __init__(self, make, model, mileage, price, pass_cap):
110         # Call the superclass's __init__ method and pass
111         # the required arguments. Note that we also have
112         # to pass self as an argument.
113         Automobile.__init__(self, make, model, mileage, price)
114
115         # Initialize the __pass_cap attribute.
116         self.__pass_cap = pass_cap
117
118     # The set_pass_cap method is the mutator for the
119     # __pass_cap attribute.
120
121     def set_pass_cap(self, pass_cap):
122         self.__pass_cap = pass_cap
123
124     # The get_pass_cap method is the accessor for the
125     # __pass_cap attribute.
126
127     def get_pass_cap(self):
128         return self.__pass_cap
```

The SUV class's __init__ method begins in line 109. It takes arguments for the vehicle's make, model, mileage, price, and passenger capacity. Just as the Car and Truck classes did, the SUV class calls the Automobile class's __init__ method (in line 113) passing the make, model, mileage, and price as arguments. Line 116 creates the `__pass_cap` attribute, initializing it to the value of the `pass_cap` parameter.

The `set_pass_cap` method in lines 121 through 122 is the mutator for the `__pass_cap` attribute, and the `get_pass_cap` method in lines 127 through 128 is the accessor for the attribute.

Program 11-6 demonstrates each of the classes we have discussed so far. It creates a `Car` object, a `Truck` object, and an `SUV` object.

Program 11-6 (car_truck_suv_demo.py)

```
# This program creates a Car object, a Truck object,
# and an SUV object.

import vehicles

def main():
    # Create a Car object for a used 2001 BMW
    # with 70,000 miles, priced at $15,000, with
    # 4 doors.
    car = vehicles.Car('BMW', 2001, 70000, 15000.0, 4)

    # Create a Truck object for a used 2002
    # Toyota pickup with 40,000 miles, priced
    # at $12,000, with 4-wheel drive.
    truck = vehicles.Truck('Toyota', 2002, 40000, 12000.0, '4WD')

    # Create an SUV object for a used 2000
    # Volvo with 30,000 miles, priced
    # at $18,500, with 5 passenger capacity.
    suv = vehicles.SUV('Volvo', 2000, 30000, 18500.0, 5)

    print('USED CAR INVENTORY')
    print('==================')

    # Display the car's data.
    print('The following car is in inventory:')
    print('Make:', car.get_make())
    print('Model:', car.get_model())
    print('Mileage:', car.get_mileage())
    print('Price:', car.get_price())
    print('Number of doors:', car.get_doors())
    print()

    # Display the truck's data.
    print('The following pickup truck is in inventory.')
```

(program continues)

Program 11-6 *(continued)*

```
    print('Make:', truck.get_make())
    print('Model:', truck.get_model())
    print('Mileage:', truck.get_mileage())
    print('Price:', truck.get_price())
    print('Drive type:', truck.get_drive_type())
    print()

    # Display the SUV's data.
    print('The following SUV is in inventory.')
    print('Make:', suv.get_make())
    print('Model:', suv.get_model())
    print('Mileage:', suv.get_mileage())
    print('Price:', suv.get_price())
    print('Passenger Capacity:', suv.get_pass_cap())

# Call the main function.
main()
```

Program Output

```
USED CAR INVENTORY
==================
The following car is in inventory:
Make: BMW
Model: 2001
Mileage: 70000
Price: 15000.0
Number of doors: 4

The following pickup truck is in inventory.
Make: Toyota
Model: 2002
Mileage: 40000
Price: 12000.0
Drive type: 4WD

The following SUV is in inventory.
Make: Volvo
Model: 2000
Mileage: 30000
Price: 18500.0
Passenger Capacity: 5
```

Inheritance in UML Diagrams

You show inheritance in a UML diagram by drawing a line with an open arrowhead from the subclass to the superclass. (The arrowhead points to the superclass.) Figure 11-2 is a UML diagram showing the relationship between the `Automobile`, `Car`, `Truck`, and `SUV` classes.

Figure 11-2 UML diagram showing inheritance

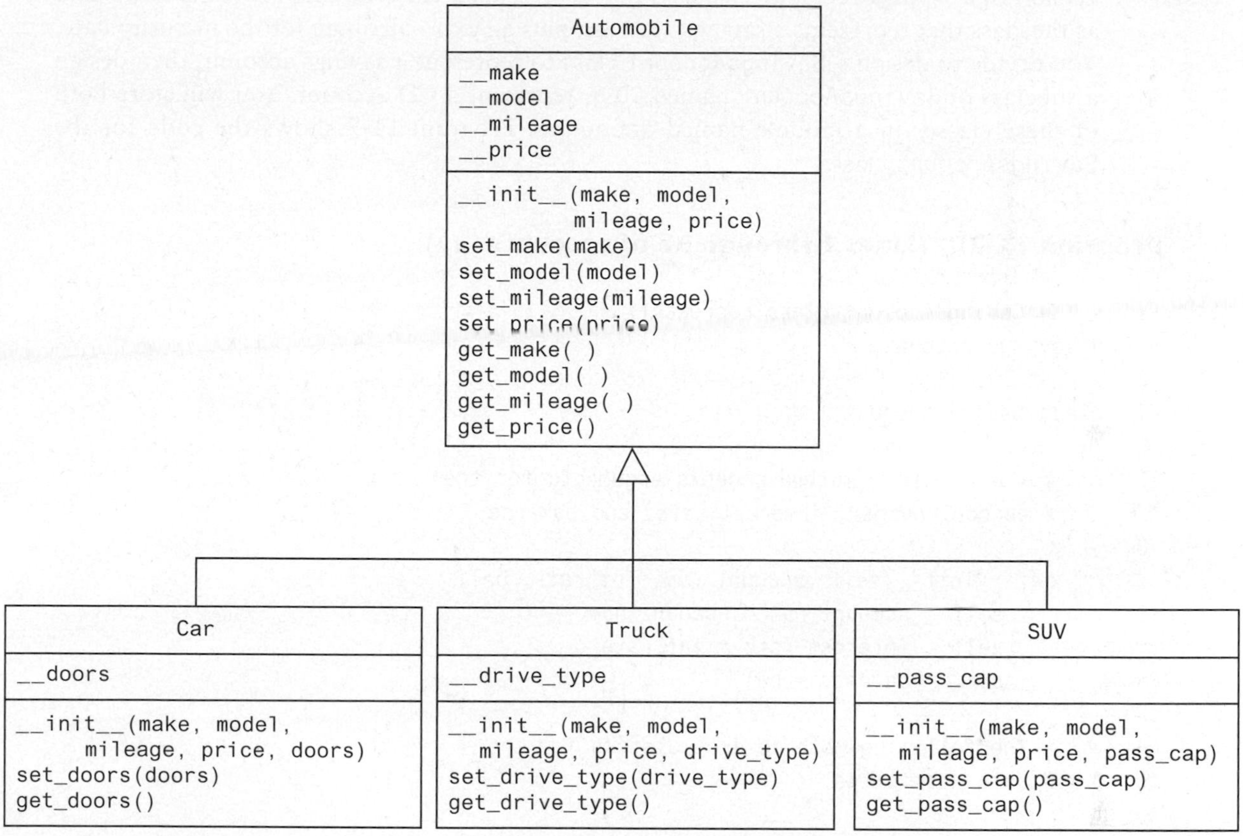

```
Automobile
---------------------------
__make
__model
__mileage
__price
---------------------------
__init__(make, model,
         mileage, price)
set_make(make)
set_model(model)
set_mileage(mileage)
set_price(price)
get_make( )
get_model( )
get_mileage( )
get_price()
```

(Car, Truck, and SUV each inherit from Automobile.)

```
Car
---------------------------
__doors
---------------------------
__init__(make, model,
    mileage, price, doors)
set_doors(doors)
get_doors()
```

```
Truck
---------------------------
__drive_type
---------------------------
__init__(make, model,
  mileage, price, drive_type)
set_drive_type(drive_type)
get_drive_type()
```

```
SUV
---------------------------
__pass_cap
---------------------------
__init__(make, model,
  mileage, price, pass_cap)
set_pass_cap(pass_cap)
get_pass_cap()
```

In the Spotlight:

Using Inheritance

Bank Financial Systems, Inc. develops financial software for banks and credit unions. The company is developing a new object-oriented system that manages customer accounts. One of your tasks is to develop a class that represents a savings account. The data that must be held by an object of this class is:

- The account number.
- The interest rate.
- The account balance.

You must also develop a class that represents a certificate of deposit (CD) account. The data that must be held by an object of this class is:

- The account number.
- The interest rate.
- The account balance.
- The account maturity date.

As you analyze these requirements, you realize that a CD account is really a specialized version of a savings account. The class that represents a CD will hold all of the same data as the class that represents a savings account, plus an extra attribute for the maturity date. You decide to design a `SavingsAccount` class to represent a savings account, then design a subclass of `SavingsAccount` named `CD` to represent a CD account. You will store both of these classes in a module named `accounts`. Program 11-7 shows the code for the `SavingsAccount` class.

Program 11-7 **(Lines 1 through 37 of `accounts.py`)**

```
# The SavingsAccount class represents a
# savings account.

class SavingsAccount:

    # The __init__ method accepts arguments for the
    # account number, interest rate, and balance.

    def __init__(self, account_num, int_rate, bal):
        self.__account_num = account_num
        self.__interest_rate = int_rate
        self.__balance = bal

    # The following methods are mutators for the
    # data attributes.

    def set_account_num(self, account_num):
        self.__account_num = account_num

    def set_interest_rate(self, int_rate):
        self.__interest_rate = int_rate

    def set_balance(self, bal):
        self.__balance = bal

    # The following methods are accessors for the
    # data attributes.

    def get_account_num(self):
        return self.__account_num

    def get_interest_rate(self):
        return self.__interest_rate

    def get_balance(self):
        return self.__balance

```

The class's `__init__` method appears in lines 9 through 12. The `__init__` method accepts arguments for the account number, interest rate, and balance. These arguments are used to initialize data attributes named `__account_num`, `__interest_rate`, and `__balance`.

The `set_account_num`, `set_interest_rate`, and `set_balance` methods that appear in lines 17 through 24 are mutators for the data attributes. The `get_account_num`, `get_interest_rate`, and `get_balance` methods that appear in lines 29 through 36 are accessors.

The `CD` class is shown in the next part of Program 11-7.

Program 11-7 (Lines 38 through 65 of `accounts.py`)

```
38  # The CD account represents a certificate of
39  # deposit (CD) account. It is a subclass of
40  # the SavingsAccount class.
41
42  class CD(SavingsAccount):
43
44      # The init method accepts arguments for the
45      # account number, interest rate, balance, and
46      # maturity date.
47
48      def __init__(self, account_num, int_rate, bal, mat_date):
49          # Call the superclass __init__ method.
50          SavingsAccount.__init__(self, account_num, int_rate, bal)
51
52          # Initialize the __maturity_date attribute.
53          self.__maturity_date = mat_date
54
55      # The set_maturity_date is a mutator for the
56      # __maturity_date attribute.
57
58      def set_maturity_date(self, mat_date):
59          self.__maturity_date = mat_date
60
61      # The get_maturity_date method is an accessor
62      # for the __maturity_date attribute.
63
64      def get_maturity_date(self):
65          return self.__maturity_date
```

The `CD` class's `__init__` method appears in lines 48 through 53. It accepts arguments for the account number, interest rate, balance, and maturity date. Line 50 calls the `SavingsAccount` class's `__init__` method, passing the arguments for the account number, interest rate, and balance. After the `SavingsAccount` class's `__init__` method executes, the `__account_num`, `__interest_rate`, and `__balance` attributes will be created and initialized. Then the statement in line 53 creates the `__maturity_date` attribute.

The `set_maturity_date` method in lines 58 through 59 is the mutator for the `__maturity_date` attribute, and the `get_maturity_date` method in lines 64 through 65 is the accessor.

To test the classes, we use the code shown in Program 11-8. This program creates an instance of the `SavingsAccount` class to represent a savings account, and an instance of the CD account to represent a certificate of deposit account.

Program 11-8 (account_demo.py)

```
# This program creates an instance of the SavingsAccount
# class and an instance of the CD account.

import accounts

def main():
    # Get the account number, interest rate,
    # and account balance for a savings account.
    print('Enter the following data for a savings account.')
    acct_num = input('Account number: ')
    int_rate = float(input('Interest rate: '))
    balance = float(input('Balance: '))

    # Create a SavingsAccount object.
    savings = accounts.SavingsAccount(acct_num, int_rate,
                                      balance)

    # Get the account number, interest rate,
    # account balance, and maturity date for a CD.
    print('Enter the following data for a CD.')
    acct_num = input('Account number: ')
    int_rate = float(input('Interest rate: '))
    balance = float(input('Balance: '))
    maturity = input('Maturity date: ')

    # Create a CD object.
    cd = accounts.CD(acct_num, int_rate, balance, maturity)

    # Display the data entered.
    print('Here is the data you entered:')
    print()
    print('Savings Account')
    print('---------------')
    print('Account number:', savings.get_account_num())
    print('Interest rate:', savings.get_interest_rate())
    print('Balance: $',
          format(savings.get_balance(), ',.2f'),
          sep='')
```

```
    print()
    print('CD')
    print('---------------')
    print('Account number:', cd.get_account_num())
    print('Interest rate:', cd.get_interest_rate())
    print('Balance: $',
          format(cd.get_balance(), ',.2f'),
          sep='')
    print('Maturity date:', cd.get_maturity_date())

# Call the main function.
main()
```

Program Output (with input shown in bold)

```
Enter the following data for a savings account.
Account number: 1234SA Enter
Interest rate: 3.5 Enter
Balance: 1000.00 Enter
Enter the following data for a CD.
Account number: 2345CD Enter
Interest rate: 5.6 Enter
Balance: 2500.00 Enter
Maturity date: 12/12/2019 Enter
Here is the data you entered:

Savings Account
---------------
Account number: 1234SA
Interest rate: 3.5
Balance: $1,000.00

CD
---------------
Account number: 2345CD
Interest rate: 5.6
Balance: $2,500.00
Maturity date: 12/12/2019
```

Checkpoint

11.1 In this section, we discussed superclasses and subclasses. Which is the general class, and which is the specialized class?

11.2 What does it mean to say there is an "is a" relationship between two objects?

11.3 What does a subclass inherit from its superclass?

11.4 Look at the following code, which is the first line of a class definition. What is the name of the superclass? What is the name of the subclass?

```
class Canary(Bird):
```

11.2 Polymorphism

CONCEPT: Polymorphism allows subclasses to have methods with the same names as methods in their superclasses. It gives the ability for a program to call the correct method depending on the type of object that is used to call it.

The term *polymorphism* refers to an object's ability to take different forms. It is a powerful feature of object-oriented programming. In this section, we will look at two essential ingredients of polymorphic behavior:

1. The ability to define a method in a superclass, then define a method with the same name in a subclass. When a subclass method has the same name as a superclass method, it is often said that the subclass method *overrides* the superclass method.
2. The ability to call the correct version of an overridden method, depending on the type of object that is used to call it. If a subclass object is used to call an overridden method, then the subclass's version of the method is the one that will execute. If a superclass object is used to call an overridden method, then the superclass's version of the method is the one that will execute.

Actually, you've already seen method overriding at work. Each subclass that we have examined in this chapter has a method named `__init__` that overrides the superclass's `__init__` method. When an instance of the subclass is created, it is the subclass's `__init__` method that automatically gets called.

Method overriding works for other class methods too. Perhaps the best way to describe polymorphism is to demonstrate it, so let's look at a simple example. Program 11-9 shows the code for a class named `Mammal`, which is in a module named `animals`.

Program 11-9 (Lines 1 through 22 of `animals.py`)

```
# The Mammal class represents a generic mammal.

class Mammal:

    # The __init__ method accepts an argument for
    # the mammal's species.

    def __init__(self, species):
        self.__species = species

    # The show_species method displays a message
    # indicating the mammal's species.

    def show_species(self):
        print('I am a', self.__species)

    # The make_sound method is the mammal's
    # way of making a generic sound.
```

```
    def make_sound(self):
        print('Grrrrr')
```

The Mammal class has three methods: __init__, show_species and make_sound. Here is an example of code that creates an instance of the class and calls these methods:

```
import animals
mammal = animals.Mammal('regular mammal')
mammal.show_species()
mammal.make_sound()
```

This code will display the following:

```
I am a regular mammal
Grrrrr
```

The next part of Program 11-9 shows the Dog class. The Dog class, which is also in the animals module, is a subclass of the Mammal class.

Program 11-9 (Lines 23 through 38 of animals.py)

```
# The Dog class is a subclass of the Mammal class.

class Dog(Mammal):

    # The __init__ method calls the superclass's
    # __init__ method passing 'Dog' as the species.

    def __init__(self):
        Mammal.__init__(self, 'Dog')

    # The make_sound method overrides the superclass's
    # make_sound method.

    def make_sound(self):
        print('Woof! Woof!')
```

Even though the Dog class inherits the __init__ and make_sound methods that are in the Mammal class, those methods are not adequate for the Dog class. So, the Dog class has its own __init__ and make_sound methods, which perform actions that are more appropriate for a dog. We say that the __init__ and make_sound methods in the Dog class override the __init__ and make_sound methods in the Mammal class. Here is an example of code that creates an instance of the Dog class and calls the methods:

```
import animals
dog = animals.Dog()
```

```
dog.show_species()
dog.make_sound()
```

This code will display the following:

```
I am a Dog
Woof! Woof!
```

When we use a Dog object to call the show_species and make_sound methods, the versions of these methods that are in the Dog class are the ones that execute. Next, look at Program 11-10, which shows the Cat class. The Cat class, which is also in the animals module, is another subclass of the Mammal class.

Program 11-9 (Lines 39 through 53 of animals.py)

```
# The Cat class is a subclass of the Mammal class.

class Cat(Mammal):

    # The __init__ method calls the superclass's
    # __init__ method passing 'Cat' as the species.

    def __init__(self):
        Mammal.__init__(self, 'Cat')

    # The make_sound method overrides the superclass's
    # make_sound method.

    def make_sound(self):
        print('Meow')
```

The Cat class also overrides the Mammal class's __init__ and make_sound methods. Here is an example of code that creates an instance of the Cat class and calls these methods:

```
import animals
cat = animals.Cat()
cat.show_species()
cat.make_sound()
```

This code will display the following:

```
I am a Cat
Meow
```

When we use a Cat object to call the show_species and make_sound methods, the versions of these methods that are in the Cat class are the ones that execute.

The `isinstance` Function

Polymorphism gives us a great deal of flexibility when designing programs. For example, look at the following function:

```
def show_mammal_info(creature):
    creature.show_species()
    creature.make_sound()
```

We can pass any object as an argument to this function, and as long as it has a `show_species` method and a `make_sound` method, the function will call those methods. In essence, we can pass any object that "is a" `Mammal` (or a subclass of `Mammal`) to the function. Program 11-10 demonstrates.

Program 11-10 **(polymorphism_demo.py)**

```
# This program demonstrates polymorphism.

import animals

def main():
    # Create a Mammal object, a Dog object, and
    # a Cat object.
    mammal = animals.Mammal('regular animal')
    dog = animals.Dog()
    cat = animals.Cat()

    # Display information about each one.
    print('Here are some animals and')
    print('the sounds they make.')
    print('--------------------------')
    show_mammal_info(mammal)
    print()
    show_mammal_info(dog)
    print()
    show_mammal_info(cat)

# The show_mammal_info function accepts an object
# as an argument, and calls its show_species
# and make_sound methods.

def show_mammal_info(creature):
    creature.show_species()
    creature.make_sound()

# Call the main function.
main()
```

(program output continues)

Program Output *(continued)*

```
Here are some animals and
the sounds they make.
--------------------------
I am a regular animal
Grrrrr
I am a Dog
Woof! Woof!
I am a Cat
Meow
```

But what happens if we pass an object that is not a `Mammal`, and not of a subclass of `Mammal` to the function? For example, what will happen when Program 11-11 runs?

Program 11-11 (wrong_type.py)

```
1  def main():
2      # Pass a string to show_mammal_info …
3      show_mammal_info('I am a string')
4
5  # The show_mammal_info function accepts an object
6  # as an argument, and calls its show_species
7  # and make_sound methods.
8
9  def show_mammal_info(creature):
10     creature.show_species()
11     creature.make_sound()
12
13 # Call the main function.
14 main()
```

In line 3, we call the `show_mammal_info` function passing a string as an argument. When the interpreter attempts to execute line 10, however, an `AttributeError` exception will be raised because strings do not have a method named `show_species`.

We can prevent this exception from occurring by using the built-in function `isinstance`. You can use the `isinstance` function to determine whether an object is an instance of a specific class, or a subclass of that class. Here is the general format of the function call:

```
isinstance(object, ClassName)
```

In the general format, *`object`* is a reference to an object, and *`ClassName`* is the name of a class. If the object referenced by `object` is an instance of *`ClassName`* or is an instance of a subclass of *`ClassName`*, the function returns true. Otherwise, it returns false. Program 11-12 shows how we can use it in the `show_mammal_info` function.

Program 11-12 (polymorphism_demo2.py)

```
# This program demonstrates polymorphism.

import animals

def main():
    # Create an Mammal object, a Dog object, and
    # a Cat object.
    mammal = animals.Mammal('regular animal')
    dog = animals.Dog()
    cat = animals.Cat()

    # Display information about each one.
    print('Here are some animals and')
    print('the sounds they make.')
    print('-------------------------')
    show_mammal_info(mammal)
    print()
    show_mammal_info(dog)
    print()
    show_mammal_info(cat)
    print()
    show_mammal_info('I am a string')

# The show_mammal_info function accepts an object
# as an argument and calls its show_species
# and make_sound methods.

def show_mammal_info(creature):
    if isinstance(creature, animals.Mammal):
        creature.show_species()
        creature.make_sound()
    else:
        print('That is not a Mammal!')

# Call the main function.
main()
```

Program Output

```
Here are some animals and
the sounds they make.
-------------------------
I am a regular animal
Grrrrr
```

(program output continues)

Program Output *(continued)*

```
I am a Dog
Woof! Woof!
I am a Cat
Meow
That is not a Mammal!
```

In lines 16, 18, and 20 we call the `show_mammal_info` function, passing references to a `Mammal` object, a `Dog` object, and a `Cat` object. In line 22, however, we call the function and pass a string as an argument. Inside the `show_mammal_info` function, the `if` statement in line 29 calls the `isinstance` function to determine whether the argument is an instance of `Mammal` (or a subclass). If it is not, an error message is displayed.

Checkpoint

11.5 Look at the following class definitions:

```
class Vegetable:
    def __init__(self, vegtype):
        self.__vegtype = vegtype
    def message(self):
        print("I'm a vegetable.")
class Potato(Vegetable):
    def __init__(self):
        Vegetable.__init__(self, 'potato')
    def message(self):
        print("I'm a potato.")
```

Given these class definitions, what will the following statements display?

```
v = Vegetable('veggie')
p = Potato()
v.message()
p.message()
```

Review Questions

Multiple Choice

1. In an inheritance relationship, the __________ is the general class.
   a. subclass
   b. superclass
   c. slave class
   d. child class

2. In an inheritance relationship, the __________ is the specialized class.
   a. superclass
   b. master class
   c. subclass
   d. parent class
3. Suppose a program uses two classes: `Airplane` and `JumboJet`. Which of these would most likely be the subclass?
   a. `Airplane`
   b. `JumboJet`
   c. Both
   d. Neither
4. This characteristic of object-oriented programming allows the correct version of an overridden method to be called when an instance of a subclass is used to call it.
   a. polymorphism
   b. inheritance
   c. generalization
   d. specialization
5. You can use this to determine whether an object is an instance of a class.
   a. the `in` operator
   b. the `is_object_of` function
   c. the `isinstance` function
   d. the error messages that are displayed when a program crashes

True or False

1. Polymorphism allows you to write methods in a subclass that have the same name as methods in the superclass.
2. It is not possible to call a superclass's `__init__` method from a subclass's `__init__` method.
3. A subclass can have a method with the same name as a method in the superclass.
4. Only the `__init__` method can be overridden.
5. You cannot use the `isinstance` function to determine whether an object is an instance of a subclass of a class.

Short Answer

1. What does a subclass inherit from its superclass?
2. Look at the following class definition. What is the name of the superclass? What is the name of the subclass?

   ```
   class Tiger(Felis):
   ```
3. What is an overridden method?

Algorithm Workbench

1. Write the first line of the definition for a `Poodle` class. The class should extend the `Dog` class.

2. Look at the following class definitions:

```
class Plant:
    def __init__(self, plant_type):
        self.__plant_type = plant_type
    def message(self):
        print("I'm a plant.")
class Tree(Plant):
    def __init__(self):
        Plant.__init__(self, 'tree')
    def message(self):
        print("I'm a tree.")
```

Given these class definitions, what will the following statements display?

```
p = Plant('sapling')
t = Tree()
p.message()
t.message()
```

3. Look at the following class definition:

```
class Beverage:
    def __init__(self, bev_name):
        self.__bev_name = bev_name
```

Write the code for a class named `Cola` that is a subclass of the `Beverage` class. The `Cola` class's `__init__` method should call the `Beverage` class's `__init__` method, passing 'cola' as an argument.

Programming Exercises

1. `Employee` and `ProductionWorker` Classes

Write an `Employee` class that keeps data attributes for the following pieces of information:

- Employee name
- Employee number

Next, write a class named `ProductionWorker` that is a subclass of the `Employee` class. The `ProductionWorker` class should keep data attributes for the following information:

- Shift number (an integer, such as 1, 2, or 3)
- Hourly pay rate

The workday is divided into two shifts: day and night. The shift attribute will hold an integer value representing the shift that the employee works. The day shift is shift 1 and the night shift is shift 2. Write the appropriate accessor and mutator methods for each class.

Once you have written the classes, write a program that creates an object of the `ProductionWorker` class and prompts the user to enter data for each of the object's data attributes. Store the data in the object, then use the object's accessor methods to retrieve it and display it on the screen.

2. `ShiftSupervisor` Class

In a particular factory, a shift supervisor is a salaried employee who supervises a shift. In addition to a salary, the shift supervisor earns a yearly bonus when his or her shift meets production goals. Write a `ShiftSupervisor` class that is a subclass of the `Employee` class you created in Programming Exercise 1. The `ShiftSupervisor` class should keep a data attribute for the annual salary, and a data attribute for the annual production bonus that a shift supervisor has earned. Demonstrate the class by writing a program that uses a `ShiftSupervisor` object.

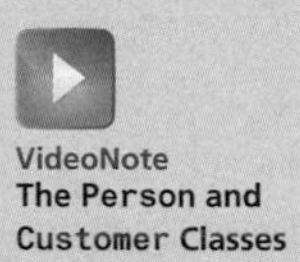
VideoNote
The Person and Customer Classes

3. `Person` and `Customer` Classes

Write a class named `Person` with data attributes for a person's name, address, and telephone number. Next, write a class named `Customer` that is a subclass of the `Person` class. The `Customer` class should have a data attribute for a customer number, and a Boolean data attribute indicating whether the customer wishes to be on a mailing list. Demonstrate an instance of the `Customer` class in a simple program.

CHAPTER

12 Recursion

TOPICS

12.1 Introduction to Recursion

CONCEPT: A recursive function is a function that calls itself.

You have seen instances of functions calling other functions. In a program, the `main` function might call function `A`, which then might call function `B`. It's also possible for a function to call itself. A function that calls itself is known as a *recursive function*. For example, look at the `message` function shown in Program 12-1.

Program 12-1 (endless_recursion.py)

```
# This program has a recursive function.

def main():
    message()

def message():
    print('This is a recursive function.')
    message()

# Call the main function.
main()
```

(program output continues)

Program Output *(continued)*

```
This is a recursive function.
This is a recursive function.
This is a recursive function.
This is a recursive function.
```

. . . and this output repeats forever!

The message function displays the string 'This is a recursive function' and then calls itself. Each time it calls itself, the cycle is repeated. Can you see a problem with the function? There's no way to stop the recursive calls. This function is like an infinite loop because there is no code to stop it from repeating. If you run this program, you will have to press Ctrl+C on the keyboard to interrupt its execution.

Like a loop, a recursive function must have some way to control the number of times it repeats. The code in Program 12-2 shows a modified version of the message function. In this program, the message function receives an argument that specifies the number of times the function should display the message.

Program 12-2 **(recursive.py)**

```
1  # This program has a recursive function.
2
3  def main():
4      # By passing the argument 5 to the message
5      # function we are telling it to display the
6      # message five times.
7      message(5)
8
9  def message(times):
10     if times > 0:
11         print('This is a recursive function.')
12         message(times - 1)
13
14 # Call the main function.
15 main()
```

Program Output

```
This is a recursive function.
This is a recursive function.
This is a recursive function.
This is a recursive function.
This is a recursive function.
```

The message function in this program contains an if statement in line 10 that controls the repetition. As long as the times parameter is greater than zero, the message 'This is a recursive function' is displayed, and then the function calls itself again, but with a smaller argument.

In line 7 the `main` function calls the `message` function passing the argument 5. The first time the function is called the `if` statement displays the message and then calls itself with 4 as the argument. Figure 12-1 illustrates this.

Figure 12-1 First two calls of the function

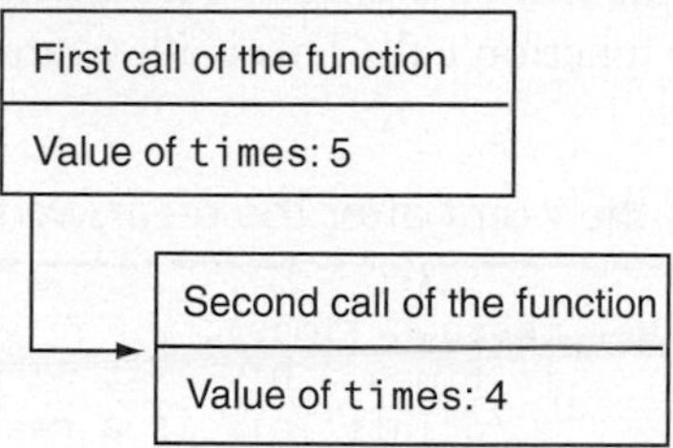

The diagram shown in Figure 12-1 illustrates two separate calls of the `message` function. Each time the function is called, a new instance of the `times` parameter is created in memory. The first time the function is called, the `times` parameter is set to 5. When the function calls itself, a new instance of the `times` parameter is created, and the value 4 is passed into it. This cycle repeats until finally, zero is passed as an argument to the function. This is illustrated in Figure 12-2.

Figure 12-2 Six calls to the `message` function

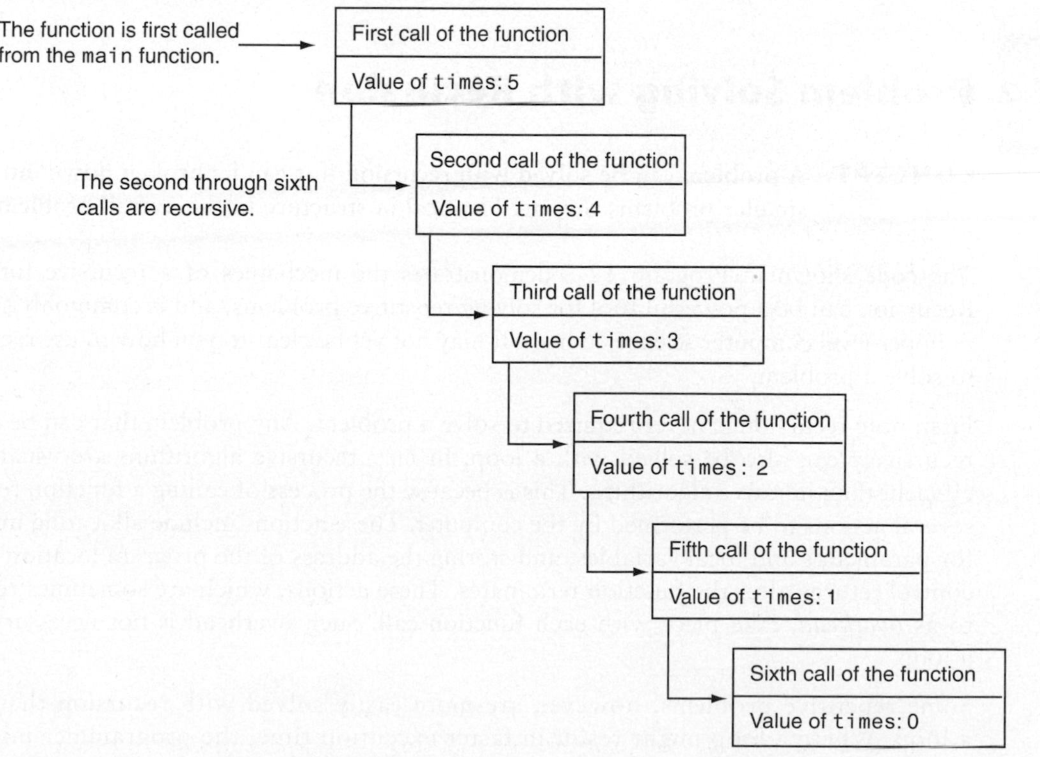

As you can see in the figure, the function is called six times. The first time it is called from the `main` function, and the other five times it calls itself. The number of times that a function calls itself is known as the *depth of recursion*. In this example, the depth of recursion is five. When the function reaches its sixth call, the `times` parameter is set to 0. At that point, the `if` statement's conditional expression is false, so the function returns. Control of the program returns from the sixth instance of the function to the point in the fifth instance directly after the recursive function call. This is illustrated in Figure 12-3.

Figure 12-3 Control returns to the point after the recursive function call

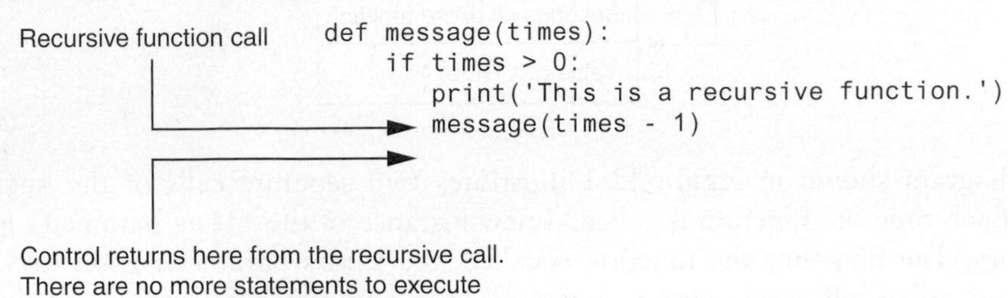

Because there are no more statements to be executed after the function call, the fifth instance of the function returns control of the program back to the fourth instance. This repeats until all instances of the function return.

12.2 Problem Solving with Recursion

CONCEPT: A problem can be solved with recursion if it can be broken down into smaller problems that are identical in structure to the overall problem.

The code shown in Program 12-2 demonstrates the mechanics of a recursive function. Recursion can be a powerful tool for solving repetitive problems, and is commonly studied in upper-level computer science courses. It may not yet be clear to you how to use recursion to solve a problem.

First, note recursion is never required to solve a problem. Any problem that can be solved recursively can also be solved with a loop. In fact, recursive algorithms are usually less efficient than iterative algorithms. This is because the process of calling a function requires several actions to be performed by the computer. These actions include allocating memory for parameters and local variables, and storing the address of the program location where control returns after the function terminates. These actions, which are sometimes referred to as *overhead*, take place with each function call. Such overhead is not necessary with a loop.

Some repetitive problems, however, are more easily solved with recursion than with a loop. Where a loop might result in faster execution time, the programmer might be able to design a recursive algorithm faster. In general, a recursive function works as follows:

- If the problem can be solved now, without recursion, then the function solves it and returns
- If the problem cannot be solved now, then the function reduces it to a smaller but similar problem and calls itself to solve the smaller problem

In order to apply this approach, first, we identify at least one case in which the problem can be solved without recursion. This is known as the *base case*. Second, we determine a way to solve the problem in all other circumstances using recursion. This is called the *recursive case*. In the recursive case, we must always reduce the problem to a smaller version of the original problem. By reducing the problem with each recursive call, the base case will eventually be reached and the recursion will stop.

Using Recursion to Calculate the Factorial of a Number

Let's take an example from mathematics to examine an application of recursive functions. In mathematics, the notation $n!$ represents the factorial of the number n. The factorial of a nonnegative number can be defined by the following rules:

If $n = 0$ then $\quad n! = 1$
If $n > 0$ then $\quad n! = 1 \times 2 \times 3 \times \ldots \times n$

Let's replace the notation $n!$ with factorial(n), which looks a bit more like computer code, and rewrite these rules as follows:

If $n = 0$ then $\quad \text{factorial}(n) = 1$
If $n > 0$ then $\quad \text{factorial}(n) = 1 \times 2 \times 3 \times \ldots \times n$

These rules state that when n is 0, its factorial is 1. When n is greater than 0, its factorial is the product of all the positive integers from 1 up to n. For instance, factorial(6) is calculated as $1 \times 2 \times 3 \times 4 \times 5 \times 6$.

When designing a recursive algorithm to calculate the factorial of any number, first we identify the base case, which is the part of the calculation that we can solve without recursion. That is the case where n is equal to 0 as follows:

If $n = 0$ then $\quad \text{factorial}(n) = 1$

This tells us how to solve the problem when n is equal to 0, but what do we do when n is greater than 0? That is the recursive case, or the part of the problem that we use recursion to solve. This is how we express it:

If $n > 0$ then $\quad \text{factorial}(n) = n \times \text{factorial}(n - 1)$

This states that if n is greater than 0, the factorial of n is n times the factorial of $n - 1$. Notice how the recursive call works on a reduced version of the problem, $n - 1$. So, our recursive rule for calculating the factorial of a number might look like this:

If $n = 0$ then $\quad \text{factorial}(n) = 1$
If $n > 0$ then $\quad \text{factorial}(n) = n \times \text{factorial}(n - 1)$

The code in Program 12-3 shows how we might design a factorial function in a program.

Program 12-3

```
# This program uses recursion to calculate
# the factorial of a number.

def main():
    # Get a number from the user.
    number = int(input('Enter a nonnegative integer: '))

    # Get the factorial of the number.
    fact = factorial(number)

    # Display the factorial.
    print('The factorial of', number, 'is', fact)

# The factorial function uses recursion to
# calculate the factorial of its argument,
# which is assumed to be nonnegative.
def factorial(num):
    if num == 0:
        return 1
    else:
        return num * factorial(num - 1)

# Call the main function.
main()
```

Program Output (with input shown in bold)

```
Enter a nonnegative integer: 4 [Enter]
The factorial of 4 is 24
```

In the sample run of the program, the `factorial` function is called with the argument 4 passed to `num`. Because `num` is not equal to 0, the `if` statement's `else` clause executes the following statement:

```
return num * factorial(num - 1)
```

Although this is a `return` statement, it does not immediately return. Before the return value can be determined, the value of `factorial(num - 1)` must be determined. The `factorial` function is called recursively until the fifth call, in which the `num` parameter will be set to zero. Figure 12-4 illustrates the value of `num` and the return value during each call of the function.

Figure 12-4 The value of num and the return value during each call of the function

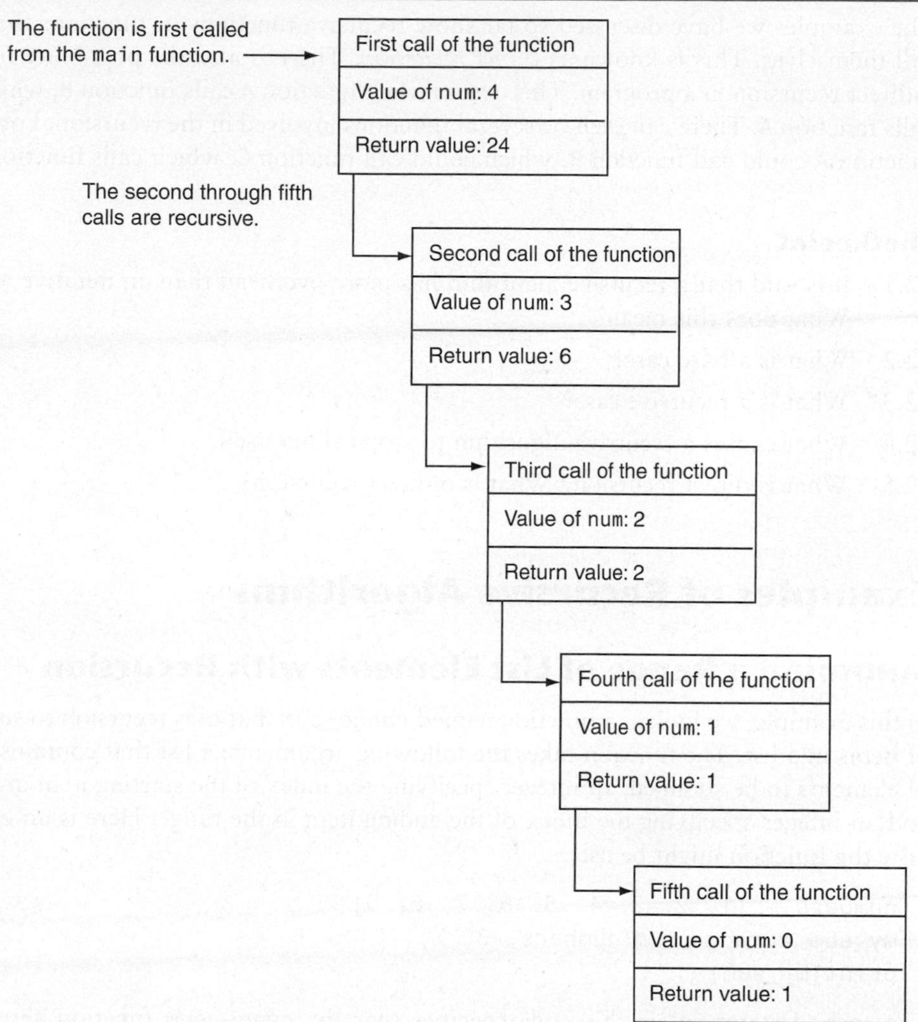

The figure illustrates why a recursive algorithm must reduce the problem with each recursive call. Eventually, the recursion has to stop in order for a solution to be reached.

If each recursive call works on a smaller version of the problem, then the recursive calls work toward the base case. The base case does not require recursion, so it stops the chain of recursive calls.

Usually, a problem is reduced by making the value of one or more parameters smaller with each recursive call. In our `factorial` function, the value of the parameter num gets closer to 0 with each recursive call. When the parameter reaches 0, the function returns a value without making another recursive call.

Direct and Indirect Recursion

The examples we have discussed so far show recursive functions or functions that directly call themselves. This is known as *direct recursion*. There is also the possibility of creating indirect recursion in a program. This occurs when function `A` calls function `B`, which in turn calls function `A`. There can even be several functions involved in the recursion. For example, function `A` could call function `B`, which could call function `C`, which calls function `A`.

Checkpoint

12.1 It is said that a recursive algorithm has more overhead than an iterative algorithm. What does this mean?

12.2 What is a base case?

12.3 What is a recursive case?

12.4 What causes a recursive algorithm to stop calling itself?

12.5 What is direct recursion? What is indirect recursion?

12.3 Examples of Recursive Algorithms

Summing a Range of List Elements with Recursion

In this example, we look at a function named `range_sum` that uses recursion to sum a range of items in a list. The function takes the following arguments: a list that contains the range of elements to be summed, an integer specifying the index of the starting item in the range, and an integer specifying the index of the ending item in the range. Here is an example of how the function might be used:

```
numbers = [1, 2, 3, 4, 5, 6, 7, 8, 9]
my_sum = range_sum(numbers, 3, 7)
print(my_sum)
```

The second statement in this code specifies that the `range_sum` function should return the sum of the items at indexes 3 through 7 in the `numbers` list. The return value, which in this case would be 30, is assigned to the `my_sum` variable. Here is the definition of the `range_sum` function:

```
def range_sum(num_list, start, end):
    if start > end:
        return 0
    else:
        return num_list[start] + range_sum(num_list, start + 1, end)
```

This function's base case is when the `start` parameter is greater than the `end` parameter. If this is true, the function returns the value 0. Otherwise, the function executes the following statement:

```
return num_list[start] + range_sum(num_list, start + 1, end)
```

This statement returns the sum of `num_list[start]` plus the return value of a recursive call. Notice in the recursive call, the starting item in the range is `start + 1`. In essence, this statement says "return the value of the first item in the range plus the sum of the rest of the items in the range." Program 12-4 demonstrates the function.

Program 12-4

```
# This program demonstrates the range_sum function.

def main():
    # Create a list of numbers.
    numbers = [1, 2, 3, 4, 5, 6, 7, 8, 9]

    # Get the sum of the items at indexes 2
    # through 5.
    my_sum = range_sum(numbers, 2, 5)

    # Display the sum.
    print('The sum of items 2 through 5 is', my_sum)

# The range_sum function returns the sum of a specified
# range of items in num_list. The start parameter
# specifies the index of the starting item. The end
# parameter specifies the index of the ending item.
def range_sum(num_list, start, end):
    if start > end:
        return 0
    else:
        return num_list[start] + range_sum(num_list, start + 1, end)

# Call the main function.
main()
```

Program Output

```
The sum of elements 2 through 5 is 18
```

The Fibonacci Series

Some mathematical problems are designed to be solved recursively. One well-known example is the calculation of Fibonacci numbers. The Fibonacci numbers, named after the Italian mathematician Leonardo Fibonacci (born circa 1170), are the following sequence:

0, 1, 1, 2, 3, 5, 8, 13, 21, 34, 55, 89, 144, 233, . . .

Notice after the second number, each number in the series is the sum of the two previous numbers. The Fibonacci series can be defined as follows:

If $n = 0$ then $\text{Fib}(n) = 0$
If $n = 1$ then $\text{Fib}(n) = 1$
If $n > 1$ then $\text{Fib}(n) = \text{Fib}(n - 1) + \text{Fib}(n - 2)$

A recursive function to calculate the *n*th number in the Fibonacci series is shown here:

```
def fib(n):
    if n == 0:
        return 0
    elif n == 1:
        return 1
    else:
        return fib(n - 1) + fib(n - 2)
```

Notice this function actually has two base cases: when *n* is equal to 0, and when *n* is equal to 1. In either case, the function returns a value without making a recursive call. The code in Program 12-5 demonstrates this function by displaying the first 10 numbers in the Fibonacci series.

Program 12-5 **(fibonacci.py)**

```
# This program uses recursion to print numbers
# from the Fibonacci series.

def main():
    print('The first 10 numbers in the')
    print('Fibonacci series are:')

    for number in range(1, 11):
        print(fib(number))

# The fib function returns the nth number
# in the Fibonacci series.
def fib(n):
    if n == 0:
        return 0
    elif n == 1:
        return 1
    else:
        return fib(n - 1) + fib(n - 2)

# Call the main function.
main()
```

Program Output

```
The first 10 numbers in the
Fibonacci series are:
1
```

```
1
2
3
5
8
13
21
34
55
```

Finding the Greatest Common Divisor

Our next example of recursion is the calculation of the greatest common divisor (GCD) of two numbers. The GCD of two positive integers x and y is determined as follows:

> If x can be evenly divided by y, then $\text{gcd}(x, y) = y$
> Otherwise, $\text{gcd}(x, y) = \text{gcd}(y, \text{remainder of } x/y)$

This definition states that the GCD of x and y is y if x/y has no remainder. This is the base case. Otherwise, the answer is the GCD of y and the remainder of x/y. The code in Program 12-6 shows a recursive method for calculating the GCD.

Program 12-6 (gcd.py)

```
# This program uses recursion to find the GCD
# of two numbers.

def main():
    # Get two numbers.
    num1 = int(input('Enter an integer: '))
    num2 = int(input('Enter another integer: '))

    # Display the GCD.
    print('The greatest common divisor of')
    print('the two numbers is', gcd(num1, num2))

# The gcd function returns the greatest common
# divisor of two numbers.
def gcd(x, y):
    if x % y == 0:
        return y
    else:
        return gcd(x, x % y)

# Call the main function.
main()
```

(program output continues)

Program Output (with input shown in bold)

```
Enter an integer: 49 [Enter]
Enter another integer: 28 [Enter]
The greatest common divisor of
these two numbers is 7
```

The Towers of Hanoi

The Towers of Hanoi is a mathematical game that is often used in computer science to illustrate the power of recursion. The game uses three pegs and a set of discs with holes through their centers. The discs are stacked on one of the pegs as shown in Figure 12-5.

Figure 12-5 The pegs and discs in the Tower of Hanoi game

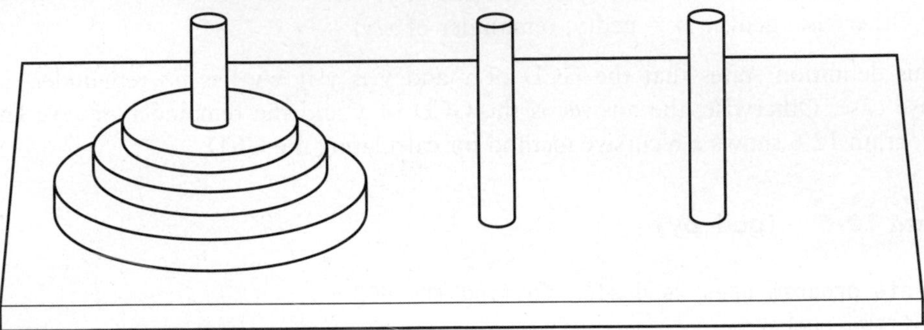

Notice the discs are stacked on the leftmost peg, in order of size with the largest disc at the bottom. The game is based on a legend where a group of monks in a temple in Hanoi have a similar set of pegs with 64 discs. The job of the monks is to move the discs from the first peg to the third peg. The middle peg can be used as a temporary holder. Furthermore, the monks must follow these rules while moving the discs:

- Only one disk may be moved at a time
- A disk cannot be placed on top of a smaller disc
- All discs must be stored on a peg except while being moved

According to the legend, when the monks have moved all of the discs from the first peg to the last peg, the world will come to an end.[1]

To play the game, you must move all of the discs from the first peg to the third peg, following the same rules as the monks. Let's look at some example solutions to this game, for different numbers of discs. If you only have one disc, the solution to the game is

[1]In case you're worried about the monks finishing their job and causing the world to end anytime soon, you can relax. If the monks move the discs at a rate of 1 per second, it will take them approximately 585 billion years to move all 64 discs!

simple: move the disc from peg 1 to peg 3. If you have two discs, the solution requires three moves:

- Move disc 1 to peg 2
- Move disc 2 to peg 3
- Move disc 1 to peg 3

Notice this approach uses peg 2 as a temporary location. The complexity of the moves continues to increase as the number of discs increases. To move three discs requires the seven moves shown in Figure 12-6.

Figure 12-6 Steps for moving three pegs

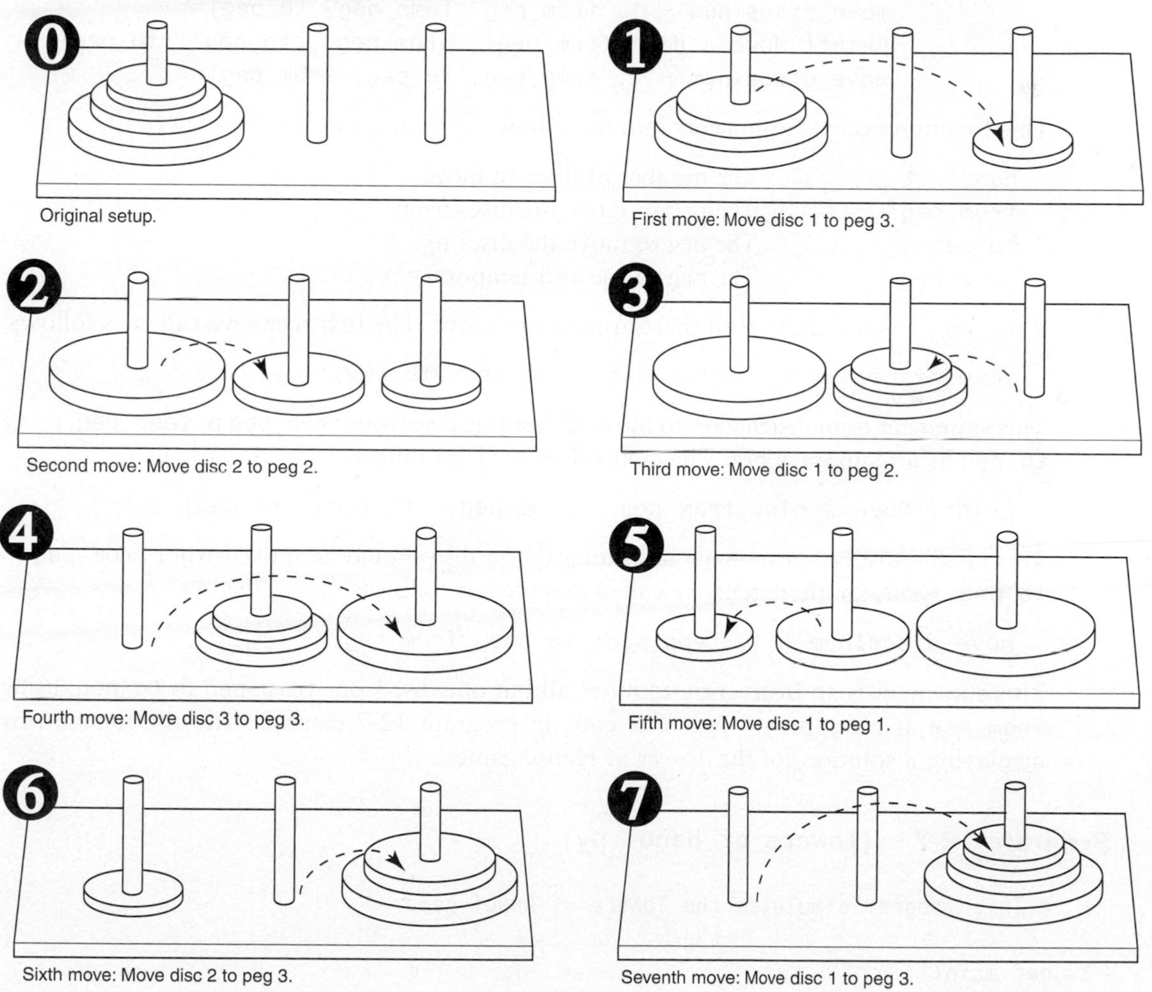

The following statement describes the overall solution to the problem:

Move n discs from peg 1 to peg 3 using peg 2 as a temporary peg.

The following summary describes a recursive algorithm that simulates the solution to the game. Notice in this algorithm, we use the variables A, B, and C to hold peg numbers.

To move n discs from peg A to peg C, using peg B as a temporary peg, do the following:
If n > 0:
Move n − 1 discs from peg A to peg B, using peg C as a temporary peg.
Move the remaining disc from peg A to peg C.
Move n − 1 discs from peg B to peg C, using peg A as a temporary peg.

The base case for the algorithm is reached when there are no more discs to move. The following code is for a function that implements this algorithm. Note the function does not actually move anything, but displays instructions indicating all of the disc moves to make.

```
def move_discs(num, from_peg, to_peg, temp_peg):
    if num > 0:
        move_discs(num - 1, from_peg, temp_peg, to_peg)
        print('Move a disc from peg', from_peg, 'to peg', to_peg)
        move_discs(num - 1, temp_peg, to_peg, from_peg)
```

This function accepts arguments into the following parameters:

num	The number of discs to move.
from_peg	The peg to move the discs from.
to_peg	The peg to move the discs to.
temp_peg	The peg to use as a temporary peg.

If num is greater than 0, then there are discs to move. The first recursive call is as follows:

```
move_discs(num - 1, from_peg, temp_peg, to_peg)
```

This statement is an instruction to move all but one disc from `from_peg` to `temp_peg`, using `to_peg` as a temporary peg. The next statement is as follows:

```
print('Move a disc from peg', from_peg, 'to peg', to_peg)
```

This simply displays a message indicating that a disc should be moved from `from_peg` to `to_peg`. Next, another recursive call is executed as follows:

```
move-discs(num - 1, temp_peg, to_peg, from_peg)
```

This statement is an instruction to move all but one disc from `temp_peg` to `to_peg`, using `from_peg` as a temporary peg. The code in Program 12-7 demonstrates the function by displaying a solution for the Tower of Hanoi game.

Program 12-7 **(towers_of_hanoi.py)**

```
# This program simulates the Towers of Hanoi game.

def main():
    # Set up some initial values.
    num_discs = 3
    from_peg = 1
    to_peg = 3
    temp_peg = 2
```

```

    # Play the game.
    move_discs(num_discs, from_peg, to_peg, temp_peg)
    print('All the pegs are moved!')

# The moveDiscs function displays a disc move in
# the Towers of Hanoi game.
# The parameters are:
#    num:        The number of discs to move.
#    from_peg:   The peg to move from.
#    to_peg:     The peg to move to.
#    temp_peg:   The temporary peg.
def move_discs(num, from_peg, to_peg, temp_peg):
    if num > 0:
        move_discs(num - 1, from_peg, temp_peg, to_peg)
        print('Move a disc from peg', from_peg, 'to peg', to_peg)
        move_discs(num - 1, temp_peg, to_peg, from_peg)

# Call the main function.
main()
```

Program Output

```
Move a disc from peg 1 to peg 3
Move a disc from peg 1 to peg 2
Move a disc from peg 3 to peg 2
Move a disc from peg 1 to peg 3
Move a disc from peg 2 to peg 1
Move a disc from peg 2 to peg 3
Move a disc from peg 1 to peg 3
All the pegs are moved!
```

Recursion versus Looping

Any algorithm that can be coded with recursion can also be coded with a loop. Both approaches achieve repetition, but which is best to use?

There are several reasons not to use recursion. Recursive function calls are certainly less efficient than loops. Each time a function is called, the system incurs overhead that is not necessary with a loop. Also, in many cases, a solution using a loop is more evident than a recursive solution. In fact, the majority of repetitive programming tasks are best done with loops.

Some problems, however, are more easily solved with recursion than with a loop. For example, the mathematical definition of the GCD formula is well suited to a recursive approach. If a recursive solution is evident for a particular problem, and the recursive algorithm does not slow system performance an intolerable amount, then recursion would be a good design choice. If a problem is more easily solved with a loop, however, you should take that approach.

Review Questions

Multiple Choice

1. A recursive function _______________.
   a. calls a different function
   b. abnormally halts the program
   c. calls itself
   d. can only be called once
2. A function is called once from a program's `main` function, then it calls itself four times. The depth of recursion is _______________.
   a. one
   b. four
   c. five
   d. nine
3. The part of a problem that can be solved without recursion is the _______________ case.
   a. base
   b. solvable
   c. known
   d. iterative
4. The part of a problem that is solved with recursion is the _______________ case.
   a. base
   b. iterative
   c. unknown
   d. recursion
5. When a function explicitly calls itself, it is called _______________ recursion.
   a. explicit
   b. modal
   c. direct
   d. indirect
6. When function A calls function B, which calls function A, it is called _______________ recursion.
   a. implicit
   b. modal
   c. direct
   d. indirect
7. Any problem that can be solved recursively can also be solved with a _______________.
   a. decision structure
   b. loop
   c. sequence structure
   d. case structure
8. Actions taken by the computer when a function is called, such as allocating memory for parameters and local variables, are referred to as _______________.
   a. overhead
   b. set up
   c. clean up
   d. synchronization

9. A recursive algorithm must _______________ in the recursive case.
   a. solve the problem without recursion
   b. reduce the problem to a smaller version of the original problem
   c. acknowledge that an error has occurred and abort the program
   d. enlarge the problem to a larger version of the original problem
10. A recursive algorithm must _______________ in the base case.
   a. solve the problem without recursion
   b. reduce the problem to a smaller version of the original problem
   c. acknowledge that an error has occurred and abort the program
   d. enlarge the problem to a larger version of the original problem

True or False

1. An algorithm that uses a loop will usually run faster than an equivalent recursive algorithm.
2. Some problems can be solved through recursion only.
3. It is not necessary to have a base case in all recursive algorithms.
4. In the base case, a recursive method calls itself with a smaller version of the original problem.

Short Answer

1. In Program 12-2, presented earlier in this chapter, what is the base case of the message function?
2. In this chapter, the rules given for calculating the factorial of a number are as follows:

   If $n = 0$ then factorial(n) $= 1$
   If $n > 0$ then factorial(n) $= n \times$ factorial($n - 1$)

   If you were designing a function from these rules, what would the base case be? What would the recursive case be?
3. Is recursion ever required to solve a problem? What other approach can you use to solve a problem that is repetitive in nature?
4. When recursion is used to solve a problem, why must the recursive function call itself to solve a smaller version of the original problem?
5. How is a problem usually reduced with a recursive function?

Algorithm Workbench

1. What will the following program display?

```
def main():
    num = 0
    show_me(num)

def show_me(arg):
    if arg < 10:
        show_me(arg + 1)
    else:
        print(arg)
main()
```

2. What will the following program display?

```
def main():
    num = 0
    show_me(num)

def show_me(arg):
    print(arg)
    if arg 10:
        show_me(arg + 1)
main()
```

3. The following function uses a loop. Rewrite it as a recursive function that performs the same operation.

```
def traffic_sign(n):
    while n > 0:
        print('No Parking')
        n = n > 1
```

Programming Exercises

1. Recursive Printing

Design a recursive function that accepts an integer argument, n, and prints the numbers 1 up through n.

2. Recursive Multiplication

VideoNote
The Recursive Multiplication Problem

Design a recursive function that accepts two arguments into the parameters x and y. The function should return the value of x times y. Remember, multiplication can be performed as repeated addition as follows:

$$7 \times 4 = 4 + 4 + 4 + 4 + 4 + 4 + 4$$

(To keep the function simple, assume x and y will always hold positive nonzero integers.)

3. Recursive Lines

Write a recursive function that accepts an integer argument, n. The function should display n lines of asterisks on the screen, with the first line showing 1 asterisk, the second line showing 2 asterisks, up to the nth line which shows n asterisks.

4. Largest List Item

Design a function that accepts a list as an argument and returns the largest value in the list. The function should use recursion to find the largest item.

5. Recursive List Sum

Design a function that accepts a list of numbers as an argument. The function should recursively calculate the sum of all the numbers in the list and return that value.

6. Sum of Numbers

Design a function that accepts an integer argument and returns the sum of all the integers from 1 up to the number passed as an argument. For example, if 50 is passed as an argument, the function will return the sum of 1, 2, 3, 4, . . . 50. Use recursion to calculate the sum.

7. Recursive Power Method

Design a function that uses recursion to raise a number to a power. The function should accept two arguments: the number to be raised, and the exponent. Assume the exponent is a nonnegative integer.

8. Ackermann's Function

Ackermann's Function is a recursive mathematical algorithm that can be used to test how well a system optimizes its performance of recursion. Design a function `ackermann(m, n)`, which solves Ackermann's function. Use the following logic in your function:

If m = 0 then return n + 1
If n = 0 then return ackermann(m − 1, 1)
Otherwise, return ackermann(m − 1, ackermann(m, n − 1))

Once you've designed your function, test it by calling it with small values for `m` and `n`.

CHAPTER

13 GUI Programming

TOPICS

13.1 Graphical User Interfaces

CONCEPT: A graphical user interface allows the user to interact with the operating system and other programs using graphical elements such as icons, buttons, and dialog boxes.

A computer's *user interface* is the part of the computer with which the user interacts. One part of the user interface consists of hardware devices, such as the keyboard and the video display. Another part of the user interface lies in the way that the computer's operating system accepts commands from the user. For many years, the only way that the user could interact with an operating system was through a *command line interface,* such as the one shown in Figure 13-1. A command line interface typically displays a prompt, and the user types a command, which is then executed.

Many computer users, especially beginners, find command line interfaces difficult to use. This is because there are many commands to be learned, and each command has its own syntax, much like a programming statement. If a command isn't entered correctly, it will not work.

In the 1980s, a new type of interface known as a graphical user interface came into use in commercial operating systems. A *graphical user interface* (*GUI*; pronounced "gooey"), allows the user to interact with the operating system and other programs through graphical elements on the screen. GUIs also popularized the use of the mouse as an input device. Instead of requiring the user to type commands on the keyboard, GUIs allow the user to point at graphical elements and click the mouse button to activate them.

Much of the interaction with a GUI is done through *dialog boxes,* which are small windows that display information and allow the user to perform actions. Figure 13-2 shows

Figure 13-1 A command line interface

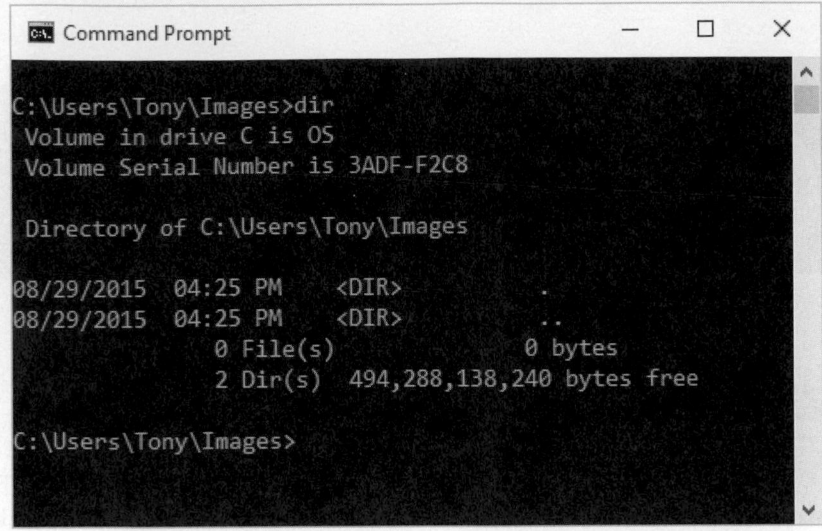

Figure 13-2 A dialog box

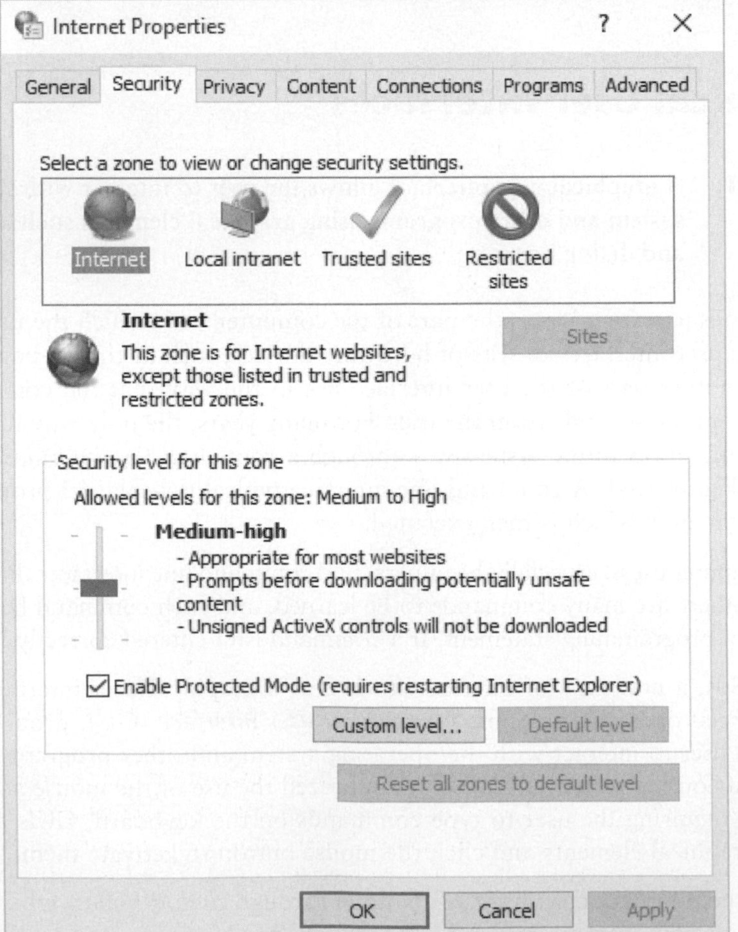

an example of a dialog box from the Windows operating system that allows the user to change the system's Internet settings. Instead of typing commands according to a specified syntax, the user interacts with graphical elements such as icons, buttons, and slider bars.

GUI Programs Are Event-Driven

In a text-based environment such as a command line interface, programs determine the order in which things happen. For example, consider a program that calculates the area of a rectangle. First, the program prompts the user to enter the rectangle's width. The user enters the width, then the program prompts the user to enter the rectangle's length. The user enters the length, then the program calculates the area. The user has no choice but to enter the data in the order that it is requested.

In a GUI environment, however, the user determines the order in which things happen. For example, Figure 13-3 shows a GUI program (written in Python) that calculates the area of a rectangle. The user can enter the length and the width in any order he or she wishes. If a mistake is made, the user can delete, the data that was entered and retype it. When the user is ready to calculate the area, he or she clicks the *Calculate Area* button, and the program performs the calculation. Because GUI programs must respond to the actions of the user, it is said that they are *event-driven*. The user causes events to take place, such as the clicking of a button, and the program must respond to the events.

Figure 13-3 A GUI program

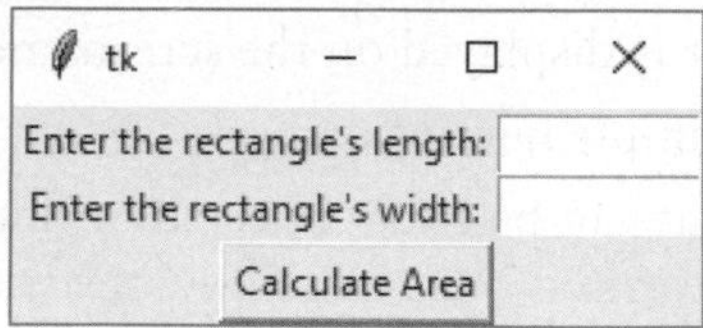

Checkpoint

13.1 What is a user interface?

13.2 How does a command line interface work?

13.3 When the user runs a program in a text-based environment, such as the command line, what determines the order in which things happen?

13.4 What is an event-driven program?

13.2 Using the tkinter Module

CONCEPT: In Python, you can use the tkinter module to create simple GUI programs.

Python does not have GUI programming features built into the language itself. However, it comes with a module named tkinter that allows you to create simple GUI programs. The name "tkinter" is short for "Tk interface." It is named this because it provides a way for Python programmers to use a GUI library named Tk. Many other programming languages use the Tk library as well.

NOTE: There are numerous GUI libraries available for Python. Because the `tkinter` module comes with Python, we will use it only in this chapter.

A GUI program presents a window with various graphical *widgets* with which the user can interact or view. The `tkinter` module provides 15 widgets, which are described in Table 13-1. We won't cover all of the `tkinter` widgets in this chapter, but we will demonstrate how to create simple GUI programs that gather input and display data.

Table 13-1 `tkinter` widgets

Widget	Description
`Button`	A button that can cause an action to occur when it is clicked.
`Canvas`	A rectangular area that can be used to display graphics.
`Checkbutton`	A button that may be in either the "on" or "off" position.
`Entry`	An area in which the user may type a single line of input from the keyboard.
`Frame`	A container that can hold other widgets.
`Label`	An area that displays one line of text or an image.
`Listbox`	A list from which the user may select an item
`Menu`	A list of menu choices that are displayed when the user clicks a `Menubutton` widget.
`Menubutton`	A menu that is displayed on the screen and may be clicked by the user
`Message`	Displays multiple lines of text.
`Radiobutton`	A widget that can be either selected or deselected. `Radiobutton` widgets usually appear in groups and allow the user to select one of several options.
`Scale`	A widget that allows the user to select a value by moving a slider along a track.
`Scrollbar`	Can be used with some other types of widgets to provide scrolling ability.
`Text`	A widget that allows the user to enter multiple lines of text input.
`Toplevel`	A container, like a `Frame`, but displayed in its own window.

The simplest GUI program that we can demonstrate is one that displays an empty window. Program 13-1 shows how we can do this using the `tkinter` module. When the program runs, the window shown in Figure 13-4 is displayed. To exit the program, simply click the standard Windows close button (×) in the upper right corner of the window.

NOTE: Programs that use `tkinter` do not always run reliably under IDLE. This is because IDLE itself uses `tkinter`. You can always use IDLE's editor to write GUI programs, but for the best results, run them from your operating system's command prompt.

Program 13-1 (empty_window1.py)

```
1  # This program displays an empty window.
2
3  import tkinter
4
5  def main():
6      # Create the main window widget.
7      main_window = tkinter.Tk()
8
9      # Enter the tkinter main loop.
10     tkinter.mainloop()
11
12 # Call the main function.
13 main()
```

Figure 13-4 Window displayed by Program 13-1

Line 3 imports the `tkinter` module. Inside the `main` function, line 7 creates an instance of the `tkinter` module's `Tk` class and assigns it to the `main_window` variable. This object is the root widget, which is the main window in the program. Line 10 calls the `tkinter` module's `mainloop` function. This function runs like an infinite loop until you close the main window.

Most programmers prefer to take an object-oriented approach when writing a GUI program. Rather than writing a function to create the on-screen elements of a program, it is a common practice to write a class with an `__init__` method that builds the GUI. When an instance of the class is created, the GUI appears on the screen. To demonstrate, Program 13-2 shows an object-oriented version of our program that displays an empty window. When this program runs it displays the window shown in Figure 13-4.

Program 13-2 (empty_window2.py)

```
# This program displays an empty window.

import tkinter
```

(program continues)

Program 13-2 *(continued)*

```
4
5  class MyGUI:
6    def __init__(self):
7      # Create the main window widget.
8      self.main_window = tkinter.Tk()
9
10     # Enter the tkinter main loop.
11     tkinter.mainloop()
12
13 # Create an instance of the MyGUI class.
14 my_gui = MyGUI()
```

Lines 5 through 11 are the class definition for the `MyGUI` class. The class's `__init__` method begins in line 6. Line 8 creates the root widget and assigns it to the class attribute `main_window`. Line 11 executes the `tkinter` module's `mainloop` function. The statement in line 14 creates an instance of the `MyGUI` class. This causes the class's `__init__` method to execute, displaying the empty window on the screen.

Checkpoint

13.5 Briefly describe each of the following `tkinter` widgets:

a) `Label`

b) `Entry`

c) `Button`

d) `Frame`

13.6 How do you create a root widget?

13.7 What does the `tkinter` module's `mainloop` function do?

13.3 Display Text with `Label` Widgets

CONCEPT: You use the `Label` widget to display text in a window.

VideoNote
Creating a Simple GUI application

You can use a `Label` widget to display a single line of text in a window. To make a `Label` widget you create an instance of the `tkinter` module's `Label` class. Program 13-3 creates a window containing a `Label` widget that displays the text "Hello World!" The window is shown in Figure 13-5.

Program 13-3 `(hello_world.py)`

```
# This program displays a label with text.

import tkinter

```

```
5  class MyGUI:
6    def __init__(self):
7        # Create the main window widget.
8        self.main_window = tkinter.Tk()
9
10       # Create a Label widget containing the
11       # text 'Hello World!'
12       self.label = tkinter.Label(self.main_window,
13                                  text='Hello World!')
14
15       # Call the Label widget's pack method.
16       self.label.pack()
17
18       # Enter the tkinter main loop.
19       tkinter.mainloop()
20
21 # Create an instance of the MyGUI class.
22 my_gui = MyGUI()
```

Figure 13-5 Window displayed by Program 13-3

The `MyGUI` class in this program is very similar to the one you saw previously in Program 13-2. Its `__init__` method builds the GUI when an instance of the class is created. Line 8 creates a root widget and assigns it to `self.main_window`. The following statement appears in lines 12 and 13:

```
self.label = tkinter.Label(self.main_window,
                           text='Hello World!')
```

This statement creates a `Label` widget and assigns it to `self.label`. The first argument inside the parentheses is `self.main_window`, which is a reference to the root widget. This simply specifies that we want the `Label` widget to belong to the root widget. The second argument is `text='Hello World!'`. This specifies the text that we want to be displayed in the label.

The statement in line 16 calls the `Label` widget's `pack` method. The `pack` method determines where a widget should be positioned and makes the widget visible when the main window is displayed. (You call the `pack` method for each widget in a window.) Line 19 calls the `tkinter` module's `mainloop` method, which displays the program's main window, shown in Figure 13-5.

Let's look at another example. Program 13-4 displays a window with two `Label` widgets, shown in Figure 13-6.

Program 13-4 (hello_world2.py)

```
# This program displays two labels with text.

import tkinter

class MyGUI:
    def __init__(self):
        # Create the main window widget.
        self.main_window = tkinter.Tk()

        # Create two Label widgets.
        self.label1 = tkinter.Label(self.main_window,
                                    text='Hello World!')
        self.label2 = tkinter.Label(self.main_window,
                               text='This is my GUI program.')

        # Call both Label widgets' pack method.
        self.label1.pack()
        self.label2.pack()

        # Enter the tkinter main loop.
        tkinter.mainloop()

# Create an instance of the MyGUI class.
my_gui = MyGUI()
```

Figure 13-6 Window displayed by Program 13-4

Notice the two `Label` widgets are displayed with one stacked on top of the other. We can change this layout by specifying an argument to `pack` method, as shown in Program 13-5. When the program runs, it displays the window shown in Figure 13-7.

Program 13-5 (hello_world3.py)

```
# This program uses the side='left' argument with
# the pack method to change the layout of the widgets.

import tkinter

class MyGUI:
    def __init__(self):
```

```
8         # Create the main window widget.
9         self.main_window = tkinter.Tk()
10
11        # Create two Label widgets.
12        self.label1 = tkinter.Label(self.main_window,
13                                    text='Hello World!')
14        self.label2 = tkinter.Label(self.main_window,
15                            text='This is my GUI program.')
16
17        # Call both Label widgets' pack method.
18        self.label1.pack(side='left')
19        self.label2.pack(side='left')
20
21        # Enter the tkinter main loop.
22        tkinter.mainloop()
23
24  # Create an instance of the MyGUI class.
25  my_gui = MyGUI()
```

Figure 13-7 Window displayed by Program 13-5

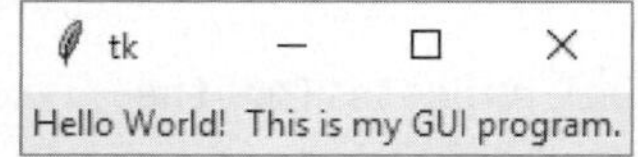

In lines 18 and 19, we call each `Label` widget's `pack` method passing the argument `side='left'`. This specifies that the widget should be positioned as far left as possible inside the parent widget. Because the `label1` widget was added to the `main_window` first, it will appear at the leftmost edge. The `label2` widget was added next, so it appears next to the `label1` widget. As a result, the labels appear side by side. The valid `side` arguments that you can pass to the `pack` method are `side='top'`, `side='bottom'`, `side='left'`, and `side='right'`.

Checkpoint

13.8 What does a widget's `pack` method do?

13.9 If you create two `Label` widgets and call their `pack` methods with no arguments, how will the `Label` widgets be arranged inside their parent widget?

13.10 What argument would you pass to a widget's `pack` method to specify that it should be positioned as far left as possible inside the parent widget?

13.4 Organizing Widgets with Frames

CONCEPT: A `Frame` is a container that can hold other widgets. You can use `Frame`s to organize the widgets in a window.

A `Frame` is a container. It is a widget that can hold other widgets. `Frames` are useful for organizing and arranging groups of widgets in a window. For example, you can place a set of widgets in one `Frame` and arrange them in a particular way, then place a set of widgets in another `Frame` and arrange them in a different way. Program 13-6 demonstrates this. When the program runs it, displays the window shown in Figure 13-8.

Program 13-6 (frame_demo.py)

```
# This program creates labels in two different frames.

import tkinter

class MyGUI:
    def __init__(self):
        # Create the main window widget.
        self.main_window = tkinter.Tk()

        # Create two frames, one for the top of the
        # window, and one for the bottom.
        self.top_frame = tkinter.Frame(self.main_window)
        self.bottom_frame = tkinter.Frame(self.main_window)

        # Create three Label widgets for the
        # top frame.
        self.label1 = tkinter.Label(self.top_frame,
                                    text='Winken')
        self.label2 = tkinter.Label(self.top_frame,
                                    text='Blinken')
        self.label3 = tkinter.Label(self.top_frame,
                                    text='Nod')

        # Pack the labels that are in the top frame.
        # Use the side='top' argument to stack them
        # one on top of the other.
        self.label1.pack(side='top')
        self.label2.pack(side='top')
        self.label3.pack(side='top')

        # Create three Label widgets for the
        # bottom frame.
        self.label4 = tkinter.Label(self.bottom_frame,
                                    text='Winken')
        self.label5 = tkinter.Label(self.bottom_frame,
                                    text='Blinken')
        self.label6 = tkinter.Label(self.bottom_frame,
                                    text='Nod')

```

```
40          # Pack the labels that are in the bottom frame.
41          # Use the side='left' argument to arrange them
42          # horizontally from the left of the frame.
43          self.label4.pack(side='left')
44          self.label5.pack(side='left')
45          self.label6.pack(side='left')
46
47          # Yes, we have to pack the frames too!
48          self.top_frame.pack()
49          self.bottom_frame.pack()
50
51          # Enter the tkinter main loop.
52          tkinter.mainloop()
53
54  # Create an instance of the MyGUI class.
55  my_gui = MyGUI()
```

Figure 13-8 Window displayed by Program 13-6

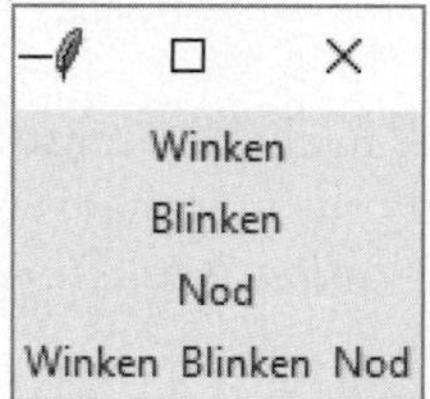

Take a closer look at lines 12 and 13:

```
self.top_frame = tkinter.Frame(self.main_window)
self.bottom_frame = tkinter.Frame(self.main_window)
```

These lines create two `Frame` objects. The `self.main_window` argument that appears inside the parentheses cause the `Frame`s to be added to the `main_window` widget.

Lines 17 through 22 create three `Label` widgets. Notice these widgets are added to the `self.top_frame` widget. Then, lines 27 through 29 call each of the `Label` widgets' `pack` method, passing `side='top'` as an argument. As shown in Figure 13-6, this causes the three widgets to be stacked one on top of the other inside the `Frame`.

Lines 33 through 38 create three more `Label` widgets. These `Label` widgets are added to the `self.bottom_frame` widget. Then, lines 43 through 45 call each of the `Label` widgets' `pack` method, passing `side='left'` as an argument. As shown in Figure 13-9, this causes the three widgets to appear horizontally inside the `Frame`.

Lines 48 and 49 call the `Frame` widgets' `pack` method, which makes the `Frame` widgets visible. Line 52 executes the `tkinter` module's `mainloop` function.

Figure 13-9 Arrangement of widgets

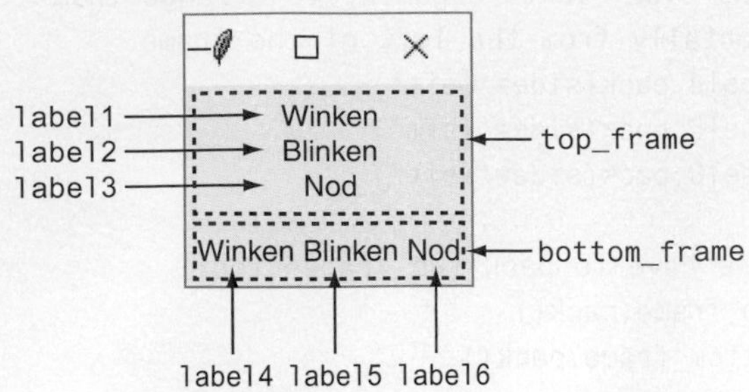

13.5 Button Widgets and Info Dialog Boxes

CONCEPT: You use the `Button` widget to create a standard button in a window. When the user clicks a button, a specified function or method is called.

VideoNote
Responding to Button Clicks

An info dialog box is a simple window that displays a message to the user, and has an OK button that dismisses the dialog box. You can use the `tkinter.messagebox` module's `showinfo` function to display an info dialog box.

A `Button` is a widget that the user can click to cause an action to take place. When you create a `Button` widget you can specify the text that is to appear on the face of the button and the name of a callback function. A *callback function* is a function or method that executes when the user clicks the button.

> **NOTE:** A callback function is also known as an *event handler* because it handles the event that occurs when the user clicks the button.

To demonstrate, we will look at Program 13-7. This program displays the window shown in Figure 13-10. When the user clicks the button, the program displays a separate *info dialog box*, shown in Figure 13-11. We use a function named `showinfo`, which is in the `tkinter.messagebox` module, to display the info dialog box. (To use the `showinfo` function, you will need to import the `tkinter.messagebox` module.) This is the general format of the `showinfo` function call:

```
tkinter.messagebox.showinfo(title, message)
```

In the general format, *`title`* is a string that is displayed in the dialog box's title bar, and *`message`* is an informational string that is displayed in the main part of the dialog box.

Program 13-7 (button_demo.py)

```
# This program demonstrates a Button widget.
# When the user clicks the Button, an
# info dialog box is displayed.
```

```

import tkinter
import tkinter.messagebox

class MyGUI:
    def __init__(self):
        # Create the main window widget.
        self.main_window = tkinter.Tk()

        # Create a Button widget. The text 'Click Me!'
        # should appear on the face of the Button. The
        # do_something method should be executed when
        # the user clicks the Button.
        self.my_button = tkinter.Button(self.main_window,
                                        text='Click Me!',
                                        command=self.do_something)

        # Pack the Button.
        self.my_button.pack()

        # Enter the tkinter main loop.
        tkinter.mainloop()

    # The do_something method is a callback function
    # for the Button widget.

    def do_something(self):
        # Display an info dialog box.
        tkinter.messagebox.showinfo('Response',
                                    'Thanks for clicking the button.')

# Create an instance of the MyGUI class.
my_gui = MyGUI()
```

Figure 13-10 The main window displayed by Program 13-7

Figure 13-11 The info dialog box displayed by Program 13-7

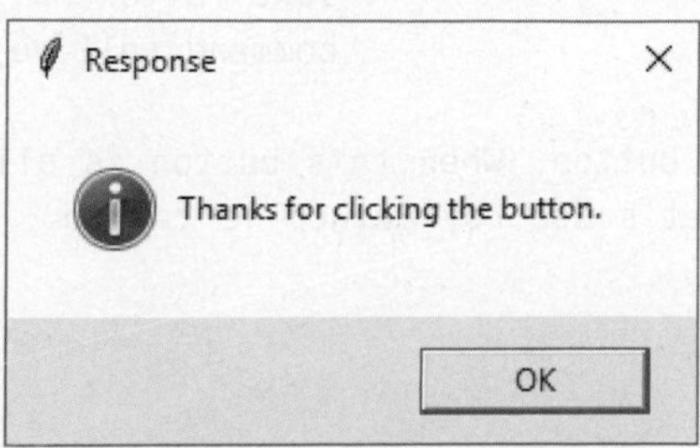

Line 5 imports the `tkinter` module, and line 6 imports the `tkinter.messagebox` module. Line 11 creates the root widget and assigns it to the `main_window` variable.

The statement in lines 17 through 19 creates the `Button` widget. The first argument inside the parentheses is `self.main_window`, which is the parent widget. The `text='Click Me!'` argument specifies that the string 'Click Me!' should appear on the face of the button. The `command='self.do_something'` argument specifies the class's `do_something` method as the callback function. When the user clicks the button, the `do_something` method will execute.

The `do_something` method appears in lines 31 through 33. The method simply calls the `tkinter.messagebox.showinfo` function to display the info box shown in Figure 13-11. To dismiss the dialog box, the user can click the OK button.

Creating a Quit Button

GUI programs usually have a *Quit button* (or an Exit button) that closes the program when the user clicks it. To create a Quit button in a Python program, you simply create a `Button` widget that calls the root widget's `destroy` method as a callback function. Program 13-8 demonstrates how to do this. It is a modified version of Program 13-7, with a second `Button` widget added as shown in Figure 13-12.

Program 13-8 (quit_button.py)

```
# This program has a Quit button that calls
# the Tk class's destroy method when clicked.

import tkinter
import tkinter.messagebox

class MyGUI:
    def __init__(self):
        # Create the main window widget.
        self.main_window = tkinter.Tk()

        # Create a Button widget. The text 'Click Me!'
        # should appear on the face of the Button. The
        # do_something method should be executed when
        # the user clicks the Button.
        self.my_button = tkinter.Button(self.main_window,
                                        text='Click Me!',
                                        command=self.do_something)

        # Create a Quit button. When this button is clicked
        # the root widget's destroy method is called.
```

```
22          # (The main_window variable references the root widget,
23          # so the callback function is self.main_window.destroy.)
24          self.quit_button = tkinter.Button(self.main_window,
25                                            text='Quit',
26                                            command=self.main_window.destroy)
27
28
29          # Pack the Buttons.
30          self.my_button.pack()
31          self.quit_button.pack()
32
33          # Enter the tkinter main loop.
34          tkinter.mainloop()
35
36      # The do_something method is a callback function
37      # for the Button widget.
38
39      def do_something(self):
40          # Display an info dialog box.
41          tkinter.messagebox.showinfo('Response',
42                                      'Thanks for clicking the button.')
43
44  # Create an instance of the MyGUI class.
45  my_gui = MyGUI()
```

Figure 13-12 The info dialog box displayed by Program 13-8

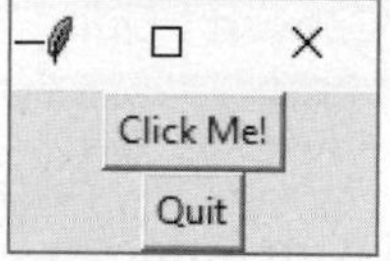

The statement in lines 24 through 26 creates the Quit button. Notice the `self.main_window.destroy` method is used as the callback function. When the user clicks the button, this method is called and the program ends.

13.6 Getting Input with the Entry Widget

CONCEPT: An `Entry` widget is a rectangular area that the user can type input into. You use the `Entry` widget's `get` method to retrieve the data that has been typed into the widget.

An `Entry` widget is a rectangular area that the user can type text into. Entry widgets are used to gather input in a GUI program. Typically, a program will have one or more `Entry` widgets in a window, along with a button that the user clicks to submit the data that he or she has typed into the `Entry` widgets. The button's callback function retrieves data from the window's `Entry` widgets and processes it.

You use an `Entry` widget's `get` method to retrieve the data that the user has typed into the widget. The `get` method returns a string, so it will have to be converted to the appropriate data type if the `Entry` widget is used for numeric input.

To demonstrate, we will look at a program that allows the user to enter a distance in kilometers into an `Entry` widget then click a button to see that distance converted to miles. The formula for converting kilometers to miles is:

$$Miles = Kilometers \times 0.6214$$

Figure 13-13 shows the window that the program displays. To arrange the widgets in the positions shown in the figure, we will organize them in two frames, as shown in Figure 13-14. The label that displays the prompt and the `Entry` widget will be stored in the `top_frame`, and their `pack` methods will be called with the `side='left'` argument. This will cause them to appear horizontally in the frame. The Convert button and the Quit button will be stored in the `bottom_frame`, and their `pack` methods will also be called with the `side='left'` argument.

Program 13-9 shows the code for the program. Figure 13-15 shows what happens when the user enters 1000 into the `Entry` widget and clicks the Convert button.

Figure 13-13 The `kilo_converter` program's window

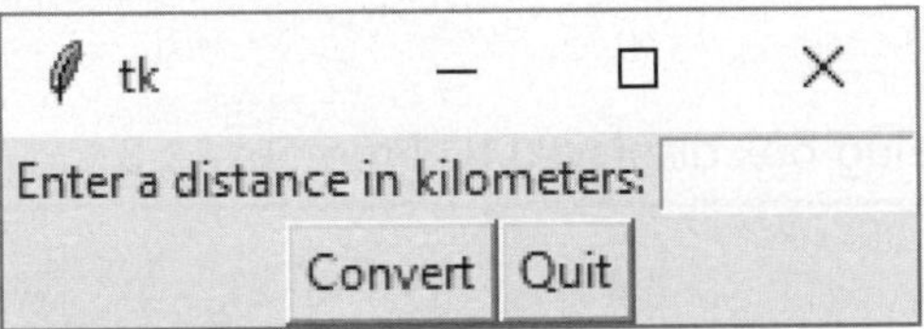

Figure 13-14 The window organized with frames

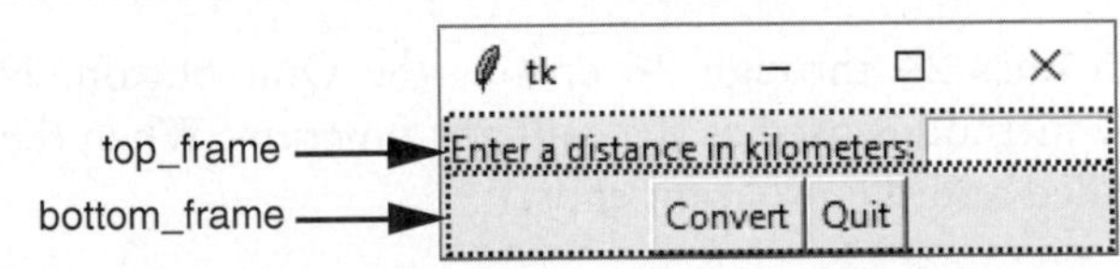

Program 13-9 (`kilo_converter.py`)

```
# This program converts distances in kilometers
# to miles. The result is displayed in an info
# dialog box.

import tkinter
import tkinter.messagebox
```

```

class KiloConverterGUI:
    def __init__(self):

        # Create the main window.
        self.main_window = tkinter.Tk()

        # Create two frames to group widgets.
        self.top_frame = tkinter.Frame(self.main_window)
        self.bottom_frame = tkinter.Frame(self.main_window)

        # Create the widgets for the top frame.
        self.prompt_label = tkinter.Label(self.top_frame,
                    text='Enter a distance in kilometers:')
        self.kilo_entry = tkinter.Entry(self.top_frame,
                                        width=10)

        # Pack the top frame's widgets.
        self.prompt_label.pack(side='left')
        self.kilo_entry.pack(side='left')

        # Create the button widgets for the bottom frame.
        self.calc_button = tkinter.Button(self.bottom_frame,
                                          text='Convert',
                                          command=self.convert)
        self.quit_button = tkinter.Button(self.bottom_frame,
                                          text='Quit',
                                          command=self.main_window.destroy)
        # Pack the buttons.
        self.calc_button.pack(side='left')
        self.quit_button.pack(side='left')

        # Pack the frames.
        self.top_frame.pack()
        self.bottom_frame.pack()

        # Enter the tkinter main loop.
        tkinter.mainloop()

    # The convert method is a callback function for
    # the Calculate button.

    def convert(self):
        # Get the value entered by the user into the
        # kilo_entry widget.
        kilo = float(self.kilo_entry.get())

```

(program continues)

Program 13-9 *(continued)*

```
54         # Convert kilometers to miles.
55         miles = kilo * 0.6214
56
57         # Display the results in an info dialog box.
58         tkinter.messagebox.showinfo('Results',
59                                     str(kilo) +
60                                     ' kilometers is equal to ' +
61                                     str(miles) + ' miles.')
62
63 # Create an instance of the KiloConverterGUI class.
64 kilo_conv = KiloConverterGUI()
```

Figure 13-15 The info dialog box

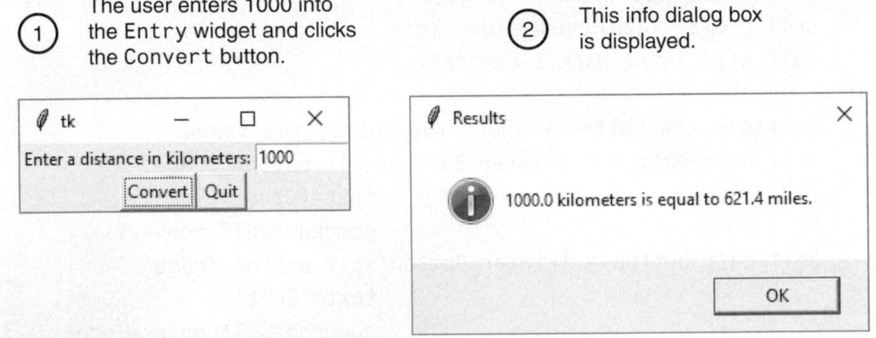

The `convert` method, shown in lines 49 through 60 is the Convert button's callback function. The statement in line 52 calls the `kilo_entry` widget's `get` method to retrieve the data that has been typed into the widget. The value is converted to a `float` then assigned to the `kilo` variable. The calculation in line 55 performs the conversion and assigns the results to the `miles` variable. Then, the statement in lines 58 through 61 displays the info dialog box with a message that gives the converted value.

13.7 Using Labels as Output Fields

CONCEPT: When a `StringVar` object is associated with a `Label` widget, the `Label` widget displays any data that is stored in the `StringVar` object.

Previously, you saw how to use an info dialog box to display output. If you don't want to display a separate dialog box for your program's output, you can use `Label` widgets in the program's main window to dynamically display output. You simply create empty `Label` widgets in your main window, then write code that displays the desired data in those labels when a button is clicked.

The `tkinter` module provides a class named `StringVar` that can be used along with a `Label` widget to display data. First, you create a `StringVar` object. Then, you create a `Label` widget and associate it with the `StringVar` object. From that point on, any value that is then stored in the `StringVar` object will automatically be displayed in the `Label` widget.

Program 13-10 demonstrates how to do this. It is a modified version of the `kilo_converter` program that you saw in Program 13-9. Instead of popping up an info dialog box, this version of the program displays the number of miles in a label in the main window.

Program 13-10 (kilo_converter2.py)

```
# This program converts distances in kilometers
# to miles. The result is displayed in a label
# on the main window.

import tkinter

class KiloConverterGUI:
    def __init__(self):

        # Create the main window.
        self.main_window = tkinter.Tk()

        # Create three frames to group widgets.
        self.top_frame = tkinter.Frame()
        self.mid_frame = tkinter.Frame()
        self.bottom_frame = tkinter.Frame()

        # Create the widgets for the top frame.
        self.prompt_label = tkinter.Label(self.top_frame,
                    text='Enter a distance in kilometers:')
        self.kilo_entry = tkinter.Entry(self.top_frame,
                                        width=10)

        # Pack the top frame's widgets.
        self.prompt_label.pack(side='left')
        self.kilo_entry.pack(side='left')

        # Create the widgets for the middle frame.
        self.descr_label = tkinter.Label(self.mid_frame,
                                         text='Converted to miles:')

        # We need a StringVar object to associate with
        # an output label. Use the object's set method
        # to store a string of blank characters.
        self.value = tkinter.StringVar()

```

(program continues)

Program 13-10 *(continued)*

```
        # Create a label and associate it with the
        # StringVar object. Any value stored in the
        # StringVar object will automatically be displayed
        # in the label.
        self.miles_label = tkinter.Label(self.mid_frame,
                                         textvariable=self.value)

        # Pack the middle frame's widgets.
        self.descr_label.pack(side='left')
        self.miles_label.pack(side='left')

        # Create the button widgets for the bottom frame.
        self.calc_button = tkinter.Button(self.bottom_frame,
                                          text='Convert',
                                          command=self.convert)
        self.quit_button = tkinter.Button(self.bottom_frame,
                                          text='Quit',
                                          command=self.main_window.destroy)

        # Pack the buttons.
        self.calc_button.pack(side='left')
        self.quit_button.pack(side='left')

        # Pack the frames.
        self.top_frame.pack()
        self.mid_frame.pack()
        self.bottom_frame.pack()

        # Enter the tkinter main loop.
        tkinter.mainloop()

    # The convert method is a callback function for
    # the Calculate button.

    def convert(self):
        # Get the value entered by the user into the
        # kilo_entry widget.
        kilo = float(self.kilo_entry.get())

        # Convert kilometers to miles.
        miles = kilo * 0.6214

        # Convert miles to a string and store it
        # in the StringVar object. This will automatically
        # update the miles_label widget.
```

```
82         self.value.set(miles)
83
84 # Create an instance of the KiloConverterGUI class.
85 kilo_conv = KiloConverterGUI()
```

When this program runs, it displays the window shown in Figure 13-16. Figure 13-17 shows what happens when the user enters 1000 for the kilometers and clicks the Convert button. The number of miles is displayed in a label in the main window.

Figure 13-16 The window initially displayed

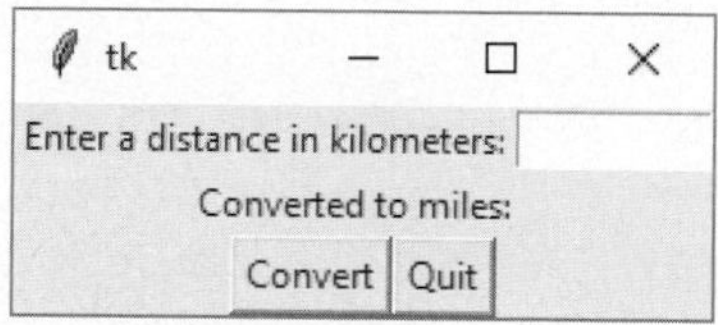

Figure 13-17 The window showing 1000 kilometers converted to miles

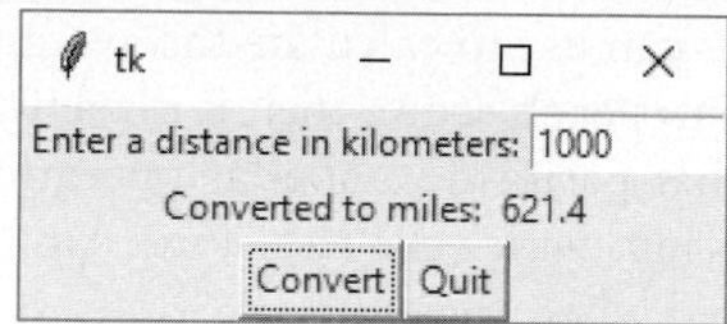

Let's look at the code. Lines 14 through 16 create three frames: `top_frame`, `mid_frame`, and `bottom_frame`. Lines 19 through 26 create the widgets for the top frame and call their `pack` method.

Lines 29 through 30 create the `Label` widget with the text `'Converted to miles:'` that you see on the main window in Figure 13-16. Then, line 35 creates a `StringVar` object and assigns it to the `value` variable. Line 41 creates a `Label` widget named `miles_label` that we will use to display the number of miles. Notice in line 42, we use the argument `textvariable=self.value`. This creates an association between the `Label` widget and the `StringVar` object that is referenced by the `value` variable. Any value that we store in the `StringVar` object will be displayed in the label.

Lines 45 and 46 pack the two `Label` widgets that are in the `mid_frame`. Lines 49 through 58 create the `Button` widgets and `pack` them. Lines 61 through 63 pack the `Frame` objects. Figure 13-18 shows how the various widgets in this window are organized in the three frames.

The `convert` method, shown in lines 71 through 82 is the Convert button's callback function. The statement in line 74 calls the `kilo_entry` widget's `get` method to retrieve the data that has been typed into the widget. The value is converted to a `float` then assigned to the `kilo` variable. The calculation in line 77 performs the conversion and assigns the results to the miles variable. Then the statement in line 82 calls the StringVar object's set method, passing miles as an argument. This stores the value referenced by miles in the StringVar object, and also causes it to be displayed in the miles_label widget.

Figure 13-18 Layout of the kilo_converter2 program's main window

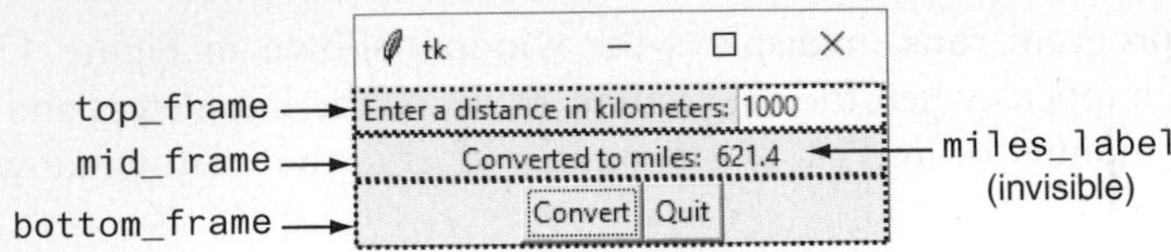

In the Spotlight:
Creating a GUI Program

Kathryn teaches a science class. In Chapter 3, we stepped through the development of a program that her students can use to calculate the average of three test scores. The program prompts the student to enter each score, then it displays the average. She has asked you to design a GUI program that performs a similar operation. She would like the program to have three Entry widgets into which the test scores can be entered, and a button that causes the average to be displayed when clicked.

Before we begin writing code, it will be helpful if we draw a sketch of the program's window, as shown in Figure 13-19. The sketch also shows the type of each widget. (The numbers that appear in the sketch will help us when we make a list of all the widgets.)

Figure 13-19 A sketch of the window

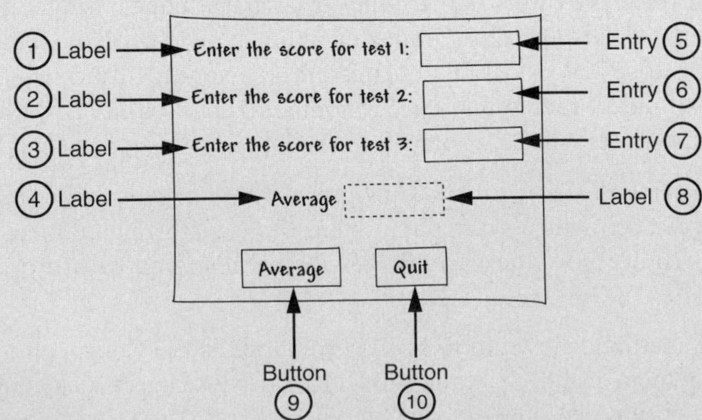

By examining the sketch, we can make a list of the widgets that we need. As we make the list, we will include a brief description of each widget, and a name that we will assign to each widget when we construct it.

Widget Number in Figure 13-19	Widget Type	Description	Name
1	`Label`	Instructs the user to enter the score for test 1.	`test1_label`
2	`Label`	Instructs the user to enter the score for test 2.	`test2_label`
3	`Label`	Instructs the user to enter the score for test 3.	`test3_label`
4	`Label`	Identifies the average, which will be displayed next to this label.	`result_label`
5	`Entry`	This is where the user will enter the score for test 1.	`test1_entry`
6	`Entry`	This is where the user will enter the score for test 2.	`test2_entry`
7	`Entry`	This is where the user will enter the score for test 3.	`test3_entry`
8	`Label`	The program will display the average test score in this label.	`avg_label`
9	`Button`	When this button is clicked, the program will calculate the average test score and display it in the `averageLabel` component.	`calc_button`
10	`Button`	When this button is clicked the program will end.	`quit_button`

We can see from the sketch that we have five rows of widgets in the window. To organize them, we will also create five `Frame` objects. Figure 13-20 shows how we will position the widgets inside the five `Frame` objects.

Figure 13-20 Using Frames to organize the widgets

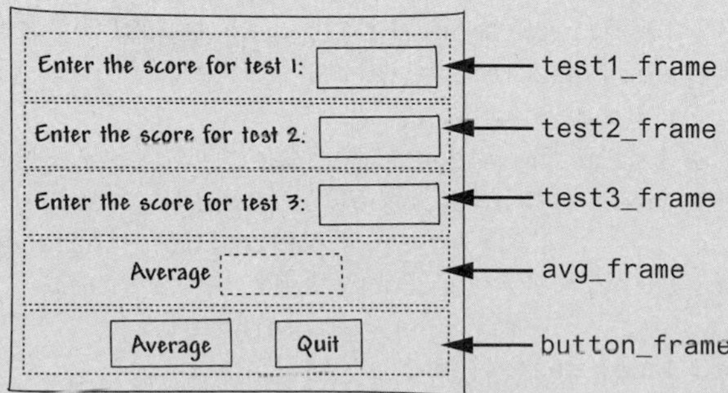

Program 13-11 shows the code for the program, and Figure 13-21 shows the program's window with data entered by the user.

Program 13-11 (test_averages.py)

```
# This program uses a GUI to get three test
# scores and display their average.

import tkinter

class TestAvg:
    def __init__(self):
        # Create the main window.
        self.main_window = tkinter.Tk()

        # Create the five frames.
        self.test1_frame = tkinter.Frame(self.main_window)
        self.test2_frame = tkinter.Frame(self.main_window)
        self.test3_frame = tkinter.Frame(self.main_window)
        self.avg_frame = tkinter.Frame(self.main_window)
        self.button_frame = tkinter.Frame(self.main_window)

        # Create and pack the widgets for test 1.
        self.test1_label = tkinter.Label(self.test1_frame,
                                         text='Enter the score for test 1:')
        self.test1_entry = tkinter.Entry(self.test1_frame,
                                         width=10)
        self.test1_label.pack(side='left')
        self.test1_entry.pack(side='left')

        # Create and pack the widgets for test 2.
        self.test2_label = tkinter.Label(self.test2_frame,
                                         text='Enter the score for test 2:')
        self.test2_entry = tkinter.Entry(self.test2_frame,
                                         width=10)
        self.test2_label.pack(side='left')
        self.test2_entry.pack(side='left')

        # Create and pack the widgets for test 3.
        self.test3_label = tkinter.Label(self.test3_frame,
                                         text='Enter the score for test 3:')
        self.test3_entry = tkinter.Entry(self.test3_frame,
                                         width=10)
        self.test3_label.pack(side='left')
        self.test3_entry.pack(side='left')

        # Create and pack the widgets for the average.
        self.result_label = tkinter.Label(self.avg_frame,
```

```
                                            text='Average:')
        self.avg = tkinter.StringVar() # To update avg_label
        self.avg_label = tkinter.Label(self.avg_frame,
                                        textvariable=self.avg)
        self.result_label.pack(side='left')
        self.avg_label.pack(side='left')

        # Create and pack the button widgets.
        self.calc_button = tkinter.Button(self.button_frame,
                                          text='Average',
                                          command=self.calc_avg)
        self.quit_button = tkinter.Button(self.button_frame,
                                          text='Quit',
                                          command=self.main_window.destroy)
        self.calc_button.pack(side='left')
        self.quit_button.pack(side='left')

        # Pack the frames.
        self.test1_frame.pack()
        self.test2_frame.pack()
        self.test3_frame.pack()
        self.avg_frame.pack()
        self.button_frame.pack()

        # Start the main loop.
        tkinter.mainloop()

    # The calc_avg method is the callback function for
    # the calc_button widget.

    def calc_avg(self):
        # Get the three test scores and store them
        # in variables.
        self.test1 = float(self.test1_entry.get())
        self.test2 = float(self.test2_entry.get())
        self.test3 = float(self.test3_entry.get())

        # Calculate the average.
        self.average = (self.test1 + self.test2 +
                        self.test3) / 3.0

        # Update the avg_label widget by storing
        # the value of self.average in the StringVar
        # object referenced by avg.
        self.avg.set(self.average)

# Create an instance of the TestAvg class.
test_avg = TestAvg()
```

Figure 13-21 The `test_averages` program window

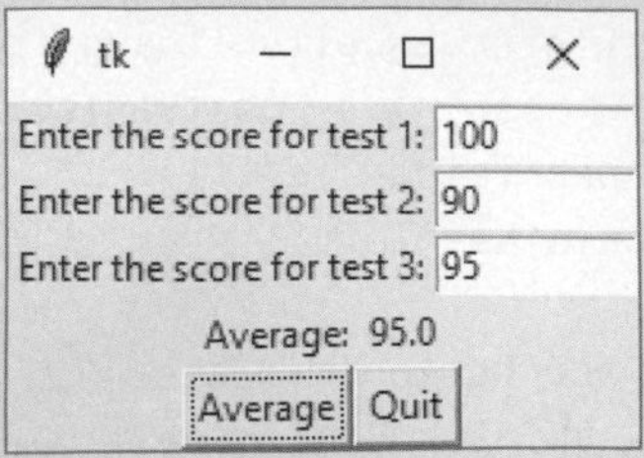

Checkpoint

13.11 How do you retrieve data from an `Entry` widget?

13.12 When you retrieve a value from an `Entry` widget, of what data type is it?

13.13 What module is the `StringVar` class in?

13.14 What can you accomplish by associating a `StringVar` object with a `Label` widget?

13.8 Radio Buttons and Check Buttons

CONCEPT: Radio buttons normally appear in groups of two or more, and allow the user to select one of several possible options. Check buttons, which may appear alone or in groups, allow the user to make yes/no or on/off selections.

Radio Buttons

Radio buttons are useful when you want the user to select one choice from several possible options. Figure 13-22 shows a window containing a group of radio buttons. A radio button may be selected or deselected. Each radio button has a small circle that appears filled in when the radio button is selected, and appears empty when the radio button is deselected.

Figure 13-22 A group of radio buttons

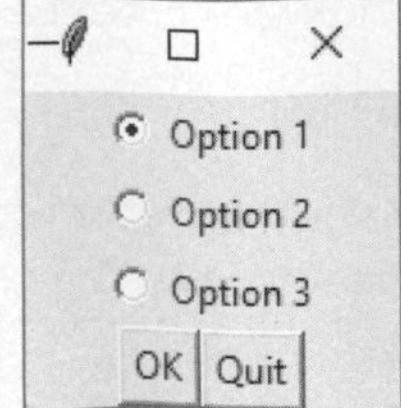

… `tkinter` module's `Radiobutton` class to create `Radiobutton` widgets. Only … `diobutton` widgets in a container, such as a `Frame`, may be selected at any time. Clicking a `Radiobutton` selects it and automatically deselects any other `Radiobutton` in the same container. Because only one `Radiobutton` in a container can be selected at any given time, they are said to be *mutually exclusive*.

NOTE: The name "radio button" refers to the old car radios that had push buttons for selecting stations. Only one of the buttons could be pushed in at a time. When you pushed a button in, it automatically popped out any other button that was pushed in.

The `tkinter` module provides a class named `IntVar` that can be used along with `Radiobutton` widgets. When you create a group of `Radiobuttons`, you associate them all with the same `IntVar` object. You also assign a unique integer value to each `Radiobutton` widget. When one of the `Radiobutton` widgets is selected, it stores its unique integer value in the `IntVar` object.

Program 13-12 demonstrates how to create and use `Radiobuttons`. Figure 13-23 shows the window that the program displays. When the user clicks the OK button, an info dialog box appears indicating which of the `Radiobuttons` is selected.

Program 13-12 (radiobutton_demo.py)

```
# This program demonstrates a group of Radiobutton widgets.
import tkinter
import tkinter.messagebox

class MyGUI:
    def __init__(self):
        # Create the main window.
        self.main_window = tkinter.Tk()

        # Create two frames. One for the Radiobuttons
        # and another for the regular Button widgets.
        self.top_frame = tkinter.Frame(self.main_window)
        self.bottom_frame = tkinter.Frame(self.main_window)

        # Create an IntVar object to use with
        # the Radiobuttons.
        self.radio_var = tkinter.IntVar()

        # Set the intVar object to 1.
        self.radio_var.set(1)

        # Create the Radiobutton widgets in the top_frame.
        self.rb1 = tkinter.Radiobutton(self.top_frame,
                                       text='Option 1',
                                       variable=self.radio_var,
                                       value=1)
```

(program continues)

Program 13-12 *(continued)*

```
        self.rb2 = tkinter.Radiobutton(self.top_frame,
                                       text='Option 2',
                                       variable=self.radio_var,
                                       value=2)
        self.rb3 = tkinter.Radiobutton(self.top_frame,
                                       text='Option 3',
                                       variable=self.radio_var,
                                       value=3)

        # Pack the Radiobuttons.
        self.rb1.pack()
        self.rb2.pack()
        self.rb3.pack()

        # Create an OK button and a Quit button.
        self.ok_button = tkinter.Button(self.bottom_frame,
                                        text='OK',
                                        command=self.show_choice)
        self.quit_button = tkinter.Button(self.bottom_frame,
                                        text='Quit',
                                        command=self.main_window.destroy)

        # Pack the Buttons.
        self.ok_button.pack(side='left')
        self.quit_button.pack(side='left')

        # Pack the frames.
        self.top_frame.pack()
        self.bottom_frame.pack()

        # Start the mainloop.
        tkinter.mainloop()

    # The show_choice method is the callback function for the
    # OK button.
    def show_choice(self):
        tkinter.messagebox.showinfo('Selection', 'You selected option ' +
                                   str(self.radio_var.get()))

# Create an instance of the MyGUI class.
my_gui = MyGUI()
```

Figure 13-23 Window displayed by Program 13-12

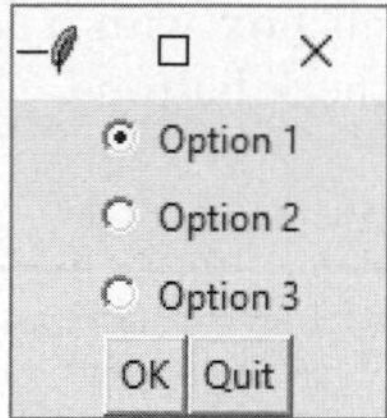

Line 17 creates an `IntVar` object named `radio_var`. Line 20 calls the `radio_var` object's `set` method to store the integer value 1 in the object. (You will see the significance of this in a moment.)

Lines 23 through 26 create the first `Radiobutton` widget. The argument `variable=self.radio_var` (in line 25) associates the `Radiobutton` with the `radio_var` object. The argument `value=1` (in line 26) assigns the integer 1 to this `Radiobutton`. As a result, any time this `Radiobutton` is selected, the value 1 will be stored in the `radio_var` object.

Lines 27 through 30 create the second `Radiobutton` widget. Notice this `Radiobutton` is also associated with the `radio_var` object. The argument `value=2` (in line 30) assigns the integer 2 to this `Radiobutton`. As a result, any time this `Radiobutton` is selected, the value 2 will be stored in the `radio_var` object.

Lines 31 through 34 create the third `Radiobutton` widget. This `Radiobutton` is also associated with the `radio_var` object. The argument `value=3` (in line 34) assigns the integer 3 to this `Radiobutton`. As a result, any time this `Radiobutton` is selected, the value 3 will be stored in the `radio_var` object.

The `show_choice` method in lines 62 through 64 is the callback function for the OK button. When the method executes, it calls the `radio_var` object's `get` method to retrieve the value stored in the object. The value is displayed in an info dialog box.

Did you notice when the program runs, the first `Radiobutton` is initially selected? This is because we set the `radio_var` object to the value 1 in line 20. Not only can the `radio_var` object be used to determine which `Radiobutton` was selected, but it can also be used to select a specific `Radiobutton`. When we store a particular `Radiobutton`'s value in the `radio_var` object, that `Radiobutton` will become selected.

Using Callback Functions with `Radiobuttons`

Program 13-12 waits for the user to click the OK button before it determines which `Radiobutton` was selected. If you prefer, you can also specify a callback function with `Radiobutton` widgets. Here is an example:

```
self.rb1 = tkinter.Radiobutton(self.top_frame,
                               text='Option 1',
                               variable=self.radio_var,
                               value=1,
                               command=self.my_method)
```

This code uses the argument `command=self.my_method` to specify that `my_method` is the callback function. The method `my_method` will be executed immediately when the `Radiobutton` is selected.

Check Buttons

A *check button* appears as a small box with a label appearing next to it. The window shown in Figure 13-24 has three check buttons.

Figure 13-24 A group of check buttons

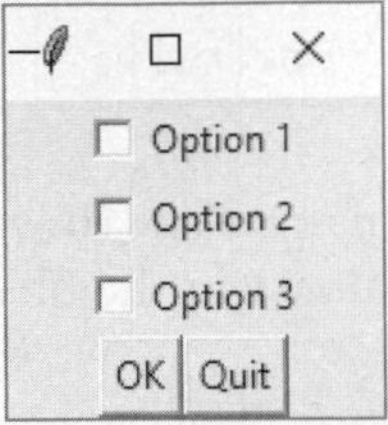

Like radio buttons, check buttons may be selected or deselected. When a check button is selected, a small check mark appears inside its box. Although check buttons are often displayed in groups, they are not used to make mutually exclusive selections. Instead, the user is allowed to select any or all of the check buttons that are displayed in a group.

You use the `tkinter` module's `Checkbutton` class to create `Checkbutton` widgets. As with `Radiobuttons`, you can use an `IntVar` object along with a `Checkbutton` widget. Unlike `Radiobuttons`, however, you associate a different `IntVar` object with each `Checkbutton`. When a `Checkbutton` is selected, its associated `IntVar` object will hold the value 1. When a `Checkbutton` is not selected, its associated `IntVar` object will hold the value 0.

Program 13-13 demonstrates how to create and use `Checkbuttons`. Figure 13-25 shows the window that the program displays. When the user clicks the OK button, an info dialog box appears indicating which of the `Checkbuttons` is selected.

Program 13-13 (checkbutton_demo.py)

```
# This program demonstrates a group of Checkbutton widgets.
import tkinter
import tkinter.messagebox

class MyGUI:
    def __init__(self):
        # Create the main window.
        self.main_window = tkinter.Tk()

        # Create two frames. One for the checkbuttons
        # and another for the regular Button widgets.
        self.top_frame = tkinter.Frame(self.main_window)
        self.bottom_frame = tkinter.Frame(self.main_window)

        # Create three IntVar objects to use with
        # the Checkbuttons.
        self.cb_var1 = tkinter.IntVar()
```

```
        self.cb_var2 = tkinter.IntVar()
        self.cb_var3 = tkinter.IntVar()

        # Set the intVar objects to 0.
        self.cb_var1.set(0)
        self.cb_var2.set(0)
        self.cb_var3.set(0)

        # Create the Checkbutton widgets in the top_frame.
        self.cb1 = tkinter.Checkbutton(self.top_frame,
                                       text='Option 1',
                                       variable=self.cb_var1)
        self.cb2 = tkinter.Checkbutton(self.top_frame,
                                       text='Option 2',
                                       variable=self.cb_var2)
        self.cb3 = tkinter.Checkbutton(self.top_frame,
                                       text='Option 3',
                                       variable=self.cb_var3)

        # Pack the Checkbuttons.
        self.cb1.pack()
        self.cb2.pack()
        self.cb3.pack()

        # Create an OK button and a Quit button.
        self.ok_button = tkinter.Button(self.bottom_frame,
                                        text='OK',
                                        command=self.show_choice)
        self.quit_button = tkinter.Button(self.bottom_frame,
                                          text='Quit',
                                          command=self.main_window.destroy)

        # Pack the Buttons.
        self.ok_button.pack(side='left')
        self.quit_button.pack(side='left')

        # Pack the frames.
        self.top_frame.pack()
        self.bottom_frame.pack()

        # Start the mainloop.
        tkinter.mainloop()

    # The show_choice method is the callback function for the
    # OK button.

```

(program continues)

Program 13-13 *(continued)*

```
    def show_choice(self):
        # Create a message string.
        self.message = 'You selected:\n'

        # Determine which Checkbuttons are selected and
        # build the message string accordingly.
        if self.cb_var1.get() == 1:
            self.message = self.message + '1\n'
        if self.cb_var2.get() == 1:
            self.message = self.message + '2\n'
        if self.cb_var3.get() == 1:
            self.message = self.message + '3\n'

        # Display the message in an info dialog box.
        tkinter.messagebox.showinfo('Selection', self.message)

# Create an instance of the MyGUI class.
my_gui = MyGUI()
```

Figure 13-25 Window displayed by Program 13-13

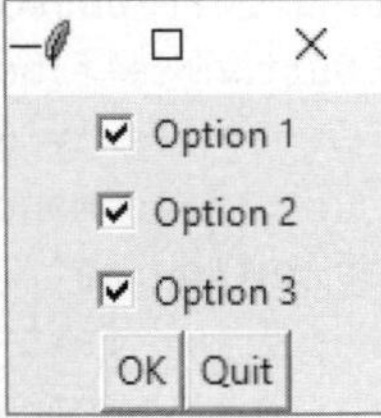

Checkpoint

13.15 You want the user to be able to select only one item from a group of items. Which type of component would you use for the items, radio buttons or check buttons?

13.16 You want the user to be able to select any number of items from a group of items. Which type of component would you use for the items, radio buttons or check buttons?

13.17 How can you use an `IntVar` object to determine which `Radiobutton` has been selected in a group of `Radiobuttons`?

13.18 How can you use an `IntVar` object to determine whether a `Checkbutton` has been selected?

13.9 Drawing Shapes with the Canvas Widget

CONCEPT: The Canvas widget provides methods for drawing simple shapes, such as lines, rectangles, ovals, polygons, and so on.

The Canvas widget is a blank, rectangular area that allows you to draw simple 2D shapes. In this section, we will discuss Canvas methods for drawing lines, rectangles, ovals, arcs, polygons, and text. Before we examine how to draw these shapes, however, we must discuss the screen coordinate system. You use the Canvas widget's *screen coordinate system* to specify the location of your graphics.

The Canvas Widget's Screen Coordinate System

The images that are displayed on a computer screen are made up of tiny dots called *pixels*. The screen coordinate system is used to identify the position of each pixel in an application's window. Each pixel has an *X* coordinate and a *Y* coordinate. The *X* coordinate identifies the pixel's horizontal position, and the *Y* coordinate identifies its vertical position. The coordinates are usually written in the form (*X*, *Y*).

In the Canvas widget's screen coordinate system, the coordinates of the pixel in the upper-left corner of the screen are (0, 0). This means that its *X* coordinate is 0 and its *Y* coordinate is 0. The *X* coordinates increase from left to right, and the *Y* coordinates increase from top to bottom. In a window that is 640 pixels wide by 480 pixels high, the coordinates of the pixel at the bottom right corner of the window are (639, 479). In the same window, the coordinates of the pixel in the center of the window are (319, 239). Figure 13-26 shows the coordinates of various pixels in the window.

Figure 13-26 Various pixel locations in a 640 by 480 window

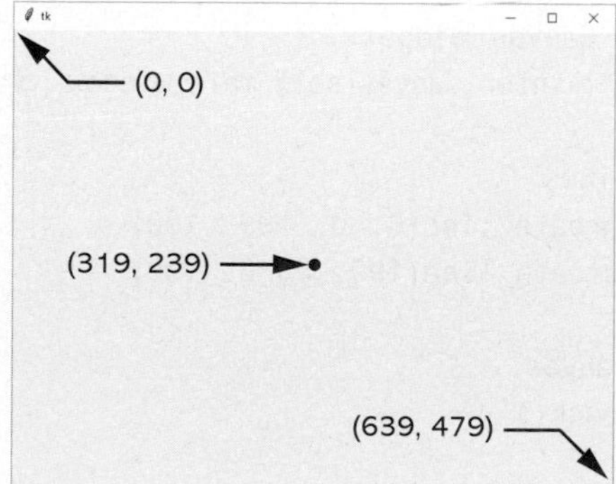

NOTE: The Canvas widget's screen coordinate system differs from the Cartesian coordinate system that is used by the turtle graphics library. Here are the differences:

- With the Canvas widget, the point (0, 0) is in the upper left corner of the window. In turtle graphics, the point (0, 0) is in the center of the window.
- With the Canvas widget, the *Y* coordinates increase as you move down the screen. In turtle graphics, the *Y* coordinates decrease as you move down the screen.

The Canvas widget has numerous methods for drawing graphical shapes on the surface of the widget. The methods that we will discuss are:

- `create_line`
- `create_rectangle`
- `create_oval`
- `create_arc`
- `create_polygon`
- `create_text`

Before discussing the details of these methods, let's look at Program 13-14. It is a simple program that uses a Canvas widget to draw lines. Figure 13-27 shows the window that the program displays.

Program 13-14 (draw_line.py)

```
# This program demonstrates the Canvas widget.
import tkinter

class MyGUI:
    def __init__(self):
        # Create the main window.
        self.main_window = tkinter.Tk()

        # Create the Canvas widget.
        self.canvas = tkinter.Canvas(self.main_window, width=200,height=200)

        # Draw two lines.
        self.canvas.create_line(0, 0, 199, 199)
        self.canvas.create_line(199, 0, 0, 199)

        # Pack the canvas.
        self.canvas.pack()

        # Start the mainloop.
        tkinter.mainloop()

# Create an instance of the MyGUI class.
my_gui = MyGUI()
```

Figure 13-27 Window displayed by Program 13-14

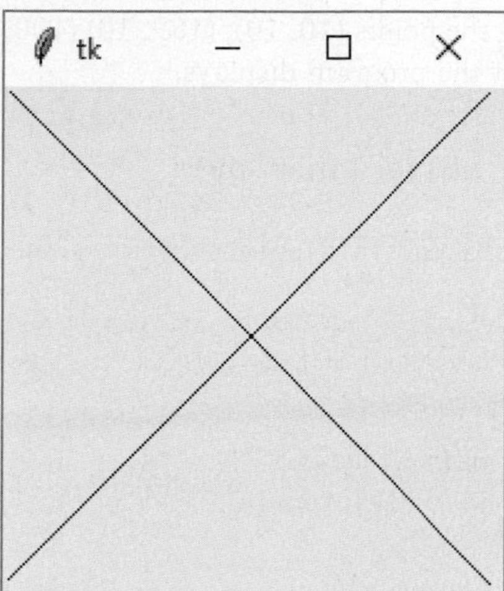

Let's take a closer look at the program. Line 10 creates the `Canvas` widget. The first argument inside the parentheses is a reference to `self.main_window`, which is the parent container to which we are adding the widget. The arguments `width=200` and `height=200` specify the size of the `Canvas` widget.

Line 13 calls the `Canvas` widget's `create_line` method, to draw a line. The first and second arguments are the (*X*, *Y*) coordinates of the line's starting point. The third and fourth arguments are the (*X*, *Y*) coordinates of the line's ending point. So, this statement draws a line on the `Canvas`, from (0, 0) to (199, 199).

Line 14 also calls the `Canvas` widget's `create_line` method, to draw a second line. This statement draws a line on the `Canvas`, from (199, 0) to (0, 199).

Line 17 calls the `Canvas` widget's `pack` method, which makes the widget visible. Line 20 executes the `tkinter` module's `mainloop` function.

Drawing Lines: The `create_line` Method

The `create_line` method draws a line between two or more points on the `Canvas`. Here is the general format of how you call the method to draw a line between two points:

```
canvas_name.create_line(x1, y1, x2, y2, options...)
```

The arguments *x1* and *y1* are the (*X*, *Y*) coordinates of the line's starting point. The arguments *x2* and *y2* are the (*X*, *Y*) coordinates of the line's ending point. In the general format, *options ...* indicates several optional keyword arguments that you may pass to the method. We will examine some of those in Table 13-2.

You saw examples of the `create_line` method being called in Program 13-14. Recall that line 13 in the program draws a line from (0, 0) to (199, 199):

```
self.canvas.create_line(0, 0, 199, 199)
```

You can pass multiple sets of coordinates as arguments. The `create_line` method will draw lines connecting the points. Program 13-15 demonstrates this. The statement in line 13 draws a line connecting the points (10, 10), (189, 10) (100, 189), and (10, 10). Figure 13-28 shows the window that the program displays.

Program 13-15 (draw_multi_lines.py)

```
1  # This program connects multiple points with a line.
2  import tkinter
3
4  class MyGUI:
5      def __init__(self):
6          # Create the main window.
7          self.main_window = tkinter.Tk()
8
9          # Create the Canvas widget.
10         self.canvas = tkinter.Canvas(self.main_window, width=200, height=200)
11
12         # Draw a line connecting multiple points.
13         self.canvas.create_line(10, 10, 189, 10, 100, 189, 10, 10)
14
15         # Pack the canvas.
16         self.canvas.pack()
17
18         # Start the mainloop.
19         tkinter.mainloop()
20
21 # Create an instance of the MyGUI class.
22 my_gui = MyGUI()
```

Figure 13-28 Window displayed by Program 13-15

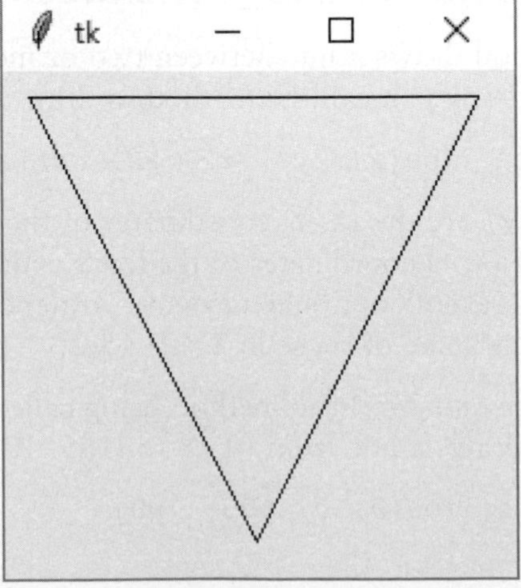

Alternatively, you can pass a list or a tuple containing the coordinates as an argument. For example, in Program 13-15, we could replace line 13 with the following code and get the same results:

```
points = [10, 10, 189, 10, 100, 189, 10, 10]
self.canvas.create_line(points)
```

There are several optional keyword arguments that you can pass to the `create_line` method. Table 13-2 lists some of the more commonly used ones.

Table 13-2 Some of the optional arguments to the `create_line` method

Argument	Description
`arrow=`*`value`*	By default, lines do not have arrowheads, but this argument causes the line to have an arrowhead at one or both ends. Specify `arrow=tk.FIRST` to draw an arrowhead at the beginning of the line, `arrow=tk.LAST` to draw an arrowhead at the end of the line, or `arrow=tk.BOTH` to draw arrowheads at both ends of the line.
`dash=`*`value`*	This argument causes the line to be a dashed line. The value is a tuple, consisting of integers, that specifies a pattern. The first integer specifies the number of pixels to draw, the second integer specifies the number of pixels to skip, and so forth. For example, the argument `dash=(5, 2)` will draw 5 pixels, skip 2 pixels, and repeat until the end of the line is reached.
`fill=`*`value`*	Specifies the color of the line. The argument's value is the name of a color, as a string. There are numerous predefined color names that you can use, and Appendix D shows the complete list. Some of the more common colors are `'red'`, `'green'`, `'blue'`, `'yellow'`, and `'cyan'`. (If you omit the `fill` argument, the default color is black.)
`smooth=`*`value`*	By default, the `smooth` argument is set to `False`, which makes the method draw straight lines connecting the specified points. If you specify `smooth=True`, the lines are drawn as curved splines.
`width=`*`value`*	Specifies the width of the line, in pixels. For example, the argument `width=5` causes the line to be 5 pixels wide. By default, lines are 1 pixel wide.

Drawing Rectangles: The `create_rectangle` Method

The `create_rectangle` method draws a rectangle on the `Canvas`. Here is the general format of how you call the method:

```
canvas_name.create_rectangle(x1, y1, x2, y2, options...)
```

The arguments *x1* and *y1* are the (*X*, *Y*) coordinates of the rectangle's upper-left corner. The arguments *x2* and *y2* are the (*X*, *Y*) coordinates of the rectangle's lower-right corner. In the general format, *options ...* indicates several optional keyword arguments that you may pass to the method. We will examine some of those in Table 13-3.

Program 13-16 demonstrates the `create_rectangle` method, in line 13. The rectangle's upper-left corner is at (20, 20), and its lower-right corner is at (180, 180). Figure 13-29 shows the window that the program displays.

Program 13-16 (draw_square.py)

```
# This program draws a rectangle on a Canvas.
import tkinter

class MyGUI:
    def __init__(self):
        # Create the main window.
        self.main_window = tkinter.Tk()

        # Create the Canvas widget.
        self.canvas = tkinter.Canvas(self.main_window, width=200, height=200)

        # Draw a rectangle.
        self.canvas.create_rectangle(20, 20, 180, 180)

        # Pack the canvas.
        self.canvas.pack()

        # Start the mainloop.
        tkinter.mainloop()

# Create an instance of the MyGUI class.
my_gui = MyGUI()
```

Figure 13-29 Window displayed by Program 13-16

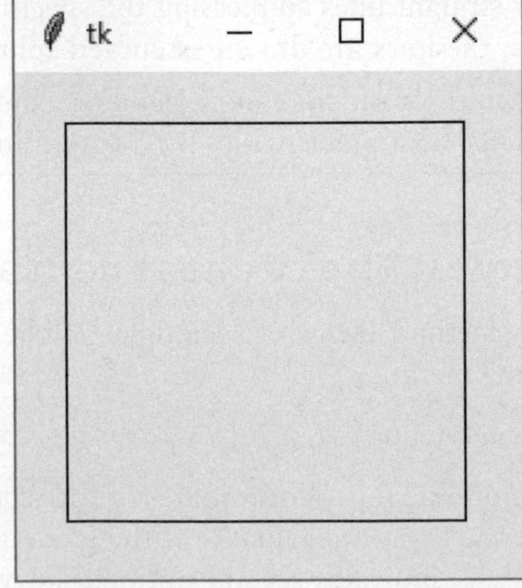

There are several optional keyword arguments that you can pass to the `create_rectangle` method. Table 13-3 lists some of the more commonly used ones.

Table 13-3 Some of the optional arguments to the `create_rectangle` method

Argument	Description
`dash=value`	This argument causes the outline of the rectangle to be a dashed line. The value is a tuple, consisting of integers, that specifies a pattern. The first integer specifies the number of pixels to draw, the second integer specifies the number of pixels to skip, and so forth. For example, the argument `dash=(5,2)` will draw 5 pixels, skip 2 pixels, and repeat until the end of the line is reached.
`fill=value`	Specifies a color with which to fill the rectangle. The argument's value is the name of a color, as a string. There are numerous predefined color names that you can use, and Appendix D shows the complete list. Some of the more common colors are `'red'`, `'green'`, `'blue'`, `'yellow'`, and `'cyan'`. (If you omit the `fill` argument, the rectangle will not be filled.)
`outline=value`	Specifies the color of the rectangle's outline. The argument's value is the name of a color, as a string. There are numerous predefined color names that you can use, and Appendix D shows the complete list. Some of the more common colors are `'red'`, `'green'`, `'blue'`, `'yellow'`, and `'cyan'`. (If you omit the `outline` argument, the default color is black.)
`width=value`	Specifies the width of the rectangle's outline, in pixels. For example, the argument `width=5` causes the line to be 5 pixels wide. By default, lines are 1 pixel wide.

For example, if we modify line 13 in Program 13-16 as follows, the program will draw a rectangle with a dashed, 3-pixel wide outline. The program's output would appear as shown in Figure 13-30.

```
self.canvas.create_rectangle(20, 20, 180, 180, dash=(5, 2), width=3)
```

Figure 13-30 Dashed, 3-pixel wide outline

Drawing Ovals: The `create_oval` Method

The `create_oval` method draws an oval, or an ellipse. Here is the general format of how you call the method:

```
canvas_name.create_oval(x1, y1, x2, y2, options...)
```

The method draws an oval that fits just inside a bounding rectangle defined by the coordinates that are passed as arguments. (*x1*, *y1*) are the coordinates of the rectangle's upper-left corner, and (*x2*, *y2*) are the coordinates of the rectangle's lower-right corner. This is illustrated in Figure 13-31. In the general format, *options ...* indicates several optional keyword arguments that you may pass to the method. We will examine some of those in Table 13-4.

Figure 13-31 An oval's bounding rectangle

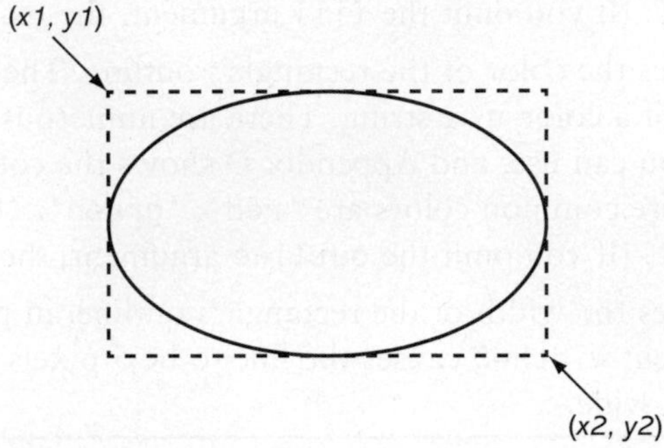

Program 13-17 demonstrates the `create_oval` method, in lines 13 and 14. The first oval, drawn in line 13, is defined by a rectangle with its upper-left corner at (20, 20) and its lower-right corner at (70, 70). The second oval, drawn in line 14, is defined by a rectangle with its upper-left corner at (100, 100) and its lower-right corner at (180, 130). Figure 13-32 shows the window that the program displays.

Program 13-17 (draw_ovals.py)

```
1  # This program draws two ovals on a Canvas.
2  import tkinter
3
4  class MyGUI:
5      def __init__(self):
6          # Create the main window.
7          self.main_window = tkinter.Tk()
8
9          # Create the Canvas widget.
10         self.canvas = tkinter.Canvas(self.main_window, width=200, height=200)
11
12         # Draw two ovals.
13         self.canvas.create_oval(20, 20, 70, 70)
14         self.canvas.create_oval(100, 100, 180, 130)
15
16         # Pack the canvas.
17         self.canvas.pack()
```

```

        # Start the mainloop.
        tkinter.mainloop()

# Create an instance of the MyGUI class.
my_gui = MyGUI()
```

Figure 13-32 Window displayed by Program 13-17

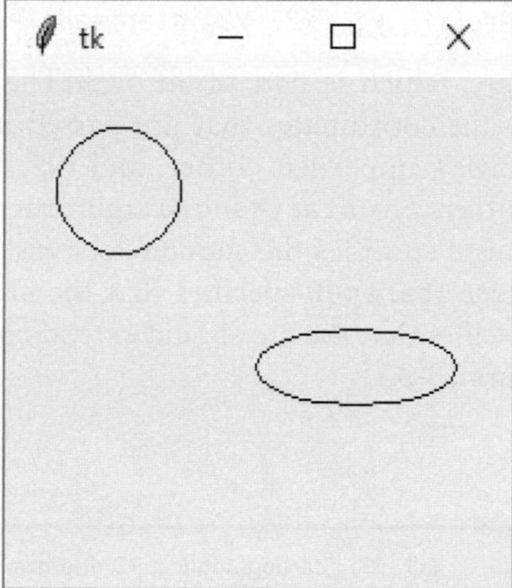

There are several optional keyword arguments that you can pass to the `create_oval` method. Table 13-4 lists some of the more commonly used ones.

Table 13-4 Some of the optional arguments to the `create_oval` method

Argument	Description
`dash=`*`value`*	This argument causes the outline of the oval to be a dashed line. The value is a tuple, consisting of integers, that specifies a pattern. The first integer specifies the number of pixels to draw, the second integer specifies the number of pixels to skip, and so forth. For example, the argument `dash=(5, 2)` will draw 5 pixels, skip 2 pixels, and repeat until the end of the line is reached.
`fill=`*`value`*	Specifies a color to fill the oval with which. The argument's value is the name of a color, as a string. There are numerous predefined color names that you can use, and Appendix D shows the complete list. Some of the more common colors are `'red'`, `'green'`, `'blue'`, `'yellow'`, and `'cyan'`. (If you omit the `fill` argument, the oval will not be filled.)
`outline=`*`value`*	Specifies the color of the oval's outline. The argument's value is the name of a color, as a string. There are numerous predefined color names that you can use, and Appendix D shows the complete list. Some of the more common colors are `'red'`, `'green'`, `'blue'`, `'yellow'`, and `'cyan'`. (If you omit the `outline` argument, the default color is black.)
`width=`*`value`*	Specifies the width of the oval's outline, in pixels. For example, the argument `width=5` causes the line to be 5 pixels wide. By default, lines are 1 pixel wide.

> **TIP:** To draw a circle, call the `create_oval` method and make all sides of the bounding rectangle the same length.

Drawing Arcs: The `create_arc` Method

The `create_arc` method draws an arc. Here is the general format of how you call the method:

```
canvas_name.create_arc(x1, y1, x2, y2, start=angle, extent=width, options...)
```

This method draws an arc, which is part of an oval. The oval fits just inside a bounding rectangle defined by the coordinates that are passed as arguments. (*x1*, *y1*) are the coordinates of the rectangle's upper-left corner, and (*x2*, *y2*) are the coordinates of the rectangle's lower-right corner. The `start=`*`angle`* argument specifies the starting angle, and the `extent=`*`width`* argument specifies the counterclockwise extent of the arc, as an angle. For example, the argument `start=90` specifies that the arc starts at 90 degrees, and the argument `extent=45` specifies that the arc should extend counterclockwise for 45 degrees. This is illustrated in Figure 13-33.

Figure 13-33 Arc properties

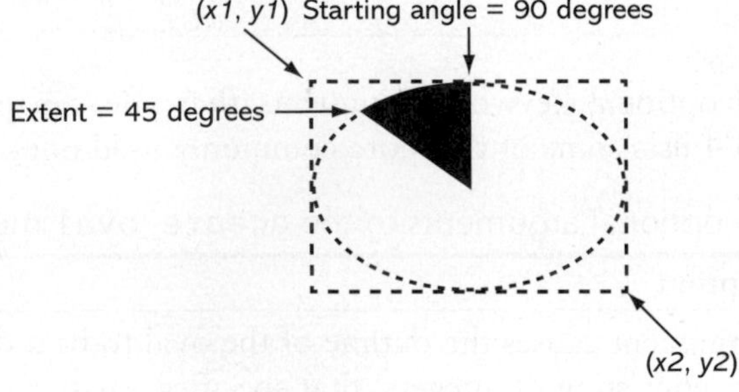

In the general format, *`options . . .`* indicates several optional keyword arguments that you may pass to the method. We will examine some of those in Table 13-5.

Program 13-18 demonstrates the `create_arc` method. The arc, drawn in line 13, is defined by a bounding rectangle with its upper-left corner at (10, 10), and its lower-right corner at (190, 190). The arc starts at 45 degrees, and extends for 30 degrees. Figure 13-34 shows the window that the program displays.

Program 13-18 (draw_arc.py)

```
1  # This program draws an arc on a Canvas.
2  import tkinter
3
```

```
class MyGUI:
    def __init__(self):
        # Create the main window.
        self.main_window = tkinter.Tk()

        # Create the Canvas widget.
        self.canvas = tkinter.Canvas(self.main_window, width=200, height=200)

        # Draw an arc.
        self.canvas.create_arc(10, 10, 190, 190, start=45, extent=30)

        # Pack the canvas.
        self.canvas.pack()

        # Start the mainloop.
        tkinter.mainloop()

# Create an instance of the MyGUI class.
my_gui = MyGUI()
```

Figure 13-34 Window displayed by Program 13-18

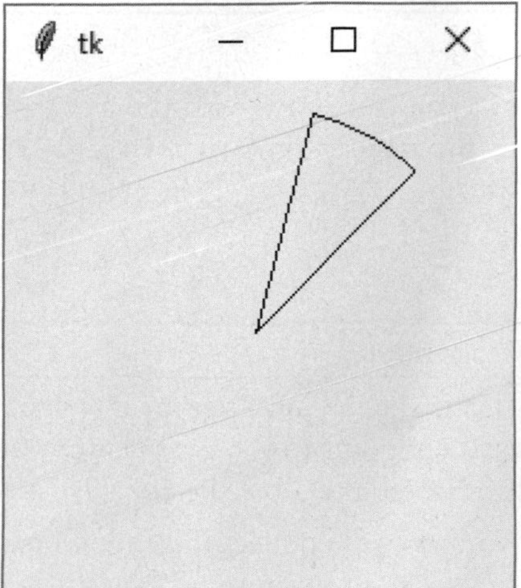

There are several optional keyword arguments that you can pass to th _arc method. Table 13-5 lists some of the more commonly used ones.

Table 13-5 Some of the optional arguments to the `create_arc` method

Argument	Description
`dash=value`	This argument causes the outline of the arc to be a dashed line. The value is a tuple, consisting of integers, that specifies a pattern. The first integer specifies the number of pixels to draw, the second integer specifies the number of pixels to skip, and so forth. For example, the argument `dash=(5, 2)` will draw 5 pixels, skip 2 pixels, and repeat until the end of the line is reached.
`fill=value`	Specifies a color with which to fill the arc. The argument's value is the name of a color, as a string. There are numerous predefined color names that you can use, and Appendix D shows the complete list. Some of the more common colors are `'red'`, `'green'`, `'blue'`, `'yellow'`, and `'cyan'`. (If you omit the `fill` argument, the arc will not be filled.)
`outline=value`	Specifies the color of the arc's outline. The argument's value is the name of a color, as a string. There are numerous predefined color names that you can use, and Appendix D shows the complete list. Some of the more common colors are `'red'`, `'green'`, `'blue'`, `'yellow'`, and `'cyan'`. (If you omit the `outline` argument, the default color is black.)
`style=value`	Specifies the style of the arc. The `style` argument can be one of the values `tkinter.PIESLICE`, `tkinter.ARC`, or `tkinter.CHORD`. See Table 13-6 for more information.
`width=value`	Specifies the width of the arc's outline, in pixels. For example, the argument `width=5` causes the line to be 5 pixels wide. By default, lines are 1 pixel wide.

There are three styles of arc you can draw with the `style=arcstyle` argument, summarized in Table 13-6. (Note the default type is `tkinter.PIESLICE`.) Figure 13-35 shows examples of each type of arc.

Table 13-6 Arc types

`style` Argument	Description
`style=tkinter.PIESLICE`	This is the default arc type. Straight lines will be drawn from each endpoint to the arc's center point. As a result, the arc will be shaped like a pie slice.
`style=tkinter.ARC`	No lines will connect the endpoints. Only the arc will be drawn.
`style=tkinter.CHORD`	A straight line will be drawn from one endpoint of the arc to the other endpoint.

-35 Types of arcs

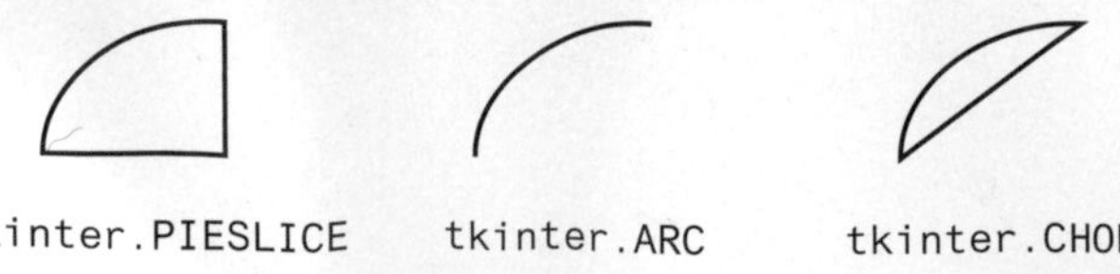

`tkinter.PIESLICE` `tkinter.ARC` `tkinter.CHORD`

Program 13-19 shows an example program that uses arcs to draw a pie chart. The program's output is shown in Figure 13-36.

Program 13-19 (draw_piechart.py)

```
# This program draws a pie chart on a Canvas.
import tkinter

class MyGUI:
    def __init__(self):
        self.__CANVAS_WIDTH = 320  # Canvas width
        self.__CANVAS_HEIGHT = 240 # Canvas height
        self.__X1 = 60             # Upper-left X of bounding rectangle
        self.__Y1 = 20             # Upper-left Y of bounding rectangle
        self.__X2 = 260            # Lower-right X of bounding rectangle
        self.__Y2 = 220            # Lower-right Y of bounding rectangle
        self.__PIE1_START = 0      # Starting angle of slice 1
        self.__PIE1_WIDTH = 45     # Extent of slice 1
        self.__PIE2_START = 45     # Starting angle of slice 2
        self.__PIE2_WIDTH = 90     # Extent of slice 2
        self.__PIE3_START = 135    # Starting angle of slice 3
        self.__PIE3_WIDTH = 120    # Extent of slice 3
        self.__PIE4_START = 255    # Starting angle of slice 4
        self.__PIE4_WIDTH = 105    # Extent of slice 4

        # Create the main window.
        self.main_window = tkinter.Tk()

        # Create the Canvas widget.
        self.canvas = tkinter.Canvas(self.main_window,
                                     width=self.__CANVAS_WIDTH,
                                     height=self.__CANVAS_HEIGHT)

        # Draw slice 1.
        self.canvas.create_arc(self.__X1, self.__Y1, self.__X2, self.__Y2,
                               start=self.__PIE1_START,
                               extent=self.__PIE1_WIDTH,
                               fill='red')

        # Draw slice 2.
        self.canvas.create_arc(self.__X1, self.__Y1, self.__X2, self.__Y2,
                               start=self.__PIE2_START,
                               extent=self.__PIE2_WIDTH,
                               fill='green')

```

```
41         # Draw slice 3.
42         self.canvas.create_arc(self.__X1, self.__Y1, self.__X2, self.__Y2,
43                                start=self.__PIE3_START,
44                                extent=self.__PIE3_WIDTH,
45                                fill='black')
46 
47         # Draw slice 4.
48         self.canvas.create_arc(self.__X1, self.__Y1, self.__X2, self.__Y2,
49                                start=self.__PIE4_START,
50                                extent=self.__PIE4_WIDTH,
51                                fill='yellow')
52 
53         # Pack the canvas.
54         self.canvas.pack()
55 
56         # Start the mainloop.
57         tkinter.mainloop()
58 
59 # Create an instance of the MyGUI class.
60 my_gui = MyGUI()
```

Figure 13-36 Window displayed by Program 13-19

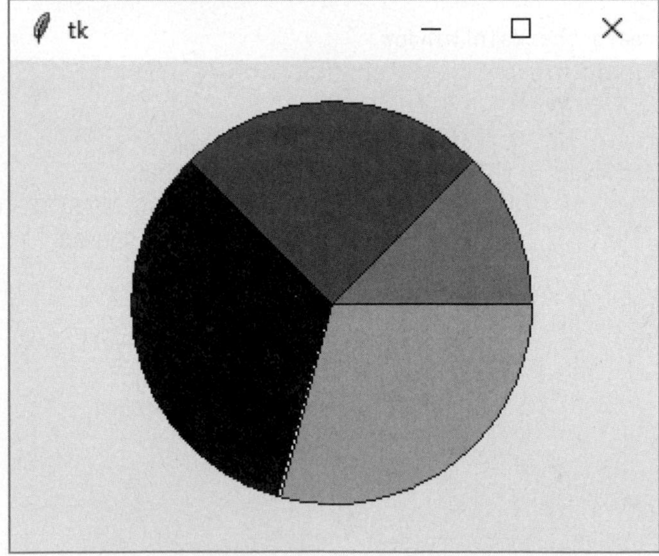

Let's take a closer look at the `__init__` method in the `MyGUI` class, in Program 13-19:

- Lines 6 and 7 define attributes for the `Canvas` widget's width and height.
- Lines 8–11 define attributes for the coordinates of the upper-left and lower-right corners of the bounding rectangle that each arc will share.

- Lines 12–19 define attributes for each of the pie slice's starting angle and extent.
- Line 22 creates the main window, and lines 25–27 create the `Canvas` widget.
- Lines 30–33 create the first pie slice, setting its fill color to red.
- Lines 36–39 create the second pie slice, setting its fill color to green.
- Lines 42–45 create the third pie slice, setting its fill color to black.
- Line 54 packs the `Canvas`, making its contents visible, and line 57 starts the `tkinter` module's `mainloop` function.

Drawing Polygons: The `create_polygon` Method

The `create_polygon` method draws a closed polygon on the `Canvas`. A polygon is constructed of multiple line segments that are connected. The point where two line segments are connected is called a *vertex*. Here is the general format of how you call the method to draw a polygon:

```
canvas_name.create_polygon(x1, y1, x2, y2, ..., options ...)
```

The arguments *`x1`* and *`y1`* are the (*X*, *Y*) coordinates of the first vertex, *`x2`* and *`y2`* are the (*X*, *Y*) coordinates of the second vertex, and so on. The method will automatically close the polygon by drawing a line segment from the last vertex to the first vertex. In the general format, *`options ...`* indicates several optional keyword arguments that you may pass to the method. We will examine some of those in Table 13-7.

Program 13-20 demonstrates the `create_polygon` method. The statement in lines 13 and 14 draws a polygon with eight vertices. The first vertex is at (60, 20), the second vertex is at (100, 20), and so on, as illustrated in Figure 13-37. Figure 13-38 shows the window that the program displays.

Program 13-20 (draw_polygon.py)

```
 1  # This program draws a polygon on a Canvas.
 2  import tkinter
 3
 4  class MyGUI:
 5      def __init__(self):
 6          # Create the main window.
 7          self.main_window = tkinter.Tk()
 8
 9          # Create the Canvas widget.
10          self.canvas = tkinter.Canvas(self.main_window, width=160, height=160)
11
12          # Draw a polygon.
13          self.canvas.create_polygon(60, 20, 100, 20, 140, 60, 140, 100,
14                                     100, 140, 60, 140, 20, 100, 20, 60)
15
16          # Pack the canvas.
17          self.canvas.pack()
```

(program continues)

Program 13-20 *(continued)*

```

        # Start the mainloop.
        tkinter.mainloop()

# Create an instance of the MyGUI class.
my_gui = MyGUI()
```

Figure 13-37 Points of each vertex in the polygon

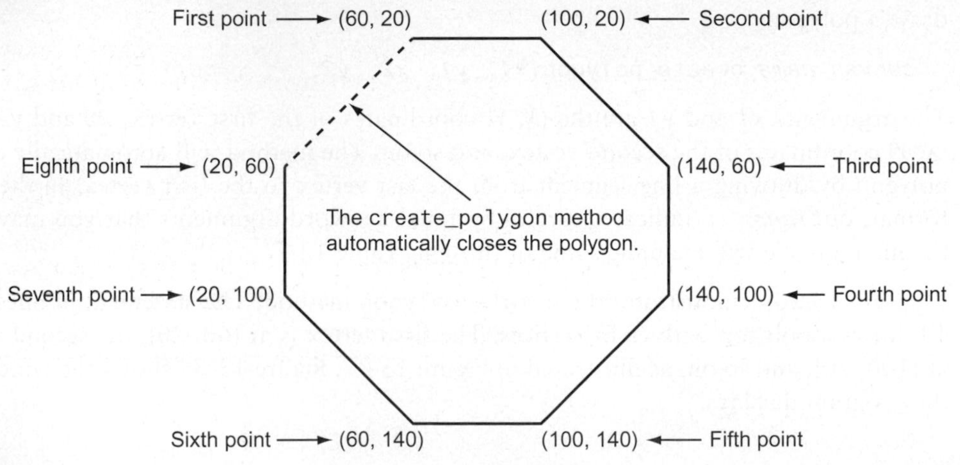

Figure 13-38 Window displayed by Program 13-20

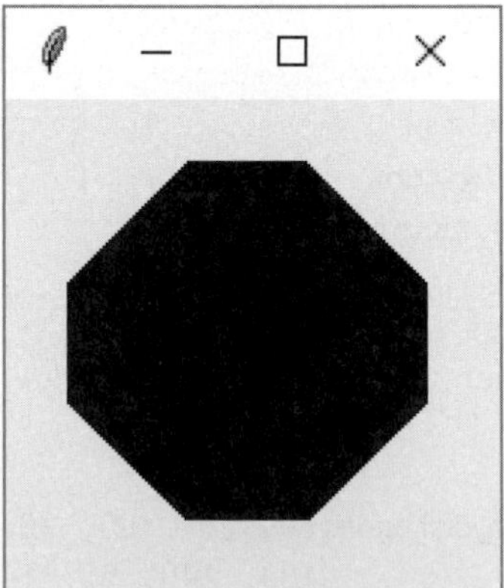

There are several optional keyword arguments that you can pass to the `create_polygon` method. Table 13-7 lists some of the more commonly used ones.

Table 13-7 Some of the optional arguments to the `create_polygon` method

Argument	Description
`dash=value`	This argument causes the outline of the polygon to be a dashed line. The first integer specifies the number of pixels to draw, the second integer specifies the number of pixels to skip, and so forth. For example, the argument `dash=(5, 2)` will draw 5 pixels, skip 2 pixels, and repeat until the end of the line is reached.
`fill=value`	Specifies a color with which to fill the polygon. The value is the name of a color, as a string. There are numerous predefined color names that you can use, and Appendix D shows the complete list. Some of the more common colors are `'red'`, `'green'`, `'blue'`, `'yellow'`, and `'cyan'`. (If you omit the `fill` argument, the polygon will be filled with black.)
`outline=value`	Specifies the color of the polygon's outline. The value is the name of a color, as a string. There are numerous predefined color names that you can use, and Appendix D shows the complete list. Some of the more common colors are `'red'`, `'green'`, `'blue'`, `'yellow'`, and `'cyan'`. (If you omit the `outline` argument, the default color is black.)
`smooth=value`	By default, the smooth argument is set to `False`, which makes the method draw straight lines connecting the specified points. If you specify `smooth=True`, the lines are drawn as curved splines.
`width=value`	The value is an integer that specifies the width of the polygon's outline, in pixels. For example, the argument `width=5` causes the outline to be 5 pixels wide. By default, the outline is 1 pixel wide.

Drawing Text: The `create_text` Method

You can use the `create_text` function to display text on the `Canvas`. Here is the general format of how you call the method:

```
canvas_name.create_text(x, y, text=text, options ...)
```

The arguments *x* and *y* are the (*X*, *Y*) coordinates of the text's insertion point, and the `text=text` argument specifies the text to display. By default, the text is centered horizontally and vertically around the insertion point. In the general format, *options . . .* indicates several optional keyword arguments that you may pass to the method. We will examine some of those in Table 13-8.

Program 13-21 demonstrates the `create_text` method. The statement in line 13 displays the text `'Hello World'` in the center of the window, at coordinates (100, 100). Figure 13-39 shows the window that the program displays.

Program 13-21 (draw_text.py)

```
1  # This program draws text on a Canvas.
2  import tkinter
3
```

(program continues)

Program 13-21 *(continued)*

```
class MyGUI:
    def __init__(self):
        # Create the main window.
        self.main_window = tkinter.Tk()

        # Create the Canvas widget.
        self.canvas = tkinter.Canvas(self.main_window, width=200, height=200)

        # Display text in the center of the window.
        self.canvas.create_text(100, 100, text='Hello World')

        # Pack the canvas.
        self.canvas.pack()

        # Start the mainloop.
        tkinter.mainloop()

# Create an instance of the MyGUI class.
my_gui = MyGUI()
```

Figure 13-39 Window displayed by Program 13-21

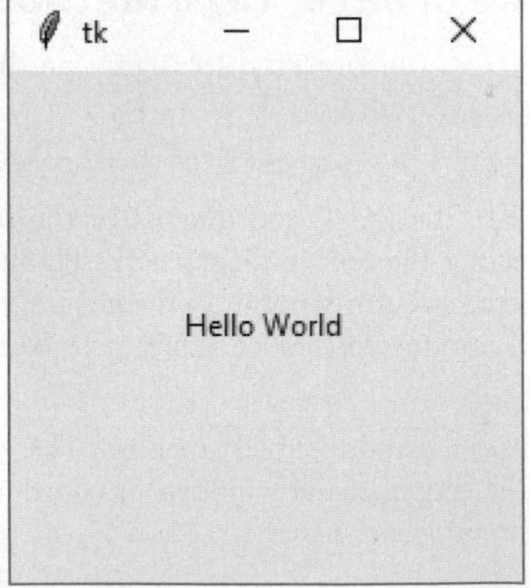

There are several optional keyword arguments that you can pass to the `create_text` method. Table 13-8 lists some of the more commonly used ones.

Table 13-8 Some of the optional arguments to the `create_text` method

Argument	Description
`anchor=value`	This argument specifies how the text is positioned relative to its insertion point. By default, the `anchor` argument is set to `tkinter.CENTER`, causing the text to be centered both vertically and horizontally around the insertion point. You can specify any of the values listed in Table 13-9.
`fill=value`	Specifies the text color. The value is the name of a color, as a string. There are numerous predefined color names that you can use, and Appendix D shows the complete list. Some of the more common colors are `'red'`, `'green'`, `'blue'`, `'yellow'`, and `'cyan'`. (If you omit the `fill` argument, the text will be black.)
`font=value`	To change the default font, create a `tkinter.font.Font` object and pass it as value of the `font` argument. (See the discussion on fonts later in this section.)
`justify=value`	If multiple lines of text are displayed, this argument specifies how the lines are justified. The values can be `tk.LEFT`, `tk.CENTER`, or `tk.RIGHT`. The default value is `tk.LEFT`.

There are nine different ways that you can position the text relative to its insertion point. You use the `anchor=position` argument to change the positioning. The different values of the argument are summarized in Table 13-9. Note the default value is `tkinter.CENTER`.

Table 13-9 anchor values

anchor Argument	Description
`anchor=tkinter.CENTER`	Causes the text to be vertically and horizontally centered around the insertion point. This is the default positioning.
`anchor=tkinter.NW`	Causes the text to be positioned, so the insertion point is at the text's upper-left corner (northwest).
`anchor=tkinter.N`	Causes the text to be positioned, so the insertion point is centered along the top edge of the text (north).
`anchor=tkinter.NE`	Causes the text to be positioned, so the insertion point is at the text's upper-right corner (northeast).
`anchor=tkinter.W`	Causes the text to be positioned, so the insertion point is at the text's left edge, in the middle (west).
`anchor=tkinter.E`	Causes the text to be positioned, so the insertion point is at the text's right edge, in the middle (east).
`anchor=tkinter.SW`	Causes the text to be positioned, so the insertion point is at the text's lower-left corner (southwest).
`anchor=tkinter.S`	Causes the text to be positioned, so the insertion point is centered along the bottom edge of the text (south).
`anchor=tkinter.SE`	Causes the text to be positioned, so the insertion point is at the text's lower-right corner (southeast).

Figure 13-40 illustrates the different anchor positions. In the figure, each line of text has a dot that represents the position of the insertion point.

Figure 13-40 Results of the various `anchor` values

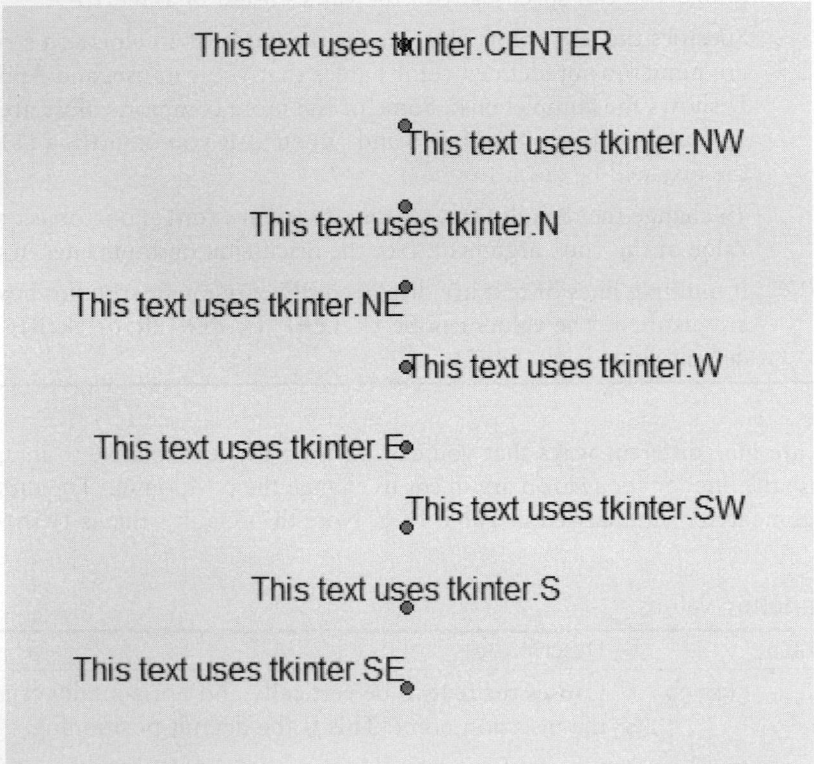

This text uses tkinter.CENTER
This text uses tkinter.NW
This text uses tkinter.N
This text uses tkinter.NE
This text uses tkinter.W
This text uses tkinter.E
This text uses tkinter.SW
This text uses tkinter.S
This text uses tkinter.SE

Setting the Font

You can set the font that is used with the `create_text` method by creating a `Font` object, and passing it as the `font=` argument. The `Font` class is in the `tkinter.font` module, so you must include the following `import` statement in your program:

```
import tkinter.font
```

Here is an example of creating a `Font` object that specifies a Helvetica 12-point font:

```
myfont = tkinter.font.Font(family='Helvetica', size='12')
```

When you construct a `Font` object, you can pass values for any of the keyword arguments shown in Table 13-10.

Table 13-10 Keyword arguments for the Font class

Argument	Description
`family=value`	This argument is a string that specifies the name of the font family, such as `'Arial'`, `'Courier'`, `'Helvetica'`, `'Times New Roman'`, and so on.
`size=value`	This argument is an integer that specifies the font size in points.
`weight=value`	This argument specifies the weight of the font. The valid values are the strings `'bold'` and `'normal'`.
`slant=value`	This argument specifies the slant of the font. If you want the font to appear slanted, specify `'italic'`. If you want the font to appear unslanted, specify `'roman'`.
`underline=value`	If you want the text to appear underlined, specify 1. Otherwise, specify 0.
`overstrike=value`	If you want the text to appear crossed-out, specify 1. Otherwise, specify 0.

The names of the font families that are available are somewhat system-dependent. To see a list of the font families that you have installed, enter the following at the Python shell:

```
>>> import tkinter
>>> import tkinter.font
>>> tkinter.Tk()
<tkinter.Tk object .>
>>> tkinter.font.families()
```

Program 13-22 shows an example of displaying text with an 18-point boldface Helvetica font. Figure 13-41 shows the window that the program displays.

Program 13-22 (font_demo.py)

```
# This program draws text on a Canvas.
import tkinter
import tkinter.font

class MyGUI:
    def __init__(self):
        # Create the main window.
        self.main_window = tkinter.Tk()

        # Create the Canvas widget.
        self.canvas = tkinter.Canvas(self.main_window, width=200, height=200)

        # Create a Font object.
        myfont = tkinter.font.Font(family='Helvetica', size=18, weight='bold')

        # Display some text.
        self.canvas.create_text(100, 100, text='Hello World', font=myfont)
```

(program continues)

Program 13-22 *(continued)*

```

        # Pack the canvas.
        self.canvas.pack()

        # Start the mainloop.
        tkinter.mainloop()

# Create an instance of the MyGUI class.
my_gui = MyGUI()
```

Figure 13-41 Window displayed by Program 13-22

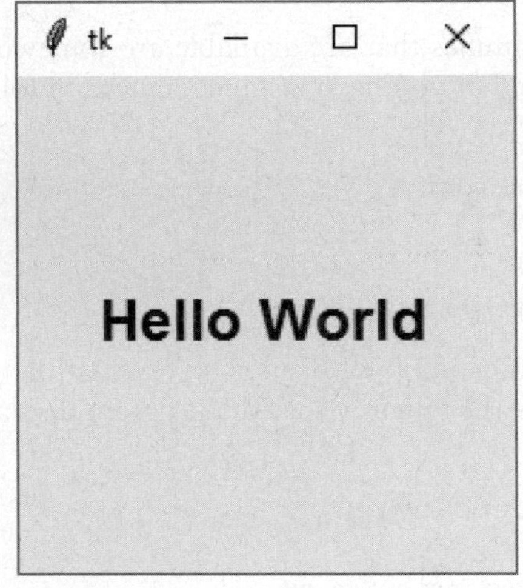

Checkpoint

13.19 In the Canvas widget's screen coordinate system, what are the coordinates of the pixel in the upper-left corner of the window?

13.20 Using the Canvas widget's screen coordinate system with a window that is 640 pixels wide by 480 pixels high, what are the coordinates of the pixel in the lower-right corner?

13.21 How is the Canvas widget's screen coordinate system different from the Cartesian coordinate system used by the turtle graphics library?

13.22 What Canvas widget methods would you use to draw each of the following types of shapes?

a) A circle
b) A square
c) A rectangle
d) A closed six-sided shape
e) An ellipse
f) An arc

Review Questions

Multiple Choice

1. The ______________ is the part of a computer with which the user interacts.
   a. central processing unit
   b. user interface
   c. control system
   d. interactivity system
2. Before GUIs became popular, the ______________ interface was the most commonly used.
   a. command line
   b. remote terminal
   c. sensory
   d. event-driven
3. A ______________ is a small window that displays information and allows the user to perform actions.
   a. menu
   b. confirmation window
   c. startup screen
   d. dialog box
4. These types of programs are event driven.
   a. command line
   b. text-based
   c. GUI
   d. procedural
5. An item that appears in a program's graphical user interface is known as a(n) ______________.
   a. gadget
   b. widget
   c. tool
   d. iconified object
6. You can use this module in Python to create GUI programs.
   a. `GUI`
   b. `PythonGui`
   c. `tkinter`
   d. `tgui`
7. This widget is an area that displays one line of text.
   a. `Label`
   b. `Entry`
   c. `TextLine`
   d. `Canvas`
8. This widget is an area in which the user may type a single line of input from the keyboard.
   a. `Label`
   b. `Entry`
   c. `TextLine`
   d. `Input`

9. This widget is a container that can hold other widgets.
   a. `Grouper`
   b. `Composer`
   c. `Fence`
   d. `Frame`
10. This method arranges a widget in its proper position, and it makes the widget visible when the main window is displayed.
    a. `pack`
    b. `arrange`
    c. `position`
    d. `show`
11. A(n) ______________ is a function or method that is called when a specific event occurs.
    a. callback function
    b. auto function
    c. startup function
    d. exception
12. The `showinfo` function is in this module.
    a. `tkinter`
    b. `tkinfo`
    c. `sys`
    d. `tkinter.messagebox`
13. You can call this method to close a GUI program.
    a. The root widget's `destroy` method
    b. Any widget's `cancel` method
    c. The `sys.shutdown` function
    d. The `Tk.shutdown` method
14. You call this method to retrieve data from an `Entry` widget.
    a. `get_entry`
    b. `data`
    c. `get`
    d. `retrieve`
15. An object of this type can be associated with a `Label` widget, and any data stored in the object will be displayed in the `Label`.
    a. `StringVar`
    b. `LabelVar`
    c. `LabelValue`
    d. `DisplayVar`
16. If there are a group of these in a container, only one of them can be selected at any given time.
    a. `Checkbutton`
    b. `Radiobutton`
    c. `Mutualbutton`
    d. `Button`

17. The __________ widget provides methods for drawing simple 2D shapes.
    a. `Shape`
    b. `Draw`
    c. `Palette`
    d. `Canvas`

True or False

1. The Python language has built-in keywords for creating GUI programs.
2. Every widget has a `quit` method that can be called to close the program.
3. The data that you retrieve from an `Entry` widget is always of the `int` data type.
4. A mutually exclusive relationship is automatically created among all `Radiobutton` widgets in the same container.
5. A mutually exclusive relationship is automatically created among all `Checkbutton` widgets in the same container.

Short Answer

1. When a program runs in a text-based environment, such as a command line interface, what determines the order in which things happen?
2. What does a widget's `pack` method do?
3. What does the `tkinter` module's `mainloop` function do?
4. If you create two widgets and call their `pack` methods with no arguments, how will the widgets be arranged inside their parent widget?
5. How do you specify that a widget should be positioned as far left as possible inside its parent widget?
6. How do you retrieve data from an `Entry` widget?
7. How can you use a `StringVar` object to update the contents of a `Label` widget?
8. How can you use an `IntVar` object to determine which `Radiobutton` has been selected in a group of `Radiobuttons`?
9. How can you use an `IntVar` object to determine whether a `Checkbutton` has been selected?

Algorithm Workbench

1. Write a statement that creates a `Label` widget. Its parent should be `self.main_ window`, and its text shoud be `'Programming is fun!'`
2. Assume `self.label1` and `self.label2` reference two `Label` widgets. Write code that packs the two widgets so they are positioned as far left as possible inside their parent widget.
3. Write a statement that creates a `Frame` widget. Its parent should be `self.main_ window`.
4. Write a statement that displays an info dialog box with the title "Program Paused" and the message "Click OK when you are ready to continue."
5. Write a statement that creates a `Button` widget. Its parent should be `self.button_ frame`, its text should be `'Calculate'`, and its callback function should be the `self. calculate` method.

6. Write a statement that creates a `Button` widget that closes the program when it is clicked. Its parent should be `self.button_frame`, and its text should be `'Quit'`.
7. Assume the variable `data_entry` references an `Entry` widget. Write a statement that retrieves the data from the widget, converts it to an `int`, and assigns it to a variable named `var`.
8. Assume that in a program, the following statement creates a `Canvas` widget and assigns it to the `self.canvas` variable:

```
self.canvas = tkinter.Canvas(self.main_window, width=200, height=200)
```

Write statements that do the following:

a) Draws a blue line from the `Canvas` widget's upper-left corner to its lower-right corner. The line should be 3 pixels wide.

b) Draws a rectangle with a red outline and a black interior. The rectangle's corners should appear in the following locations on the `Canvas`:
   - Upper-left: (50, 50)
   - Upper-right: (100, 50)
   - Lower-left: (50, 100)
   - Lower-right: (100, 100)

c) Draws a green circle. The circle's center-point should be at (100, 100), and its radius should be 50.

d) Draws a blue-filled arc that is defined by a bounding rectangle with its upper-left corner at (20, 20), and its lower-right corner at (180, 180). The arc should start at 0 degrees, and extend for 90 degrees.

Programming Exercises

1. Name and Address

VideoNote
The Name and Address Problem

Write a GUI program that displays your name and address when a button is clicked. The program's window should appear as the sketch on the left side of Figure 13-42 when it runs. When the user clicks the Show Info button, the program should display your name and address, as shown in the sketch on the right of the figure.

Figure 13-42 Name and address program

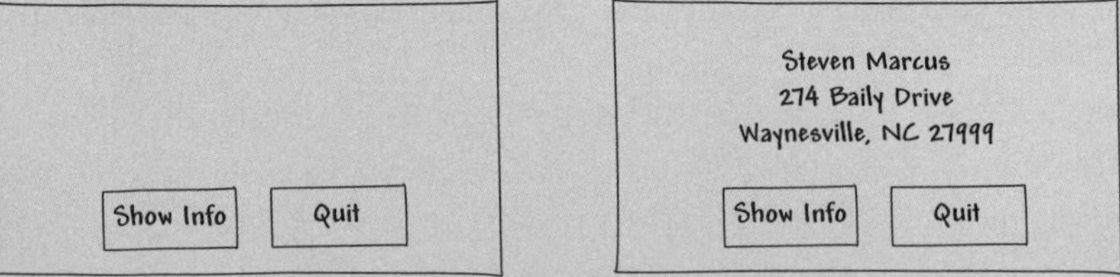

2. Latin Translator

Look at the following list of Latin words and their meanings:

Latin	English
sinister	left
dexter	right
medium	center

Write a GUI program that translates the Latin words to English. The window should have three buttons, one for each Latin word. When the user clicks a button, the program displays the English translation in a label.

3. Miles Per Gallon Calculator

Write a GUI program that calculates a car's gas mileage. The program's window should have `Entry` widgets that let the user enter the number of gallons of gas the car holds, and the number of miles it can be driven on a full tank. When a *Calculate MPG* button is clicked, the program should display the number of miles that the car may be driven per gallon of gas. Use the following formula to calculate miles-per-gallon:

$$MPG = \frac{miles}{gallons}$$

4. Celsius to Fahrenheit

Write a GUI program that converts Celsius temperatures to Fahrenheit temperatures. The user should be able to enter a Celsius temperature, click a button, then see the equivalent Fahrenheit temperature. Use the following formula to make the conversion:

$$F = \frac{9}{5}C + 32$$

F is the Fahrenheit temperature, and C is the Celsius temperature.

5. Property Tax

A county collects property taxes on the assessment value of property, which is 60 percent of the property's actual value. If an acre of land is valued at $10,000, its assessment value is $6,000. The property tax is then $0.75 for each $100 of the assessment value. The tax for the acre assessed at $6,000 will be $45.00. Write a GUI program that displays the assessment value and property tax when a user enters the actual value of a property.

6. Joe's Automotive

Joe's Automotive performs the following routine maintenance services:

- Oil change—$30.00
- Lube job—$20.00
- Radiator flush—$40.00
- Transmission flush—$100.00
- Inspection—$35.00
- Muffler replacement—$200.00
- Tire rotation—$20.00

Write a GUI program with check buttons that allow the user to select any or all of these services. When the user clicks a button, the total charges should be displayed.

7. Long-Distance Calls

A long-distance provider charges the following rates for telephone calls:

Rate Category	Rate per Minute
Daytime (6:00 A.M. through 5:59 P.M.)	$0.07
Evening (6:00 P.M. through 11:59 P.M.)	$0.12
Off-Peak (midnight through 5:59 A.M.)	$0.05

Write a GUI application that allows the user to select a rate category (from a set of radio buttons), and enter the number of minutes of the call into an `Entry` widget. An info dialog box should display the charge for the call.

8. This Old House

Use the `Canvas` widget that you learned in this chapter to draw a house. Be sure to include at least two windows and a door. Feel free to draw other objects as well, such as the sky, sun, and even clouds.

9. Tree Age

Counting the growth rings of a tree is a good way to tell the age of a tree. Each growth ring counts as one year. Use a `Canvas` widget to draw how the growth rings of a 5-year-old tree might look. Then, using the `create_text` method, number each growth ring starting from the center and working outward with the age in years associated with that ring.

10. Hollywood Star

Make your own star on the Hollywood Walk of Fame. Write a program that displays a star similar to the one shown in Figure 13-43, with your name displayed in the star.

Figure 13-43 Hollywood star

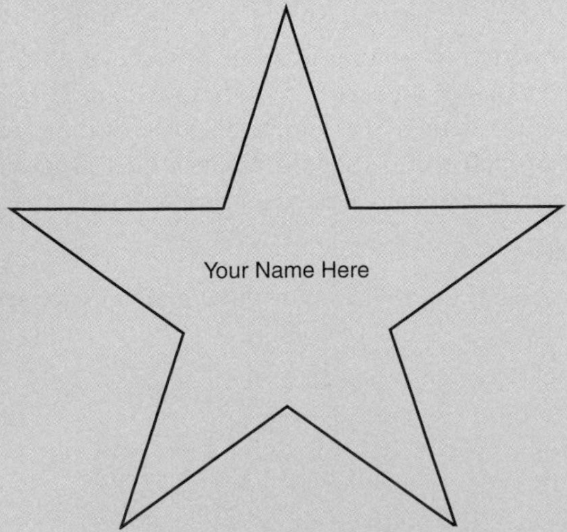

11. Vehicle Outline

Using the shapes you learned about in this chapter, draw the outline of the vehicle of your choice (car, truck, airplane, and so forth).

12. Solar System

Use a `Canvas` widget to draw each of the planets of our solar system. Draw the sun first, then each planet according to distance from the sun (Mercury, Venus, Earth, Mars, Jupiter Saturn, Uranus, Neptune, and the dwarf planet, Pluto). Label each planet using the `create_text` method.

APPENDIX

A Installing Python

Downloading Python

To run the programs shown in this book, you will need to install Python 3.0, or a later version. You can download the latest version of Python from www.python.org/downloads. This appendix discusses installing Python for Windows. Python is also available for the Mac, Linux, and several other platforms. Links to download versions of Python for these systems are shown on the Python download site at www.python.org/downloads.

TIP: Keep in mind that there are two *families* of Python that you can download: Python 3.*x* and Python 2.*x*. The programs in this book work only with the Python 3.*x* family.

Installing Python 3.*x* For Windows

When you visit the Python download site at www.python.org/downloads, you should download the latest version of Python 3.*x* that is available. Figure A-1 shows how the download site appeared at the time this was written. As you can see in the figure, Python 3.5.2 was the latest version at that time.

Figure A-1 Download the latest Python version

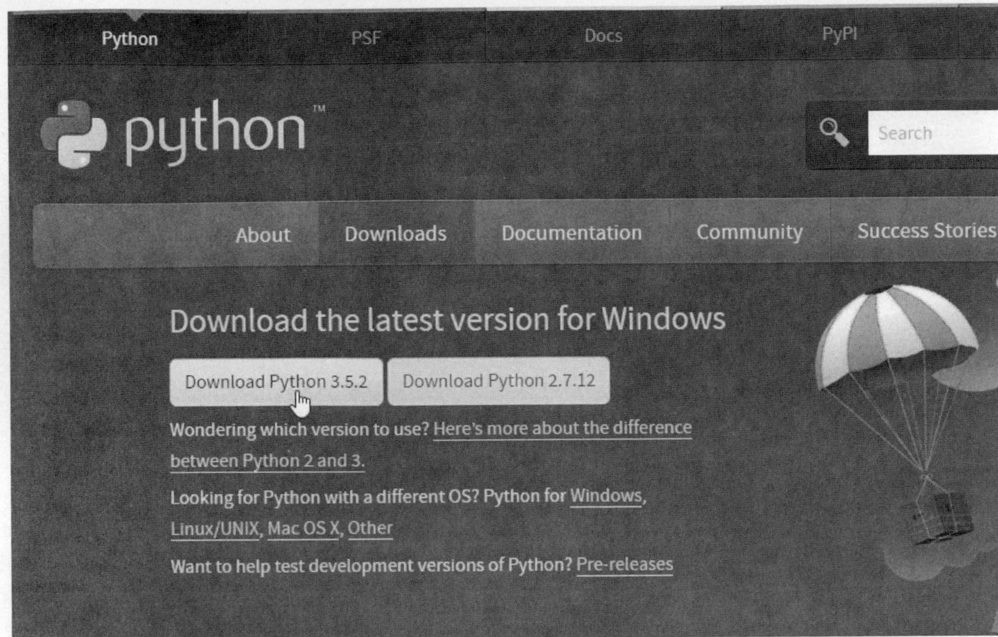

Once you have downloaded the Python installer, you should execute it. Figure A-2 shows the installer for Python 3.5.2. It is highly recommended that you check both options at the bottom of the screen: *Install launcher for all users*, and *Add Python 3.x to PATH*. Once you have done that, click *Install Now*.

Figure A-2 Python installer

Next, Windows will prompt you with a message such as "Do you want to allow this app to make changes to your device?" Click *Yes* to proceed with the installation. When the installation has finished, you will see the message "Installation was successful." Click the Close button to exit the installer.

APPENDIX

B Introduction to IDLE

IDLE is an integrated development environment that combines several development tools into one program, including the following:

VideoNote
Introduction to IDLE

- A Python shell running in interactive mode. You can type Python statements at the shell prompt and immediately execute them. You can also run complete Python programs.
- A text editor that color codes Python keywords and other parts of programs.
- A "check module" tool that checks a Python program for syntax errors without running the program.
- Search tools that allow you to find text in one or more files.
- Text formatting tools that help you maintain consistent indentation levels in a Python program.
- A debugger that allows you to single-step through a Python program and watch the values of variables change as each statement executes.
- Several other advanced tools for developers.

The IDLE software is bundled with Python. When you install the Python interpreter, IDLE is automatically installed as well. This appendix provides a quick introduction to IDLE, and describes the basic steps of creating, saving, and executing a Python program.

Starting IDLE and Using the Python Shell

After Python is installed on your system, a Python program group will appear in your Start menu's program list. One of the items in the program group will be titled *IDLE (Python GUI)*. Click this item to start IDLE, and you will see the Python Shell window shown in Figure B-1. Inside this window, the Python interpreter is running in interactive mode, and at the top of the window is a menu bar that provides access to all of IDLE's tools.

Figure B-1 IDLE shell window

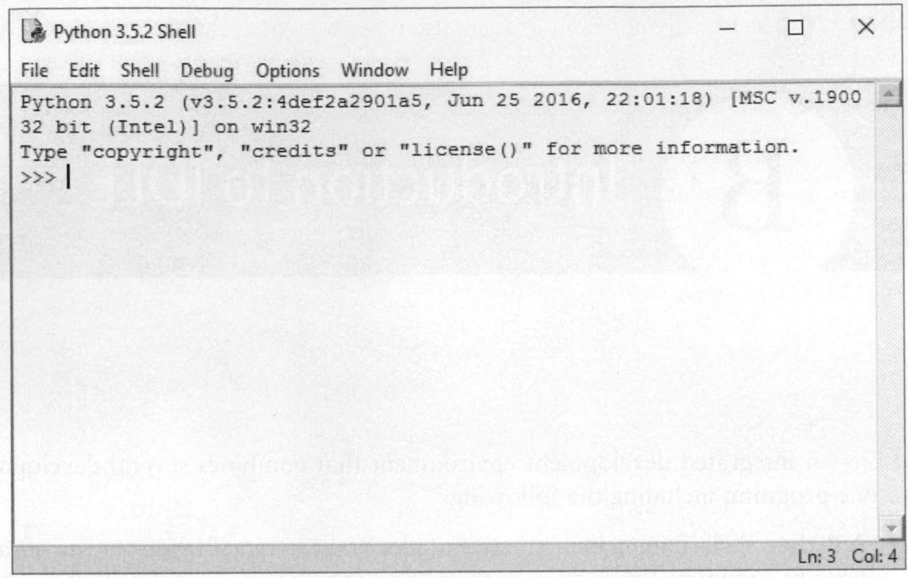

The >>> prompt indicates that the interpreter is waiting for you to type a Python statement. When you type a statement at the >>> prompt and press the Enter key, the statement is immediately executed. For example, Figure B-2 shows the Python Shell window after three statements have been entered and executed.

Figure B-2 Statements executed by the Python interpreter

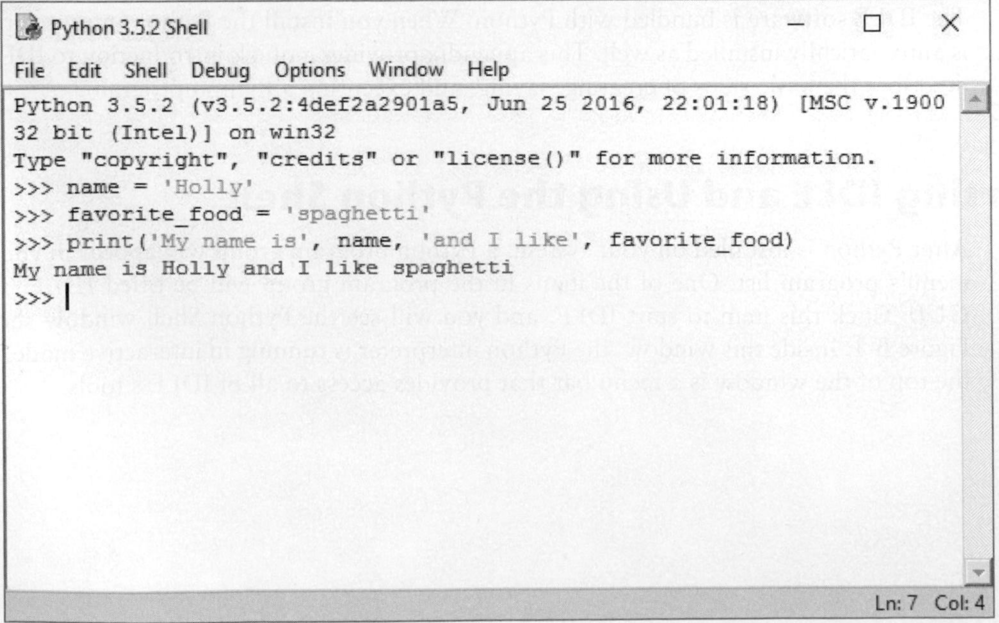

When you type the beginning of a multiline statement, such as an `if` statement or a loop, each subsequent line is automatically indented. Pressing the Enter key on an empty line indicates the end of the multiline statement and causes the interpreter to execute it. Figure B-3 shows the Python Shell window after a `for` loop has been entered and executed.

Figure B-3 A multiline statement executed by the Python interpreter

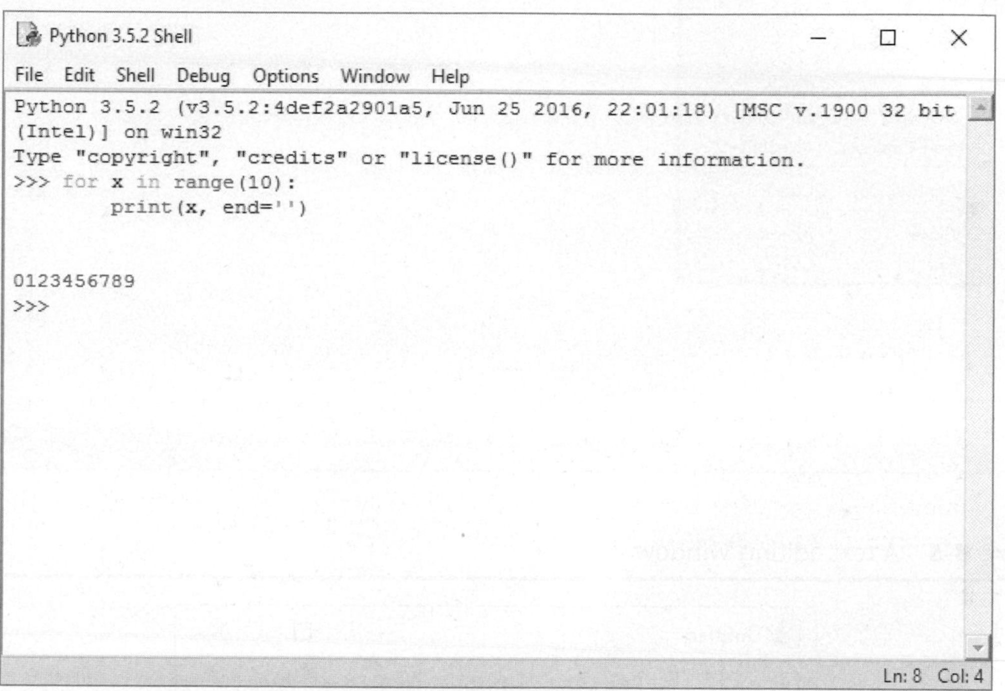

Writing a Python Program in the IDLE Editor

To write a new Python program in IDLE, you open a new editing window. As shown in Figure B-4, you click File on the menu bar, then click New File on the dropdown menu. (Alternatively, you can press Ctrl+N.) This opens a text editing window like the one shown in Figure B-5.

Figure B-4 The File menu

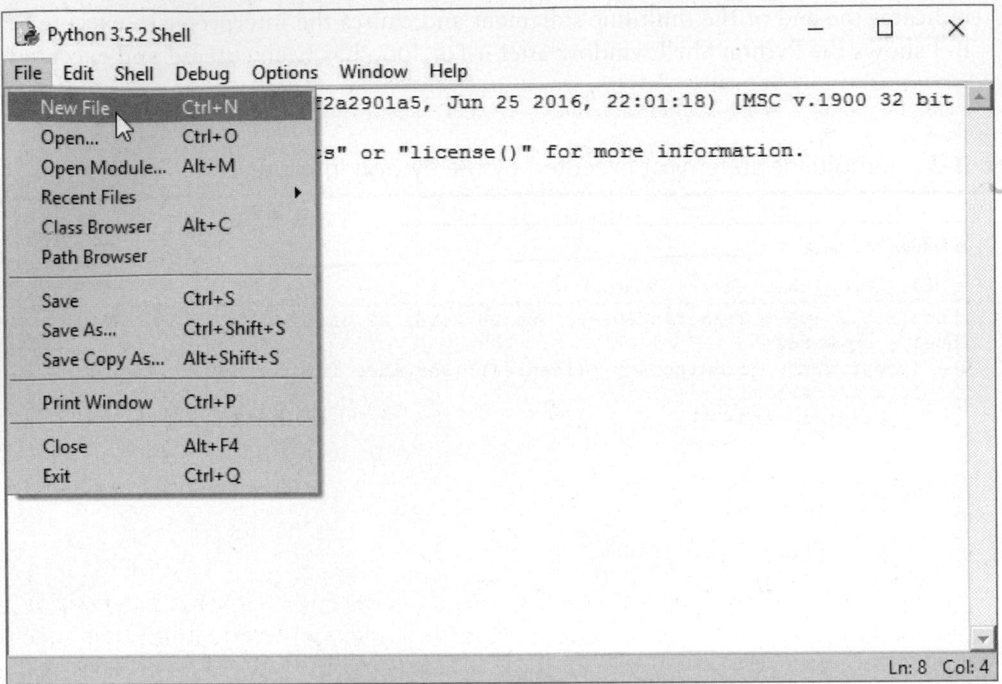

Figure B-5 A text editing window

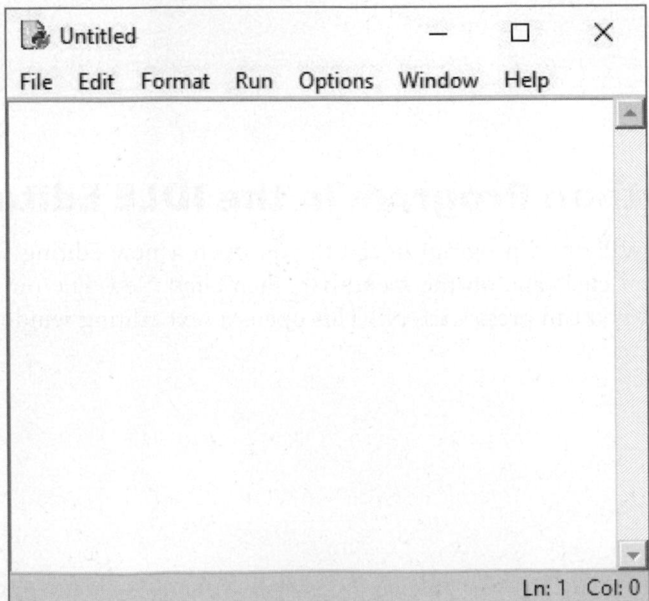

To open a program that already exists, click File on the menu bar, then click Open. Simply browse to the file's location and select it, and it will be opened in an editor window.

Color Coding

Code that is typed into the editor window, as well as in the Python Shell window, is colorized as follows:

- Python keywords are displayed in orange.
- Comments are displayed in red.
- String literals are displayed in green.
- Defined names, such as the names of functions and classes, are displayed in blue.
- Built-in functions are displayed in purple.

TIP: You can change IDLE's color settings by clicking Options on the menu bar, then clicking Configure IDLE. Select the Highlighting tab at the top of the dialog box, and you can specify colors for each element of a Python program.

Automatic Indentation

The IDLE editor has features that help you to maintain consistent indentation in your Python programs. Perhaps the most helpful of these features is automatic indentation. When you type a line that ends with a colon, such as an `if` clause, the first line of a loop, or a function header, then press the Enter key, the editor automatically indents the lines that are entered next. For example, suppose you are typing the code shown in Figure B-6. After you press the Enter key at the end of the line marked①, the editor will automatically indent the lines that you type next. Then, after you press the Enter key at the end of the line marked②, the editor indents again. Pressing the Backspace key at the beginning of an indented line cancels one level of indentation.

Figure B-6 Lines that cause automatic indentation

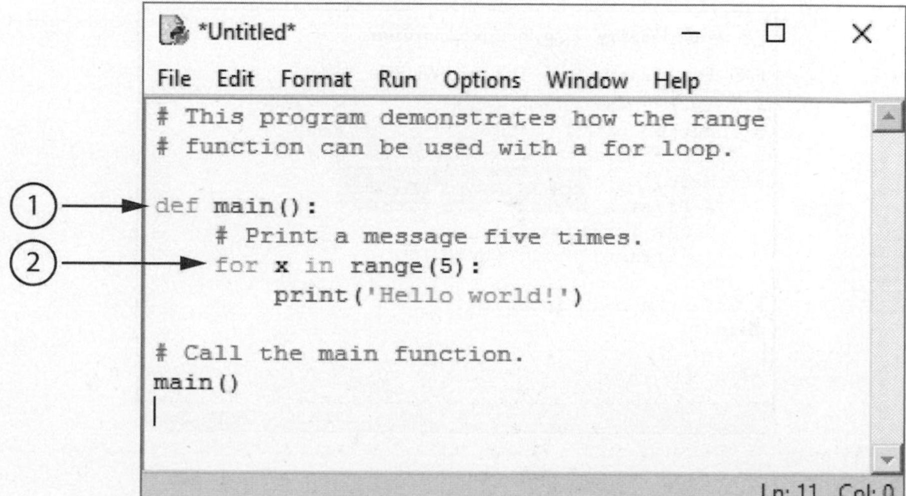

By default, IDLE indents four spaces for each level of indentation. It is possible to change the number of spaces by clicking Options on the menu bar, then clicking Configure IDLE. Make sure Fonts/Tabs is selected at the top of the dialog box, and you will see a slider bar that allows you to change the number of spaces used for indentation width. However, because four spaces is the standard width for indentation in Python, it is recommended that you keep this setting.

Saving a Program

In the editor window, you can save the current program by selecting any of these operations from the File menu:

- Save
- Save As
- Save Copy As

The Save and Save As operations work just as they do in any Windows application. The Save Copy As operation works like Save As, but it leaves the original program in the editor window.

Running a Program

Once you have typed a program into the editor, you can run it by pressing the F5 key, or as shown in Figure B-7, by clicking Run on the editor window's menu bar, then clicking Run Module. If the program has not been saved since the last modification was made, you will see the dialog box shown in Figure B-8. Click OK to save the program. When the program runs, you will see its output displayed in IDLE's Python Shell window, as shown in Figure B-9.

Figure B-7 The editor window's Run menu

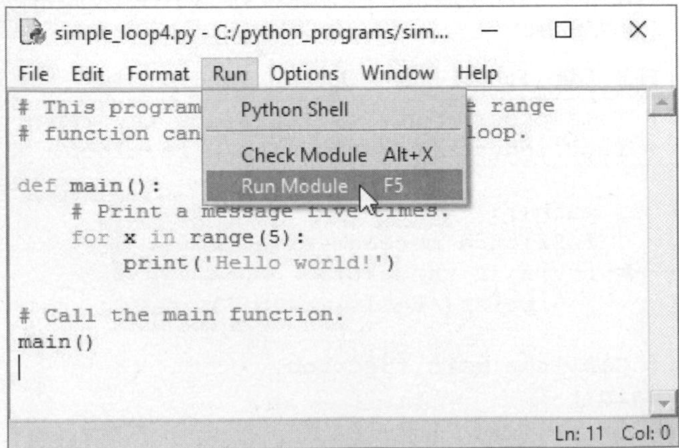

Figure B-8 Save confirmation dialog box

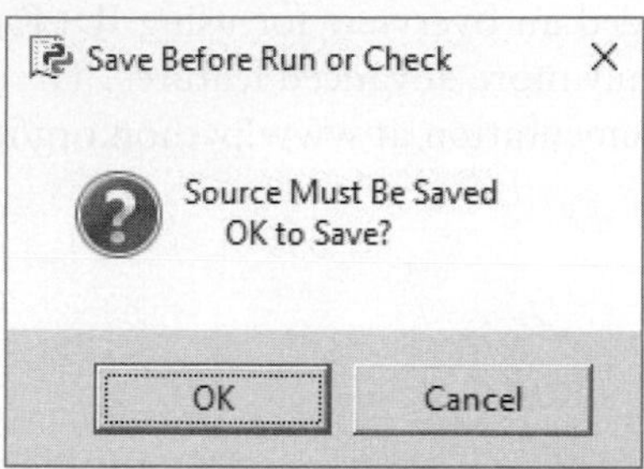

Figure B-9 Output displayed in the Python Shell window

```
Python 3.5.2 Shell
File Edit Shell Debug Options Window Help
Python 3.5.2 (v3.5.2:4def2a2901a5, Jun 25 2016, 22:01:18) [MSC v.1900 32 bit
(Intel)] on win32
Type "copyright", "credits" or "license()" for more information.
>>>
================ RESTART: C:\python_programs\simple_loop4.py ================
=
Hello world!
Hello world!
Hello world!
Hello world!
Hello world!
>>>
Ln: 10 Col: 4
```

Program output

If a program contains a syntax error, when you run the program you will see the dialog box shown in Figure B-10. After you click the OK button, the editor will highlight the location of the error in the code. If you want to check the syntax of a program without trying to run it, you can click Run on the menu bar, then click Check Module. Any syntax errors that are found will be reported.

Figure B-10 Dialog box reporting a syntax error

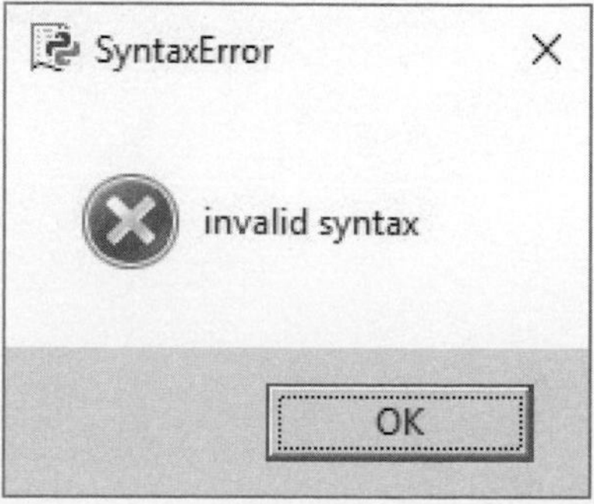

Other Resources

This appendix has provided an overview for using IDLE to create, save, and execute programs. IDLE provides many more advanced features. To read about additional capabilities, see the official IDLE documentation at www.python.org/idle

APPENDIX C The ASCII Character Set

The following table lists the ASCII (American Standard Code for Information Interchange) character set, which is the same as the first 127 Unicode character codes. This group of character codes is known as the *Latin Subset of Unicode*. The code columns show character codes, and the character columns show the corresponding characters. For example, the code 65 represents the letter A. Note that the first 31 codes, and code 127, represent control characters that are not printable.

Code	Character	Code	Character	Code	Character	Code	Character	Code	Character
0	NUL	26	SUB	52	4	78	N	104	h
1	SOH	27	Escape	53	5	79	O	105	i
2	STX	28	FS	54	6	80	P	106	j
3	ETX	29	GS	55	7	81	Q	107	k
4	EOT	30	RS	56	8	82	R	108	l
5	ENQ	31	US	57	9	83	S	109	m
6	ACK	32	(*Space*)	58	:	84	T	110	n
7	BEL	33	!	59	;	85	U	111	o
8	Backspace	34	"	60	<	86	V	112	p
9	HTab	35	#	61	=	87	W	113	q
10	Line Feed	36	$	62	>	88	X	114	r
11	VTab	37	%	63	?	89	Y	115	s
12	Form Feed	38	&	64	@	90	Z	116	t
13	CR	39	'	65	A	91	[	117	u
14	SO	40	(	66	B	92	\	118	v
15	SI	41	)	67	C	93	]	119	w
16	DLE	42	*	68	D	94	^	120	x
17	DC1	43	+	69	E	95	_	121	y
18	DC2	44	'	70	F	96	`	122	z
19	DC3	45	–	71	G	97	a	123	{
20	DC4	46	.	72	H	98	b	124	|
21	NAK	47	/	73	I	99	c	125	}
22	SYN	48	0	74	J	100	d	126	~
23	ETB	49	1	75	K	101	e	127	DEL
24	CAN	50	2	76	L	102	f		
25	EM	51	3	77	M	103	g		

APPENDIX

D Predefined Named Colors

These are the defined color names that can be used with the turtle graphics library, `matplotlib`, and `tkinter`.

'snow'	'ghost white'	'white smoke'
'gainsboro'	'floral white'	'old lace'
'linen'	'antique white'	'papaya whip'
'blanched almond'	'bisque'	'peach puff'
'navajo white'	'lemon chiffon'	'mint cream'
'azure'	'alice blue'	'lavender'
'lavender blush'	'misty rose'	'dark slate gray'
'dim gray'	'slate gray'	'light slate gray'
'gray'	'light grey'	'midnight blue'
'navy'	'cornflower blue'	'dark slate blue'
'slate blue'	'medium slate blue'	'light slate blue'
'medium blue'	'royal blue'	'blue'
'dodger blue'	'deep sky blue'	'sky blue'
'light sky blue'	'steel blue'	'light steel blue'
'light blue'	'powder blue'	'pale turquoise'
'dark turquoise'	'medium turquoise'	'turquoise'
'cyan'	'light cyan'	'cadet blue'
'medium aquamarine'	'aquamarine'	'dark green'
'dark olive green'	'dark sea green'	'sea green'
'medium sea green'	'light sea green'	'pale green'
'spring green'	'lawn green'	'medium spring green'

(*continued*)

'green yellow'	'lime green'	'yellow green'
'forest green'	'olive drab'	'dark khaki'
'khaki'	'pale goldenrod'	'light goldenrod yellow'
'light yellow'	'yellow'	'gold'
'light goldenrod'	'goldenrod'	'dark goldenrod'
'rosy brown'	'indian red'	'saddle brown'
'sandy brown'	'dark salmon'	'salmon'
'light salmon'	'orange'	'dark orange'
'coral'	'light coral'	'tomato'
'orange red'	'red'	'hot pink'
'deep pink'	'pink'	'light pink'
'pale violet red'	'maroon'	'medium violet red'
'violet red'	'medium orchid'	'dark orchid'
'dark violet'	'blue violet'	'purple'
'medium purple'	'thistle'	'snow2'
'snow3'	'snow4'	'seashell2'
'seashell3'	'seashell4'	'AntiqueWhite1'
'AntiqueWhite2'	'AntiqueWhite3'	'AntiqueWhite4'
'bisque2'	'bisque3'	'bisque4'
'PeachPuff2'	'PeachPuff3'	'PeachPuff4'
'NavajoWhite2'	'NavajoWhite3'	'NavajoWhite4'
'LemonChiffon2'	'LemonChiffon3'	'LemonChiffon4'
'cornsilk2'	'cornsilk3'	'cornsilk4'
'ivory2'	'ivory3'	'ivory4'
'honeydew2'	'honeydew3'	'honeydew4'
'LavenderBlush2'	'LavenderBlush3'	'LavenderBlush4'
'MistyRose2'	'MistyRose3'	'MistyRose4'
'azure2'	'azure3'	'azure4'
'SlateBlue1'	'SlateBlue2'	'SlateBlue3'
'SlateBlue4'	'RoyalBlue1'	'RoyalBlue2'
'RoyalBlue3'	'RoyalBlue4'	'blue2'
'blue4'	'DodgerBlue2'	'DodgerBlue3'
'DodgerBlue4'	'SteelBlue1'	'SteelBlue2'
'SteelBlue3'	'SteelBlue4'	'DeepSkyBlue2'
'DeepSkyBlue3'	'DeepSkyBlue4'	'SkyBlue1'
'SkyBlue2'	'SkyBlue3'	'SkyBlue4'

'LightSkyBlue1'	'LightSkyBlue2'	'LightSkyBlue3'
'LightSkyBlue4'	'SlateGray1'	'SlateGray2'
'SlateGray3'	'SlateGray4'	'LightSteelBlue1'
'LightSteelBlue2'	'LightSteelBlue3'	'LightSteelBlue4'
'LightBlue1'	'LightBlue2'	'LightBlue3'
'LightBlue4'	'LightCyan2'	'LightCyan3'
'LightCyan4'	'PaleTurquoise1'	'PaleTurquoise2'
'PaleTurquoise3'	'PaleTurquoise4'	'CadetBlue1'
'CadetBlue2'	'CadetBlue3'	'CadetBlue4'
'turquoise1'	'turquoise2'	'turquoise3'
'turquoise4'	'cyan2'	'cyan3'
'cyan4'	'DarkSlateGray1'	'DarkSlateGray2'
'DarkSlateGray3'	'DarkSlateGray4'	'aquamarine2'
'aquamarine4'	'DarkSeaGreen1'	'DarkSeaGreen2'
'DarkSeaGreen3'	'DarkSeaGreen4'	'SeaGreen1'
'SeaGreen2'	'SeaGreen3'	'PaleGreen1'
'PaleGreen2'	'PaleGreen3'	'PaleGreen4'
'SpringGreen2'	'SpringGreen3'	'SpringGreen4'
'green2'	'green3'	'green4'
'chartreuse2'	'chartreuse3'	'chartreuse4'
'OliveDrab1'	'OliveDrab2'	'OliveDrab4'
'DarkOliveGreen1'	'DarkOliveGreen2'	'DarkOliveGreen3'
'DarkOliveGreen4'	'khaki1'	'khaki2'
'khaki3'	'khaki4'	'LightGoldenrod1'
'LightGoldenrod2'	'LightGoldenrod3'	'LightGoldenrod4'
'LightYellow2'	'LightYellow3'	'LightYellow4'
'yellow2'	'yellow3'	'yellow4'
'gold2'	'gold3'	'gold4'
'goldenrod1'	'goldenrod2'	'goldenrod3'
'goldenrod4'	'DarkGoldenrod1'	'DarkGoldenrod2'
'DarkGoldenrod3'	'DarkGoldenrod4'	'RosyBrown1'
'RosyBrown2'	'RosyBrown3'	'RosyBrown4'
'IndianRed1'	'IndianRed2'	'IndianRed3'
'IndianRed4'	'sienna1'	'sienna2'
'sienna3'	'sienna4'	'burlywood1'

(continued)

'burlywood2'	'burlywood3'	'burlywood4'
'wheat1'	'wheat2'	'wheat3'
'wheat4'	'tan1'	'tan2'
'tan4'	'chocolate1'	'chocolate2'
'chocolate3'	'firebrick1'	'firebrick2'
'firebrick3'	'firebrick4'	'brown1'
'brown2'	'brown3'	'brown4'
'salmon1'	'salmon2'	'salmon3'
'salmon4'	'LightSalmon2'	'LightSalmon3'
'LightSalmon4'	'orange2'	'orange3'
'orange4'	'DarkOrange1'	'DarkOrange2'
'DarkOrange3'	'DarkOrange4'	'coral1'
'coral2'	'coral3'	'coral4'
'tomato2'	'tomato3'	'tomato4'
'OrangeRed2'	'OrangeRed3'	'OrangeRed4'
'red2'	'red3'	'red4'
'DeepPink2'	'DeepPink3'	'DeepPink4'
'HotPink1'	'HotPink2'	'HotPink3'
'HotPink4'	'pink1'	'pink2'
'pink3'	'pink4'	'LightPink1'
'LightPink2'	'LightPink3'	'LightPink4'
'PaleVioletRed1'	'PaleVioletRed2'	'PaleVioletRed3'
'PaleVioletRed4'	'maroon1'	'maroon2'
'maroon3'	'maroon4'	'VioletRed1'
'VioletRed2'	'VioletRed3'	'VioletRed4'
'magenta2'	'magenta3'	'magenta4'
'orchid1'	'orchid2'	'orchid3'
'orchid4'	'plum1'	'plum2'
'plum3'	'plum4'	'MediumOrchid1'
'MediumOrchid2'	'MediumOrchid3'	'MediumOrchid4'
'DarkOrchid1'	'DarkOrchid2'	'DarkOrchid3'
'DarkOrchid4'	'purple1'	'purple2'
'purple3'	'purple4'	'MediumPurple1'
'MediumPurple2'	'MediumPurple3'	'MediumPurple4'
'thistle1'	'thistle2'	'thistle3'
'thistle4'	'gray1'	'gray2'

'gray3'	'gray4'	'gray5'
'gray6'	'gray7'	'gray8'
'gray9'	'gray10'	'gray11'
'gray12'	'gray13'	'gray14'
'gray15'	'gray16'	'gray17'
'gray18'	'gray19'	'gray20'
'gray21'	'gray22'	'gray23'
'gray24'	'gray25'	'gray26'
'gray27'	'gray28'	'gray29'
'gray30'	'gray31'	'gray32'
'gray33'	'gray34'	'gray35'
'gray36'	'gray37'	'gray38'
'gray39'	'gray40'	'gray42'
'gray43'	'gray44'	'gray45'
'gray46'	'gray47'	'gray48'
'gray49'	'gray50'	'gray51'
'gray52'	'gray53'	'gray54'
'gray55'	'gray56'	'gray57'
'gray58'	'gray59'	'gray60'
'gray61'	'gray62'	'gray63'
'gray64'	'gray65'	'gray66'
'gray67'	'gray68'	'gray69'
'gray70'	'gray71'	'gray72'
'gray73'	'gray74'	'gray75'
'gray76'	'gray77'	'gray78'
'gray79'	'gray80'	'gray81'
'gray82'	'gray83'	'gray84'
'gray85'	'gray86'	'gray87'
'gray88'	'gray89'	'gray90'
'gray91'	'gray92'	'gray93'
'gray94'	'gray95'	'gray97'
'gray98'	'gray99'	

APPENDIX E More About the `import` Statement

A module is a Python source code file that contains functions and/or classes. Many of the functions in the Python standard library are stored in modules. For example, the `math` module contains various mathematical functions, and the `random` module contains functions for working with random numbers.

In order to use the functions and/or classes that are stored in a module, you must import the module. To import a module, you write an `import` statement at the top of your program. Here is an `import` statement that imports the `math` module:

```
import math
```

This statement causes the Python interpreter to load the contents of the `math` module into memory, making the functions and/or classes that are stored in the `math` module available to the program. To use any item that is in the module, you must use the item's *qualified name*. This means that you must prefix the item's name with the name of the module, followed by a dot. For example, the `math` module has a function named `sqrt` that returns the square root of a number. To call the `sqrt` function, you would use the name `math.sqrt`. The following interactive session shows an example:

```
>>> import math
>>> x = math.sqrt(25)
>>> print(x)
5.0
>>>
```

Importing a Specific Function or Class

The previously shown form of the `import` statement loads the entire contents of a module into memory. Sometimes you want to import only a specific function or class from a module. When this is the case, you can use the `from` keyword with the `import` statement, as shown here:

```
from math import sqrt
```

This statement causes only the sqrt function to be imported from the math module. It also allows you to call the sqrt function without prefixing the function's name with the name of the module. The following interactive session shows an example:

```
>>> from math import sqrt
>>> x = sqrt(25)
>>> print(x)
5.0
>>>
```

You can specify the names of multiple items, separated with commas, when you use this form of the import statement. For example, the import statement in the following interactive session imports only the sqrt function and the radians function from the math module:

```
>>> from math import sqrt, radians
>>> x = sqrt(25)
>>> a = radians(180)
>>> print(x)
5.0
>>> print(a)
3.141592653589793
>>>
```

Wildcard Imports

A wildcard import statement loads the entire contents of a module. Here is an example:

```
from math import *
```

The difference between this statement and the import math statement is that the wildcard import statement does not require you to use the qualified names of the items in the module. For example, here is an interactive session that uses a wildcard import statement:

```
>>> from math import*
>>> x = sqrt(25)
>>> a = radians(180)
>>>
```

And, here is an interactive session that uses the regular import statement:

```
>>> import math
>>> x = math.sqrt(25)
>>> a = math.radians(180)
>>>
```

Typically, you should avoid using the wildcard import statement because it can lead to name clashes when you are importing several modules. A *name clash* occurs when a program imports two modules that have functions or classes with the same name. Name clashes do not occur when you are using the qualified names of a module's functions and/or classes.

Using an Alias

You can use the as keyword to assign an *alias* to a module when you import it. The following statement shows an example:

```
import math as mt
```

This statement loads the math module into memory, assigning the module the alias mt. To use any of the items that are in the module, you prefix the item's name with the alias, followed by a dot. For example, to call the sqrt function, you would use the name mt.sqrt. The following interactive session shows an example:

```
>>> import math as mt
>>> x = mt.sqrt(25)
>>> a = mt.radians(180)
>>> print(x)
5.0
>>> print(a)
3.141592653589793
>>>
```

You can also assign an alias to a specific function or class when you import it. The following statement imports the sqrt function from the math module, and assigns the function the alias square_root:

```
from math import sqrt as square_root
```

After using this import statement, you would use the name square_root to call the sqrt function. The following interactive session shows an example:

```
>>> from math import sqrt as square_root
>>> x = square_root(25)
>>> print(x)
5.0
>>>
```

In the following interactive session, we import two functions from the math module, giving each of them an alias. The sqrt function is imported as square_root, and the tan function is imported as tangent:

```
>>> from math import sqrt as square_root, tan as tangent
>>> x = square_root(25)
>>> y = tangent(45)
>>> print(x)
5.0
>>> print(y)
1.6197751905438615
```

APPENDIX F

Installing Modules with the pip Utility

The Python standard library provides classes and functions that your programs can use to perform basic operations, as well as many advanced tasks. There are operations, however, that the standard library cannot perform. When you need to do something that is beyond the scope of the standard library, you have two choices: write the code yourself, or use code that someone else has already written.

Fortunately, there are thousands of Python modules, written by independent programmers, that provide capabilities that the standard Python library does not offer. These are known as *third-party modules*. A large collection of third-party modules exists at the website pypi.python.org, which is known as the *Python Package Index*, or *PyPI*.

The modules that are available at PyPI are organized as packages. A *package* is simply a collection of one or more related modules. The easiest way to download and install a package is with the `pip` utility. The `pip` utility is a program that is part of the standard Python installation, beginning with Python 3.4. To install a package on a Windows system with the `pip` utility, you must open a command prompt window, and type a command following this format:

```
pip install package_name
```

package_name is the name of a package that you want to download and install. If you are running a Mac or a Linux system, you must use the `pip3` command instead of the `pip` command. In addition, you will need superuser privileges to execute the `pip3` command on a Mac or Linux system, so you will have to prefix the command with `sudo`, as shown here:

```
sudo pip3 install package_name
```

Once you enter the command, the `pip` utility will start downloading and installing the package. Depending on the size of the package, it may take a few minutes to complete the installation process. Once the process is finished, you can typically verify that the package was correctly installed by starting IDLE and entering the command

```
>>> import package_name
```

where *package_name* is the name of the package that you installed. If you do not see an error message, you can assume the package was successfully installed.

In Chapter 7, you will explore a popular third-party package named `matplotlib`. You can use the `matplotlib` package to create charts and graphs.

APPENDIX

G Answers to Checkpoints

Chapter 1

1.1 A program is a set of instructions that a computer follows to perform a task.

1.2 Hardware is all the physical devices, or components, of which a computer is made.

1.3 The central processing unit (CPU), main memory, secondary storage devices, input devices, and output devices

1.4 The CPU

1.5 Main memory

1.6 Secondary storage

1.7 Input device

1.8 Output device

1.9 The operating system

1.10 A utility program

1.11 Application software

1.12 One byte

1.13 A bit

1.14 The binary numbering system

1.15 It is an encoding scheme that uses a set of 128 numeric codes to represent the English letters, various punctuation marks, and other characters. These numeric codes are used to store characters in a computer's memory. (ASCII stands for the American Standard Code for Information Interchange.)

1.16 Unicode

1.17 Digital data is data that is stored in binary, and a digital device is any device that works with binary data.

1.18 Machine language

1.19 Main memory, or RAM

1.20 The fetch-decode-execute cycle

1.21 It is an alternative to machine language. Instead of using binary numbers for instructions, assembly language uses short words that are known as mnemonics.

1.22 A high-level language

1.23 Syntax

1.24 A compiler

1.25 An interpreter

1.26 A syntax error

Chapter 2

2.1 Any person, group, or organization that is asking you to write a program

2.2 A single function that the program must perform in order to satisfy the customer

2.3 A set of well-defined logical steps that must be taken to perform a task

2.4 An informal language that has no syntax rules and is not meant to be compiled or executed. Instead, programmers use pseudocode to create models, or "mock-ups," of programs.

2.5 A diagram that graphically depicts the steps that take place in a program

2.6 Ovals are terminal symbols. Parallelograms are either output or input symbols. Rectangles are processing symbols.

2.7 `print('Jimmy Smith')`

2.8 `print("Python's the best!")`

2.9 `print('The cat said "meow"')`

2.10 A name that references a value in the computer's memory

2.11 `99bottles` is illegal because it begins with a number. `r&d` is illegal because the & character is not allowed.

2.12 No, it is not because variable names are case sensitive.

2.13 It is invalid because the variable that is receiving the assignment (in this case `amount`) must appear on the left side of the = operator.

2.14 `The value is val.`

2.15 `value1` will reference an `int`. `value2` will reference a `float`. `value3` will reference a `float`. `value4` will reference an `int`. `value5` will reference an `str` (string).

2.16 0

2.17 `last_name = input("Enter the customer's last name: ")`

2.18 `sales = float(input('Enter the sales for the week: '))`

2.19 Here is the completed table:

Expression	Value
`6 + 3 * 5`	21
`12 / 2 - 4`	2
`9 + 14 * 2 - 6`	31
`(6 + 2) * 3`	24
`14 / (11 - 4)`	2
`9 + 12 * (8 - 3)`	69

2.20 4

2.21 1

2.22 If you do not want the `print` function to start a new line of output when it finishes displaying its output, you can pass the special argument `end = ' '` to the function.

2.23 You can pass the argument `sep=` to the `print` function, specifying the desired character.

2.24 It is the newline escape character.

2.25 It is the string concatenation operator, which joins two strings together.

2.26 65.43

2.27 987,654.13

2.28 (1) Named constants make programs more self-explanatory, (2) widespread changes can easily be made to the program, and (3) they help to prevent the typographical errors that are common when using magic numbers.

2.29 `DISCOUNT_PERCENTAGE = 0.1`

2.30 0 degrees

2.31 With the `turtle.forward` command.

2.32 With the command `turtle.right(45)`

2.33 You would first use the `turtle.penup()` command to raise the turtle's pen.

2.34 `turtle.heading()`

2.35 `turtle.circle(100)`

2.36 `turtle.pensize(8)`

2.37 `turtle.pencolor('blue')`

2.38 `turtle.bgcolor('black')`

2.39 `turtle.setup(500, 200)`

2.40 `turtle.goto(100, 50)`

2.41 `turtle.pos()`

2.42 `turtle.speed(10)`

2.43 `turtle.speed(0)`

2.44 To fill a shape with a color, you use the `turtle.begin_fill()` command before drawing the shape, then you use the `turtle.end_fill()` command after the shape is drawn. When the `turtle.end_fill()` command executes, the shape will be filled with the current fill color.

2.45 With the `turtle.write()`command

Chapter 3

3.1 A logical design that controls the order in which a set of statements execute

3.2 It is a program structure that can execute a set of statements only under certain circumstances.

3.3 A decision structure that provides a single alternative path of execution. If the condition that is being tested is true, the program takes the alternative path.

3.4 An expression that can be evaluated as either true or false

3.5 You can determine whether one value is greater than, less than, greater than or equal to, less than or equal to, equal to, or not equal to another value.

3.6

```
if y == 20:
x = 0
```

3.7

```
if sales >= 10000:
    commissionRate = 0.2
```

3.8 A dual alternative decision structure has two possible paths of execution; one path is taken if a condition is true, and the other path is taken if the condition is false.

3.9 `if-else`

3.10 When the condition is false

3.11 z is not less than a.

3.12 Boston
New York

3.13
```
if number == 1:
    print('One')
elif number == 2:
    print('Two')
elif number == 3:
    print('Three')
else:
    print('Unknown')
```

3.14 It is an expression that is created by using a logical operator to combine two Boolean subexpressions.

3.15 F
T
F
F
T
T
T
F
F
T

3.16 T
F
T
T
T

3.17 The `and` operator: If the expression on the left side of the `and` operator is false, the expression on the right side will not be checked.
The `or` operator: If the expression on the left side of the `or` operator is true, the expression on the right side will not be checked.

3.18
```
if speed >= 0 and speed <= 200:
    print('The number is valid')
```

3.19
```
if speed < 0 or speed > 200:
    print('The number is not valid')
```

3.20 `True` or `False`

3.21 A variable that signals when some condition exists in the program

3.22 You use the `turtle.xcor()` and `turtle.ycor()` functions.

3.23 You would use the `not` operator with the `turtle.isdown()` function, like this:
```
if turtle.isdown():
    statement
```

3.24 You use the `turtle.heading()` function.

3.25 You use the `turtle.isvisible()` function.

3.26 You use the `turtle.pencolor()` function to determine the pen color. You use the `turtle.fillcolor()` function to determine the current fill color. You use the `turtle.bgcolor()` function to determine the current background color of the turtle's graphics window.

3.27 You use the `turtle.pensize()` function.

3.28 You use the `turtle.speed()` function.

Chapter 4

4.1 A structure that causes a section of code to repeat

4.2 A loop that uses a true/false condition to control the number of times that it repeats

4.3 A loop that repeats a specific number of times

4.4 An execution of the statements in the body of the loop

4.5 Before

4.6 None. The condition `count < 0` will be false to begin with.

4.7 A loop that has no way of stopping and repeats until the program is interrupted.

4.8
```
for x in range(6):
    print('I love to program!')
```

4.9
```
0
1
2
3
4
5
```

4.10
```
2
3
4
5
```

4.11
```
0
100
200
300
400
500
```

4.12
```
10
9
8
7
6
```

4.13 A variable that is used to accumulate the total of a series of numbers

4.14 Yes, it should be initialized with the value 0. This is because values are added to the accumulator by a loop. If the accumulator does not start at the value 0, it will not contain the correct total of the numbers that were added to it when the loop ends.

4.15 `15`

4.16
```
15
5
```

4.17 a) `quantity += 1`
b) `days_left -= 5`
c) `price *= 10`
d) `price /= 2`

4.18 A sentinel is a special value that marks the end of a list of items.

4.19 A sentinel value must be unique enough that it will not be mistaken as a regular value in the list.

4.20 It means that if bad data (garbage) is provided as input to a program, the program will produce bad data (garbage) as output.

4.21 When input is given to a program, it should be inspected before it is processed. If the input is invalid, then it should be discarded and the user should be prompted to enter the correct data.

4.22 The input is read, then a pretest loop is executed. If the input data is invalid, the body of the loop executes. In the body of the loop, an error message is displayed so the user will know that the input was invalid, and then the input read again. The loop repeats as long as the input is invalid.

4.23 It is the input operation that takes place just before an input validation loop. The purpose of the priming read is to get the first input value.

4.24 None

Chapter 5

5.1 A function is a group of statements that exist within a program for the purpose of performing a specific task.

5.2 A large task is divided into several smaller tasks that are easily performed.

5.3 If a specific operation is performed in several places in a program, a function can be written once to perform that operation, and then be executed any time it is needed.

5.4 Functions can be written for the common tasks that are needed by the different programs. Those functions can then be incorporated into each program that needs them.

5.5 When a program is developed as a set of functions in which each performs an individual task, then different programmers can be assigned the job of writing different functions.

5.6 A function definition has two parts: a header and a block. The header indicates the starting point of the function, and the block is a list of statements that belong to the function.

5.7 To call a function means to execute the function.

5.8 When the end of the function is reached, the computer returns back to the part of the program that called the function, and the program resumes execution at that point.

5.9 Because the Python interpreter uses the indentation to determine where a block begins and ends

5.10 A local variable is a variable that is declared inside a function. It belongs to the function in which it is declared, and only statements in the same function can access it.

5.11 The part of a program in which a variable may be accessed

5.12 Yes, it is permissible.

5.13 Arguments

5.14 Parameters

5.15 A parameter variable's scope is the entire function in which the parameter is declared.

5.16 No, it does not.

5.17 a. passes by keyword argument
b. passes by position

5.18 The entire program

5.19 Here are three:

- Global variables make debugging difficult. Any statement in a program can change the value of a global variable. If you find that the wrong value is being stored in a global variable, you have to track down every statement that accesses it to determine where the bad value is coming from. In a program with thousands of lines of code, this can be difficult.
- Functions that use global variables are usually dependent on those variables. If you want to use such a function in a different program, you will most likely have to redesign it so it does not rely on the global variable.
- Global variables make a program hard to understand. A global variable can be modified by any statement in the program. If you are to understand any part of the program that uses a global variable, you have to be aware of all the other parts of the program that access the global variable.

5.20 A global constant is a name that is available to every function in the program. It is permissible to use global constants. Because their value cannot be changed during the program's execution, you do not have to worry about its value being altered.

5.21 The difference is that a value returning function returns a value back to the statement that called it. A simple function does not return a value.

5.22 A prewritten function that performs some commonly needed task

5.23 The term "black box" is used to describe any mechanism that accepts input, performs some operation (that cannot be seen) using the input, and produces output.

5.24 It assigns a random integer in the range of 1 through 100 to the variable `x`.

5.25 It prints a random integer in the range of 1 through 20.

5.26 It prints a random integer in the range of 10 through 19.

5.27 It prints a random floating-point number in the range of 0.0 up to, but not including, 1.0.

5.28 It prints a random floating-point number in the range of 0.1 through 0.5.

5.29 It uses the system time, retrieved from the computer's internal clock.

5.30 If the same seed value were always used, the random number functions would always generate the same series of pseudorandom numbers.

5.31 It returns a value back to the part of the program that called it.

5.32 a) `do_something`
b) It returns a value that is twice the argument passed to it.
c) 20

5.33 A function that returns either `True` or `False`

5.34 `import math`

5.35 `square_root = math.sqrt(100)`

5.36 `angle = math.radians(45)`

Chapter 6

6.1 A file to which a program writes data. It is called an output file because the program sends output to it.

6.2 A file from which a program reads data. It is called an input file because the program receives input from it.

6.3 (1) Open the file. (2) Process the file. (3) Close the file.

6.4 Text and binary. A text file contains data that has been encoded as text using a scheme such as ASCII. Even if the file contains numbers, those numbers are stored in the file as a series of characters. As a result, the file may be opened and viewed in a text editor such as Notepad. A binary file contains data that has not been converted to text. As a consequence, you cannot view the contents of a binary file with a text editor.

6.5 Sequential and direct access. When you work with a sequential access file, you access data from the beginning of the file to the end of the file. When you work with a direct access file, you can jump directly to any piece of data in the file without reading the data that comes before it.

6.6 The file's name on the disk and the name of a variable that references a file object.

6.7 The file's contents are erased.

6.8 Opening a file creates a connection between the file and the program. It also creates an association between the file and a file object.

6.9 Closing a file disconnects the program from the file.

6.10 A file's read position marks the location of the next item that will be read from the file. When an input file is opened, its read position is initially set to the first item in the file.

6.11 You open the file in append mode. When you write data to a file in append mode, the data is written to the end of the file's existing contents.

6.12

```
outfile = open('numbers.txt', 'w')
for num in range(1, 11):
    outfile.write(str(num) + '\n')
outfile.close()
```

6.13 The `readline` method returns an empty string (`''`) when it has attempted to read beyond the end of a file.

6.14

```
infile = open('numbers.txt', 'r')
line = infile.readline()
while line != '':
    print(line)
    line = infile.readline()
infile.close()
```

6.15

```
infile = open('data.txt', 'r')
for line in infile:
    print(line)
infile.close()
```

6.16 A record is a complete set of data that describes one item, and a field is a single piece of data within a record.

6.17 You copy all the original file's records to the temporary file, but when you get to the record that is to be modified, you do not write its old contents to the temporary file. Instead, you write its new, modified values to the temporary file. Then, you finish copying any remaining records from the original file to the temporary file.

6.18 You copy all the original file's records to the temporary file, except for the record that is to be deleted. The temporary file then takes the place of the original file. You delete the original file and rename the temporary file, giving it the name that the original file had on the computer's disk.

6.19 An exception is an error that occurs while a program is running. In most cases, an exception causes a program to abruptly halt.

6.20 The program halts.

6.21 `IOError`

6.22 `ValueError`

Chapter 7

7.1 `[1, 2, 99, 4, 5]`

7.2 `[0, 1, 2]`

7.3 `[10, 10, 10, 10, 10]`

7.4
```
1
3
5
7
9
```

7.5 `4`

7.6 Use the built-in `len` function.

7.7
```
[1, 2, 3]
[10, 20, 30]
[1, 2, 3, 10, 20, 30]
```

7.8
```
[1, 2, 3]
[10, 20, 30, 1, 2, 3]
```

7.9 `[2, 3]`

7.10 `[2, 3]`

7.11 `[1]`

7.12 `[1, 2, 3, 4, 5]`

7.13 `[3, 4, 5]`

7.14
```
Jasmine's family:
['Jim', 'Jill', 'John', 'Jasmine']
```

7.15 The `remove` method searches for and removes an element containing a specific value. The `del` statement removes an element at a specific index.

7.16 You can use the built-in `min` and `max` functions.

7.17 You would use statement b, `names.append('Wendy')`. This is because element 0 does not exist. If you try to use statement a, an error will occur.

7.18 a) The `index` method searches for an item in the list and returns the index of the first element containing that item.
b) The `insert` method inserts an item into the list at a specified index.
c) The `sort` method sorts the items in the list to appear in ascending order.
d) The `reverse` method reverses the order of the items in the list.

7.19 The list contains 4 rows and 2 columns.

7.20
```
mylist = [[0, 0, 0, 0], [0, 0, 0, 0],
          [0, 0, 0, 0], [0, 0, 0, 0]]
```

7.21
```
for r in range(4):
    for c in range(2):
        print(numbers[r][c])
```

7.22 The primary difference between tuples and lists is that tuples are immutable. That means that once a tuple is created, it cannot be changed.

7.23 Here are three reasons:

- Processing a tuple is faster than processing a list, so tuples are good choices when you are processing lots of data and that data will not be modified.
- Tuples are safe. Because you are not allowed to change the contents of a tuple, you can store data in one and rest assured that it will not be modified (accidentally or otherwise) by any code in your program.
- There are certain operations in Python that require the use of a tuple.

7.24 `my_tuple = tuple(my_list)`

7.25 `my_list = list(my_tuple)`

7.26 Two lists: one holding the *X* coordinates of the data points, and the other holding the *Y* coordinates.

7.27 A line graph

7.28 Use the `xlabel` and `ylabel` functions.

7.29 Call the `xlim` and `ylim` functions, passing values for the `xmin`, `xmax`, `ymin`, and `ymax` keyword arguments.

7.30 Call the `xticks` and `yticks` functions. You pass two arguments to these functions. The first argument is a list of tick-mark locations, and the second argument is a list of labels to display at the specified locations.

7.31 Two lists: one containing the *X* coordinates of each bar's left edge, and another containing the heights of each bar, along the *Y* axis.

7.32 The bars will be red, blue, red, and blue.

7.33 You pass a list of values as an argument. The `pie` function will calculate the sum of the values in the list, then use that sum as the value of the whole.

Then, each element in the list will become a slice in the pie chart. The size of a slice represents that element's value as a percentage of the whole.

Chapter 8

8.1
```
for letter in name:
    print(letter)
```

8.2 0

8.3 9

8.4 An `IndexError` exception will occur if you try to use an index that is out of range for a particular string.

8.5 Use the built-in `len` function.

8.6 The second statement attempts to assign a value to an individual character in the string. Strings are immutable, however, so the expression `animal[0]` cannot appear on the left side of an assignment operator.

8.7 `cde`

8.8 `defg`

8.9 `abc`

8.10 `abcdefg`

8.11
```
if 'd' in mystring:
    print('Yes, it is there.')
```

8.12
```
little = big.upper()
```

8.13
```
if ch.isdigit():
    print('Digit')
else:
    print('No digit')
```

8.14 `a A`

8.15
```
again = input('Do you want to repeat ' +
              'the program or quit? (R/Q) ')
while again.upper() != 'R' and again.upper() != 'Q':
    again = input('Do you want to repeat the ' +
                  'program or quit? (R/Q) ')
```

8.16 `$`

8.17
```
for letter in mystring:
    if letter.isupper():
        count += 1
```

8.18
```
my_list = days.split()
```

8.19
```
my_list = values.split('$')
```

Chapter 9

9.1 Key and value

9.2 The key

9.3 The string `'start'` is the key, and the integer 1472 is the value.

9.4 It stores the key-value pair `'id' : 54321` in the `employee` dictionary.

9.5 `ccc`

9.6 You can use the `in` operator to test for a specific key.

9.7 It deletes the element that has the key 654.

9.8 `3`

9.9
```
1
2
3
```

9.10 The `pop` method accepts a key as an argument, returns the value that is associated with that key, and removes that key-value pair from the dictionary. The `popitem` method returns a randomly selected key-value pair, as a tuple, and removes that key-value pair from the dictionary.

9.11 It returns all a dictionary's keys and their associated values as a sequence of tuples.

9.12 It returns all the keys in a dictionary as a sequence of tuples.

9.13 It returns all the values in the dictionary as a sequence of tuples.

9.14 Unordered

9.15 No

9.16 You call the built-in `set` function.

9.17 The set will contain these elements (in no particular order): `'J'`, `'u'`, `'p'`, `'i'`, `'t'`, `'e'`, and `'r'`.

9.18 The set will contain one element: 25.

9.19 The set will contain these elements (in no particular order): `'w'`, `' '`, `'x'`, `'y'`, and `'z'`.

9.20 The set will contain these elements (in no particular order): 1, 2, 3, and 4.

9.21 The set will contain these elements (in no particular order): `'www'`, `'xxx'`, `'yyy'`, and `'zzz'`.

9.22 You pass the set as an argument to the `len` function.

9.23 The set will contain these elements (in no particular order): 10, 9, 8, 1, 2, and 3.

9.24 The set will contain these elements (in no particular order): 10, 9, 8, `'a'`, `'b'`, and `'c'`.

9.25 If the specified element to delete is not in the set, the `remove` method raises a `KeyError` exception, but the `discard` method does not raise an exception.

9.26 You can use the `in` operator to test for the element.

9.27 `{10, 20, 30, 100, 200, 300}`

9.28 `{3, 4}`

9.29 `{1, 2}`

9.30 `{5, 6}`

9.31 `{'a', 'd'}`

9.32 `set2` is a subset of `set1`, and `set1` is a superset of `set2`.

9.33 The process of converting the object to a stream of bytes that can be saved to a file for later retrieval.

9.34 `'wb'`

9.35 `'rb'`

9.36 The `pickle` module

9.37 `pickle.dump`

9.38 `pickle.load`

Chapter 10

10.1 An object is a software entity that contains both data and procedures.

10.2 Encapsulation is the combining of data and code into a single object.

10.3 When an object's internal data is hidden from outside code and access to that data is restricted to the object's methods, the data is protected from accidental corruption. In addition, the programming code outside the object does not need to know about the format or internal structure of the object's data.

10.4 Public methods can be accessed by entities outside the object. Private methods cannot be accessed by entities outside the object. They are designed to be accessed internally.

10.5 The metaphor of a blueprint represents a class.

10.6 Objects are the cookies.

10.7 Its purpose is to initialize an object's data attributes. It executes immediately after the object is created.

10.8 When a method executes, it must have a way of knowing which object's data attributes it is supposed to operate on. That's where the `self` parameter comes in. When a method is called, Python automatically makes its `self` parameter reference the specific object that the method is supposed to operate on.

10.9 By starting the attribute's name with two underscores

10.10 It returns a string representation of the object.

10.11 By passing the object to the built-in `str` method

10.12 An attribute that belongs to a specific instance of a class

10.13 10

10.14 A method that returns a value from a class's attribute but does not change it is known as an accessor method. A method that stores a value in a data attribute or changes the value of a data attribute in some other way is known as a mutator method.

10.15 The top section is where you write the name of the class. The middle section holds a list of the class's fields. The bottom section holds a list of the class's methods.

10.16 A written description of the real-world objects, parties, and major events related to the problem

10.17 If you adequately understand the nature of the problem you are trying to solve, you can write a description of the problem domain yourself. If you do not thoroughly understand the nature of the problem, you should have an expert write the description for you.

10.18 First, identify the nouns, pronouns, and pronoun phrases in the problem domain description. Then, refine the list to eliminate duplicates, items that you do not need to be concerned with in the problem, items that represent objects instead of classes, and items that represent simple values that can be stored in variables.

10.19 The things that the class is responsible for knowing and the actions that the class is responsible for doing

10.20 In the context of this problem, what must the class know? What must the class do?

10.21 No, not always

Chapter 11

11.1 A superclass is a general class, and a subclass is a specialized class.

11.2 When one object is a specialized version of another object, there is an "is a" relationship between them. The specialized object "is a" version of the general object.

11.3 It inherits all the superclass's attributes.

11.4 `Bird` is the superclass, and `Canary` is the subclass.

11.5 I'm a vegetable.
I'm a potato.

Chapter 12

12.1 A recursive algorithm requires multiple method calls. Each method call requires several actions to be performed by the JVM. These actions include allocating memory for parameters and local variables and storing the address of the program location where control returns after the method terminates. All these actions are known as overhead. In an iterative algorithm, which uses a loop, such overhead is unnecessary.

12.2 A case in which the problem can be solved without recursion

12.3 Cases in which the problem is solved using recursion

12.4 When it reaches the base case

12.5 In direct recursion, a recursive method calls itself. In indirect recursion, method A calls method B, which in turn calls method A.

Chapter 13

13.1 The part of a computer and its operating system with which the user interacts

13.2 A command line interface typically displays a prompt, and the user types a command, which is then executed.

13.3 The program

13.4 A program that responds to events that take place, such as the user clicking a button

13.5 a) `Label`—An area that displays one line of text or an image
b) `Entry`—An area in which the user may type a single line of input from the keyboard
c) `Button`—A button that can cause an action to occur when it is clicked
d) `Frame`—A container that can hold other widgets

13.6 You create an instance of the `tkinter` module's `Tk` class.

13.7 This function runs like an infinite loop until you close the main window.

13.8 The `pack` method arranges a widget in its proper position, and it makes the widget visible when the main window is displayed.

13.9 One will be stacked on top of the other.

13.10 `side=-left-`

13.11 You use an `Entry` widget's `get` method to retrieve the data that the user has typed into the widget.

13.12 It is a string.

13.13 `tkinter`

13.14 Any value that is stored in the `StringVar` object will automatically be displayed in the `Label` widget.

13.15 You would use radio buttons.

13.16 You would use check buttons.

13.17 When you create a group of `Radiobuttons`, you associate them all with the same `IntVar` object. You also assign a unique integer value to each `Radiobutton` widget. When one of the `Radiobutton` widgets is selected, it stores its unique integer value in the `IntVar` object.

13.18 You associate a different `IntVar` object with each `Checkbutton`. When a `Checkbutton` is selected, its associated `IntVar` object will hold the value 1. When a `Checkbutton` is deselected, its associated `IntVar` object will hold the value 0.

13.19 (0, 0)

13.20 (139, 479)

13.21 With the `Canvas` widget, the point (0, 0) is in the upper-left corner of the window. In turtle graphics, the point (0, 0) is in the center of the window. Also, with the `Canvas` widget, the *Y* coordinates increase as you move down the screen. In turtle graphics, the *Y* coordinates decrease as you move down the screen.

13.22 a) `create_oval`
b) `create_rectangle`
c) `create_rectangle`
d) `create_polygon`
e) `create_oval`
f) `create_arc`

Index

I

U

V

W

Z

Credits

Cover Image © Westend61 GmbH/Alamy Stock Photo

Figure 1.2a pg. 3 © iko/Shutterstock

Figure 1.2b pg. 3 © Nikita Rogul/Shutterstock

Figure 1.2c pg. 3 © Feng Yu/Shutterstock

Figure 1.2d pg. 3 © Chiyacat/Shutterstock

Figure 1.2e pg. 3 © Eikostas/Shutterstock

Figure 1.2f pg. 3 © tkemot/Shutterstock

Figure 1.2g pg. 3 © Vitaly Korovin/Shutterstock

Figure 1.2h pg. 3 © Lusoimages/Shutterstock

Figure 1.2i pg. 3 © jocic/Shutterstock

Figure 1.2j pg. 3 © Best Pictures/Shutterstock

Figure 1.2k pg. 3 © Peter Guess/Shutterstock

Figure 1.2l pg. 3 © Aquila/Shutterstock

Figure 1.2m pg. 3 © Andre Nitsievsky/Shutterstock

Figure 1.3 pg. 4 Courtesy of US Army Historic Computer Images

Figure 1.4 pg. 4 © Creativa/Shutterstock

Figure 1.5 pg. 5 © Garsya/Shutterstock

Chapter 1 Microsoft screenshots - SEE MICROSOFT AGREEMENT FOR FULL CREDIT.

Chapter 6 Microsoft screenshots - SEE MICROSOFT AGREEMENT FOR FULL CREDIT.

Chapter 8 Microsoft screenshots - SEE MICROSOFT AGREEMENT FOR FULL CREDIT.

Chapter 9 Microsoft screenshots - SEE MICROSOFT AGREEMENT FOR FULL CREDIT.

Chapter 13 Microsoft screenshots - SEE MICROSOFT AGREEMENT FOR FULL CREDIT.